The Origins of the Slavic Nations

The latest developments in the countries of eastern Europe, including the rise of authoritarian tendencies in Russia and Belarus, as well as the victory of the democratic "Orange Revolution" in Ukraine, pose important questions about the origins of the East Slavic nations and the essential similarities or differences between their cultures. This book traces the origins of the modern Russian, Ukrainian, and Belarusian nations by focusing on premodern forms of group identity among the Eastern Slavs. It also challenges attempts to "nationalize" the Rus' past on behalf of existing national projects, laying the groundwork for a new understanding of the premodern history of Russia, Ukraine, and Belarus. The book covers the period from the Christianization of Kyivan Rus' in the tenth century to the reign of Peter I and his eighteenth-century successors, by which time the idea of nationalism had begun to influence the thinking of East Slavic elites.

SERHII PLOKHY is Professor of History and associate director of the Peter Jacyk Centre at the University of Alberta. His numerous publications on Russian and Ukrainian history include *The Cossacks and Religion in Early Modern Ukraine* (2001), and *Unmaking Imperial Russia: Mykhailo Hrushevsky and the Writing of Ukrainian History* (2005).

The Origins of the Slavic Nations

Premodern Identities in Russia, Ukraine, and Belarus

Serhii Plokhy

CAMBRIDGE
UNIVERSITY PRESS

947
P72σ

CAMBRIDGE UNIVERSITY PRESS
Cambridge, New York, Melbourne, Madrid, Cape Town, Singapore, São Paulo

Cambridge University Press
The Edinburgh Building, Cambridge CB2 2RU, UK

Published in the United States of America by Cambridge University Press, New York

www.cambridge.org
Information on this title: www.cambridge.org/9780521 864039

© Cambridge University Press 2006

First published 2006

Printed in the United Kingdom at the University Press, Cambridge
Cau

A catalogue record for this book is available from the British Library

ISBN-13 978-0-521-86403-9 hardback
ISBN-10 0-521-86403-8 hardback

To Maryna

Contents

Preface

I did not intend to write this book. I was working on another project pertaining to modern history when questions related to the premodern identities of the Eastern Slavs slowly but surely took over most of my time and attention. Looking at the major modern narratives of East Slavic history, I suddenly realized that perceptions of the premodern Russians, Ukrainians, and Belarusians, both in their homelands and in the West, are still shaped by the views of national historians and the paradigms they created. While historians studying individual periods and topics of East Slavic history have made significant progress over the past century, the main national paradigms have survived both Soviet repression and the emigration of the bearers of national historiographic traditions to the West. Since the fall of the USSR, those paradigms have reappeared in the East Slavic lands and even blossomed on the ruins of Soviet historiography.

"Has anybody done better since the Depression?" asked the wife of an acquaintance of mine who was preparing a talk on the Ukrainian national historian, Mykhailo Hrushevsky (1866–1934). "Well, frankly, no," was the answer he gave. I asked myself the same question, broadening its range from Hrushevsky to the entire field of Russian, Ukrainian, and Belarusian historiography. I also had to extend the chronological scope of the question, starting not with the Depression but with the Russo-Japanese War of 1904–5 and the Revolution of 1905 in the Russian Empire. It was then that Hrushevsky published the first twentieth-century outline of Ukrainian history; the patriarch of Russian historiography, Vasilii Kliuchevsky, began to issue his *Survey of Russian History*; and Belarusian national historiography began to emerge from the shell of Russian imperial history. The answer to my question was equally negative. In the last hundred years, no one had done it better, nor had any approach to the "nationalization" of the past improved significantly on the achievements of those two outstanding scholars. In the end, I could not resist the urge to take a fresh look at the dominant versions of premodern Russian, Ukrainian, and Belarusian history and try to denationalize and update them according to the standards of contemporary historical scholarship. In order to do so, it turns out, I had to write this book.

I could not have written it without the support offered me (intentionally or not) by many individuals and institutions – at times they, too, were under the impression that I was working on a different project altogether. I would like to offer individual thanks to those who helped me most. My special thanks go to Myroslav Yurkevich for his support, tactful advice, and thorough editing of my Ukrainglish prose. Advice from Roman Szporluk, Blair Ruble, Terry Martin, and Timothy Snyder was instrumental in shaping the scope of this book and my analytical approach. So were the comments of Volodymyr Kulyk, who, for good reason, advised me against writing this work. I am also grateful to Frank E. Sysyn and Zenon E. Kohut for sharing their insights on the history of early modern Ukrainian texts and identities, as well as books and copies of articles from their personal libraries. Also very helpful were discussions with Natalia Yakovenko, Charles J. Halperin, Michael S. Flier, and Edward L. Keenan on early modern Russian and Ukrainian identities. Paul Bushkovitch, Simon Franklin, Valerie Kivelson, Don Ostrowski, Oleksii Tolochko, Olena Rusyna, and Michael Moser read individual chapters of the book and gave me excellent advice on how to improve them. I would also like to thank participants in the Workshop on Cultural Identities at the University of Alberta – John-Paul Himka, Jelena Pogosjan, Natalia Pylypiuk, Oleh Ilnytzkyj, Heather Coleman, and Peter Rolland – for their comments on chapters originally presented at meetings of the workshop. Parts of chapters 7 and 8 originally appeared in my article "The Two Russias of Teofan Prokopovyč," published in *Mazepa e il suo tempo. Storia, cultura, società / Mazepa and His Time: History, Culture, Society* (Alessandria, 2004), pp. 334–66. I thank Giovanna Brogi Bercoff for her advice on the content of the article and the editor of the volume, Giovanna Siedina, for permission to reprint parts of it in this book.

I am also greatly indebted to participants in the Humanities Program of the American Council of Learned Societies in Belarus, Russia, and Ukraine, especially to the members of the Carnegie Selection Committee with whom I was privileged to work in 2003–6: Andrzej Tymowski, William Rosenberg, Joan Neuberger, and administrative assistant Olga Bukhina. My work in the program gave me a unique opportunity to meet with leading Russian, Ukrainian, and Belarusian scholars working on topics closely related to the subject of this book. My research was sponsored by a grant from the Ukrainian Studies Fund, Inc. (New York), and I would like to express my deep appreciation to the director of the Fund, Roman Procyk, for supporting this project. I thank Michael Watson, commissioning editor for history at Cambridge University Press, for guiding the manuscript through the review and acceptance process. At CUP my thanks also go to Isabelle Dambricourt, Jackie Warren, and Jacqueline French for their help with the editing of the manuscript. I am also grateful to the two anonymous reviewers of the book, whose suggestions I took into account in preparing the final version of the manuscript. I would also like to acknowledge the kind assistance of Viktor Brekhunenko, who helped me with copyright issues in Ukraine. As always, I thank Peter Matilainen for his help in solving computer problems. My special thanks go to my family in Canada and Ukraine.

Note on transliteration, dates, and translations

In the text of this book, the modified Library of Congress system is used to transliterate Russian, Ukrainian, and Belarusian personal names and toponyms. This system omits the soft sign (ь) and, in masculine personal names, the final "й" (thus, for example, Ostrozky, not Ostroz'kyi). In bibliographic references, the full Library of Congress system (ligatures omitted) is used, and the titles of publications issued after 1800 are given in modernized spelling. Toponyms are usually transliterated from the language of the country in which the designated places are currently located. As a rule, personal names are given in forms characteristic of the cultural traditions to which the given person belonged. If an individual belonged to (or is claimed by) more than one national tradition, alternative spellings are given in parentheses. In this case, as in the use of specific terminology related to the history of the Eastern Slavs and titles of east European officials and institutions, I follow the practice established by the editors of the English translation of Mykhailo Hrushevsky's *History of Ukraine-Rus'*.[1]

The Julian calendar used by the Eastern Slavs until 1918 lagged behind the Gregorian calendar used in the Polish-Lithuanian Commonwealth and western Europe (by ten days in the sixteenth and seventeenth centuries and by eleven days in the eighteenth century). Dates in this study are generally given according to the Julian calendar; where both styles appear concurrently, the Gregorian-calendar date is given in parentheses, e.g., 13 (23) May.

Translations within the text are my own unless a printed source is cited.

---

[1] Cf. editorial prefaces and glossary in Mykhailo Hrushevsky, *History of Ukraine-Rus'*, ed. Frank E. Sysyn et al., vol. VII (Edmonton and Toronto, 1999), xix–xxvi, liii–lvi.

Maps

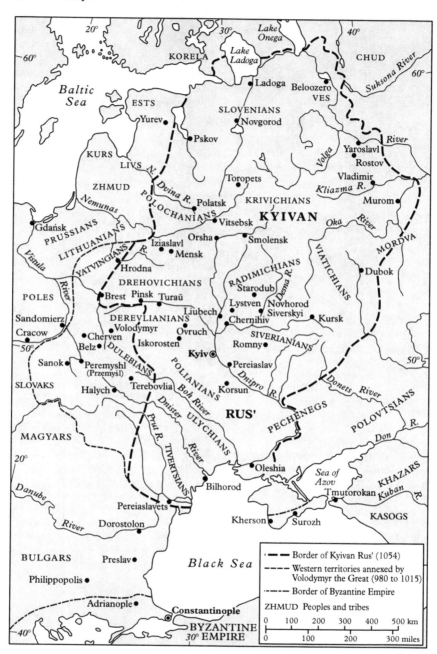

1. Kyivan Rus'
(Source: Zenon E. Kohut, Bohdan Y. Nebesio, and Myroslav Yurkevich, *Historical Dictionary of Ukraine* [Lanham, Maryland, Toronto, Oxford: Scarecrow Press, 2005].)

2. Rus' principalities ca. 1100
(Source: *The Cambridge Encyclopedia of Russia and the Former Soviet Union* [Cambridge, 1994].)

3. Muscovy in the fifteenth–sixteenth centuries
(Source: *The Cambridge Encyclopedia of Russia and the Former Soviet Union* [Cambridge, 1994].)

4. Lands of the Polish-Lithuanian Commonwealth in the sixteenth–
eighteenth centuries
(Source: *Encyclopedia of Ukraine*, ed. Volodymyr Kubijovyč and Danylo
Husar Struk, vol. IV [Toronto: University of Toronto Press, 1993].)

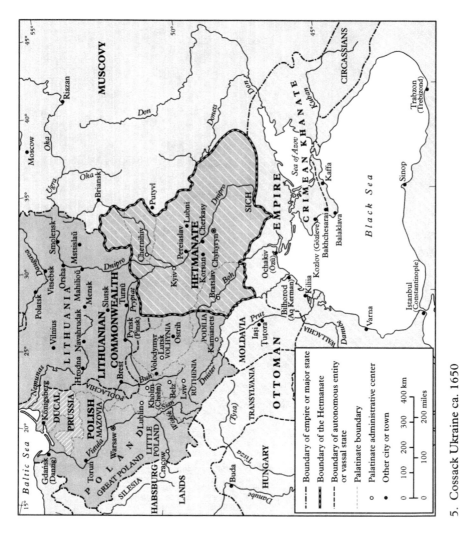

5. Cossack Ukraine ca. 1650

(Source: Mykhailo Hrushevsky, *History of Ukraine-Rus'*, ed. Frank E. Sysyn et al., vol. IX, bk. 1 [Edmonton and Toronto: Canadian Institute of Ukrainian Studies Press, 2005].)

6. The Cossack Hetmanate in the mid-eighteenth century
(Source: Zenon E. Kohut, *Russian Centralism and Ukrainian Autonomy:
Imperial Absorption of the Hetmanate, 1760s–1830s* [Cambridge, Mass.:
Harvard Ukrainian Research Institute, 1988).]

Introduction

The disintegration of the USSR in 1991 and the emergence of fifteen independent nation-states on its ruins demonstrated to the outside world that the Soviet Union was not Russia, despite the best efforts of the Western media to convince its readers to the contrary by using the two terms interchangeably for decades. Political developments in the post-Soviet space indicated that the definition of the USSR as Russia was wrong not only in relation to the non-Slavic republics of the former Soviet Union but also with regard to the Ukrainians and Belarusians, the East Slavic cousins of the Russians. Each of the three newly independent states manifested its own character and chose its own path in the turbulent transition from communism. After a lengthy period of political uncertainty and economic chaos, Russia opted for the construction of a strong state with clear authoritarian tendencies and assumed the role of a regional superpower. Belarus, after a brief period of democratic development, refused to reform its political and economic system and took refuge in Soviet-style ideology and Stalin-era authoritarianism. Ukraine, on the other hand, after long hesitation between East and West, underwent a popular revolution in defense of democratic principles and embarked on a pro-Western course with the goal of joining the European Union. For all the salient differences between these three post-Soviet nations, they have much in common when it comes to their culture and history, which goes back to Kyivan (Kievan) Rus', the medieval East Slavic state based in the capital of present-day Ukraine.

Soviet historians often portrayed Kyivan Rus' as the common cradle of the three East Slavic nations. According to that logic, not unlike the builders of the Tower of Babel, the Eastern Slavs originally constituted one Old Rus' nationality or ethnicity that spoke a common language. It was only the Mongol invasion that divided the people of Rus' and set them on separate paths of development, which eventually led to the formation of three modern nations. The competing view, advanced by imperial Russian historians and shared by some authors in present-day Russia, claims Kyivan Rus' history for one indivisible Russian nation, of which

Ukrainians and Belarusians are considered mere subgroups, distinguished not by separate cultures and languages but by variants of Russian culture and dialects of the Russian language. Ukrainian national historiography, on the contrary, treats Kyivan Rus' as an essentially Ukrainian state and claims that the differences between Russians and Ukrainians were apparent and quite profound even then. That viewpoint finds some support among Belarusian historians, who seek the roots of their nation in the history of the Polatsk principality of Kyivan times. Who is right and who is wrong? What are the origins of the three modern East Slavic nations? These are the questions that informed my research and discussion of the origins of modern Russia, Ukraine, and Belarus.[1]

There is little doubt in my mind that the Kyivan-era project involving the construction of a single identity had a profound impact on the subsequent identities of all the ethnic groups that constituted the Kyivan state. That project defined the parameters of the Rus' legacy, which still forms the basis of the cultural commonalities between the three East Slavic nations. I regard the post-Kyivan Eastern Slavs as a group of distinct communities that possessed and developed their own identities. The number of my premodern East Slavic communities that emerged on the ruins of the Kyivan state is smaller than seventy-two – the number of peoples into which God divided humankind by assigning different languages to the audacious constructors of the Tower of Babel. But it is certainly greater than the number of nationalities or ethnicities suggested either by the proponents of one Old Rus' (alternatively, Russian) nationality or by those who claim that there were three separate East Slavic nations from the very beginning. The approach that I have taken in studying the historical roots of the modern Russians, Ukrainians, and Belarusians is based on the identification and reconstruction of lost structures of group identity among the Eastern Slavs. I am particularly interested in those types of identity that can be interpreted as more or less distant precursors of modern national identity. My point of departure is the assumption that there can be no ethnicity or nation without a distinct identity, and finding the roots of that identity is in many ways tantamount to uncovering the roots of the nation itself.

This book covers the period from the tenth-century Christianization of Kyivan Rus' to the mid-eighteenth century, when the idea of nationalism

---

[1] On the competing interpretations of Kyivan Rus' history in modern Russian, Ukrainian, and Belarusian historiography, see Andrew Wilson, *The Ukrainians: Unexpected Nation* (New Haven and London, 2000), pp. 1–11; Taras Kuzio, "Historiography and National Identity among the Eastern Slavs: Towards a New Framework," *National Identities* 3, no. 2 (2001): 109–32. A detailed discussion of these interpretations appears in the historiographic sections of each of the eight chapters of this book.

had begun to influence the thinking of East Slavic elites. As noted in the preface, the idea of writing this book came out of my dissatisfaction with the treatment of the premodern history of the Eastern Slavs in current historical literature. University textbooks and popular literature on the subject are still dominated by concepts formed at the turn of the twentieth century and rooted in "primordialist" efforts to read the modern nation back into the past. My book challenges attempts to "nationalize" the East Slavic past on behalf of existing modern nations by focusing on the development of premodern identities.

History as a scholarly discipline took shape in the era of nationalism. That factor alone burdened all the major narratives of the era with the task of nationalizing the pre-1800 past and thereby legitimizing the rise and continuing existence of modern nations and nation-states. This approach met with serious criticism in the second half of the twentieth century, primarily on the part of "modernists" – historians and social scientists who argued that there were no nations prior to the modern era.[2] In the ongoing debate between modernists and "primordialists" I take the side of the former, subscribing at the same time to the critique of the "modernists" by the "revisionists," who seek the origins of nationhood in premodern times or point out the ethnic origins of modern nations. Following in the footsteps of John A. Armstrong, Anthony D. Smith, Adrian Hastings, and other "revisionists," I claim that the origins of modern nations are to be found in premodern national communities, or ethnicities, which I often call "nationalities" (in the tradition of East Slavic historiography) and to which Smith refers as *ethnies*.[3] I adopt Adrian Hastings's definition of ethnicity as a "group of people with a shared cultural identity and spoken language." I also subscribe to his broad definition of the nation as "a far more self-conscious community" that, being "[f]ormed from one or more ethnicities, and normally identified by a literature of its own . . . possesses or claims the right to political identity and autonomy as a people, together with the control of specific territory . . . in a world thought of as one of nation states."[4]

[2] Among the most influential "modernist" works of the last few decades are Ernest Gellner, *Nations and Nationalism* (Oxford, 1983); Benedict Anderson, *Imagined Communities: Reflections on the Origins and Spread of Nationalism* (London, 1983); and Eric Hobsbawm, *Nations and Nationalism since 1780* (Cambridge, 1990).

[3] See Anthony D. Smith, *The Ethnic Origins of Nations* (Oxford, 1986). For other attempts to extend the life of nations to premodern times, see John A. Armstrong, *Nations before Nationalism* (Chapel Hill, NC, 1982) and Anthony W. Marx, *Faith in Nation: Exclusionary Origins of Nationalism* (New York, 2003).

[4] Adrian Hastings, *The Construction of Nationhood: Ethnicity, Religion and Nationalism* (Cambridge, 1997), pp. 1–4.

Although premodern ethnicities were of course different from nations of the modern era, I argue that the identities associated with both types of community were products of very similar identity-building projects. In that sense I agree with Anthony D. Smith's assertion that constituent elements of premodern "identities and cultures – the myths, memories, symbols, and values – can often be adapted to new circumstances by being accorded new meanings and new functions" within the framework of nation-building projects.[5] The essentials of premodern ethnicity, which, according to Smith, include a collective name, a common myth of origins, a shared history, a distinctive culture, association with a particular territory, and a sense of solidarity, are very similar to the constituent elements of nations,[6] and so, I would argue, are the two types of identity. Not only does national identity develop out of the constituent elements of ethnic identity, but the latter is often defined by loyalty to common culture and mythology, as well as to common political institutions, which some students of the subject reserve for modern national identity alone. It was the realization of this close connection between ethnic (proto-national) and national types of identity that led me to study them in tandem. That connection also prompted me to use the term "ethnonational" as the basic category of my analysis, since it is applicable to premodern and modern identity-building projects alike.

In my research on the history of Eastern Slavic identities, I have drawn on methods developed both by "modernists" and by "revisionists." The idea that the national narratives whereby modern societies define themselves are products of the "nationalization" of the past by historians of the nineteenth and early twentieth centuries comes directly from the modernist arsenal. I also accept the definition of nations as "imagined communities" proposed by the "modernist" Benedict Anderson and subscribe to his maxim that national identities are formulated and sustained in cultural texts. Unlike the "modernists," however, I extend this approach to the study of premodern communities, stressing the medieval and early modern origins of nations and national ideologies. In that sense, this book is a contribution to the growing "revisionist" literature that posits the existence of nations before nationalism. It renationalizes the past by stressing the importance of the ethnonational factor in premodern history. At the same time, it declines to read modern nationalism back into the past and rejects "primordialist" assumptions about the millennial history of present-day nations. Instead, I delve into the construction of medieval and early modern identities and track changes in their structures and meanings. In the process, I attempt to show how the

---

[5] Smith, *The Ethnic Origins of Nations*, p. 3.   [6] Ibid., pp. 22–31.

imagined communities of the premodern era differed from their modern-day successors.

My approach to "identity," a concept central to the book, is "soft" in the sense defined by Rogers Brubaker and Frederick Cooper. It is influenced by poststructuralist and postmodernist thought and generally conforms to the definition of the term adopted in recent studies on ethnicity and nationalism. Thus I understand identity as a phenomenon that manifests itself in collective and individual consciousness and action. I also regard it as a "situationalist" phenomenon, a constantly changing construct produced by the interaction of a number of discourses. Crucial to my approach, as noted above, is the assumption that every ethnic or national community must have a concept of common identity to qualify for the status of either ethnicity or nation.[7]

The terms "ethnicity" and "nationality," like most terms used in present-day social analysis, are inventions of modern times. In studying the Eastern Slavs, nineteenth-century linguists and ethnologists identified three major ethnic groups or, in their terminology, nationalities: Great Russian, Little Russian (Ukrainian), and Belarusian. But they also admitted major linguistic and cultural differences within those nationalities, and often the lack of clearly defined borders between them. The conclusion that emerges from an examination of the linguistic and ethnographic material is quite simple. The ethnic classifications themselves were the result of outside interference – in other words, they were constructed – while the borders of those ethnicities were created by stressing the differences between nationalities and downplaying the fault lines within them. My research suggests that the division of communities into ethnicities and nations is not always a very helpful analytical tool. On the level of identity-building projects and collective identities, the line between the two is blurred, and the division of human history into ethnic and national phases simplifies and distorts that history more than it promotes understanding.

Consequently, as explained above, I often fuse the two categories by applying the term "ethnonational" in the text of this book. I have also adopted the practice of categorizing nations as modern and premodern, introducing "premodern nation" along with "ethnicity" as one of the main terms of my analysis. I use this term to denote premodern communities that acquired many but not all of the characteristics of the modern nation. At various times, nations have been defined in terms of culture, language, religion, territory, and polity, to list the most obvious factors.[8]

---

[7] See Rogers Brubaker and Frederick Cooper, "Beyond 'Identity,'" *Theory and Society* 29 (2000): 1–47, here 1–8.

[8] On the changing meanings of "nation," see Liah Greenfeld, *Nationalism: Five Roads to Modernity* (Cambridge, Mass., 1992), pp. 4–9.

Thus, while drawing a distinction between premodern communities and modern nations, I do not shy away from the term "nation," which occurs in some of my early modern sources, in discussing the premodern history of the Eastern Slavs. I employ "nation" quite consistently when discussing developments after the turn of the seventeenth century, as I consider the Ruthenian and Muscovite communities of the time to be the first East Slavic groups that possessed the characteristics of a premodern nation. They constituted a type of community that did not offer membership in its ranks to the whole population of its territory, limiting it to members of the elite, but managed to formulate its identity outside (or concurrently with) the concept of loyalty to the ruler or dynasty.

Dealing with premodern East Slavic identities means following the development of a number of Rus' identities. In spite of their profound differences, the creators and bearers of all these identities connected them with the name of Rus', which denotes both the land and the people. For the sake of clarity, I use different names for these various types of Rus'-based identities. While I refer to most of the medieval East Slavic identities as Rus' or Rus'ian, I follow established English-language practice in switching from "Rus'" to "Ruthenia" when discussing Ukraine and Belarus after the incorporation of the Rus' lands into the Kingdom of Poland and the Grand Duchy of Lithuania in the second half of the fourteenth century. I switch from "Rus'" to "Muscovy" to denote the territories of Northeastern and Northwestern Rus' that were annexed to the Grand Duchy of Moscow in the second half of the fifteenth century. I speak of Ukrainian (Little Russian) identity starting with the second half of the seventeenth century, and I refer to (Great) Russian and Russian imperial identities from the beginning of the eighteenth century.

The political and ecclesiastical elites whose members were largely responsible for the identity-building projects discussed in this book left a significant number of texts that shed light on the development of ethnonational identity. The effect of those elite projects can be measured by their impact on communal identities, and it is here that problems begin to multiply. In many cases, no full investigation of that impact can be undertaken for lack of sources. Although I have tried to pay as much attention as possible to manifestations of ethnonational identity among rank-and-file members of East Slavic communities, the book often focuses on elites and their efforts to construct and implement ethnonational projects. Thus I am entirely in accord with the approach adopted recently by Simon Franklin and Emma Widdis in their interpretation of Russian identities as texts written by "producers of culture." They write:

It is these culturally inscribed Russias that are our focus here. It would of course be nice to know what proportion of the wider population might have heard of or associated themselves with which aspects of which type of identity at which time. By and large, however, we try to steer clear of the trap of taking the populace for granted when attributing an identity to it, and such speculations are beyond our scope.[9]

When it comes to "identity texts" produced by elites, it is worth noting that political and religious institutions, with which those elites were closely associated, generally tend to sustain identities that justify their existence and present their view of the world. There is also a tension between central and local institutions. Thus it is hardly surprising that in the fifteenth century chroniclers sponsored by the Muscovite metropolitans promoted the unity of the Rus′ lands under Moscow, while chroniclers working under the auspices of the Lithuanian princes emphasized the unity of the Lithuanian land and Lithuanian Rus′. It would certainly be wrong to treat ethnonational identities in isolation from political, religious, and other types of loyalties constructed and sustained by early modern societies. This book focuses mainly on ethnic and national identities, but other types of identity, such as religious, political, and social, are discussed as well, usually in connection with the formation of the former. The study of their interaction suggests that up to the late eighteenth century ethnonational identities were secondary to other types of identity and loyalty, such as those based on family, clan, social group, region, dynasty, and religion. This does not mean, however, that ethnonational identity did not exist before that period or did not contribute significantly to the formation of collective and individual self-consciousness in premodern societies.

Given the focus of this book on builders and producers of identity, the main analytical category that I employ in my research is the identity-building project. In my discussion of East Slavic identities, I show how they were constructed by means of diverse efforts that created reservoirs of collective memory, images, and symbols. The first such undertaking examined in the book is the Rus′ project of the Kyivan period, which served as the basis for most of the later competing projects developed by the East Slavic elites. These included the Muscovite project, matched on the opposite side of the Mongol boundary by the Ruthenian project of the Ukrainian and Belarusian elites. In eastern Europe, the second half of the seventeenth century saw the beginnings of the first modern national project, that of Russian imperial identity, with blurred

[9] Simon Franklin and Emma Widdis, "All the Russias . . .?" in *National Identity in Russian Culture: An Introduction*, ed. edem (Cambridge, 2004), pp. 1–8, here 3.

boundaries between its imperial and national components. I argue that it was fully formed in the first decades of the century, during the era of the Petrine reforms. The construction of Ukrainian Cossack identity, which laid the foundations for the Ukrainian national project of the modern era, was completed at about the same time. The Ruthenian identity that developed in the Grand Duchy of Lithuania prepared the ground for the nineteenth-century Belarusian national project. By the end of the eighteenth century, literary works written in languages very close to modern Russian and Ukrainian had emerged from the cocoon of bookish Church Slavonic.

The questions posed in this book are largely informed by historiographic tradition. Every chapter begins with a discussion of different viewpoints concerning a given problem, while in the conclusions I return to the historiographic problems posed at the beginning. Since the book is addressed to an English-speaking Western audience, the historiographic sections pay special attention to the presentation and critique of approaches developed by Russian and Soviet historians, which still frame Western interpretations of the subject to a significant degree. Although I often discuss in great detail the pluses and minuses of each historiographic approach, my purpose is not to pick winners and losers in historiographic debate but to go beyond the national paradigms that have largely shaped historical discussions over the last two centuries in order to present a fresh view of the subject. The only way to assess the validity of historiographic tradition is to check its main assumptions and conclusions against the evidence of the sources, which take center stage in my investigation. The reader should therefore be prepared to encounter many excerpts from a great diversity of historical sources. Selecting sources in a narrative that covers almost a millennium is a challenging task in itself, and different approaches are required to deal with twelfth-century chronicles and eighteenth-century bureaucratic correspondence. Still, I believe that direct access to the voices of the past helps the reader make sense of complex historiographic concepts from which s/he is separated by layers of cultural insulation.

Owing to the scarcity of modern research directly related to my topic, each chapter of the book deals with a limited number of identity-related issues that have some basis in the historiographic tradition. In discussing these issues, I try to reconstruct the main stages of development of East Slavic identities on the basis of the available data. Provocative questions posed in this book, such as the one on who has the better claim to the Kyivan Rus' heritage, may strike specialists in the field as overly simple and anachronistic. Nevertheless, they are highly relevant to ongoing public debate about the premodern history of the Eastern Slavs and often helpful in tackling a number of "historiographically correct" questions with which specialists are concerned. My approach to the subject is twofold. First, I seek to deconstruct the existing "nation-based" narrative of East Slavic history. Long before I began to write this book, that narrative was questioned in specific studies on individual periods of East Slavic history. For example, debates on the Old Rus' nationality of Kyivan times undermined the concept of one Rus' nation, while research on early modern Belarus and Ukraine questioned the existence of separate Ukrainian and Belarusian identities in the sixteenth and early seventeenth centuries. Yet there has been no systematic effort to reevaluate the entire historical paradigm. My other major goal, and a risky one at that, is to suggest a new outline of the development of East Slavic identities and thus prepare the ground for a reconceptualization of the premodern history of Russia, Ukraine, and Belarus. I hope that both attempts will stimulate new research on the history of East Slavic identities and lead eventually to a new synthesis of the history of the Eastern Slavs.

Finally, a few words about the structure of the book, whose focus on the development of premodern identity-building projects has led me to depart from the conventions of traditional Russian, Ukrainian, and Belarusian national histories. Chapter 1, which considers the origins of Rus', is followed by a discussion of the changing meanings of the term "Rus' Land" during the appanage period (chapter 2). A Great Russian narrative would continue by focusing on Muscovy, but chapter 3 of this work is devoted to Rus' identities in the Grand Duchy of Lithuania: judging by available sources, the concept of the Rus' Land was adopted in the Rus' territories under Lithuanian control much earlier than in the lands under Mongol suzerainty. A work on Ukrainian or Belarusian history would go on to discuss Ruthenian identity, but that topic is deferred here to chapter 5, while the intervening chapter 4 is concerned with the development of Muscovite identity, forged between the fourteenth and sixteenth centuries. Knowledge of that process is indispensable to understanding the transformation of Lithuanian Rus' loyalties into the Ruthenian identity of the sixteenth and seventeenth centuries. The multiple lines of my narrative meet in chapter 6 ("Was there a reunification?") and then divide into separate but related streams: chapter 7 discusses the construction of imperial Russian identity, while chapter 8 deals with the metamorphoses of Ruthenian identity in the Muscovite state (including the Hetmanate) and the Commonwealth in the late seventeenth and early eighteenth centuries. The conclusions summarize the results of my research and discuss their bearing on present-day concerns.

1   The origins of Rus'

The history of Kyivan (Kievan) Rus', the medieval East Slavic state that existed between the tenth and thirteenth centuries and extended from the Baltic in the north to the Black Sea in the south, and from the Carpathian Mountains in the west to the Volga River in the east, has remained at the center of Russia's search for identity ever since the emergence of historical studies as a scholarly discipline in the Russian Empire. In fact, the first historiographic debate in the empire, which took place in the 1740s and pitted one of the founders of historical studies in Russia, G. F. Müller, against Russia's preeminent scientist and linguist, Mikhail Lomonosov, focused on Kyivan Rus' history. At the core of that debate, which subsequently became known as the "Varangian Controversy," was the question of whether the first Kyivan princes and the state they created were Germanic (Varangian) or "Russian" (East Slavic). The debate has now been going on for more than two centuries, gaining new impetus in the years of World War II and the Cold War, and turning on the definition of Russian identity and that of other Eastern Slavs vis-à-vis the West.[1]

With the rise of the Ukrainian movement in the Russian Empire in the 1840s, the history of Kyivan Rus' turned into a battleground between followers and opponents of the Slavist Mikhail Pogodin. According to Pogodin's theory, Kyiv and its environs were originally settled by Great Russian tribes that migrated north after the Mongol invasion of the mid-thirteenth century. Only after this migration, claimed Pogodin, did the "Little Russians" or Ukrainians settle the area. At stake was the question of Russian and Ukrainian historical identity and which of the two East Slavic nations had the better claim to the legacy of the Kyivan Rus' princes. The twentieth century added a new twist to the debate,

---

[1] On the origins of the Varangian controversy and the uses of history in the eighteenth-century Russian Empire, see Hans Rogger, *National Consciousness in Eighteenth-Century Russia* (Cambridge, Mass., 1960), pp. 186–52, and Vera Tolz, *Russia* (London and New York, 2001), pp. 50–53. For the history of the debate, see I. P. Shaskol'skii, *Normanskaia teoriia v sovremennoi burzhuaznoi nauke* (Moscow and Leningrad, 1965), and A. A. Khlevov, *Normanskaia problema v otechestvennoi istoricheskoi nauke* (St. Petersburg, 1997).

dividing scholars who argued that Kyivan Rus' was the common homeland of the Eastern Slavs and the cradle of the "Old Rus'" nationality from
those who claimed the Kyivan past on behalf of the Russian or Ukrainian
nation.[2]

Was Kyivan Rus' the product of the activities of the Vikings/
Norsemen/Varangians, or was it a state not only populated mainly by
Eastern Slavs but also created and ruled by them? And if the latter
was the case, then who had the better claim to Kyivan Rus' – the Russians or the Ukrainians and Belarusians (separately or together)? The
first question has lost its political urgency because of the outcome of
post-communist nation-building in eastern Europe, but it has not disappeared altogether. Since the dissolution of the USSR and the demise of
the notoriously anti-Normanist Soviet historiography, historians in that
part of the world are no longer obliged to oppose the Normanist thesis on
ideological grounds. Nevertheless, after Russia's brief flirtation with the
West in the early 1990s, the West resumed its traditional role of "other"
in Russian national consciousness, thereby reviving the anti-Normanist
trend in Russian historiography and popular literature.[3] The dissolution
of the USSR has well and truly revived the East Slavic contest for the
legacy of Kyivan Rus'. The view that the Ukrainians were the true heirs
to the Rus' legacy, which was confined to Ukrainian émigré publications
in the West before 1991, has gained a new lease on life in independent
Ukraine on both the academic and the popular levels. In Ukrainian public
discourse, Kyivan Rus' emerged as the first Ukrainian state, the images
of Rus' princes appeared on Ukrainian bank notes, and the symbol of
the Kyivan princes, the trident, was adopted as the coat of arms of independent Ukraine. Cathedrals and monasteries dating back to the times
of Kyivan Rus' and destroyed by the Bolshevik regime were restored by
the Kyiv city authorities, as was the monument to the first Christian
princess, Olha (Olga), in downtown Kyiv. These aggressive efforts on the
part of the Ukrainian public to reclaim the legacy of the Kyivan Rus' past
encouraged Belarusian intellectuals to renew their search for the origins
of their nation in the same historical period and turn their attention to

---

[2] For the origins of the debate, see Jaroslaw Pelenski, "The Ukrainian-Russian Debate over
the Legacy of Kievan Rus'," in idem, *The Contest for the Legacy of Kievan Rus'* (Boulder,
Colo., 1998), pp. 213–27; Olga Andriewsky, "The Russian-Ukrainian Discourse and the
Failure of the 'Little Russian Solution,' 1782–1917," in *Culture, Nation, and Identity:
The Ukrainian-Russian Encounter (1600–1945)*, ed. Andreas Kappeler, Zenon E. Kohut,
Frank E. Sysyn, and Mark von Hagen (Edmonton and Toronto, 2003), pp. 182–214.

[3] For a recent example of the latter, see a volume of almost eight hundred pages by the
extremely prolific Russian writer and amateur historian A. L. Nikitin, *Osnovaniia russkoi
istorii* (Moscow, 2001).

the Principality of Polatsk, an autonomous realm in the empire of the Kyivan princes.[4]

Exploring the ethnocultural identities of Kyivan Rus' remains an important task for anyone who seeks to place the age-old debates on the national character of Kyivan Rus' into broader historical perspective and test their main assumptions against what we now know about the medieval history of Rus'. The present chapter approaches this question by examining the identity project that was endorsed by the elites of Kyivan Rus' and found expression in the Rus' chronicles and other surviving literary works of the period. It asks questions about the primary loyalty of those elites (to their tribe, city, principality, state, and dynasty) and goes on to explore the ethnic, political, religious, cultural, and other levels of Rus' identity. It also tries to distinguish the loyalties of those who inhabited the center of the Kyivan realm from those of dwellers on the periphery. Such a differentiation seems particularly important for any attempt to reconstruct the identity of the Kyivan Rus' elites in all its complexity and attain a fuller understanding of the ethnocultural and political roots of the nations known today under the common name of Eastern Slavs.

What was Kyivan Rus'?

An answer to this simple question, as to most questions about medieval East Slavic history, is not readily available, and the one we can provide is quite complex and incomplete. The term itself comes from imperial Russian historiography and was created to distinguish one historical period within the imperial Russian narrative from another (that is, Kyivan from Muscovite). It helped underline existing differences between these two periods of "all-Russian" history and as such was gladly accepted in Ukrainian historiography, whose twentieth-century representatives fought hard to remove the history of Kyivan Rus' from the imperial historical narrative. Currently, "Kyivan Rus'" is used mainly to define the state

---

[4] On debates about Kyivan Rus' in post-1991 Ukraine, see Andrew Wilson, *The Ukrainians: Unexpected Nation* (New Haven and London, 2000), pp. 1–20. For the interpretation of the history of Polatsk and the Polatsk principality in Soviet and post-1991 Belarusian historiography, see G. V. Shtykhov, *Drevnii Polotsk, IX–XIII vv.* (Minsk, 1975); idem, *Goroda Polotskoi zemli (IX–XIII vv.)* (Minsk, 1978); idem, "U istokov belorusskoi narodnosti," *Ruthenica* (Kyiv) 1 (2002): 85–88; Uladzimir Arloŭ, *Taiamnitsy polatskai historyi* (Minsk, 1994). For a discussion of the genesis of the Belarusian nation and an account of the Polatsk principality as the first Belarusian state in post-Soviet Belarusian historiography, see Rainer Lindner, *Historyki i ŭlada. Natsyiatvorchy ptratsès i histarychnaia palityka ŭ Belarusi XIX–XX st.* (Minsk, 2003), pp. 445–53 (Lindner's book was originally published in German under the title *Historiker und Herrschaft: Nationsbildung und Geschichtspolitik in Weißrussland im 19. und 20. Jahrhundert* [Munich, 1999]).

established in the tenth century by princes of the Rurikid dynasty that disintegrated into a number of polities after the Mongol invasion of the mid-thirteenth century. As the first known Kyivan princes and members of their retinues had non-Slavic or, more precisely, Scandinavian names – Rorik (Rurik), from whom the Rurikid dynasty took its name, Helgi (Oleh/Oleg), Ingvar (Ihor/Igor), Helga (Olha/Olga), and so on – there is good reason to believe that the polity known today as Kyivan Rus′ was one of the many "nation-building" enterprises undertaken by the Norsemen in medieval Europe.

In all likelihood, the Scandinavian rulers appeared in Kyiv sometime in the late ninth or early tenth century and very soon found themselves at the head of a growing empire. Kyiv reached the height of its power in the late tenth and early eleventh centuries, when it was ruled by three of its most famous princes, Sviatoslav the Brave, St. Volodymyr (Vladimir) the Great, and Yaroslav the Wise. Prince Sviatoslav ruled between 945 and 972 (prior to 957 under the regency of his mother, Olha, who was the first Christian member of the dynasty). He became known for his victories over the neighbors of Rus′, including Byzantium, but despite his Slavic name (Sviatoslav was the first in his dynasty to have a non-Scandinavian name), he had little attachment to the Rus′ realm, and, judging by the chronicler's account, planned to move his capital to the Danube. His son Volodymyr, who ruled between 980 and 1015, felt much more attached to Kyiv. He considerably extended the boundaries of the realm and cemented it ideologically by introducing Byzantine Christianity as the official religion of the land ca. 988. Volodymyr's son Yaroslav, who ruled (with interruptions) between 1015 and 1054, reunited the realm after a period of fratricidal wars. He supported the development of Christian culture and learning and turned Kyiv into a "Constantinople on the Dnipro [Dnieper]" but also fought a war with Byzantium and distanced his realm from it by installing the first Rus′-born metropolitan in Kyiv.

After the death of Yaroslav in 1054, the freshly built empire gradually began to disintegrate into a number of smaller principalities ruled by members of the Rurikid dynasty. In the second half of the eleventh century, that process had not yet reached its peak and was somewhat delayed by Yaroslav's eldest sons. Early in the twelfth century, Yaroslav's grandson, Prince Volodymyr Monomakh, who ruled Kyiv between 1113 and 1125, managed to restore the unity of the realm and the authority of its Kyivan prince. But his success proved temporary, and soon after Monomakh's death the feuds resumed. The power of Kyiv was eroded by the growing strength of the local princes, who developed into semi-autonomous or fully independent rulers by the end of the century. The disintegration of the formerly centralized Kyivan state was partly responsible for the ease with which the Mongols conquered Rus' in a number of military campaigns between 1237 and 1240. Most historians regard the Mongol invasion as the single event that formally closed the period of East Slavic history known as the era of Kyivan Rus'.[5]

What we know about Kyivan Rus' today is based primarily on the account of its history presented in the earliest Rus' historical narrative, the Primary Chronicle, which has survived in compilations dating from the fourteenth and fifteenth centuries. Most students of the chronicle assume that Nestor, a monk of the Kyivan Cave Monastery, composed (or edited) its text ca. 1113. There have been numerous and generally successful attempts to find or reconstruct the sources used by the author of the Primary Chronicle, including Byzantine chronicles and Slavic literary works. The most optimistic assessments suggest that chronicle writing began in Kyiv as early as the tenth century, but that hypothesis runs counter to the most authoritative theory on the subject, developed in the first decades of the twentieth century by Aleksei Shakhmatov. He dated the emergence of chronicle writing in Kyiv to the 1030s, assuming that it was associated with the activities of the Kyiv metropolitanate and the clergy of St. Sophia's Cathedral. From there, chronicle writing evidently moved to the Kyivan Cave Monastery: the first autobiographical entry in the Primary Chronicle, under the year 1051, states that one of its authors was admitted to the monastery at the age of seventeen. It is assumed today that the Primary Chronicle is based on an earlier account comprising Kyivan and Novgorodian narratives (the earliest of them apparently not divided into annual entries) that was compiled in Kyiv in the 1090s. The author of the Primary Chronicle (presumably Nestor) edited the earlier account, supplemented it with annual entries for the last decade of the eleventh century and the first decade of the twelfth, and added an introduction whose opening sentence, "This is the Tale of Bygone Years," supplied the name by which the chronicle is known in modern scholarship. Further additions and revisions were made in the second decade of the twelfth century, first at the Vydubychi Monastery in Kyiv

---

[5] For general surveys of the period, see Mykhailo Hrushevsky, *History of Ukraine-Rus'*, ed. Frank E. Sysyn et al., vol. I, *From Prehistory to the Eleventh Century* (Edmonton and Toronto, 1997); Simon Franklin and Jonathan Shepard, *The Emergence of Rus, 750–1200* (London and New York, 1996); J. L. I. Fennell, *The Crisis of Medieval Russia* (London and New York, 1983); Oleksii Tolochko and Petro Tolochko, *Kyïvs'ka Rus'*, vol. IV of *Ukraïna kriz' viky* (Kyiv, 1998). For the treatment of Kyivan Rus' history in English-language syntheses of Russian and Ukrainian history, see Nicholas V. Riasanovsky, *A History of Russia*, 6th edn (New York and Oxford, 2000), pp. 23–62; Janet Martin, *Medieval Russia, 980–1584* (Cambridge, 1996), pp. 1–133; Orest Subtelny, *Ukraine: A History* (Toronto, 1988), pp. 19–54; Paul R. Magocsi, *A History of Ukraine* (Toronto, 1996), pp. 51–104.

during the rule of Volodymyr Monomakh and later in Novgorod, where Mstyslav, the son of Monomakh, probably oversaw the editorial process.[6]

This reconstruction of the earliest history of Rus' chronicle writing is largely based on hypothesis, and many questions still remain unanswered. What does seem clear is that the Primary Chronicle was not the work of a single author but of a number of editors and compilers.[7] It is also apparent that the chronicle was as much a work of literary art as it was a political and cultural statement, for the chroniclers' knowledge of "bygone years" was limited at best. The authors of the Primary Chronicle had ample opportunity to reconstruct events long gone and vanished from the memory of contemporaries, as well as to report on current developments, in a manner that fitted their own agendas and the needs of their sponsors. Those agendas and needs often differed from one chronicler and prince to another. Thus, when a new author took on the compilation of the chronicle, the process of editing, censoring, and correcting its text would begin anew. As a result, when it comes to the structure of its narrative, the Primary Chronicle often reads like a postmodern text. It can easily be compared to a historical archive – a repository of earlier texts of various provenance whose narrative lines often were not reconciled with one another and could even be flatly contradictory. "One should not, however," warns Simon Franklin, "imagine the chronicle as an unedited scrap book, a random assemblage of whatever snippets happened to be available. The compiler had a coherent approach to Providential history, a coherent perspective on native history, and a critical concern for accuracy." According to Franklin, the chronicler successfully adapted the traditions of Byzantine historical writing to his own purposes. He accepted the principles of Byzantine historical chronology and found a place for Rus' in the Byzantine time map. He also incorporated the local historical tradition into a Christian interpretation of history borrowed from Byzantine sources. The contradictions in his narrative lines, obvious to the modern eye, were not regarded as such by the medieval author, for

---

[6] For an English translation of the text of the tale in its Laurentian (Suzdal or Northeastern Rus' version), see The Russian Primary Chronicle: Laurentian Text, ed. and trans. Samuel Hazzard Cross and Olgerd P. Sherbowitz-Wetzor (Cambridge, Mass., 1953). For a discussion of the earliest stages of Kyivan chronicle writing, see A. A. Shakhmatov, Razyskaniia o drevneishikh russkikh letopisnykh svodakh (St. Petersburg, 1908); M. D. Priselkov, Istoriia russkogo letopisaniia XI–XV vv. (Leningrad, 1940); B. A. Rybakov, Drevniaia Rus': skazaniia, byliny, letopisi (Moscow, 1963); A. K. Aleshkovskii, Povest' vremennykh let (Moscow, 1971); A. G. Kuz'min, Nachal'nye ètapy drevnerusskogo letopisaniia (Moscow, 1977); V. K. Ziborov, O letopisi Nestora. Osnovnoi letopisnyi svod v russkom letopisanii XI v. (St. Petersburg, 1995).

[7] On the ambiguity of the term "author" in relation to medieval texts, see Riccardo Picchio, "Compilation and Composition: Two Levels of Authorship in the Orthodox Slavic Tradition," Cyrillomethodianum 5 (1981): 1–4.

whom the numerous stories of the baptism of Rus' did not derive from free human will but manifested a divine plan for the Land of Rus'.[8]

Most importantly for our discussion, the Primary Chronicle speaks in many voices and reveals multiple identities – a fact that can only be welcomed, given the overall scarcity of sources on the period. The preservation of the chronicle text in a number of versions in regional, non-Kyivan compilations enhances its potential as a source for the study of the development of Rus' identities, not only in the capital but also "on the ground," in the peripheral principalities of the Rurikid realm.

The elusive nationality

When it comes to the present-day understanding of Russian history, the concept that dominates the interpretation of issues related to the ethnic identity of Kyivan Rus' remains that of one Rus' or Russian nationality.[9] During the nineteenth and early twentieth centuries, the view of the East Slavic past as the history of one all-Rus' nationality extended to all periods of East Slavic history. The emergence of Ukrainian and Belarusian national historiographies in the twentieth century resulted in the division of the common all-Russian historical account into national Russian, Ukrainian, and Belarusian narratives. The only exception, as noted in the introduction to the present work, seems to be the history of Kyivan Rus', which in most textbooks of east European history, both in Russia and in the West, continues to be seen not only as the common starting point of the history of the three East Slavic nations but also as the home of one all-Rus' nationality. In the West, this problem is treated quite differently in the specialized literature on Kyivan Rus' and in general surveys of Russian history. For example, in their innovative survey of Rus' before 1200, Simon Franklin and Jonathan Shepard draw a clear distinction between "Rus" and "Russia": "The story of the land of the Rus could continue in one direction towards modern Russia, or in other directions towards, eventually, Ukraine or Belarus. The land of the Rus is none of these, or

---

[8] See Franklin and Shepard, *The Emergence of Rus*, pp. 317–19. Cf. Simon Franklin, "Borrowed Time: Perceptions of the Past in Twelfth-Century Rus'," in idem, *Byzantium-Rus-Russia: Studies in the Translation of Christian Culture* (Aldershot, Hampshire and Burlington, Vermont, 2002), no. XVI, pp. 157–71. On the nature of Byzantine historicism, see S. S. Averintsev, "Poriadok kosmosa i poriadok istorii v mirovozzrenii rannego srednevekov'ia. (Obshchie zamechaniia)," in *Antichnost' i Vizantiia*, ed. L. A. Freidberg (Moscow, 1975), pp. 266–87.

[9] For a survey of pertinent historiographic concepts, see Taras Kuzio, "Historiography and National Identity among the Eastern Slavs: Towards a New Framework," *National Identities* 3, no. 2 (2001): 109–32, here 113–22.

else it is a shared predecessor of all three."[10] But that is not the approach taken by Nicholas V. Riasanovsky in his *History of Russia*, the most popular Western textbook on the subject. He begins his chapter on the origins of the Kyivan state with the following statement: "The problem of the origin of the first Russian state, that of Kiev, is exceedingly complex and controversial."[11]

The origins of the theory of one Rus' nationality as the main agent of Kyivan Rus' history can be traced back to the writings of the father of twentieth-century Russian historiography, Vasilii Kliuchevsky. A number of Russian scholars, including Aleksandr Presniakov, contributed to the development of that concept.[12] Not until Soviet times, however, was it truly launched on its career. It was fully formulated by the Leningrad scholar Vladimir Mavrodin in his work on the formation of the Old Rus' state, published in 1945 in an atmosphere of strong anti-German sentiment and Soviet wartime patriotism. The book treated the East Slavic population of Kyivan Rus' as a unified ethnocultural category, defined as "nationality" (*narodnost'*).[13] The term "Old Rus' nationality" and the concept denoted by it served, *inter alia*, to establish Russia's claim to the historical legacy of Kyivan Rus' and therefore survived the demise of Soviet historiography. It is quite popular in Russia today, accepted even by such authors as Valentin Sedov, who is prepared go as far back as the middle of the first millennium BC in searching for the origins of the Russians, Ukrainians, and Belarusians, and who recognizes the Ukrainians (in line with Mykhailo Hrushevsky's argument) as the heirs of the sixth-century Antes.[14] Even in Ukraine, where the authors of general surveys seem to embrace Hrushevsky's interpretation of the ethnic history of Kyivan

---

[10] Franklin and Shepard, *The Emergence of Rus*, p. xvii. Cf. Simon Franklin, "Russia in Time," in *National Identity in Russian Culture: An Introduction*, ed. Franklin and Emma Widdis (Cambridge, 2004), pp. 11–29, here 12.

[11] Riasanovsky, *A History of Russia*, p. 25.

[12] See V. O. Kliuchevskii, *Sochineniia*, vol. I (Moscow, 1956), pp. 32–34, 42–43, 94–95, 128–29, 147, 152–53, 204–5; A. E. Presniakov, *Lektsii po russkoi istorii*, vol. I, *Kievskaia Rus'* (Moscow, 1938; repr. The Hague, 1966), pp. 1–11.

[13] The term *drevnerusskaia narodnost'* (Old Russian nationality), coined by Mavrodin to denote the population of Kyivan Rus', competed with two other terms suggested respectively in 1943 and 1944 by A. D. Udaltsov: *drevnerusskii narod* (Old Russian people) and *obshcherusskaia narodnost'* (all-Russian nationality). Mavrodin's variant combined elements of both formulas, obscuring the genetic link of the concept of Old Rus' nationality with its all-Russian prototype of the turn of the twentieth century. On Mavrodin and his role in creating the concept of Old Rus' nationality, see Nataliia Iusova, "'Problema davn'orus'koï narodnosti' v pratsi V. V. Mavrodina 'Obrazovanie drevnerusskogo gosudarstva' (1945 r.)," *Ruthenica* (Kyiv) 1 (2002): 152–63.

[14] See Valentin Sedov, "Drevnerusskaia narodnost' i predposylki ee differentsiatsii," *Ruthenica* 1 (2002): 70–73. Cf. idem, *Slaviane v rannem srednevekov'e* (Moscow, 1995); idem, *Drevnerusskaia narodnost'* (Moscow, 1999).

Rus', the concept appears to be alive and well in the writings of such students of the period as Petro Tolochko.[15]

There are nevertheless serious problems with the term and the concept itself. In Russia, for example, Igor Danilevsky recently questioned the role of the state in the formation of the Old Rus' nationality (he uses the term in quotation marks) and expressed doubt whether Kyivan Rus' authors had any "national consciousness" at all. He also criticized the use of the ethnonym "Russians" by some of his colleagues in referring to the East Slavic population of Kyivan Rus'.[16] In Ukraine, Oleksii Tolochko stated that it would be a waste of effort to search Kyivan Rus' history for any "people" unified by biological, linguistic, and cultural factors; he suggested instead that the "Old Rus' nationality" be conceived not as an ethnocultural entity but as an imagined community in the sense defined by Benedict Anderson.[17]

When applying the idea of an Old Rus' nationality to the history of the Kyivan realm, its proponents generally avoid discussing the chronological boundaries within which that nationality was formed, while those who do so face the problem of squeezing its formation into an unreasonably short period of time. In most accounts, the "window of opportunity" is slightly more than fifty years in length, extending from the formation of the Kyivan Rus' territory under Volodymyr and Yaroslav, accompanied by the gradual Christianization of the realm (an all-important factor in the argument of proponents of this concept), to the early twelfth century, when the sources provide indisputable evidence of the progressive disintegration of the Rus' state and the identity that could plausibly be associated with its existence. Thus Aleksandr Rogov and Boris Floria, who offer the most consistent discussion of the development of ethnic, cultural, and

---

[15] Taras Kuzio states that in today's Ukraine "Kyivan Rus' is described as either a proto-Ukrainian state *in toto* or as a common but loose eastern Slavic state until the twelfth century. No current in Ukrainian historiography can accept that Kyivan Rus' was the first Russian state" ("Historiography and National Identity," p. 125). On the existence of one Rus' nationality, see Petro Tolochko's chapter on the ethnic development of Rus' from the ninth to the twelfth century in Tolochko and Tolochko, *Kyïvs'ka Rus'*, pp. 287–309. In this particular work, the term used to define the notion of Old Rus' nationality is "Old Rus' ethnocultural communality (*spil'nist'*)." The same term is applied consistently by Petro Tolochko's younger colleague Volodymyr Rychka (see his *Kyïvs'ka Rus': problema etnokul'turnoho rozvytku (konfesiinyi aspekt)* [Kyiv, 1994]). Another Ukrainian author, Yurii Pavlenko, uses the term "Old Rus' macro-ethnic entity" with reference to the same concept. See his "Teoretyko-metodolohichni zasady doslidzhennia etnohenezu skhidnoslov'ians'kykh narodiv u tsyvilizatsiinomu konteksti," *Ruthenica* 1 (2002): 9–24, here 22.

[16] See Igor' Danilevskii, "Drevnerusskaia gosudarstvennost' i 'narod Rus'': vozmozhnosti i puti korrektnogo opisaniia," *Ab Imperio* (Kazan), 2001, no. 3: 147–68.

[17] See Aleksei (Oleksii) Tolochko, "Voobrazhennaia narodnost'," *Ruthenica* 1 (2002): 112–17, here 115.

political identities in Kyivan Rus', find themselves in difficulty when seeking a chronological space in which to "park" the formation of the Old Rus' nationality. In searching for manifestations of an all-Rus' identity in the writings of the Kyivan era, they indicate a period from the mid-eleventh century to the beginning of the twelfth as the time when the term "Rus' Land" began to be applied to the Rurikid realm as a whole. The problem with that interpretation becomes apparent at the end of the article, when, in their effort to explain the local sympathies and even bias of the author of the Primary Chronicle, Rogov and Floria identify this same period as a time of growing separatist feeling among the Rus' elites – a process allegedly manifested in the revival of old tribal loyalties and reflected in the chronicle.[18]

Once scholars proceed from a discussion of factors that may or may not have been involved in the formation of the Old Rus' nationality to an analysis of sources that are supposed to reflect the existence of the all-Russian (East Slavic) identity, they encounter impassable obstacles in their way. If it is possible to find numerous examples of loyalty to what we today would call a Rus' state, there is very little evidence that Kyivan Rus' authors had a well-defined identity setting them apart from the non-Slavic subjects of the Rus' princes. This was one of the conclusions of Nikita Tolstoi, who was among the first to pose the question about the identity of Nestor, the presumed author of the Primary Chronicle. Tolstoi concluded that East Slavic (he called it "Russian") consciousness was a marginal component of the chronicler's identity.[19]

Owing to the scarcity of sources, recent discussions of the identity of Kyivan Rus' have focused mainly on the identity of Nestor the Chronicler. The question of whether Nestor the Hagiographer, a monk known from the Patericon of the Kyivan Cave Monastery, was indeed the author of the chronicle or wrote only a number of *Lives* of the monastery's fathers is still open for discussion. Some scholars claim that the very notion of Nestor the Chronicler is a product of the imaginations of fifteenth-century monks at the Cave Monastery. Others continue to defend the traditional view,

[18] The selection and interpretation of sources on the basis of which Rogov and Floria reached their conclusion about the application of the term "Rus' Land" to the whole Rurikid realm seems no less problematic. All of them except the *Sermon* (*Slovo*) of Metropolitan Ilarion bear clear indications of later (post-twelfth-century) revisions, while Ilarion's *Sermon*, contrary to the statements of Rogov and Floria, does not refer to "all the Rus' Land." See A. I. Rogov and B. N. Floria, "Formirovanie samosoznaniia drevnerusskoi narodnosti (po pamiatnikam drevnerusskoi pis'mennosti X–XII vv.)," in *Razvitie ètnicheskogo samosoznaniia slavianskikh narodov v èpokhu rannego srednevekov'ia* (Moscow, 1982), pp. 96–119, here 109–10; cf. 117.

[19] See N. I. Tolstoi, "Ètnicheskoe samopoznanie i samosoznanie Nestora Letopistsa, avtora 'Povesti vremennykh let,'" in *Issledovaniia po slavianskomu istoricheskomu iazykoznaniiu. Pamiati professora G. A. Khaburgaeva* (Moscow, 1993), pp. 4–12.

claiming that Nestor the Hagiographer and Nestor the Chronicler were one and the same.[20] Under these circumstances, the question lately posed by students of the Primary Chronicle about the "self-consciousness" of its author takes on a provocative double or even triple meaning. Was Nestor the Hagiographer also the author/editor of the Primary Chronicle? Did the work have one author or many? What can we say about the identity (or identities) of the author (or authors) of the chronicle?

The last question seems especially pertinent to our discussion. Fortunately, it can be dealt with irrespective of whether Nestor the Hagiographer was the author of the chronicle or not, or whether there was one author or more. We can treat the chronicle as a text that speaks in many voices and try to figure out what identities those voices represent. This approach has been tried in the last few decades by a number of scholars, although some of them believed that they were discussing the multiple identities of one chronicler – Nestor. Probably the first to approach the question was V. D. Koroliuk, who argued that the chronicler's historical outlook was defined by the impact of European (actually, Byzantine) education, Rus′ learning, and the idea of Slavic unity.[21] Other scholars count more layers of the chronicler's identity. Tolstoi, for example, held that there were five main levels of Nestor's "self-consciousness," including religious (Christian), intertribal (all-Slavic), intermediary tribal ("Russian" or East Slavic), particular tribal (Polianian), and statist, with the last expressed in Nestor's loyalty to the Rus′ Land.[22] Tolstoi's ideas were further developed by Viktor Zhivov, who probed the interrelations between Tolstoi's five levels of the chronicler's "self-consciousness." In so doing, he treated the religious and particular tribal levels as basic ones, on which foundation other levels of identity were constructed.[23] Also directly related to the discussion of Nestor's identity is Simon Franklin's recent summary of the "different categories of narrative [and] different criteria for constructing time" fused into one "historical" identity by the Rus′ bookmen of the late eleventh and early twelfth centuries. According to Franklin, these categories included "a dynastic story of Scandinavian

[20] For a restatement of the traditional view concerning the author of the Primary Chronicle, see Ziborov, *O letopisi Nestora*. For the revisionist view, see Oleksii Tolochko, "Nestor-litopysets′: bilia dzherel odniieï istoriohrafichnoï tradytsiï," *Kyïvs′ka starovyna*, 1996, nos. 4–5: 11–34.

[21] See V. D. Koroliuk, "K voprosu o slavianskom samosoznanii v Kievskoi Rusi i u zapadnykh slavian," in *Istoriia, kul′tura, fol′klor i ètnografiia slavianskikh narodov. Doklady sovetskoi delegatsii. VI Mezhdunarodnyi s′ezd slavistov* (Moscow, 1968), pp. 98–113.

[22] See Tolstoi, "Ètnicheskoe samopoznanie i samosoznanie Nestora Letopistsa."

[23] See V. M. Zhivov, "Ob ètnicheskom i religioznom samosoznanii Nestora Letopistsa," in *Slovo i kul′tura. Pamiati Nikity Il′icha Tolstogo*, vol. II (Moscow, 1998), pp. 321–37, here 329.

origins, an ethnic story of Slavonic origins, a conversion story of 'Greek' origins; a chronological framework of biblical origins, and a providential story justifying their own place in the overall scheme of time."[24]

How many identities (or levels of one identity) did the author or authors of the Primary Chronicle possess, and what impact did they have on his/their interpretation of the past? Did that identity really include the elements described above and, if so, was it limited to the above-mentioned five components, or did it represent a more complex and multilevel construct? We shall approach the question of the "hybrid" identity of the author of the Primary Chronicle by examining several legends that can be interpreted as vehicles facilitating the chronicler's search for the origins of his own identity.

Choosing an identity

"This is the tale of bygone years regarding the origin of the land of Rus', the first princes of Kyiv, and from what source the land of Rus' had its beginning," read the first lines of the Primary Chronicle.[25] Further reading indicates that its author (like some of his predecessors, no doubt) was struggling to bring together in one text a number of sometimes parallel and sometimes conflicting narratives of the origins of what he considered to be the "Rus' Land." One of those narratives was the history of the Rurikid princes who ruled the land; another was an ethnic history of Rus' through which the lineage of the princes of Kyiv could be introduced into the nation-based cosmographic history of the world developed by Byzantine authors of the time. To achieve his goal, the chronicler had to chart a course through a number of political and ethnocultural spheres and find a place for his princes, people and land in a number of imagined communities of the era. Each of those spheres endowed the author of the Primary Chronicle and the heroes of his narrative with different kinds of identity, all of which had to be at least partly reconciled and adjusted to one another.

What were those spheres? The Primary Chronicle contains stories about its main heroes' choice of three such identities. One was defined by the concept of belonging to a political entity, another by the idea of belonging to a broader Slavic world and sharing its language, culture, and letters, and the third by Christian belief and learning as received predominantly but not exclusively from Byzantium. Characteristically, the

---

[24] Franklin, "Russia in Time," p. 15.

[25] Adapted from *The Russian Primary Chronicle*, p. 51. Here and throughout the book, in quotations from English translations of primary sources, I use the Ukrainian form, "Kyiv," not "Kiev," when referring to the capital of Ukraine.

Primary Chronicle presents numerous and often conflicting stories of how the Rus' came to participate in all those communities. What strikes one in most of these stories is their common element. It is the princes and tribesmen with whom the chronicler associates himself who choose the community to which they are to belong, not the other way around. Thus the story told by the chronicler is that of his people's search for identity.

This certainly applies to the political identity of Rus', which was dynastic in origin. According to the Primary Chronicle, once upon a time a conglomerate of Slavic (Slovenians and Krivichians) and Finno-Ugric (Chud and Ves) tribes overthrew their overseas princes, the Varangians, and decided to become masters of their own destiny. It appears that very soon thereafter they confronted a set of problems familiar to any post-colonial nation: the richness of the land failed to deliver prosperity to the people, while lack of experience in self-government led to the collapse of the established order and the onset of internal strife. Under these circumstances, the newly independent tribes mustered a sufficient consensus in favor of going to their former overlords and asking them to take back their subjects. As might be expected, their submission was not unconditional. They wanted the overlords to abide by certain rules and judge them according to laws – and their conditions were apparently accepted. The chronicler presents the results of the joint Slavic and Finno-Ugric effort to ensure the arrival of medieval peacekeepers and nation-builders as follows:

They accordingly went overseas to the Varangian Rus': these particular Varangians were known as Rus', just as some are called Swedes, and others Normans, English, and Gotlanders, for they were thus named. The Chud, the Slovenians, the Krivichians, and the Ves then said to the people of Rus', "Our land is great and rich, but there is no order in it. Come to rule and reign over us." They thus selected three brothers, with their kinfolk, who took with them all of the Rus' and migrated.[26]

Thus, by selecting rulers who agreed to their conditions, the conglomerate of Finno-Ugric and Slavic tribes chose their new name and dynasty – all-important components of their identity.

Also freely chosen was another important component of that identity, the Eastern Christian religion. The Primary Chronicle includes a number of competing and contradictory stories about the baptism of Rus', but the longest, most prominent and elaborate of them explicitly says that the whole process was the result of a free choice made by the Rus', not by someone who chose them. Volodymyr, a descendant of Varangian warriors and prince of Kyiv, made the decision on behalf of the Rus'. The

[26] Adapted from *The Russian Primary Chronicle*, p. 59.

chronicler describes Volodymyr's choice of faith in terms no less colorful than those in his account of the invitation to the Varangians by the disillusioned tribesmen of the Novgorod region. Among those who allegedly tried to persuade Volodymyr to accept their religion were the Muslim Bulgars, the (Western) Christian Germans, the Judaic Khazars, and the (Eastern) Christian Greeks. Volodymyr, who, according to the chronicler, had six hundred wives and eight hundred concubines before accepting Christianity, was especially pleased to hear the words of the Muslim envoys about the endorsement of polygamy by their religion but refused to accept the conditions and limitations imposed by Islam. "Volodymyr listened to them," wrote the chronicler, "for he was fond of women and indulgence, regarding which he listened with pleasure. But circumcision and abstinence from pork and wine were disagreeable to him. 'Drinking,' said he, 'is the joy of Rus'. We can not exist without that pleasure.'"[27] Volodymyr sent envoys to all the lands from which the proselytizers had come to him. Eventually he decided to accept Eastern Christianity, as his envoys were particularly impressed by the glamor and beauty of the Byzantine churches.

The reader of the Primary Chronicle could learn about one more choice of identity made by his ancestors. It was revealed to him at numerous places in the text that the core Rus' tribes, which had acquired their name from the Varangians, were in fact Slavs who shared a common language, letters, and culture with numerous Slavic tribes to the west. According to the chronicler, the creation of the Slavic alphabet and the translation of Christian writings from Greek into Slavic took place at the initiative of three Slavic princes, Rostislav, Sviatopolk, and Kotsel, who ruled among the Moravians and sent their envoys to the Byzantine emperor, asking him for "teachers who can make known to us the words of the scriptures and their sense."[28] That was the beginning of the mission of SS. Cyril and Methodius to the Slavs, which resulted in the creation of the Cyrillic alphabet and the dissemination of Old Slavic writings in Bulgaria and Rus'. There is good reason to believe that the source of this tale in the Primary Chronicle is a text of either West Slavic (Czech) or South Slavic (Bulgarian) origin and that the initial goal of its author was to establish the equality of status of the Old Slavic literary language with Greek and Latin.[29] For the author of the Primary Chronicle, that Czech or Bulgarian

---

[27] Ibid., p. 97.   [28] Ibid., p. 62.

[29] There is a substantial literature on the subject, beginning with Aleksei Shakhma-tov's "Skazanie o prelozhenii knig na slavianskii iazyk," in *Zbornik v slavu Vatroslava Jagića* (Berlin, 1908), pp. 172–88. For recent contributions on the topic, see B. N. Floria, "Skazanie o prelozhenii knig na slovenskii iazyk. Istochniki, vremia i mesto napisaniia," *Byzantinoslavica* 46 (1985): 121–30; V. M. Zhivov, "Slavia Christiana i

legend could perform a number of different functions, including the presentation of the Rus' church as part of the larger Christian world, which included Rome. After all, it called St. Paul an apostle not only to the Slavs but also to the Rus'. The legend could also explain to readers of the Primary Chronicle how the Rus', who had acquired their name by inviting Varangian princes to rule them and their religious identity by choosing Byzantine Christianity, had become part of a world that might be called *Slavia Christiana*.

Should we trust these accounts of the medieval search for belonging? Not necessarily. First, the Primary Chronicle contains a number of contending versions of the origins of the Rus' Land, the baptism of Rus', and the apostolic origins of its Christian faith. Second, we know perfectly well that whatever problems former subjects encounter, they do not go back to their former overlords voluntarily; belief systems are not chosen by statesmen on the basis of the quality of church frescos; and alphabets are created by proselytizers, not at the initiative of those who are proselytized. Apart from that, there are good reasons to question the historical accuracy of all three tales. It is a well-established fact that the Varangians penetrated the Finno-Ugric and East Slavic territories by military conquest, not by invitation, while the episodes of choosing the faith and creating the Slavic alphabet find parallels in other literary traditions.[30] Should we then reject these legends entirely? By no means. Apart from the possibility that they reflect elements of historical reality, they represent a unique source for the study and understanding of what we may call the "hybrid" identity of the Rus' elites.

By retelling these tales, the authors and editors of the Primary Chronicle were explaining to their contemporaries how the mighty Rus' – who, judging by the writings of their first native-born metropolitan, Ilarion, took pride in being known in all parts of the earth – had exchanged their rulers and gods for a foreign name, dynasty, religion, and letters. Even more importantly for us, the chronicler's version of events made it appear that his ancestors chose all these voluntarily. In researching and reinterpreting the past, the chronicler was in fact providing historical legitimacy for the complex political and ethnocultural identity shared by his contemporaries. By the time of the writing and editing of the Primary Chronicle,

istoriko-kul'turnyi kontekst *Skazaniia o russkoi gramote*," in *Russkaia dukhovnaia kul'tura*, ed. L. Magarotto and D. Rizzi (Trent, 1992), pp. 71–125; Horace Lunt, "What the Rus' *Primary Chronicle* Tells Us about the Origin of the Slavs and of Slavic Writing," *Harvard Ukrainian Studies* 19 (1995): 335–57.

[30] On literary parallels of Prince Volodymyr's choice of faith as described in the Primary Chronicle, see Peter A. Rolland, "And Beauty Shall Save a Prince: Orthodox Theology and Kyjevan Texts," *Paleoslavica* 10 (*Zlatyie vrata. Essays Presented to Ihor Ševčenko on His Eightieth Birthday by His Colleagues and Students*, vol. 2), no. 2 (2002): 197–202.

elements of Slavic identity coexisted peacefully in the minds of its authors and editors with the legacy of the Scandinavian conquerors of the Slavs, as did pride in the glorious deeds of the pre-Christian Rus' (who often opposed the Byzantine Christians) with loyalty to Byzantine Christianity.

Mixing identities

If indeed Rus', Slavic, and Christian identities coexisted in the mind of the author of the Primary Chronicle, how did they interact with one another? Did they form one "hybrid" identity, and, if so, what were its main characteristics?

Let us begin our discussion of the question with an analysis of the chronicler's treatment of all-Slavic history. The Slavic theme was one of the most important in the chronicler's search for the origins of the Rus' Land. In the tradition of Christian ethnography, it allowed him to link his ancestors with the biblical account of the origins of world history and the tale of Noah's ark. Modeling his account on the Byzantine chronicles, the Kyivan author wrote that as the three sons of Noah divided the earth between them, one of the brothers, Japheth, was allotted the western and northern territories, which included the area north of the Black Sea, extending from the Danube in the west to the Volga in the east. According to the chronicler, the Slavs not only settled in Japheth's realm but were also descendants of his, linked with Noah's son through the biblical Noricians. The chronicler defined the Slavs as *iazyk* (people/nation, literally "tongue") on the basis of the language they used.[31] They had originally settled in the Danube region but then migrated to other parts of eastern Europe, with different Slavic tribes taking distinct names from the territories they settled.

It is generally accepted that the author of the Primary Chronicle borrowed the story of the Danube settlement of the Slavs, like the one about the creation of the Cyrillic alphabet, from a West or South Slavic source. He attempted to fit his people into the context created by that story. Literary sources about other Slavs and the common language they used came to the Rus' with the first Christian missionaries, who used Old Slavic texts to disseminate their message and declared the Rus' Slavs to be part of the broader Slavic world. The author of the Primary Chronicle clearly accepted the division of the Slavs into different tribes, but, on the basis of his own experience, he also tried to group some of those tribes into larger

---

[31] In medieval Rus' texts, *iazyk* is used to denote both language and people. In the latter case, it often implies the linguistic particularity of a given people. For the meaning of *iazyk* in Rus' texts, see V. V. Kolesov, *Mir cheloveka v slove drevnei Rusi* (Leningrad, 1986), pp. 132–36.

entities. He defined the tribes of Polianians, Lutichians, Mazovians, and Pomorians as descendants of the Liakhs (Poles). If this was indeed the chronicler's innovation, and not something he borrowed from one of his sources, his motive is quite clear. In his time, there was a centralized Polish state with which the Rus' had close military, diplomatic, commercial and other relations, and he was not satisfied with the mere division of the Slavs into minor tribes. Another large Slavic tribal group present in the Primary Chronicle is the Rus' Slavs. It consisted of the Dnipro Polianians, Derevlianians, Siverianians, and others, with the notable exception of the Radimichians and Viatichians, whom the chronicler regarded as descendants of the Liakhs. It is well known that the Viatichians remained beyond the control of the Rus' princes longer than any other Slavic tribe and resisted Christianization long after its acceptance in Kyiv. This probably meant that they were perceived as ethnically somewhat different from the rest of the Rus' Slavs, even though the chronicler notes that the pre-Christian Viatichians, Radimichians, and Siverianians had the same customs. Thus the picture of the Slavic world borrowed from foreign texts was revised and rendered more complex by the author of the Primary Chronicle in order to reflect the realities of the Rus' state and its relations with its neighbors.

As noted above, the Slavs were defined in the Primary Chronicle as a separate people on the basis of the language and grammar they used. The chronicler also knew another definition of a people, based not on linguistic but on religious criteria. Quoting from the chronicle of the Byzantine author Georgios Hamartolos, the Kyivan writer stated that each people had its own law or custom and asserted that the Christian people had its own Christian customs. According to the Primary Chronicle, Christian customs replaced those that existed among the Slavic tribes before the baptism of Rus', and thus, one might assume, turned them into one people (this is the impression one gains on encountering the chronicler's counterpositions of "us" [Christians] to the pagan Polovtsians).[32] The Kyivan author defined the Christian people/community, to which the Rus' Slavs belonged according to the logic of the chronicle, in the broadest possible terms. More often than not it included both Eastern and Western Christendom, as the chronicler often showed equal respect for Rome and

[32] See *The Russian Primary Chronicle*, pp. 57–58. Cf. *Povest' vremennykh let*, pt. 1, *Tekst i perevod* (Moscow and Leningrad, 1950), pp. 115–16. The most authoritative edition of the Primary Chronicle has recently been produced by Donald Ostrowski and published by the Harvard Ukrainian Research Institute. See the *Povest' vremennykh let: An Interlinear Collation and Paradosis*, comp. and ed. Donald Ostrowski; associate editor David Birnbaum; senior consultant Horace G. Lunt, Harvard Library of Early Ukrainian Literature, Texts, vol. 10, pts. 1–3 (Cambridge, Mass., 2003).

Constantinople. He declared St. Paul an apostle to the Rus', quoted the words of the pope of Rome in defense of the Slavic alphabet, and sent St. Andrew on a tour of Europe from Sinope to Rome. At the same time, in the legend about St. Volodymyr's choice of faith, the chronicler (or his source) made a clear statement in favor of Eastern Christianity. There is little doubt that different legends were included in the text of the Primary Chronicle by various authors and editors at different times. But the survival of all these legends, both pro-Western and pro-Eastern, as parts of a single text indicates the presence of a common factor that appealed to the early twelfth-century editors of the chronicle. That factor may have been the idea of the apostolic origins of Rus' Christianity, which found its best expression in the chronicle legend of St. Andrew visiting the site of the future capital of Rus', predicting its great future, and erecting a cross on the hills where Kyiv would be built. This explicit claim of apostolic status for the Kyivan church helped the chronicler present the Rus' as one of the original and most valuable members of the Christian people in spite of their very late entrance into the Christian community.

The ideas of Slavic ethnolinguistic unity and the unity of the Christian world emphasized the links between the core population of the Rus' realm and the rest of eastern Europe, a significant part of which found itself under the Byzantine cultural veil. At the same time, the Slavic idea poorly fitted the requirements of the Rus' "nation-building project." It defined the enemies of Rus' in the West, the Christian Poles or Liakhs, as relatives, while separating the Rus' Slavs from their non-Slavic countrymen, the Finno-Ugric tribes of Merians, Muroma, Cheremisians, Mordva, and others, not to mention the legendary initiators of the invitation to the Varangians, the Chud and Ves. Thus the non-Slavic tribes that were part of the Rus' realm and, in the chronicler's words, were paying tribute to Rus', were defined by him as peoples separate from the Slavs. Every non-Slavic tribe was referred to as a people (*iazyk*), for the chronicler believed that they all used different languages. That privilege was denied to the individual Slavic tribes, as their different customs apparently did not suffice to make them separate peoples. Apart from the non-Slavic tribes of the Rus' realm, the historical Varangians, allegedly the original bearers of the name of Rus', were also left outside the *Slavia Christiana*, the ethnocultural circle defined by membership in the Slavic and Christian world.[33]

As the text of the Primary Chronicle suggests, the concept of Rus' turned out to be very helpful in bringing together Slavic and Finno-Ugric,

---

[33] See the chronicler's description of the Rus' tribes in *The Russian Primary Chronicle*, p. 55. Cf. *Povest' vremennykh let*, p. 13.

Christian and non-Christian subjects under the sway of the Kyivan princes and separating them from their ethnic brethren and coreligionists outside the realm. For this to succeed in the long term, however, it was necessary that the name of Rus′, derived from the region's Varangian past, acquire strong and clear Slavic and Christian characteristics. The author of the Primary Chronicle struggled to meet that demand by seeking to reconcile different versions of the political and religious history of his homeland. Apart from the legend about the invitation to the Varangians, he offered a story about the rule of the local dynasty in Kyiv. There were at least three different versions of the baptism of Rus′: by the apostle Andrew, who blessed the land; by the Varangian warriors Askold and Dir, whose army accepted Christianity after its attack on Byzantium; and, finally, by Prince Volodymyr of Kyiv himself. As his narration of the pre-Christian history of Rus′ indicates, the chronicler saw no contradiction between loyalty to the pre-Christian Rus′ princes who gained glory through their campaigns against Byzantium and to his Byzantine coreligionists. In one instance, following the Byzantine chronicles, the author of the Primary Chronicle even referred to the attackers as the "godless Rus′," but in general he clearly took pride in the victories of the pagan princes Oleh and Sviatoslav over the "Greeks." In his effort to link the Varangian and Slavic past of Rus′, the chronicler reminds his readers again and again that the Rus′ and the Slavs are the same. "But the Slavs and the Rus′ are one people (*iazyk*), for it is because of the Varangians that the latter became known as Rus′, though originally they were Slavs."[34] Thus, by amalgamating the Varangian name and dynastic tradition, the Christian law/custom, and the Slavic language of the majority population of the Rus′ realm, the chronicler was turning the subjects of the Kyivan princes into a new people that became known as the people of Rus′.

As far as we know, the existence of such a people was originally proclaimed in the mid-eleventh century by the first native-born metropolitan of Kyiv, Ilarion, who wrote about the Rus′ *iazyk*, using that term to define his people.[35] Ilarion anticipated a later generation of chroniclers in its attempts to master the Byzantine conceptual arsenal and discursive practices. He was the first known author to place Rus′ and the Rus′ Land within the context of Christian time and space, borrowed by the Rus′ elites from Byzantium and deeply rooted in Mediterranean historiography. As Franklin notes, Ilarion "laid the foundations for the myth of collective

---

[34] Adapted from *The Russian Primary Chronicle*, p. 63. Cf. *Povest′ vremennykh let*, pp. 23, 219.

[35] For an English translation of Ilarion's *Sermon*, see Ilarion, "Sermon on Law and Grace," in *Sermons and Rhetoric of Kievan Rus′*, trans. and with introduction by Simon Franklin (Cambridge, Mass., 1991), pp. 3–30.

Christian identity for the Rus."[36] That identity project was further developed and elaborated in the writings of "Nestor," whose name stands for the Rus' chroniclers of the late eleventh and early twelfth centuries in general.

From tribe to people

For the chronicler, the term "Rus'" was originally associated with the "Varangians," but later in his narrative he clearly distinguished the two groups. He used the term "Rus'" for Scandinavians, while "Varangians," in his usage, represented a mixture of Scandinavians, Slavic, and Finno-Ugric warriors who composed the retinue of the Rus' princes. Essential to the chronicler's effort to blend the Varangians and Slavs into one people, the Rus', was the history of one of the East Slavic tribes, the Polianians. Expounding his argument that the Slavs and the Rus' were one and the same, the chronicler wrote: "While some Slavs were termed Polianians, their speech (rich') was still Slavic. They were known as Polianians because they lived in the fields, but they had the same Slavic language (iazyk)."[37] Thus the author of the Primary Chronicle clearly treated the Rus', Slavs, and Polianians as the same people. Who were the Polianians of the Primary Chronicle? Judging by its text, there were two kinds of Polianians. The first were listed along with the Lutichians, Mazovians, and Pomorians as part of the "Liakh" group of Slavic tribes. These Liakh Polianians were mentioned only once. When they cropped up again in the chronicler's discussion of Slavic settlement along the Danube, he simply replaced them with "the Polianians, who are now called the Rus'."[38]

Throughout the rest of the Primary Chronicle, the Kyivan author treated the Rus' Polianians as a Slavic group that settled along the Dnipro River. He further specified their location in his description of the apostle Andrew's journey along the Dnipro, claiming that the Polianians lived in their own settlements on the hills (elsewhere he wrote that they lived in the fields, apparently failing to note the contradiction between these statements). When St. Andrew reached the Polianian region, he allegedly pointed to the hills and addressed his disciples as follows: "'See ye these hills? So shall the favor of God shine upon them that on this spot a great city shall arise, and God shall erect many churches therein.' He drew near the hills, and having blessed them, he set up a cross."[39] Thus it was the Polianian territory and, by extension, the Polianians themselves who

---

[36] Franklin and Shepard, *The Emergence of Rus*, p. 213.
[37] Adapted from *The Russian Primary Chronicle*, p. 63. Cf. *Povest' vremennykh let*, pp. 23, 219.
[38] *The Russian Primary Chronicle*, p. 62.   [39] Ibid., p. 54.

were blessed by the apostle Andrew. If the chronicler's account is to be believed, the first apostolic baptism of the Rus' was that of the Polianians. Comparing Polianian pre-Christian customs with those of other Rus' Slavs, the chronicler (who apparently did not consider it important to describe the customs of the Rus' non-Slavs) characterized them as "mild and peaceful," alluding to some of the most important Christian virtues. He also wrote that unlike other tribes, such as the Derevlianians, Radimichians, Viatichians, Krivichians, and Siverianians, the Polianians had marriage customs even before their baptism. The chronicler openly mocked other Slavic tribes. Apparently he considered the Viatichians the most barbaric of the lot, as they still maintained their pagan traditions at the time the Primary Chronicle was written.[40] He also slighted the Novgorodian Slovenians, ridiculing their saunas in his account of St. Andrew's visit to their lands.[41]

According to the chronicler, the Polianians had their own ruling dynasty established by the three brothers Kyi, Shchek, and Khoryv, who founded the city of Kyiv. He rejected legends that presented Kyi as a simple ferryman and insisted on his princely status. Once the Kyi dynasty died out, the Polianians paid tribute to the Khazars. Then they were ruled by the Varangian warriors Askold and Dir, who established their control over the "Polianian Land" with the help of their fellow Varangians. Eventually these warriors were killed by the army of another Varangian, Oleh, who acted on behalf of the young Varangian prince Ihor, son of Rurik – the legendary founder of the Rus' dynasty. Since Askold and Dir were allegedly members of Rurik's retinue and established their rule over Kyiv without his consent (Rurik apparently allowed them to go to Constantinople but not to settle in Kyiv), the chronicler did not condemn Oleh's treacherous murder of the two Varangian warriors. He went on to state that those who came to Kyiv as part of Oleh's army received the name of Rus'. They included not only Varangians but also representatives of Slavic and Finno-Ugric tribes – the Novgorod Slovenians, Krivichians, Meria, Chud, and Ves – all of whom, except the Meria, had issued the original invitation to the Varangian princes, according to another legend recorded by the chronicler.[42] Thus, if one assumes that the chronicler's account indeed reflects certain historical realities, the term "Rus'," originally used to denote the Varangians, eventually spread to the retinue recruited from Slavic and non-Slavic tribes that came under Varangian control. According to the chronicler, once Oleh established his seat in Kyiv he proclaimed it "the mother of Rus' cities," in other words, the capital of Rus'. Novgorod was supposed to pay tribute to the rulers of

---

[40] Ibid., p. 56.   [41] Ibid., p. 54.   [42] Ibid., pp. 60–61; cf. 59.

Kyiv. Then it was the Polianians' turn to accept the name of "Rus'." Having given this account, the chronicler evidently felt justified in declaring that the Rus', the Slavs, and the Polianians were one and the same.[43]

As we try to put the chronicler's diverse terminology into some order, it becomes only too obvious that he was far from consistent in his choice of terms and names. Although he conflates the Slavs, Polianians, and Rus' into one group (as noted above), in a subsequent passage he does not hesitate to list the Rus', Varangians, Polianians, Slovenians, Krivichians, and other tribes as separate entities.[44] Still, the early disappearance of the name of the Polianians – the chronicler's favorites among the Eastern Slavs – from the chronicle text indicates that the chronicler did indeed consider them to be the same as the Rus'. The Polianians' western neighbors, the Derevlianians, and toponyms derived from their name are mentioned in the chronicler's discussion of the rule of Volodymyr the Great, under the year 988, and were also known to the continuators of the Primary Chronicle.[45] The chronicler mentions the Siverianians, the Polianians' neighbors to the northeast, under the year 1024.[46] But there is not a word about the Polianians in the discussion of these periods of Rus' history – they are last mentioned by the chronicler under the year 944!

The disappearance of the Polianians and the blending of their tribal name with the political designation "Rus'," and later with the Kyivans, a name derived from their principal city (similarly, the Siverians eventually became known as Chernihovians, the Slovenians as Novgorodians, and so on), seems plausible enough, given that their territory became the center of the Rus' realm and was thus closely associated with the name of the polity. Suspicion is aroused, however, by the lack of archaeological evidence distinguishing the Polianians of the chronicle from their immediate neighbors. What the archaeologists have found is a series of burials associated with the so-called "retinue culture," which is distinguishable in social but not ethnocultural terms from burials on the territory of other tribes mentioned in the Primary Chronicle. Suspicion is heightened even more when one takes into account the minuscule territory allocated to that allegedly powerful tribe by the chronicler, who assigns huge territories to other Rus' groups. Were the Polianians indeed a separate tribe on a par with the Derevlianians, Slovenians and others, as the

---

[43] Ibid., p. 63.

[44] Ibid., p. 72. For a recent discussion of the interrelation of the terms "Rus'," "Varangians," and "Polianians" in the Primary Chronicle, see V. Ia. Petrukhin, *Nachalo étnokul'turnoi istorii Rusi IX–XI vekov* (Smolensk, 1995), pp. 69–82.

[45] Petrukhin, *Nachalo étnokul'tumoi istorii Rusi IX–XI vekov*, p. 119; *Litopys Rus'kyi za ipats'kym spyskom*, ed. and trans. Leonid Makhnovets' (Kyiv, 1989), p. 189.

[46] See *The Russian Primary Chronicle*, p. 135.

chronicler maintains, or were they merely a local Slavic population that acquired a separate identity by falling under the control of the Varangians earlier than neighboring tribes? By mixing with Scandinavians and representatives of other Slavic and non-Slavic groups that constituted the retinue of the first Kyivan princes, that population might indeed have taken on the cosmopolitan characteristics of those who inhabited the capital of a huge empire and then looked down on their "uncultured" brethren. Such a postulate finds support in Constantine VII Porphyrogenitus's description of Rus' rule in Kyiv in the mid-tenth century, as well as in the archaeological data.[47] The linguistic hypothesis according to which the language spoken in Kyiv and region was "all-Rus'" in the sense that it reflected features of a number of Rus' dialects also points in that direction.[48] If that was indeed the case, then the author of the Primary Chronicle had every right to claim at the beginning of the twelfth century that the Rus', Slavs, and Polianians were one and the same.

Thus our rereading of the Primary Chronicle undermines some scholars' belief in the chronicler's highly developed tribal identity. It is hard to imagine that Nestor or, for that matter, any other author or editor of the chronicle could have thought of himself as belonging to a tribe that had ceased to exist, even in his own imagination, at least a century and a

[47] On the difficulty of locating Polianian archaeological monuments and the assumption that Kyiv was not the center of any particular tribe but the intertribal center of a vast realm, see Tolochko and Tolochko, Kyïvs'ka Rus', pp. 32–35. The authors also suggest that the very existence of Rus' Polianians and Slovenians could be a figment of the chronicler's imagination, as he needed those phantom tribes in order to establish a link between Scandinavian and Slavic Rus' (ibid., pp. 34–35). Although this hypothesis finds some support in textual analysis of the Primary Chronicle, it requires further investigation. If it is correct, then one might suggest that the above-mentioned tribes also perform another function within the parameters of Nestor's narrative, linking the Rus' Slavs with the Danube Slavs who appear in the South Slavic texts used by the chronicler. The name of the Slovenians corresponds to that of Slavs in general in sources that also use the name "Polianians" to designate one of the West Slavic tribes. But the hypothesis can more easily be applied to the Polianians than to the Slovenians. After all, if the Polianians disappear from the Primary Chronicle after the entry for 944 – a completely mythical time for the author of the chronicle and his contemporaries – the Slovenians are present in the account of the rule of Yaroslav the Wise under the year 1034, almost a century later, much closer to the times of the virtual Nestor and his contemporaries, when chronicle writing supposedly emerged in Kyiv (see The Russian Primary Chronicle, p. 136). Moreover, references to the Slovenians appear in the Rus' Law.

[48] Aleksei Shakhmatov first suggested this hypothesis in his Vvedenie v kurs istorii russkogo iazyka, pt. 1 (Petrograd, 1916), pp. 81–83. It was subsequently accepted by Mykhailo Hrushevsky, who wrote about the all-Ukrainian and even all-Slavic character of the language spoken in Kyiv (see his "Poraionne istorychne doslidzhennia Ukraïny i obsliduvannia Kyïvs'koho uzla," in Kyïv ta ioho okolytsi v istoriï ta pam'iatkakh [Kyiv, 1926], pp. 1–23, here 22). For a critique of the hypothesis, see V. V. Nimchuk, "Literaturni movy Kyïvs'koï Rusi," in Istoriia ukraïns'koï kul'tury, vol. I (Kyiv, 2001), pp. 694–708.

half before his own times. A comparison with modern historiography can help elucidate this point. It may be assumed that the Polianians were the chronicler's heroes, just as the Antes were the heroes of Mykhailo Hrushevsky in his reconstruction of early Ukrainian history. Yet Hrushevsky had a Ukrainian identity, not an Antean one, even though he considered the Antes to be the first known ancestors of the Ukrainian ethnos. The same probably applied to the author of the Primary Chronicle, for whom the Polianians represented the ancient past. There were no Polianians in his own time, nor was there a Polianian identity. That is why he never tired of repeating that the Rus' (a people, not a territorial or political alliance) and the Polianians were one and the same. The ethnic Rus' replaced the tribal Polianians as the protagonists of the Primary Chronicle from the beginning of the tenth century and continued to dominate the narrative until its very end. Thus, if the chronicler associated himself with a particular group, that group was not tribal but ethnocultural and territorial, and its name was Rus'.

The Rus' Land

"What is the origin of the Land of Rus'?" As noted above, this was one of the major questions addressed by the author of the Primary Chronicle, who appears to have been no less preoccupied than modern historians with the vexed question of origins. Yet the chronicler has us at a considerable disadvantage in dealing with the question, not only because we are much further removed in time from the subject of our research but also because we do not fully understand what the author of our main historical source had in mind when he wrote about the "Rus' Land." Did he mean the state, the people, the territory, or all of these? Present-day scholars agree that the term could apply to them all.

What also remains blurred is the geographical and thus the ethno-political extent of the Rus' Land. Was it the territory around Kyiv, all the possessions of the Kyivan princes, or something in between? Students of the Primary Chronicle noted long ago that its author referred to the Rus' Land in narrow and broad senses. The first included the core possessions of the Kyivan princes – the Kyiv, Chernihiv, and Pereiaslav territories. The Rus' Land in the broad sense extended to the farthest regions under Kyiv's control. When and how did these two concepts come into existence? Historians are divided on which came first, the "narrow" or the "broad" concept of the Rus' Land. One group, which includes the author of the fundamental monograph on the issue, A. N. Nasonov, claims that the term was originally used in relation to the Southern Rus' and only later extended to the whole territory of the Kyivan state.[49] Another group, represented by such scholars as D. S. Likhachev and A. V. Soloviev, claims that the term originally applied to the whole territory of the Rus' state, and only in the twelfth century, with the growing decentralization of Kyivan Rus', did it come to designate the land around Kyiv.[50]

What does the text of the Primary Chronicle tell us about the meaning of the term "Rus' Land," and does it help resolve the controversy that began half a century ago? To begin with, we should note that the evidence of the chronicle itself is very confusing. The author of the chronicle dated the emergence of the "Rus' Land" to 852, which he regarded as the year of a Rus' expedition against Constantinople, taking his information from the Byzantine chronicle of Georgios Hamartolos.[51] He apparently found some additional information about the Rus' in the texts of the treaties of 907 and 944 between Rus' and Byzantium. Both of them defined Rus' as the lands of Kyiv, Chernihiv, and Pereiaslav, only occasionally adding other Rus' towns to this triad (the treaty of 907 lists Polatsk, Rostov, and Liubech among those other towns).[52] But there is serious doubt that the dates attached to the texts of these treaties are reliable. Indeed, there is good reason to believe that the treaties are at least partly the result of later creative editing of original texts, either by the author of the Primary Chronicle or by his predecessors. For example, the text of the Rus' treaty of 911 with Byzantium, which is considered more reliable than the other two, does not include a list of Rus' towns. Besides, we know very well that neither in 907 nor in 944 could Chernihiv and Pereiaslav be regarded as major centers of the Rurikid realm. The archaeological and historical data, including the Primary Chronicle itself, indicate that until the end of the tenth century the territories around Chernihiv and Pereiaslav either were not settled at all or were beyond the control of the Kyivan princes. It has also been argued that princely centers were established in those territories only in the early eleventh century, at least a hundred years after the treaty of 907.[53]

---

[49] For a summary of Nasonov's argument, see his concluding remarks in "*Russkaia zemlia*" i obrazovanie territorii drevnerusskogo gosudarstva. Istoriko-geograficheskoe issledovanie (Moscow, 1951), pp. 216–20.

[50] See D. S. Likhachev's commentary in *Povest' vremennykh let* 2: 239–40; Alexander Soloviev, "Der Begriff 'Rußland' im Mittelalter," in *Studien zur älteren Geschichte Osteuropas* (Graz and Cologne, 1956), pp. 149–50. Cf. Charles J. Halperin, "The Concept of the Russian Land from the Ninth to the Fourteenth Centuries," *Russian History* 2 (1975): 29–38.

[51] See *The Russian Primary Chronicle*, pp. 58. Cf. Tolochko and Tolochko, *Kyïvs'ka Rus'*, pp. 25, 60–61.

[52] See *The Russian Primary Chronicle*, pp. 64, 74.

[53] See Tolochko and Tolochko, *Kyïvs'ka Rus'*, p. 122.

Does this mean that the Rus' Land, with its centers in Kyiv, Chernihiv, and Pereiaslav, was a mere figment of someone's imagination? Apparently, with regard to the tenth and even the early eleventh centuries, it does. The area on the left bank of the Dnipro, where the Chernihiv and Pereiaslav districts (*volosti*) were located, was attached to the Kyiv realm quite late, in the early eleventh century, as a result of the energetic colonization policy of Prince Volodymyr. According to the chronicler, the area was fortified and colonized by settlers from other parts of the realm: Slovenians, Krivichians, Chud, and Viatichians, who were the last East Slavic tribe to come under Kyiv's control. As Oleksii Tolochko has recently pointed out, this ethnically mixed conglomerate, which had little other identity than "people of the Rus' prince," found itself in a situation that made it much easier to forget about tribal differences than in other parts of the Rus' realm and forge a new Rus' identity in a fierce confrontation with the nomadic "other."[54] Such, in all likelihood, were the origins of the concept of the Rus' Land in the narrow sense. Two of the three centers of that land, Chernihiv and Pereiaslav, rose to prominence only after the death of Volodymyr. Chernihiv, for example, unexpectedly became the capital of half of Rus' when Volodymyr's son Mstyslav made it his seat in 1024. Pereiaslav's real rise to prominence occurred even later and was associated with the activities of Prince Volodymyr Monomakh at the end of the eleventh century.

It was only after the death of Yaroslav the Wise that the three princely sees of Kyiv, Chernihiv, and Pereiaslav become the most prized possessions of the Rurikid clan. According to the Primary Chronicle, Yaroslav assigned them to his eldest sons. Although the question of whether Yaroslav's will ever existed is open for discussion, the chronicler's information about the rule of his three eldest sons in those cities has not aroused suspicion among scholars.[55] Kyiv, Chernihiv, and Pereiaslav were designated as the only three patrimonies of the whole Rus' Land at the Liubech congress of Rus' princes in 1097. By that time, the era of unchallenged rule of the Kyivan princes over the entire Rus' realm had already passed. The princes quarreled and fought with one another over the *volosti*, which were in short supply owing to the slow pace of the Rus' state's territorial expansion (it almost came to a halt in the times of Yaroslav the Wise). The congress established a new political order whereby the Kyivan prince emerged as the supreme arbiter but not the authoritative ruler of the realm. Instead, real power was concentrated in the hands of the heirs of Yaroslav's three eldest sons, the princes of Kyiv, Chernihiv, and Pereiaslav. Those huge principalities were designated as

[54] Ibid., p. 121.   [55] Ibid., p. 177.

patrimonies or unconditional possessions of the princes who held power there at that time, while the rest of the Rurikid clan found itself in conditional possession of lands that could be taken away from them by the three senior princes. As some of the Rurikids now became more equal than others, so did Rus' defined in the narrow sense of the term, which was in the unconditional possession of the princes of Kyiv, Chernihiv, and Pereiaslav, while the other Rus', more broadly defined, was conditionally held by the less fortunate members of the clan.

It appears that in the post-Liubech Rus' world the concept of the Rus' Land and the idea of its defense against the incursions of the steppe nomads (of whom the Polovtsians were strongest at that time) became an extremely important ideological construct. As the power of the Kyivan princes continued to decline, this idea became essential for enhancing the solidarity of the Rurikid clan, mobilizing their forces in support of the common cause and keeping the dispossessed princes in line by emphasizing the common good. It seems that there was one prince who benefited most from the concept of the "Rus' Land" as the common property of the Rurikids. His name was Volodymyr Monomakh, and in the late eleventh and early twelfth centuries he was the prince of Pereiaslav. Monomakh's prominence in the struggle with the steppe nomads made him one of the most popular Rus' princes and allowed him to take power as the new prince of Kyiv in 1113 in defiance of the Liubech provisions. One might assume that Monomakh's skillful exploitation of the concept of the unity of the Rus' Land helped him recentralize the Rus' realm once he became prince of Kyiv. This could explain the importance of that idea in the text of the Primary Chronicle, which is believed to have been composed, edited, and reedited in Kyiv during the first five years of Monomakh's rule.[56]

What does this detour into the political history of Rus' tell us about the meaning that the term "Rus' Land" acquired in the text of the Primary Chronicle? First of all, it indicates that the concept itself, in both its narrow and broader senses, may have been a product of the political thinking of the post-Yaroslav era, when princely feuds threatened or tore apart the unity of the formerly unified realm. Under these circumstances, the concept of the Rus' Land was supposed to help prevent the breakup of the Rus' polity and was fully exploited to that end by the author of the Primary Chronicle. As Viktor Zhivov has recently noted, two-thirds of the references to the "Rus' Land" in the chronicle (there are more than sixty altogether) pertain to events after the rule of Yaroslav, and only one-third concern earlier periods. It is only in the final portion of the chronicle

---

[56] Ibid., pp. 198–213.

that references to the Rus' Land take on the very specific connotation of preserving the unity of the Rurikid realm as a political entity.[57] Does this mean that the concept of the Rus' Land – the main "hero" of the Primary Chronicle, with the discussion of whose origins the narrative begins – was read back by the chronicler into the events of early Rus' history? Most probably, it does. But does it also mean that the concept itself was the product of the political thinking of the early twelfth century and that the chronicler had to "implant" it into his discussion of events in the second half of the eleventh century? Probably not. There is reason to believe that the concept was already present in earlier versions of the chronicle. Moreover, there is a reference to the Rus' Land in the *Sermon* of Metropolitan Ilarion, which comes from the mid-eleventh century.[58]

What was the chronological relation between the narrow and broad senses of the term "Rus' Land"? Did the former replace the latter, or was it the other way around? As noted earlier, this question has preoccupied many scholars of the chronicle over the last fifty years. Unfortunately, we must leave it unanswered. As the text of the Primary Chronicle that we possess today was produced in the early decades of the twelfth century, when there appears to have been general agreement that "Rus' Land" meant the territory around Kyiv, Chernihiv, and Pereiaslav, we can only guess whether the term really had a broader meaning in the eleventh century or, most particularly, in the tenth. What we can assert is that in the overwhelming majority of cases the Rus' Land as the "protagonist" of the Primary Chronicle and the object of the chronicler's primary loyalty meant the triangle of Kyiv, Chernihiv, and Pereiaslav. For the most part, as Nasonov has shown convincingly, it did not include the rest of the Kyivan realm.

The Rus' Land of the chronicle was predominantly Slavic in ethnic composition, as were the Polianians, but there was a fair admixture of Scandinavians and Finno-Ugrians. The chronicler listed representatives of Varangians, Slovenians, Krivichians, and even Meria and Chud among Oleh's conquerors of Kyiv in 882 [6390]. He also named some of them (Slovenians, Krivichians, and Chud), along with the Viatichians, as settlers of the steppes to the south of Kyiv and on the left bank of the Dnipro in Volodymyr's times.[59] These were the territories around Kyiv, Chernihiv, and Pereiaslav – lands not assigned by the chronicler to any tribe except the Polianians. They constituted the Rus' Land of the chronicle in the narrow meaning of the term, and they were the homeland

---

[57] See Zhivov, "Ob ètnicheskom i religioznom samosoznanii Nestora Letopistsa," pp. 330–31.

[58] See Ilarion, "Sermon on Law and Grace," p. 18.

[59] See *The Russian Primary Chronicle*, pp. 60–61, 119.

of the chronicler and his Rus' people. The identity produced by loyalty to that land had little to do with the statist level of Nestor's identity as defined by Nikita Tolstoi. The chronicler's dominant level of identity was not tribal, nor was it statist in the sense of loyalty to the whole Rurikid realm. Instead, his Rus' Land identity was territorially rooted in the Kyiv-Chernihiv-Pereiaslav triangle – the shared territory of the Rurikid clan.

The "outer Rus'"

As early as the second half of the tenth century, the Byzantines were faced with the problem of distinguishing between the Rus' territories per se and the lands controlled by the Rus' princes. Thus, in his *De administrando imperio*, Constantine VII Porphyrogenitus wrote about Rus' proper and "outer Rus'."[60] The Rus' chronicler, unfortunately, did not develop a special terminology to distinguish between those two notions. Like any resident of a metropolis, he usually confused the name of his homeland with the name of the empire that it ruled. In that regard he resembled his modern-day successors. When nineteenth-century St. Petersburg historians referred to "Russia," did they mean Russia per se, the lands of the Eastern Slavs, or the Russian Empire, which included large parts of the Caucasus and Central Asia? Only the context in which the term was used would allow us to determine its exact meaning. This observation is equally valid for works of the twelfth and the twenty-first centuries.

If the concept of the Rus' Land in its narrow meaning was a product of the political thinking and development of the second half of the eleventh century, so must have been the main components of the chronicler's identity associated with that concept. But how long did the concept and its associate identity manage to survive? It appears that for the remainder of the pre-Mongol period of Rus' history, the city of Kyiv, though weakened and declining in power, continued to serve as the imagined center of the Rus' Land and a valued prize in the wars waged by the non-Kyivan princes for dominance in the Rus' Land. The chroniclers therefore continued, albeit with little success, to call upon the princes to look to the welfare of the Rus' Land and maintain its unity. They also continued to locate the Rus' Land within the boundaries of the Kyiv, Chernihiv, and Pereiaslav triangle and refer to its rulers as princes of Rus'. The authors of the Kyiv Chronicle, the early thirteenth-century continuation of the Primary Chronicle, were consistent in treating Chernihiv and Pereiaslav as parts of the Rus' Land, while excluding Smolensk, Polatsk, Vladimir on the

---

[60] Nasonov, *"Russkaia zemlia" i obrazovanie territorii drevnerusskogo gosudarstva*, p. 31.

Kliazma, and the lands of the Derevlianians and the Viatichians.[61] Thus
the identity associated with the concept of the Kyiv-Chernihiv-Pereiaslav
Rus' was clearly alive and well in Kyiv throughout the twelfth and early
thirteenth centuries, while the other lands ruled by the Rurikids were
viewed merely as possessions, not as part of the Rus' Land per se.

Regarding the Rus' Land as his home territory, the author of the Primary Chronicle divided the rest of the Rus' realm into lands as well: the
Novgorod Land, the Smolensk Land, the Polatsk Land, the Suzdal Land,
and so on. In the text of the chronicle, this classification replaced the previous division of Rus' into tribal districts. Most of the tribes, not unlike the
Polianians, figure only in the chronicler's account of events taking place in
the tenth century. Although the names of the territories allegedly settled
by those tribes are still to be encountered in the description of eleventh-
century developments, they also eventually disappear from the text of
the chronicle. (It is not entirely impossible that toponyms current in the
chronicler's day were transformed in his imagination into the names of
tribes that allegedly settled those territories in ancient times.) The chronicler renamed some tribes according to the places they settled: for example, the Polianians-Rus' became Kyivans, the Slovenians Novgorodians,
and the Krivichians Polatsians. The Meria, whose lands were colonized
by the Slavs, turned into Rostovians, and so on. Other tribes, such as the
Ulychians and Tivertsians, disappeared from the narrative altogether.
Many tribes gave rise to more than one new name: the Siverianians, for
instance, were eventually replaced by the Novhorodians (named after
Novhorod-Siverskyi) and Kurskians. The existence of the Rus' Land did
not in and of itself prevent the Kyivans, Chernihovians, and Pereiaslavians
from having distinct identities in the Kyivan chronicles. Thus the division of the Rurikid realm into semi-independent principalities became
the main parameter identifying its population. These new local identities
represented the new political structure of the Kyivan state, not the former
tribal and cultural divisions – a clear gain, at first glance, for the cause
of Rus' ethnocultural unity. Yet the Rus' conglomerate was moving ever
closer to disintegration along new political fault lines, jeopardizing the
whole unity project of the Kyivan political and intellectual elites.[62]

[61] See the evidence summarized in Nasonov, "*Russkaia zemlia*" *i obrazovanie territorii
drevnerusskogo gosudarstva*, p. 29, and A. N. Robinson, *Literatura drevnei Rusi v liter-
aturnom protsesse srednevekov'ia, XI–XIII vv.* (Moscow, 1980), pp. 227–28.
[62] I am siding here with Anton Gorsky, who argues against Valentin Sedov's hypothesis
that the twelfth-century lands evolved on the basis and within the boundaries of the
former tribes. Gorsky has demonstrated that the term "land" was applied in the twelfth
century to semi-independent principalities whose territories were formed with no direct
reference to the lands of the former tribes. See Anton Gorskii, "O drevnerusskikh 'zemliakh,'" *Ruthenica* (Kyiv) 1 (2002): 55–63. Cf. Sedov, *Drevnerusskaia narodnost'*.

So far we have discussed the identity of the author of the Primary Chronicle, which to some degree mirrored that of the Kyivan secular and religious elites. What of the interests and identities of those outside Kyiv, or, to be more precise, outside the Rus' Land in the narrow sense? There are clear indications that the old elites in the tribal lands annexed by Ihor, Volodymyr, and Yaroslav to the Rurikid realm did not like the economic exploitation or the political and cultural "Rusification" imposed on them by the new rulers with the help of the sword. The Derevlianians killed Ihor in the tenth century, the Polatsk princes maintained the de facto independence of their realm well into the eleventh century, and the Viatichians continued their resistance to forced Christianization until the early twelfth century, killing Christian missionaries sent to them from the Kyivan Caves. Dispossessed princes of the Rurikid clan, who had no right or opportunity to acquire patrimonies in the Kyiv-Chernihiv-Pereiaslav triangle, were busy creating their own patrimonies outside the Rus' Land. To what degree can all these events be regarded as manifestations of the separate identities of local elites? Did the members of those elites associate themselves with the Rus' Land in the narrow sense, like the Kyivan chronicler, or did they reject that association? It is hard to give any definite answer to this question, for Kyiv long remained the major, if not the only, center of learning and chronicle writing in the Rus' lands, and most of what we know about Rus' identity comes from writings produced by Kyivans in the interests of Kyivans. But the situation clearly changed in the twelfth century as the power of Kyiv declined and chronicle writing proliferated in other centers.

Today we have chronicle complexes produced in the three main centers of Rus' outside the Kyiv-Chernihiv-Pereiaslav realm. They come from Novgorod, Vladimir-Suzdal Rus', and Galicia-Volhynia, where chronicle writing was conducted in the thirteenth and fourteenth centuries with the support of the local princes. To be sure, chronicles were also written elsewhere in Rus', including the two other centers of the Rus' Land, Chernihiv, and Pereiaslav, but these are the complexes that have survived. What do they tell us about local identities in the land that Constantine Porphyrogenitus called "outer Rus'"?[63] First of all, there are clear indications that the chroniclers in those centers were very well aware that their territories did not belong to the Rus' Land per se. Very important in this regard is the case of Novgorod, one of the two original centers of the Kyivan state. It appears that neither foreign writers nor Kyivan chroniclers nor the Novgorodians themselves considered their realm to be part

---

[63] The question of which Rus' centers besides Kyiv belonged to "inner" Rus' and which ones besides Novgorod to "outer" Rus' continues to be discussed. See Petrukhin, *Nachalo ètnokul'turnoi istorii Rusi*, pp. 62–69.

of the Rus' Land. Constantine Porphyrogenitus, for his part, regarded Novgorod as part of "outer Rus'." He had good reason to do so, for the Novgorodians continued to pay tribute to Kyiv up to the beginning of the eleventh century – a tribute from which the Rus' territory around Kyiv was exempt, indicating that the Novgorodians belonged to the category of tribes dependent on the Rus' princes. The author of the Primary Chronicle listed the Novgorod Slovenians as part of Rus', but not of the Rus' Land. The Kyivan chronicler mentions the Slovenians for the last time in his account of the rule of Yaroslav the Wise and then refers to the local population as Novgorodians, but the latter fared no better than the Slovenians when it came to the membership of their territory in the Rus' Land. The Novgorod chroniclers, for their part, referred to their land as the Novgorod country (*oblast'*) and never (prior to the Mongol invasion) confused it with Rus' or the Rus' Land to the south.[64]

To be sure, the Rurikid princes who ruled in the "outer" Rus' of the twelfth and early thirteenth centuries knew perfectly well that although they did not belong to the Rus' Land per se, they were part of the Rus' realm. Their membership in the Rurikid clan legitimized their rule on the periphery. Moreover, interference in their affairs by Kyivan princes and metropolitans, as well as their own attempts to take control of Kyiv, kept them aware of their ties with the center. The sense of belonging to a common entity was also nurtured by what Benedict Anderson (referring to a much later period) has called "pilgrimages" within the territory of an "imagined community." According to Oleksii Tolochko, in the case of Rus' such "pilgrimages" included the constant rotation of princes and their retinues between the princely centers and Orthodox clergymen between church eparchies.[65] True, after the Liubech Congress the territory in which the princes of a given branch of the Rurikid clan were allowed to make their "pilgrimages" was dramatically reduced, leading to the creation of new, much smaller "imagined communities," but the church continued its former practices. The most prominent princes also maintained an interest in the affairs of potential allies and rivals.

Christian Rus'

A reading of the Primary Chronicle indicates that despite its author's primary loyalty to the Rus' Land in the narrow sense, he also had a clearly defined "all-Rus'" identity and cared deeply about the unity of

---

[64] On the use of the term "Rus'" in the Novgorod chronicles, see *Davnia istoriia Ukraïny*, ed. Petro Tolochko et al., vol. III (Kyiv, 2000), pp. 486–87.
[65] See Tolochko, "Voobrazhennaia narodnost'," pp. 112–17.

the Rurikid realm. It is quite apparent why Monomakh and other Kyivan princes before and after him sought to preserve the unity of Rus', but why was the author of the Primary Chronicle so concerned about it? The answer is not so simple as might appear at first glance. The explanation that chronicle writing simply reflected the sympathies and interests of the princely patron, which was quite popular among scholars at the turn of the twentieth century, has not withstood the criticism advanced by subsequent research. Clearly, while the chronicler took the interests of the princes into account, he often served not only as a sympathetic recorder of the princes' deeds but also as their principled critic. His main loyalty did not lie with the princes. The Primary Chronicle, as well as the earlier chronicles on which it was based, was not written at the princely court but in the Kyivan Cave Monastery, and it was the interests of that monastery, the metropolitan see, and the church in general that counterbalanced the chronicler's loyalty to a particular prince. He judged the prince's deeds by the standard of Christian principles and the interests of the Rus' Land, which brings us back to the question of why those interests were so important to the author of the Primary Chronicle.

The short (and therefore simplified) answer to this question is that the interests of the largest monastery in the capital of the Rus' realm, as well as those of the church as a whole, represented by the "Metropolitan of All Rus'," coincided with the interests of the Kyivan princes. They all wished to preserve the unity of the state and the dominant role of Kyiv, which was the basis of their status, power, and wealth. The threat to them emanated not only, or even predominantly, from the Polovtsians, in opposition to whom the concept of the Rus' Land had been constructed (or reconstructed) in the second half of the eleventh century, but above all from the other centers of the formerly unified realm. In the eleventh century, cathedrals of St. Sophia based on the Constantinople model were built not only in Kyiv but also in Novgorod and Polatsk. After 1024, Prince Mstyslav of Chernihiv began building the largest cathedral in Rus', which was meant to surpass even that of St. Sophia in Kyiv. The worst was yet to come. In 1162, Prince Andrei Bogoliubsky of Vladimir in Northeastern Rus' sent an embassy to Constantinople, lobbying for a separate metropolitan see in Vladimir. Seven years later, Bogoliubsky's armies sacked Kyiv, devastating it as never before. Not even St. Sophia was spared, to say nothing of other churches and monasteries. This was a development that the authors and editors of the Primary Chronicle could not have foreseen, but arguably, even at the turn of the twelfth century, they had good reason to be "patriots" of Rus', encouraging princes to preserve its unity.

The Kyivan church, among whose spokesmen in the court of posterity is the author of the Primary Chronicle, was one of many instruments that helped establish and maintain the unity of the Rurikid realm. Even if we do not take at face value the chronicler's stories about Volodymyr's pre-Christian attempts to create a pantheon of pagan gods, or question the significance of those initiatives as an important step toward the religious unification of his realm,[66] we may assume that he faced the real problem of unifying the vast territories of his newly conquered domain by means of a common belief system. If so, then Christianity was a much better tool for dealing with the problem than some ad hoc pan-East Slavic pantheon. The unifying function of the Christian church was already apparent in the name of the Kyiv metropolitanate, whose official appellation was the "Metropolitanate of Rus'," derived not from the city in which it was located but from the people and the country subject to its spiritual authority.[67] The church and its hierarchs were dependent on the good will of the princes, who on occasion could appoint their own metropolitans without formal approval from Constantinople, as Yaroslav the Wise did in 1051 and Iziaslav Mstyslavovych in 1147. Even more important was the fact that until the twelfth century the church received its main income in the form of tithes from the revenues collected by the prince. The fragmentation of political power in the second half of the twelfth century also resulted in the devolution of economic and ecclesiastical power.[68] Once it became apparent that princely feuds were beginning to undermine the unity of the Rus' church, Constantinople began to treat the Kyivan metropolitans as metropolitans of all Rus'.[69]

The metropolitan see and the Kyivan monasteries benefited from that devolution, as they acquired the right to own land and thus established their own economic base, but they also acquired new rivals. Not only were new bishoprics created in the new princely centers, but additional metropolitanates (albeit titular and short-lived) arose in Chernihiv and Pereiaslav, the two other centers of the Rus' Land. Some of the best-known polemical works of the Kyivan Rus' period are associated with

---

[66] On the history of the "pantheon" legend, see Tolochko and Tolochko, *Kyïvs'ka Rus'*, pp. 105–8.

[67] See Omeljan Pritsak, "Kiev and All of Rus': The Fate of a Sacral Idea," *Harvard Ukrainian Studies* 10, nos. 3–4 (December 1986): 279–300, here 282.

[68] On the position of the church in Kyivan Rus', see Andrzej Poppe, *The Rise of Christian Russia* (London, 1982); Ia. N. Shchapov, *Gosudarstvo i tserkov' Drevnei Rusi, X–XIII vv.* (Moscow, 1989); O. P. Motsia, "Relihiia i tserkva," in *Istoriia ukraïns'koï kul'tury*, ed. P. P. Tolochko et al., vol. I (Kyiv, 2001), pp. 768–90.

[69] On the introduction of the concept of "all Rus'" into official ecclesiastical discourse, see Simon Franklin, "Diplomacy and Ideology: Byzantium and the Russian Church in the Mid Twelfth Century," in idem, *Byzantium-Rus-Russia*, no. VIII, pp. 145–50.

efforts on the part of Kyiv-based clerics (or those close to Kyiv) to combat religious dissent, which emerged under the protection of local princes and bishops on the periphery of the state. Klymentii Smoliatych's *Poslanie* (Epistle) cannot be properly understood without taking account of the ecclesiastical struggle and the opposition to his election as metropolitan (1147) on the part of the hierarchs of Novgorod and Smolensk, who allied themselves with Constantinople against him. Bishop Kyryl of Turaŭ (Turiv) is known, among other things, for his attack on the Reverend Fedor, who was Prince Andrei Bogoliubsky's candidate for bishop of the projected independent eparchy.[70]

Among the numerous identity-building projects initiated in the realm of the Rurikids with its Christianization was the introduction of Church Slavonic as a literary language. It was based on the dialect of Macedonian spoken by Slavs near the city of Thessalonica, the home of the missionaries to the Slavs, SS. Cyril and Methodius, and originally served (to borrow Ihor Ševčenko's expression) as a "tool for translation from the Greek." It became established as a literary language in the second half of the ninth century. Old Slavonic gradually incorporated elements of the Slavic languages spoken in the newly Christianized regions of eastern Europe, including Bulgaria. From there it spread to Rus′, where it became the language of education and church liturgy. By the twelfth century it had acquired enough local East Slavic characteristics to allow modern scholars to define it as a distinct language, Church Slavonic. Some linguists argue that Church Slavonic coexisted with the so-called Old Rus′ literary language in which secular documents and chronicles, including the Primary Chronicle, were written. Whatever the extent of the difference, there is little doubt that by the early twelfth century the Slavic languages had successfully replaced Greek as the official medium of Rus′ secular and ecclesiastical government. They were accepted and used all over Kyivan Rus′, helping to create a common literary culture among the secular and ecclesiastical elites. The monopoly of Church Slavonic in liturgical practice meant that the Christianization of the non-Slavic population of Rus′ was accompanied by and promoted the Slavicization of the Finno-Ugric and other non-Slavic subjects of the Rurikid princes. It also helped unify the linguistic practices of their Slavic subjects.[71]

---

[70] On the writings of Klymentii Smoliatych and Kyryl of Turaŭ and their political and religious context, see Simon Franklin's introduction to *Sermons and Rhetoric of Kievan Rus′*, pp. xiii–cix.

[71] See Ihor Ševčenko, "Byzantium and the Slavs," in his *Ukraine between East and West: Essays on Cultural History to the Early Eighteenth Century* (Edmonton and Toronto, 1996), pp. 12–26, here 21; George Y. Shevelov, "Church Slavic," in *Encyclopedia of Ukraine*, vol. I (Toronto, 1984), pp. 488–89; Nimchuk, "Literaturni movy Kyïvs′koï Rusi." On the "nativization" of Rus′ culture from the turn of the twelfth century, see Franklin and Shepard, *The Emergence of Rus*, pp. 313–17.

What language (or languages) did the Slavic population of Kyivan Rus' speak? The answer to this question is extremely important to the modern debate on who has the best claim to Kyivan Rus' – the Russians, Ukrainians or Belarusians. Linguists seem to agree that all three modern languages form a group separate from the West and South Slavic languages. They also agree on the general model of development of the Slavic languages from a common Slavic to particular national languages. At this point, disagreement begins. The most politically loaded question is whether the East Slavic languages developed directly from a Slavic proto-language or whether there was an intermediate stage in the form of a common East Slavic language. Another bone of contention is the issue of periodization in linguistic development. Prior to the Revolution of 1917, the majority of Russian linguists, who, like Aleksei Shakhmatov, also turned out to be proponents of the imperial idea of all-Russian unity, argued in favor of the existence of a common all-Russian language. That approach became the only one acceptable in official Soviet linguistics, with Soviet authors dating the earliest stages of the disintegration of the common idiom and the emergence of separate Russian, Ukrainian, and Belarusian languages to the fourteenth century. A number of Ukrainian scholars, including George (Yurii) Shevelov, refused to subscribe to that theory and traced the origins of separate East Slavic languages back to the seventh and eighth centuries. Discussion of the problem continues, but for present purposes it is fair to suggest that whatever the languages spoken by the Slavic population of Kyivan Rus', the introduction and use of Old Slavonic and, later, Church Slavonic (and Old Rus') as a common literary medium could not help but retard the development and eventual formation of distinct East Slavic languages.[72]

Thus it would appear that the language in which the author(s) of the Primary Chronicle wrote, their membership in the church, their location in a monastery in the capital of the Rurikid realm, and their closeness to the secular and spiritual powers of Kyivan Rus' all helped turn them into proponents of all-Rus' unity.

Who has the better claim?

What does all this mean for the modern debate about the ethno-national character of Kyivan Rus'? Were Hrushevsky and his followers right to assert the proto-Ukrainian character of Kyivan Rus' and represent Galician-Volhynian Rus' as the true heir of Kyiv, while denying that

---

[72] For a summary of current discussion about the spoken language of Kyivan Rus', see Magocsi, *A History of Ukraine*, pp. 100–102; Vasyl' Nimchuk, "Mova," in *Istoriia ukraïns'koï kul'tury*, I: 683–94.

right to the proto-Russian Suzdal principality? Or does the evidence favor Mikhail Pogodin, Aleksei Sobolevsky, and other Russian historians and linguists, who believed that the entire population of the core area of Kyivan Rus' abandoned it sometime in the thirteenth century to migrate to the North and later participated in the formation of the modern Russian nation?

With regard to the nineteenth- and early twentieth-century controversy, the latest research, above all the results of archaeological excavations, shows that there was no significant outmigration from the Kyiv region to the North (or, for that matter, to the West, as Vasilii Kliuchevsky assumed), and that the local population remained in the area. Our reading of the twelfth-century chronicles indicates that the early Rus' identity was attached to and based upon the concept of the Rus' Land in the narrow sense, limited to the territory around Kyiv, Chernihiv, and Pereiaslav. Only later was the name of the Rus' Land adopted by elites outside this "inner" Rus'. Thus it can be argued that the concept of Rus' and, consequently, the original Rus' identity was the product of elites and populations that later helped form the Ukrainian nation. But this is as far as one can go on the basis of the available data in endorsing Hrushevsky's viewpoint.

Our rereading of the sources shows no sign of an identity that might define the population of what is now Ukrainian territory (the Rus' Land per se and Galicia-Volhynia) as a single entity in opposition to a "non-Ukrainian" other. No such identity existed at the time. The same applies to the type of identity that existed in the territories of present-day Russia and Belarus during the Kyivan Rus' era. There were significant differences between the political structures (and the identities based upon them) in the two proto-Russian polities of Novgorod and Suzdal. Nor can one speak of a sense of unity between them, as opposed to the other Rus' lands, in the period prior to the Mongol invasion. When it comes to Belarus, historians of that country can and do look to the history of the Krivichians and the Principality of Polatsk for the origins of the modern Belarusian nation. They are probably as justified in doing so as are Ukrainian historians in searching for the origins of "their" polities in the Kyivan Rus' conglomerate, but, once again, no "all-Belarusian" identity existed at the time, even in prototype. The history of the Polatsk principality, like that of the Rus' Land around Kyiv, Chernihiv, and Pereiaslav, or the Suzdal principality, can serve as a good beginning for modern national narratives but is a poor starting point if one is looking for the construction sites of modern national identities.

Does this mean that Kliuchevsky and his followers in the Soviet Union and in the West were more correct than their opponents in claiming that

Kyivan Rus' history was the product of a single Old Rus' nationality? Wrong again. Nikita Tolstoi, whose work on the multiple identities of the author of the Primary Chronicle has been noted above, was perfectly right to identify the East Slavic component as the weakest of all the levels of Nestor's ethnopolitical consciousness. Ethnic affinity played a role in the development of the sense of Rus' unity, but that role was marginal even among the Kyivan elites, to say nothing of those of "outer" Rus'. Even their political loyalty as we know it from twelfth-century sources was to their lands of Rus', Suzdal, Novgorod, Polatsk, and so on, not to the Rurikid realm. If East Slavic identity was so weak among the Slavic elites, it is hard to imagine that it was any stronger among the population at large. The fact that we can now distinguish a number of East Slavic tribes on the basis of archaeological evidence indicates that their differences in material culture were quite significant as well. The only exception is represented by the medieval melting pots – meeting grounds for representatives of various East Slavic and non-Slavic tribes – that emerged in newly colonized areas on the borderlands of the Rurikid realm.

What proponents of the idea of one Rus' nationality often forget is that Kyivan Rus' was not only an East Slavic state. Varangians and Finno-Ugric tribes were as important in its creation and development as the Eastern Slavs – a factor that was not overlooked by the author of the Primary Chronicle. Thus, even if we think of Kyivan Rus' as an "imagined community," the image we get is not one of an Old Rus' nationality (itself the product of the modern historical imagination) but of a multiethnic imperial elite whose identity was quite different from that of the rest of the population. Indeed, it is generally accepted that even at the peak of their power, the prince and church of Kyivan Rus' had at best a limited capacity to invest their subjects with a sense of common belonging. As the Ukrainian scholar Natalia Yakovenko correctly suggests, assuming the existence of one Old Rus' nationality on the basis of a common intellectual tradition among the Rus' literati is as misleading as it would be to assume the existence of one "Latin nationality" on the basis of the tradition of Latin schooling in western Europe.[73]

What all this tells us about the competing national interpretations of Kyivan Rus' history is that the national paradigm per se is not very help-ful in our search for the origins of East Slavic identities. This is not to deny that the paradigm played an important role in the effort to bet-ter understand the history of Kyivan Rus'. Originally, when the concept of all-Russian nationality was introduced into the study of Kyivan Rus',

[73] Natalia Iakovenko, *Narys istoriï Ukraïny z naidavnishykh chasiv do kintsia XVIII stolittia* (Kyiv, 1997), pp. 53–59.

it undermined the dominance of the dynastic approach to the history of the Kyivan realm and opened new prospects for historical research. When Ukrainian and Belarusian scholars challenged the concept of all-Russian nationality, they rightly questioned the level of ethnic homogeneity in the Kyivan Rus' state and its capacity to create a single nationality out of diverse ethnic and tribal strata of population. Even today, it would appear that the national paradigm has not exhausted its creative potential to inform questions and studies pertaining to the history of cultural identities in the region. On the other hand, it is clear that simply replacing one nationality with three as a subject of research does not solve the problem of the complex ethnocultural identity shared at one time or another by the inhabitants of Kyivan Rus'. Our own discussion of Kyivan Rus' identities shows that they were in constant flux, often looking to the past for justification of the particular structure of that identity at any given time.

Modern historians in search of the origins of their own changing identities (and seeking legitimacy for them as well) continue to disagree in their interpretations of the ethnocultural history of Kyivan Rus'. What seems beyond doubt, however, is that the Kyivan intellectuals succeeded in creating an identity-building model – one that endowed the Rus' elite with a sense of common identity extending beyond the boundaries of the Rus' Land in the narrow sense. The Kyivan state left a strong legacy in the region in terms of historical memory, law, religion, and ultimately identity, which was adopted in one form or another by all its former subjects. Most importantly for our discussion, that state left a tradition of usage of the name of Rus' and thus a lasting reason to recover and reinvent the Rus' identity for generations to come.

2   What happened to the Rus′ Land?

The period from the mid-thirteenth to the late fifteenth century is probably the least researched in the history of the Eastern Slavs. Yet the events of
that time gave rise to extremely important developments in the ethnocultural history of the region that led, according to most scholars, to growing
differentiation among the East Slavic ethnonational communities. Soviet
historians claimed that this was the period in which one all-Rus′ nationality ceased to exist and the three East Slavic nationalities were formed.
There are also a number of other questions pertaining to the period that
seem vital to modern-day national narratives. Did the final disintegration of Kyivan Rus′ and the establishment of appanage principalities in
its place lead to the fragmentation of Rus′ identity, bring out already
existing differences, or have no serious impact on the sense of Rus′ unity
developed in Kyivan times? I address this question by examining changes
in the concept of the Rus′ Land after the dissolution of the Kyivan state.
What happened to the sense of commonality of the Rurikid princes and
the Rus′ elites when they lost control over the Kyiv-Chernihiv-Pereiaslav
triangle and had no common patrimony to care about? To answer this
question, I shall consider changes in the treatment of the concepts of
Rus′ and the Rus′ Land as markers of political, territorial, and ethnocultural communities in regions that were rarely considered to be part
of the Rus′ Land in Kyivan times but became carriers and strong promoters of Rus′ identity during the appanage period. These were the
Principality of Galicia-Volhynia in the thirteenth and early fourteenth
centuries and the Vladimir-Suzdal Land, where I shall follow developments until the end of the fourteenth century (including a discussion
of mainly fifteenth-century sources). Not only was the concept of the
Rus′ Land (in one form or another) adopted in these polities during the
period in question, but it was also passed on to subsequent generations
as an important element of the prevailing system of political and cultural
values.

The heirs of Kyiv

The "official" end of Kyivan Rus', as treated in modern historiography, came with the Mongol invasion of 1237–40, which began a new era in East Slavic history. For most historians, the Mongol invasion serves as a turning point at which Russian history begins to follow one path, while the histories of Ukraine and Belarus take another. The major factor influencing this divergence was that from the mid-thirteenth century Northeastern Rus' found itself under Mongol rule, while the rest of the Rus' territories, following a much shorter encounter with the Mongols as overlords, came under the control of Lithuanian princes and Polish kings.

The political history of the Ukrainian and Belarusian lands in the thirteenth and fourteenth centuries is a process of coexistence and competition between several larger and smaller principalities that emerged from the ruins of Kyivan Rus'. The state that stands out in the multifaceted political history of the region is the Principality of Galicia-Volhynia. In 1199, when the author of the Kyiv Chronicle wrote his last entry, this powerful new polity emerged in the westernmost part of the Rurikid realm. The principalities of Halych and Volodymyr in Volhynia were brought together under the rule of Prince Roman Mstyslavych. The new superprincipality included the districts (*volosti*) of Halych (the town that gave its name to the Land of *Halychyna* – Galicia), Peremyshl (Przemyśl), Zvenyhorod, Terebovlia, Volodymyr in Volhynia, Lutsk, and Belz. Although Prince Roman managed to extend his power to Kyiv, his death in 1205 not only put an end to the Galician-Volhynian princes' control of Kyiv but also initiated a forty-year conflict that saw the active involvement of Polish and Hungarian rulers in the principality's affairs. The brief period of Prince Roman's supreme power later served as a point of departure for chroniclers of his son Danylo, who restored the unity of the principality and established – or, as more optimistic scholars suggest, restored – the tradition of chronicle writing in the region. Ironically, the text of the Galician-Volhynian Chronicle, whose composition began under Danylo in the 1250s, omits (in its present incomplete form) the rule of Roman Mstyslavych, the prince to whom it refers as "the autocrat of all Rus'."

The Mongol invasion hardly affected Danylo's ascendancy as a regional ruler. On the one hand, he lost control over Kyiv, which he ruled through a voevoda (military governor) on the eve of the Mongol attack of 1240. On the other hand, in 1245, in the wake of the Mongol campaign, he managed to restore the unity of Galicia-Volhynia (or Volhynia-Galicia, as some scholars believe the principality should be called). Danylo subdued the powerful local boyars, ensuring the political stability of the realm.

He conducted a skillful foreign policy, playing off the Poles and Hungarians in the west against the Mongols in the east and becoming the only Rus' prince who dared to engage the Mongols militarily after 1240. Danylo was unable to secure the independence of his principality from the Mongols, but he ensured its unity until his death in 1265. It was only after his demise that the unity of his realm was broken and the principality divided into Galician and Volhynian parts. As Danylo's nephew Volodymyr Vasylkovych of Volhynia, apparently a great lover of learning, continued to support the chronicle writing promoted by his uncle, we have a relatively good account of developments in Galicia-Volhynia throughout most of the thirteenth century. After 1290, however, when the Galician-Volhynian Chronicle ends, "Cimmerian darkness" (in Mykhailo Hrushevsky's phrase) descends on the territory.

We know very little about political events and especially about their reception by local elites in most of the fourteenth and early fifteenth centuries, until chronicle writing by Rus' clerics resumed in the Grand Duchy of Lithuania sometime in the 1440s. What little is known from foreign sources allows scholars to conclude that in the early fourteenth century Galicia-Volhynia was reestablished as a unified polity by Prince Yurii I. His two sons, the last Rurikids at the helm of the principality, were killed in the first half of the 1320s, allegedly while fighting the Lithuanians. Power was then assumed by the elected Prince Yurii (Bolesław) II, who was killed by the local boyars in 1340. That was the year in which Prince Liubart of Lithuania established himself in Volhynia, while Galicia, after a brief period of rule by the local boyar Dmytro Detko, succumbed (along with western Volhynia) to King Casimir III of Poland in 1339. Although Hungarian kings also claimed the region, it remained under Polish control from 1387. The former principality, whose name of "Rus'" was by now firmly established in the minds of its domestic elites and neighbors alike, remained a bone of contention in Polish-Hungarian relations until the 1420s.[1]

While Galicia-Volhynia was nominally dependent on the Mongols only until the turn of the fourteenth century, Northeastern Rus' experienced their rule until the mid-fifteenth century. Initially, the Mongols treated the Suzdal-Vladimir Land, along with Kyiv and Chernihiv in the south

---

[1] On the history of the Galician-Volhynian principality and its territories in the thirteenth and fourteenth centuries, see A. M. Andriiashev, *Ocherk istorii Volynskoi zemli do kontsa XIV stoletiia* (Kyiv, 1887); Ivan Lynnychenko, *Suspil'ni verstvy Halyts'koi Rusy XIV–XV vv.* (Lviv, 1899); Mykhailo Hrushevs'kyi, *Istoriia Ukraïny-Rusy*, vols. II–IV (repr. Kyiv, 1992–93); V. T. Pashuto, *Ocherki po istorii Galitsko-Volynskoi Rusi* (Moscow, 1950); Ivan Kryp'iakevych, *Halyts'ko-Volyns'ke kniazivstvo* (Kyiv, 1984); Mykola Kotliar, *Halyts'ko-Volyns'ka Rus'* (Kyiv, 1998).

and Novgorod and Pskov in the northwest, as a separate Rus' realm. They controlled it through grand princes dependent on the khans. The Rus' lands were obliged to recognize the sovereignty of the khans (later the khans of the Golden Horde – Qipchaq Khanate – and the Great Horde), pay taxes, and provide military support for their campaigns. The khans played off the princes of one appanage principality against another, usually offering the grand-princely title to a ruler strong enough to collect tribute for them, but that game could succeed only as long as the Horde itself was strong. The grand princes took advantage of any internal strife in the Horde to strengthen their grip on the Rus' principalities. The greatest success in this enterprise went to the princes of Moscow, an insignificant town at the time of the Mongol invasion that did not even have its own princely line of succession. It acquired one in the second half of the thirteenth century, and the claim has often been made that Moscow's ascendancy over the initially much more powerful principality of Tver was due to the prudence and energy of its princes. In 1317, as Prince Yurii of Moscow married a sister of the khan of the Golden Horde, the grand-princely title and the power associated with it passed for the first time from Tver to Moscow.

Since Moscow was at first weaker than Tver, the khans readily supported the Muscovite princes. One of them was Ivan Kalita, who ruled as grand prince from 1331 to 1340 and not only strengthened and extended his realm but also turned Moscow into the seat of the metropolitans of all Rus' (1325). Another very successful prince was Dmitrii Ivanovich (known since the sixteenth century as Donskoi), the central figure of the Muscovite and later Russian historical myth of the Battle of Kulikovo Field (1380). It took place at the time of a major feud within the Golden Horde. Dmitrii rallied the support of a number of Rus' princes and confronted Mamai, a contestant for the throne of the Golden Horde who was assisted by the princes of Riazan. The battle has been heralded in historical and literary works as a major victory for Rus' arms and the turning point in the liberation of the Rus' lands from the "Tatar yoke." Yet recent research shows that the victory attributed to Dmitrii by later tradition was less than decisive.[2] In any case, the battle did not affect the balance of power in the region, for in a few short years Dmitrii had to abandon Moscow and flee from advancing Tatar troops led by Khan Tokhtamysh. What seems more reliable is the claim that the battle increased the prestige of the prince of Moscow among his peers. Moreover, the literature

[2] For a discussion of the importance of Dmitrii's victory, see Donald Ostrowski, *Muscovy and the Mongols: Cross-Cultural Influences on the Steppe Frontier, 1304–1589* (Cambridge, 1998), pp. 155–56.

about the battle firmly established the notion of the Rus' Land (a name now applied to the territory of Northeastern Rus') as an object of loyalty for local elites and turned it into a rallying cry for those who wanted to deliver Northeastern Rus' from the rule of the Qipchaq khans.[3]

One, two, or three? Counting the nationalities

At different times, the chroniclers of both Galicia-Volhynia and Suzdal-Vladimir claimed that their particular principality was in fact the Rus' Land and that their contemporaries residing in it were Rus' people. Does this mean that elites of both principalities shared one ethnonational identity and that the Rus' identity was dominant in the hierarchy of political and cultural identities of the period? Scholars have been arguing this question for centuries, with many Russian historians giving an essentially positive answer. As noted in the previous chapter, before the notion of one all-Russian nationality was confined to the chronological limits of Kyivan Rus', it ruled supreme over all periods of East Slavic history, and the Galician-Volhynian past, as well as that of the other Ukrainian and Belarusian territories, was conceptualized in Russian imperial historiography as the history of Russia and the Russian people. That interpretation of East Slavic history, which was advanced by Vasilii Kliuchevsky, had a profound impact on the Western historiography of Russia and eastern Europe.

The major challenge to this interpretation was posed in the early twentieth century by Mykhailo Hrushevsky, who removed not only Ukrainian but also Belarusian history from the Russian grand narrative. His claim that Galicia-Volhynia was the most legitimate successor to Kyivan Rus' turned out to be crucial to the Ukrainian deconstruction of the all-Russian narrative at the turn of the twentieth century and is a cornerstone of the contemporary Ukrainian historical narrative.[4] The history of another

[3] On the history of Northeastern Rus' from the thirteenth to the fifteenth century, see John Fennell, *The Crisis of Medieval Russia* (London and New York, 1983), and respective chapters in the general histories by Nicholas V. Riasanovsky, *A History of Russia*, 6th edn.; (New York and Oxford, 2000); Janet Mortin, *Medieval Russia, 980–1584* (Cambridge, 1996); and Gregory L. Freeze, ed., *Russia: A History* (Oxford and New York, 1997). On the relation of Northeastern Rus' history to that of Kyivan Rus', see Ihor Ševčenko, "Rival and Epigone of Kiev: The Vladimir-Suzdal' Principality," in idem, *Ukraine between East and West*, pp. 56–68.

[4] See Mykhailo Hrushevsky, *The Traditional Scheme of "Russian" History and the Problem of a Rational Organization of the History of the East Slavs*, ed. Andrew Gregorovich (Winnipeg, 1965); repr. in *Mykhailo Hrushevsky: Ukrainian-Russian Confrontation in Historiography*, ed. Lubomyr R. Wynar (Toronto, New York, and Munich, 1988), pp. 35–42. On Hrushevsky's role in the deconstruction of the Russian imperial narrative, see Serhii Plokhy, *Unmaking Imperial Russia: Mykhailo Hrushevsky and the Writing of Ukrainian History* (Toronto, 2005).

(significantly smaller) heir to Kyivan glory, the Polatsk principality, eventually became paramount to the Belarusians' search for the medieval roots of their national sovereignty. Soviet historiography eventually adopted a compromise position, maintaining that the united all-Rus' nationality split into smaller groups after the disintegration of Kyivan Rus'. According to this version, the Old Rus' nationality was replaced by distinct Russian, Ukrainian, and Belarusian nationalities, which began to take shape in the fourteenth century. The Soviet view was based on the findings of linguists who claimed that this was the period in which separate East Slavic languages began to crystallize.[5] The thesis that the formation of all three nationalities began at about the same time corresponded to the official dogma of the equality of the Soviet peoples and was further justified by means of the Soviet Marxist truism that nationalities and, subsequently, nations came into existence primarily as a result of economic development.

It would be incorrect to state that all Soviet historians subscribed to this historiographic scheme. In the 1970s, the Russian scholar Valentin Sedov sought Belarusian origins in the early history of their relations with the Baltic tribes – an encounter that took place well before the times of Kyivan Rus'. In Ukraine, Fedir Shevchenko, who was removed from his position as director of the Institute of Archaeology in 1972 on a charge of following the historical scheme of Mykhailo Hrushevsky, apparently refused to learn his lesson. In an essay on the formation of the Ukrainian nationality published as part of a multivolume academic history of Ukraine (1979), he dated the beginning of the first stage of that formation to the second half of the twelfth century.[6] In Russia, some leading representatives of

<hr />

[5] For the treatment of the history of the Russian language in Soviet literature, see R. I. Avanesov, "Voprosy razvitiia russkogo iazyka v ėpokhu formirovaniia i dal'neishego razvitiia russkoi (velikorusskoi) narodnosti," in *Voprosy formirovaniia russkoi narodnosti i natsii*, ed. N. M. Druzhinin and L. V. Cherepnin (Moscow and Leningrad, 1958), pp. 155–91. Soviet views on the formation of the Ukrainian and Belarusian languages are summarized by Anna Khoroshkevich in Vladimir Pashuto, Boris Floria, and Khoroshkevich, *Drevnerusskoe nasledie i istoricheskie sud'by vostochnogo slavianstva* (Moscow, 1982), pp. 77–79.

[6] Shevchenko's periodization ran counter to the views of such prominent Russian scholars as Boris Rybakov, who dated the disintegration of the Old Rus' nationality to the fourteenth and fifteenth centuries. The Ukrainian scholar's security against possible accusations of nationalist deviation lay, apparently, in the views of such Russian scholars as Lev Cherepnin, who were prepared to speak of "preconditions" for the creation of the three East Slavic nationalities existing as early as the twelfth century, citing the "feudalization" of Rus' as the background for that process (see L. V. Cherepnin, "Istoricheskie usloviia formirovaniia russkoi narodnosti do kontsa *XV v.*," in *Voprosy formirovaniia russkoi narodnosti i natsii*, pp. 7–105). Shevchenko also claimed (apparently in order to defend himself against further official attack) that the formation of the Ukrainian nationality was not fully achieved until the mid-seventeenth century. See idem, "Formuvannia ukraïns'koï narodnosti," in *Istoriia Ukraïns'koï RSR*, vol. I, bk. 2 (Kyiv, 1979), pp. 186–97.

Soviet historiography silently ignored the official scheme in favor of the Russocentric paradigm. The authors of the "collective monograph" *The Old Rus' Heritage and the Historical Fate of the Eastern Slavs* (1982) revived the prerevolutionary and World War II-era practice of using the term "Russians" to denote all three East Slavic nationalities. Vladimir Pashuto, for example, referred to the thirteenth-century population of Kyivan Rus' as "Russian people," while Boris Floria called the seventeenth-century inhabitants of Ukraine and Belarus a "Russian population."[7] Given the existence of such centrifugal and mutually exclusive tendencies within the supposed monolith of Soviet historiography, it is hardly surprising that once party control over historiography was lifted with the advent of glasnost, the artificial uniformity of Soviet historians' views on the ethnogenesis of the Eastern Slavs became a thing of the past.

After the disintegration of the USSR, a number of Ukrainian and Belarusian scholars revived theories previously suppressed by the Soviet establishment about the early (pre-Kyivan) origins of their nations.[8] Russian scholars such as the distinguished linguist Oleg Trubachev took the opposite tack, seeking to establish the common origins of the three East Slavic peoples and languages.[9] Once the excitement of independence and the shock of disintegration faded away, most scholars found themselves subscribing to a somewhat looser version of the old Soviet paradigm. In general, they accept the view that the formation of the East Slavic nationalities took place between the thirteenth and sixteenth centuries. Within this broad consensus, however, there are distinct emphases depending on the individual historian and the historiographic school s/he represents.[10] As noted in the previous chapter, most Ukrainian scholars reject the concept of one Rus' nationality. Still, they are inclined to regard the thirteenth century as the point of origin of separate East Slavic nationalities,

---

[7] Pashuto, Floria, and Khoroshkevich, *Drevnerusskoe nasledie i istoricheskie sud'by vostochnogo slavianstva*, pp. 5–6, 20, 196. For the continuation of that practice in post-Soviet Russian historiography, see A. I. Dvornichenko, *Russkie zemli Velikogo kniazhestva Litovskogo (do nachala XVI veka). Ocherki istorii obshchiny, soslovii, gosudarstvennosti* (St. Petersburg, 1993).

[8] In Belarus, A. I. Mikulich applied genetics to the study of Belarusian ethnogenesis. He concluded that of the twelve genes analyzed in his study, Belarusians differ from Lithuanians by two genes, from Russians by three, from Ukrainians by four, and from Poles by six. See G. V. Shtykhov, "U istokov belorusskoi narodnosti," *Ruthenica* (Kyiv) 1 (2002): 85–88, here 87–88. Cf. his "Drevnerusskaia narodnost': realii i mif," in *Trudy VI Mezhdunarodnogo kongressa slavianskoi arkheologii. Ėtnogenez i kul'turnye kontakty slavian*, vol. III (Moscow 1997), pp. 376–85.

[9] See O. N. Trubachev, *V poiskakh edinstva* (Moscow, 1992).

[10] For a discussion of the formation of the Belarusian nation in contemporary Belarusian historiography, see Henadz' Sahanovich, *Narys historyi Belarusi* (Minsk, 2001), pp. 175–82, and I. U. Chakvin, "Etnichnyia pratsesy u XIV – pershai palove XVII st.," in *Belarusy. Vytaki i ėtnichnae razvitstsė*, vol. IV (Minsk, 2001), pp. 48–170.

indicating the complete disintegration of the Kyivan realm and the different political conditions prevailing in the various Rus' lands.[11] Most Russian scholars, by contrast, continue to believe in the existence of one Old Rus' nationality. Some of them, like Boris Floria, are inclined to extend its life all the way to the end of the sixteenth century. His observations on the subject are especially important for our discussion, as he bases them on the study of early modern East Slavic identities. Floria regards the turn of the fifteenth century as a period in which preconditions for the formation of separate East Slavic nationalities had only begun to emerge.[12]

Which of the contemporary historians revising the old Soviet paradigm to meet new political and scholarly challenges has the better claim? Having discussed the strengths and weaknesses of the concept of Old Rus' nationality in the previous chapter, we hardly need to return to this problem. But the question of when separate East Slavic identities developed (out of one identity-building project or otherwise) deserves our further attention. Should we regard the political calamities of the thirteenth and fourteenth centuries as the true starting point? As promised at the beginning of the chapter, this question and related issues will be approached by way of an analysis of the notions of Rus' and the Rus' Land as they developed in the territories of the former Kyivan state.

Galicians into Rus'ians

The authors of the Galician-Volhynian Chronicle, who constructed their narrative in the second half of the thirteenth century, regarded their princes and their principality as the lawful continuators and heirs of the Kyivan princes and the Kyivan state. So did the authors of the modern Ukrainian national narrative. But when did the Galician-Volhynian elites and their neighbors to the east and west begin to think of their land as part of Rus'? My answer to this question is probably as surprising as it is controversial. It appears that the process of identification with Rus' was fully completed only after the Kyivan state had succumbed to the Mongol invasion. Impossible? Let us see what the sources have to say about it.

[11] See Mykola Kotliar writing in a Soviet-style "collective monograph," *Istoriia Ukraïny* (Kyiv, 1997), pp. 47–48, and Natalia Iakovenko, *Narys istoriï Ukraïny z naidavnishykh chasiv do kintsia XVIII stolittia* (Kyiv, 1997), pp. 53–59.
[12] See Boris Floria, "O nekotorykh osobennostiakh razvitiia ètnicheskogo samosoznaniia vostochnykh slavian v èpokhu srednevekov'ia – rannego novogo vremeni," in *Rossiia-Ukraina: istoriia vzaimootnoshenii*, ed. A. I. Miller, V. F. Reprintsev, and B. N. Floria (Moscow, 1997), pp. 9–38. Cf. idem, "Istoricheskie sud'by Rusi i ètnicheskoe samosoznanie vostochnykh slavian v XII–XV vekakh. (K voprosu o zarozhdenii vostochnoslavianskikh narodnostei)," *Slavianovedenie*, 1993, no. 2: 53–55.

Since we have both Kyivan and local Galician-Volhynian chronicles (which, together with the Primary Chronicle, constitute the Hypatian Codex), we can trace the Galician-Volhynian elites' acquisition of the Rus′ name and identity from two vantage points. The fact that the first voice belongs to the twelfth century while the second comes from the thirteenth (more precisely, its latter part) complicates our task. Nevertheless, compared with the exclusively Kyivan perspective on Rus′ presented by the authors of the Primary Chronicle and the complete silence of the fourteenth-century sources with regard to the history of the region, the stereo sounds that we can extract from the chronicles covering the history of the Galician-Volhynian principality are a true boon to anyone interested in the study of its political, military, economic, religious, and cultural history.

Let us begin investigating the identities of the Galician-Volhynian elites by listening to the Kyivan voices. According to the author of the Primary Chronicle, the territory of the future principality was settled by a number of tribes. Among them were the Dulibians, Buzhanians, and Volhynians, who resided in Volhynia, and the Ulichians, Tivertsians, and Croats, who lived in Galicia and neighboring territories. Like some other Rus′ tribes, certain of those mentioned as having settled the future territory of the Galician-Volhynian principality were probably little more than a figment of the chronicler's imagination. For example, the Buzhanians, who according to the chronicler were replaced by the Volhynians, are mentioned only once. Most of the other tribes disappear very early in the chronicler's narrative.[13] We have a much better understanding of the region's history from the late tenth century, when the power of the Kyivan princes was extended to the western edge of the future Galician Land – the town of Peremyshl (Przemyśl). Under 981, the Primary Chronicle reports on Volodymyr's campaign against the Poles, which resulted in the capture of "their towns" Peremyshl and Cherven. As the chronicler notes, they remained under Rus′ control until his own time.[14] Volhynia first emerges in the Primary Chronicle as a separate land only in the last quarter of the eleventh century, while the Galician Land was not known to the author of that chronicle as a distinct entity and was first mentioned by the authors of the Kyiv Chronicle under the year 1152.[15]

If in the first half of the eleventh century Galicia (the "Cherven towns") and Volhynia were the bone of contention between Prince Yaroslav the Wise of Kyiv and the Poles, in the second half of the century the Rurikids

---

[13] See the discussion of the Primary Chronicle's account of the "Galician-Volhynian" tribes in Kotliar, *Halyts′ko-Volyns′ka Rus′*, pp. 18–28.

[14] Under the same year, the chronicler reported Volodymyr's victory over the Viatichians.

[15] See Kotliar, *Halyts′ko-Volyns′ka Rus′*, p. 28.

themselves began fighting over them, with the Kyivan princes squaring off against their Volhynian and Galician counterparts. The princely congress of Liubech in 1097 assigned Volodymyr in Volhynia, Peremyshl, and Terebovlia in Galicia to individual representatives of the Rurikid clan. It failed, however, to put an end to internecine warfare: the Kyivan and Volodymyr-Volhynian princes plotted against Vasylko of Terebovlia and blinded him. That act of violence, committed by the Rurikid princes against one of their own, allegedly made Volodymyr Monomakh exclaim: "Such a crime as this has never been perpetrated in the Rus' Land either in the time of our grandfathers or in that of our fathers."[16]

Curiously enough, despite his invocation of a discourse of loyalty to the Rus' Land in connection with the war that broke out in Galicia and Volhynia, the author of the Primary Chronicle did not consider those territories to be part of the Rus' Land per se. They were "under Rus'," as he noted in the entry for 981, but that did not make them part of Rus' or of the Rus' Land in the narrow meaning of the term. The chronicler was worried instead that the redistribution of princely possessions in that part of the Rurikid empire would change the balance of power in the Rus' Land (narrowly conceived), making it an easy target for the Polovtsians, who might destroy it completely. There are numerous statements to that effect in the pages of the Primary Chronicle. Its continuators, the authors of the Kyiv Chronicle, give much more evidence that in the twelfth century neither Volhynia nor Galicia was considered part of the Rus' Land per se. In the entry for 1144, describing the campaign launched by the Kyivan prince Vsevolod against Volodymyr of Halych, the chronicler noted that Vsevolod's troops (Rus' regiments) included detachments from the Rus' Land around Kyiv, Chernihiv, and Pereiaslav, while Volodymyr's troops were "Galicians."[17] The fact that Vsevolod's army also included Polish detachments did not change the general attitude of the chronicler, who regarded Halych and the Galicians as outsiders. The same applies to the entry for 1152, when another Kyivan prince, Iziaslav, now accompanied by Hungarian troops, attacked Volodymyr of Halych. According to the chronicle, Iziaslav addressed his men as follows: "Brothers and retainers! God has never exposed the Rus' Land and the sons of Rus' to dishonor! They have won their honor everywhere, and today, brothers, we shall all see to it. May God grant that we win our honor in these lands and before foreign peoples."[18] In all likelihood, the "foreign peoples" mentioned by

---

[16] Adapted from *The Russian Primary Chronicle: Laurentian Text*, ed. and trans. Samuel Hazzard Cross and Olgerd P. Sherbowitz-Wetzor (Cambridge, Mass., 1953), p. 191. Cf. A. K. Aleshkovskii, *Povest' vremennykh let* (Moscow, 1971), p. 174.

[17] See *Polnoe sobranie russkikh letopisei* (henceforth *PSRL*), vol. II, *Ipat'evskaia letopis'*, 2nd edn (St. Petersburg, 1908; repr. Moscow, 1962), col. 315.

[18] Ibid., cols. 448–49.

the chronicler were the Hungarians, not the Galicians, but the reference
to the Rus' Land and its sons clearly showed that the Galicians were not
included in either of those concepts. Moreover, after the conclusion of a
peace treaty between the warring parties, the Hungarian king demanded
that Prince Volodymyr return the captured "Rus' towns" to Iziaslav. The
towns in question were in the Rus' Land per se, and it was there, according
to the chronicler, that Iziaslav returned from the Galician Land after the
end of the campaign.[19]

So much for the Kyivan chroniclers' assignment of identity to the
inhabitants of Volhynia and Galicia. But what about the self-identification
of the Volhynian and Galician elites? It would appear that the authors of
the Galician-Volhynian Chronicle followed (at least initially) the historiographic tradition of referring to the Kyiv region as the Rus' Land to
the exclusion of all other parts of the Rurikid realm. One might assume
that their use of the term also reflected the reality "on the ground," or at
least corresponded to their contemporaries' usage. Under the year 1231,
the chronicler reports on Prince Danylo of Halych taking possession
of the town of Torchesk, which is characterized as part of the Rus' Land.[20]
The entry for 1234 describes an attack by the Polovtsians, who "came
to Kyiv and plundered the Rus' Land."[21] Recording the sack of Kyiv
by the Mongols in 1240, the chronicler states that "the Rus' Land was
filled with enemies (ratnykh)."[22] Interestingly enough, after the fall of
Kyiv to the Mongols the Galician-Volhynian Chronicle makes no direct
reference to the Rus' Land in the narrow sense, meaning references that
can be limited indisputably to the Kyivan Land. It is difficult to avoid
the impression that the Mongols delivered the final blow to that concept,
at least when it comes to the use of the term in the southwestern part
of the Rurikid realm. But what happened to the very notion of the Rus'
Land? Did it vanish entirely, or did it acquire a new meaning under new
circumstances?

The notion of the Rus' Land certainly did not disappear. Instead, it
took on new political and geographical dimensions, including Galicia
and Volhynia as integral parts. The tendency to extend the meaning of the
term is apparent in the chronicler's account of events that long preceded
the Mongol invasion of Rus'. For example, he treats the struggle for the
possession of Galicia-Volhynia after the death of Roman Mstyslavych

---

[19] Ibid., col. 452.
[20] For a critical edition of the text of the Galician-Volhynian Chronicle, see *Halyts'ko-
Volyns'kyi litopys. Doslidzhennia. Tekst. Komentar*, ed. Mykola Kotliar (Kyiv, 2002).
For an English translation, see *The Hypatian Codex*, pt. 2, *The Galician-Volhynian
Chronicle*, trans. George A. Perfecky (Munich, 1973). Cf. *Halyts'ko-Volyns'kyi litopys*,
p. 95.
[21] Ibid., p. 97.   [22] Ibid., p. 101.

in the early thirteenth century as a time of "great disorder . . . in the Rus′ Land."[23] The Galician Land is identified with the Rus′ Land in the chronicle account of the conflict over Halych between Danylo and the Hungarian King Béla IV in 1230. On the one hand, the chronicler reports in his description of the conflict that in order to defend the town of Halych, Danylo mobilized the whole Galician Land. On the other hand, he writes that one of the Galician boyars (an enemy of Danylo's) called upon the Hungarians: "Come out against Halych and take the Rus′ Land."[24] In his account of developments after the Mongol sack of Kyiv, the chronicler frequently uses the term "Rus′ Land" with reference to territories from Kyiv in the east to the Polish and Hungarian borders in the west. Danylo's voevoda in Kyiv allegedly advised the Mongols to move on and attack Hungary, for he saw how the Rus′ Land was suffering at the hands of the invaders. According to the chronicler's account, Danylo found refuge from the Mongols in Hungary and then in Poland, where he met family members who had had to leave the Rus′ Land. Danylo himself allegedly waited for news that the Mongols had left the Rus′ Land before he returned there.[25] It is interesting that by the Rus′ Land, the chronicler understood the towns of Dorohychyn, Berestia, and Kholm, to which Danylo returned after his temporary exile.

It would appear that the secret of how the chronicler's mind transformed Galicia and Volhynia into the Rus′ Land in its new extended boundaries was quite simple. Since the Galician-Volhynian princes took possession of parts of the traditional Rus′ Land without relinquishing control over Galicia and Volhynia, they extended the concept to their entire realm. Thus the chronicler called Prince Roman Mstyslavych the "autocrat (*samoderzhets*) of all Rus′" or "autocrat of the whole Rus′ Land."[26] Danylo, who acquired Kyiv on the eve of the Mongol invasion and installed his voevoda there, was also referred to in the chronicle entry for 1250 as the former grand prince who, "together with his brother, ruled the Rus′ Land, Kyiv, Volodymyr, and Halych, and other lands."[27] Thus, according to the chronicler, Kyiv remained the core of the Rus′ Land, but its two peripheral centers were now located in the west, not in the east: Chernihiv was replaced in the new scheme by Volodymyr in Volhynia, while Halych, the capital of Galicia, took the place of Pereiaslav. Danylo's deeds were compared with those of such Rurikid princes as Sviatoslav the Brave and Volodymyr the Great as the chronicler sought to establish that Danylo had been the first in the Rus′ Land to fight the Czechs.[28]

[23] Ibid., p. 77.   [24] Ibid., p. 92.   [25] Ibid., p. 102.
[26] Ibid., p. 77.   [27] Ibid., p. 109.   [28] Ibid., p. 114.

The application of the term "Rus' Land" to the Galician-Volhynian principality gradually displaced chronicle references based on the names of particular towns and lands.[29] The warriors of the Galician-Volhynian princes also increasingly began to figure not as Galicians, Volodymyrians or Peremyshlianians but as men of Rus', especially when they were mentioned along with actual "foreigners" (Poles and Hungarians). The Rus' and the Liakhs are mentioned as adversaries in Danylo's campaign of 1243 and as two constituent parts of the armies that he led against the Polish prince Władysław in 1229 and against the Yatvingians in 1248.[30] Reporting on the confrontation between Bolesław of Poland and the Rus' princes Vasylko and Shvarno in 1266, the chronicler refers to the two parties involved as the Liakhs and the Rus'.[31] Thus Danylo's army, and probably the general population of Galicia-Volhynia, from which it was recruited, were increasingly regarded by the chroniclers not just as a populace under the control of the Rus' princes but as part of the Rus' people itself.

As the official titles of the rulers of Galicia-Volhynia might suggest, the fourteenth century saw the further penetration of the term "Rus'" into local political discourse. The tradition of its use in the official titles of Galician-Volhynian princes can be traced back to Prince Danylo, who was called "rex Ruthenorum" in the papal bulls of 1246–48. His heirs, Princes Andrii and Lev, who jointly ruled the newly reunited principality of Galicia-Volhynia in the first decades of the fourteenth century, were referred to in their own documents as "leaders of the whole land of Rus', Galicia and Lodomeria, by the grace of God." Separate references to Galicia and Volhynia (usually known in Latin as "Lademirie," a name derived from that of its main city, Volodymyr) showed that these two parts of Danylo's principality had recently existed as separate entities. This is also apparent in the title of one of the brothers, Andrii, who was referred to in his own edicts as "leader of Lodomeria and lord of Rus'," with the latter term denoting Galicia. Yurii II, the last independent ruler of Galicia-Volhynia, usually styled himself "leader and lord of Rus'" or "leader of all Little Rus'," thereby applying the term "Rus'" to his entire realm and stressing its unity. The end of the independent existence of Galicia-Volhynia and the division of its lands between Polish and Hungarian kings

---

[29] This is the impression conveyed by the references to Galicians, meaning inhabitants of the town of Halych and the Halych district. The Volhynian and Kholm-based chroniclers cease to mention Galicians, who had earlier been among the main heroes or, better, antiheroes of their narrative, after the description of events of the 1240s that led to Danylo's restoration of a united Galician-Volhynian principality. Earlier, the Galicians, sometimes called "the godless," are often counterposed to the "good" inhabitants of Volodymyr in Volhynia (see, e.g., ibid., p. 77).

[30] Ibid., pp. 90–93, 105–6, 110–11.   [31] Ibid., p. 130.

(who took Galicia) and the Lithuanian prince Liubartas (who annexed Volhynia) saw a return to the earlier practice of applying the term "Rus'" to Galicia alone. In the titles and official documentation of Polish and Hungarian kings, Galicia was often referred to as the "Kingdom of Rus'" in recognition of its history of independent existence and its special status within the Polish and Hungarian realms. After 1387, the status of Galicia in the Kingdom of Poland was gradually reduced to that of a land (*terra*). In time, it constituted the core area of a palatinate that existed until the partitions of Poland in the late eighteenth century. Interestingly, the name of the land and palatinate of Rus' remained unchanged until the end of the era.[32]

Galician Rus' and its others

As the Rus' identity gradually made its way into the consciousness of the Galician-Volhynian elites, what were their attitudes and perceptions with regard to their "others"? I shall seek an answer to this question by analyzing the chronicler's attitudes toward the Poles in the west, the Polovtsians and, later, the Mongols to the south and east, and, finally, the other Rus' principalities to the north and northeast.

The Poles, or "Liakhs," as the chronicler called them, are among the most frequently mentioned representatives of the Rus' "other" in the Galician-Volhynian Chronicle. The manifold relations of the Galician-Volhynian princes with their Polish neighbors to the west – wars as well as alliances; conflicts as well as marriages – made the Poles a familiar presence to the inhabitants of southwestern Rus'. The border separating the Rus' from the Poles did not negate the sense of a certain commonality between them. In some documentary references, such as the list of peoples invited by Danylo to settle his new capital of Kholm, Poles were even excluded from the category of "foreigners" (*inoplemennyky*).[33] Was this the continuation of a tradition established in the Primary Chronicle of regarding the Poles as fellow Slavs, or did it indicate that the inhabitants of Galicia-Volhynia understood the Polish language and culture more easily than those of their other non-Rus' neighbors? Both factors probably

---

[32] There is an extensive literature on the official titulature of the rulers of Galicia-Volhynia. For the most recent discussion of the historical evidence and literature on the subject, see Iaroslav Isaievych, "On the Titulature of Rulers in Eastern Europe," in *Synopsis: A Collection of Essays in Honour of Zenon E. Kohut* (Edmonton and Toronto, 2005), pp. 219–44.

[33] In the Galician-Volhynian Chronicle, that term is reserved almost exclusively for the Mongols and only occasionally applied to the Poles and Hungarians.

played a role in shaping the chronicler's attitudes toward the Poles.[34] What can be said with certainty is that religion was only occasionally a deciding factor in drawing the line between the two communities. According to the chronicler, Danylo accepted a royal crown from the envoys of the pope after the Polish princes convinced him that they would support his actions against the Mongols. Further justifying Danylo's act, the chronicler wrote that Pope Innocent IV condemned those who denigrated the "Greek faith" and planned to convene a council to reunite the divided churches, clearly regarding the latter as a positive prospect.[35] Mykhailo Hrushevsky was certainly right in suggesting that political antagonism resulting from military confrontation in the Polish-Rus' borderlands preceded religious (Orthodox-Catholic) hostility.[36]

The recognition of religious affinity and commonality between the Rus' and their Western neighbors, shared by the authors of the Rus' chronicles,[37] gave way to a strong sense of religious distinctiveness and animosity when nomadic neighbors to the south and east were involved.[38] In the Primary Chronicle, the opposition of the Rurikid princes to the steppe nomads already figured as a powerful device to help construct the Rus' identity. If the author of the Primary Chronicle counterposed the Rus' princes and the Rus' Land to a specific ethnopolitical enemy, the Polovtsians, whom he called "foreigners," his continuators usually referred to the steppe adversaries of Rus' as "pagans."[39] That term not only accompanied the actual name of a given people but also often replaced it. For

---

[34] The deterioration of relations between Western and Eastern Christianity affected Rus' only in the 1230s. It had no impact on the Galician and Volhynian princes, a fact fully reflected in the Galician-Volhynian Chronicle. There is an extensive literature on the relations of the Galician-Volhynian princes with Rome and their Catholic neighbors; for the most recent contribution, see Boris Floria, *U istokov religioznogo raskola slavianskogo mira (XIII vek)* (St. Petersburg, 2004). On the attitudes of the authors of the Galician-Volhynian Chronicle toward Catholicism, see ibid., pp. 198–205.

[35] See *Halyts'ko-Volyns'kyi litopys*, p. 116.

[36] See Hrushevs'kyi, *Istoriia Ukraïny-Rusy*, vol. VI (repr. Kyiv, 1995), pp. 297–98.

[37] One of the best examples of this in the Primary Chronicle is to be found in the legend about St. Paul as an apostle to the Rus'. The authors of the Kyiv Chronicle regarded Prince Iziaslav of Kyiv and King Géza II of Hungary as rulers who behaved according to the Christian code of ethics ("you act in a Christian manner," *PSRL*, II: 453), while the author of the Galician-Volhynian Chronicle uses the same terms to characterize the Orthodox and Polish Roman Catholic clergy (*popovi*) and Orthodox and Roman Catholic churches (*tserkva*) (*Halyts'ko-Volyns'kyi litopys*, p. 140).

[38] On the treatment of the steppe nomads in medieval Rus' sources, see Leonid Chekin, "The Godless Ishmaelites: The Image of the Steppe in Eleventh–Thirteenth Century Rus'," *Russian History* 19 (1992): 9–28.

[39] An interesting example of the "updating" of the Primary Chronicle's ethnopolitical terminology occurs in an addition to its text in the sixteenth-century Voskresensk Chronicle. There, a reference to the Polovtsians as "pagans" is added to the account of Volodymyr Monomakh's expedition against the Polovtsians in 1111. See *Povest' vremennykh let*, p. 192.

example, the Kyiv Chronicle's first reference to the Polovtsians identifies them as "pagans" with no further elaboration of whom the chronicler had in mind.[40] The religious component of the new image of the Polovtsians becomes especially clear in the chronicler's account of the Polovtsian attack on Rus' in the summer of 1179. He writes: "In that year, in the month of August, foreigners came to the Rus' Land, godless Ishmaelites. Accursed Hagarites, the filthy brood of a devil, Satanic in nature, named Konchak, who inflicted evil on true Orthodox Christians."[41]

The authors of the Galician-Volhynian Chronicle transferred this harsh characterization of the Polovtsians as godless infidels to their successors in the Black Sea steppes, the Mongols, or Tatars, as they became known in the Rus' literary tradition. The first incursion of the Mongols into that region, which led to the Battle of the Kalka River (1223), was described by the chronicler as a manifestation of "godless Moabites, called Tatars."[42] In the chronicle account of Batu's attacks on the Rus' principalities in 1237–40, the Mongols were characterized not only as "foreigners" but also as "godless Ishmaelites," "godless Hagarites," and "godless Tatars."[43] As in the case of the Polovtsian attacks on Rus', the chroniclers regarded the Mongol invasion as punishment for the sins of the Christians. The chronicler reconciled himself to the Rus' princes' submission to the power of the Mongols but was vehemently opposed to the notion of accepting their religion. That was the main burden of the chronicler's account of the death of Prince Mykhail of Chernihiv, who was allegedly killed by the Mongols for refusing to convert to their faith. He reportedly said to Batu: "If God has delivered us and our land into your hands because of our sins, we make obeisance to you and pay our respects to you. As for the law of your fathers and your fiat, which is repugnant to God, we do not make obeisance."[44] The protagonist of the chronicle, Prince Danylo, is praised by the chronicler for refusing to make obeisance to the sacred bush, as Prince Yaroslav Vsevolodovych of Vladimir-Suzdal had allegedly done at Mongol insistence. Yet Danylo apparently agreed to drink fermented mare's milk (*kumys*), an act that made him a Tatar in Batu's eyes.[45] Probably it was a lesser evil to accept a new political identity than a new religious one, thereby abandoning Christianity.[46]

[40] *PSRL*, II: 286.   [41] Ibid., col. 612.
[42] See *Halyts'ko-Volyns'kyi litopys*, p. 85.   [43] Ibid., pp. 99–101.
[44] Ibid., p. 105. On Mykhail of Chernihiv, see Martin Dimnik, *Mikhail, Prince of Chernigov and Grand Prince of Kiev, 1224–1246* (Toronto, 1981).
[45] See *Halyts'ko-Volyns'kyi litopys*, p. 109.
[46] The chronicler recorded numerous examples of the Galician-Volhynian princes' negative view of the Mongols as "pagans." He was also displeased that the Mongols forced the princes to participate in their campaign against Poland in 1287 (ibid., p. 139).

If the Galician-Volhynian elites were separated by political, ethnic, and religious differences from the Poles, Hungarians, and Czechs in the west and nomadic peoples to the south, how did they view their relations with the other Rus' principalities – the Rus' Land that had been baptized by St. Volodymyr, an act to which they continued to refer in the Galician-Volhynian Chronicle? What we know about the period attests that the leaders of the Rurikid clan continued to maintain close relations, as shown by the marriage of Danylo's daughter to the son of Yaroslav of Suzdal. Nevertheless, it would appear that the Mongol invasion became a major turning point in the self-perception of the Rus' princes. The text of the Galician-Volhynian Chronicle, compiled in the second half of the thirteenth century, gives ample evidence of that impact. Once the Mongols took direct control of most of the Rus' Land, the senior representatives of the Rurikid clan all but lost the object of their common loyalty, whether they were in Galicia-Volhynia or in Vladimir-Suzdalia. The discourse of the common good of the Rus' Land disappeared from the pages of the chronicle, whose territorial coverage also became much more narrow. This became particularly apparent when Danylo's chroniclers were replaced by those of Volodymyr Vasylkovych, whose political horizons were essentially limited to Volhynia and its immediate neighbors. Scholars have long regretted this change of perspective, but for us it is the best evidence of the gradual shrinking of the world of the Rurikid elites after the Mongol invasion. Their political ambitions changed profoundly, from competing for rule over the Rus' Land in the Kyiv region to maintaining control over their own patrimonies.

What happened in Galicia-Volhynia was a transfer of the old concept of the Rus' Land to the new entity, ruled by the heirs of Roman Mstyslavych and his two sons, Danylo and Vasylko. As we have seen, the chroniclers of Danylo and Vasylko's son Volodymyr successfully applied the term "Rus' Land" to the territory of Galicia-Volhynia.[47] Indeed, they tended to apply it exclusively to their principality. Volodymyr's chroniclers treated only the descendants of Roman Mstyslavych as princes of Rus', denying that title to other Rurikids. In the chronicle account of the Lithuanian campaign of 1275, three Galician-Volhynian princes, Lev, Mstyslav, and Volodymyr, are called "Rus' princes" to the exclusion of all the other Rurikids who took part in the expedition,[48] including the "trans-Dnipro"

[47] Omeljan Pritsak, who has noted the new meaning acquired by the term "Rus'" in Galicia-Volhynia, argues that the Galician author of the chronicle was much more willing to call his land "Rus'" than was his Volhynian continuator. See Pritsak, "Kiev and All of Rus': The Fate of a Sacral Idea," *Harvard Ukrainian Studies* 10, nos. 3–4 (December 1986): 279–300, here 287–88.

[48] See *Halyts'ko-Volyns'kyi litopys*, pp. 131–32. The chronicler referred to Lev, Mstyslav, and Volodymyr alternately as "Rus'" or "Volhynian" princes (ibid., pp. 137–40).

princes of Briansk and Smolensk, as well as the princes of Pinsk and
Turaŭ. The failure to apply the term "Rus′ princes" to the rulers of Turaŭ,
a town traditionally considered to be part of the Rus′ Land proper, is
particularly telling.[49] It serves to indicate the almost total appropriation
of the Rus′ name by the Galician-Volhynian elites toward the end of the
thirteenth century, when the Galician-Volhynian Chronicle underwent
its final revision.

As Kyiv and the Rus′ Land (in the narrow meaning of the term) became
less effective in exercising their leading role – a tendency reinforced by the
Mongol invasion – references to them in the text of the Galician-Volhynian
Chronicle gradually disappeared. One of the chronicle's concluding sections, the panegyric to Prince Volodymyr Vasylkovych of Volhynia, also
attests to the decline of Kyiv's symbolic importance on the political and
cultural map of the new Rus′ Land. In the chronicle list of churches that
Volodymyr Vasylkovych built during his reign or supported with donations, none is located in Kyiv, although there are references to churches in
Volodymyr, Peremyshl, Lutsk, Liuboml, and even Chernihiv in the trans-
Dnipro region. Clearly, the times when princely servitors from Rostov
had made major donations to the Kyivan Cave Monastery (recorded in
the Kyiv Chronicle under the year 1130) were long gone.[50] Besides, the
Kyivan clergy itself was fleeing the city. Among those who took part in the
funeral of Volodymyr Vasylkovych, the chronicle mentions the hegumen
of the Cave Monastery, Ahapyt – a possible indication that he had either
moved to Volhynia or was staying there at the time of the prince's death.
We know for certain that within a few years the metropolitan of Kyiv himself abandoned his seat forever and moved to Northeastern Rus′. He took
with him the title of metropolitan of all Rus′, helping to transfer the Rus′
name to the Vladimir-Suzdal principality, but not before the Galician-
Volhynian princes had appropriated that Kyivan "brand." Although their
powerful principality, restored by Danylo in 1245, disintegrated after his
death in 1264, both constituents of the former super-principality retained
the Rus′ identity.

The Rus′ Land of the north

When and under what circumstances was the name of the Rus′ Land
adopted in Northeastern Rus′, and what were the political underpinnings

---

[49] For a reference to Turaŭ as one of the districts of the Kyivan Land, see the entry for
1155 in the Kyiv Chronicle (*Litopys Rus′kyi*, p. 265).
[50] Ibid., p. 184.

and ideological significance of that process? It is difficult if not impossible to give an exact answer to the first part of this question. What remains beyond doubt, however, is that the chroniclers of Northeastern Rus', the authors of the so-called Laurentian Codex,[51] were much slower than their Galician-Volhynian counterparts to apply the term "Rus' Land" to their realm, which they usually called the "Suzdal Land." Under the year 1249, they recorded that the Mongol khan had awarded Kyiv and all the Rus' Land to Aleksandr Nevsky, adding that Vladimir on the Kliazma was given to his brother Andrei. Thus for them the Rus' Land was still centered in Kyiv, not in Vladimir. They clearly distinguished their land from the Rus' Land around Kyiv, as they did the two Pereiaslavs – one in the Rus' Land, which they called Pereiaslav-Russkii, and the other in Northeastern Rus', known as Pereiaslav-Zalesskii.[52] According to Charles J. Halperin, the name of the Rus' Land was adopted in Northeastern Rus' sometime between 1293 and 1328, with the process fully complete by 1340. It appears that after 1310 the chroniclers all but ceased to use the term "Suzdal Land," replacing it with "Rus' Land."[53]

Halperin bases his observations on the data of the Trinity Chronicle, the earliest of the Moscow chronicles known to scholars. The portion written by native chroniclers covered events in Northeastern Rus' from 1305, the year that ended the narrative of the Laurentian Codex, to 1408 – the period in which, according to Halperin, the *translatio* of the concept of

---

[51] The Laurentian Codex is a compilation (like the Hypatian Codex) that includes the text of the Primary Chronicle but then shifts to the history of Northeastern Rus' and covers it up to 1305. The surviving copy of the codex was made by monks of the Nizhegorod Cave Monastery in Northeastern Rus' in 1377.

[52] See the geographical index and references to both Pereiaslavs in *Lavrent'evskaia letopis'*, *PSRL*, vol. I (Moscow, 1962). There was a third Pereiaslav in the Riazan Land, already known to the compiler of the Laurentian Codex but much more familiar to his fourteenth-century continuators.

[53] See Halperin, "The Concept of the Russian Land"; idem, "The Russian Land and the Russian Tsar: The Emergence of Muscovite Ideology, 1380–1408," *Forschungen zur osteuropäischen Geschichte* (Berlin) (1976): 7–103 (the latter article being a revised and augmented version of the former); idem, "The Concept of *Russkaia zemlia* and Medieval National Consciousness from the Tenth to the Fifteenth Centuries," *Nationalities Papers* 8, no. 1 (Spring 1981): 75–86. My discussion of the historical evidence generally follows Halperin's selection of sources. My summary excludes the data provided by the "Slovo o pogibeli Russkoi zemli," as I believe that Halperin offers sufficient evidence to rule out this text as a product of the writing done in Northeastern Rus'. I have also omitted the "Povest' o razorenii Batyem Riazani" from my discussion, as that work is not known from the medieval compilations. For the text of the "Povest'" as it appears in a sixteenth-century codex, see V. P. Adrianova-Peretts, ed., *Voinskie povesti drevnei Rusi* (Moscow and Leningrad, 1949). Nor do I comment on the *Tale of Ihor's Campaign*, whose authenticity has been placed in serious doubt by students of the text. For the most recent discussion of the issue, see Edward L. Keenan, *Josef Dobrovský and the Origins of the* Igor' Tale (Cambridge, Mass., 2003).

the Rus' Land from the Dnipro to the Volga region actually took place.[54] There is nevertheless a serious problem with the Trinity Chronicle – it no longer exists, for the original manuscript perished in the fire of Moscow in 1812, when Napoleon paid an unsolicited visit to the former Russian capital. No copy of the famous chronicle was made, although extensive quotations from it appeared in the *History of the Russian State*, published after the Napoleonic Wars by the official historian of Russia, Nikolai Karamzin. On the basis of these citations, M. D. Priselkov reconstructed the text of the lost chronicle, filling in the text between quotations with borrowings from other, obviously later, chronicles that in his highly informed opinion were closest to the lost text of the Trinity Chronicle.[55] It was on this reconstructed text of the chronicle that Halperin based his conclusions. Although Priselkov's authority remains unchallenged, it is clear that observations made on the basis of his reconstruction rather than on the actual text of the chronicle are hypothetical. In his later studies, Halperin declined to treat Priselkov's reconstruction of the Trinity Chronicle as an authentic and reliable source and even criticized other scholars for doing so.[56] Nevertheless, Halperin's earlier conclusions regarding the time when the concept of the Rus' Land was transferred to Suzdalia were never revised and are clearly in need of reexamination, given the hypothetical nature of Priselkov's reconstruction of the Trinity Chronicle.

This applies, for example, to the chronicle entry for 1293, regarded as the first application of the idea of the Rus' Land to Northeastern Rus'. The entry does not belong to Karamzin's citations from the Trinity Chronicle but is one of Priselkov's borrowings from the Simeon Chronicle, written no earlier than the late fifteenth century and preserved in a sixteenth-century copy.[57] In fact, all but three references to the Rus' Land in the reconstructed text of the Trinity Chronicle come from Priselkov's borrowings, not from Karamzin's citations. Of these three, two were not directly attributed by Karamzin to the Trinity Chronicle but interpreted as such by Priselkov himself. There is only one unquestionable reference

---

[54] For a brief discussion of the Trinity Chronicle and its relation to the later chronicles of Northeastern Rus', see L. L. Murav'eva, *Letopisanie Severo-Vostochnoi Rusi XIII–XV veka* (Moscow, 1983), pp. 21–41.

[55] See Priselkov's reconstruction of the text of the Trinity Chronicle in his *Troitskaia letopis'. Rekonstruktsiia teksta* (Moscow and Leningrad, 1950).

[56] See Charles J. Halperin, "'Text and Textology': Salmina's Dating of the Chronicle Tales about Dmitrii Donskoi," *Slavonic and East European Review* 79, no. 2 (April 2001): 248–63.

[57] Priselkov used the Chronicle as a basis for his reconstruction of the text of the Trinity Chronicle between 1177 and 1305 (see Priselkov's introduction to his *Troitskaia letopis'*, pp. 41–44). On the Simeon Chronicle, see Murav'eva, *Letopisanie Severo-Vostochnoi Rusi*, p. 23.

to the Rus' Land in the original text of the Trinity Chronicle as it is known today from Karamzin's notes. That reference occurs in the entry for 1332 and is related to a famine that afflicted the Rus' Land.[58] Although the entry in question has been sandwiched between two others that discuss events in and around Moscow, its actual content does not allow one to conclude that the chronicler had in mind that particular region when he was writing about the Rus' Land. It is difficult to say whether the chronicler was referring to the area around Moscow, the whole Suzdal Land, all of Rus' irrespective of the Mongolian-Lithuanian border, or the Kyiv region affected by the famine. Thus the portions of the Trinity Chronicle preserved in Karamzin's notes do not give us enough grounds to say anything definitive about the usage of the term "Rus' Land" in Northeastern Rus' during the fourteenth century – the period in which, according to Halperin, the *translatio* of the term actually took place. One of Halperin's sources – the earliest version of the *Life of Metropolitan Petr*, which he dates to the 1320s–30s, or the period when the *translatio* was supposed to be all but complete – indicates that at the time Moscow was still considered part of the Suzdal Land, not of the Rus' Land. In his later study, Halperin extended the "transitional period" by a decade, from 1340 to the mid-fourteenth century,[59] but this extension does not appear to solve the problem, as the only reference to the Rus' Land in the authentic text of the Trinity Chronicle, even if it actually pertains to Moscow, dates from 1408 or later (as the chronicle was completed after that year).

Ironically, despite the abundance of chronicle data, the fourteenth century seems to be as obscure to those studying the history of Northeastern Rus' as it is to those working on Southwestern Rus'. In the southwest, the demise of independent Rus' polities in the course of the fourteenth century led to the disappearance of chronicle writing. Until the fifteenth century, there was no political agency interested in revising and reediting the existing chronicles. In the northeast, where local chronicle writing flourished in the fourteenth century, it was dealt a major blow in the fifteenth, when Moscow monopolized the process. Moscow scribes included data from the chronicles of subordinate appanage principalities in their own chronicles, revising those accounts according to the requirements of a grand-princely power and the political ambitions of the Moscow-based metropolitans. Thus, by and large, we have access only to a late,

---

[58] See Priselkov, *Troitskaia letopis'*, entries for the years 1308 (p. 353), 1328 (p. 359), and 1332 (p. 361).

[59] See Halperin, "The Concept of the Russian Land," p. 35; cf. idem, "The Russian Land and the Russian Tsar," p. 66.

predominantly fifteenth-century Muscovite point of view on the events of the fourteenth century in Northeastern Rus'.[60]

Where should we go from here? Can we use other written sources to determine whether the Moscow scribes actually employed the concept of the Rus' Land prior to the fifteenth century? The literary works of the so-called Kulikovo cycle should certainly be considered for that purpose. These writings, which laud the victory of Grand Prince Dmitrii Ivanovich (known from the sixteenth century as Donskoi) over Tatar forces led by Mamai at the Kulikovo Field in August 1380, include the *Slovo o zhitii i prestavlenii velikogo kniazia Dmitriia Ivanovicha* (Oration Concerning the Life and Passing of Grand Prince Dmitrii Ivanovich), the *Skazanie o Mamaevom poboishche* (Tale of the Battle with Mamai), and the famous epic *Zadonshchina* (The Battle beyond the Don), which was either based on the *Tale of Ihor's Campaign* or influenced it. All of them dwell on the Rus' Land as an object of common loyalty for the prince of Moscow, his allies and subjects. A reading of these sources allowed Halperin not only to support his hypothesis that by the mid-fourteenth century the myth of the Rus' Land had been fully adopted in Moscow but also to argue that by the end of that century it was already subordinate to the myth of the Muscovite ruler.[61] That might indeed have been the case if the literary works in question had been written immediately or shortly after the Battle of Kulikovo Field. But were they?

Donald Ostrowski, for one, has serious doubts in that regard. Citing the findings of the Russian scholar M. A. Salmina and his own research on anti-Tatar motifs in the literature of the period, Ostrowski claims that those works could not have been written before the 1440s.[62] Halperin, who questioned Salmina's dating, did not challenge Ostrowski's dating of the works of the Kulikovo cycle.[63] Yet Ostrowski's conclusions shift the end of Halperin's *translatio* period by a hundred years, to the mid-fifteenth century. Most scholars seem to agree that the texts of the Kulikovo cycle already existed in one form or another by the second half of the fifteenth century. If that is so, then it might be assumed that by that time "the Rus' Land" had indeed been adopted as the name of Northeastern Rus': the polity of the Muscovite princes had successfully taken over for its

---

[60] On the history of chronicle writing in Northeastern Rus', see Murav'eva, *Letopisanie Severo-Vostochnoi Rusi*. On the rewriting and reconstruction of major ideological myths in Muscovite Rus', see Andreas Ebbinghaus, "Reception and Ideology in the Literature of Muscovite Rus'," in *Culture and Identity in Muscovy, 1359–1584*, ed. A. M. Kleimola and G. D. Lenhoff (Moscow, 1997), pp. 68–83.

[61] See Halperin, "The Concept of the Russian Land," pp. 36–38. Cf. idem, "The Russian Land and the Russian Tsar," pp. 69–78.

[62] See Ostrowski, *Muscovy and the Mongols*, pp. 155–63.

[63] See Halperin, "'Text and Textology,'" pp. 254–55.

own purposes the concept of the Rus' Land, which prior to the Mongol invasion of the mid-thirteenth century had been applied predominantly to the Kyiv-Chernihiv-Pereiaslav triangle in the Dnipro region.

From Kyiv to Moscow

What was the political rationale and ideological meaning of the concept of the Rus' Land as it emerges from the works of the Kulikovo cycle, and what can that cycle tell us about the identity projects that were under way in Northeastern Rus' of the period?

One of the meanings of the concept of the Rus' Land in fifteenth-century Mongol Rus' can be reconstructed on the basis of the *Life of St. Sergii of Radonezh* (ca. 1418), arguably one of the earliest works of the Kulikovo cycle. According to the author of the *Life*, Sergii, one of the principal saints of Russian Orthodoxy, directly associated in later historical tradition with Prince Dmitrii Donskoi, was born "in the Rus' Land in the Grand Princedom of Tver during the reign of Grand Prince Dmitrii Mikhailovich, in the time of the Most Reverend Archbishop Petr, Metropolitan of All Rus'." The reader of the *Life* was then informed that Sergii's family resided in Rostov and the Rostov area (*oblast'*). Thus the Rus' or Rus' Land of the author of the *Life* included a number of oblasts ruled by various grand princes (apart from this mention of the grand prince of Tver, there are references in the text to Grand Princes Ivan Danilovich and Dmitrii Ivanovich of Moscow); in terms of church jurisdiction, it was part of the Metropolitanate of All Rus'. Such is the concept of the Rus' Land as it emerges from a text that is thought to have been written in the first decades of the fifteenth century.[64]

What was known to the author of the *Life of St. Sergii of Radonezh* as the Rus' Land was often referred to by other authors as the "Land of All Rus'." The so-called *Short Chronicle Tale* about the Kulikovo battle, most probably composed between 1449 and 1462 and later included in the Simeon Chronicle, presented Prince Dmitrii Donskoi as the protector of the "Land of All Rus'." In the tale, that land emerges as an important object of loyalty and is discussed along with the Polovtsian Land, the Tatar Land, and the Riazan Land. There is little doubt that in this particular context it included the territories whose inhabitants were loyal to

---

[64] For excerpts from the *Life of St. Sergii of Radonezh*, see *Khrestomatiia po drevnei russkoi literature*, comp. N. K. Gudzii (Moscow, 1973), pp. 196–203. On the cult of St. Sergii, which apparently became very popular in the mid-fifteenth century, see David B. Miller, "The Cult of St. Sergius of Radonezh and Its Political Uses," *Slavic Review* 52, no. 4 (1993): 680–99; Pierre Gonneau, "The Trinity-Sergius Brotherhood in State and Society," in *Culture and Identity in Muscovy*, pp. 116–45, here 137–44.

Dmitrii Donskoi as grand prince. In the hierarchy of the grand prince's own loyalties, as presented in the tale, the "Land of All Rus'" also occupied an important place. In the list of possessions and institutions that Dmitrii intended to protect from Tatar invasion, it followed Moscow, to which the chronicler referred as the prince's patrimony, and the church, which the chronicler probably served. Indeed, the "Land of All Rus'" is mentioned in the tale much more frequently than the prince's patrimony of Moscow, which was certainly part of that land. Other centers of the "Land of All Rus'" mentioned in the tale included Pereiaslavl, Kostroma, and Vladimir.[65]

For a better understanding of how the Moscow-ruled Rus' Land replaced the notion of the Kyiv-based one, we may turn to contemporary accounts of the lives of two saints, Stefan of Perm and Dmitrii Donskoi, the hero of Kulikovo. The first of these lives, traditionally attributed to Epifanii Premudryi (the Wise), probably dates from the period between 1396, the year of the death of Stefan of Perm, and 1420, the approximate year of Epifanii's demise, even though it first appears in a manuscript of 1480. The dating of the second monument is no less tentative. Although it is believed that the first version of the *Oration Concerning the Life and Passing of Grand Prince Dmitrii Ivanovich*[66] was written soon after the prince's death in 1389, the text that has actually come down to us bears the marks of later editing. Thus, some scholars tend to date the *Oration* to the first half of the fifteenth century[67] and others to the 1470s, when the work was first included in the Muscovite chronicles.[68]

Generally speaking, it is fair to assume that if the *Life of St. Stefan of Perm* gives us an idea of how the Rus' Land was regarded by authors of Mongol Rus', the *Oration* represents the views of the post-Mongol period.

[65] See excerpts from the Simeon Chronicle in Priselkov, *Troitskaia letopis'*, pp. 419–21. The *Expanded Chronicle Tale*, which was included, along with other compilations, in the *Novgorod IV Chronicle*, also defined Moscow as the patrimony of Prince Dmitrii. For excerpts from the *Novgorod IV Chronicle*, see *Povesti o Kulikovskoi bitve*, ed. M. N. Tikhomirov, V. F. Rzhiga, and L. A. Dmitriev (Moscow, 1959), pp. 30–40.

[66] For the text of the *Oration*, see *Pamiatniki literatury drevnei Rusi. XIV – seredina XV veka* (Moscow, 1981), pp. 208–29. For a discussion of the monument, see Harvey Goldblatt, "Confessional and National Identity in Early Muscovite Literature: The Discourse on the Life and Death of Dmitrii Ivanovich Donskoi," in *Culture and Identity in Muscovy*, pp. 84–115.

[67] See Halperin, "The Russian Land and the Russian Tsar," pp. 69–78.

[68] See Ostrowski, *Muscovy and the Mongols*, pp. 161, 178. Since the author of the *Oration* often speaks of the "Land of All Rus'" and identifies Dmitrii as its tsar, it is clear that the text was at least heavily revised (if not actually written) in the second half of the fifteenth century, or even later, when the title of tsar came to be applied to the Muscovite princes. The earliest copies of the *Oration* date from the period after 1481. See Gail Lenhoff, "Unofficial Veneration of the Danilovichi in Muscovite Rus'," in *Culture and Identity in Muscovy*, pp. 391–416, here 408–9.

That era saw a dramatic expansion of the power of the Muscovite princes, who annexed Tver and Novgorod and began to compete with the Grand Duchy of Lithuania for Rus' territories under its control. The authors of the *Life* and the *Oration* had very different notions of the location and extent of the Rus' Land, as we can readily see from their treatment of an excerpt from Metropolitan Ilarion's *Sermon* in which the eleventh-century cleric calls upon his listeners/readers to praise Prince Volodymyr, the ruler of the Rus' Land.[69] Writing, apparently, in the late fourteenth or early fifteenth century, Epifanii Premudryi stated: "the Greek [land praises] the apostle Andrew; the Rus' Land [praises] Grand Prince Volodymyr, who baptized it; Moscow blesses and honors Metropolitan Petr as a new miracle-worker; the Rostov Land its Bishop Leontii; you, Bishop Stefan, the Perm Land praises and honors. . . ."[70] For this author, then, Moscow was not part of the Rus' Land, which did not extend either to Rostov or to Perm. A different picture emerges from the *Oration*, presumably written in the late fifteenth century, whose author also used a quotation from Ilarion's *Sermon* to extol his hero, Prince Dmitrii. He describes Prince Volodymyr as a saint "praised by Kyiv and its neighboring towns," while noting that Prince Dmitrii was praised by all the Rus' Land.[71] The way in which the concept of the "Land of All Rus'" emerges from the pages of the *Oration* indicates quite clearly that it does not include Kyiv. In fact, the notion of the Rus' Land was dissociated from Kyiv and attached to Moscow and the realm ruled by its princes in the last decades of the fifteenth century. Apparently, the new Rus' Land also included Rostov and Perm. The dominance of saints based in particular lands was passing, while the day of the all-Rus' (Muscovite) saints was clearly dawning, as shown by the elevation of Grand Prince Dmitrii Donskoi of Moscow to that status in the *Oration*.

The geographical limits of the Rus' Land and the central status of that notion within the hierarchy of Muscovite loyalties become clearly apparent in the most famous monument of the Kulikovo cycle, the so-called *Zadonshchina*. In this epic, preserved in a number of versions dating from the 1470s to the 1520s, the Rus' Land emerges as a territory based in

---

[69] See *Sermons and Rhetoric of Kievan Rus'*, trans. and with introduction by Simon Franklin (Cambridge, Mass., 1991), pp. 3–30.

[70] Adapted from Halperin, "The Russian Land and the Russian Tsar," p. 77.

[71] See ibid., p. 77. The *Admonition of Metropolitan Petr*, apparently written in the fourteenth century, uses the same quotation from the *Sermon* of Metropolitan Ilarion but avoids references to "lands," focusing instead on towns. There Moscow, which acquired its saint in Metropolitan Petr, is listed along with Kyiv, which "took pride" in the Rus' martyr princes SS. Borys and Hlib. See Jaroslaw Pelenski, "The Origins of the Muscovite Ecclesiastical Claims to the Kievan Inheritance," in idem, *The Contest for the Legacy of Kievan Rus'* (Boulder, Colo., 1998), pp. 61–76, here 63.

Moscow and its surroundings (especially Serpukhov and Kolomna). It does not include the Riazan Land, whose prince opposed Dmitrii Donskoi and sided with the Tatars. Yet it refers to a broader area than the immediate surroundings of Moscow, which the epic calls the *Zalesskaia zemlia*, or the land beyond the forest. On occasion, the notion of the Rus' Land also extends as far as "Great Novgorod." Most importantly, in *Zadonshchina* the Rus' Land moves from third place in the hierarchy of princely loyalties (as presented in the *Short Chronicle Tale*) to first place. According to the author of *Zadonshchina*, not only the Northern Rus' princes but also those of Lithuania were prepared to fight for the Rus' Land, the Orthodox faith, and (occasionally) for the wrongs done to Prince Dmitrii.[72] The rise of the Rus' Land in the hierarchy of princely loyalties is accompanied by its treatment as the patrimony of the grand prince. For example, in the *Oration Concerning the Life and Passing of Grand Prince Dmitrii Ivanovich*, the Rus' Land, not Moscow, is mentioned twice as the patrimony of the prince of Moscow.[73] According to *Zadonshchina*, the Rus' princes joined Dmitrii against Mamai to fight for their patrimony, otherwise designated in the epic as the "Rus' Land."[74]

The works of the Kulikovo cycle reflect in significant detail the transformation of the notion of the Rus' Land from the common patrimony of the Kyivan princes to the exclusive patrimony of the princes of Moscow. It would appear that the Galician-Volhynian princes were the first not only to assert themselves as belonging to the Rus' Land but also to advance their exclusive right to that concept. The northeastern rulers – the main rivals of the Galician-Volhynian princes in claiming possession of Kyiv during the decades prior to the Mongol attack – were slower to make their claims. One might assume that Prince Andrei Bogoliubsky's effort to develop a rival center in Suzdal during the twelfth century was a factor that slowed the adoption of the name and concept of the Rus' Land in Northeastern Rus'. As the transformation of St. Aleksandr Nevsky from "son of Suzdal" to "son of Rus'" in early modern Muscovite literature well attests,[75] the core of that new entity lay in the lands of the Vladimir-Suzdal Principality. From that perspective, Halperin is certainly right in asserting that "in part, the political and intellectual ancestor of Muscovy was

---

[72] See "Slovo Sofoniia riazantsa o velikom kniazi Dmitrii Ivanoviche i brate ego Vladimire Ondreeviche," in *Povesti o Kulikovskoi bitve*, pp. 9–17.

[73] See Jaroslaw Pelenski, "The Origins of the Official Muscovite Claims to the Kievan Inheritance," in idem, *The Contest for the Legacy of Kievan Rus'*, pp. 77–101, here 86.

[74] See "Slovo Sofoniia riazantsa," p. 10.

[75] On the cult of St. Aleksandr Nevsky, see Mari Mäki-Petäys, "Warrior and Saint: The Changing Image of Alexander Nevsky as an Aspect of Russian Imperial Identity," in *Imperial and National Identities in Pre-revolutionary, Soviet and Post-Soviet Russia*, ed. Chris J. Chulos and Johannes Remy (Helsinki, 2002), pp. 45–69.

not eleventh-century Kyiv, but twelfth-century Suzdalia."[76] One might add that the Suzdal Land also served as the immediate forerunner of the notion of the Rus' Land in the political discourse of Northeastern Rus'.

Local identities

As the princes of Moscow and their bookmen adopted the concept of the Rus' Land for their territories as one of the basic elements of their identity, what was happening to the identity of their subjects, especially those living outside the former Suzdal Land? It is difficult to answer this question satisfactorily, given the revising and editing of the local chronicles that were eventually merged into the Moscow codices. Nevertheless, there exist chronicle entries that avoided complete rewriting by the Moscow editors, as well as hagiographic and other writings of the fifteenth century composed outside Moscow, and Muscovite texts that take account of the views of people from the newly acquired territories. They support the assumption that the acquisition of a common identity was no simple process and that loyalties to particular lands presented a formidable obstacle to the Moscow-sponsored identity.

Novgorod was of course among the strongest bastions of local identity, and it is hardly surprising that its chroniclers, despite subsequent censorship by Moscow editors, best represent the non-Muscovite regional identity of the period. According to the Novgorodian chronicles, the local elites changed their minds about the relation of their territory to the Rus' Land. The entries dealing with pre-Mongol history positioned Novgorod outside the Rus' Land, which was based in Kyiv, but records of developments in the second half of the thirteenth century expressed a different attitude. For the first time, the author of a Novgorod chronicle claimed the name of the Rus' Land for the territory that he and his predecessors had earlier termed the Novgorod oblast in the entry for 1263. In that entry, the recently deceased Prince Aleksandr Nevsky was praised for his efforts on behalf of "Novgorod and all the Rus' Land." There was another shift in the entries on the fourteenth century. The entry for 1327, which discussed the Tatar attack on Northeastern Rus', clearly distinguished the Rus' Land (which included Tver, Kashin, and Torzhok) from Novgorod.[77]

As a rule, the fourteenth- and fifteenth-century Novgorodians did not consider their realm part of the Rus' Land, which they often referred to as

---

[76] See Halperin, "The Russian Land and the Russian Tsar," p. 67.

[77] See Charles J. Halperin, "Novgorod and 'Novgorodian Land,'" *Cahiers du monde russe* 40, no. 3 (July–September 1999): 345–64, here 353. Cf. *Davnia istoriia Ukraïny*, ed. Petro Tolochko et al., vol. III (Kyiv, 2003), p. 487.

the Low Country (*Niz* or *Nizovskaia zemlia*). The Low Country included the possessions of the Moscow princes (formerly the Suzdal Land), the Riazan Land, and the Principality of Tver, to list the most important polities of the region. Novgorod and its sister republic of Pskov, which was in the Novgorodian sphere of influence, were outside the bounds of the Rus' Land.[78] According to the chroniclers, the "Novgorod men" fought and died not for the Rus' Land, like the Moscow princes, but for St. Sophia, the holy protectress of Novgorod and the patroness of their cathedral, which was the seat of their archbishop and the symbol of what they called "Great Novgorod."[79] As Halperin argues, the Novgorodians never developed a concept of the Novgorodian Land, since they lacked the essential underpinning for such a political idea, namely, a local dynasty. Nevertheless, it is well known that even after annexation to the Muscovite realm, the Novgorodians preserved their separate identity. For example, treaties between Novgorod and Livonia signed after the formal takeover of the republic by Moscow spoke of "Novgorodian merchants" and "Novgorodians" in general, not of Rus' merchants or "Rus'ians."[80] Judging by the troubled history of Moscow–Novgorod relations, the Novgorodians not only possessed a distinct identity but also often harbored strong anti-Muscovite feelings. They were not alone, as grievances against Moscow were also expressed by representatives of local elites in territories that had never enjoyed autonomy comparable to Novgorod's or lost it long before the fifteenth century.

Clear signs of strong local identity and resentment of Moscow are apparent in the *Lives* of St. Sergii of Radonezh and St. Stefan of Perm. As noted earlier, the author of the *Life of St. Stefan* (whether he was Epifanii or not) did not regard Moscow, Rostov, and Perm as parts of the Rus' Land, which in his opinion was still based in Kyiv. He also distinguished himself as an ardent loyalist of the Perm Land and a critic of Moscow and the Muscovites (*moskvichi*), who possessed the earthly remains of

[78] The positioning of Novgorod outside the Rus' Land was characteristic not only of the views of "insiders," i.e., the Novgorodian chroniclers, but also of such "outsiders" as Patriarch Dionisios of Constantinople, who wrote in 1467 that he had sent envoys to "the Land of All Rus' and to Great Novgorod." See E. V. Beliakova, "K istorii uchrezhdeniia avtokefalii Russkoi tserkvi," in *Rossiia na putiakh tsentralizatsii. Sbornik statei*, ed. D. S. Likhachev et al. (Moscow, 1982), pp. 152–56, here 155.

[79] For numerous references to the Rus' Land as a territory that excluded Novgorod and Pskov while including Moscow and Tver, see *The Chronicle of Novgorod, 1016–1471* (London, 1914; repr. Hattiesburg, Miss., 1970), pp. 125, 128, 129, 131, 136, 156, 159, 167, 171, 179. This is a translation of *Novgorodskaia letopis' po sinodal'nomu kharateinomu spisku*, vol. II (St. Petersburg, 1888).

[80] See N. A. Kazakova, "O polozhenii Novgoroda v sostave Russkogo gosudarstva v kontse XV – pervoi polovine XVI v.," in *Rossiia na putiakh tsentralizatsii*, pp. 156–59.

St. Stefan and did not want them to be in the Perm Land.[81] The author
or editor of the *Life of St. Sergii*, unlike the author of the *Life of St. Stefan*,
assumed that Rostov was indeed part of the Rus′ Land but pulled no
punches when it came to describing how Moscow, under Grand Prince
Ivan Kalita, had annexed the Rostov Land, where the parents of St. Sergii
resided. This is the picture he presents:

and not a few of them, the people of Rostov, gave their possessions to the Muscovites under duress and suffered wounds to their bodies because of this, with
reproach [to the Muscovites], and went away empty-handed, for they were the
image of utter destitution, as they had not only been stripped of their possessions
but had also suffered wounds to their flesh and dolefully bore and endured those
sores on their bodies.

The author of the *Life of St. Sergii* accused the minions of the Muscovite
prince not only of expropriating the possessions of the Rostov boyar elite
and persecuting its members but also of attacking the local bishop. "And
there was great fear among all who heard and saw this, not only in the town
of Rostov but also in all its outlying areas," writes the author, concluding
his description of the violent takeover, which left long and bitter memories
among those who survived it.[82]

Toward the "all-Rus′" identity

In his study of the interrelation between early modern identity and the
minting of coins by the princes of Moscow, Thomas S. Noonan made an
important observation on the nature of Muscovite identity in the fourteenth and fifteenth centuries. He wrote:

One of the major elements in the formation of a Muscovite state was the success of
the Muscovite grand princes in creating a "national Muscovite" identity and then
imposing this new identity on the conquered peoples of other Rus′ lands. Those
who came under Muscovite control were not just subjects who had obligations
to their Muscovite overlords. They were gradually assimilated into an emergent
imperial, Muscovite society and forced to assume a new identity. Residents of
Novgorod, Tver′, and Riazan slowly but surely became Muscovites.[83]

---

[81] On the anti-Moscow sentiments of the author of the *Life*, see Goldblatt, "Confessional
    and National Identity in Early Muscovite Literature," pp. 102–4.
[82] See "Zhitie Sergiia Radonezhskogo," in *Khrestomatiia po drevnei russkoi literature*,
    pp. 196–203, here 196–99. For the complex history of the annexation of the Rostov
    principality by Moscow, see V. A. Kuchkin, *Formirovanie gosudarstvennoi territorii Severo–
    Vostochnoi Rusi v X–XIV vv.* (Moscow, 1984), pp. 264–82.
[83] Thomas S. Noonan, "Forging a National Identity: Monetary Politics during the Reign
    of Vasilii I (1389–1425)," in *Culture and Identity in Muscovy*, p. 496.

The territorial growth of Muscovy resulted from two policies that involved sizable migrations of population. One of them was the attraction and invitation of elites from territories conquered or otherwise acquired to the service of the grand prince, a long process that sometimes took decades.[84] Another strategy involved the resettlement of elites from troublesome areas such as Novgorod.[85] Migration within the realm of the Moscow princes, whether it involved individuals or large masses of people, was clearly a cause of great stress. Thus, the author of the *Life of St. Sergii* complains about the relocation of St. Sergii's family from Rostov to Radonezh, while the author of *The Life of St. Stefan* makes a point of noting how difficult it was for the young St. Stefan "to leave his homeland and all his existing property" in Ustiug, located in what the author called the Dvina Land, and move to the capital of the neighboring principality of Rostov.[86] On the other hand, increased mobility and "pilgrimages" within the territory ruled by the Moscow princes clearly helped create a sense of broader identity. The fact that St. Sergii, the son of refugees from Rostov, could become one of the most venerated saints in Moscow, while St. Stefan, a native of Ustiug, could be turned into an apostle of the Perm Land, shows that a broader trans-regional identity-building project was clearly at work in the rapidly expanding Muscovite realm. The creation of an all-Muscovite pantheon of saints that brought together SS. Petr of Moscow, Sergii of Radonezh, Stefan of Perm, Leontii of Rostov, Kirill of Beloozero, and other local saints can be dated to the fifteenth century.[87] By the end of that century, the refusal of Novgorodians to venerate Muscovite saints was already viewed (or at least could be interpreted) as a sign of heresy.[88] The canonization of thirty-nine saints by

---

[84] The complete integration of the Tver nobility into the Muscovite social structure was achieved as late as the 1540s. On the incorporation of the Tver region into Muscovy, see Boris Floria, "O putiakh politicheskoi tsentralizatsii russkogo gosudarstva (na primere Tverskoi zemli)," in *Obshchestvo i gosudarstvo feodal'noi Rossii. Sbornik statei, posviashchennyi 70-letiiu akademika L'va Vladimirovicha Cherepnina,* ed. V. I. Pashuto (Moscow, 1975), pp. 280–91. On political ideas in fifteenth-century Tver, see Charles J. Halperin, "Tverian Political Thought in the Fifteenth Century," *Cahiers du monde russe et soviétique* 18, no. 3 (July-September 1997): 267–73.

[85] On the interrelations between migration and identity in Muscovy, see Janet Martin, "Mobility, Forced Resettlement and Regional Identity in Moscow," in *Culture and Identity in Muscovy,* pp. 431–49.

[86] See "Zhitie Stefana Permskogo," in *Khrestomatiia po drevnei russkoi literature,* pp. 188–96, here 189.

[87] See Richard D. Bosley, "The Changing Profile of the Liturgical Calendar in Muscovy's Formative Years," in *Culture and Identity in Muscovy,* pp. 26–38, here 36–38.

[88] See Ruslan Skrynnikov, "Russkaia tserkov' v XV–XVI vv. Vzaimootnosheniia Moskvy i Novgoroda," in *Culture and Identity in Muscovy,* pp. 543–56, here 545–46.

Metropolitan Makarii between 1547 and 1549 could only further the cause of "national" unification.[89]

An important idea that symbolized and enhanced the unification project was the old Kyivan concept of "all Rus'," which appeared in the writings of the Kulikovo cycle as the "Land of All Rus'." The concept, borrowed from ecclesiastical discourse, was not only important to the Rus' princes competing for the grand-princely title but was also accepted by their Mongol overlords. As far as is known today, the term first appeared in the title of the grand princes of Rus' after Metropolitan Maximos's departure for Northeastern Rus' in 1299. It served to enhance the power of the grand princes of Vladimir over the other Rus' princes under Mongol suzerainty. The first to use it was Grand Prince Mikhail of Tver. Ivan Kalita occasionally included references to "all Rus'" in his title – after all, the metropolitan of Rus' was now resident in Moscow. That practice was continued by his heirs, including Semen Ivanovich and Dmitrii Donskoi.[90] Vasilii I (1389–1425) was the first prince of Moscow to style himself "Ruler of All Rus'" on his coins. Ironically, we learn about this from coins struck in Moscow between 1389 and 1399 whose reverse bears the inscription: "Sultan Tokhtamysh: Long may he live!" Not only was the grand prince of all Rus' not an independent ruler, but his "all Rus'" was limited at best to the territory controlled by the Golden Horde.[91] Still, it is fair to assume that the concept of "all Rus'" as embodied in the titles of the grand princes of Moscow, with all its limitations, enhanced the sense of Rus' unity among the khans' Orthodox subjects.

The identity that linked St. Sergii and St. Stefan in spite of all the dislocations that they and their families endured was that of Rus'. St. Stefan, for example, was described by his hagiographer as "a Rus'ian by birth (*rodom rusin*) and a Slav by language," while St. Sergii, it was

---

[89] It appears that this was the case even when Makarii helped "reactivate" local cults, which were revived as constituent parts of the Muscovite pantheon. On Moscow's involvement in the promotion of local saints in Tver, see Isolde Thyrêt, "Accounts of the Transfer of Relics and Cults of Saints in Muscovite Russia: Saints Arsenii and Mikhail of Tver'," paper submitted to a conference on "The Modern History of Eastern Christianity: Transitions and Problems," Harvard University, 26–27 March 2004.

[90] See A. A. Gorskii, *Russkie zemli v XII–XIV vekakh. Puti politicheskogo razvitiia* (Moscow, 1996), p. 102. Cf. Anna Khoroshkevich, "Otrazhenie predstavlenii o regionakh vseia Rusi i Rossiiskogo tsarstva v velikokniazheskoi i tsarskoi titulature XVI v.," in *Die Geschichte Rußlands im 16. und 17. Jahrhundert aus der Perspektive seiner Regionen*, ed. Andreas Kappeler (Vienna, 2004), pp. 102–27, here 106–8; Aleksandr Filiushkin, "Vgliadyvaias' v oskolki razbitogo zerkala: Rossiiskii diskurs Velikogo kniazhestva Litovskogo," *Ab Imperio*, 2004, no. 4: 561–601.

[91] On Vasilii's coinage and the meaning of "All Rus'," see Noonan, "Forging a National Identity," p. 496.

claimed, had been born in the Rus' Land. Despite their strong sense of distinct identity, the authors of the Novgorod Chronicle still referred to their own people as "Rus'ian Novgorodians."[92] The merchant Afanasii Nikitin, a native of Moscow's main competitor, Tver, who traveled to the Muslim East and India, emerges from his travel notes as a representative of a people called Rus'ians (*russkie*) dwelling in a polity known as Rus', which comprised various lands. He regarded himself above all as a Rus' Christian.[93] This strong sense of a hybrid Rus' and Christian identity allowed the inhabitants of Northeastern and Northwestern Rus' to distinguish themselves not only from "foreigners" outside the Rus' lands but also from non-Slavs and non-Christians within the Muscovite realm. That distinction becomes particularly apparent when one reads the *Life of St. Stefan*, the "apostle" to the non-Slavic and non-Christian people of Perm who created the Perm alphabet and written language. Born a Rus'ian, according to his *Life*, and thus a native to the Slavic language and the Christian faith, St. Stefan "taught himself the Perm language and created a new Perm grammar, and devised a previously unknown alphabet for the needs of the Perm language [people], as required, and translated Rus'ian books into the Perm language."[94] Christian, Slavonic and Rus'ian markers of identity are counterposed here to Perm paganism, Perm language, and Perm ethnicity.

The Rus' identity of the local elites of Northeastern and Northwestern Rus' was based on common or similar linguistic and cultural practices. Historical and literary tradition, as represented first in local and then in centralized chronicle writing, was another significant factor. A common religious tradition embodied in ecclesiastical structure, liturgy, and daily practice was also important in maintaining a sense of Rus' unity. So was a common political culture, which was shared by local Rus' elites throughout the appanage period. The political structure that maintained and reinforced Rus' unity was the Mongol state, which treated the Rus' territories under its control as a unit and usually looked to the grand prince to represent its interests there. Under these circumstances, the office of grand prince symbolized the principle of the unity of Mongol Rus'. Even as the Rus' princes competed with one another for supreme office, they were inadvertently creating a common political space that reinforced the existing sense of unity. As the khans became too weak to check the growth of the political and military clout of the Moscow

---

[92] See *The Chronicle of Novgorod*, p. 131.

[93] The account of Nikitin's journey was included in the Sofiia II Chronicle under the year 1475. It was published separately as *Khozhdenie za tri moria Afanasiia Nikitina, 1466–1472*, 2nd edn (Moscow and Leningrad, 1958).

[94] "Zhitie Stefana Permskogo," p. 190.

princes, the latter emerged as "gatherers" of the Rus′ lands under their auspices.

It is important to note in this context that until the end of the fifteenth century, both under the Mongols and under the Moscow princes who replaced the khans as actual rulers of the region, the borders of Mongol or, later, Muscovite Rus′ as a political entity also generally marked the geographical boundaries of Rus′ identity as it developed in the north-eastern and northwestern parts of the former Kyivan realm. On the one hand, Moscow and Novgorod were aware that most of the Grand Duchy of Lithuania was settled by the Rus′. On the other hand, Muscovite and Novgorodian authors usually referred to those Rus′ cousins, whether allies or enemies, as Lithuanians, while their territories were called the Lithuanian Land. The author of the *Expanded Chronicle Tale* about the Battle of Kulikovo Field showed great animosity toward the troops led in support of Mamai by the Lithuanian Grand Duke Jogaila, addressing them as "pagan Lithuanians."[95] The fact that Jogaila probably also led Orthodox Rus′ detachments never occurred to the chronicler. The same tendency is apparent in the writings of Sofonii of Riazan. The alleged author of *Zadonshchina*, by contrast, was positively disposed toward the Grand Duchy of Lithuania. In his narrative he does not mention Jogaila at all, stressing instead the role played in the battle by his two brothers, Andrii and Dmytro, who, together with the voevoda Dmytro of Volhynia, fought on the side of Dmitrii Donskoi. While Sofonii claims that they were fighting for the Rus′ Land and the Christian faith, as well as to avenge the wrongs done to Dmitrii, in *Zadonshchina* they are clearly associated with Lithuania and the Lithuanian Land and are not identified as Rus′ princes or sons of Rus′.[96] Political divisions clearly helped shape the boundaries of Rus′ identity as it developed in Muscovite Rus′ during the fifteenth century.

The many faces of Rus′

What does all this mean for the historiographic debate on the ethnogenesis of the Eastern Slavs? Should we speak of one Rus′ nationality that maintained its integrity until the end of the sixteenth century? Does it make more sense to accept the view that by the fourteenth and fifteenth centuries there were three East Slavic nationalities? Should we hold to the notion that there were only two (Lithuanian and Northeastern) East Slavic nationalities at the time? Nor should we overlook the belief that

---

[95] See excerpts from the *Novgorod IV Chronicle* in *Povesti o Kulikovskoi bitve*, pp. 30, 38.
[96] See "Slovo Sofoniia riazantsa," p. 11.

three separate East Slavic nationalities (or at least their precursors) existed before and during the times of Kyivan Rus'. Traditionally, most attempts to reconstruct the ethnonational history of eastern Europe during the late medieval and early modern eras have either completely ignored the identity-based evidence or used it selectively to demonstrate the validity of a specific theory advanced by a particular author. Indeed, if used selectively, the sources can yield sufficient evidence to support any of the above-mentioned theories. Lacunae in the sources complicate the issue even further by allowing the construction of daring historiographic hypotheses. Little wonder that the debate goes on. Is the glass half empty or half full?

It must be admitted that for most of this period there were voices advocating both all-Rus' solidarity and the distinctiveness of a number of East Slavic groups that can be defined in local, political, and proto-national terms. The real question, though, is not whether these loyalties and identities actually existed but how they coexisted with one another and what status they held in the broader set of identities of the Rus' elites in a given region and at a given time. Any answer to these questions should take into account the paramount importance of local identities in the premodern world of East Slavdom. When speaking of the period between the thirteenth and fifteenth centuries, local identity should be regarded as central to a number of broader identities, for which it served as a nucleus. Among these, I would single out polity-based identities. How strong were these identities, and how did they relate to the local ones? Naturally, the answers to these questions cannot be constant but would have to be adjusted for every geographical area and historical period.

The concept of Rus' political identity represented by the notion of the Rus' Land was hybrid in nature and cannot be treated in isolation from local (tribe- or land-based) dynastic and cultural loyalties. How does one distinguish Rus' political identities from ethnocultural ones in writings of the twelfth and thirteenth centuries? It is quite clear that the military conquest of a territory and its political inclusion in the Rurikid realm (in other words, its subordination to the Rus' princes) invested it with a new polity-based name and identity. As time passed, political, religious, and cultural identities intermixed. Were Smolensk merchants called Rus' because they considered themselves (and were considered by others) to be part of the Rus' ethnos or because, not necessarily being of Slavic origin, they were ruled by the Rus' princes and shared in the Rus' "political" identity? Was the definition of one group of Eastern Slavs as Muscovites and another as Lithuanians a manifestation of those groups' political, ethnic or cultural identity? Nikita Tolstoi helped put the question of ethnic identity into a much broader cultural and political context in his study of the consciousness of the author of the Primary Chronicle, but that approach has never been applied to the study of later periods of East Slavic history.

With regard to Rus' identity, it would doubtless be correct to say that it was always in flux and highly fragmented. Nevertheless, there seems to be an irrepressible urge on the part of both scholars and nation-builders to assume that similarity of name implies similarity of identity, irrespective of time and place. It is this approach that allows Aleksandr Solzhenitsyn, for example, to posit the existence of Russian identity in Lviv in the mid-nineteenth century on the grounds that the local council during the Revolution of 1848 was called the Rus'ka Rada. In actual fact, Rus' meant very different things to different people at different times. Depending on the period under consideration and the context in which they appear, such terms as "Rus'" and "the Rus' Land" can indicate either the unity or the diversity of individual Rus' territories and elites. The sense of Rus' unity was partly reflected in the interest expressed by local chroniclers in the affairs of other Rus' territories: Kyivans recorded events in Northeastern (Suzdal-Vladimir) and Northwestern (Novgorod) Rus', and vice versa. Not unlike the Kyivan chroniclers, those writing outside the center had not only a narrow but also a broader understanding of Rus'. In an entry for 1216, the author of a Suzdal chronicle included the lands of Halych, Kyiv, Smolensk, Chernihiv, Novgorod, and Riazan as constituent parts of Rus'.

It would appear that the Mongol invasion helped preserve the sense of Rus' unity by forcing elites throughout the Rurikid realm to think of their appanage principalities first and foremost as part of the Rus' Land. First of all, close contact with the Mongol "other" must have promoted a sense of all-Rus' solidarity, which had all but disappeared during feudal conflicts among the Rurikid princes in the decades leading up to the invasion. Under these circumstances, regarding one's land as part of a larger Rus' opposed to the Mongols must have become more important and politically advantageous than rivalry with the princes of the Rus' Land around Kyiv, Chernihiv and Pereiaslav. Second, with the destruction of Kyiv in 1240, not only the former capital and title of the prince of Kyiv but the Rus' name itself was up for grabs. The Mongols never questioned the existence of the "imagined community" of Rus' and even invested the Rus' princes with the title of grand prince of Rus'. If a prince wanted to claim that title, he had to declare his realm, whether Suzdal, Vladimir, or Moscow, to be not just part of some "outer Rus'" but the Rus' Land itself. Different princes and local elites followed a variety of strategies in advancing their claims to the Rus' heritage.

Although the Rurikid realm and its various principalities were known to local and foreign observers alike as "Rus'" long before the Mongol invasion, the application of the name "Rus' Land" to parts of the former Kyivan realm is documented only in sources of the post-Kyivan Rus' period. While the concept of the Rus' Land was based on a common historical, religious, legal, and cultural heritage, the term was applied differently in various regions of the former Rurikid realm and produced identities that differed significantly from one another. The application of the historically, politically, and legally loaded term "Rus' Land" to a given principality (to the exclusion of the rest of Rus', which was thereby "othered") may be viewed as a manifestation of that multifarious reality.[97] The spread of the ethnonym "Rus'" throughout the territories that once constituted the domain of the Rurikids and were affected by the political, legal, and religious culture of that dynasty indicates that the sense of unity did not disappear altogether, but the strenuous efforts of the Rurikid princes to rein in the centrifugal aspirations of local elites show that commonality was not to be taken for granted. Local identity, rooted in loyalty to particular lands, was predominant. And it was land by land, principality by principality, that the Rurikids' more aggressive neighbors took over their patrimony. It is hard to overcome the impression that the main promoters of Rus' identity at the time were not the Rurikid princes and their ideologists but the patriarchs of Constantinople, who fought hardest, as will be shown below, to preserve the name and unity of the Rus' metropolitanate.

[97] On the tendency to identify only particular Rus' polities as the "Rus' Land" between the thirteenth and fifteenth centuries, see Floria, "Istoricheskie sud'by Rusi," pp. 46–61.

3   The Lithuanian solution

Whose state was the Grand Duchy of Lithuania?

The late thirteenth and early fourteenth centuries witnessed a dramatic geopolitical change in eastern Europe. While the Mongols took over the eastern and northern parts of the former Kyivan realm, the rest of the region, with the notable exception of Galicia, eventually found itself within the boundaries of the Grand Duchy of Lithuania. That process reached its pinnacle during the rule of Grand Dukes Gediminas (1316–41) and Algirdas (1345–77), whose power extended to most of present-day Belarus, Ukraine, and even some parts of Russia. By the mid-fifteenth century, the ratio of Lithuanian ethnic territories to those settled by Eastern Slavs in the Grand Duchy of Lithuania was 1:12.[1] In the fourteenth century most of the Rurikid princes in the southwestern part of the former Kyivan realm were either deposed or forced to recognize the authority of the Grand Duke of Lithuania. Most scholars assume that the political takeover was largely peaceful, but there are sources that indicate major military confrontations between the Lithuanians and the Rus'. A case in point is the alleged capture of Kyiv by Gediminas, reported in a much later chronicle account.[2] Unfortunately, we have very few sources from the fourteenth century to rely on.

Gediminas was probably the first Lithuanian ruler to call himself *Rex Letvinorum et Ruthenorum* and refer to his realm as *regnum Letuinorum et (multorum) Ruthenorum*. His son Algirdas added to his title the Rus' designation "grand prince" (*velykyi kniaz'*).[3] Rus'ian terminology became

---

[1] See Olena Rusyna, *Ukraïna pid tataramy i Lytvoiu*, vol. VI of *Ukraïna kriz' viky* (Kyiv, 1998), pp. 43–55. According to some projections, the Lithuanians of the Grand Duchy found themselves outnumbered two to one, or perhaps even four to one, by their East Slavic neighbors. See Daniel Stone, *The Polish-Lithuanian State, 1386–1795*, vol. IV of *A History of East Central Europe* (Seattle and London, 2001), p. 12.

[2] For conflicting interpretations of the chronicle account, see S. C. Rowell, *Lithuania Ascending: A Pagan Empire within East-Central Europe, 1295–1345* (Cambridge, 1994), pp. 94–111; Rusyna, *Ukraïna pid tataramy i Lytvoiu*, pp. 43–55.

[3] See Rowell, *Lithuania Ascending*, pp. 63–66.

an important element in the titles of Lithuanian princes and in the definition of their state. It clearly reflected local conditions, as most of the lands ruled by Gediminas and his successors were former territories of Kyivan Rus'. From its new subjects the Lithuanian state adopted important elements of administration and jurisprudence, as well as the literary language used in the grand duke's chancellery. The chancellery itself was often staffed with Orthodox scribes, while Orthodoxy became the religion of choice for Algirdas's numerous descendants.[4]

Although the Lithuanian state was extremely successful in taking control of the Rus' lands and thus gradually emerged as a formidable competitor of the Mongols, it was less effective in resisting the aggression of the Teutonic Knights and, later, in standing up to the growing might of the Grand Principality of Moscow. The Lithuanian elites met both challenges by forging a closer alliance with the Kingdom of Poland. The Union of Kreva (1385), which resulted in the election of Grand Prince Jogaila of Lithuania as king of Poland (under the name Władysław II), established a personal union between the two states that later became a dynastic union. During the reign of the last Jagellonian, Sigismund Augustus, the Union of Lublin (1569) ended the independent existence of the Lithuanian state by making it an autonomous duchy in the Polish-ruled "Commonwealth of Two Nations." One result of the union was the official redistribution of the Rus' lands between the two partners in the Commonwealth. Most of today's Ukraine became subject to the Kingdom of Poland, while today's Belarus remained within the boundaries of the duchy.[5]

This chapter focuses on the Rus' lands that found themselves within the boundaries of the Grand Duchy of Lithuania in the second half of the fourteenth century. The existing sources give very little information regarding the identity of the Rus' population at large. Another limitation imposed by the sources is that we cannot follow in any detail the development of elite identity in any given territory throughout the period (that is,

---

[4] On the Lithuanian annexation of the Rus' lands, see Jaroslaw Pelenski, "The Contest between Lithuania and the Golden Horde in the Fourteenth Century for Supremacy over Eastern Europe," in idem, *The Contest for the Legacy of Kievan Rus'* (Boulder, Colo., 1998), pp. 131–50; E. Gudavicius, *Mindaugas* (Vilnius, 1998); A. K. Kraŭtsevich, *Stvarennie Velikaga kniastva Litoŭskaga* (Rzeszów, 2000).

[5] On the history of the Grand Duchy of Lithuania and its Rus' lands, aside from the above-mentioned literature, see Matvei Liubavskii, *Ocherk istorii Litovsko-russkogo gosudarstva do Liublinskoi unii vkliuchitel'no* (Moscow, 1910; repr. The Hague, 1966); V. T. Pashuto, *Obrazovanie Litovskogo gosudarstva* (Moscow, 1959); Henryk Łowmiański, *Studia nad dziejami Wielkiego Księstwa Litewskiego* (Poznań, 1983); Feliks Shabul'do, *Zemli Iugo-Zapadnoi Rusi v sostave Velikogo kniazhestva Litovskogo* (Kyiv, 1987); Jerzy Ochmański, *Historia Litwy*, 3rd edn (Wrocław, 1990); M. M. Krom, *Mezh Rus'iu i Litvoi: zapadnorusskie zemli v sisteme russko-litovskikh otnoshenii kontsa XV – pervoi treti XVI v.* (Moscow, 1995). For an English translation of selected chapters from Krom's book, see *Russian Studies in History* 40, no. 4 (Spring 2002): 9–93.

from the beginning of the thirteenth century to the Union of Lublin). The Galician-Volhynian Chronicle covers the thirteenth century, but then we lose our main source of information. We are thus obliged to zigzag in pursuit of sources from western Ukraine to Smolensk and Lithuania, where chronicle writing began sometime in the mid-fifteenth century. The only area that remains in focus despite these geographical shifts is Volhynia, but no local chronicle writing went on there in the fourteenth century, and there appears to have been little in the fifteenth. Other sources help fill the gap, but they are incomplete and, for the earlier period, not very numerous. The scarcity of sources has left this field open to rampant speculation and given rise to quite a few contradictory concepts and theories, especially when it comes to the history of identities.

Was the Grand Duchy of Lithuania primarily a Lithuanian state, or was it in fact a Lithuanian-Rus' polity, or even a Rus'-Lithuanian one, given that Eastern Slavs accounted for most of its population? And who were those Eastern Slavs? Were they Belarusians and Ukrainians, or were they "Russians," as imperial Russian historiography claimed? One of the dominant trends in Belarusian national historiography claims most of the historical legacy of the Grand Duchy for the Belarusian nation. This claim gave rise to major disputes between Lithuanian and Belarusian historians and political elites. After the disintegration of the USSR, the latter claimed for Belarus not only the Lithuanian capital of Vilnius (in Belarusian, Vilnia) but also the current coat of arms of Lithuania, which shows a mounted equestrian with a raised sword – a symbol deeply rooted in the history of the Grand Duchy.[6] For Ukrainian historians, their country's association with the Grand Duchy is a fairly marginal episode, a sideshow to their historical narrative, which focuses primarily on the exploits of Kyivan princes and Zaporozhian Cossacks. Not so for Russian historiography. As Aleksandr Filiushkin has recently observed, Russian interest in the history of the Duchy was often driven by the need to legitimize the partitions of Poland, the suppression of the Polish uprisings of the nineteenth century, and the annexation of Lithuania, western Belarus, and western Ukraine in the aftermath of the Molotov-Ribbentrop Pact of 1939.[7]

---

[6] On the twentieth-century Polish-Lithuanian-Belarusian contest for Vilnius/Vilnia, see Timothy Snyder, *The Reconstruction of Nations: Poland, Ukraine, Lithuania, Belarus, 1569–1999* (New Haven and London, 2003), pp. 52–102.

[7] See Aleksandr Filiushkin, "Vgliadyvaias' v oskolki razbitogo zerkala," *Ab Imperio*, 2004, no. 4: 561–601. The same issue of *Ab Imperio* contains essays by Darius Vilimas, Giedrė Mickūnaitė, Igor Mrazaliuk, and Dmitrii Vyrskii on the image of the Grand Duchy of Lithuania in the present-day Lithuanian, Ukrainian, and Belarusian historical imaginations, as well as Filiushkin's interview with Hieronim Grala on the reception of the Grand Duchy of Lithuania in Polish historiography and society.

Not surprisingly, then, Soviet historiography followed in the footsteps of tsarist-era Russian imperial historiography. Muted debate on whether the Grand Duchy was a legitimate "gatherer" of Rus' lands in the fourteenth to sixteenth centuries, as the Grand Principality of Muscovy was officially considered to be, began in the Russian Empire and continued in the USSR until the 1980s.[8] The perestroika years and the Yeltsin period in Russian politics promoted a view of the Grand Duchy as a tolerant and federalist European alternative to the tradition of Muscovite autocracy – an interpretation advocated during the "constitutional" period of Russian imperial history by Vasilii Kliuchevsky's successor at Moscow University, Matvei Liubavsky, and developed during the Soviet period in the works of Anna Khoroshkevich.[9] It is hard to say whether this reading of the Grand Duchy's history, already in decline because of the growing "nationalization" of Russian historiography and its focus on the history of the Russian state and nation, will survive the coming changes in Russian politics and the growing alienation between the three East Slavic societies. What can be said with greater assurance is that the effort to identify Westernized "Russians" in the history of the Grand Duchy, coupled with the inability of scholars writing in Russian to distinguish the "Russians" of the Grand Duchy terminologically from those inhabiting the modern Russian nation, will continue to hinder research on the political and cultural history of the region. This observation is probably even more applicable to contemporary English-language historiography. Although there are alternatives in English to the practice of calling the Rus' population of the Grand Duchy "Russian," Slavic studies in the West continue to be influenced by the imperial-era view that the Grand Duchy of Lithuania belongs to "Russian" history. Textbooks on Russian history repeat this view: the author of the best known of them, Nicholas Riasanovsky, refers to the Grand Duchy of Lithuania as a "Lithuanian-Russian state" and to its East Slavic population as "Russians."[10]

[8] See, for example, Vladimir Pashuto's critique of the views of Igor Grekov in Pashuto, Boris Floria, and Anna Khoroshkevich, *Drevnerusskoe nasledie i istoricheskie sud'by vostochnogo slavianstva* (Moscow, 1982), pp. 28–29. Following the Russian prerevolutionary tradition, Grekov was inclined to see the Grand Duchy as a predominantly East Slavic state and thus a legitimate competitor of Muscovy. Pashuto, developing the Soviet-era paradigm that treated the Grand Duchy as a Lithuanian feudal state (the Lithuanian Soviet Socialist Republic was part of the USSR, and the socialist Lithuanian nation could not be completely deprived of its history, as had been the case prior to 1917), denied any legitimacy to Grekov's claim and regarded the Lithuanian "gathering" of Rus' lands as outright aggression.

[9] See Liubavsky's introduction to his *Ocherk istorii Litovsko-russkogo gosudarstva*, pp. 1– 4. For an assessment of the trend inspired by Liubavsky in Russian historiography of the 1990s, as well as literature on the subject, see Filiushkin, "Vgliadyvaias' v oskolki razbitogo zerkala."

[10] For Riasanovsky's interpretation of the history of the Grand Duchy of Lithuania in the context of Russian history, see his *History of Russia* (Oxford and New York, 1977), pp. 146–56.

Among the important historiographic problems pertaining to the history of East Slavic identities is the role of the Lithuanian experience in enhancing distinctiveness among different groups of the Rus' population. The long-held Soviet view that distinct East Slavic nationalities were formed in the course of the fourteenth and fifteenth centuries has recently been challenged by Boris Floria. According to him, the Rus' elites of the Commonwealth and Muscovy only began to regard each other as distinct entities in the late sixteenth and early seventeenth centuries. But even then, in Floria's opinion, there was no irreversible separation. Floria also questions the grounds for speaking of a distinct Belarusian (and, by implication, Ukrainian) ethnic identity prior to the seventeenth century,[11] thereby reviving the discussion that began in Ukrainian historiography in the 1930s about the existence of a common Ukrainian-Belarusian nationality during the early modern period.[12] In Belarus, Ihar Marzaliuk, a leading authority on matters pertaining to premodern Belarusian identities, seems unimpressed by Floria's denial of a distinct medieval and early modern identity to the Belarusians. Marzaliuk often equates manifestations of Rus'/Ruthenian identity on the territory of what is now Belarus with those of Belarusian identity.[13] In Ukraine, by contrast, some of Floria's ideas have made inroads into current historiography.[14] The debate on the role of the Lithuanian factor in shaping premodern East Slavic identities is still going on, and my discussion of the issue seeks to contribute to this scholarly debate, which has obvious political implications.

[11] See Boris Floria, "O nekotorykh osobennostiakh razvitiia ètnicheskogo samosoznaniia vostochnykh slavian v èpokhu srednevekov'ia–rannego novogo vremeni," in *Rossiia-Ukraina: Istorii vzaimootno-shenii*, ed. A. I. Miller, V. F. Reprintsev, and B. N. Floria (Moscow, 1997), pp. 9–38, and Floria's polemic against A. S. Kotliarchuk on this point in idem, "Nekotorye soobrazheniia ob ètnicheskom samosoznanii predkov sovremennykh belorussov (v sviazi so stat'ei A. S. Kotliarchuka)," in *Rus'-Litva-Belarus'. Problemy natsional'nogo samosoznaniia v istoriografii i kul'turologii* (Moscow, 1997), pp. 92–94. In his post-1991 publications, Floria refers to the Rus' population of the Grand Duchy and of the later Polish-Lithuanian Commonwealth as "Russians," putting the term (though not consistently) in quotation marks.

[12] See Myron Korduba, "Die Entstehung der ukrainischen Nation," in *Contributions à l'histoire de l'Ukraine au VIIe Congrès International des Sciences Historiques* (Lviv, 1933), pp. 19–67; Ivan Kryp'iakevych, "Do pytannia pro natsional'nu svidomist' ukraïns'koho narodu v kintsi XVI – na pochatku XVII st.," *Ukraïns'kyi istorychnyi zhurnal*, 1966, no. 2: 82–84.

[13] See Ihar A. Marzaliuk, *Liudzi daŭniai Belarusi: ètnakanfesiinyia i satsyia-kul'turnyia stereotypy (X–XVII st.)* (Mahilioŭ, 2003). For a detailed critique of Marzaliuk's general approach to the problem of early modern Belarusian ethnic, social, cultural, and religious stereotypes, see Henadz' Sahanovich, "Pryvid natsyi ŭ imhle stereatypaŭ," *Belaruski histarychny ahliad* 10, nos. 1–2 (2003): 281–318.

[14] For the application of Floria's approach to the ethnogenesis of the Eastern Slavs (save for his concept of an Old Rus' nationality) in Ukrainian historiography, see Rusyna, *Ukraïna pid tataramy i Lytvoiu*, pp. 273–80.

Those friendly Lithuanians

Why did the Rus' elites submit to the Lithuanian princes? What happened to the Rus' pride of the Kyivan era and the resolve with which western Rus' opposed the power of the Mongols? Historians give a variety of answers to this question, most of which pertain to the consequences of the political disintegration of the Kyivan state and the favorable conditions that the Lithuanian princes were prepared to offer the local Rus' elites. But what about group identities and images of Lithuanians and Mongols that the Rus' elites developed over time? Did they play any role in the process? I shall approach this question by focusing on the image of the Lithuanians as it emerges from the Galician-Volhynian Chronicle – the only Rus' chronicle that pays substantial attention to the Lithuanian neighbors of the Eastern Slavs.[15]

The Lithuanians and their next-door neighbors, the Yatvingians, were already known to the authors of the Primary Chronicle and the Kyiv Chronicle. The author of the former noted under the year 1040 that the Lithuanians had been conquered by Yaroslav the Wise. In an introduction to the chronicle written in the early twelfth century, the Lithuanians are listed among the tribes that lived in the realm of Japheth and paid tribute to Rus'.[16] Thus for the author of the Primary Chronicle the Lithuanians figured as subjects conquered by the Kyivan princes who lived peacefully under Rus' suzerainty thereafter. A somewhat different image of the Lithuanians emerges from the Kyiv Chronicle, which often refers to the military campaigns of the Rus' princes against the Lithuanians. One such campaign, recorded under the year 1132, resulted not only in the burning of Lithuanian settlements but also in heavy casualties among the Kyivans who took part in the expedition. The latter did not leave the area with the main army and were attacked by Lithuanians who emerged from hiding once the principal Rus' forces had departed.[17] The Lithuanians of the Kyiv Chronicle were clearly a different lot – rebellious people who required considerable attention from the Kyivan princes. A much more aggressive image of these same Lithuanian tribes emerges from the pages of the Galician-Volhynian Chronicle: they are first mentioned under the year 1205, during the feudal struggle in Galicia-Volhynia, when they attacked the Cherven towns and Volhynia in

[15] For a discussion of the Galician-Volhynian Chronicle's coverage of Lithuanian history and a synopsis of the reports of other Rus' chronicles on the Lithuanians, see Michael Moser, "Stereotipy Litvy i svedeniia o nei v drevneishikh vostochnoslavianskikh letopisiakh: Novgorodskaia I, Lavrent'evskaia i Ipat'evskaia letopisi – do kontsa XIII veka," *Studia Slavica Academiae Scientiarum Hungaricae* 49, nos. 3–4 (2004): 229–80.

[16] See *The Russian Primary Chronicle*, pp. 52, 55, 138.

[17] See *Polnoe sobranie russkikh letopisei* (henceforth *PSRL*), vol. II (Moscow, 1962), p. 294.

league with the Yatvingians.[18] Thus the former tributaries and rebellious subjects were on the offensive and often acted as an invading force from that point on.[19]

The authors of the Galician-Volhynian Chronicle were much more closely acquainted with the Lithuanians, especially their princes, than their predecessors had been. Princes Danylo, Vasylko, and their sons not only waged wars with their Lithuanian counterparts but also allied themselves with them against Poles and Tatars. They were also related by marriage and had both friends and enemies among the Lithuanian princes. Moreover, there is a hypothesis that the authors of the chronicle may have drawn on records kept in Navahrudak or some other major center of Lithuanian Rus'.[20] It would appear that in the eyes of the chroniclers the major factor distinguishing the Lithuanians from Galicia-Volhynia's other immediate neighbors, the Poles, was religion. Judging by the chronicle account, Prince Danylo even appealed to the principle of Christian solidarity when calling upon the Poles to join forces with him against the pagan Lithuanians. Prince Vasylko garnered special praise from the chronicler for his victories over the pagans, who included the Lithuanians and Yatvingians. The chronicler also praised such Lithuanian princes as Vaišelga (Vaišalgas, Vaišvilkas, Voishelk) who accepted Christianity and were clients of the Galician-Volhynian rulers, while castigating those, such as Traidenis, who remained pagan and hostile.[21]

The case of Mindaugas, the "Lithuanian grand prince" and "autocrat of the whole Lithuanian Land," as the chronicler calls him, shows that being Christian was insufficient to obtain a positive characterization in the chronicle. The kind of Christianity (Eastern or Western) adopted by a Lithuanian ruler and the nature of his relations with the Galician-Volhynian princes were no less important factors. Mindaugas was generally in conflict with the Galician-Volhynian princes. Accordingly, the chronicler casts Mindaugas's conversion in a negative light: the Lithuanian prince was insincere, for he continued his pagan practices, and the baptism that he accepted on the advice of Andreas, the master of the Riga Knights, led to the defeat of the Christianization project in Lithuania.[22] The chronicler's ideal Lithuanian prince was Mindaugas's son Vaišelga,

---

[18] Ibid., col. 721.

[19] It appears that derogatory remarks in the Rus' sources about Lithuanians emerging from marshes and woods into the light of day (see Rusyna, *Ukraïna pid tataramy i Lytvoiu*, pp. 42–43) actually belong to a later period. As noted earlier, the dating of one of those sources, the *Slovo o pogibeli Russkoi zemli*, to the thirteenth century remains questionable.

[20] See Rowell, *Lithuania Ascending*, p. 32.This hypothesis, first suggested by Vladimir Pashuto, has been questioned by other scholars, including Mykola Kotliar. See his *Halyts'ko-Volyns'kyi litopys XIII st.* (Kyiv, 1993), pp. 131–32.

[21] See Moser, "Stereotipy Litvy," pp. 237–42.   [22] See *PSRL*, II: 813–18, 858–60.

who accepted Christianity in Rus', became an Orthodox monk and even attempted to go to Mount Athos. Moreover, Vaišelga was very friendly toward the Galician-Volhynian princes. He was installed as grand prince of Lithuania with the help of Rus' troops and allegedly referred to Prince Vasylko as his father, while calling Danylo's son Shvarno his brother. It was to the latter that Vaišelga transferred his authority over the Lithuanian Land. The chronicler openly condemned Prince Lev, another son of Danylo's, who killed Vaišelga.[23]

What we know today from reading the Galician-Volhynian Chronicle indicates the growth of Lithuanian power in the region during the thirteenth century, which extended the Lithuanian princes' rule or influence over territories traditionally settled by Eastern Slavs, including Hrodna (Horadnia), Navahradak, and Polatsk. It also sheds light on the competition between Galician-Volhynian and Lithuanian princes for some of those territories and indicates the existence of close contacts between the two elites. It is clear that the Rus' princes had no reservations about establishing matrimonial ties with Lithuanian princely families, while local Rus' elites were often prepared to replace Rurikid princes with Lithuanian ones. The cities' practice of inviting (originally Rurikid) princes to rule them was a perfect vehicle for bringing the more powerful Lithuanian princes to the Rus' lands if the local boyars wished to do so, although this change of princely guard was not a straightforward process. Sometimes the local princes gave only nominal recognition to the suzerainty of their Lithuanian counterparts, who in turn (as was the case with Vaišelga) could be vassals of the Galician-Volhynian princes.[24] The process of replacing Rurikid princes with Lithuanian ones could last for generations and go back and forth, as was the case in Polatsk.[25]

The Galician-Volhynian Chronicle was composed prior to the triumphal march of the Lithuanian princes across the Rus' lands in the fourteenth century and remained largely untainted by retrospective emphasis on the importance of the Lithuanian factor in the region. Data from the chronicle suggest a number of reasons why that "friendly" takeover took place and identify some of the cultural mechanisms involved in the process. Religion was certainly one of them, but a careful reading of

---

[23] Ibid., cols. 867–70. On the treatment of Vaišelga in the Rus' chronicles, see David M. Goldfrank, "The Lithuanian Prince-Monk Vojšelk: A Study of Competing Legends," *Harvard Ukrainian Studies* 11, nos. 1–2 (June 1987): 44–76; Moser, "Stereotipy Litvy," pp. 241–42.

[24] Prince Iziaslav of Polatsk recognized the suzerainty of Vaišelga, who in turn was a client of the Galician-Volhynian princes. The replacement of Vaišelga by Shvarno as grand prince of Lithuania further complicated the situation but probably smoothed the transition.

[25] See Sahanovich, *Narys historyi Belarusi*, pp. 64–65; Rowell, *Lithuania Ascending*, pp. 83–87.

the sources indicates that the acceptance of Christianity, more specifically Orthodoxy, by the Lithuanian princes was not indispensable. True,
many Lithuanian princes, especially in the fourteenth century, "went
native" and accepted the Orthodoxy of their new subjects. In the thirteenth century, however, the inhabitants of the so-called Black Rus' along
the Nemunas (Nieman) River often preferred pagan Lithuanian princes
to Christian Rurikids from Galicia-Volhynia. The authors of the Galician-
Volhynian Chronicle would drop such epithets as "godless" with regard
to the Lithuanians if they allied themselves with Rus' princes or served
in their armies.[26] Thus the acceptance of Christianity by the Lithuanian
princes was probably an important but not a necessary condition for the
submission of local elites.

What seems much more significant in this context is that the Lithuanian
princes who emerged from the ruins of the Kyivan empire shared the same
political culture as their former Rus' masters and were often willing to pay
the cultural price for their dominance by accepting Rus' folkways. Their
situation was very different from that of the Mongols, who at first were not
only distinguished from the Rus' princes by their political culture but also
insisted (or so the Christians feared) on the acceptance of their religion.
Besides, the Mongols were a real alternative to the Rurikid princes only
in the southern and eastern parts of the former Kyivan realm, while in the
lands of present-day Belarus they appeared only sporadically, mostly in
support of their Galician-Volhynian vassals when the latter were fighting
the Lithuanians. The ancestors of the modern Belarusians never experienced the Mongol invasion per se: instead, they had to choose between
the growing power of the Lithuanian princes and the declining strength
of the Rurikid princes of Galicia-Volhynia. The process presented dramatically in modern historical narratives as ethnic subjugation probably
amounted to little more than the replacement of local elites descended
from the Scandinavian ruling clan, by then completely nativized, with
Lithuanian elites, for whom most of that process still lay ahead.

Staying Rus'ian

The narratives of the thirteenth century show that the Rus' component
was important to the identity of ruling elites in the lands of present-day
Belarus. There, as in the Rus' lands generally, Rus' identity was based
on an intricate web of political, religious, cultural, and local loyalties.
The interrelation between these elements of elite identity can be reconstructed on the basis of a number of diplomatic accords. Among them is

[26] See Moser, "Stereotipy Litvy."

a treaty concluded in 1229 by Prince Mstyslav Davydovych of Smolensk
with Riga, Gotland, and a number of German cities. There the terms
Rus' and *Rusin* are intermixed with *Smolensk* and *Smolnianin*. In the text
of the treaty, the "Latin language/people" are the counterparts of *Rus'*,
latynin or *nemchin* of *Rusin*, and *Ryzhanin* of *Smolnianin*.[27] If terms based
on the name of Smolensk can be defined in this context as political or
local names, terms based on the name "Rus'" should be seen as reflecting ethnocultural and religious rather than political identities. Lithuanian
penetration of the Rus' territories began at a time when not only the Rus'
elites but also their subjects had begun to cast off their old tribal loyalties
and accept some form of Rus' identity. The case of the Krivichians, an
East Slavic tribe that settled significant parts of present-day Belarus, is
particularly instructive in that regard. The Krivichians showed surprising tenacity in maintaining their separate identity; unlike many other East
Slavic tribes, they never disappeared from the text of the Primary Chronicle. They were also mentioned by the authors of its continuation, the
Kyiv Chronicle, where one can still read about the Krivichian princes in
the entry for 1162.[28] Toponyms based on the name of the Krivichians –
a clear indication of enduring identity and its recognition by neighbors –
were still emerging on the borders of the territories settled by them in the
twelfth and thirteenth centuries, but by the fourteenth century they had
yielded to place-names based on the ethnonym of Rus'.[29]

As in the case of Galicia-Volhynia and Northeastern Rus', the Belarusian territories may not have been regarded as part of the Rus' Land in the
narrow sense of the term but were certainly considered to belong to it in
the broader sense. That was the case with the Polatsk principality, which
managed to avoid absorption by Rus' for most of the pre-Mongol period.
Given the special status of the Polatsk Land, Volodymyr the Great considered it important to marry one of its princesses. Polatsk was one of the
three Rus' cities, along with Kyiv and Novgorod, in which a cathedral of
St. Sophia was built, and the Polatsk principality remained out of reach
of the sons of Yaroslav the Wise, who divided Rus' among themselves

---

[27] The treaty is known in two versions, one from Gotland and the other from Riga. Both
are published in A. F. Vishneŭski and Ia. A. Iukho, *Historyia dziarzhavy i prava Belarusi
ŭ dakumentakh i matèryialakh* (Minsk, 2003), pp. 15–23. The division of the world in the
treaty text into Rus' and Latin peoples reminds one of Natalia Yakovenko's observation
(noted in chapter 1 of this book) that it is as misleading to speak of the existence of one
Old Rus' nationality as it would be to infer the existence of one Latin nationality from
the practice of Latin schooling in western Europe.
[28] See *PSRL*, II: 521.
[29] See I. U. Chakvin, "Etnanimichnyia aikonimy Belarusi – krynitsa histarychnai pamiatsi
naroda," in *Nash Radavod* (Hrodna), 1996, no. 7: 121–23. The last known reference to
the Krivichian land in foreign narratives dates from the fourteenth century. See Vladimir
Pashuto, "Letopisnaia traditsiia o 'plemennykh kniazheniiakh' i variazhskii vopros," in
Letopisi i khroniki. 1973 (Moscow, 1974), p. 110.

after his death.[30] Does all this mean that the Polatsk elites felt their distinctness from the rest of Rus' more strongly than the inhabitants of other principalities? Probably it does. But can we then go on to say that they did not regard themselves (even before the Mongol invasion) as part of the Rus' Land in the broad sense? Certainly not.

Quite telling in that regard is a comparison of an incident involving princes of Polatsk recorded in the Kyiv Chronicle under the year 1140 with the above-mentioned treaty of 1229. In the first case, we learn about Grand Prince Mstyslav of Kyiv arresting two princes of Polatsk and sending them to Constantinople for their refusal to go to the Rus' Land and assist him with his campaign against the Polovtsians.[31] In the second case, the parties to the treaty refer to Smolensk, Polatsk, and Vitsebsk as parts of the Rus' Land. The Polatsk principality is also referred to as the Rus' Land in a treaty signed in 1264 by Gerden, the Lithuanian prince of Polatsk and Vitsebsk.[32] If the Polatsk realm was not part of the Rus' Land for the twelfth-century Kyivan prince, for the thirteenth-century Rus' and Lithuanian princes it certainly was, or, more precisely, it was one of a number of Rus' lands. Treaties concluded by Polatsk with Riga and other trading centers of the Baltic littoral in the late thirteenth and early fourteenth centuries suggest that the Polatsk Land was regarded by its elites as a separate polity and part of the broadly defined Rus' lands. Its inhabitants were called "Rusins" or "Polatskians," as opposed to the Germans (*nemtsy*) or "Ryzhanins" of Riga.[33]

A different system of political names and ethnonyms was employed by the authors of the peace treaty of 1338 between Gediminas, the alleged Lithuanian "gatherer" of the Rus' lands, and the Master of the Livonian Knights, Eberhard Mannheim. Gediminas was called the *koningh* of Lithuania whose power extended over the Lithuanians and the Rus' inhabiting the Lithuanian and Rus' Lands. It was in the name of those two lands and peoples that Gediminas concluded the treaty. The document was also approved by the Orthodox bishop of Polatsk, the Lithuanian princes of Polatsk and Vitsebsk, and the elites of the two cities. Nevertheless, their cities and lands were not mentioned in the treaty (as they had been in the previous trade agreements), being represented

---

[30] See Oleksii Tolochko and Petro Tolochko, *Kyïvs'ka Rus'*, vol. IV of *Ukraïna kriz' viky* (Kyiv, 1998), pp. 178, 184.

[31] See *PSRL*, II: 303.

[32] See the text of the circular in *Polotskie gramoty XIII – nachala XVI veka*, comp. A. L. Khoroshkevich, 4 vols. (Moscow, 1977–82), I: 35–36.

[33] Aside from Gerden's circular letter of 1264, see also the letter of 1300 from the Polatsk Orthodox bishop to the Riga authorities and the treaty of 1330 between Polatsk and Riga in *Belorussiia v ėpokhu feodalizma. Sbornik dokumentov i materialov v trekh tomakh*, vol. I, nos. 24 and 25 (Minsk, 1959), pp. 82–83. For the texts of other Polatsk documents of that period, see *Polotskie gramoty*.

instead by the general term "Rus' Land." Although it is risky to discern order in terminological usage at a time when it often did not exist, it might be assumed nevertheless that in this context the term "Rus' Land" was employed not only as an ethnocultural but also as a political designation of part of the Lithuanian state. The disappearance of the names of separate principalities from the text of the treaty and the endorsement of the notion of the Rus' Land as a counterpart of the Lithuanian Land could not but promote the loyalty of the Rus' elites to the idea of a broader Rus' community.[34]

The Lithuanian princes' acceptance of the concept of the Rus' Land as a legitimate counterpart of the Lithuanian Land appears to have been a short-lived phenomenon that did not survive the first union of the Grand Duchy with the Kingdom of Poland. While the Rus' ethnocultural identity was becoming increasingly established in the consciousness of Rus' elites and commoners alike (as attested by the Rus'-derived toponyms in Belarus), the political component of that identity was manifestly disappearing. It can be argued that with no distinct political entity to support it, the concept of the Rus' Land as a legal entity was being steadily transformed from a current political notion into a historical one. The references to Rus' in the official titulature of Grand Prince (and subsequently king) Władysław-Jogaila of Poland were concerned with his historical rights to the Rus' lands of the Grand Duchy and the Kingdom of Poland (Galicia and western Podilia). But the act of union between the two polities concluded in 1385 at Kreva (another toponymic memorial to the Krivichian past of a significant portion of present-day Belarus) listed only two parties to the agreement, the Kingdom of Poland and the Grand Duchy. The Rus' lands were mentioned only once, along with the Lithuanian lands, as territories that Władysław pledged to attach to the Kingdom of Poland.[35] In Władysław's letter of 1387 granting his brother Skirgaila control of a significant portion of the Grand Duchy, there was no mention of the Rus' Land or its particular status. There were references to the Lithuanian principality (*kniazhen'e*) and the Lithuanian Land, but none to the Rus' Land, even though Skirgaila was gaining control not only of Trakai in Lithuania but also of Polatsk in present-day Belarus.[36]

At a time when the political component of Rus' identity was losing ground along with the decline in the power and status of the Rurikid

[34] For the text of the treaty, see *Polotskie gramoty*, III: 102–7. For examples of Gediminas's treatment of the Rus' population of his realm as a distinct linguistic and religious group, see Marzaliuk, *Liudzi daŭniai Belarusi*, p. 48.

[35] For the text of the Union of Kreva, see *Akta unii Polski z Litwą, 1385–1791*, ed. S. Kutrzeba and W. Semkowicz (Cracow, 1932), no. 1, pp. 1–3. For a Belarusian translation, see Vishneŭski and Iukho, *Historyia dziarzhavy i prava Belarusi*, pp. 32–34.

[36] For the text of the letter, see *Polotskie gramoty*, I: 50–54. Cf. Vishneŭski and Iukho, *Historyia dziarzhavy i prava Belarusi*, pp. 35–37.

princes, who had first brought that identity to the region in the tenth and eleventh centuries, Rus' identity in general received an unexpected boost from the sudden mobilization of its religious component. As long as the Lithuanian princes were willing to accept Orthodoxy – the Rus' brand of Christianity – or remained pagan, the religious component of their identity remained largely dormant, or at least did not serve to differentiate the Rus' and Lithuanian elites. As noted above, the local elites did not regard the Lithuanian princes as "other," and they were often chosen to rule Rus' principalities in preference to the Orthodox Rurikids. In Lithuania proper, Orthodoxy was confined to the major cities, but in Rus' it claimed numerous members of the Lithuanian princely elite.[37] That situation changed dramatically after the Union of Kreva, which required the pagan Lithuanians to convert to Roman Catholicism. Jogaila himself accepted not only a new name but also a new faith, as did those of his brothers who were not yet Christian, but those who were Orthodox refused a second baptism. With that, the problem seemed resolved, but it reappeared in 1413, when the Union of Horodło replaced the personal union between Poland and Lithuania with a dynastic one. The new union gave the Lithuanian nobles a broad range of privileges on condition that they become Catholics. These privileges did not extend to the Orthodox princely and nobiliary class.[38] A legal barrier had been erected between the Poles and Lithuanians on the one hand and the Rus' nobility on the other. It had nothing to do with the local (land) identity of the inhabitants of the Polatsk Land or Volhynia; instead, it united them on the basis of religious identity while distinguishing them from the Lithuanians. Moreover, the religious discrimination introduced by the Union of Horodło helped distinguish the Rus' nobility in the Grand Duchy from the Rurikid princes and their boyars outside it, in Tver, Pskov, Novgorod, and Moscow, where there was no such discrimination.

The Unions of Kreva and Horodło effectively reversed the course of cultural development in the Grand Duchy of Lithuania. If there had previously been clear indications of the political, religious, and cultural Rus'ianization of the Lithuanian elites, from the late fourteenth century there were equally clear signs that the process had come to an end. Moreover, the formerly dominant Rus' cultural tradition suddenly found itself competing with an equally developed, if not superior, cultural product. With the support of the central authorities, that product not only removed

---

[37] On the situation of the Orthodox Church in the Grand Duchy of Lithuania, see Rowell, *Lithuania Ascending*, pp. 149–50, 180–88.

[38] For the Latin text of the resolutions of the Horodło Diet and a discussion of the discriminatory measures of the Diet decree, see Liubavskii, *Ocherk istorii Litovsko-russkogo gosudarstva*, pp. 58–61, appendix 1, pp. 297–302.

the Lithuanian elites from the Rus' sphere of influence but also made inroads into the ranks of the Rus' elites themselves.[39]

The Rus' princes and nobles gained an opportunity to show their dissatisfaction with the government's discriminatory measures and test their new-found sense of Rus' solidarity during the feudal war that began in the Grand Duchy of Lithuania after the death of Grand Prince Vytautas. In 1430 Prince Švitrigaila, who was appointed by his brother Władysław II to replace Vytautas, soon found himself in conflict with a powerful opposition composed of Polish nobles. The issue was who – the Kingdom of Poland or the Grand Duchy – had the better claim to Podilia (in present-day Ukraine). In a conflict that saw Władysław siding with the Poles, Švitrigaila appealed for support to the Teutonic Knights and the dissatisfied Rus' nobles, whom he provided with a legitimate means of challenging the political and cultural status quo. They turned out to be Švitrigaila's strongest supporters in his contest for power with Władysław's new protégé, Prince Žygimantas, who began trying to satisfy all sides. The Poles received Podilia, while the Orthodox were promised the same privileges as those guaranteed to the Catholics by the Horodło decree. But this attempted compromise failed. Władysław apparently did not confirm the extension of the Horodło privileges, while the Rus' nobles in eastern Podilia prevented the transfer of their lands to Poland. Besides, only the Lithuanian lands of the Grand Duchy recognized Žygimantas as their ruler, while the Rus' lands continued to support Švitrigaila.

In 1434 Žygimantas extended the Horodło privileges to the Orthodox nobles by a decree of his own that he later confirmed more than once. In combination with other political and military measures, it swayed the loyalties of the Rus' nobles. From 1434 we see the movement of those elites away from Švitrigaila – first in what are now the Ukrainian lands, and later in Belarus. Švitrigaila's adherence to the Catholic faith and his execution (by burning at the stake) of Metropolitan Gerasim, who had allegedly been involved in a failed attempt to deliver Smolensk to Žygimantas, did not enhance the prince's popularity among the Orthodox nobles. Nevertheless, he did not lose their support entirely. Some of them, like Oleksander Chartoryisky, took part in the assassination of Žygimantas in 1430 in the hope of reinstalling Švitrigaila as grand prince of Lithuania, but by that time the latter's career was clearly over.[40]

---

[39] The deterioration of Rus' cultural supremacy in the Grand Duchy of Lithuania as a result of consecutive unions with the Kingdom of Poland was decried by numerous East Slavic historians, including the Ukrainian Mykhailo Hrushevsky. See his *Istoriia Ukraïny-Rusy*, vol. IV (Kyiv, 1993), pp. 180–84, 256–65, 338–423.

[40] The decree of 1434, which pertained to the Lithuanian and Rus' lands of the Grand Duchy (*terras nostras Lithvania et Russie*), was mainly intended to prevent a confrontation between the peoples (*populos*) inhabiting those lands. It has been argued that the decree

The developments just described – the original support for Švitrigaila among the Rus' nobles who suffered discrimination, the extension of privileges to them by Žygimantas, and the coincidence of the promulgation of Žygimantas's decree with the first major defection of the Rus' nobles from Švitrigaila – may be seen as events linked to the mobilization of Rus' identity during the 1430s. We know that the decade preceding the crisis of the 1430s also saw the rise of Lithuanian ethnic identity, which found expression in Vytautas's characterization of Lithuania (Aukštaitija) and Samogitia as "one language and one people."[41] Polish observers also interpreted the original conflict between Władysław and Švitrigaila in ethnic and religious terms. One of them, Bishop Zbigniew Oleśnicki, wrote in 1430 to the papal representative at the Council of Basel that Švitrigaila had gained the support of the Rus' nobles by promising to raise the status of their Orthodox faith and to heed their advice once he became grand prince. Oleśnicki believed that the Lithuanian Catholics were prepared to reconcile Władysław and Švitrigaila, but that the Rus' nobles, whose preponderance over the Lithuanians he attributed to Švitrigaila's support, did not want peace for fear that their religion would suffer and their influence would be diminished.[42]

Another indication that the ethnoreligious factor played a major role in the conflict can be found in texts of Rus' provenance, especially in the so-called Chronicle of the Grand Duchy of Lithuania, an early version of which has been preserved as part of the Suprasl Chronicle.[43] The former was most probably written in the course of the 1430s in Smolensk, in the milieu of the local bishop and later metropolitan Gerasim. That victim of Švitrigaila's auto-da-fé came originally from Moscow, served as bishop of Volodymyr in Volhynia, and was a close collaborator of Švitrigaila and

of 1434 concerned only the Orthodox nobles of Lithuania proper, which included Black Rus' and the Brest region, while the privileges granted by Žygimantas in 1434 were in fact extended to the rest of the Orthodox nobles of the Grand Duchy by the much later decree of 1447 (see Liubavskii, *Ocherk istorii Litovsko-russkogo gosudarstva*, pp. 60–75). For the interpretation of the events of the 1430s in present-day Belarusian and Ukrainian historiography, see Sahanovich, *Narys historyi Belarusi*, pp. 95–100; Rusyna, *Ukraïna pid tataramy i Lytvoiu*, pp. 108–18.

[41] See Jerzy Ochmański, "The National Idea in Lithuania from the Sixteenth to the First Half of the Nineteenth Century: The Problem of Cultural-Linguistic Differentiation," *Harvard Ukrainian Studies* 10, nos. 3–4 (December 1986): 301–15, here 303–4.

[42] See Mykhailo Hrushevs'kyi, *Istoriia ukraïns'koï literatury*, vol. V (Kyiv, 1926–27; repr. New York, 1960), pp. 71–72. On Švitrigaila's wars of the 1430s as a manifestation of the Lithuanian-Rus' conflict, see also Henryk Łowmiański, *Studia nad dziejami Wielkiego Księstwa Litewskiego* (Poznań, 1983), pp. 413–24. On the support offered to Švitrigaila by Rus' elites, see A. Iu. Dvornichenko, *Russkie zemli Velikogo kniazhestva Litovskogo: ocherki istorii obshchiny, soslovii, gosudarstvennosti* (St. Petersburg, 1993), pp. 206–9.

[43] For a brief English-language survey of Lithuanian chronicle writing, see Rowell, *Lithuania Ascending*, pp. 41–43. Much more detailed accounts are available in T. Sushyts'kyi, *Zakhidno-rus'ki litopysy iak pam'iatky literatury*, 2 vols. (Kyiv, 1921–29); Nikolai Ulashchik, *Vvedenie v izuchenie belorussko-litovskogo letopisaniia* (Moscow, 1985).

his protégé as metropolitan.[44] The author of the Chronicle of the Grand Duchy of Lithuania did not conceal his sympathy for Švitrigaila, although even he condemned the prince for his execution of Gerasim and saw that act as the source of all the misfortunes that later befell his hero. He also introduced a strong ethnic element into the interpretation of the wars of succession of the 1430s. His narrative evinces a powerful sense of Rus' identity that is not to be found in the official Lithuanian and Polish documents on which we have had to rely so far.

First of all, the Grand Duchy emerges from the pages of the chronicle as a continuation of and a legitimate heir to Kyivan Rus'.[45] Secondly, according to the chronicler, and contrary to what we know from other sources, there was not only a Lithuanian but also a Rus' principality/grand-princely office (*kniazhen'e*) in the Grand Duchy of Lithuania. Both were held by Vytautas, but after his death Žygimantas was installed by the Lithuanians as grand prince of Vilnius and Trakai, while Švitrigaila was granted the Grand Principality of Rus' by the Rus' princes and boyars. The chronicler regarded the conflict between the two princes as a war between Rus' and Lithuania, with Rus' troops fighting the Lithuanian (*Lytva*) forces. Perhaps naturally for a Smolensk author, the chronicler considered his land to belong to the core area of the imagined Grand Principality of Rus': thus he reported that Švitrigaila was installed as grand prince of Rus' once he came to Polatsk and Smolensk. He also stated that Žygimantas took over the two princely offices (of Lithuania and Rus') after Smolensk, Polatsk, and Vitsebsk surrendered to him. Although there is reason to believe that the chronicler's concept of Rus' was not limited to these territories and, at a minimum, also included Kyiv, whose prince Mykhailo is listed as a supporter of Švitrigaila and to which the grand prince retreated after his campaigns against Lithuania, the chronicler's direct references to Rus' are limited to the Smolensk, Polatsk, and Vitsebsk principalities. Nor does his Rus' extend to the ethnic Belarusian territories that were included in the Grand Duchy proper and did not constitute semi-autonomous lands (principalities) such as Polatsk and Smolensk.[46]

If the authors of the Primary and Kyivan Chronicles saw the center of the Rus' Land in Kyiv, the authors of the Galician-Volhynian Chronicle found it in Halych and Volodymyr, the authors of the Kulikovo cycle imagined it around Moscow, and the Smolensk authors considered their

---

[44] On the composition of the chronicle, see Hrushevs'kyi, *Istoriia ukraïns'koï literatury*, V: 162–73.

[45] See Igor' Marzaliuk, "Velikoe kniazhestvo Litovskoe v istoricheskoi pamiati belorusov-rusinov: ot srednevekov'ia k modernu," *Ab Imperio*, 2004, no. 4: 539–60.

[46] See the text of the Suprasl Chronicle in *PSRL*, vol. XXXV, *Letopisi belorussko-litovskie* (Moscow, 1980), pp. 57–58.

own territory the center of the virtual Grand Principality of Rus'. Over the years there developed more than one image of Rus', the Rus' Land, and the Rus' principality. Multiplicity also meant fragmentation. The only institution whose mere existence could remind the Rus' elites of their former unity and glorious past was the Metropolitanate of Rus'. The migrations of the higher clergy within the former Kyivan realm and the maintenance of a common liturgical language and church practices also helped preserve a sense of common identity long after the disappearance of the unified political structure. Still, despite extensive contacts between the various centers of Rus' Orthodoxy, they were slowly growing apart in the course of the fourteenth and early fifteenth centuries.

The division of the Rus' church

The disintegration of the formerly unified realm and its common religious identity was reflected in the jurisdictional history of the Rus' church and the official titles of its leaders. As noted in chapter 1, they initially bore the title of "Metropolitan of Rus'," a rare exception to the Byzantine practice of titling bishops after the capital cities over which they presided. With the political fragmentation of the Kyivan realm in the second half of the twelfth century, the heads of the church who resided in Kyiv received the title of "Metropolitan of All Rus'." Although that term referred not to the territory but to the people, the change of title suggested that the metropolitan's authority extended to all the lands of the Rurikid realm. But the Mongol invasion and the continuing fragmentation of the realm further affected the status of the church, necessitating changes in ecclesiastical jurisdiction and metropolitans' titles. The policies of the rulers of Galicia-Volhynia, the Lithuanian grand dukes and the grand princes of Moscow, all of whom competed for control over the formerly united metropolitanate, informed and influenced those changes. Once Metropolitan Maximos left Kyiv for Northeastern Rus' in 1299, and the Metropolitanate of Halych was established in the next few years, it became officially known as the Metropolitanate of Little Rus'. As discussed above,[47] the term made its way into the title of the last Galician prince, Yurii II (1325–40), who occasionally styled himself *Dux totius Russiae Minoris*. The grand dukes of Lithuania also established their own metropolitanate ca. 1317. It is generally regarded as an attempt by Gediminas to gain control over his Orthodox subjects and isolate them from the foreign influence of the metropolitans of all Rus' and Little Rus'.[48]

---

[47] See chapter 2 of this book.   [48] See Rowell, *Lithuania Ascending*, pp. 151–61.

Contrary to general belief, the name of the city of Kyiv was not incorporated into the title of the Rus' metropolitans until the mid-fourteenth century. That innovation resulted from a fierce struggle between Moscow and Vilnius for control over the Metropolitanate of All Rus'. The name of Kyiv first appears in the title of the metropolitan of all Rus' in documents drawn up in Constantinople in 1354, possibly as a result of promises made by Grand Duke Algirdas of Lithuania to convert to Orthodoxy if the metropolitan see were moved from Moscow back to Kyiv. It may also be related to what some historians consider an attempt on the part of Kyivan elites to demonstrate their opposition to Algirdas and play an independent role in church politics. They did so by welcoming Metropolitan Feodorit, who had been consecrated in Bulgaria and was never recognized by Constantinople. One of the Kyivan princes, Volodymyr Olherdovych (Algirdaitis), later even insisted on his historical right to nominate metropolitans. It was probably in response to these developments in the Grand Duchy that the patriarch of Constantinople added the name of Kyiv to the title of the next metropolitan of all Rus', the Muscovite candidate Aleksii. Like his predecessors, Aleksii resided in Moscow but now bore the title of metropolitan of Kyiv. The practice seemed strange and apparently was not welcomed in Moscow: by all accounts, Aleksii avoided using his full title. But Constantinople insisted, and Aleksii's successor, Metropolitan Pimen, is known to have combined references to Kyiv and Great Rus' (not all Rus') in his title, styling himself "Metropolitan of Kyiv and Great Rus'." The new title reflected the de facto partition of the Metropolitanate of All Rus'.[49]

Constantinople probably reserved the title "Metropolitan of Kyiv and All Rus'" for a metropolitan who would be accepted by Moscow and Vilnius alike. The patriarchs of Constantinople tried to prevent the fragmentation of the metropolitanate, for local princes could easily cut ecclesiastical ties with Constantinople, as they had done in Bulgaria in the thirteenth century and would do in Serbia in the fifteenth century. Even more pressing was the threat that new metropolitanates created at the insistence of Polish or Lithuanian rulers would enter into union with Rome. Thus the patriarchs were receptive to pleas and gifts from Moscow. As a rule, they agreed to the creation of new metropolitanates only if there was no other way to satisfy the feuding princes, but sought to restore the unity of the Rus' church once conditions improved.[50] Since 1354,

[49] Rusyna, *Ukraïna pid tataramy i Lytvoiu*, pp. 208–10; G. M. Prokhorov, *Rus' i Vizantiia v ėpokhu Kulikovskoi bitvy. Stat'i*, 2nd edn (St. Petersburg, 2000), pp. 242–44.

[50] On the motives for Constantinople's pro-Muscovite policies, see Ihor Ševčenko, "The Policy of the Byzantine Patriarchate in Eastern Europe in the Fourteenth Century," in idem, *Ukraine between East and West*, pp. 69–91.

Lithuanian Rus' had been subject to Metropolitan Roman, who was consecrated in Constantinople. Because the prince of Kyiv did not recognize Roman's jurisdiction, he was obliged to establish his seat in Navahrudak. In 1375 Metropolitan Cyprian was consecrated as Roman's successor with the title "Metropolitan of Kyiv and Lithuania" but was later styled "Metropolitan of Little Rus' and Lithuania." Unlike his predecessor, he managed to establish his seat in Kyiv. He also secured the support of both Vytautas in Lithuania and Vasilii II in Muscovy. Cyprian managed to prevent the patriarch of Constantinople from consecrating the new metropolitan of Halych (the see was restored in 1371 at the insistence of Casimir IV of Poland, who took over Galicia) and reestablished his control of Novgorod. After 1392 he began to style himself "Metropolitan of Kyiv and All Rus'."[51]

As he sought to reunite the divided metropolitanate under his authority, Cyprian emerged as a leading proponent of all-Rus' unity. In his letters to the prince of Moscow, who initially denied him access to Mongol Rus', Cyprian insisted that his jurisdiction extended to "all the Rus' Land" and that he should have access to his churches not only in the Grand Duchy but also in Northeastern Rus'.[52] For him, "all the Rus' Land" meant the traditional territory of the Metropolitanate of All Rus', including not only the Grand Duchy and Mongol Rus' but also Novgorod and Galicia. It becomes apparent from the *Life of Metropolitan Petr*, which was edited by Cyprian, that he regarded Galicia (which was under Polish-Hungarian suzerainty at the time of writing/editing) as part of the Volhynian Land, which in turn was part of the Rus' Land. Cyprian's restoration of the unity of the Kyiv metropolitanate and the resumption of chronicle writing at the metropolitan's court (the famous Trinity Chronicle was produced at Cyprian's initiative) doubtless enhanced the sense of all-Rus' unity. The veneration of saints such as Metropolitan Petr, who came from Galicia, probably had the same effect.[53]

The unity of the metropolitanate was nevertheless short-lived, as the fifteenth century brought about its final division. After Cyprian's death, Vytautas and Vasilii resumed their struggle for control of the metropolitanate. The new metropolitan, Photius, lived in Moscow, and in 1415

[51] On Metropolitan Cyprian and his activities, see ibid., pp. 263–84. On the history of metropolitans' titles and the ideological meaning of changes in them, see Oneljan Pritsak, "Kiev and All of Rus': The Fate of a Sacral Idea," *Harvard Ukrainian Studies* 10, nos. 3/4 (December, 1986): 279–300; Andrei Pliguzov, "On the Title 'Metropolitan of Kiev and All Rus'," *Harvard Ukrainian Studies* 15, nos. 3/4 (1991): 340–53.

[52] See Cyprian's letter of 23 June 1378 in G. M. Prokhorov, *Rus' i Vizantiia v èpokhu Kulikovskoi bitvy. Povest' o Mitiae*, 2nd edn (St. Petersburg, 2000), pp. 398–410, here 399.

[53] For the text of the *Life of Metropolitan Petr*, see ibid., pp. 413–37.

Vytautas insisted on the election of Gregory Tsamblak, a nephew of the deceased Cyprian, as the new metropolitan of Kyiv. This amounted to a de facto restoration of the Lithuanian metropolitanate, although Vytautas claimed to be reestablishing Kyiv as the seat of the Metropolitanate of All Rus'. In justifying the election of his candidate, who was actually excommunicated by the patriarch of Constantinople, Vytautas employed a patriotic discourse, presenting himself as the defender of the Rus' church and Rus' honor against a metropolitan who resided in Moscow, neglecting his pastoral duties in the Grand Duchy, and against the corrupt practices of Constantinople itself. Tsamblak was elected metropolitan by an episcopal council representing Lithuanian and Galician Orthodox parishes that considered themselves fully entitled to consecrate a pastor for their fatherland (otechestvo).

The death of Metropolitan Tsamblak in 1419 led to the reunification of the all-Rus' metropolitanate under the jurisdiction of a metropolitan residing in Moscow. But unity was restored for less than twenty years. The division became final in the mid-fifteenth century with the refusal of the Moscow hierarchs to accept the decisions of the Union of Florence (1439), which declared the jurisdictional subordination of the Orthodox ecumene to Rome: the Orthodox were to accept Catholic dogma while retaining their rituals.[54] While the Moscow Orthodox, supported by their grand prince, refused to follow Metropolitan Isidore into union with Rome and even forced him to leave the country, the Orthodox eparchies of the Grand Duchy stood by their spiritual leader, although they did little or nothing to make the union of Catholicism and Orthodoxy effective in their realm. The split widened when the Muscovite hierarchs elected a new head of their church, Metropolitan Iona, in 1448 without the agreement of Constantinople, while King Casimir IV of Poland, who was also Grand Duke of Lithuania, supported Gregory the Bulgarian, a disciple of Isidore. Gregory was consecrated metropolitan of Kyiv and all Rus' (1458) by the pope with the consent of the Uniate patriarch of Constantinople. In 1467 Gregory was confirmed in that post by the new anti-Uniate patriarch of Constantinople, thereby ending the new metropolitanate's flirtation with the idea of church union.[55] Thus the

---

[54] On the Union of Florence and its reception in the Kyiv metropolitanate, see Oskar Halecki, *From Florence to Brest, 1439–1596*, 2nd edn (New York, 1968); Borys A. Gudziak, *Crisis and Reform: The Kyivan Metropolitanate, the Patriarchate of Constantinople, and the Genesis of the Union of Brest* (Cambridge, Mass., 1998), pp. 43–58.

[55] For a discussion of the contest between Muscovy and the Grand Duchy for control over the Rus' metropolitanate and its final division in the mid-fifteenth century, see John Fennell, *A History of the Russian Church to 1448* (London and New York, 1995); Pelenski, *The Contest for the Legacy of Kievan Rus'*, pp. 61–76; Vasyl' Ul'ianovs'kyi, *Istoriia tserkvy ta relihiinoï dumky v Ukraïni*, vol. I (Kyiv, 1994), pp. 24–42; Mykola Chubatyi, *Istoriia Khrystyianstva na Rusy-Ukraïni* (Rome and New York, 1965), pp. 643–713; Rusyna, *Ukraïna pid tataramy i Lytvoiu*, pp. 205–26; Rowell, *Lithuania Ascending*, pp. 163–69.

major outcome of the controversy was not the pro forma acceptance of the Union by the Orthodox eparchies of the Grand Duchy but the division of the formerly unified Rus' metropolitanate into two parts, one based in Moscow and the other theoretically in Kyiv, but actually in Navahrudak, in close proximity to the capital of the Grand Duchy, Vilnius. The last Kyivan institution that fostered a sense of unity among the heirs of medieval Rus' was now gone, giving rise to a variety of religious cultures and loyalties on the former territory of Kyivan Rus'.

Kyiv was in one part of the divided metropolitanate, while Moscow, the actual seat of the "Metropolitan of Kyiv and All Rus'," was in the other. Metropolitan Iona of Moscow, after going back and forth on including the name of Kyiv in his official title, eventually dropped it in 1461, remaining "Metropolitan of All Rus'." This was probably a response to the arrival in the Grand Duchy of Gregory the Bulgarian, who used the title "Metropolitan of Kyiv and All Rus'." Although Iona dropped the name of Kyiv from his title, he never got around to replacing "All Rus'" with "Great Rus'" – the term used in Metropolitan Pimen's title. The ability and willingness of church leaders to recognize and adjust to the new realities certainly had their limits. Gregory the Bulgarian also never dropped the reference to "All Rus'" in his title in favor of Lithuania or Little Rus'. Thus both metropolitans claimed jurisdiction over the whole territory of the now defunct Rus' metropolitanate. Arguably, they set an example for their secular counterparts, the grand dukes of Lithuania and the grand princes of Moscow, who fiercely contested the Rus' lands extending between their core possessions in the late fifteenth and early sixteenth centuries.

The boundaries of Rus'

The division of Orthodox Rus' into two metropolitanates, which became irreversible in the second half of the fifteenth century, could only reinforce the kind of thinking that first manifested itself in 1415, when the Orthodox hierarchs of Poland and Lithuania elected Gregory Tsamblak metropolitan of their "fatherland." This term, used in the council's letter, was applied to what are now the Ukrainian and Belarusian lands (including Smolensk) and may be regarded as one of the first manifestations of a united Polish and Lithuanian Rus' identity counterposed to that of Mongol Rus'.[56] The transformation of loyalty to the princely patrimony into loyalty to a common fatherland (*otechestvo*) was potentially a decisive step toward the formation of a new protonational identity. The term (in its new meaning) was probably suggested by Tsamblak himself. It was first

[56] See Rusyna, *Ukraïna pid tataramy i Lytvoiu*, pp. 213–15.

used to define the notion of "fatherland" in Rus' texts produced by the circle of Metropolitan Cyprian's Bulgarian disciples, who used *otechestvo* to denote the metropolitan's homeland of Bulgaria.[57] If the term did in fact originate with Tsamblak, that may account for its lack of currency in Rus' literary works of the period. It was an import whose significance the Rus' literati were apparently not yet ready to appreciate.

The alienation of the two Ruses was aggravated by the growing competition between Vilnius and Moscow for the "gathering" of the Rus' lands. Indicative of changes that occurred during the fifteenth century in the thinking of the Orthodox literati about the place of Lithuanian Rus' in the broader world is the textual history of the *Eulogy for Vitold* (Vytautas), originally composed in the milieu of a native of Moscow, the bishop of Smolensk and metropolitan of Lithuania, Gerasim. The earliest text of the *Eulogy* is to be found in a manuscript commissioned by Gerasim in 1428. There the author of the *Eulogy* presented Vytautas not only as the ruler of the Grand Principality of Lithuania and Rus' (making no distinction between them, in contrast to the Chronicle of the Grand Duchy of Lithuania) but also as the suzerain of a group of other grand principalities that the author called "all the Rus' Land." What he meant by this term becomes clear from the following statement, in which the grand princes of Moscow, Tver, and Riazan, as well as the states of Novgorod and Pskov, are listed as rulers and polities that "served" Vytautas. The author of the *Eulogy* also characterized those polities as belonging to the Rus' people (*iazyk*). "Simply speaking, the whole Rus' people rendered homage and gifts to him," wrote the anonymous author.[58] Thus, according to the author of the *Eulogy*, "all the Rus' Land" meant the Rus' people and included (apart, it would seem, from the Rus' lands of the Grand Duchy of Lithuania) the Rus' principalities and republics to the north and east of the Grand Duchy. Such was the view of a person close to the Moscow-born hierarch Gerasim, who would become both a strong supporter and a victim of Švitrigaila, the imagined "grand prince of Rus'."

By the mid-fifteenth century, the *Eulogy* was incorporated into the Chronicle of the Grand Duchy of Lithuania, which was edited several times in the course of the fifteenth and sixteenth centuries.[59] The text

---

[57] On the medieval and early modern usage of the term *otechestvo*, see V. V. Kolesov, *Mir cheloveka v slove drevnei Rusi* (Leningrad, 1986), pp. 242–46.

[58] See excerpts from the 1428 version of the *Eulogy* in Hrushevs'kyi, *Istoriia ukraïns'koï literatury*, V: 164–65. Cf. his "Pokhvala v. kn. Vytovtu," in idem, *Tvory u 50 tomakh*, vol. V (Lviv, 2003), pp. 50–65.

[59] For the textual history of the *Eulogy*, see Sushyts'kyi, *Zakhidno-rus'ki litopysy*, II: 292–305.

of the *Eulogy* was significantly revised as well, giving us an opportunity to examine the changes that took place in the minds of the Rus' literati after 1428. One of the most interesting changes directly related to our discussion is the removal from the text of the *Eulogy* of a passage about the Rus' grand princes who served Vytautas and of a reference to them and their realms as part of the Rus' people. The statement about the Rus' Land ruled by Vytautas survived the revisions but remained without explanation. It was devoid of connection with the concept of the Rus' people, allowing one to treat it as a reference to the Rus' lands within the boundaries of the Grand Duchy of Lithuania. The passage about the grand princes of Moscow, Tver, Riazan, and the republics of Novgorod and Pskov did not disappear from the text of the *Eulogy*, but it was moved alongside the reference to the rulers of Moldavia, Bessarabia, and Bulgaria paying their respects to Vytautas.[60] The "other Rus'" appears to have been removed from the list of ethnolinguistic relatives of Lithuanian Rus' and added to the list of Orthodox coreligionists, reflecting a possible change in the attitude of the Lithuanian Rus' literati to the Rus' and Orthodox world outside their homeland. It is important not to read too much into this rearrangement of the text of the monument, made at a time when ethnic and religious identities were closely intertwined and "Rus'" often also meant Orthodox, but it is also dangerous to ignore it entirely.

There was more to follow. From the 1440s, the Lithuanian chroniclers began referring to the Rus' territories of the Grand Duchy as "all the Rus' land," while calling the inhabitants of Northeastern Rus' "Muscovites."[61] The refusal of the Lithuanian Rus' literati to treat the inhabitants of Northeastern Rus' not only as fellow Rus' but even as coreligionists is exemplified in the so-called Short Volhynian Chronicle, which includes a description of the Battle of Orsha (1514) between the Muscovite and Lithuanian-Rus' armies and a panegyric to Prince Kostiantyn Ivanovych Ostrozky, who led the army of the Grand Duchy in the battle. The author of the panegyric considered the war to have been provoked by the aggression of Grand Prince Vasilii Ivanovich of Moscow, who was allegedly motivated by greed when he invaded the patrimony of Sigismund I, king of Poland and grand prince of Lithuania and Rus'(as he was referred to in the panegyric, according to prevailing practice). According to the chronicle, the battle was waged by Lithuanian warriors against

---

[60] The changes to the text of the *Eulogy* included a mention of the grand princes of Moscow separately from the other Rus' grand princes, not as servitors but as friends of Vytautas. See *PSRL*, XXXV: 58–59.

[61] See Marzaliuk, *Liudzi daŭniai Belarusi*, pp. 52–53.

the men of the grand prince of Moscow, who were referred to as Muscovites (*moskvichi*), while the term "Rus'" was reserved for Lithuanian Rus'. Several times the Grand Duchy was called the Grand Principality of Lithuania and Rus', while the Volhynian troops in Ostrozky's army were referred to as "the valiant Lithuanian and Rus' warriors." Not only was the word "Rus'" never applied to the Muscovites, their prince and state, but Prince Ostrozky was praised for defending the "Christian churches of God" against them. It was the services rendered by Prince Ostrozky to his Lithuanian sovereign that won him special acclaim from the author of the panegyric.[62]

The long wars waged between Muscovy and the Grand Duchy of Lithuania for control of the Rus' lands turned particularly ferocious as the sixteenth century dawned. Those conflicts must have strengthened the loyalty of the Rus' subjects of the Grand Duchy to a sovereign whom they also considered to be a Rus' prince and to a state that they continued to regard as not only Lithuanian but also Rus'ian. In the final analysis, different political loyalties and dynastic thinking overcame the potential for cultural solidarity between the two Ruses. Once Tver, Novgorod, and Pskov had been subjected to the grand princes of Moscow, the enemy was easily identifiable in political terms as Muscovy. In diplomatic negotiations of the 1490s and early 1500s, the Lithuanian diplomats questioned the right of Ivan III to be called "Sovereign of All Rus'."[63] After the loss of Smolensk to Muscovy, Lithuania refused to recognize the addition of Smolensk to the title of the grand princes of Moscow. It also avoided the phrase "Sovereign of All Rus'" in the grand prince's title, preferring to address him as grand prince of Moscow, which drew protests from the Muscovites. In Lithuanian diplomatic usage, Muscovite Rus' figured not as Rus' but as Muscovy – the term that became dominant in European accounts of Muscovy and its people.[64] The war also helped create the image of an enemy devoid of cultural characteristics that could be regarded as linking the two Ruses: language, ethnicity, and religion. The

---

[62] Ibid., pp. 125–26. The Muscovite-Lithuanian conflicts of the early sixteenth century, particularly the Battle of Orsha, served as a starting point for the dissemination of a negative image of Muscovites in central and western Europe by authors in the employ of Polish elites or closely associated with them. (Poland was then linked to Lithuania by a dynastic union.) See Marshall T. Poe, *"A People Born to Slavery." Russia in Early Modern European Ethnography, 1476–1748* (Ithaca and London, 2000), pp. 19–22.

[63] On the debates over the title of Ivan III and its geopolitical implications at the time, see Filiushkin, "Vgliadyvaias' v oskolki razbitogo zerkala."

[64] See Anna Khoroshkevich, "Otrazhenie predstavlenii o regionakh vseia Rusi i Rossiiskogo tsarstva v velikokniazheskoi i tsarskoi titulature XVI v.," in *Die Geschichte Rußlands im 16. und 17. Jahrhundert aus der Perspektive seiner Regionen*, ed. Andreas Kappeler (Vienna, 2004), pp. 102–27, here 113–19. On the name and image of Muscovy in European accounts of the period, see Poe, *"A People Born to Slavery,"* pp. 11–38.

defections of Rus' princes from Muscovy to Lithuania were greatly eased by the existing cultural affinity between Lithuanian and Muscovite Rus', but the motives behind them should be sought in the political aspirations of individual princes, not in culturally based agendas.[65] The tragic fate that awaited the defectors in Moscow, along with growing differences in the political status of nobles in the Grand Duchy of Lithuania and the Grand Principality of Moscow, eventually deterred Rus' princes from defecting to "tyrannical" Muscovy.[66]

Between the land and the duke

The Chronicle of the Grand Duchy of Lithuania (1430s) demonstrates the level of vitality and mobilization of the Rus' identity in the Grand Duchy of Lithuania in the late fourteenth and early fifteenth centuries. At the same time, it attests to the "Lithuanization" of that identity under the influence of political realities that could not be eliminated just by imagining a virtual Grand Principality of Rus'. The fact that the chroniclers not only praised Vytautas at the expense of Władysław but also favored him over the princes of Kyiv and Smolensk indicates that their loyalty to Vytautas and the Grand Duchy took priority over their allegiance either to the Polish king – the head of the united Polish-Lithuanian state – or to the Rus' princes and their appanages.

A clear indication of the Lithuanization of Rus' identity can also be found in the manner in which chroniclers used the term "Lithuanian Land." It had two senses for them – one broad, covering all the lands of the Duchy, including those of Rus'; the other narrow, pertaining mainly to the ethnic Lithuanian territories. In the chronicle description of Švitrigaila's wars of the 1430s, the term was used mostly in its narrow sense, although even there it also included the lands of Black Rus'. In the broader sense (encompassing the whole territory of the Grand Duchy), the term "Lithuanian Land" was employed in chronicle descriptions of Tatar attacks on what today are Ukrainian territories. For example, in his account of the battle between Vytautas and the Tatars at the Vorskla River in 1399, the chronicler wrote that the Tatars raided the "Lithuanian Land" all the way to Lutsk.[67]

Why the "Lithuanian Land"? Lithuanian chroniclers borrowed the tale about the Battle of the Vorskla River from the chronicles of Northeastern

---

[65] On the princely defections, see Oswald P. Backus, *Motives of West Russian Nobles in Deserting Lithuania for Moscow, 1377–1514* (Lawrence, Kans., 1957).

[66] See Olena Rusyna (Elena Rusina), "Obshchnost' neskhozhego: Rossiiskoe gosudarstvo i Velikoe kniazhestvo Litovskoe v XIV – seredine XVI st." Unpublished manuscript.

[67] See *PSRL*, XXXV: 52, 57–58.

Rus', leaving references to the Lithuanian Land unchanged. When changes were finally introduced in the sixteenth century, the Lithuanian Land was replaced with references not to the Volhynian and Kyiv lands but to the Grand Duchy of Lithuania.[68] Clearly, when the Tatar "other" was involved, all the territories of the Grand Duchy were considered "Lithuanian Land": the political name covered all regions of the state. When it was a matter of internal strife, the territories of the Grand Duchy were divided along historical and ethnocultural lines, with the Rus' lands counterposed to the Lithuanian lands. The latter also included the lands that did not have autonomous status within the Grand Duchy.

Rus' identity in the Grand Duchy was influenced not only by progressive Lithuanization but also by the continuing existence and occasional activization of local (land) identities. Far from dissipating, those identities manifested themselves strongly in the pages of the chronicles, which often incorporated lengthy narratives originally composed in the individual lands and bearing the marks of local identity. Especially telling in this regard is a long fragment on the history of the Podolian Land that found its way into the Chronicle of the Lithuanian Grand Princes. Written after 1430, it presents the story of the Lithuanian-Polish struggle for Podilia from the viewpoint of the Lithuanian princes. So strong was local identity at the time that the narrative makes no reference whatever to the Rus' Land, while its principal subject, the Podolian Land, is given the same prominence as the Lithuanian Land.[69]

A historical compilation dating from the turn of the sixteenth century, known as the Short Kyivan Chronicle, introduces another object of local patriotism, the Volhynian Land, which is treated on a par with the Liakh Land. Its inhabitants, the "Volhynians," figure as prominently in the chronicle as the Lithuanians (*Lytva*). The Rus' Land is mentioned twice, but its relation to the Volhynian Land remains unclear. The first mention of the Rus' Land in the Short Kyivan Chronicle is associated with the raids of pagan warriors and is followed by a report on a local Kyivan event – a possible survival of the practice of identifying the Kyiv region with the Rus' Land. The second reference pertains to the killing of the Kyivan metropolitan Makarii by the Tatars. The chronicler exclaims that nothing of the kind had occurred in the Rus' Land since its baptism. Since the metropolitan was killed near Mazyr, which was considered to be part of the Kyivan Land during the Lithuanian era, it is not clear whether

---

[68] Ibid., pp. 139, 161. On the textual history of the tale, see Pelenski, "The Contest between Lithuania and the Golden Horde," p. 149.

[69] Pelenski, "The Contest between Lithuania and the Golden Horde," pp. 65–67. Cf. Hrushevs'kyi, *Istoriia ukraïns'koï literatury*, V: 169–70.

the chronicler was using "Rus′ Land" in the narrow or the broad sense of the term. In any case, it was the Volhynian and not the Rus′ Land that served as the "protagonist" of the Short Kyivan Chronicle.

Our reading of the early modern "Lithuanian" chronicles leaves the impression that chroniclers working in Smolensk and present-day Belarus used the term "Rus′" to refer primarily to their own territories, excluding lands to the south, while southern authors focused almost entirely on the history of their own lands, showing little (if any) interest in the notion of Rus′ advanced by their northern counterparts. Could it be that, like the Galician-Volhynian princes of the thirteenth century who limited the concept of the Rus′ Land to their principality, the Smolensk-Polatsk-Vitsebsk elites of the fifteenth century identified the concept of Rus′ with their realms alone? That seems to have been the tradition established in the Rus′ lands at least since the fourteenth century.[70] Could this also mean that there were significant differences of identity between the local proto-Belarusian and proto-Ukrainian elites in the fifteenth and early sixteenth centuries? The scarcity of sources at our disposal does not allow us to draw any definite conclusions in that regard, but what we know today about the political history of the region indicates very clearly that regional identity in the Grand Duchy was indeed highly developed.

The Lithuanian grand dukes were by no means as successful in establishing their authority over the whole realm as were the Kyivan princes at the pinnacle of their power. This becomes even more apparent when the Grand Duchy of Lithuania is compared with the neighboring Grand Principality of Moscow, whose princes were not only effective in centralizing power but also very successful in incorporating the appanage principalities of the Northeast and the Rus′ republics of the Northwest into the Muscovite political structure. It was a different picture altogether in the Grand Duchy of Lithuania.[71] The speed and ease with which the duchy grew in the thirteenth and fourteenth centuries had its negative

[70] See Boris Floria, "Istoricheskie sud′by Rusi i ėtnicheskoe samosoznanie vostochnykh slavian v XII–XV vekakh. (K voprosu o zarozhdenii vostochnoslavianskikh narodnostei)," *Slavianovedenie*, 1993, no. 2: 46–61. Cf. Marzaliuk, *Liudzi daŭniai Belarusi*, pp. 48–49.

[71] As noted above, there is a significant, mostly recent, literature comparing political and social institutions and practices in the Grand Duchy of Lithuania and the Grand Principality of Moscow. See, for example, M. E. Bychkova, *Russkoe gosudarstvo i Velikoe kniazhestvo Litovskoe s kontsa XV veka do 1569 g. Opyt sravnitel′no-istoricheskogo izucheniia politicheskogo stroia* (Moscow, 1996); M. M. Krom, "Rossiia i Velikoe kniazhestvo Litovskoe. Dva puti v istorii," *Angliiskaia naberezhnaia: Ezhegodnik Sankt-Peterburgskogo nauchnogo obshchestva istorikov i arkhivistov*, 4 (2000): 73–100; Hieronim Grala, "Diacy i pisarze: wczesnonowożytny aparat władzy w Państwie Moskiewskim i Wielkim Księstwie Litewskim (XVI – pocz. XVII w.)," in *Modernizacja struktur władzy w warunkach opóźnienia*, ed. Marian Dygo et al. (Warsaw, 1999), pp. 73–91; Rusyna (Rusina), "Obshchnost′ neskhozhego."

long-term effect – the preservation of extensive local rights and privileges that undermined the unity of the state. Only insignificant parts of the Rus' lands – mainly the western regions of present-day Belarus – were incorporated into the Grand Duchy proper, while the rest constituted autonomous lands and principalities. The lands of Polatsk, Vitsebsk, Smolensk, Volhynia, and Kyiv were autonomous, and the principalities of Polisia and Chernihiv enjoyed even greater independence. Even after the local princes were deposed (in Kyiv that did not happen until 1471), their lands remained autonomous of the center, preserved their boundaries, and maintained their political, legal, and economic privileges. The rights of the grand duke were restricted, while the autonomy and special status of the lands were confirmed and extended through numerous edicts issued by the grand princes in the course of the fifteenth and sixteenth centuries. All this strengthened the appanage-era tradition of not only acting but also thinking locally, and, as a result, promoted regional loyalty and identity.[72]

Language and people

The sixteenth century brings us the first clearly identifiable personal voices that speak through the medium of personal correspondence, diaries, and printed books. Those voices extend our capacity to examine the identities of the region and help us identify much more clearly the milieu that produced and shared them. Among the fresh voices of the early sixteenth century, by far the most interesting is that of Frantsishak Skaryna (1490–1551?), a native of Polatsk and a graduate of Cracow and Padua universities. Between 1517 and 1522, first in Prague and then in Vilnius, he issued in Cyrillic a number of predominantly religious publications, including twenty-three books of the Old Testament. Skaryna was not the first printer to issue Cyrillic-alphabet books in Church Slavonic (the first such publications appeared in Cracow in the 1490s), nor was he the first to introduce the vernacular into Church Slavonic texts of the Bible (manuscripts of that kind had circulated in the Rus' lands at least since the fifteenth century). He was, however, the first to explain why he was doing so. The ideas expressed by Skaryna in the prefaces to his publications indicate a major revolution in the self-identification of the Rus'

---

[72] On the variety of methods employed by the Lithuanian princes to acquire Rus' lands, see Rowell, *Lithuania Ascending*, pp. 84–88, 93, 115–16. On the strength of regionalism in the Grand Duchy of Lithuania, see Liubavskii, *Ocherk istorii Litovsko-Russkogo gosudarstva*, pp. 76–88. For a discussion of social change in the Rus' lands of the Grand Duchy, see Dvornichenko, *Russkie zemli Velikogo kniazhestva Litovskogo*.

elites of the Grand Duchy in the first decades of the sixteenth century under the influence of the Reformation.[73]

Skaryna, who is believed to have switched from Orthodoxy to Catholicism and then to Protestantism, defined his primary loyalties not in confessional but in cultural and ethnolinguistic terms as he attempted to make Scripture more understandable to the common folk of the "Rus' people/language." In the course of his life, Skaryna defined himself in a number of ways: Lithuanian – a marker of his political identity, Rus'ian – an indicator of his cultural identity, and Polatskian – a term derived from his birthplace that served to denote his local identity. It was the mobilized Rus' identity that seems to have been the driving force behind Skaryna's publications, which heralded the advance of new thinking in the hitherto stagnant world of Orthodox Rus' learning. They show the importance of the Reformation not only for the development of the vernacular languages, overshadowed until then by the dominance of Church Slavonic in church life and by chancery Ruthenian in the political and legal practice of the Grand Duchy of Lithuania, but also for the introduction into public discourse (invigorated by the spread of the printed word) of concepts accompanying the rise of modern nations. Among the notions that Skaryna's writings popularized in the Rus' lands of the Grand Duchy of Lithuania were the concepts of loyalty to one's homeland (place of origin) and devotion to one's people. He wrote about the special affection that people felt for the place of their birth. Skaryna also noted that he himself had been born into the Rus' people (*iazyk*) and called upon his readers to render their services to the simple Rus' folk. In order to make the text of the Bible understandable to them, he printed vernacular words in the margins of his books, including the first – the Church Slavonic version of the Psalter.[74]

From the viewpoint of ethnocultural identity, the revolutionary element of Skaryna's prefaces and afterwords was his emphasis on the common good of the Rus' people, a community that he defined in ethnolinguistic terms. The term that he applied to it (*iazyk*) was the one used centuries earlier by the writers of Kyivan Rus', including Metropolitan Ilarion, who wrote about the Rus' people in the mid-eleventh century.[75] The major difference between Skaryna and Ilarion was that for the eleventh-century author, there was no clear distinction between the Rus' people and the

---

[73] On Skaryna, see *Belorusskii prosvetitel' Frantsisk Skorina i nachalo knigopechataniia v Belorussii i Litve* (Moscow, 1979).

[74] See Frantsishak Skaryna, *Tvory. Pradmovy, kazanni, pasliasloŭi, akafisty, paskhaliia* (Minsk, 1990), pp. 18–37. Cf. Hrushevs'kyi, *Istoriia ukraïns'koï literatury*, V: 119–29.

[75] See Ilarion, "Sermon on Law and Grace," in *Sermons and Rhetoric of Kievan Rus'*, trans. and with an introduction by Simon Franklin (Cambridge, Mass., 1991), pp. 3–29.

Rus' Land. For Skaryna, the Rus' people was an ethnocultural entity that did not depend on a specific political structure. It was sustained not by the power of the ruler but by the loyalty of the "brethren" to whom Skaryna made his appeal. It also included the "simple people" – a new object of loyalty and devotion unknown to earlier authors, who catered to the interests of the princes. Unlike his successors of the early seventeenth century, who wrote at a time of profound confessionalization of Rus' society, Skaryna saw no contradiction between his non-Orthodox religious affiliation and his clearly articulated Rus' identity.

One of the problems that Skaryna's writings pose today is the vagueness of the geographic boundaries of the Rus' people with which he identified himself. Where did his homeland and his people begin and end? Were they bounded by the city of Polatsk, the Polatsk Land, the Rus' lands of the Grand Duchy, the entire Grand Duchy of Lithuania, or the Rus' lands within and outside the Grand Duchy? Or did they lie somewhere else within the boundaries of these political and ethnocultural entities? The most obvious markers of Skaryna's identity, his self-identification as a native of Polatsk and Lithuania, indicate the Rus' lands of the Grand Duchy of Lithuania (probably to the exclusion of those belonging to the Lithuanian principality proper) as his homeland. Skaryna's appeal to a largely Orthodox audience, with no mention of the Orthodox ruler of Muscovy, marks another limit of his Rus' space: it probably ended at the Muscovite-Lithuanian border. Skaryna, who published his books after the Battle of Orsha and more than sixty years after the final division of the Kyiv metropolitanate, could not help but be influenced by the growing divisions between Lithuanian and Muscovite Rus'. Even so, he may well have regarded the Orthodox of Muscovy as part of his extended audience. Whatever meaning – broad or narrow – Skaryna attributed to the term "Rus' people (*iazyk*)," his interest in the vernacular promoted the introduction of elements of the spoken language (in his case, a variant of Old Belarusian) into print, thereby implicitly undermining not only the dominance of Church Slavonic as the common literary language of Eastern Slavs but also the broader concept of a single Rus' people.

The divisive union

The final act in the history of the Grand Duchy of Lithuania took place at the Lublin Diet of 1569, which transformed the dynastically linked Kingdom of Poland and Grand Duchy of Lithuania into a new united polity, the Polish-Lithuanian Commonwealth. Modern historians of Russia, Ukraine, and Belarus have seen the Union of Lublin as an act that opened the door to Polish cultural and religious expansion in the east and drastically diminished the influence of the Rus' element in the new state. What seems to have been overlooked is the positive long-term impact of the union on the Ukrainian and Belarusian identity-building projects. By bringing the Ukrainian lands of the Grand Duchy into the Kingdom of Poland, the architects of the union "reunited" them in one political structure with other Ukrainian territories, Galicia and western Podilia, which had been part of the kingdom since the fourteenth century. In that sense the Union of Lublin revived the glory days of the Galician-Volhynian principality, when for a short period most of the Ukrainian ethnic territories were united in a single state. The union also established the border – which still survives, with minor modifications – between Ukrainian and Belarusian Polisia. Does this mean that the union resulted from the desire of sixteenth-century Ukrainian elites to reunite with their brethren to the west and separate them from the culturally related but still distinct proto-Belarusians to the north? Or was it the other way around: did the border established between the kingdom and the duchy in 1569 influence the nation-building process of the two East Slavic peoples? Or does the answer lie somewhere between these alternatives?

A reading of the sources pertaining to the Union of Lublin shows that the East Slavic factor did indeed play a crucial role in the outcome of the Diet of 1569. The decisive influence, however, came not from the Rus' elites of the Grand Duchy but from Muscovite Rus', whose military advances during the Livonian War (1558–83) forced the Lithuanian elites to seek closer cooperation with Poland. In trying to prevent the possible loss of Ukrainian and Belarusian territories to Muscovy, the Lithuanian elites unexpectedly lost a portion of them to their new partner in the Commonwealth, the consolation being that they remained within the same state. Another drawback to this arrangement was that the Lithuanians all but lost their independence to the Poles. But the Lithuanian elites were in no position to oppose the explicit will of the king and could not control the desire of the Rus' nobility to partake of the freedoms offered to their counterparts in the Kingdom of Poland. The Rus' delegates from Volhynia (until then part of the Grand Duchy) were less than decisive in their opposition to the union. The same was true of the Kyivan nobility when the Polish authorities claimed the Kyivan Land as well, stressing the need to protect their new Volhynian possessions from invasion by the Crimean Tatars. The embattled Lithuanian deputies who had originally left the Diet in protest against the Polish takeover found themselves obliged to return and consent to the union for fear that even more of the

Rus' lands would be lost if they did not do so. As a result, the Lithuanians retained the territories of what would later become Belarus.[76]

Did the Union of Lublin come down to the result of Muscovite aggression, Lithuanian weakness, Polish greed, and the Rus' nobility's desire to get a better deal from the Poles? Was there nothing in it that could be regarded as a manifestation of protonational identity? There are some traces of that as well. The Lithuanians, for example, showed dogged loyalty to their state, whose integrity they tried to preserve by all possible means. The Rus' delegates of the Volhynian and Kyivan lands showed a degree of loyalty to their ethnocultural community. Stating that they represented "a nation so respectable that we will yield to no other nation on earth,"[77] they demanded and received guarantees regarding the status and territorial possessions of their princes, legal privileges guaranteed by the Lithuanian Statute, language rights, and religious freedoms – all that on top of the new social status and privileges received by the Ruthenian nobility. While these were impressive achievements, they were all demanded and granted on a regional basis: there was little articulation of a common Rus' position. Soon after the union, for example, the culturally Polonized Rus' elites of Podlachia (another East Slavic "Lithuanian" land that joined the Commonwealth) asked the central authorities to change the language of official documentation from chancery Ruthenian to Polish, as they could no longer understand the former.

Rus' religious and cultural identity certainly existed, but it did not depend on the solidarity of Rus' elites throughout the Grand Duchy. The assertion of the rights and privileges of individual lands was sufficient. Nor do we encounter manifestations of Rus' deputies' loyalty to their former polity, the Grand Duchy, in the deliberations of the Lublin Diet (after all, they were about to cease being "Lithuanians") or to the ethnocultural community of "Lithuanian Rus'." It appears that the nobles rendered their primary loyalty to the ruler, not to the Lithuanian state. Since the Union of Lublin did not result in a change of ruler, the local elites regarded boundary adjustments as a secondary matter, so long as

---

[76] For a discussion of the political, economic and military factors that led to the Union of Lublin, as well as its ideological justification, see Jaroslaw Pelenski, "The Incorporation of the Ukrainian Lands of Kievan Rus' into Crown Poland (1569): Socio-Material Interest and Ideology (A Reexamination)," in idem, *The Contest for the Legacy of Kievan Rus'*, pp. 151–88.

[77] See a quotation from the Diet speech of Prince Kostiantyn Vyshnevetsky of Volhynia in Natalia Iakovenko, *Narys istoriï Ukraïny z naidavnishykh chasiv do kintsia XVIII stolittia* (Kyiv, 1997), pp. 121–22. On the attitude of the Ukrainian princes and the Volhynian nobility toward the Lublin takeover, see Karol Mazur, "Nieznana petycja szlachty wołyńskiej do króla w dobie sejmu lubelskiego 1569 r.," *Sotsium. Al'manakh sotsial'noï istoriï* (Kyiv) 2 (2003): 41–56.

the historical boundaries of a given land and its "ancient rights" were not violated. Nor did the Podlachians, Volhynians, and Kyivans show any interest in banding together with their fellow Ruthenians in Galicia. After the Union of Lublin, when Volhynians and Kyivans began to encounter Galicians on a more or less continuous basis, they viewed them as foreigners (*panove zahranychnyky*). It was the Poles, not the Rus' delegates to the Diet, who indicated the former status of Kyiv as capital of the country in making their case for its incorporation into the Commonwealth. The Kyivans and Volhynians themselves left little evidence of their feelings about the whole undertaking.[78]

What is known today from the chronicles and official documents of the Grand Duchy nevertheless permits the assumption that the lands transferred to the Kingdom of Poland as a result of the Union of Lublin were somewhat different from the rest of the Lithuanian Rus' lands. First of all, they were among the least integrated into the Lithuanian state. As early as 1392, for example, the Volhynian nobles acquired the same rights as those of their counterparts in the Lviv Land on the other side of the Polish-Lithuanian border. The Kyivan Land, ruled by the Ruthenized descendants of Algirdas, was by far the most independent of all the territorial units of the Grand Duchy. The Kyivan princes and boyars often found themselves in opposition to the central authorities. During the wars of the 1430s they were staunch supporters of Švitrigaila. According to the later chronicles, some of them were involved in the assassination of Grand Prince Žygimantas in 1440. In 1481 they plotted to kill another grand duke so as to replace him with one of their own. In 1508 the Kyivan nobles supported the revolt of Mykhailo Hlynsky in the hope of restoring the Kyiv principality. Even if some of these accounts were actually fabrications of a later period, their presence in sixteenth-century chronicles suggests that there was indeed a tradition of Kyivan "alienation" from the main centers of power in the Grand Duchy of Lithuania.[79] The Kyivans fell into line only as they became more dependent on their

---

[78] Pelenski's argument that religious and national considerations were of secondary importance to participants in the Lublin Diet, including those from the Rus' territories (p. 173), is shared by other scholars. Inge Auerbach, for example, while disagreeing with Pelenski on the number of Rus' delegates unwilling to take an oath of loyalty to Poland, states that "it is still too early to speak of nationalism or even a sense of community" among them. See her "Identity in Exile: Andrei Mikhailovich Kurbskii and National Consciousness in the Sixteenth Century," in *Culture and Identity in Muscovy, 1359–1584*, ed. A. M. Kleimola and G. D. Lenhoff (Moscow, 1997), pp. 11–25, here 18.

[79] For a discussion of the chronicle evidence, see Olena Rusyna, "Vid Kuzmyshchi-kyianyna do kyianyna Skobeika (modeliuvannia smerti v khronitsi Bykhovtsia)," *Sotsium* (Kyiv) 1 (2002): 37–54; eadem, "On the Kyivan Princely Tradition from the Thirteenth to the Fifteenth Centuries," *Harvard Ukrainian Studies* 18, nos. 3–4 (December 1994): 175–90, here 182.

Volhynian neighbors to the west. Symbolic of that dependence was Hlynsky's defeat at the hands of an army led by a scion of a Volhynian princely
family, Prince Kostiantyn Ivanovych Ostrozky. It was in the decades leading up to the Union of Lublin that the Volhynian princes acquired either
complete or partial control not only of their own land but also of western Podilia and the Kyivan Land. Thus the Volhynian delegates in Lublin
favored the incorporation of the Kyivan Land into the Kingdom of Poland
along with their own land.[80]

It appears that the Union of Lublin, which terminated the independent existence of the Grand Duchy of Lithuania and had such a profound impact on nation-building in eastern Europe, became possible not
because of any ethnic self-assertion on the part of the Rus' elites but
because of the dominance of local (land) and regional (trans-land) identities in the Rus' territories of the Grand Duchy.[81]

The triumph of local identity?

The Grand Duchy of Lithuania helped produce a new type of Rus' identity. It also created conditions for the first manifestation of Rus' solidarity
based not on the principle of the dynastic state but of ethnocultural unity.
That type of solidarity underlay Rus' elite involvement in Švitrigaila's wars
of the 1430s. It also manifested itself in the perception of Muscovites as
"others," which was readily adopted in Lithuanian Rus'. Boris Floria's
observation that this occurred only in the late sixteenth and early seventeenth centuries relies on the recording of that attitude in numerous
sources of the period. Signs of the "othering" of the Muscovites are indeed
readily apparent in the avalanche of polemical works that partly preceded
but mostly followed the Union of Brest (1596). Still, the dearth of such
sources before the end of the sixteenth century should not lead one to
conclude that the Lithuanian Rus' elites did not regard Northeastern
Rus' as an "other" in earlier periods. As argued earlier in this chapter,
such an attitude toward the Muscovites can be traced back at least to the
writings celebrating Prince Ostrozky's victory over Muscovite troops at
Orsha (1514). There is also ample evidence to suggest that even earlier,
by the last decades of the fifteenth century, Lithuanian Rus' elites often

---

[80] On the Volhynian and Kyivan lands, apart from the relevant sections of Yakovenko's
Narys istoriï Ukraïny, see also Dvornichenko, *Russkie zemli Velikogo kniazhestva Litovskogo*,
pp. 94–106.

[81] Like some other lands of the Grand Duchy of Lithuania, the Volhynian and Kyivan
lands enjoyed autonomous status, protected by special decrees and privileges. On this
special status, the political attitudes of local elites, and their relation to the decisions of
the Lublin Diet, see Dvornichenko, *Russkie zemli Velikogo kniazhestva Litovskogo*, pp. 91–
101, 121–24.

regarded Northeastern Rus' as an "other" or, more precisely, a combination of multiple "others" referred to as Novgorodians, Pskovians,
Tverians, and so on.

In essence, Lithuanian Rus' identity was a hybrid of loyalty to the semi-
centralized Lithuanian polity and to the distinct Rus' cultural heritage and
folkways. As such, it served as an umbrella for the distinct identities of
the various Rus' lands on what are now Ukrainian and Belarusian territories. In political terms, the Lithuanian Rus' identity was based on
the medieval and early modern concept of loyalty to the ruler. It was
further strengthened by loyalty to distinct political (and, from the fifteenth century, ecclesiastical) institutions that separated Lithuanian Rus'
from Polish (Galician) and Mongol or post-Mongol (Northeastern) Rus'.
Although the idea of all-Rus' unity was not completely lost, especially
among the ecclesiastical literati on whose evidence we often (and sometimes exclusively) rely in our discussion, it was marginalized by the hybrid
Rus'-Lithuanian identity, called forth and developed by the existence of
a Lithuanian state. The disappearance of Novgorod, Pskov, and Tver
as independent polities and the unification of Mongol Rus' under the
leadership of Moscow helped solidify the political and cultural border
between Lithuanian and post-Mongol Rus', while the wars between the
two culturally and historically related communities for control over the
Rus' lands turned them into quintessential "others."

The problem with the Lithuanian Rus' identity, produced by the political development of the Grand Duchy, was its inchoate character. While
it was strong enough to build a sizable fence, if not a full-fledged wall,
between Lithuanian and Muscovite Rus', and even to build solidarity
between the Rus' lands under the jurisdiction of the grand duke, it failed
to produce a sense of loyalty sufficient to prevent Rus' princes from
leaving for Muscovy in the early sixteenth century or joining the Kingdom of Poland in the second half of that century. At the Lublin Diet of
1569, the Lithuanian delegates justified their concessions to the Poles
with references to their duty to their fatherland, the Grand Duchy,[82] but
the concept itself was neither well developed nor in any way central to
the political discourse of the time. Whatever the positive feelings of the
Rus' elites toward the Lithuanian state, they were overruled by estate-
and culture-based interests, protected and maintained on a regional
basis.

If we look back from the perspective of 1569 at the political and cultural history of western and southwestern Rus' from the thirteenth to

---

[82] See an excerpt from the Act of the Union of Lublin in *Belorussiia v ėpokhu feodalizma.
Sbornik dokumentov i materialov v trekh tomakh*, vol. I (Minsk, 1959), p. 150.

the sixteenth century, it appears that the development of the region was most influenced by local identities based in towns and lands. The Rurikid princes fought a losing battle against local elites for the first two centuries of that period. Their attempts to integrate a number of lands into one polity and forge a regional Rus' political identity were short-lived. The Principality of Galicia-Volhynia, the mighty regional successor to Kyivan Rus', eventually disintegrated into a number of smaller and therefore weaker principalities. Once the Rurikids associated themselves with the more powerful foreign rulers through matrimonial ties, the dynastic and patrimonial principles that legitimized war and peace among the princes and undergirded the concept of loyalty to the Rus' Land were compromised, opening the door to foreign takeover. As the princes fought for their patrimonies and called on local leaders for support, the boyars and urban elites made their choices on the basis of their own interests and those of their cities and lands. Frequently the local elites decided to get rid of their Rurikid princes and replace them with Lithuanian, Polish, or Hungarian rulers. The incorporation of the Rus' lands into the Grand Duchy of Lithuania and their existence within that highly decentralized state did very little to challenge the supremacy of local ties in the overall structure of elite identities. As Grand Duke Aleksander noted in 1495 in connection with the appointment of his viceroy in Vitsebsk, "we do not introduce new things and do not touch the old ones."[83] Occasionally, as in the 1430s, the discriminatory religious practices of the Lithuanian state would arouse the Rus' elites to joint opposition, but that solidarity faded away when official pressure was reduced. The conclusion of the Union of Lublin is one of many examples of the importance of local identity in Lithuanian Rus'.

As we have seen, the concept of loyalty to the grand prince and the state that he embodied was secondary to the prevailing local identities of the day. But what about broader elite identities that transcended individual lands? It is in the existence of such identities that present-day historians see precursors of the modern Ukrainian and Belarusian nations. There is certainly a sizable body of evidence attesting to the existence of regional identities, encompassing more than one land, in the late medieval and early modern periods. The tendency of the Smolensk-based chronicler of the mid-fifteenth century to refer to Smolensk, Polatsk, and Vitsebsk as the Rus' Land, to the exclusion of the other Rus' territories, has already been noted. It is also clear from the preceding discussion that the Volhynian and Kyivan elites maintained an interest in each other's affairs, a

---

[83] Quoted in Rowell, *Lithuania Ascending*, p. 116.

tendency that can be traced back to the times of the Galician-Volhynian principality. In general, however, these overarching regional identities turned out to be as weak as state- and culture-based ones when confronted with loyalties to individual lands. The latter ruled supreme in the region throughout late medieval times and for a significant part of the early modern period.

4   The rise of Muscovy

The title that I have chosen for this chapter is reminiscent of the one often used in textbooks on Russian history to denote the emergence of the Moscow principality as the leading force in Northeastern Rus' – the rise of Moscow. Here I apply this cliché in a broader sense, covering not only the rise to prominence of the Principality of Moscow and its rulers but also the creation under their leadership of a unified state known in Western ethnography of the fifteenth and sixteenth centuries and present-day Western scholarship as Muscovy.

What was the ethnonational identity of early modern Muscovite Rus'? Was it as fragmented and local in nature as the identity of Lithuanian Rus'? Edward L. Keenan's interpretation of Muscovite history suggests that ethnic identity as it existed among the secular Muscovite elites was much less important than clan loyalty, and that those elites had much more in common with Turkic and Lithuanian elites than with the Muscovite peasantry.[1] Nancy Shields Kollmann has reached similar conclusions in her study of social identities in early modern Russia: "The boundaries of identity in pre-modern times were not fixed but fluid, the content of identity was not national but local and personal. And this was the case regardless of how strong a learned discourse a given social body might have possessed about community and society."[2] It is hard to disagree with this statement, which, apart from being based on a thorough study of the sources, is particularly convincing because it places Muscovy in the same category as most early modern European countries. Recently, however, Valerie Kivelson has made a strong case for the existence of

---

[1] Edward L. Keenan, "Royal Russian Behavior, Style and Self-Image," in *Ethnic Russia in the USSR: The Dilemma of Dominance*, ed. Edward Allworth (New York, 1980), pp. 3–16.

[2] Nancy Shields Kollmann, "Concepts of Society and Social Identity in Early Modern Russia," in *Religion and Culture in Early Modern Russia and Ukraine*, ed. Samuel H. Baron and Nancy Shields Kollmann (DeKalb, Ill., 1997), pp. 34–51, here 44. On the connection between the concept of honor and social identity in Muscovy, see Kollmann's monograph *By Honor Bound: State and Society in Early Modern Russia* (Ithaca and London, 1999), pp. 58–63.

powerful horizontal and vertical bonds in Muscovite society that qualify it, in her opinion, for the status of a political community or even a nation.[3] Acknowledging that "learned discourses" do not tell the whole story, we shall take Kivelson's argument into consideration and subject the discourses of the period to closer scrutiny, for it is there that identity- and nation-building projects took shape and the roots of later national identities are to be found.

In this chapter I seek the origins of modern Russian identity in the discourses created by Muscovite elites of the late fifteenth and sixteenth centuries. I begin with the declaration of political independence by Ivan III and end with the rule of his grandson, Ivan the Terrible – officially the first tsar on the Muscovite throne and often also regarded as the creator of a truly multiethnic Muscovite state – the immediate precursor of the Russian Empire. Ivan IV used his diplomatic skills and later often employed brute force to unite his country, relentlessly persecuting local elites and suppressing anything that smacked of opposition to central control. In many ways, the events of the Time of Troubles – the period of social upheaval and foreign intervention in the first two decades of the seventeenth century – can be regarded as consequences of the changes introduced by Ivan the Terrible. That period, which lies outside the scope of the present chapter, inaugurated a new era in Muscovite history – one that was free (insofar as the past ever relaxes its grip) from the impact, consequences, blessings, and curses of Mongol rule. The Time of Troubles found its reflection in numerous texts expressing the new concepts and structures of Great Russian (Muscovite) identity. Muscovite views of themselves and their neighbors in the late sixteenth and early seventeenth centuries will therefore be addressed in the following chapters.[4]

Muscovy and its rulers

In the course of the fourteenth century, the princes of Moscow all but monopolized the office of grand prince of Vladimir, but the final victory of Moscow in the contest for supremacy in Mongol Rus' can be dated only to the mid-fifteenth century. It coincided with the disintegration of the Golden Horde and the creation of smaller khanates in its place, which

---

[3] See Valerie Kivelson, "Muscovite 'Citizenship': Rights without Freedom," *Journal of Modern History* 74 (September 2002): 465–89.

[4] For a survey of the period, apart from the general works on Russian history cited earlier, see Robert O. Crummey, *The Formation of Muscovy, 1304–1613* (London and New York, 1987). For a recent interpretation of the era and new literature on the subject, see Nancy Shields Kollmann, "Russia," in *The New Cambridge Medieval History*, vol. VII, *c. 1415– c. 1500* (Cambridge, 1998), pp. 748–70.

left the princes of Moscow stronger and better positioned than anyone else to take advantage of the decline of Mongol (Qipchaq) power. After a prolonged dynastic crisis that resulted in wars of succession (1420s–50s), Moscow again emerged as the primary "gatherer of the Rus' lands" under Mongol tutelage. In the process, the principality turned itself into a new power in the region and constructed a new type of identity for its secular and religious elites. These developments are closely associated with Grand Prince Ivan III, who ruled from 1462 to 1505.

The first ruler of Moscow to be installed without the formal approval of the Horde, he gained a place of honor in Muscovite and, later, Russian historical tradition next to Dmitrii Donskoi for overthrowing Mongol supremacy. This signal development was allegedly the result of a confrontation (which failed to develop into a full-blown battle) between Ivan's troops and the army of Khan Ahmed of the Great Horde at the Ugra River in 1480. But that confrontation, which took place a century after the Battle of Kulikovo Field, had even less effect on actual relations between the Horde and the Rus' principalities than its forerunner. Indeed, Ivan III was criticized by his contemporaries for his indecisiveness and failure to attack the Tatars. Although Muscovy continued to pay hidden tribute to the successors of the Golden Horde for generations to come, the Ugra incident subsequently entered Russian historical annals as the official end of the "Tatar yoke." If he did not actually throw off Mongol supremacy, Ivan III should nevertheless be credited with policies that established Muscovy as an independent state and a new superpower in the region. In 1485 he took control of Moscow's ancient rival Tver, and in 1489 of Novgorod. Expansion continued under his son, Vasilii III (1505–33). In 1510, not long after Ivan's death, the republic of Pskov succumbed to Muscovite rule, and in 1520 Riazan, the last independent Great Russian principality, was absorbed by Moscow. Wars with the Grand Duchy of Lithuania that began in the last decades of the fifteenth century and continued into the next brought control of Smolensk, which was officially recognized as part of Muscovite territory in 1522.

Ivan III and Vasilii III were the founders of the new Muscovite state. Under their rule, the old princely system of government rapidly adjusted to new conditions. A bureaucracy was formed, governors assigned to individual territories, the elites of the newly acquired lands incorporated into a class of princely servitors, a system of service-tenure estates (*pomest'e*) created and, last but not least, the army, which had relied on the support of the appanage princes, was reformed to reduce the ruler's dependence on the princely and boyar elite. It was also during the tenure of Ivan and Vasilii that a new type of ideology was developed and employed in the interests of the dynasty and the autocratic state it had created. The major goal of the new ideology, presented in numerous historical and literary works of the period, was to legitimize the power of the Muscovite rulers both internally and externally. The marriage of Ivan III to Sophia Pale-ologina, the niece of the last Byzantine emperor, which was orchestrated by the papacy, and the recognition of Vasilii III as tsar by Emperor Maxi-milian in 1514 were important elements of the new ideological program. The search for a new legitimacy was fulfilled in 1547, when Ivan IV was officially installed on the Muscovite throne with the title of tsar.

Ivan IV the Terrible (1533–84) inherited a rising state that was nev-ertheless beset with numerous problems resulting from the rapid expan-sion of the late fifteenth and early sixteenth centuries, as well as from strife between boyar groupings that he had witnessed in childhood. Ivan entered the Muscovite political scene as a great negotiator and peace-maker, convoking assemblies of the land (*zemskie sobory*) and seeking to establish ties with local elites. He initiated an ambitious program of reforms, ranging from central and local administration to the system of landholding, from the law code to the military and the church. He was also a successful empire-builder, adding to his Russian (*Rossiiskoe*) tsar-dom two other tsardoms, those of Kazan (1552) and Astrakhan (1556). Ivan's problems began when he turned his army westward. The Livo-nian War that he began in 1558 promised easy prey, and indeed in a few years the Livonian Order was defeated and disbanded, while the tsar's troops took Polatsk away from its Lithuanian masters. The success of Muscovite arms in Livonia alarmed the tsar's western neighbors. First Lithuania entered the war, then Poland (after the Union of Lublin in 1569). Sweden and Denmark also joined the camp of Muscovy's ene-mies. Polatsk was recaptured and Narva lost, leaving Ivan the Terrible with little choice but to turn to the papacy for intervention and media-tion, exploiting Rome's undying hope of involving Muscovy in the war with the Ottomans and converting it to Catholicism. The papacy com-plied, sending the Jesuit Antonio Possevino as its legate to negotiate peace with the Polish-Lithuanian Commonwealth in 1582. Ivan found himself obliged to accept the harsh treaty conditions, losing not only what he had gained at the beginning of the war but also the foothold on the Baltic littoral that his grandfather had acquired after subjecting Novgorod and its possessions to Muscovite rule.

By that time Ivan was gravely ill, while his country was devastated not only by the prolonged and disastrous war but also by the policy of *oprich-nina*. In pursuing it, Ivan set aside part of the Muscovite realm for himself, introducing a separate administration and army (*oprichniki*) in an appar-ent attempt to establish his unlimited rule and build a utopian authori-tarian state. The experiment, which lasted from 1564 to 1571, exhausted the country's material and human resources as hundreds if not thousands of members of the nobiliary elite and inhabitants of cities such as Novgorod fell victim to the terror introduced by the tsar and implemented by his troops. Explanations of the terror range from those that blame the tsar's apparently erratic and illogical behavior on his illness to those that see a certain logic in all the zigzags of his policy and attribute them to a carefully crafted plan. An interpretation advanced recently by the St. Petersburg scholar Ruslan Skrynnikov explains the *oprichnina* by the tsar's inability to honor his social contract with the elites and reward them for their service with new land grants. Under those circumstances, Ivan allegedly had to resort to brute force in order to ensure the loyalty of the elites and force them to fulfill their obligations to the state.[5] The jury is still out on Ivan himself, his puzzling behavior and contradictory policies. It might be argued, however, that Ivan the Terrible left his state more centralized than he found it, with a political and ethnocultural identity stronger and more distinct than those of its imagined "others." While Ivan's policies can be blamed for creating preconditions for the social upheavals of the Time of Troubles, they also helped Muscovy survive as a state united and indivisible.

The search for origins

Ivan the Terrible strongly believed in the Kyivan roots of his dynasty and the state. So did dozens of historians who applied his belief to the process of nation formation, turning to Kyiv in search of the origins of the Great Russian nation as a whole. The first historian to challenge the "traditional" scheme of Russian history, which closely linked – not to say lumped together – the history of Kyivan and Mongol (later Muscovite) Rus', was not the Ukrainian Mykhailo Hrushevsky but the Russian Pavel Miliukov. Having studied the monuments of Muscovite historical thought and culture, Miliukov rejected the prevailing view of the Principality of Moscow as a continuator of Kyivan Rus'. In his view, that historical link was constructed in the times of Ivan III to satisfy prevailing political objectives. Miliukov also argued that prior to the sixteenth century the defining level of Rus' political and cultural life was local (*oblastnoi*). Not until the turn of the sixteenth century did the Muscovite literati manage to produce the unifying political concept that Miliukov was prepared

---

[5] See Ruslan Skrynnikov, *Tsarstvo terrora* (St. Petersburg, 1992). On Ivan the Terrible, see also Edward L. Keenan, "Ivan IV and the 'King's Evil': Ni muka li to budet?" *Russian History* 20 (1993): 5–13; idem, *The Kurbskii-Groznyi Apocrypha: The Seventeenth-Century Genesis of the "Correspondence" Attributed to Prince A. M. Kurbskii and Tsar Ivan IV* (Cambridge, Mass., 1971); Andrei Pavlov and Maureen Perrie, *Ivan the Terrible* (London, 2003).

to accept as the starting point of Great Russian history.[6] Miliukov's views influenced Hrushevsky, whose deconstruction of the "traditional" scheme of Russian history was the most systematic such effort in his day;[7] they also influenced Matvei Liubavsky and other students of Lithuanian Rus', who saw more continuity between the political and legal development of Kyivan and Lithuanian Rus' than between Kyiv and Moscow. Miliukov's ideas also found followers in the ranks of historians of Russia, including Aleksandr Presniakov, who sought the origins of the Great Russian state in the history of Northeastern rather than Kyivan Rus'.[8] Still, Miliukov's interpretation remained marginal in twentieth-century Russian historiography, overshadowed by the much more traditional view of Russian and East Slavic history formulated by his famous professor, Vasilii Kliuchevsky.

In his lectures on Russian history, originally written in the 1880s and published in the first two decades of the twentieth century, Kliuchevsky defined his subject as the history of the Russian state and "nationality," which was divided into Great Russian and Little Russian branches. He believed in the existence of one Rus' nationality in Kyivan times and dated the formation of its Great Rus'ian branch (often referred to as a nationality in its own right) to the period between the mid-fifteenth and early seventeenth centuries. Kliuchevsky characterized the following period, from the early seventeenth to the mid-nineteenth century, as that of the gathering of the various parts of the "Russian nationality" under the auspices of one "all-Russian authority."[9] The emergence of the Eurasian school among Russian émigrés in the 1920s did very little to challenge Kliuchevsky's belief in the unity of the Russian nationality, for the Eurasianists, led by Nikolai Trubetskoi, dissociated Kyiv not from the history of the Great Russian people but only from that of the Muscovite state, which they traced back to the empire of Genghis Khan.[10] After flirting with non-Russian nationalisms in the 1920s, the reformed

---

[6] See Pavel Miliukov, *Glavnye techeniia russkoi istoricheskoi mysli*, vol. I (Moscow, 1898); idem, *Ocherki po istorii russkoi kul'tury*, 2 vols. (St. Petersburg, 1896–97).

[7] On Hrushevsky's interpretation of Miliukov's views and his critique of the "traditional" scheme of Russian history, see my *Unmaking Imperial Russia: Mykhailo Hrushevsky and the Writing of Ukrainian History* (Toronto, Buffalo, and London, 2005), pp. 95–116.

[8] See A. E. Presniakov's discussion of the "traditional" scheme and the historiography of the problem in his *Lektsii po russkoi istorii*, vol. I, *Kievskaia Rus'* (Moscow, 1938; repr. The Hague, 1966), pp. 1–11. The volume contains the texts of lectures delivered by Presniakov between 1907 and 1916.

[9] See V. O. Kliuchevskii, *Sochineniia*, vol. I, *Kurs russkoi istorii*, pt. 1 (Moscow, 1956), pp. 32–34.

[10] See Nikolai Trubetskoi's programmatic article of 1925, "The Legacy of Genghis Khan: A Perspective on Russian History not from the West but from the East," in Nikolai Trubetzkoy, *The Legacy of Genghis Khan and Other Essays on Russian Identity*, ed. Anatoly Liberman (Ann Arbor, 1991), pp. 161–232.

and highly centralized Soviet historical establishment also returned to the Kliuchevsky-based paradigm of East Slavic history.

Soviet scholarship of the 1920s and 1930s largely marginalized, if it did not entirely abandon, research on the political "superstructure" and political ideas, while stressing the importance of the economic factor in the development of nationalities and their transformation into nations. Under late Stalinism, the history of the "centralized Russian state" again became the focus of scholarly attention, counterbalanced by the preponderance of economic determinism in the Soviet interpretation of Russian nation-building. Thus Soviet historians considered the turn of the sixteenth century an important milestone in the formation of the Russian (Great Russian) nation but were careful to note that the process was not completed in that period. Anna Pankratova, one of the official leaders of Soviet historiography at the time, wrote in that regard: "In the late fifteenth and early sixteenth centuries the Russian lands were already united in a single state, although the formation of the Russian nation was not yet a completed process. In his book *On Marxism in Linguistics*, a work of genius, Comrade Stalin indicates that nationalities developed into nations only 'with the appearance of capitalism; with the liquidation of feudal disaggregation and the formation of a national market.'"[11] In their interpretation of the history of Russian nationhood, Stalin and his Soviet followers would now be considered "modernists." They certainly believed in the ethnic origins of nations but were not prepared to admit their existence before the dawn of industrial (in their interpretation, capitalist) society.

As the Soviet regime switched from class-based to nation-based discourse in its efforts to legitimize its existence, the history of the Russian nation attracted increasing attention on the part of the Soviet academic establishment. In 1952 a special interdisciplinary commission was created by the Academy of Sciences of the USSR to study the formation of the Russian nationality and nation. By the end of the decade it had published a collection of papers on the subject. Although the introduction to the volume still contained numerous references to the works of Stalin, some of the contributions were well-researched and generally interesting attempts to reconstruct the history of Russian nation-building.[12] Especially pertinent to our discussion is the lengthy essay of almost one hundred pages by Lev Cherepnin, a leading authority on premodern Russia. Cherepnin focuses on the historical circumstances pertaining to the formation of the

[11] Anna Pankratova, *Velikii russkii narod*, 2nd edn ([Moscow], 1952), p. 19.
[12] "Ot redaktsii," in *Voprosy formirovaniia russkoi narodnosti i natsii. Sbornik statei*, ed. N. M. Druzhinin and L. V. Cherepnin (Moscow and Leningrad, 1958), pp. 3–6.

Russian nationality up to the end of the fifteenth century, with special attention to socioeconomic factors. Unlike his colleague L. V. Danilova, who limited herself mainly to a discussion of those factors, Cherepnin also dealt with changes in the political structure and self-identification of the Muscovite elites.[13]

Cherepnin saw preconditions for the formation of the three East Slavic nationalities in the twelfth and thirteenth centuries. In his view, the Great Russian nationality was formed in the course of the fourteenth and fifteenth centuries. He accepted the existence of one Rus' nationality during the Kyivan period but rejected the views of scholars like Boris Rybakov, who claimed that it existed until the fourteenth and fifteenth centuries. Also mistaken, in Cherepnin's opinion, were those scholars who claimed that only the Mongol invasion prevented the consolidation of the Rus' nationality into a centralized nation-state, for that implied the existence of elements of capitalism in Kyivan Rus' as early as the thirteenth century, which was contrary to the Soviet historiographic paradigm. Cherepnin maintained that the disintegration of one Rus' nationality into three East Slavic ones was the result of feudalization. According to Cherepnin's logic, feudalization and the introduction of the appanage system were inevitable and, for a time, even progressive factors of historical development.[14]

The "Marxist-Leninist" thesis that human society progressed from lower social formations to higher ones allowed Cherepnin to reject the traditional Russian view of the disintegration of one Rus' nationality as a major national tragedy. Cherepnin was also critical of Dmitrii Likhachev's efforts to revive and legitimize the traditional interpretation within the parameters of Soviet class-based discourse. The renowned literary scholar held the feudal elites ("ruling classes of feudal society") responsible for the disintegration of Rus', while presenting the popular masses ("working classes of the population") as guardians of all-Rus' unity. Not surprisingly, since Cherepnin based his analysis on the theory of progressive social formations and rejected the Mongol invasion as the crucial factor in the disintegration of the Rus' nationality, he also refused to admit the role of the Mongols in the formation of the Great Russian nationality. According to him, the "Tatar yoke" complicated the formation of all three East Slavic nationalities by forcing them to fight for their national independence. It

[13] See L. V. Cherepnin, "Istoricheskie usloviia formirovaniia russkoi narodnosti do kontsa XV v." in *Voprosy formirovaniia russkoi narodnosti i natsii*, pp. 7–105. Cf. L. V. Danilova, "Istoricheskie usloviia razvitiia russkoi narodnosti v period obrazovaniia i ukrepleniia tsentralizovannogo gosudarstva v Rossii," in *Voprosy formirovaniia russkoi narodnosti i natsii*, pp. 106–54.

[14] Cherepnin, "Istoricheskie usloviia," pp. 54–55.

also retarded the formation of the Great Russian nationality by separating Southern and Southeastern Rus′ from Northeastern Rus′. While rejecting certain elements of the "Tatar yoke" myth in favor of the social formation paradigm, Cherepnin remained a hostage of the negative assessment of Mongol rule in traditional Russian historiography.[15]

While Soviet historians searched for the origins of the Rus′ nationality by invoking "objective laws" of historical development, literary scholars promoted a more traditional interpretation of Russian nation-building. Some of them, like Likhachev, sought to push the creation of the Russian nationality (if not nation) as far back in history as possible. If for most historians the reign of Ivan III witnessed the creation of the centralized Russian state, for Likhachev it was the time when the Russian national state took shape. He dated the "cultural revival" of the Russian people and the rise of their national identity (*pod′em narodnogo samosoznaniia*) to the times of Dmitrii Donskoi – the period immediately after the Battle of Kulikovo Field (1380).[16] Writing in the 1960s, another literary scholar, G. M. Prokhorov, saw the Kulikovo battle as giving rise not only to Russian national consciousness but also to the actual formation of the Russian people per se. He claimed that the fourteenth century witnessed the rise of two peoples that managed to form their respective states, the Ottoman Turks and the Great Russians.[17]

From the 1960s, the Kulikovo battle turned into the starting point of Great Russian history and a symbol of Russian nationalism not only in the writings of literary scholars but also in the novels of Russian writers and the historical imagination of numerous proponents of the Russian national and religious revival. Aleksandr Solzhenitsyn wrote in one of his short stories about a pilgrimage to Kulikovo Field. In the years 1980–82, faced with the need to promote Russian patriotism after the invasion of Afghanistan and respond to the rise of the Solidarity movement in Poland, the Soviet authorities jumped on the bandwagon and allowed a prolonged commemoration of the six-hundredth anniversary of the Kulikovo battle. Ironically, given the conditions of the Cold War, public discussion of the event that presumably put a stop to aggression from the East took on a pronounced anti-Western character. The celebrations were regarded as a Great Russian (not all-Soviet or East Slavic) commemoration, while the Ukrainians were allowed (not without some reluctance on the part of the

---

[15] Ibid., pp. 76–79.

[16] See D. S. Likhachev, *Natsional′noe samosoznanie drevnei Rusi. Ocherki iz oblasti russkoi literatury XI–XVII vv.* (Moscow and Leningrad, 1945), pp. 68–81.

[17] See G. M. Prokhorov, "Ėtnicheskaia integratsiia v Vostochnoi Evrope v XIV veke (ot isikhastskikh sporov do Kulikovskoi bitvy)," in idem, *Rus′ i Vizantiia v ėpokhu Kulikovskoi bitvy. Stat′i*, 2nd edn (St. Petersburg, 2000), pp. 5–43, here 5.

all-Union authorities) to invent and celebrate the 1,500th anniversary of
Kyiv in 1982. While the official historical paradigm stressed the unity
of the East Slavic peoples, the politics of festivals, driven by republican
writers' unions and national intelligentsias, cast history in a different
light: if the Battle of Kulikovo Field belonged to Russia, then the Kyiv
anniversary belonged to Ukraine.[18]

The disintegration of the USSR and the end of Communist Party control over historical scholarship has led to the formation (or reformation)
of historical theories that challenge the Soviet scheme of the development
of East Slavic nationalities. Some of them solve the problem of the ethnicity of Kyivan Rus' and thus the beginnings of Great Russian history
by claiming that in the ninth century ancient Kyiv was conquered by the
Novgorodians, who turned it into the capital of a Great Russian state.
Others treat the Russian nation as a super-ethnos consisting of a number
of sub-ethnoses (including the Little Russian one), which amounts to
little more than the application of a new vocabulary to the pre-1917 concept of one Russian nation. There have also been attempts to revive some
of Miliukov's theories and treat Rus' prior to the creation of the centralized Muscovite state as a collection of multiple lands and regions,[19] but
generally the use of "Russian" interchangeably with "Great Russian" and
the application of the former term to the Rus' lands in the premodern era
makes it all too easy for Russian authors to confuse the meanings of those
terms, even inadvertently. The result is a vicious circle: the underdevelop-
ment of ethnic terminology in Russian historical literature, which has no
separate term for the premodern population of Ukraine and Belarus, hinders the development of a productive discussion of ethnogenesis and the
construction of Russian identity in Russian historiography, which until
recently had little incentive to develop such a terminology.[20]

The idea of the ethnic unity of the Eastern Slavs and the strong sense
of such unity on the part of the Muscovite elites has found a formidable
Western opponent in the person of Edward L. Keenan. He has also undermined a number of basic assumptions about early modern Russian history

---

[18] On the public debate in the USSR regarding the celebrations of the six-hundredth
anniversary of the Kulikovo battle, see Yitzhak M. Brudny, *Reinventing Russia: Russian Nationalism and the Soviet State, 1953–91* (Cambridge, Mass., and London, 2000),
pp. 181–91.

[19] See Elena Zubkova and Aleksandr Kupriianov, "Vozvrashchenie k 'russkoi idee': krizis
identichnosti i natsional'naia istoriia," in *Natsional'nye istorii v sovetskom i postsovetskikh
gosudarstvakh*, ed. K. Aimermakher and G. Bordiugov (Moscow, 1999), pp. 299–328,
here 321–22.

[20] See the recent debate between Russian and Ukrainian historians on terminological issues
in *Ukraina i sosednie gosudarstva v XVII veke. Materialy mezhdunarodnoi konferentsii*, ed.
Tatiana Yakovleva (St. Petersburg, 2004), pp. 215–32.

that are current in Russian historiography. Among them is the paradigm, shared by imperial, Soviet, and post-Soviet historiography, of the reunification of Rus' (or Russia and Ukraine) in the mid-seventeenth century. Keenan has particularly questioned the extent of interest in Kyivan history and tradition among the Muscovite secular elites of the sixteenth century. He notes the lack of sources indicating that those elites either cared about or shared a sense of commonality with the other Eastern Slavs to the degree postulated in modern historiography. Keenan also suggests that the claims of the Muscovite tsars to the Rus' lands as part of their patrimony had little to do with their sense of belonging to a common East Slavic ethnos.[21] Some ideas of the Russian Eurasianists have been further developed by Donald Ostrowski. He has successfully challenged the myth of the "Tatar yoke" and persuasively identified numerous borrowings of the Muscovite political elite and society from their Qipchaq overlords.[22] The history of Muscovite secular and religious claims to the Kyivan heritage has been thoroughly reconstructed by Jaroslaw Pelenski.[23]

These and numerous other works by Western authors continue the revisionist trend initiated by Pavel Miliukov in the late nineteenth century and offer a good basis for our present attempt to challenge the "traditional" scheme of the formation of the Russian nation. I shall begin with a close look at the origins of one of the founding myths of modern Russia, that of the Tatar yoke.

The "Tatar yoke"

The rule of the Qipchaq khans over the vast territories of Northeastern Rus' has given rise to ongoing historiographic debate about the Mongol impact on Russian history. That debate is closely linked to the formation of modern Russian identity – more specifically, its Eastern edifice. The Western-oriented Russian historiography of most of the eighteenth and nineteenth centuries continued the tradition established by the Muscovite chronicles of viewing the Tatars as infidels, while treating the period of Mongol rule as an aberration from the normal course of Russian history,

[21] See Edward L. Keenan, "On Certain Mythical Beliefs and Russian Behaviors," in *The Legacy of History in Russia and the New States of Eurasia*, ed. S. Frederick Starr (Armonk, NY, 1994), pp. 19–40; idem, "Muscovite Perceptions of Other East Slavs before 1654 – An Agenda for Historians," in *Ukraine and Russia in Their Historical Encounter*, ed. Peter J. Potichnyj, Marc Raeff, Jaroslaw Pelenski, and Gleb N. Žekulin (Edmonton, 1992), pp. 20–38.
[22] See Donald Ostrowski, *Muscovy and the Mongols: Cross-Cultural Influences on the Steppe Frontier, 1304–1589* (Cambridge, 1998).
[23] See Jaroslaw Pelenski, *The Contest for the Legacy of Kievan Rus'* (Boulder, Colo., 1998).

calling it the "Tatar yoke" and denying any Mongol impact on Russia. Such historians rejected Western notions about the Asiatic nature of Russian authoritarianism, maintaining that Russia had saved the West from Mongol barbarism. As Russia's pro-Western orientation and the negative connotations of Orientalism expired in the flames of the Revolution of 1917, a Eurasian school of historians and political thinkers stressed the Asiatic pedigree of the Russian state tradition and indicated the tremendous, often positive, impact of Mongol suzerainty on the development of Russia. Soviet historiography continued the imperial historical tradition, portraying the Tatars as invaders and basically refusing to incorporate the research of Oriental studies specialists into the Russian historical narrative. The division between "Russianists" and "Orientalists" with regard to the "Mongol period" of Russian history continues to exist in post-Soviet historiography.[24]

A close examination of the political, administrative, and military institutions of post-Mongol Muscovy makes it difficult to reject the argument of Russian Eurasianists and Western scholars like Keenan and Ostrowski that the early modern Russian state was much more a product of its recent Mongol experience than of the chronologically and geographically removed Kyivan past. It is true that Northeastern Rus' always distinguished itself from the "Horde" and that Muscovite centralization was undertaken not with the encouragement of the khans but against their will. Nevertheless, long habituation to Mongol rule led Muscovy to adopt a number of important elements of its political culture and thinking, as well as its social and economic practices. Such borrowings included the concept that all the land belonged to the ruler; the structure of the boyar council; the system of dual administration, in which regional military and civil power was concentrated in the hands of representatives of the center; the institution of *mestnichestvo*, which made the servitor's status dependent on that of his family; and the granting of land on condition of military service (*pomest'e*). The Mongols also had a profound impact on the structure and tactics of the Muscovite military. All these institutions and practices, often shared with Eastern lands as distant as China, helped shape the basic features of Muscovy as a political, social, and economic entity. They also helped differentiate the Eastern Slavs with regard to their understanding of the Byzantine and Kyivan traditions. Northeastern Rus' emerged from the period of Mongol rule strong and

---

[24] For an assessment of the historiographic tradition and the current state of research on the Golden Horde in Russian historiography, see Charles J. Halperin, "Omissions of National Memory: Russian Historiography on the Golden Horde as Politics of Inclusion and Exclusion," *Ab Imperio*, 2004, no. 3: 131–44.

united but also very different from those parts of the Rus' that did not experience the long rule of the khans.[25]

Ironically, there was probably no other institution that benefited as much from the "Tatar yoke" as the Orthodox Church. It was not only tolerated by the steppe rulers but also privileged with regard to taxation. One can even speak of a quasi-alliance between the Golden Horde and the Rus' metropolitanate for most of the period of Tatar rule over Northern Rus'. One of the underpinnings of these close relations was the actual alliance between the Byzantine emperors and the Qipchaq khans, which was sealed by a number of marriages and lasted from the second half of the thirteenth century until the fall of Constantinople to the Ottomans in 1453. The Greek metropolitans of Rus' were careful to follow the Constantinople line and maintain friendly relations with the khans. When Metropolitan Maximos abandoned Kyiv for Northeastern Rus' at the turn of the fourteenth century, he was not only moving to a more secure and economically prosperous location but also establishing himself in the heartland of the Rus' possessions of Byzantium's ally, the Mongol khan. The close ties between the Golden Horde and Byzantium should be considered at least partly responsible for the refusal of most patriarchs of Constantinople to divide the Rus' metropolitanate or move its seat to the Grand Duchy of Lithuania. Only a few pro-Western patriarchs were willing to entertain the demands of the Lithuanian and Polish rulers to establish separate metropolitanates in their realms.[26]

No wonder that the church ruled by Constantinople supported those Rus' princes who favored collaboration with the Mongols. If in Galicia-Volhynia the chroniclers of the second half of the thirteenth century did not conceal their negative attitude toward the Horde, in Northeastern Rus' we see no sign of opposition or negative characterization of the Mongols in local chronicle writing. Such traits become apparent only in the mid-fifteenth century, when the Principality of Moscow and the Rus' church began to emerge from the shadow of their respective suzerains, the Golden Horde and the patriarchate of Constantinople. The first to achieve that new degree of independence was the church, which (apparently without opposition from the Horde) rejected the conditions of the Union of Florence. That union brought Byzantium closer to the West, distancing it from its eastern ally. The irony of the situation was that the

---

[25] For a discussion of the Mongol impact on the Muscovite state and society, see Ostrowski, *Muscovy and the Mongols*, pp. 36–132; Jaroslaw Pelenski, "State and Society in Muscovite Russia and the Mongol-Turkic System in the Sixteenth Century," in idem, *The Contest for the Legacy of Kievan Rus'*, pp. 228–43.

[26] See Ostrowski, *Muscovy and the Mongols*, p. 138; Prokhorov, "Ėtnicheskaia integratsiia v Vostochnoi Evrope," pp. 5–43, here 22–29.

church, once freed from the tutelage of Constantinople, began to engage in anti-Tatar propaganda as its own interests dictated. Thus, when Grand Prince Vasilii II of Moscow agreed to the installation of a new autocephalous metropolitan in 1448 without the blessing of Constantinople, the church reciprocated by supporting the prince against his rival, Dmitrii Shemiaka, accusing the latter of pro-Tatar and anti-Rus' policies. The tradition of ecclesiastical support for Tatar rule was effectively broken. As Ostrowski has recently argued, the new anti-Tatar spirit of the church soon found expression in the chronicles and other writings produced at the metropolitan court and among churchmen in general.[27] The new myth of Rus' resistance to Mongol rule was born in the late fifteenth and early sixteenth centuries, with Prince Dmitrii Donskoi serving as its main protagonist. It was advanced, developed, and disseminated not only in the chronicles but also in the literary and hagiographic works of the Kulikovo cycle.

The myth of resistance to Mongol rule on the part of the Rus' princes and church hierarchs was later complemented by the myth of the "Tatar yoke," which vilified the Golden Horde and its practices. The term itself came into existence quite late. It cannot be traced back further than the last quarter of the sixteenth century, when it appears in one of the Western descriptions of Muscovy. It gained popularity only in the seventeenth century and apparently entered Muscovite literature through the intermediacy of Kyivan literati in the second half of that century.[28] The two motifs in combination effectively served as a founding myth of Muscovy and the Great Russian nation. The latter, according to that myth, came into existence as a result of centuries of heroic struggle to preserve its Kyivan heritage from obliteration by the oppressive Mongol regime. In the nineteenth century, Aleksandr Pushkin would claim that Russia had shielded and saved the West from the horrors of a Mongol invasion. The West, by that logic, was greatly indebted to Russia.

Rediscovering Kyiv

Another founding myth of the Muscovite state was that of its Kyivan origins. In the mid-fifteenth century, as Muscovite metropolitans dropped the name of Kyiv from their official title, while Moscow-based literati denied the ancient capital of Rus' central status in the Rus' Land, replacing it in that capacity with Moscow, nothing seemed to indicate a possible

---

[27] See Ostrowski, *Muscovy and the Mongols*, pp. 139–63.
[28] For a critique of the myth of the "Tatar yoke," see ibid., pp. 244–48; Keenan, "On Certain Mythical Beliefs," pp. 25–26.

revival of interest in the heritage of ancient Kyiv among the Moscow elites. Nevertheless, the second half of the fifteenth century witnessed just such a revival, influenced by factors of a religious and political nature. The first of these was interest in the roots of Rus' Christianity, generated by polemics over the Union of Florence, the division of the Rus' metropolitanate, and the de facto autocephaly of its Muscovite portion. The second factor was the emergence of Muscovy as a fully independent polity that had thrown off the power of the Qipchaq khanate and was looking for historical justification of its new status. In both cases, the search for a usable past led to Kyiv or through Kyiv to Byzantium, making the history of Kyivan Rus' more important to the Moscow elites than ever before. Finally, Moscow's claims to Tver, Novgorod, and Pskov, as well as to Smolensk and other Rus' territories of the Grand Duchy of Lithuania, also inspired interest in Kyiv and made it important to stress the dynastic connection between the princes of Moscow and St. Volodymyr.

The groundwork for the revival of Muscovy's interest in the Kyivan past was laid by Metropolitan Cyprian, the most "all-Rus'ian" of all metropolitans in terms of his actual pastoral experience, and by his successor, Metropolitan Fotii. The first half of the fifteenth century saw the introduction into the Muscovite church calendar of a number of feasts directly related to Kyiv and the Kyivan origins of Rus' Orthodoxy. These included the feasts of St. Olha, St. Antonii of the Kyivan Cave Monastery, and the Varangian martyrs. The fifteenth-century Muscovite church calendar also included feasts of St. Volodymyr and the dedication of the Church of St. George in Kyiv, as well as two feasts devoted to SS. Borys and Hlib.[29] When it comes to Muscovite texts, the first indications of the new interest in Kyivan times on the part of the Muscovite literati appear in the late 1450s and 1460s. They are to be found in polemical works concerning the Union of Florence that discuss St. Volodymyr and his role in the baptism of Rus'.[30] Among the works of the Kulikovo cycle, the earliest to evince strong interest in the Kyivan past is the *Oration* on the life of Dmitrii Ivanovich (1470s). Dmitrii Donskoi is presented there not only as the grandson of Grand Prince Ivan Kalita, the "gatherer of the Rus' Land," but also as the "fruitful branch and fine flower of Tsar Volodymyr (Vladimir), the new Constantine, who baptized the Rus' Land; a relative of the new miracle workers Borys and Hlib."[31] References to the Kyivan

[29] See Richard D. Bosley, "The Changing Profile of the Liturgical Calendar in Muscovy's Formative Years," in *Culture and Identity in Muscovy, 1359–1584*, ed. A. M. Kleimola and G. D. Lenhoff (Moscow, 1997), pp. 35–37.

[30] See Jaroslaw Pelenski, "The Origins of the Official Muscovite Claims to the Kievan Inheritance," in idem, *The Contest for the Legacy of Kievan Rus'*, pp. 87–88.

[31] "Slovo o zhitii i prestavlenii Velikogo kniazia Dmitriia Ivanovicha," in *Khrestomatiia po drevnei russkoi literature*, comp. N. K. Gudzii (Moscow, 1973), pp. 180–88, here 180. The

past in the *Oration* also find parallels in the chronicles of the period, which helps to explain the timing and significance of the new interest in the Kyivan heritage.

According to Pelenski, the compilers of the Muscovite Codex of 1472 not only included the *Oration* in their compilation but also extended the Kyivan princely line from Rurik and St. Volodymyr all the way to Ivan III. This was done in the entry for 1471 and spelled out in statements made during negotiations between the Novgorodians and Muscovite envoys. The latter allegedly stated on behalf of the tsar:

> From antiquity you, the people of Novgorod, have been my [Tsar Ivan III's] patrimony, from our grandfathers and our ancestors, from Grand Prince Volodymyr, the great grandson of Rurik, the first grand prince in our land, who baptized the Rus' land. And from that Rurik until this day, you have recognized only one ruling clan (*rod*) of those grand princes, first those of Kyiv, then Grand Prince Vsevolod [III] Yurievich, [and Grand Prince] Dmitrii [Ivanovich Donskoi] of Vladimir. And from that grand prince until my time, we, their kin, have ruled over you, and we bestow [our mercy] upon you, and we protect you against [all adversaries], and we are free to punish you if you do not recognize us according to the old tradition.[32]

This statement may be regarded as one of the first expressions of the *translatio* theory that postulated the transfer of power in the Rus' lands from Kyiv to Vladimir on the Kliazma and then to Moscow. The Moscow politicians and scribes needed such a theory to legitimize their claims to Novgorod, but apparently it also had an actual political connection with Kyiv. In their efforts to play off the Grand Duchy of Lithuania against Muscovy, the Novgorodians invited Prince Mykhailo Olelkovych of Kyiv to rule them, and it is possible that Muscovite literati produced the *translatio* argument in order to offset the historical arguments advanced by supporters of the Kyivan prince.[33] If that was indeed the case, then from its very inception the *translatio* theory not only established a link between Moscow and Kyiv but also did so at Kyiv's expense, excluding the Kyivan

---

Kyivan theme, in the form of numerous references to Kyivan princes and personages, was also developed in other works of the Kulikovo cycle written contemporaneously with the *Oration* and later. *Zadonshchina*, for example, contains references not only to St. Volodymyr but also to Rurik's son Ihor, Yaroslav the Wise, and the legendary Boian, the Kyivan minstrel who also appears in the *Tale of Igor's Campaign*. See "Slovo Sofoniia riazantsa o velikom kniazi Dmitrii Ivanoviche," in *Povesti o Kulikovskoi bitve*, ed. M. N. Tikhomirov, V. F. Rzhiga, and L. A. Dmitriev (Moscow, 1959), p. 9.

[32] Adapted from Pelenski, "The Origins of the Official Muscovite Claims," p. 90.

[33] Ibid., p. 90. On the Novgorod and Pskov communities' practice of inviting princes from the Grand Duchy of Lithuania, see Anna Khoroshkevich, "Istoricheskie sud'by belorusskikh i ukrainskikh zemel' v XIV – nachale XVI v.," in Vladimir Pashuto, Boris Floria, and Khoroshkevich, *Drevnerusskoe nasledie i istoricheskie sud'by vostochnogo slavianstva* (Moscow, 1982), pp. 140–41.

(and, by extension, Lithuanian) princes from the official genealogy of the ruling house of Rus'.

The appearance in the chronicles of Moscow's claim to the Kyivan heritage prepared the way for Ivan III's assumption of the title of autocrat of all Rus' in relations with the Grand Duchy of Lithuania in the early 1490s. The new rhetoric proved useful in Moscow's ongoing contest with Lithuania for Rus' territories in the borderlands of the two states, which included Kyiv. In a treaty concluded with the Habsburgs in 1490, Muscovite diplomats included a reference to a war that Ivan III might wage for the "Kyivan principality." Indeed, by the 1490s, the border skirmishes that characterized Lithuanian-Muscovite relations in the 1480s had given way to open warfare. It ended in 1494 with a treaty that stipulated not only Lithuanian recognition of Moscow's annexation of Novgorod and Tver but also provisional recognition of Ivan III as sovereign of all Rus'. The resumption of hostilities in the years 1500–1503 led to the Muscovite conquest of a number of new Rus' territories, including Chernihiv, in close proximity to Kyiv (a reference to Chernihiv was added even earlier to the official title of Ivan III). Muscovite diplomats consistently claimed as the tsar's patrimony the "entire Rus' Land, Kyiv, Smolensk, and other towns."[34] Rus' princes such as Mykhailo Hlynsky were leaving Lithuania for Moscow, and it seemed that another war might well put Muscovy in control of the capital of Kyivan Rus' itself. Only the victory of Lithuanian troops led by Kostiantyn Ostrozky at Orsha in 1514 halted the Muscovite advance and stabilized the border between the two countries.[35]

Muscovite literati of the late fifteenth and early sixteenth centuries found it important to establish the link with Kyiv not only in order to justify Muscovy's territorial acquisitions in the west but also to give substance to the new title of tsar claimed by the Muscovite rulers. That title symbolized their independence of the khans, making them equal in status with their former sovereigns, and established a claim to power comparable to that of the west European emperors. Although the title of tsar did not officially replace that of grand prince as the main designation of

---

[34] On the use of the new title in Muscovy's relations with Novgorod and Lithuania, with Muscovite diplomatic references to Lithuanian Rus' as Ivan III's patrimony, see Aleksandr Filiushkin, "Vgliadyvaias' v oskolki razbitogo zerkala: Rossiiskii diskurs Velikogo Kniazhestva Litovskogo," Ab Imperio, 2004, no. 4: 561–601.

[35] For a brief survey of Muscovite-Lithuanian relations in this period, see Janet Martin, Medieval Russia, 980–1584 (Cambridge, 1996), pp. 303–8; for a detailed discussion, see A. A. Zimin, Rossiia na poroge novogo vremeni (Ocherki politicheskoi istorii Rossii pervoi treti XVI veka) (Moscow, 1972); Mikhail Krom, Mezh Rus'iu i Litvoi: zapadnorusskie zemli v sisteme russko-litovskikh otnoshenii kontsa XV – pervoi treti XVI v. (Moscow, 1995). On the formulation of Muscovite claims to Kyiv, see Floria, "Drevnerusskie traditsii i bor'ba vostochnoslavianskikh narodov za vossoedinenie," in Pashuto, Floria, and Khoroshkevich, Drevnerusskoe nasledie, pp. 171–72.

the Muscovite ruler until the coronation of Ivan the Terrible in 1547, it was occasionally used by his grandfather, Ivan III, and recognized by the Holy Roman Emperor Maximilian I as the legitimate title of Ivan III's father, Vasilii III. It was apparently during Vasilii's reign that a political and historical treatise known as the *Tale of the Princes of Vladimir* was written – a work that presented the Muscovite rulers as heirs of Emperor Constantine Monomachos of Byzantium and Augustus Caesar of Rome. The authors of the *Tale* in fact followed the argument first developed in the early sixteenth century (and rejected by the Lithuanian authorities) by Metropolitan Spiridon-Savva of Kyiv, a native of Tver. Apparently under the influence of theories about the Roman origins of the Lithuanians, Spiridon-Savva rooted the genealogy of the Rurikid princes in the imperial Roman past and advanced a hypothesis about the Byzantine origins of the Muscovite princes' claim to tsardom.[36]

The authors of the *Tale of the Princes of Vladimir* found Kyivan history useful in establishing both connections, for it linked the rulers of Moscow with Augustus not only through Constantine Monomachos (an uncle of Prince Volodymyr Monomakh of Kyiv) but also through an alleged relative of Rurik named Prus. It also introduced Lithuanian genealogical legends into the Muscovite grand narrative, facilitating the incorporation of Lithuanian Rus' elites into Muscovite society. Under the apparent influence of Muscovite servitors descended from the princely house of Gediminas (including the Belskys, Trubetskois, and Mstislavskys), the authors of the *Tale* dropped Spiridon-Savva's story about Gediminas having been enserfed to one of the Rus' princes and identified him as a descendant of the Rurikids. Thanks to the *Tale*, the imperial heritage was symbolized by the so-called cap of Monomakh – a crown of Central Asian provenance that was claimed, in light of the new genealogical theory, to have been inherited by the princes of Moscow from their Kyivan ancestor Volodymyr Monomakh. Thus Kyivan history became central to the founding myth of the Muscovite monarchy and was featured prominently in Muscovite chronicles of the early sixteenth century.[37]

A number of factors, including the emergence of Muscovy as a state in its own right in the late fifteenth century, the need to provide historical

---

[36] On the treatment of Lithuanian genealogical legends by Spiridon-Savva and the authors of the *Tale*, see Olena Rusyna, "Kyiv-Troia: peredistoriia ta istoriï mifolohemy," in eadem, *Studiï z istoriï Kyieva ta kyïvs'koï zemli* (Kyiv, 2005), pp. 240–63, here 243–51.

[37] On the *Skazanie o kniaziakh Vladimirskikh* (Tale of the Princes of Vladimir) and the Monomakh legend, see Ostrowski, *Muscovy and the Mongols*, pp. 171–76. On the Kyivan theme in the Muscovite chronicles, see Floria, "Drevnerusskie traditsii," pp. 163–67. On the importance of the Kyivan connection for constructing the genealogy of the Muscovite Rurikids, see Norman W. Ingham, "Genealogy and Identity in the Rhetoric of Muscovite Rulership," in *Culture and Identity in Muscovy*, pp. 166–80.

legitimacy for the independent power of its rulers, and its annexation of formerly semi-autonomous Rus′ polities and Rus′ lands of the Grand Duchy of Lithuania, influenced the resurgence of interest in the Kyivan heritage among the Muscovite literati. The same factors led to a reconceptualization of the notion of the Rus′ Land, which was now understood to include Kyiv itself and all the lands once ruled by the Kyivan princes. In the second half of the sixteenth century, some Muscovite authors even referred to Moscow as a second Kyiv.[38] But what was the extent of that identification with Kyiv? Was it limited to a few literati and diplomats, or did it affect broader circles of the Muscovite elite? Edward L. Keenan, who was the first to ask this question, maintains that the court elite of the late fifteenth and sixteenth centuries was much closer in culture and tradition to the Tatar khanates than to the Kyivan heritage and that there is "no reason to believe that they were driven by, or for that matter were even aware of, any theoretical or ideological program that admonished them to reunite east Slavs under the banner of restored Kyivan heritage."[39] Donald Ostrowski disagrees with some of Keenan's arguments but generally accepts his view that the court did not consider itself attached to Kyivan tradition in any major way. In Ostrowski's opinion, it was the church leadership that imposed the Kyivan connection on the secular elites in an attempt to distance the newly independent state and its ruling stratum from its Tatar past.[40] Whether that was so or not, there was hardly a better way for the Muscovite elites to dissociate themselves from their recent Tatar past than to stress the Roman, Byzantine and, inevitably, Kyivan roots of the Muscovite dynasty.

The discourse of tsardom

The Grand Principality of Moscow officially became a tsardom with the solemn inauguration of Ivan IV the Terrible in 1547. This is the year and event with which general surveys of Russian history conventionally begin the history of the Muscovite tsardom (my computer program insistently corrects "tsardom" to "stardom," and in this case the use of either term can probably be justified). But that is not how contemporaries of Ivan the Terrible and the next several generations of Muscovites perceived Muscovy's rise to tsardom. Moreover, both seventeenth-century historical tradition and popular memory associated the transformation of Muscovy into a tsardom not with Ivan's consecration as ruler but with his conquest

---

[38] See Olena Rusyna, "Kyïv iak Sancta Civitas u moskovs′kii ideolohiï ta politychnii praktytsi XIV–XVI s.," in eadem, *Studiï z istoriï Kyieva*, pp. 172–99, here 190.

[39] Keenan, "On Certain Mythical Beliefs and Russian Behaviors," p. 25.

[40] See Ostrowski, *Muscovy and the Mongols*, pp. 169–70.

of the Khanate of Kazan, which took place five years later (1552).[41] Characteristically, when Ivan asked the patriarch of Constantinople to confirm his new title in 1557, he also cited the conquest of the Khanates of Kazan and Astrakhan (1552–56) as grounds for his request. The same argument was advanced when Muscovy sought to convince its western neighbors to accept its ruler's new title. What Ivan and his contemporaries regarded as the beginning of the tsardom is often treated by modern scholars as the beginning of the empire. The conquest of Kazan is a key event in both interpretations of Russian history. In a virtual dialogue across the centuries, equivalence has been established between the terms "tsar" and "emperor," "tsardom" and "empire." While the sixteenth-century tyrant saw his annexation of the Tsardom of Kazan as proof that he himself was tsar, modern historians see the annexation of ethnically non-Slavic Kazan as proof that Muscovy was turning not only into a tsardom but also into a multinational empire.[42]

What both perspectives appear to overlook are the historical precedents for these developments. It was Ivan III, the grandfather of Ivan the Terrible, who was the first to install his own candidate as tsar of Kazan in 1487, and it was the latter's father, Vasilii III, who extended Muscovy's patronage over the Kazan tsardom. Both rulers occasionally called themselves tsars, including references to Bulgar on the Volga or Kazan in their titles.[43] As for the multiethnic character of the Muscovite state, the inhabitants of Kazan were not the first non-Slavs to be engulfed by Muscovy. The gathering of the "Rus' lands," not unlike the "gathering" of the Mongol ones, often meant accepting the non-Slavic subjects of Rus' princes as well. The *Life of St. Stefan of Perm* gives a good idea of the problems faced by fourteenth-century missionaries working among non-Slavic and non-Christian inhabitants of Mongol Rus'. That category of the population increased dramatically after the annexation of the Novgorodian Land. Thus it appears that the view of the mid-sixteenth century as a period of Muscovy's "imperialization" is not free of pitfalls. Geoffrey

---

[41] See Pelenski, "State and Society in Muscovite Russia," p. 237; L. N. Pushkarev, "Otrazhenie istorii Russkogo tsentralizovannogo gosudarstva v ustnom narodnom tvorchestve XVI–XVII vv.," in *Rossiia na putiakh tsentralizatsii. Sbornik statei*, ed. D. S. Likhachev et al. (Moscow, 1982), pp. 250–55.

[42] Pelenski subscribes to this view when he states: "Until 1552 it [Muscovy] had primarily existed as a Great Russian state . . . Subsequently Russia ceased to be regarded as a single homogeneous country and began to be viewed as an empire (state of states) composed of a diversity of tsardoms, lands and cities" ("State and Society in Muscovite Russia," p. 237).

[43] See Anna Khoroshkevich, "Otrazhenie predstavlenii o regionakh vseia Rusi i Rossiiskogo tsarstva v velikokniazheskoi i tsarskoi titulature XVI v.," in *Die Geschichte Rußlands im. 16 und 17. Jahrhundert aus der Perspektive seiner Regionen*, ed. Andreas Kappeler (Vienna, 2004), pp. 102–27, here 119–26.

Hosking, for example, acknowledges that by 1552 "Muscovite Rus′ was already a multinational state" and regards the conquest of Kazan as the moment "when Muscovy set out on its career of empire by conquering and annexing for the first time a non-Russian sovereign state."[44] One can certainly accept this interpretation of the conquest of Kazan (if "Russian" is understood to mean "East Slavic"), but is that how the Muscovite elites of the period saw it?

Of course, contemporaries did not have our advantage of hindsight and were unaware that Kazan would be followed by Astrakhan, western Siberia, and eventually Central Asia. Besides, the Muscovite elites of the age of Ivan the Terrible thought (or, better, articulated their thoughts) not exclusively but primarily in terms of polities and dynasties. Thus the annexation of the Volga khanates was considered an addition of two new tsardoms to the tsardom of Rus′. They also thought in religious terms. The major distinction between the annexation of Kazan and Novgorod was religious: in the first case, the Muscovites were dealing with a non-Christian Muslim state, while the Novgorodians were merely suspected of corrupting Christianity. Other than that, the difference between the two cases (to be discussed below) was not as dramatic in the minds of the Muscovite elites as one would imagine today. Not only did the annexation of Kazan have its roots in the earlier annexation of Novgorod and other Rus′ polities, but so did the official justification of the takeover. In both cases the Muscovite elites relied on the old and well-developed concept of patrimony or, more specifically, the patrimonial rights of Muscovite rulers to a given territory. As the case of Kazan demonstrates, that concept was blind to ethnicity and religion, neither of which mattered very much to the tsar, who considered himself a descendant of Augustus and a German by nationality.[45]

It has often been noted in the literature that the claims of the Muscovite rulers to particular Rus′ lands on the basis of their alleged patrimonial rights had little to do with their vision of the East Slavic commonality of those lands.[46] Ivan the Terrible considered Livonia to be his patrimony, as he did the Kazan khanate. Although in his official documents Ivan the Terrible counted separately the years of his Russian (*Rosiiskoe*), Kazan,

---

[44] Geoffrey Hosking, *Russia: People and Empire, 1552–1917* (London, 1998), p. 3.

[45] Ivan the Terrible allegedly stated to his English goldsmith (later quoted by Giles Fletcher): "I am no Russe; my ancestors were German." See A. M. Kleimola, "Genealogy and Identity among the Riazan′ Elite," in *Culture and Identity in Muscovy*, pp. 284–302, here 284–85.

[46] In Keenan's opinion, the Muscovite rulers' claims of patrimonial rights can be translated into modern diplomatic language as "we have certain historical interests in this region." See Keenan, "On Certain Mythical Beliefs and Russian Behaviors," p. 24; idem, "Muscovite Perceptions of Other East Slavs," pp. 25–26.

and Astrakhan rule, there was no separate installation of the ruler for newly annexed tsardoms. That practice indicates the continuation of a tradition whereby the rulers of Moscow added to their titles the name of every new land, principality, or country that they conquered or acquired. In their correspondence the tsar and his diplomats supported those claims by invoking the acquired rights of Ivan III and Vasilii III. Thus there was no major change in the legitimization of the tsar's power and the extent of his realm after the conquest of Kazan.

Nor did the Muscovites neglect the Kyivan connection of their dynasty and the patrimonial rights associated with it. In 1548, during negotiations with Lithuanian envoys concerning recognition of Ivan the Terrible's title of tsar, Muscovite diplomats alleged that Ivan had inherited it from his ancestor Volodymyr Monomakh of Kyiv. The Lithuanians were reluctant to accept this argument, noting that Kyiv belonged to Lithuania, whose ruler had the titular right to the "Kyivan tsardom."[47] This "territorial" argument did little to change Muscovite dynastic and patrimonial thinking on the issue. As Pelenski has shown, the Kyivan theme was also exploited to justify Ivan IV's conquest of Kazan. It was not used by diplomats but by authors of chronicles composed at the tsar's court (such as the Nikon and Lviv Chronicles) and in works written at the chancellery of the Orthodox Church under the supervision of Metropolitan Makarii. According to one such work, the *Stepennaia kniga* (Book of Degrees), "the Kazan Land, which was called the Bulgar Land before, was ruled from antiquity by Rus' sovereigns, beginning with Grand Prince Rurik, who collected tribute as far as the Volga River, and as far as the Caspian Sea and the Kama River."[48]

The authors of the *Book of Degrees* were very liberal indeed in their interpretation of the data that they found in the Primary Chronicle. They extended the territory of the Cheremisians and Mordva, who paid tribute to the Rus' princes, from the Oka River all the way to the Kama River and the Caspian Sea. They claimed Astrakhan by the simple expedient of identifying it as the Kyivan-era Principality of Tmutarakan.[49] Some Muscovite authors established the patrimonial rights of Ivan the Terrible to Kazan by tracing his lineage through Dmitrii Donskoi to Volodymyr Monomakh and St. Volodymyr himself. Others, like the author of *Kazanskaia istoriia* (The History of Kazan), claimed that Kazan was founded in the Rus' Land, or even stated that the territory was settled by the Rus',

---

[47] See Rusyna, "Kyiv iak *Sancta Civitas*," pp. 189–90.
[48] Adapted from Jaroslaw Pelenski, "Muscovite Imperial Claims to the Kazan Khanate (Based on the Muscovite Theory of Succession to the Lands of Kievan Rus')," in idem, *The Contest for the Legacy of Kievan Rus'*, pp. 189–212, here 194.
[49] Ibid., pp. 196–99.

thereby introducing an ethnic argument to justify the Muscovite annexation. What seems most important in all these cases is that both at court
and in church the literati were legitimizing the annexation of Kazan as
they had the previous annexation of Novgorod – by invoking the Kyivan
roots of the Moscow dynasty.

But was the conquest of Kazan regarded by contemporaries as a major
ethnonational development? It is difficult to answer this question in general, and perhaps impossible to do so without relying on later evidence.
In the times of Peter I, there was a popular picture (*lubok*) depicting the
funeral of the Kazan Cat conducted by mice, showing that the conquest of
Kazan, formerly a powerful and dangerous enemy (the cat), was remem-
bered and celebrated by the Muscovite folk long after the actual event.
The same motif shows that the popular perception of mid-sixteenth-
century developments was not limited to the conquest of Kazan. The
Kazan Cat is also depicted as the Astrakhan and Siberian Cat, indicating
that the main divide between the Muscovites (the mouse) and the Tatars
(the cat) was along ethnocultural lines, not along the borders of sixteenth-
century polities.[50] What we know today about the incorporation of Tatar
elites into Muscovite society after the conquest of Kazan and Astrakhan
indicates that the ethnic distinctiveness of the Tatars long delayed their
full integration into the Muscovite political structure. Since they were
culturally alien to the Muscovite elites, the act of swearing allegiance to
the Muscovite tsar – which guaranteed other local elites full participation in Muscovite political life – was just the beginning for them, for only
conversion to Orthodoxy could put them on the road to full Muscovite
"citizenship." To achieve it, however, they had to become "Rus'ians" not
only politically and religiously but also culturally.[51]

The age of Ivan IV brought large population shifts as Novgorodian
boyars, craftsmen, and merchants, Kazan elites, and senior Muscovite
servitors were forced to move around the country and in and out of the
oprichnina lands. This large-scale resettlement caused major shifts of identity. The Muscovite state was quite successful in promoting service-based
identities, recruiting elites from different parts of the country. Although

---

[50] See the reproduction of the Kazan Cat *lubok* in Robin Milner-Gulland, *The Russians*
(Oxford, 1997), p. 174. On the meaning of the *lubok* composition, see Said Faizov,
"Probuzhdenie imperii v tsarstvovanie Alekseia Mikhailovicha (ofitsial'naia ideologiia
Moskvy i fol'klor)," in *Ukraina i sosednie gosudarstva v XVII veke*, pp. 145–59.

[51] On the role of ethnic and religious factors in the incorporation of Tatar elites into Muscovite society, see Michael Khodarkovsky, "Four Degrees of Separation: Constructing
Non-Christian Identities in Muscovy," in *Culture and Identity in Muscovy*, pp. 248–66,
here 248–49; Janet Martin, "Multiethnicity in Muscovy: A Consideration of Christian
and Muslim Tatars in the 1550s–1580s," *Journal of Early Modern History* 5, no. 1 (2001):
1–23.

relocated princes and boyars used every opportunity to go home, in the long run they tended to lose their regional identities and acquire new ones. In official documents, military units were now identified not by the names of the appanage principalities or provinces from which they were recruited but by the names of their commanders. Local identities became less important than provincial ones, but ethnocultural ones showed no decline. The culturally distinct Muslim elites of the Kasimov khanate, Kazan, and Astrakhan became the only exceptions to that rule. Unlike the elites of other regions, their troops and individual representatives fully maintained their distinct identity in official documentation.[52] Marginalized or ignored in the tsar's pronouncements and religious and historical works of the time, ethnicity and culture certainly mattered in the daily administration of the state and the everyday life of the tsar's subjects.

The paradoxes of the new Jerusalem

In their search for manifestations of Muscovite identity, historians are often fascinated by broad religious concepts that may or may not have had currency in the top echelons of early modern Muscovite society and may or may not have reflected and influenced the identity of broader circles of Muscovites. In this regard, the concept that has attracted most attention in the scholarly literature is that of Moscow as the Third Rome. Most modern-day scholars who accept the existence of the theory trace its origins to a letter from the Pskov monk Filofei to Grand Prince Vasilii III exhorting him to defend true Orthodoxy against heresy. Since the first two Romes (the Eternal City itself and Constantinople) had succumbed to heresy, argued Filofei, Moscow (the Third Rome) had to protect itself and safeguard the true faith, for there would be no fourth Rome. Filofei's theory lent religious legitimacy to the view of the Muscovite princes as heirs of the Byzantine emperors – a view enhanced not only by the Monomakh legend but also by the marriage of Ivan III to the niece of the last Byzantine emperor, Sophia Paleologina. It also portrayed Muscovy as the last bastion of true Christianity and placed special responsibility for protecting it on the shoulders of the Muscovite rulers.[53] Although students

---

[52] See Janet Martin, "Mobility, Forced Resettlement and Regional Identity in Moscow," in *Culture and Identity in Muscovy*, pp. 431–49.

[53] On the theory of Moscow as the Third Rome, see David M. Goldfrank, "Moscow, the Third Rome," in *The Modern Encyclopedia of Russian and Soviet History*, ed. Joseph L. Wieczynski, vol. XXIII (Gulf Breeze, Fla., 1981), pp. 118–21; N. V. Sinitsyna, *Tretii Rim. Istoriki i évoliutsiia russkoi srednevekovoi kontseptsii (XV–XVII vv.)* (Moscow, 1998); Paul Bushkovitch, "The Formation of a National Consciousness in Early Modern

of the era have spilled gallons of ink in their discussions of the theory of
Moscow as the Third Rome, the fact remains that until the end of the
sixteenth century we encounter no evidence that this theory was popular
or well known in Muscovy – a fact that allowed Keenan to dismiss it as
"little more than a scholarly misunderstanding."[54]

Why, then, has so much attention been paid to this concept in the
literature? Partly because there are clear indications in sixteenth-century
sources that the Muscovite rulers in general and Ivan the Terrible in
particular regarded their own faith and church as the only true ones
in the world. That view was of course reinforced by the actual separation of Muscovite Orthodoxy from the rest of the Christian world (both
Catholic and Orthodox) after the Union of Florence.[55] However, if there
was ever a theory that systematized and legitimized that view, then it
was the concept of Moscow as a new Jerusalem (alternatively, Israel),
not as a Third Rome. The first reference to Moscow as a new Jerusalem
appears in a letter to Ivan III from Archbishop Vassian Rylo, written after
Ivan's confrontation with the Tatars at the Ugra River in 1480. References to Muscovy as a new Israel are also to be found in sixteenth- and
seventeenth-century texts, including the *Book of Degrees* and the writings of Ivan Timofeev on the Time of Troubles.[56] Secular and spiritual
leaders of Muscovy were influenced by the image of Moscow as a new
Jerusalem. Boris Godunov planned the reconstruction of Moscow along
the architectural lines of Jerusalem, while Patriarch Nikon had his own
vision of Moscow's destiny as a new Jerusalem.[57] Over time, that concept

Russia," *Harvard Ukrainian Studies* 10, nos. 3–4 (December 1986): 355–76, here 358–
63; Ostrowski, *Muscovy and the Mongols*, 219–43. For the impact of Byzantine tradition
on Muscovite political practices, see ibid., pp. 164–218. On the influence of the Byzantine heritage on Muscovy after the fall of Constantinople, see Ihor Ševčenko, "Byzantium
and the East Slavs after 1453," in idem, *Ukraine between East and West: Essays on Cultural
History to the Early Eighteenth Century* (Edmonton and Toronto, 1996), pp. 92–111.

[54] Keenan, "On Certain Mythical Beliefs and Russian Behaviors," p. 26.

[55] For a survey of sixteenth-century Muscovite Orthodoxy, see Crummey, *The Formation
of Muscovy*, pp. 116–42; Paul Bushkovitch, *Religion and Society in Russia: The Sixteenth
and Seventeenth Centuries* (New York and Oxford, 1992), pp. 10–50; Ostrowski, *Muscovy
and the Mongols*, pp. 144–63.

[56] See Paul Bushkovitch, "Pravoslavnaia tserkov' i russkoe natsional'noe samosoznanie
XVI–XVII vv.," *Ab Imperio*, 2003, no. 3: 1017–18.

[57] On the concept of Moscow as a new Jerusalem and its reflection in Muscovite political
thought, architecture, art, and ritual, see Andrei Batalov and Aleksei Lidov, *Ierusalim v
russkoi kul'ture* (Moscow, 1994); Daniel B. Rowland, "Moscow – the Third Rome or the
New Israel," *Russian Review* 55 (1996): 591–614; Joel Raba, "Moscow – the Third Rome
or the New Jerusalem," *Forschungen zur osteuropäischen Geschichte* 50 (1995): 297–308;
and Michael S. Flier, "Court Ceremony in an Age of Reform: Patriarch Nikon and the
Palm Sunday Ritual," in *Religion and Culture in Early Modern Russia and Ukraine*, ed.
Samuel H. Baron and Nancy Shields Kollman (DeKalb, Ill., 1997), pp. 73–95.

was used both to stress the exclusivity of Muscovite Christianity and to promote ties with foreign Orthodox communities. The former tendency appears to have predominated in the sixteenth century.

Belief in the uniqueness and ultimate truth of Muscovite Orthodoxy fostered the growth of a distinct Muscovite identity. In the realm of international relations, it served not only to establish a clearly defined border between Muscovy and its immediate neighbors (including the Rus' lands of the Grand Duchy of Lithuania and, later, the Polish-Lithuanian Commonwealth) but also to legitimize aggression against them. The Muscovite literati used the religious factor to justify the conquest of Novgorod as well as Kazan. For example, an entry about Ivan III's conquest of Novgorod in 1471 that was added to a Novgorodian chronicle during the rule of his grandson, Ivan the Terrible, read as follows: "Grand Prince Ioan Vasilievich [Ivan III] marched with a force against Novgorod the Great because of its wrongdoing and lapsing into Latinism."[58] But nothing can compare to the Orthodox zeal with which the clergy and the lay servitors of Ivan the Terrible attacked the Muslim faith of the defenders of Kazan. The religious rage unleashed against the "infidel" Tatars showed that since its liberation from Byzantine control and dependency on the khans, the Muscovite church had managed not only to recover the plenitude of the anti-pagan and anti-Mongol vocabulary of its medieval polemicists but also significantly to enrich it. The theme of the eternal struggle between Christianity and Islam informed Metropolitan Makarii's epistles on the eve of the campaign, as well as the subsequent coverage of the Kazan War in the Muscovite chronicles. One of them, composed at the court of the tsar himself, asserted:

And with God's grace and because of the great faith of the Orthodox tsar Ivan Vasilievich, and on account of his heart's desire, God turned over to him the godless Kazan Tatars, and our pious Sovereign destroyed their Muslim faith, and he demolished and devastated their mosques, and he enlightened with his piety their dark places, and he erected God's churches there and introduced Orthodoxy, and he established there an archbishopric and many clergymen in the churches desiring God's love on account of his faith.[59]

The chronicler was not exaggerating. An archbishopric was indeed established in Kazan, and in a dramatic departure from the religious tolerance of the khans of the Golden Horde, their former Christian subjects initiated a brutal campaign to convert the heirs of their former rulers

[58] Adapted from *The Chronicle of Novgorod, 1016–1471* (London, 1914; repr. Hattiesburg, Miss., 1970), p. 205.
[59] Quoted in Pelenski, "Muscovite Imperial Claims to the Kazan Khanate," p. 196.

to Orthodoxy. This was certainly a case in which the Mongol Empire did not serve the tsars of Muscovy as an example for building their own polity: for a while they were clearly tempted by the model of a monoconfessional state rather than that of a multiethnic empire. In 1556, writing to Archbishop Gurii of the newly founded archbishopric of Kazan, Ivan treated the conversion of non-Christians as a divinely ordained duty of the church.[60] The theme of pan-Christian struggle against Islam also appeared in the correspondence between Ivan the Terrible and his main adversary in the Livonian War, King Stefan Batory of Poland. In a letter sent to the king in 1581, Ivan repeatedly invoked the Muslim theme, either attacking Batory for the alleged violation of his oath – which was not permitted even in Muslim states, according to the tsar – or pointing out that the spilling of Christian blood was the desire of the Muslims, or suggesting that by continuing the war and weakening both Rus' and the Lithuanian lands, the king was betraying Christianity to the Muslims (besermenom).[61]

Ivan's sense of religious superiority was not limited to his treatment of the Muslim "infidels." At times it is difficult to avoid the impression that he did not consider even Stefan Batory to be fully Christian. In a letter of 1579 to Batory, the tsar wrote as follows: "But you have lived in a Muslim state, and the Latin faith is [only] half-Christian, and your lords believe in the iconoclastic Lutheran heresy. And now we hear that the Arian faith is beginning to be practiced openly in your land."[62] Here we see references to the Muslim faith of the Ottomans, to whom Stefan's homeland of Transylvania was a vassal; an assault on Catholicism as quasi-heretical; and an attack on Reformation communities of faith that associates them with earlier Christian heresies. To be sure, Ivan IV was not the only Muscovite who regarded other Christian denominations as not entirely Christian or blatantly heretical. The author of the *Tale of the Expedition of Stefan Batory to the City of Pskov* called Stefan a "godless Lithuanian king" and counterposed him to the Orthodox tsar and sovereign Ivan the Terrible.[63] Wartime conditions naturally made it easier to vilify the enemy, but if the fortunes of war turned against Muscovy, as was the case in 1581, official rhetoric became considerably more tolerant. Once Ivan IV decided to play the anti-Ottoman and anti-Muslim card in an attempt

[60] On non-Christians in early modern Russia, see Khodarkovsky, "Four Degrees of Separation," p. 258.

[61] See "Poslanie pol'skomu koroliu Stefanu Batoriiu 1581 goda," in *Pamiatniki literatury Drevnei Rusi. Vtoraia polovina XVI veka,* comp. L. A. Dmitrieva and D. S. Likhachev (Moscow, 1986), pp. 180–217, here 186, 204, 208.

[62] Ibid., pp. 172–77, here 172.

[63] See "Povest' o prikhozhdenii Stefana Batoriia na grad Pskov," in *Pamiatniki literatury Drevnei Rusi,* pp. 400–477, here 422, 424.

to enlist papal support for ending the war, he had to modulate his self-righteous effusions. The above-mentioned references to Stefan Batory as a Christian ruler, which come from that period, occur in a letter in which Ivan sought to convince Stefan of his own religious tolerance and that of his state. The tsar even hinted that the "Latin" and "Greek" faiths might indeed be one and the same.

Ivan's arguments in that regard are of particular interest to our discussion, not so much because of his rhetorical about-face as because of the connection that they reveal between religion and Muscovy's westward expansion into non-Rus' and non-Orthodox territories. The tsar's statement was a reaction to the claim allegedly made by Polish-Lithuanian envoys that Livonia should be subject to Stefan, since it was a Catholic land and he was a Catholic ruler. Ivan countered by pointing out that the envoys were at odds with the teachings of the pope and the decisions of the Council of Florence to the effect that the Latin and Greek faiths were identical. The tsar stopped short of adopting that point of view himself but asserted that the Polish nobility was violating papal injunctions by compelling people to convert from the Greek faith to the Latin, while there were no forcible conversions from Catholicism to Orthodoxy in Muscovy. "But among us there are those who profess the Latin faith," wrote the tsar, "and we do not sunder them from the Latin faith by force but keep them in our favor (*zhalovanii*) on equal terms with our own people, favoring each with the honor that he deserves according to his noble descent and service, and they profess whatever faith they wish."[64]

The tsar was clearly very pragmatic and flexible when it came to the acquisition of new territories. He considered Livonia to be his patrimony (*otchina*), and the realization that it was settled by Catholic Germans rather than Orthodox Rus' did not appear to concern him unduly.[65] Although the official discourse of the government and the Orthodox Church treated Protestants as worse enemies of true Christianity than Catholics, Ivan and his successors were prepared to accept the realities of a confessionalized Europe, where Muscovy found allies against the Catholic Commonwealth mainly among Protestant rulers. It also appears that the tsar was prepared to show his non-Orthodox Christian subjects and guests a degree of tolerance that his Western counterparts in countries affected by the Reformation were unable to guarantee. At least the tsar was able to assure English merchants of their personal safety and the security of their merchandise, something that Queen Elizabeth could not guarantee to foreign merchants in England, who were routinely insulted

[64] See "Poslanie pol'skomu koroliu Stefanu Batoriiu 1581 goda," p. 204.
[65] Ibid., p. 200.

and attacked by her Anglican subjects.[66] The aggressive proselytism of the 1550s was more the exception than the rule of tsarist policy in the Muslim East. The fact that it took five years to pacify and secure the Kazan khanate, where the anti-Islamic program was fully applied, apparently taught Ivan a lesson. Moreover, the Crimean khan and especially the Ottoman sultan, who regarded themselves as protectors of Islam in the region, had to be assured that Muscovite expansion along the middle and lower Volga was not a threat to their religion. In time, Moscow's religious policy in the East evolved from an all-out Christian offensive to peaceful proselytism and relative tolerance of Islam.[67] In 1567, when the Crimean khan Devlet Giray demanded that Ivan cede Kazan and Astrakhan to the Crimea, as they belonged to the Muslim world and were ruled by khans of the Giray dynasty, the tsar responded that those khanates were part of his patrimony and that he already ruled one Muslim "yurt," the Kasimov khanate, implying that religious differences would not define the limits of his realm.[68]

Ivan IV apparently never abandoned his belief that the Greek faith was the only true religion, but neither did he allow the religious rhetoric of his churchmen to determine his policy in the borderlands for any significant length of time and jeopardize the potential growth of his state. As Andreas Kappeler has pointed out, Muscovite expansion in the East was long distinguished from the overseas expansion of the European powers by its lack of serious interest in missionary activity.[69] Ultimately, in its religious policy in the borderlands, Moscow was more a second Sarai – the capital of the Golden Horde – than a Third Rome or a new Jerusalem. It is probably fair to assume that the policy of religious tolerance and pragmatism inherited by Muscovy from its former Tatar masters was at least partly

---

[66] For a comparison of degrees of religious tolerance accorded to foreign merchants in sixteenth-century England and Muscovy, see Maria Salomon Arel, "Don't Ask, Don't Tell: Merchant Diasporas, Xenophobia, and the Issue of Faith in Muscovite Russia," paper presented at a conference on "The Modern History of Eastern Christianity: Transitions and Problems," Harvard University, 26–27 March 2004. On the different interpretations of the principles of religious tolerance held by English and Muscovite dissidents, see Anna Yu. Seregina and Mikhail V. Dmitriev, "Two Views on Religious Toleration in the Sixteenth Century: Robert Persons and *Starets* Artemij," in *Etre catholique – être orthodoxe – être protestant: Confessions et indentités culturelles en Europe médiévale et moderne*, ed. M. Derwicz and M. V. Dmitriev (Wrocław, 2003), pp. 89–109.

[67] See Khodarkovsky, "Four Degrees of Separation," pp. 258–60. The next wave of state-sponsored Christian proselytism in Muscovy's eastern borderlands did not ensue until the early eighteenth century. See Andreas Kappeler, *The Russian Empire: A Multiethnic History*, trans. Alfred Clayton (Harlow, 2001), pp. 52–56.

[68] See Michael Khodarkovsky, *Russia's Steppe Frontier: The Making of a Colonial Empire, 1500–1800* (Bloomington and Indianapolis, 2002), pp. 115–16.

[69] See Kappeler, *The Russian Empire*, pp. 55–56.

responsible for the spectacular success of eastward Muscovite expansion in the course of the sixteenth and seventeenth centuries.

Rus' versus Lithuania

In theory, the Livonian War (1558–83), which enlisted numerous Rus' detachments on the Lithuanian side, including the first regular regiment of Dnipro Cossacks to fight in any international conflict, gave the combatants on the Muscovite side a unique opportunity to express what they thought about their ethnic and religious brethren on the other side of the border. They could either shame and condemn the Lithuanian Rus' for attacking their own or try to enlist their support and turn them into a "fifth column" in the war against Catholic Poland-Lithuania. Paradoxically (from the present-day viewpoint, of course) we see no attempt on the part of Muscovite strategists or literati to seize that opportunity. The discourse employed by the Muscovite side in negotiations with the Grand Duchy of Lithuania remained focused on the patrimonial and dynastic rights of the Muscovite ruler.[70]

The lack of attention to Lithuanian (from 1569 Polish-Lithuanian) Rus' in official documents and literary works concerning the Livonian War seems highly anomalous if one takes into account the references in the very same documents to the Kyivan roots of the Muscovite dynasty and church. Whether we take the letters of Ivan the Terrible to Stefan Batory, in which the tsar points to his Rurikid origins in order to prove his superiority to the elected king, or Metropolitan Makarii's *Velikie minei-chetii* (Great Menology), with its entries on SS. Mykhail and Fedir of Chernihiv and the killing of Batu, which stress the all-Rus' theme in the anti-Tatar resistance, or the *History of Kazan*, where the Kyivan descent of Ivan the Terrible is used to justify his conquest of the khanate,[71] all these texts are evidence of the unquestionable importance of the Kyivan heritage for the self-identification of the Muscovite elite. It appears that the "rediscovery" of Kyiv by the Muscovite literati in the late fifteenth century and the incorporation of the Kyivan past into the official genealogy of the Muscovite rulers in the early decades of the sixteenth century had made it an integral part of Muscovite mythology and historical identity by the second half of the century. Ivan the Terrible believed in this virtual past, as did his subjects – at least those who bothered to take up

---

[70] See Filiushkin, "Vgliadyvaias' v oskolki razbitogo zerkala."

[71] See "Poslanie pol'skomu koroliu Stefanu Batoriiu 1579 goda," p. 176; "Iz Velikikh minei-chet'ikh Makariia," in *Pamiatniki literatury drevnei Rusi. Vtoraia polovina XVI veka*, pp. 478–549, here 484–88, 496, 524; "Istoriia o Kazanskom tsarstve," in *Khrestomatiia po drevnei russkoi literature*, pp. 276–85, here 278.

a pen and set down their views for posterity. By the latter half of the sixteenth century, such writers were no longer limited to the literati at the tsar's or the metropolitan's court but included exiles such as Andrei Kurbsky, or Rus′ nobles in Tatar captivity such as the alleged author of the *History of Kazan*.

Why, then, did the Muscovites not apply this historical knowledge to establish a connection (whether positive or negative) with their Rus′ brethren in Poland-Lithuania? This seeming paradox can be explained in a number of ways. First of all, if the Muscovites waged war for Kyivan territories at the turn of the sixteenth century, they no longer did so in the second half of that century, which gave them much less incentive to engage in a dialogue on rights to the Kyivan heritage. Secondly, the sense of ethnic solidarity was never very strong among the Muscovite elites. Nor do we see any clear attempt on the part of the tsar to protect the Rus′ people or the Orthodox religion in the Catholic Commonwealth – a pretext successfully used by his successors on the Russian throne in the seventeenth and eighteenth centuries. In his letters to Stefan Batory, Ivan the Terrible never mentioned the Rus′ nationality or the Orthodox religion of many of Batory's East Slavic subjects. He referred to Rus′ inhabitants in the borderlands of the Grand Duchy of Lithuania by the names of their towns, e.g., "Orshanians" and "Dubrovlianians," whom he also called "your [Batory's] borderland people (*ukrainnye liudi*)."[72] Nor were the Muscovites eager to think in confessional terms: true religion ended for them, by and large, at the borders of the tsar's realm. In fact, Ivan the Terrible was reluctant to discuss the split between the Christian East and West without the blessing of the metropolitan, as shown by the Muscovite records of his meeting with the papal legate Antonio Possevino in 1582.[73]

The relation of sixteenth-century Muscovites to ancient Kyiv was in many ways akin to the attitude of early modern Christians toward Israel. The latter looked to the biblical Jews for inspiration and compared themselves to the Jews in Egyptian captivity but failed to make a positive connection between the Jews of Israel whom they worshipped and the Jews of their homeland whom they vilified and persecuted. In the case of the Jews, there was of course a turning point – the crucifixion of Jesus Christ – when

---

[72] See "Poslanie pol′skomu koroliu Stefanu Batoriiu 1579 goda," p. 212.

[73] See Keenan, "Muscovite Perceptions of Other East Slavs," pp. 24–29; cf. Ostrowski, *Muscovy and the Mongols*, pp. 211–12. Paul Bushkovitch has recently challenged the leading role of the Muscovite secular rulers in general and Ivan IV in particular in selecting the hierarchs of the Muscovite church. See his article "The Selection and Deposition of the Metropolitan and Patriarch of the Orthodox Church in Russia, 1448–1619," in *Être catholique – être orthodoxe – être protestant*, pp. 123–50.

Christians ceased to regard them as good and associated them with evil, but there seems to have been no such turning point for Muscovites with regard to the Kyivans. One might assume, of course, that the early modern Kyivans' political allegiance to non-Rus' and non-Orthodox kings, as well as their refusal to follow the Muscovite church into schism with Constantinople after the Union of Florence, made them less than kosher to the taste of mid-sixteenth-century Muscovites, including their tsar, who was descended on his mother's side from the Hlynskys (Glinskys), a family of Orthodox refugees from Lithuania. The Muscovite sources are silent on that score, but one is struck by the tremendous difference in the attitude of official Muscovite discourse toward the medieval Kyivan princes and the early modern Rus' in Lithuania. If the former were their own, the latter were "other." For the Muscovites, the most important borders of the era were defined by dynasty and the patrimonial state, not by ethnicity and religion.

Few examples better demonstrate the complex sense of alienation between the two branches of Rus' than the "Lithuanian" journey of Andrei Kurbsky, who experienced the divide at first hand. Kurbsky, one of the Muscovite military commanders who stormed the walls of Kazan in 1552, switched sides in 1564. During the tsar's new war in the west, he followed in the footsteps of dozens of fifteenth-century princes who fled to Lithuania in order to escape unfavorable political circumstances in Muscovy. The way in which Kurbsky was treated by his old sovereign (Ivan IV) and his new one (Sigismund Augustus) after his defection speaks volumes about the different concepts of loyalty to the ruler in Muscovy and the Grand Duchy of Lithuania. Ivan IV treated Kurbsky's defection as treason (interpreted as "treason to the Motherland" by such scholars as Likhachev), while his negotiations on entering the Habsburg service in 1569 were apparently viewed with understanding in the Grand Duchy, provoking no negative reaction at court.[74] If Muscovy demanded loyalty to the person of the ruler, in the Grand Duchy of Lithuania the individual noble had the right to choose his suzerain in peacetime.[75] Nevertheless, Kurbsky felt himself to be a foreigner in Lithuanian Rus', where he settled after his flight from Muscovy. Even if one disregards the *History of Ivan IV*, a work attributed to Kurbsky in which the author calls himself "a stranger

---

[74] See Auerbach, "Identity in Exile: Andrei Mikhailovich Kurbskii and National Consciousness in the Sixteenth Century" in *Culture and Identity in Muscovy*, pp. 11–25, here 14–17.

[75] Prince Dmytro Vyshnevetsky, the legendary sixteenth-century founder of Zaporozhian Cossackdom, could freely return to the court of Sigismund Augustus after having offered his "voluntary services" to Ivan IV. On Vyshnevetsky, known in Ukrainian folklore as Baida, see Mykhailo Hrushevsky, *History of Ukraine-Rus'*, ed. Frank E. Sysyn et al., vol. VII (Edmonton and Toronto, 1999), pp. 88–98.

and newcomer here,"[76] there is enough evidence to state that Kurbsky's neighbors regarded him as a foreigner. They called him a "Muscovite," a term that he disliked: on at least one occasion, it provoked a fight with an "assailant." Not even Kurbsky's marriage to a Volhynian woman, his active participation in regional politics, his service as a Volhynian delegate to the 1573 Diet, or his defense of Orthodoxy against the advances of the Reformation could change his peers' perception of him as a foreigner. His opposition to Western influences and linguistic Polonization eventually put him on a collision course with his Volhynian patron, Prince Kostiantyn (Vasyl) Ostrozky, the son of the hero of Orsha.[77]

A sense of otherness vis-à-vis Polish-Lithuanian Rus′ was clearly expressed by the author of the *Tale of the Expedition of Stefan Batory to the City of Pskov*, which described the Muscovite defense of the city in 1581.[78] The events of the siege, as well as the text of the *Tale*, indicate a new-found sense of loyalty toward the rulers of Moscow on the part of a city that they had taken over as recently as the early sixteenth century. At that time, the anonymous Pskovian author of the *Skazanie o Pskovskom vziatii* (Narrative of the Annexation of Pskov) stressed that since the very beginnings of the Rus′ Land, Pskov had not been ruled by princes and mourned the loss of the city's liberties, now that it had been "captured not by infidels but by its own coreligionists."[79] By contrast, his successor, the author of the *Tale of the Expedition of Stefan Batory*, not only believed that Pskov belonged to the Rus′ Land and shared the same religion as Muscovy but also had no misgivings about the Muscovite rulers, praising

[76] See *Prince A. M. Kurbsky's History of Ivan IV*, ed. and trans J. L. I. Fennell (Cambridge, 1965). For excerpts from the work, see Andrei Kurbskii, "Istoriia o Velikom kniaze Moskovskom," in *Pamiatniki literatury Drevnei Rusi. Vtoraia polovina XVI veka*, pp. 218–399 (original and translation into modern Russian), here 376. For arguments against the authenticity of the "History," see Edward L. Keenan, "Putting Kurbskii in His Place, or: Observations and Suggestions concerning the Place of the *History of the Grand Prince of Muscovy* in the History of Muscovite Literary Culture," *Forschungen zur osteuropäischen Geschichte* 24 (1978): 131–62. Following Keenan, I consider Kurbsky's "History" to be the product of Moscow-based bookmen of the 1670s. Signs of the work's later provenance include the author's (or authors') use of the term "fatherland" (*otechestvo*) in reference to the Muscovite state, which is uncharacteristic of sixteenth-century writings in Muscovy and the Rus′ lands of the Commonwealth.

[77] See Auerbach, "Identity in Exile," pp. 18–22. For Likhachev's description of Kurbsky's act as treason to his motherland, see the introduction to *Pamiatniki literatury Drevnei Rusi. Vtoraia polovina XVI veka*, "Na puti k novomu literaturnomu soznaniiu," pp. 5–14, here 9.

[78] On the discourse employed by the tsar's court and the Orthodox Church during the Polatsk campaign of 1562–63, see Sergei Bogatyrev, "Battle for Divine Wisdom. The Rhetoric of Ivan IV's Campaign against Polotsk," in *The Military and Society in Russia, 1450–1917*, ed. Eric Lohr and Marshall Poe (Leiden, 2002), pp. 325–63.

[79] See "Skazanie o Pskovskom vziatii," in *Khrestomatiia po drevnei russkoi literature*, pp. 257–60.

Ivan the Terrible and his ancestors for having defended their subjects against infidel invaders. He also showed some acquaintance with ideas reminiscent of the notion of Moscow as the Third Rome, which originated in Pskov. He especially praised "[our] Christian tsar, who occupies the highest throne installed by God for all four corners of the universe, maintaining the holy Christian faith and ordaining that it be held firmly and kept unblemished."[80] The author of the *Tale* regarded the siege of Pskov as an action in defense of the Orthodox Christian faith on the part of an Orthodox tsar who was being attacked by a godless "Lutheran king."

The case of Smolensk, acquired by the Muscovites in the early sixteenth century and recently discussed by Mikhail Krom, indicates the role of economic and social factors that induced the townsfolk of the former "Lithuanian" cities to accept the rule of a new sovereign, the tsar of Muscovy.[81] The tale of the siege of Pskov gives us a better understanding of the discursive strategies applied by sixteenth-century literati in order to promote the change of loyalties and identities.

The Pskov conflict was portrayed by the anonymous author of the *Tale* as a confrontation between the Rus' Land, led by the Russian (*rossiiskii*) tsar, and the Lithuanian Land, led by the "Lithuanian king" Stefan Batory (less often identified as a Pole).[82] Pskov was of course part of the Rus' Land and the tsar's patrimony, and its defenders were prepared to die "at the hands of the Lithuanians." "But we shall not," wrote the author, "betray our sovereign's city of Pskov to the Polish king Stefan."[83] Quite strangely for a Pskovian author, whose land had a long tradition of independent relations with the Grand Duchy of Lithuania, the author of the *Tale* not only failed to distinguish between Lithuania and the Kingdom of Poland, referring to the Commonwealth and its ruler as the Lithuanian Land and the Lithuanian king, but also never distinguished between the "Lithuanians" and Rus' warriors in Batory's army. For him, all the attackers were Lithuanian and all indistinguishably evil – not a surprising attitude for someone who perhaps survived the siege but had no direct contact with the enemy.

The author's treatment of themes related to Rus' lands of the Grand Duchy of Lithuania goes some way toward explaining his ethnocultural blindness. The *Tale* contains two references to the city of Polatsk that

[80] "Povest' o prikhozhdenii Stefana Batoriia na grad Pskov," p. 400.
[81] See Mikhail Krom, "Mestnoe samosoznanie i tsentralizovannoe gosudarstvo: Smolensk v XVI veke," in *Die Geschichte Rußlands*, pp. 128–36.
[82] Batory was also called "the Lithuanian leader of the accursed and most arrogant people (*iazyk*)" ("Povest' o prikhozhdenii Stefana Batoriia na grad Pskov," p. 444).
[83] Ibid, p. 448.

are highly illuminating in this regard. In the first reference, Polatsk is characterized as a former Lithuanian city that was captured by the tsar, with no reference to the Rus′ origins of the city or its inhabitants. In the second reference, the author mentions a Polatsk musketeer who defected to the defenders of Pskov. He is described as a "former Rus′ian" who came from the "Lithuanian army."[84] The musketeer had probably served in Polatsk when it was under the tsar's rule, but according to the logic of the narrative, ceased to be "Rus′ian" as soon as he found himself under Lithuanian command. The same was apparently true of Polatsk itself, which could be regarded as a Rus′ian city only as long as it remained under the tsar's jurisdiction.

In using the terms "Lithuanian" and "Rus′ian," the author of the *Tale* resorted to political rather than ethnic categories. It appears that in the understanding of Muscovite literati of that period, the identity of a person or place depended upon the established political authority. Since the Polish-Lithuanian Rus′ were under Lithuanian rule, they were to be regarded as "Lithuanians." In order to be considered Rus′ian in the eyes of the Muscovite elites, they would have had to be not only Orthodox in religion but also subject to the Orthodox tsar. This was also the way in which the Muscovite Rus′ were regarded by their cousins on the other side of the border. It was not only ethnic Poles and Lithuanians who applied the political designation "Muscovites" to the Muscovite Rus′ but also their next of kin, the Polish-Lithuanian Rus′ians, who reserved the "Rus′ian" designation for themselves. Political identity reigned supreme on both sides of the Rus′-Rus′ border.

The origins of Great Rus′

Let us summarize some of the arguments presented in this chapter and try to answer the question of where one should seek the origins of Great Rus′.

Muscovite Rus′ seems to be the first polity to which we can trace the identity of Russia, one of the three modern East Slavic nations. In embryonic form, Muscovite Rus′ exhibits some basic features of the identity project – attitudes toward authority, political institutions, individual rights, religion, and the "other" – that influenced the formation of what historians of the mid-twentieth century used to call "the Russian mind." It appears that the formation of a distinct ethnonational identity took place much sooner in Muscovite Rus′ than in Polish-Lithuanian Rus′, where local loyalties were dominant among the Rus′ elites of the mid-sixteenth

---

[84] Ibid., pp. 406, 462.

century, and where we cannot identify parallel embryonic features of the later Ukrainian and Belarusian identities. Consequently, a comparison of the political and ethnocultural factors that influenced identity formation in Southwestern and Northeastern Rus' should help explain the faster development of the Muscovite Rus' identity-building project.

One should begin by stressing the importance of Mongol rule for the process of identity formation in Northeastern Rus'. In that regard, it seems appropriate to extend the Eurasianist argument about the importance of the Mongol impact on the Muscovite political structure and economy to the sphere of ethnonational identity. The Mongol invasion did not obstruct or complicate (as Cherepnin assumed) the formation of the "Great Russian nationality." On the contrary, it created all-important preconditions for shaping the nature and boundaries of that nationality. It defined the extent of future Great Russian territory in the southwest and in the east; it also lumped the Novgorodians, with their West Slavic dialects, together with a largely East Slavic population in one political entity. Furthermore, Mongol dominance gave the elites of those territories a sense of unity by defining their political homeland as an autonomous realm of the Golden Horde ruled by the grand prince of Rus'. All this can be seen as a head start in the identity-building project that Rus' lands beyond Mongol control clearly lacked. Even when they were "reunited" within one Lithuanian state, the Rus' lands there never constituted a separate grand principality (the goal that the Rus' elites sought to attain in the time of Švitrigaila). Moreover, their elites' political ambitions were never confined to a Rus' ghetto, as they were allowed to participate in governing the whole Lithuanian state – a privilege that significantly retarded the development of a separate identity.

When the Mongols finally realized the danger of a united Rus' and tried to undermine it by granting the title of grand prince to several Rus' princes at once, it was too late to stop the consolidation of Northeastern Rus' under the leadership of one princely house. Thus the emergence of an autochthonous Muscovite state and dynasty should be seen as another indirect consequence of Mongol rule that helped the nation-building project in the Northeast. The growing centralization of Muscovy in the course of the sixteenth century helped forge a united identity that replaced the multiple identities of the appanage principalities. The lack of authentic sources for most of the fourteenth century hinders the search for the origins of Mongol Rus' identity, but it also spotlights the middle and second half of the fifteenth century, when the earliest copies of monuments of the Kulikovo cycle were produced, as a period of active construction of that identity. The fifteenth-century struggle for liberation from Tatar suzerainty provided the rising Muscovite state and its elites not only with a common cause but also with a founding myth that, according to the rules of the genre, was projected into the past, in this case to the 1380s.

The separation of the Muscovite church from the rest of the Orthodox world after the Union of Florence promoted the development of a separate ethnocultural identity among the Muscovite elites. The occasional allusions of Muscovite literati to the theory of the Third Rome should be regarded as manifestations of a "fortress mentality," which has proved highly effective as a nation-building instrument. Separated by their Christian faith from the Muslims and infidels in the East, by their Orthodox beliefs from the Catholics and Lutherans in the West, and by their rift with Constantinople from the Ruthenian Orthodox, who continued to recognize the jurisdiction of the ecumenical patriarch, the Muscovites of the late fifteenth and sixteenth centuries were in a highly advantageous position to form an identity of their own. The church not only separated them from the rest of the world but also broke down old local loyalties by introducing a national pantheon of saints and centralizing the ecclesiastical administration, which proceeded to institute nationwide reforms.

The new independent status of the dynasty, state, and church required legitimization, as did the Muscovite princes' annexation of new Rus' and non-Rus' territories. It was here that the Kyivan origins of the Muscovite Rus' literary tradition proved especially useful, allowing the Muscovite literati to establish links with the glorious past of the Kyivan state, Byzantium and Rome. The concept of the Rus' Land, which the Rus' chroniclers originally applied to Kyiv and the surrounding area, was later appropriated by Northeastern Rus' to designate the Suzdal Land and then by Muscovy to denote all its new possessions, including Novgorod, Pskov and even Kazan. Preoccupied with the search for the origins of the Muscovite dynasty, the literati working at the courts of the tsar and the metropolitan made Kyiv an essential part of the official historical narrative and thereby created a basis for diplomatic recognition of the tsar's new titles and territorial acquisitions, but they seem to have done very little to enhance a feeling of commonality between the elites of Muscovite and Lithuanian Rus'.

The evidence discussed in this chapter appears to confirm the conclusion reached at the end of the nineteenth century by Pavel Miliukov: Great Russian history per se, at least when it comes to self-identification and ethnopolitical identity, begins with the reign of Ivan III. It was in his time that the Muscovite literati created the underpinnings of Muscovite Rus' identity as an exclusive and unifying structure. The sixteenth century (designated by Edward L. Keenan as the period in which Muscovite political culture attained synthesis)[85] witnessed the acceptance of that identity by broad circles of the Muscovite elite, from the tsar himself to his boyars and servitors. This was, in effect, the birth of a new early modern nation, defined by Valerie Kivelson as "a collectivity that is broadly inclusive of the whole political community, as opposed to partial or local community."[86] We lack sufficient documentation of the importance of horizontal links in the sixteenth-century Muscovite nation, but there is plenty of evidence indicating the importance of vertical links, especially those leading from the tsar at the top to his numerous subjects at the bottom. Not unlike the dynastic narrative that was central to the Muscovite ideological construct of the period, the person of the tsar was central to the political and communal fabric of Muscovite society and, by extension, to its political, social, and religious identity.[87] The macro- and microcosms of Muscovite identity revolved around the person of the tsar, who, regardless of his sometimes bizarre behavior (as was the case with Ivan IV), was imagined by his literati not as a tyrannical autocrat but as a meek ruler governing his realm in harmony with the boyars. [88]

The complex of symbols and ideas defining the identity of Muscovite Rus' was the first powerful unifying project since the demise of Kyivan Rus'. Both the Kyivan and the Muscovite projects were undertaken by strong rulers who wanted to legitimize their power and were prepared to commit significant intellectual resources to that end. The two identity-building projects were as different as the states that gave rise to them. While both were based on the concept of dynastic legitimacy and employed the notion of the Rus' Land to mobilize elite loyalty, these components worked differently in the two polities. If in Kyiv the Rus' Land stood for the common patrimony of the Rurikid princes and claimed the loyalty of the whole clan, in Moscow it referred to the patrimony of the grand prince (a term and an office unknown to the Kyivans) and was used to promote the loyalty of dependent princes and servitor elites to the grand prince. If the Rus' Land of the Kyivan scribes did not infringe on the individual patrimonies of the Rurikid princes (outside the boundaries of the Rus' Land per se), the Rus' Land of the Muscovite literati swallowed one patrimony after another, jumped the boundary of the Suzdal-Vladimir Land, and took in the new territories annexed to the grand prince's patrimony – the Muscovite state. Its actual borders were those of the Grand Principality of Moscow.

[85] See Edward L. Keenan, "Muscovite Political Folkways," *Russian Review* 45 (1986): 115–81.
[86] Kivelson, "Muscovite 'Citizenship,'" p. 470.   [87] Ibid., pp. 469–74.
[88] See Bushkovitch, "The Formation of a National Consciousness," pp. 363–68.

As the dynasty, the patrimonial state, and the "true" religion stopped at the border with Lithuania, so did the identity of Muscovite Rus'. Bound by politics and state boundaries, the two Rus' identities became increasingly separate. As Muscovite territory expanded to meet the eastern boundaries of the Grand Duchy of Lithuania and open warfare developed between the two states in the late fifteenth century, it became difficult for the opposing sides to insist on the Rus' commonality underlying their "Lithuanian" and "Muscovite" identities. Paul Bushkovitch describes the situation that resulted from the crystallization of differences between the Muscovites and other Eastern Slavs as follows:

During the sixteenth and early seventeenth century Russian national consciousness was in some respects clearer than in the nineteenth century. Unlike the conservative (and many liberal) Russians of the last century, the men of the sixteenth century did not confuse Russians with Eastern Slavs. The tsar in Moscow ruled over *Rus'*, *Rossiia,* or the *Russkaia zemlia,* and his people were the *Rus'*. The Eastern Slavs of Poland-Lithuania were generally called *Litva* or (if Cossacks) *Cherkassy.*[89]

As Muscovy developed into a multiethnic and multireligious empire, forging closer ties between Slavs and non-Slavs, Christians and Muslims within its borders than with fellow Orthodox Slavs across the Muscovite-Lithuanian border, the two Ruses grew even further apart.

[89] Ibid., pp. 355–56.

The late sixteenth and early seventeenth centuries or, more precisely, the eight decades between the Union of Lublin (1569) and the beginning of the Khmelnytsky Uprising (1648) are often treated as a distinct period in the history of Poland, Lithuania, Ukraine, and Belarus. If the starting point requires little introduction, since it was marked by the creation of the Polish-Lithuanian Commonwealth, the terminus certainly needs some explanation. The Cossack uprising of 1648, led by Hetman Bohdan Khmelnytsky, spread to most of the Ukrainian territories and took in a significant part of the Belarusian lands. More than previous Cossack revolts, it shook the Commonwealth, resulting in the loss of much of its territory and inaugurating a long series of wars that eventually led to the decline of the Polish-Lithuanian state. The uprising also marked the end of Polish-Lithuanian eastward expansion and set off a long Muscovite drive to the West that saw Russian troops enter Paris in 1813 and the Red Army occupy Berlin in 1945. More immediately important for our discussion is that the uprising brought about the first prolonged encounter between Muscovite and Polish-Lithuanian Rus', which led to their political union. The Khmelnytsky Uprising and its long-term consequences must be viewed as a result of the interaction of various political, social, religious, and cultural factors that were not in place in 1569. The same period saw the formation of a new type of identity that was to have an important effect on subsequent developments.

Polish-Lithuanian Rus'

The post-Lublin era became a period of dramatic political, social, and cultural change in the Rus' territories of the recently established Commonwealth. Sigismund II Augustus (1548–72), the "father" of the Lublin "takeover," turned out to be the last monarch of the Jagellonian dynasty, whose representatives had ruled Poland and Lithuania since the late fourteenth century and brought about their political union. After the brief tenure of Henri de Valois of France (1573–75) and the successful rule

161

of the Transylvanian prince Stefan Batory (1576–86), elected kings from the Swedish Vasa dynasty – Sigismund III (1587–1632), Władysław IV (1632–48), and John Casimir (1648–68) – ruled the Commonwealth until the second half of the seventeenth century. Under Sigismund III, the Commonwealth intervened in Muscovy during the Time of Troubles and extended its eastern territories as far as Chernihiv.

Important geopolitical shifts and changes in state boundaries were accompanied by great social transformations. The Commonwealth nobility took advantage of the interregnums of the 1570s to win official guarantees of its extensive rights and privileges. As a result, major socioeconomic shifts took place in the Rus' lands, although princes such as the powerful Kyivan palatine Kostiantyn Ostrozky managed to withstand competition from the newly empowered nobility and enhance their status and power. Cities grew in number and strength as a result of increased trade and the colonization of steppe areas in the southeastern part of the realm. Demand for grain on European markets promoted the creation of huge latifundia that depended on corvée labor. Peasants, for their part, sought to avoid labor obligations by moving eastward into the Ukrainian steppes (as did burghers fleeing the imposition of new taxes) and joining bands of steppe freebooters and tradesmen known as Cossacks. Landowning nobles, often accompanied by Jewish leaseholders, followed the fugitives eastward and managed to impose the taxes and obligations that the latter had fled in the first place. The Cossacks, their ranks augmented by new arrivals mainly from the territories of present-day Ukraine and Belarus, rose in revolt. Using the standing army originally recruited to fight the Crimean Tatars, as well as the troops of the local magnates, the government sought to prevent new fugitives from gaining access to the Lower Dnipro region – the stronghold of Cossackdom – and suppressed their rebellions. But this policy was successful only until 1648, when the Khmelnytsky Uprising overwhelmed the Commonwealth forces.

In addition to these political and social changes, the sixteenth-century Reformation caused a great ideological, religious, and cultural upheaval in eastern Europe. The Commonwealth, where the last Jagellonian ruler was favorably disposed to the Reformation, became a breeding ground for Lutheranism (accepted by Ducal Prussia and embraced by burghers throughout the Polish-Lithuanian state) and Calvinism (which gained many converts among the nobility), as well as a safe haven for religious dissidents of all stripes. But the Commonwealth also became a major battleground between Protestantism and Catholicism once the latter embarked on the road of ecclesiastical reform. When the first Jesuits entered the Commonwealth in the 1560s, their attention was attracted not only by the growing number of Calvinists among the Catholic nobility but also by the Orthodox Ruthenians, who were being courted at the time by representatives of Protestant confessions. A local union of Catholicism and Orthodoxy, defined along the lines approved by the Union of Florence (1439) and limited to the boundaries of the Commonwealth, emerged as a possible solution to religious tensions. It was advocated by proponents of the Counter-Reformation as a way to stop the eastward advance of Protestantism and bring new faithful under the jurisdiction of Rome to replace those lost to the Reformation in central Europe. Pro-union propaganda initiated by the Polish Jesuits had its effect: by the end of the sixteenth century, the Orthodox hierarchy had not only embraced the idea of church union but also asked the king and the Catholic Church to facilitate the transfer of the Ruthenian Orthodox from the jurisdiction of Constantinople to that of Rome.

Orthodoxy, which had been the majority religion in the Grand Duchy, became a minority faith in the Commonwealth after the Union of Lublin. The advance of the Reformation and the general confessionalization of religious life forced it to compete on the open market of religious ideas, where it was clearly at a disadvantage. With little or no support from Constantinople (or Moscow, for that matter), lacking educational institutions and a disciplined clergy, the Orthodox Church was losing its elite to Protestantism and Catholicism alike. Its luminaries, such as Prince Kostiantyn Ostrozky, not only intermarried with non-Orthodox but maintained close relations with papal nuncios and flirted with the idea of church union. The movement for church renewal, initiated by Orthodox burghers organized in religious brotherhoods, threatened the power of the Orthodox hierarchs, who were further confused by the conflicting orders and decrees issued by Patriarch Jeremiah II of Constantinople during his visit to the Commonwealth in the late 1580s. The half-hearted attempts of the hierarchy to reform the church on their own by increasing ecclesiastical discipline, taking control of the press, and reining in the rebellious brotherhoods eventually gave way to direct negotiations with state and church authorities concerning union with Rome.

In December 1595, Pope Clement VIII received two representatives of the Ruthenian hierarchy, Bishops Kyryl Terletsky and Ipatii Potii, in Rome. The Ruthenian Orthodox were accepted into the church of Rome on condition of affirming Catholic dogma; they were allowed to retain the Eastern Christian liturgy. The union was to be confirmed by a church council upon the bishops' return to the Commonwealth. Ironically, union with Rome split the Kyiv metropolitanate and its faithful. In October 1596, two councils – one pro-union, the other anti-union – took place in the town of Brest on the Ukrainian-Belarusian-Polish border. The latter council included representatives of the Eastern patriarchs, two

Orthodox bishops, numerous priests, delegates from Orthodox brotherhoods, and nobles led by the most powerful opponent of the union, Prince Kostiantyn Ostrozky. The Commonwealth authorities nevertheless recognized the Uniate Church as the only legal Eastern Christian religious body under their jurisdiction. They outlawed the Orthodox Church, which nevertheless retained the loyalty of much of Ruthenian (Ukrainian-Belarusian) society. The government could not physically liquidate the rebellious church, partly because of guarantees of religious freedom given to the Commonwealth nobility of all denominations. Nobiliary diets and dietines turned into arenas of religious dispute between Orthodox nobles on the one hand and representatives of the Catholic government and the Uniate hierarchy on the other. The Union of Brest also provoked religious polemics in Ukraine and Belarus, with Polish Catholic and Ruthenian Uniate authors opposing Ruthenian Orthodox ones. The Union made more progress in the Belarusian lands, while Orthodoxy remained the majority religion among the elites in Ukraine, the power base of the two Orthodox bishops who refused to join the Union and of its main nobiliary opponent, Prince Ostrozky.

Another factor that made Ukraine friendlier toward Orthodoxy than Belarus was the presence of the Zaporozhian Cossacks. After the death of Prince Ostrozky, the Zaporozhian Host emerged as the main protector of the persecuted church. In 1620 Cossack support was crucial for the consecration of a new Orthodox hierarchy by Patriarch Theophanes of Jerusalem, and the city of Kyiv, which lay within the Cossack sphere of influence, developed into a new center of Orthodox learning. The idea of defending Orthodoxy against the Polish-Lithuanian government became an important ideological postulate for the Cossacks, who shook the Commonwealth with their uprisings, beginning with the revolt of Kryshtof Kosynsky in 1591–93. In 1596, allegedly at Ostrozky's instigation, Severyn Nalyvaiko led the Cossacks in pillaging the properties of supporters of the Union, including Bishop Terletsky. The Cossack uprising of 1630 featured religious demands as important elements of its program. During the interregnum of 1632, the Polish government was finally obliged to recognize the legitimacy of the Orthodox hierarchy and the existence of two Eastern Christian churches, Uniate and Orthodox, in the Commonwealth. This was a tacit admission that the Union had failed to gain the allegiance of most of the Orthodox population of the Commonwealth and, instead of promoting religious unity, had created dissension in the state.

Official recognition of the Orthodox hierarchy spelled the end of close cooperation between rebellious Cossackdom and the Orthodox Church. It also ensured that the revival of Orthodoxy and its reform undertaken by the new Orthodox metropolitan of Kyiv, Petro Mohyla (1632–47), was politically loyal to the Commonwealth and deferential to the dominant Polish culture. What it failed to do, however, was to end the Cossack uprisings, which were fueled by the continuing administrative and economic penetration of the magnates into the Dnipro region originally settled by the Cossacks, the constant replenishment of their ranks by runaway peasants and burghers, and the government's refusal to recognize the Cossacks as a distinct privileged estate. Thus, in 1637–38, a new uprising shook the foundations of political and social order in Ukraine. It was provoked by the government's construction of a fortress above the Dnipro rapids and its blocking of access to the *Sich* – the Cossack stronghold beyond the rapids – as well as by an official ban on Cossack military expeditions against the Ottomans on the Black Sea. By building the fortress, the government sought to buy off both local magnates and the Ottoman Porte, which was threatening the Commonwealth with retaliation for Cossack attacks on its shores. Instead, the Commonwealth authorities ended up with a new Cossack uprising on their hands. The revolt was brutally suppressed, and Polish officers were put in charge of the Cossack troops. On the other hand, the Cossacks were recognized de facto as a separate estate with special rights and privileges, although membership in that estate was severely restricted. Ukraine entered a period known in Polish historiography as the "golden peace." As subsequent events would show, it was only a lull before the storm. The Cossack uprising of 1648 was an epochal event that created a completely different political and cultural situation in the region.[1]

The period between the Union of Lublin and the Khmelnytsky Uprising not only witnessed major political, social, and religious change in the Ukrainian and Belarusian lands but also saw the emergence of group loyalties that created a strong sense of commonality among the elites of the region.

---

[1] On the history of the Ukrainian and Belarusian territories of the Commonwealth in the sixteenth and seventeenth and centuries, see Mykhailo Hrushevsky, *History of Ukraine-Rus'*, vols. VII and VIII (Edmonton and Toronto, 1999–2002); Henadz' Sahanovich, *Narys historyi Belarusi* (Minsk, 2001), pp. 205–65; Natalia Iakovenko, *Narys istoriï Ukraïny z naidavnishykh chasiv do kintsia XVIII stolittia* (Kyiv, 1997), pp. 119–76. For individual topics in the history of the region, see David Frick, *Meletij Smotryc'kyj* (Cambridge, Mass., 1995); Linda Gordon, *Cossack Rebellions: Social Turmoil in the Sixteenth-Century Ukraine* (Albany, NY, 1983); Borys A. Gudziak, *Crisis and Reform: The Kyivan Metropolitanate, the Patriarchate of Constantinople, and the Genesis of the Union of Brest* (Cambridge, Mass., 1998); Serhii Plokhy, *The Cossacks and Religion in Early Modern Ukraine* (Oxford, 2001); Ihor Ševčenko, *Ukraine between East and West: Essays on Cultural History to the Early Eighteenth Century* (Edmonton and Toronto, 1996); Frank E. Sysyn, *Between Poland and the Ukraine: The Dilemma of Adam Kysil, 1600–1653* (Cambridge, Mass., 1985).

Was there a Polish noble nation?

The importance of the Union of Lublin (1569) for the historical fate of the Eastern Slavs has long been underestimated in Russocentric narratives of east European history. Under Soviet tutelage, the Ukrainian and Belarusian historical narratives, which paid considerable attention to the union of 1569, were demoted to the status of appendixes to the Great Russian historical narrative, disguised as the history of (the peoples of) the USSR. The emergence of independent East Slavic states after the breakup of the USSR inspired efforts to reconceptualize the history of the region, which entailed a new focus on the Union of Lublin. A similar process has taken place in the West, where there is now greater willingness to go beyond the Russocentric paradigm in conceptualizing the history of the region. Recently, in his long-range reexamination of the development of east European nations and national movements, Timothy Snyder even took the Union of Lublin as his starting point. He wrote in that regard:

1569 is an untraditional starting point. National histories of Poland, Lithuania, Belarus, Ukraine, or Russia usually begin with the medieval period, and trace the purportedly continuous development of the nation to the present. To recognize change, it is best to accept the unmistakable appearance of a single early modern nation in the vast territories of the early modern Commonwealth, then consider its legacies to modern politics.[2]

Did the Union of Lublin indeed inaugurate not only a new era in east European history but also the emergence of a new early modern nation? And if so, what nation was it? Snyder states that "1569 marks the creation of the early modern Polish nation." He explains that term as follows:

The nation of this Commonwealth was its nobility, Catholic, Orthodox, and Protestant. United by common political and civil rights, nobles of Polish, Lithuanian, and East Slavic origin alike described themselves, in Latin or Polish, as "of the Polish nation." They took for granted that, in the natural order of things, the language of state, speech, literature, and liturgy would vary. After the Commonwealth's partition by rival empires in the eighteenth century, some patriots recast the nation as the people, and nationality as the language they spoke.[3]

The idea that the Polish-Lithuanian Commonwealth had a "noble nation" crossing ethnic and religious bounds is not a Western invention. It was popularized in Poland after World War II by a host of scholars, including Stanisław Kot and Janusz Tazbir, two prominent authorities on

---

[2] See Timothy Snyder, *The Reconstruction of Nations: Poland, Ukraine, Lithuania, Belarus, 1569–1999* (New Haven and London, 2003), p. 3.
[3] Ibid., p. 1.

early modern Polish history. It was disseminated in the West in numerous works by Andrzej Walicki, a leading specialist in Polish and Russian intellectual history.[4] In twentieth-century historiography it became the basis for treating the Polish historical experience as unique in European history, since it had seen the formation of a civic nation in Europe long before the modern age. According to this school of thought, the Commonwealth was a cradle of democracy (albeit limited to the noble estate), civic patriotism, and exceptional tolerance. Not all these claims can be reconciled with historical fact.

In the history of the Commonwealth, one can certainly find numerous manifestations of broad solidarity, extending across ethnic and religious boundaries, among the nobiliary elites. The Union of Lublin is one of the best-known instances of such solidarity. Nevertheless, these horizontal links were often broken, and vertical links between social estates developed in particular ethnocultural communities. In Ruthenian society, this process began on the eve of the Union of Brest and continued for decades afterward. To be sure, the concept of the Polish "noble nation" is a useful analytical model that puts special emphasis on the character of the Commonwealth's political system, takes account of the nobiliary monopoly on political participation, and stresses the equality of members of the Commonwealth nobility, irrespective of ethnocultural background. But this model also tends to overlook and thus distort the development of ethnocultural identities in the multiethnic state, which was largely responsible for the decline of the Commonwealth's historical fortunes after the Khmelnytsky Uprising of the mid-seventeenth century. More fundamentally, one may ask whether a Polish "noble nation" actually existed in the sixteenth- and seventeenth-century Commonwealth or whether it was a useful invention of later times.

As David Althoen has recently argued, the image of the Polish "noble nation" is indeed a creation of the modern era. His research shows that sixteenth-century Poles imagined their nation (and nations in general) as linguistic and cultural entities, not political ones. Nor did they believe that only nobles were entitled to participate in the nation, or at least no such idea was formulated until modern times. The nobles' reference to themselves as a "noble nation" was an awkward translation from the Latin that actually meant "of noble origin" and had nothing to do with the concept of "nation." When it comes to the nobles' alleged loyalty to their "noble

---

[4] See Janusz Tazbir's most recent statement on this question in his *Kultura szlachecka w Polsce. Rozkwit – upadek – relikty* (Poznań, 2002), pp. 87–105 ("Świadomość narodowa szlachty"). See also Andrzej Walicki, *The Enlightenment and the Birth of Modern Nationhood: Polish Political Thought from Noble Republicanism to Tadeusz Kościuszko*, trans. Emma Harris (Notre Dame, Ind., 1989).

nation" in preference to the ethnolinguistic one, Althoen maintains that this was also a product of nineteenth-century Polish thought, which by no means reflected the hierarchy of identities shared by early modern elites of the Polish-Lithuanian Commonwealth. Althoen's research not only deconstructs a number of historiographic myths but also shows how they were created to promote the formation of a "big" Polish nation in the nineteenth century.[5] In light of the latest findings, the work of Józef Andrzej Gierowski deserves special attention. He was the first to conceptualize the Commonwealth not as a state of one (Polish) or two (Polish and Lithuanian) nations but as a polity of many nations.[6] The work done in the last few decades by Frank E. Sysyn and David Frick in North America and Teresa Chynczewska-Hennel and Mirosław Czech in Poland also undermines the established interpretation of early modern national identity in the Polish-Lithuanian state.[7] The development of a strong Ruthenian identity among the nobiliary stratum, which is demonstrated by these studies, challenges the view that a multiethnic and multicultural Polish nation existed in the sixteenth and seventeenth centuries. Judging by the recent research of Natalia Yakovenko, only Ruthenian princes and magnates could easily cross national and religious boundaries in the Commonwealth, intermarrying with the Catholic and Protestant aristocracy of Poland and Lithuania, while the Ruthenian nobility was confined to a closed and very traditional space defined by local culture and Eastern Christian tradition.[8] The known examples of nobiliary, Cossack, and

---

[5] See David Althoen, "*Natione Polonus* and the *Naród Szlachecki*: Two Myths of National Identity and Noble Solidarity," *Zeitschrift für Ostmitteleuropa-Forschung* 52, no. 4 (2003): 475–508. Cf. idem, "That Noble Quest: From True Nobility to Enlightened Society in the Polish-Lithuanian Commonwealth, 1550–1830," Ph.D. dissertation, University of Michigan, 2001.

[6] See the tribute to him in *Rzeczpospolita wielu narodów i jej tradycje*, ed. Andrzej K. Link-Lenczowski and Mariusz Markiewicz (Cracow, 1999).

[7] See Frank E. Sysyn, "Ukrainian-Polish Relations in the Seventeenth Century: The Role of National Consciousness and National Conflict in the Khmelnytsky Movement," in *Poland and Ukraine: Past and Present*, ed. Peter J. Potichnyj (Edmonton and Toronto, 1980), pp. 55–82; idem, "Concepts of Nationhood in Ukrainian History Writing, 1620–1690," *Harvard Ukrainian Studies* 10, nos. 3–4 (1986): 393–423; idem, "The Cossack Chronicles and the Development of Modern Ukrainian Culture and National Identity," *Harvard Ukrainian Studies* 14, nos. 3–4 (1990): 593–607; Frick, *Meletij Smotryc'kyj*, pp. 229–45; Teresa Chynczewska-Hennel, *Świadomość narodowa szlachty ukraińskiej i kozaczyzny od schyłku XVI do połowy XVII st.* (Warsaw, 1985); eadem, "The National Consciousness of Ukrainian Nobles and Cossacks from the End of the Sixteenth to the Mid-Seventeenth Century," *Harvard Ukrainian Studies* 10, nos. 3–4 (December 1986): 377–92. See also Mirosław Czech, "Świadomość historyczna Ukraińców pierwszej połowy XVII w. w świetle ówczesnej literatury polemicznej," *Slavia Orientalis* 38, nos. 3–4 (1989): 563–84, and Plokhy, *The Cossacks and Religion*, pp. 145–75.

[8] See Natalia Iakovenko, "Relihiini konversiï: sproba pohliadu zseredyny," in eadem, *Paralel'nyi svit. Doslidzhennia z istoriï uiavlen' ta idei v Ukraïni XVI–XVII st.* (Kyiv, 2002), pp. 13–79.

burgher participation in the development of Ruthenian identity also challenge the myth of a socially inclusive multiethnic Commonwealth nation.
Thus the Commonwealth hardly constitutes an exception to the general
rule of the early modern period, when the term "nation" was applied to
ethnocultural communities and not political nations, which only came
into existence in the nineteenth century.

Gente Ruthenus, natione Polonus

One of the objects of Althoen's criticism is the popularity among scholars of early modern Poland of the formula *gente Ruthenus, natione Polonus*,
which is generally attributed to the prominent sixteenth-century political writer Stanisław Orzechowski (Stanislav Orikhovsky, 1513–66).[9] This
formula has been used to argue that ethnic Ruthenian identity was subordinate to Polish national identity, turning a Ruthenian noble into a
political Pole. Andrzej Walicki attested to the importance of that formula
for the traditional view of the early modern Polish nation when he wrote:

The nation of the gentry was conceived as a political, not an ethnic community, and it was precisely this that made it powerfully attractive to the gentry
of the entire Commonwealth, irrespective of their ethnicity and language. An
influential sixteenth-century writer, Stanisław Orzechowski was not mistaken in
attributing this integrating effect to the attractiveness of Polish liberties. Significantly, he was not a native Pole but a Polonized Ukrainian who described himself
as "gente Ruthenus, Natione Polonus – politically a Pole, although ethnically a
Ruthenian."[10]

By writing *natione* with a capital letter and *gens* with a small one, Walicki
(consciously or not) manifested his belief in the priority of the former over
the latter. But no such distinction existed in the sixteenth-century Commonwealth or, for that matter, in Europe generally, as both terms were
used interchangeably. Even more important, *gens* corresponded to the
present-day idea of "nation" as often as did *natio*, which also pertained to
an individual's lineage. Althoen, who was unable to locate Orzechowski's
famous phrase in any of his writings, noted that historians who used the
phrase never provided an exact citation for it.[11] One might add that there
is a certain stretching of evidence in Walicki's statement (and the tradition it represents), which seeks to demonstrate the full participation of

---

[9] On Orzechowski and his writings, see Jerzy Starnawski's introduction to his edition of
Stanisław Orzechowski, *Wybór pism* (Wrocław et al., 1972), pp. iii–lxxxiii.
[10] Andrzej Walicki, *Poland between East and West: The Controversies over Self-Definition and
Modernization in Partitioned Poland*, The August Zaleski Lectures, Harvard University,
18–22 April 1994 (Cambridge, Mass., 1994), p. 10.
[11] See Althoen, "*Natione Polonus*," pp. 494–99.

the ethnic Ruthenian nobility in the Polish political nation. If anything, Orzechowski was a Ukrainized Pole, not a Polonized Ukrainian.

Orzechowski is an interesting case for our study of the transformation of ethnonational identities in the Commonwealth, both because of the popularity of his writings in mid-sixteenth-century Poland-Lithuania and because of the attention devoted to him by Polish (and, subsequently, Ukrainian) scholars, who claim him for their respective national literary canons. Who was Orzechowski in his own eyes, if he was not *gente Ruthenus, natione Polonus*? Orzechowski's life and writings demonstrate, probably better than those of anyone else, the impact of the Reformation on mobilizing and transforming ethnonational identities in the Kingdom of Poland on the eve of its takeover of the Grand Duchy of Lithuania. Having been born in 1513 of a Catholic father and an Orthodox mother in the Peremyshl area of the Rus' palatinate, the young Orzechowski was sent to study in Vienna. Fleeing the advancing Ottoman armies in 1529, he came to Wittenberg, where he became a student of Martin Luther and Philip Melanchthon and accepted their teachings. Orzechowski then visited Rome, where he was impressed by the arguments mustered in defense of Roman Catholic doctrine by Cardinal Gasparo Contarini. After three years under the tutelage of Cardinal Hieronymus Ghinucci, Orzechowski returned to Galicia in 1543 a committed Catholic, except on the issue of celibacy. In that regard he continued to adhere to Luther's teachings and strongly promoted the idea of a married priesthood, pointing out the existence of such a tradition in the Ruthenian (Orthodox) and Armenian churches. When Orzechowski became a Catholic priest at his father's insistence, he married in defiance of his bishop. As a result, he was defrocked and even excommunicated by the Catholic Church. Only the support of fellow Galician nobles saved him from the confiscation of his lands. The church authorities eventually reinstated him in the priesthood, but his marriage was never recognized by Rome.[12]

Orzechowski was one of the most prolific political writers of his era. Many of his works were devoted to two subjects: the issue of celibacy and the need to defend the Commonwealth against the Ottoman threat. The treatment of both themes was informed by his own experience. In the first case, his partly Ruthenian and Orthodox background (his maternal grandfather was an Orthodox priest) gave him an excellent platform from which to argue in favor of the institution of the married clergy without falling into the "heresy" of Luther. In the second case, Orzechowski's membership in the nobiliary estate of the Rus' palatinate, more vulnerable

---

[12] Orzechowski relates his life story in his letter of 10 December 1564 to Cardinal Giovanni Francesco Commendone (Orzechowski, *Wybór pism*, pp. 620–41).

to Crimean and Ottoman attack than any other Polish province, gave him the authority to demand the direct involvement of the whole kingdom in the defense of the region. In arguing these matters, Orzechowski left numerous expressions of his Ruthenian identity. More often than not he signed his writings "Stanisław Orzechowski Roxolanus," the latter designation being synonymous with "Ruthenian." In a letter to the pope, he identified himself as follows: "I am of the Scythian people and of the Ruthenian nation (*gente Scytha, natione Ruthena*). But in a certain way I am of the Sarmatian [nation], for Rus', which is my *patria*, is located in European Sarmatia."[13] In his Polish writings, Orzechowski presented himself both as a Ruthenian and as a Pole, using the term *patria* in relation to Rus' and Poland and thereby signaling that both were important elements of his identity. But what was the relationship between them? Althoen argues that Orzechowski referred more often to his Ruthenian than to his Polish identity. He resorted to the latter while abroad or when addressing the Polish nobility and its needs in general. His Polishness was associated with his membership in the Polish nobility and symbolized by the coat of arms inherited from his Polish ancestors. Orzechowski considered himself "Roxolanus" or Ruthenian, meaning that his immediate ancestors as well as his family name were products of Ruthenian history and life. Althoen interprets the phrase *gente Roxolanus, natione vero Polonus*, which he found in Orzechowski's writings, as "a Ruthenian by nationality, but also a Pole by descent."[14]

What were the main components of Orzechowski's Ruthenian identity? Was it linked to territory? Or was it defined (and, if so, to what degree) by religion, language, culture, and social status? Instructive in that regard is Orzechowski's long letter to the papal nuncio in Poland, Giovanni Francesco Commendone, written on 10 December 1564. There Orzechowski designates Rus' (not Poland) as his fatherland, limiting its territory to the foothills of the Carpathian Mountains along the Dnister (Dniester) River and thereby giving the strong impression that his *patria* more or less coincided with the borders of the Rus' palatinate. Judging by the letter, Orzechowski's fatherland was settled by people who were more warriors than scholars. They had accepted the Christian faith from Constantinople during the rule of Prince Volodymyr. Orzechowski divides his people into the nobility, most of which accepted Catholicism, and the common folk, who maintained the Greek rite. His reference to Volodymyr can be seen as an indication that his people's homeland was not limited to Galicia, but the author himself does not make this observation. On the

---

[13] Cited in Althoen, "That Noble Quest," p. 123. Cf. idem, "*Natione Polonus*," p. 493.
[14] Althoen, "*Natione Polonus*," pp. 499–504.

contrary, adopting a regional (as opposed to an ethnocultural) Ruthenian identity, Orzechowski claims that his people fell under strong Latin influence when they were taken over by Poland. Orzechowski never defines his people in linguistic terms, but his comment that its limited education was either in Latin or Slavic, which was used for church services and legislation, points in the direction of Church or Chancery Slavonic as the medium of the indigenous culture. Orzechowski's narrative indicates that he associated himself first and foremost with the people of Rus', not with the Polish presence in the area. On the other hand, the population of his Rus' was multiethnic and multiconfessional. It was blended into one people by the Polish kings, who allowed intermarriage between representatives of different religions. Thus, claimed Orzechowski, his ancestors, the Polish nobles, could marry Ruthenian women, settle in the Ruthenian village of Orikhivtsi, and become Ruthenian warriors. By this logic, Poles turned into Ruthenians by marrying local women and settling in Rus'.[15]

Does this autobiographical account bring us closer to an understanding of Orzechowski's Ruthenian identity? I would argue that it does. It appears that a particular local and cultural identity strongly stamped Orzechowski as a Ruthenian, and the designation "Roxolanus," which he often added to his last name, served as an important marker of both types of identity on the territory of the Polish state. But that designation apparently had little meaning outside Poland. Thus, when traveling abroad, Orzechowski defined himself as a Pole (that is, an inhabitant of the Kingdom of Poland), as he did when being introduced to Cardinal Contarini in Rome. He explained this in a letter of 1549 to Paolo Ramusio of Venice, pointing out that his relatives Stanisław Wapowski and Stanisław Drohojowski were considered Poles in Rome, since Rus' was a province of Poland.[16] Recent research on the Polish system of government and the political culture of the Polish nobility notes the paramount importance of local political structures and loyalties in the sixteenth-century Commonwealth.[17] The palatinate of Rus' was certainly an object of such loyalty for the local nobility. Unlike most other Polish palatinates, it also possessed

---

[15] Orzechowski wrote the letter in Latin. For a Polish translation, see idem, *Wybór pism*, pp. 620–41. For a Ukrainian translation, see *Ukraïns'ka literatura XIV–XVI st.*, ed. V. L. Mykytas' (Kyiv, 1988), pp. 155–66.

[16] This letter was also written in Latin. For a Polish translation, see Orzechowski, *Wybór pism*, pp. 92–97, here 94. For a Ukrainian translation, see *Ukraïns'ka literatura XIV–XVI st.*, pp. 152–55, here 153.

[17] See Andrzej Zajączkowski, *Szlachta polska. Kultura i struktura*, 2nd edn (Warsaw, 1993); Antoni Mączak, *Klientela. Nieformalne systemy władzy w Polsce i Europie XVI–XVIII w.* (Warsaw, 1994).

a different history, ethnic composition, and religious tradition – a legacy embraced and cherished by Orzechowski. Judging by his writings, he was particularly devoted to the Rus' religion. It has been argued, quite correctly, that Orzechowski had a vested interest in stressing the Orthodox roots of his family and the Eastern Christian tradition of his homeland, as he needed to legitimize his marriage and ensure that his children would be able to inherit his nobiliary status and property.[18] It should be stressed nevertheless that in making his case, Orzechowski did not invent anything that was not already there in cultural and political terms. Instead, he chose arguments that the local nobility could readily understand. Orzechowski's particular situation only gave him an extra incentive to articulate a sense of belonging that must have been shared by quite a few of his fellow "Ruthenians."

Orzechowski's case attests to the strength of Ruthenian identity in the Rus' territories of the Kingdom of Poland and its capacity to assimilate the new masters of the situation, the Polish nobles. Clearly, Rus' identity was strong enough to cross ethnic, linguistic, and cultural bounds. But that identity stopped at the borders of the Kingdom of Poland: Orzechowski's writings show that the Ruthenized Poles were unwilling or unable to make a connection with Rus' identity in the Grand Duchy of Lithuania. As Orzechowski put it in his letter to the pope (1551), his *patria* was surrounded by Dacia on the right, Poland on the left, Hungary in front, and Scythia (Tataria) at the back.[19] All that was about to change in 1569 – three years after Orzechowski's death.

The drive to the east

The Union of Lublin presented the Polish political elites both in the Rus' palatinate and outside it with a new situation. They had to redefine their identity (especially in the palatinate) vis-à-vis the new Rus' possessions of the Kingdom of Poland, as well as the Rus' lands of the Grand Duchy, which, for all its autonomy, drew much closer to Poland in political terms than ever before. Should that palatinate-based identity be extended to include the Rus' territories of the Kingdom or the whole Commonwealth, or should it be reserved to the palatinate, while the other Rus' territories continued to be defined in their own regional terms? It would appear that the latter solution was the one originally favored by Polish political and religious elites. As the future Catholic archbishop of

---

[18] See Althoen, *"Natione Polonus,"* pp. 497–99.
[19] Quoted in Althoen, "That Noble Quest," p. 123.

Lviv, Jan Dymitr Solikowski, wrote in 1573, "in the joint kingdom there sit the Pole, the Lithuanian, the Prussian, the Ruthenian (*Rusak*), the Masurian, the Samogitian, the Livonian, the Podlachian, the Volhynian, and the Kyivan."[20] In 1573 the name *Rusak* was still reserved for inhabitants of the Rus' palatinate. It would soon spread to other Rus' territories, including Volhynia and the Kyiv region. In the vanguard of change were those who had to deal with features of Rus' society such as religion and customs, which crossed regional boundaries.

Instructive in this regard was the change in the territorial scope of union between the Roman Catholic and Orthodox churches as envisioned on the eve of the Union of Lublin. The idea was originally proposed by Benedykt Herbest, who, like Orzechowski, was a Roman Catholic from the Rus' palatinate. A graduate of the Cracow Academy, he visited his homeland in 1566 and had extensive discussions with representatives of the Catholic, Orthodox, and Armenian clergy. The next year he published a short book, *Showing the Way*, in which he advocated union of the two churches as a solution to the crisis created by the advance of the Reformation. He wrote: "now that the Germans have turned away from Peter of Rome, perhaps the Lord will unite [the people] with us in our Rus', as he has done in the Indies."[21] Herbest was writing first and foremost about the Rus' palatinate, which was most probably the "Rus'" that he wanted to unite with Rome. His suggestion was made three years before the Union of Lublin: soon afterwards, the idea of religious union was reformulated to include all the Rus' territories encompassed by the newly created Commonwealth.

That task was undertaken by the Polish Jesuit Piotr Skarga, who taught for a year at the Jesuit College in Vilnius and produced a book entitled *On the Unity of the Church of God under One Shepherd and on the Greek Separation from That Unity*. The book was written ca. 1574 and published in 1577. Skarga expanded the idea of church union to the "outer Rus'" of the Polish-Lithuanian Commonwealth, addressing his argument to the "Ruthenian peoples," although he never clarified what he meant by the term. Since Skarga divided Rus' into Red (Galicia) and White (central and eastern Belarus), he may have divided the Ruthenian population into similar categories. He may also have thought of the inhabitants of the Grand Duchy of Lithuania and the palatinates of Rus', Volhynia, Bratslav, and Kyiv as separate Ruthenian peoples. It seems quite clear, however,

[20] Quoted in Tazbir, *Kultura szlachecka w Polsce*, p. 101.

[21] Benedykt Herbest, "Wypisanie drogi," in Michał Wiszniewski, *Historia literatury polskiej*, vol. VII (Cracow, 1845), pp. 569–81, here 579. On Herbest, see Oleksander Sushko, "Predtecha tserkovnoï uniï 1596 r. Benedykt Herbest," *Zapysky Naukovoho tovarystva im. Shevchenka* 53 (1903): 1–71; 55 (1903): 72–125; 61 (1904): 126–77.

that Skarga's "Ruthenian peoples" inhabited a territory far larger than the Rus' palatinate, and that the Muscovites were not included.[22] Thus, on the one hand, the Rus' population of the Commonwealth was viewed as a conglomerate of distinct peoples (not unlike Solikowski's Ruthenians and Volhynians). On the other hand, they were regarded as composite parts of a Rus' entity sharing the same religion – a reality reflected in the fact that Skarga also employed the term "Ruthenian people" (in the singular) in his book.

Skarga was not alone in considering Rus' a conglomerate of Ruthenian peoples. The same approach was taken by Maciej Stryjkowski, the author of the Polish-language *Chronicle of Poland, Lithuania, Samogitia and All Rus'* (1582). Stryjkowski identified distinct Ruthenian and Volhynian peoples but, unlike Skarga, counted Muscovites and "Lithuanian Belarusians" among the Rus' peoples (in a section devoted to the history of Black and White Rus') and acknowledged Muscovy as part of historical Rus'.[23] Still, he focused mainly on Polish-Lithuanian Rus'. Stryjkowski's major theme was the history of the Lithuanian and Rus' princes, peoples, and territories. He was close to the Ruthenian princely families, and, unlike another author of the period, Michael the Lithuanian, declined to treat Ruthenians as inferior to ethnic Lithuanians, who were allegedly descended from the Romans. An important aspect of Stryjkowski's narrative was the Sarmatian myth, which held that all the peoples of the Polish-Lithuanian Commonwealth were descended from the ancient Sarmatians. The *Chronicle* profoundly influenced subsequent Polish, Lithuanian, and Ruthenian works on Rus' history,[24] slowing down the separation of the Lithuanian and Ruthenian historical narratives that began in the early sixteenth century. Polish writers used its ideas and data to incorporate Rus' history into the Polish historical narrative, while Lithuanian and Ruthenian authors stressed the separate roots and distinct histories of Lithuania and the Rus' lands vis-à-vis Poland.

---

[22] For the text of Skarga's book, see *Russkaia istoricheskaia biblioteka*, vol. VII (St. Petersburg, 1882), pp. 223–580. For a discussion of Skarga's use of the term "Ruthenian peoples," see my book (S. N. Plokhii), *Papstvo i Ukraina: politika rimskoi kurii na ukrainskikh zemliakh v XVI–XVII vv.* (Kyiv, 1989), pp. 13–17. On Skarga, see Janusz Tazbir, *Piotr Skarga – szermierz kontrreformacji* (Warsaw, 1983).

[23] See Maciej Stryjkowski, *Kronika Polska, Litewska, Żmódzka i wszystkiej Rusi* (Warsaw, 1846; repr. Warsaw, 1985), pp. 107–11.

[24] On the image of Rus' in Stryjkowski's *Chronicle*, see P. Borek, "Ruś w Kronice Macieja Strykowskiego," *Mediaevalia Ucrainica: mental'nist' ta istoriia idei* 5 (1998): 57–67. For Stryjkowski's influence on the historiography of the region, see A. I. Rogov, "Maciej Stryjkowski i historiografia ukraińska XVII wieku," *Slavia Orientalis* 14, no. 4 (1965): 311–29; Eugenija Ulčinaite, "Literatura neołacińska jako świadectwo litewskiej świadomości narodowej," in *Łacina w Polsce. Zeszyty naukowe*, ed. Jerzy Axer, nos. 1–2, *Między Slavia Latina i Slavia Orthodoxa* (Warsaw, 1995), pp. 37–39.

The first of these two approaches was taken by Sebastian Fabian Klonowic, the author of the Latin poem *Roxolania*, which was published in Cracow in 1586.[25] Like Herbest and Skarga, Klonowic was an ethnic Pole. Although he was not a native of the region, he spent most of his adult life as a city official in Lublin on the Polish-Ruthenian ethnic border. He dedicated his *Roxolania* to the city council of Lviv, where he apparently spent some time before moving to Lublin in 1572. In the tradition of Renaissance ethnography, *Roxolania* celebrated the character and folkways of the inhabitants of Ruthenia (*Russia* in the original), which was depicted as the ultimate land of milk and honey.[26] Its inhabitants, the *Russis*, were treated by the author as a distinct, somewhat remote, primitive and mysterious people (*gens*) descended from the biblical Japheth who might have been known in the past as the Bastarnae, Sauromatians, Illyrians, or Hamaxobians. They were united by religion and way of life. Klonowic does not say explicitly whether he included the non-Ruthenian inhabitants of Ruthenian towns such as Lviv among the *Russis*, but his listing of those towns gives a good idea of his geographic conception of the land described in *Roxolania*.

Klonowic begins with Lviv and goes on to Zamość, Kyiv, Kamianets, Lutsk, Buzk, Sokal, Horodlo, Belz, Peremyshl, Drohobych, Kholm, and Krasnostav (elsewhere he also devotes substantial attention to Lublin). Thus Klonowic's Ruthenia included not only the territories of the Rus' palatinate but also the newly acquired lands of Volhynia and Kyiv. With the exception of Podlachia, it included all the ethnic Ruthenian territories that ended up within the boundaries of the Kingdom of Poland after the Union of Lublin.[27] Lviv remained the center of that Ruthenia, but Kyiv is a close second as regards the length of Klonowic's description.

---

[25] For the Latin text, accompanied by a Polish translation, see Sebastian Fabian Klonowic, *Roxolania/Roksolania czyli ziemie Czerwonej Rusi*, ed. and trans. Mieczysław Mejor (Wrocław, 1996). On Klonowic, see Halina Wiśniewska, *Renesansowe życie i dzieło Sebastiana Fabiana Klonowicza* (Lublin, 1985).

[26] On Renaissance ethnography and the interest of European ethnographers in eastern Europe and Muscovy, see Marshall T. Poe, *"A People Born to Slavery." Russia in Early Modern European Ethnography, 1476–1748* (Ithaca and London, 2000), pp. 11–38. Klonowic was among the founders of the Polish literary tradition of treating Rus' as a land of ancient practices, mysteries, and wonders. On the development of that tradition, see Joanna Partyka, "'Głębokie ruskie kraje' w oczach staropolskiego encyklopedysty," in *Mazepa and His Time: History, Culture, Society*, ed. Giovanna Siedina (Alessandria, 2004), pp. 291–300.

[27] Cf. the political and ethnic maps of the sixteenth-century Polish-Lithuanian Commonwealth in *The Historical Atlas of Poland*, ed. Władysław Czapliński and Tadeusz Ładogórski (Warsaw and Wrocław, 1986), pp. 20–21, 23. In one case Klonowic defines Ruthenia (*Russia*) as a country extending from the Black Sea in the south to the Arctic Ocean in the north but otherwise regards the Muscovite Rus' as a separate people whom he calls *Moschi*.

Thus Klonowic extended the concept of Lviv-centered *Russia* as far east as Kyiv, which he considered part of Black Rus'. Kyiv is depicted in *Roxolania* as the capital of the old Rus' princes, a bastion in the war against the Tatars, and the site of miraculous caves in which the remains of Rus' heroes are preserved uncorrupted. "Moreover, for an inhabitant of Black Rus'," wrote Klonowic, "Kyiv means as much as ancient Rome to a Christian."[28] If Orzechowski's Rus'/Ruthenia/Roxolania was limited to the Rus' palatinate, for Klonowic it included the latter but was not limited to it. On the other hand, unlike Skarga, Klonowic restricted his *Russia*/Roxolania to lands within the Kingdom of Poland. Significantly, the Rus' of both Skarga and Klonowic included the Volhynian and Kyivan lands, where a new regional power center was emerging in the second half of the sixteenth century.

The return of the dynasty

That center was the Volhynian city of Ostrih, the seat of the powerful Prince Kostiantyn (Vasyl) Ostrozky.[29] He was the son of the hero of Orsha (1514), Prince Kostiantyn Ivanovych Ostrozky, grand hetman of the Grand Duchy of Lithuania. In the second half of the sixteenth century, the Volhynian princes in general and the Ostrozkys in particular established full control over their native Volhynia and the adjoining Kyivan Land. The formal equalization of the legal status of the nobility proclaimed under the Union of Lublin did not affect their power, as they maintained their princely titles and felt quite secure at the top of a pyramid consisting of hundreds of minor noble clients economically and politically dependent on them. Ostrozky was virtually an uncrowned king of the Volhynia, Bratslav, and Kyiv lands, where informal networks of power and the characteristic political regionalism of the Polish-Lithuanian Commonwealth were strongest.[30] Yet the Union of Lublin presented the Ostrozky clan and other Volhynian princely families with the challenge of legitimizing their authority over their now legally equal clients from the ranks of the petty nobility. They also needed to rationalize their often recalcitrant attitude toward the king and their dominant role in the Ukrainian lands east of Volhynia.

---

[28] Klonowic, *Roxolania*, p. 100: "Praeterea Nigro tanti Kiiovia Russo est, quanti Christicolis Roma vetusta fuit."

[29] On Ostrozky, see Teresa Chynczewska-Hennel, "Ostrogski, Konstanty Wasyl, książe (ok. 1526–1608)," in *Polski słownik biograficzny*, ed. Władysław Konopczyński et al., vol. 24, fasc. 3 (1979): 489–95.

[30] On regionalism in the Ukrainian lands of the Commonwealth, see Sysyn, *Between Poland and the Ukraine*, pp. 21–22.

As noted above, before the Union of Lublin the dominant level of identity among the Rus' elites of the Grand Duchy of Lithuania was local. Thus the Volhynian elites of the mid-sixteenth century seem to have regarded themselves as Volhynians first, although they fully appreciated their membership in the broader community. The Volhynian noble Vasyl Zahorovsky, who wrote his testament in Tatar captivity in 1577, wanted his children to be taught Rus' grammar and did not want them to forsake the Rus' language and traditions or the Greek religious rite, but he considered himself primarily a loyal son of the Volhynian Land, which marked the boundaries of his main socioeconomic contacts and interests.[31] In the following year, when a print shop established in his native land issued a Rus' grammar, its introduction defined Ostrih as a city in the Volhynian Land, with no reference to Rus', the Kingdom of Poland, or the Polish-Lithuanian Commonwealth.[32] Local identity continued to rule the day.

This was about to change somewhat with the realization of the major project of Prince Ostrozky and the circle of literati around him – the publication of the first Slavonic Bible in 1580–81. The introduction to the Bible still referred to Ostrih as a city in the Volhynian Land, but there were also clear signs of a new and much broader identity. The same introduction shows that the literati assembled by Ostrozky saw their patron not only as a Volhynian magnate but also as an heir of the Kyivan Rurikids and a lawful ruler of Rus'. This was a dramatic change from the panegyrists' treatment of his famous father, the hero of Orsha. If the senior Ostrozky was praised for services rendered to his overlord, the Polish king and Lithuanian grand prince Sigismund I, the junior one was lauded as a protector of the Orthodox Church and thus a continuator of the work of Emperor Constantine and the Kyivan princes St. Volodymyr and Yaroslav.[33] Herasym Smotrytsky, the likely author of the verse introduction to the Ostrih Bible, wrote in that regard:

> For Volodymyr enlightened his nation by baptism,
> While Kostiantyn brought them light with the writings of holy
>   wisdom. . . .
> Yaroslav embellished Kyiv and Chernihiv with church buildings,
> While Kostiantyn raised up the one universal church with writings.[34]

In the preface to the Ostrih Bible, written by Smotrytsky on Ostrozky's behalf, the manuscript used for the edition was traced back to the version

---

[31] For the text of Zahorovsky's testament, see *Ukraïns'ka literatura XIV–XVI st.*, pp. 167–84.

[32] For the text of the introduction to the grammar of 1578, see ibid., p. 199.

[33] See Plokhy, *The Cossacks and Religion*, pp. 154–55.

[34] See Herasym Smotryts'kyi, "Vsiakoho chynu pravoslavnyi chytateliu," in *Ukraïns'ka literatura XIV–XVI st.*, p. 461.

translated from the Greek in the days of St. Volodymyr. It was also claimed to have been acquired from another Rurikid, Ivan the Terrible, the Commonwealth's adversary in the Livonian War, whom Smotrytsky/Ostrozky called a "sovereign and grand prince pious and most resplendent in Orthodoxy."[35] The editors of the Ostrih Bible were consciously establishing parallels and connections between Ostrozky and the Rurikids but were not yet prepared to declare the prince a Rurikid and a direct descendant of St. Volodymyr. Smotrytsky did so in 1587 in the dedication to his book *The Key to the Kingdom of Heaven*, which called Oleksander, the son of Kostiantyn Ostrozky, an heir and descendant of St. Volodymyr.[36]

The uncrowned king of Rus' had now emerged as the lawful heir of the Kyivan princes. The "sons of the Eastern Church who belong to the Rus' nation (*narod*)" to whom Ostrozky addressed his Bible first and foremost had now acquired a legitimate dynast who was willing to protect their church and, by extension, their nation. That theme was further developed in numerous panegyrics and works devoted to members of Ostrozky's family and their relatives, the Zaslavskys, in the late sixteenth and early seventeenth centuries. The transformation of the Volhynian princes into heirs of Kyivan rulers and protectors of Rus' was accomplished by writers who generally came from the pre-1569 Kingdom of Poland, as did Smotrytsky and Demian Nalyvaiko, the brother of the famous Cossack leader Severyn Nalyvaiko. As Natalia Yakovenko has recently shown, the vast majority of sixteenth- and seventeenth-century panegyrists were non-Orthodox and not even ethnic Ruthenians (the latter accounted for only six of the forty-seven identified by Yakovenko). They were predominantly Polish Catholics (thus it would appear to be no accident that the first references to the Kyivan origins of the Ostrozky princely family appeared in the 1570s in Polish rather than Ruthenian sources).[37]

The new aspirations of the Ostrozkys were articulated, legitimized, and disseminated not only by Polish writers but also with the aid of "Polish" ideas. There were two different agendas advocated by two groups

[35] See Smotryts'kyi, "[Persha peredmova do Ostroz'koï Bibliï 1581 r.]," in *Ukraïns'ka literatura XIV–XVI st.*, p. 202.

[36] See Smotryts'kyi, "Kliuch tsarstva nebesnoho," in *Ukraïns'ka literatura XIV–XVI st.*, p. 213. On the development of the genealogical legend of the Ostrozkys, see Leonid Sobolev, "Genealogicheskaia legenda roda kniazei Ostrozhskikh," *Slavianovedenie*, 2001, no. 2: 32–33.

[37] Out of forty-seven panegyrics analyzed by Yakovenko, only six were written by Ruthenian authors, while Polish authors, mostly clients or servants of the princely family, accounted for thirty-nine. See Natalia Iakovenko, "Topos 'z'iednanykh narodiv' u panehyrykakh kniaziam Ostroz'kym i Zaslavs'kym (bilia vytokiv ukraïns'koï identychnosti)," in eadem, *Paralel'nyi svit*, pp. 232–69, here 239–42.

of panegyrists. The first was promoted by such Orthodox Ruthenians as Herasym Smotrytsky, who stressed Ostrozky's connection not just with the Kyivan princely dynasty but with St. Volodymyr, the baptizer of Rus', in particular. They obviously counted on Ostrozky's support for the Orthodox Church and the Ruthenian nation. In so doing, they created a virtual space for Polish-Lithuanian Rus' at the center of *Slavia Orthodoxa* – a conglomerate of Slavic-speaking Orthodox countries. Along with the Ruthenian people, that broader entity was the addressee of the Ostrih Bible.[38] The Muscovite component of that world was not forgotten by the authors of the introduction, who informed their readers that the biblical text had been delivered to Ostrih from Moscow with the consent of Ivan the Terrible. That world was also represented in Ostrih by Muscovite emigrants hostile to the tsar – Prince Andrei Kurbsky, Ostrozky's adviser on matters of religion, and the printer of the Bible, Ivan Fedorov.[39] To be sure, Smotrytsky and the other Ostrih literati did not envision Muscovy as part of their virtual homeland, but they saw it as an important part of their cultural identity. If there was no principality left for Kostiantyn Ostrozky to rule within the Polish-Lithuanian Commonwealth, there was a separate religion and ecclesiastical structure to protect and a separate people to lead. Unlike his real or imagined Rurikid ancestors and relatives, Ostrozky was emerging willy-nilly as the leader of a new type of community defined not by the boundaries of the prince's realm but by those of ethnicity, language, culture, and religion.

Ostrozky's Polish Catholic literary servants worked within a very different paradigm. In the well-established tradition of Polish historical writing, they positioned their patron not in the context of *Slavia Orthodoxa*, Rus', or the Commonwealth but within the cultural space of the Kingdom of Poland. Not unlike Klonowic, they were prepared to extend the boundaries of Orzechowski's Ruthenia far to the east, but not beyond the borders of the kingdom. As Natalia Yakovenko has shown, Ostrozky's rule over Rus' was legitimized in the Polish historical context by associating the Ostrozky line with a figure of Polish legend known as Rus. According to the Polish chronicles, that name belonged to the brother of Czech and Lech (alternatively, son of Lech), the founders of the Czech and Polish

---

[38] See Smotryts'kyi, "[Persha peredmova do Ostroz'koï Bibliï 1581 r.]," pp. 200, 202.

[39] On Fedorov, see Iaroslav Isaievych, *Ivan Fedorov i vynyknennia drukarstva na Ukraïni*, 2nd edn (Lviv, 1983). There is an abundance of literature on Fedorov – the result of the work of dozens of scholars contributing to the "Fedoroviana" industry, which in the eyes of the Soviet authorities of the 1950s–80s was intended to demonstrate the beneficent cultural influence of Muscovy on Ukraine. In fact, it served to legitimize research on the early modern cultural history of Ukraine, Belarus, and Lithuania, which was otherwise regarded with suspicion by the Soviet authorities.

states. Thus the genealogical legend of the Ostrozkys was neatly incorporated into the Polish founding myth. The separation of that legend from
the historical tradition of the Grand Duchy of Lithuania was achieved
by presenting the Ostrozkys as heirs not to Gediminas but to Danylo of
Halych. Some panegyrists called him "Danylo Ostrozky" and portrayed
the thirteenth-century prince as the ruler of Volhynia, Belz, Kyiv, and
Halych, while his son Lev (also referred to as Ostrozky) was identified as
the founder of Lviv.[40] The Polish literati were in fact erasing the border
between Polish and Lithuanian Rus' of the pre-1569 era and moving it to
the boundary established by the Union of Lublin. Ironically, in so doing,
they were emerging as successors to the Galician-Volhynian chroniclers
of the thirteenth century, whose concept of Rus' also included Galicia,
Volhynia, and the Dnipro territories.

At the center of the historical space constructed by the Ruthenian and
Polish clients of the Ostrozkys (for all their undoubted differences) was,
of course, the princely house of the Ostrozkys – heirs of the glorious rulers
of Kyivan Rus' and uncrowned kings of the new Ruthenia.

The church union

All over Europe, the advance of the Reformation and the political and
religious turmoil that accompanied it gave local elites and aristocratic
clans new opportunities to legitimize their struggle for privileges accru-
ing to their social estate and region. In this regard, the Polish-Lithuanian
Commonwealth presents a classic example of local princes using a "rebel
religion" to achieve their political goals. The acceptance of the Lutheran
Reformation by Ducal Prussia, a dependency of Poland, brought Reformation ideas directly into the realm of the Polish kings. By the mid-
sixteenth century, the aristocrats of Little Poland and Lithuania were
embracing Calvinism. The Roman curia, for its part, was seeking to rein-
vigorate Polish Catholicism through the intervention of its nuncios and
the activities of the newly arrived Jesuits.[41] The idea of an ecclesiastical
union of Roman Catholicism and Orthodoxy was in the air. Meanwhile,
the Orthodox burghers of Lviv were trying to revive their church so as
to counter the advances of Protestantism and reformed Catholicism. In
Rus', representatives of all religious trends and churches were hoping for

[40] See Iakovenko, "Topos 'z'iednanykh narodiv,'" pp. 246–51, 254.
[41] For a short history of (and literature on) the Polish Reformation and Counter-
Reformation, see Jerzy Kłoczowski, *A History of Polish Christianity* (Cambridge, 2000),
pp. 84–163. On the role of the Jesuits in promoting the church union in the Commonwealth, see Jan Krajcar, "Jesuits and the Genesis of the Union of Brest," *Orientalia
Christiana Periodica* 44 (1978): 131–53.

support from the most powerful figure in the land, Prince Kostiantyn Ostrozky, who was also a possible candidate for the Polish throne. Piotr Skarga even dedicated the first edition of his pro-union treatise, *On the Unity of the Church of God* (1577), to Ostrozky, but the prince apparently ordered the entire print run bought up and destroyed. He had his own ideas about what position he would take in the religious turmoil of the time. While Calvin was busy turning Geneva into a Protestant Rome, Ostrozky made his Ostrih an Orthodox Geneva by establishing a school and a printing press. Clearly, he was thinking on a grand scale. In 1584 he even toyed with a plan to move the seat of the patriarch of Constantinople to Ostrih.[42]

The event that truly demonstrated Ostrozky's power in Ruthenian society and mobilized it along religious lines was the Union of Brest (1596), which declared the subordination of the Kyiv metropolitanate to Rome. The Union, encouraged by Polish Catholics close to Rome, conceived by the Ruthenian Orthodox hierarchy, supported by the king, and welcomed by the pope, proved a major disappointment to its authors and supporters. Instead of helping to unify the state and facilitate the eastward advance of Catholicism, it turned out to be a source of social strife and religious conflict. It would appear that the Kingdom of Poland lost its only chance to ensure a peaceful amalgamation of its Catholic and Orthodox populations even before it united with the Grand Duchy of Lithuania at Lublin. In 1555, when after decades of confrontation central Europe worked out the peacemaking principle *cuius regio, eius religio* at Augsburg, the Polish Diet suggested a reform of the Roman Catholic Church in Poland so as to make it more attractive and perhaps acceptable to Protestants and Orthodox alike. Orzechowski's earlier ideas about the reconciliation of the Catholic and Orthodox churches (expressed in his tract *Baptismus Ruthenorum* in 1544) and the permissibility of clerical marriage made their way into the Diet resolutions of 1555, which suggested that the clergy be allowed to marry, since it was "allowed by the Greeks, the Ruthenians, and the Bulgarians, and used to be practiced in the Western Church." The Diet deputies also asked Rome to allow the Eucharist to be administered to the laity in two species ("as it was once practiced at the beginning of the history of the Church and as it is now still practiced by the Greeks, the Bulgarians, and the Ruthenians").[43] Rome rejected this "made in Poland" solution – a development that split Polish society. In the long run, it also alienated the Orthodox lands of the

---

[42] On Ostrozky's activities and religious attitudes, see Jan Krajcar, "Konstantin Basil Ostrozskij and Rome in 1582–84," *Orientalia Christiana Periodica* 35, no. 1 (1969): 193–213, here 201; Gudziak, *Crisis and Reform*, pp. 119–42.

[43] See Kłoczowski, *A History of Polish Christianity*, p. 101.

Commonwealth from its Catholic core and helped turn the former not only into a center of Orthodox opposition to royal power but also into a breeding ground of radical forms of Polish Protestantism.[44]

The Ruthenian community itself emerged from the church councils of Brest (as noted above, there were two of them – one for proponents of the union, the other for its critics) bitterly divided, with most of the clergy and lay patrons of the church (but not the hierarchy) opposing the union. The ensuing controversy resulted in an explosion of polemical writings whereby Rus' truly entered the age of the Reformation.[45] Some religious treatises of the period provide unique information on the state and development of Rus' group identity. What seems quite clear from a reading of early polemical works by proponents and opponents of the Union (both groups included ethnic Ruthenians and Poles) is that the notions of Orthodoxy and Ruthenian ethnicity were closely associated in the eyes of Ruthenians and their non-Ruthenian counterparts alike. The term "Rus'" was applied both to the church and to the national community, covering all social strata of Ruthenian society. Ruthenian identity of the period, like the image of Rus' in the Commonwealth generally, had clear ethnoconfessional characteristics. After all, Skarga appealed in his writings to the Rus' peoples, not to the Orthodox. The same category was of central importance in Herasym Smotrytsky's *Key to the Kingdom of Heaven*. In court documents of the period, Orthodox priests were routinely called Ruthenian, while Roman Catholic priests were identified as Polish.[46] Jan Szczęsny Herburt, a Polish Catholic opponent of the Union and a Ruthenian by regional identity, manifested this connection between Rus' nationality and religion in 1613, when he accused the enemies of Orthodoxy of trying to create a situation in which there would be "no Rus' in Rus'."[47]

The interests of Rus' became the trump card in the polemics that followed the Union of Brest. The contending parties justified their attitudes and actions by claiming to promote the interests of the Ruthenian nation (*rus'kyi narod*), which they clearly distinguished from the Polish nation

---

[44] On the spread of radical Reformation ideas in Ukraine, see George H. Williams, "Protestants in the Ukraine during the Period of the Polish-Lithuanian Commonwealth," *Harvard Ukrainian Studies* 2, no. 1 (March 1978): 41–72; no. 2 (June 1978): 184–210.

[45] For a brief survey of the struggle over church union and an interpretation of the ensuing reforms in terms of the confessionalization paradigm, see my *Cossacks and Religion*, pp. 77–99.

[46] See the reference to a court case of 1585 in Iakovenko, "Relihiini konversiï," p. 35.

[47] See Jan Szczęsny Herburt, *Zdanie o narodzie Ruskim*, repr. in *Z dziejów Ukrainy*, ed. Wacław Lipiński (Cracow, 1912), pp. 92–96. The same formula was used in a speech delivered in defense of the Orthodox Church by the Roman Catholic prince Krzysztof Zbaraski at the diet of 1623 (Iakovenko, "Relihiini konversiï," p. 46).

(*naród polski*) on the basis of its religion, culture, and language. Debates over the Union also helped reinforce the existing boundary between the Commonwealth Rus' and Muscovy and their versions of Orthodoxy. The pre-1596 tendency of lay Orthodox literati in the Commonwealth to define themselves as part of a larger Rus' (including Muscovy) faded away as the boundaries of the Kyiv metropolitanate defined the religious battleground for all parties involved. In his anti-union letters from Mount Athos in Greece to the Orthodox inhabitants of the "Liakh Land," the Orthodox polemicist Ivan Vyshensky defined the Ukrainian and Belarusian territories as Little Rus'.[48] This old Greek term, originally used to denote the Halych metropolitanate, now helped give a name and identity to the Orthodox population of Poland-Lithuania in the larger world of *Slavia Orthodoxa*. The notion of Little Rus' superseded the boundary between the Rus' population of the Kingdom of Poland and the Grand Duchy of Lithuania. At the same time, it distinguished that imagined world from the other Orthodox Slavic lands. It was subject to different circumstances and found itself under constant attack. If in the religious sphere the Orthodox Ruthenians needed a separate term to distinguish themselves from Muscovite Rus', no such term was required in secular discourse, where the ethnonym Ruthenian (*rus'kyi*) was counterposed to the political name "Muscovite." For pro-Uniate and anti-Uniate authors alike, these were two separate nations.

While all parties to the debate agreed on the distinctiveness of the Ruthenians vis-à-vis the Poles and Muscovites, they disagreed on their true interests and how they could best be served. The Orthodox clearly associated the Ruthenian nation and its tradition with themselves. They claimed all the historical privileges granted by Lithuanian and Polish rulers to Rus' and its church, regarding any attack on the Orthodox Church as an offensive against the Rus' nation, its rights and freedoms. The Union was declared a new invention – a notion that had clear negative connotations in the public discourse of the time – divorced from the traditions of the old (meaning true and Orthodox) Rus'. The Uniates, for their part, challenged the exclusive Orthodox claim to the Rus' name and fought hard to limit the number of Orthodox participants in the debate.[49] They directed their fire mainly against the Rus' Protestants, who advocated the use of the vernacular (as opposed to Church Slavonic) in church liturgy and publications; more importantly, the Protestants sided with the Orthodox in the conflict with the Commonwealth authorities over the church union. In the eyes of Ipatii Potii, an architect of the Union and

---

[48] See Ivan Vyshens'kyi, "Knyzhka," in *Ukraïns'ka literatura XIV–XVI st.*, pp. 306–68, here 306–7, 333–37.
[49] See my *Cossacks and Religion*, pp. 149–52.

later metropolitan of the Uniate Church, the Protestants did not belong to Rus′ and had no business interfering in what he regarded as an internal Ruthenian dispute.[50] According to Uniate polemicists, the Rus′ converts to Roman Catholicism had also banished themselves from the Ruthenian nation: by going directly to the Catholic Church and bypassing the Union, they had embarked on the road of cultural Polonization.[51] The Orthodox, by contrast, recognized the legitimacy of the Catholic Rus′ while denying it to the Uniates. Clearly, the monoconfessional model of Rus′ to which the Ruthenian literati had subscribed prior to the Union of Brest was in deep crisis. The architects of the Union failed to win the loyalty of most of the Ruthenian elites, and the restoration of the Orthodox hierarchy in 1620 made it unrealistic to expect a healing of the split in the near future.

The division of Rus′ into two churches and confessions troubled many Ruthenian intellectuals, including the son of Herasym Smotrytsky, Meletii, an Orthodox polemicist and church figure who was deeply concerned about the interests of the Ruthenian nation. Looking for a way out of the religious conflict that resulted in the killing of the Uniate archbishop of Polatsk, Yosafat Kuntsevych (1623), Smotrytsky, who was then an Orthodox archbishop and Kuntsevych's rival in Belarus, first turned for support and guidance to Constantinople. Disappointed in the offerings of the Orthodox East to struggling Rus′, Smotrytsky eventually accepted the Union himself. In the process he changed his polemical arguments but remained devoted to the ultimate good of the Ruthenian nation.[52] His own experience turned him into a strong opponent of internecine religious conflict, which he called "the struggle of Rus′ with Rus′." Smotrytsky was probably the first Ruthenian intellectual who attempted to break the vicious circle of ethnoconfessional identity and dissolve the strong connection between Rus′ ethnicity and Rus′ religion. "Whoever changes his faith does not immediately also degenerate from his blood," wrote Smotrytsky, "whoever from the Ruthenian nation becomes of the Roman faith does not become immediately a Spaniard or an Italian by birth; rather he remains a noble Ruthenian as before. For it is not the faith that makes a Ruthenian a Ruthenian, a Pole a Pole, or a Lithuanian a Lithuanian, but Ruthenian, Polish, and Lithuanian blood and birth."[53]

---

[50] See Petro Kraliuk, *Osoblyvosti vyiavu natsional′noï svidomosti v ukraïns′kii suspil′nii dumtsi 16 – pershoï polovyny 17 st.* (Lutsk, 1996), pp. 71–73.

[51] On Uniate arguments to that effect, see Ihar I. Marzaliuk, *Liudzi daŭniai Belarusi: ètnakanfesiinyia i satsyia-kul′turnyia stereotypy (X–XVII st.)* (Mahilioŭ, 2003), pp. 84–85.

[52] On Smotrytsky, see Frick, *Meletij Smotryc′kyj.*

[53] Smotrytsky, *Verificatia niewinności* (Vilnius, 1621), p. 60 (quoted in Frick, *Meletij Smotryc′kyj*, p. 235). For a discussion of Smotrytsky's views on the "Ruthenian nation," see ibid., pp. 229–38.

Thus Smotrytsky directly attacked the Orthodox postulate that anyone who abandoned Orthodoxy ceased to be a Ruthenian – a view advanced by Ivan Vyshensky, among others. Smotrytsky was clearly ahead of his time: in the confessionalizing Ruthenian society of the early seventeenth century, Vyshensky's model of the Ruthenian nation was more acceptable than Smotrytsky's multiconfessional one.

Nobiliary Rus'

The concept of the Ruthenian nation that became central to public discourse in the aftermath of the Union of Brest was contested not only by a variety of religious groups but also by different social strata. They included princes, nobles, clergymen, and burghers, all of whom spoke in the name of Rus' and claimed to be protectors of the Ruthenian nation.

The princes' concept of Rus', created with the help of Polish intellectuals, ironically reached its culmination when the most powerful Ruthenian princely family, the Ostrozkys, had virtually died out, while the others not only accepted another religion but also lost most of their former power and became all but irrelevant to the subsequent development of Rus'. The Polish panegyrists do not appear to have been taken aback by the princes' abandonment of Orthodoxy, which was so closely identified with Rus'.[54] Indeed, this made it easier for representatives of Polish Catholic learning to appropriate Rus' history and territory as integral parts of a broader Commonwealth identity that included Poles, Lithuanians, and Ruthenians. Not unlike Orzechowski in the mid-sixteenth century, these Polish writers of the early seventeenth century were proud of the Ruthenian past and strongly identified themselves with Rus' regional identity. They exalted their princely patrons by establishing their descent from ancient Kyivan princes. Thus the last of the Ostrozkys, a Roman Catholic named Janusz, was linked by his panegyrist Sebastian Sleszkowski to Rus, the brother of Lech and Czech, and Kyi, the legendary founder of Kyiv (1612).[55] Jan Dąbrowski, the author of the poem *Camoenae Borysthenides*

---

[54] Among the princes, the percentage of marriages outside their confession appears to have diminished from approximately 50 percent in the period 1540–1615 to 29 percent in the years 1616–50. By 1616 most princely families had already abandoned Orthodoxy and married within their new confession (predominantly Roman Catholicism). By that time the confessionalization of religious life in the Commonwealth was well advanced, making interconfessional marriages and families an exception to the general rule. These developments reduced the number of interconfessional marriages not only among the princes but also among the Ruthenian nobility in general. According to Yakovenko's calculations, they declined from 16 percent (1581–1615) to 12 percent (1616–50) (Iakovenko, "Relihiini konversii," p. 36).

[55] See Natalia Iakovenko, "Latyna na sluzhbi kyievo-rus'koï istoriï (*Camoenae Borysthenides*, 1620 rik)," in eadem, *Paralel'nyi svit*, pp. 270–95, here 292.

(1620), which introduced the new Catholic bishop of Kyiv to the riches of Rus′ history and tradition, even commended Janusz for abandoning Orthodoxy. Nor did he forget to mention that the current palatine of Kyiv, the ethnic Pole and Catholic Tomasz Zamojski, was married to Kateryna Ostrozka, which established his Ruthenian credentials.[56] Genealogical arguments ruled the day as the culturally Polonized Rus′ princes continued to be lauded by their panegyrists as representatives and protectors of Rus′, whose historical and cultural space was thus appropriated by the Polish nation-building project.[57]

While the princes continued to encourage their panegyrists to seek the sources of their Rus′ identity in Kyivan times, the Rus′ nobility was constructing its own model of Ruthenian identity. As might be expected, that model was based on the Union of Lublin, which guaranteed them the same rights as those of the princes and equalized them with the Polish nobility. Like their Polish counterparts, the Rus′ nobles referred to themselves as part of the noble *narod*: as in Polish, the term referred not to a people but to birth (that is, descent or lineage).[58] In the religious debates of the 1620s, they called themselves the "Ruthenian noble *narod*," thereby manifesting their membership in the Ruthenian nobility. The notion of the "Ruthenian noble *narod*" paralleled that of the Polish noble *naród* and became a crux of the religious debates, for the Orthodox nobility treated the advance of the Union and royal persecution of the Orthodox Church as an attack on their estate rights, which had been guaranteed (so went the argument) by the conditions of the Union of Lublin and the decrees of Polish kings. It was argued that under the terms of the Union, the Ruthenian nation (*narod*) had been attached to the Polish one as "equal to equal and free [nation] to free [nation]." It was also claimed that those rights had been given by the Commonwealth to Orthodox and Catholic Rus′, as there was no other (meaning Uniate) Rus′ at the time. Thus any expansion of the Union or the property rights of the Uniate Church at the expense of the Orthodox was a violation of the estate rights of

[56] For an often erroneous Ukrainian translation of this Latin poem, see *Ukraïns′ka poeziia XVII stolittia (persha polovyna). Antolohiia*, comp. V. V. Iaremenko, ed. O. V. Lupii (Kyiv, 1988), pp. 93–119. For an analysis of the poem, see Ihor Ševčenko, "Poland in Ukrainian History," in idem, *Ukraine between East and West*, pp. 112–30, here 124–26; Iakovenko, "Latyna na sluzhbi kyievo-rus′koï istoriï."

[57] On the treatment of Janusz Ostrogski (Ostrozky) and the Zaslavsky princes – heirs of the Ostrozkys and protectors of the Uniate Church – in panegyrical literature, see Iakovenko, "Topos 'z′iednanykh narodiv,'" pp. 248–54.

[58] Members of a nobiliary dietine convoked at Berestechko in March 1573 described themselves as follows: "We the councillors, dignitaries, land and castle officials and the whole knighthood of the noble nation [descent], citizens of the Volhynian land." See Petro Sas, *Politychna kul′tura ukraïns′koho suspil′stva (kinets′ XVI – persha polovyna XVII st.)* (Kyiv, 1998), pp. 44–45.

the Orthodox nobles. These arguments were most cogently presented by
Lavrentii Drevynsky in a speech at the Diet of 1621 and by the unknown
authors of the *Supplication* issued by the Orthodox on the eve of the Diet
of 1623.[59]

For the purposes of our discussion, probably the most important outcome of the religious debates provoked by the restoration of the Orthodox
hierarchy in 1620 was the articulation of the concept of the Ruthenian
nation not only as a separate entity but also as an equal partner of the
Polish and Lithuanian nations. That concept was first presented in documents attributed to the Orthodox nobility and further developed in the
writings of Orthodox intellectuals, including the most talented of them,
Meletii Smotrytsky. The Orthodox argument, intended to serve the purposes of the new religious, political, and ethnocultural situation, rested on
a highly "creative" interpretation of the rights granted to the Ruthenian
palatinates – more specifically, to the Ruthenian nobility of those palatinates – at the Lublin Diet of 1569. The rights guaranteed to individual
palatinates entering the Kingdom of Poland were now used to defend the
rights of the Orthodox Church throughout the Commonwealth, including the Ruthenian lands of the Grand Duchy. Although the concept of the
Ruthenian nation as an equal partner in the Commonwealth was clearly
the product of nobiliary thinking, Orthodox authors, especially Smotrytsky, did their best to extend those rights to a much broader spectrum of
Ruthenian society. To that end, they treated the nobility as an estate that
included not only the gentry but also the princes – the leaders of Ruthenian society (at least at the time of the Union of Lublin). The clergy,
the burghers, and even the Cossacks were also included under this broad
umbrella.

A good example of this expanded treatment of the rights acquired by
the Ruthenian nobility at Lublin occurs in the Polish-language pamphlet
Justification of Innocence (1623), which is usually attributed to Smotrytsky.[60] According to the *Justification*,

For those above-mentioned honorable deeds and audacious acts of courage that
the noble Ruthenian nation rendered to the Grand Dukes, their Lords, [and]
Their Majesties the Kings of Poland, it has been given the freedom by them to
sit in senatorial dignity equally with the two, Polish and Lithuanian, nations, to
give counsel concerning the good of their states and their own fatherland, and
to enjoy all the dignities, prerogatives, the call to offices, freedoms, rights, and

[59] See extensive quotations from both documents and a discussion of their contents in
Mykhailo Hrushevs'kyi, *Istoriia ukraïns'koï literatury*, vol. VI (Kyiv, 1995), pp. 201–7,
272–91.

[60] For a discussion of Smotrytsky's use of the term "Ruthenian nation" and the multiple
meanings that he attributed to it, see Frick, *Meletij Smotryc'kyj*, pp. 232–34. Cf. Kraliuk,
Osoblyvosti vyiavu, pp. 76–80.

liberties of the Kingdom of Poland. This was given to it as equal to equal and free [nation] to free Polish nation, united and incorporated in joint honor and unity of corporate body: to the princes and nobles, the nobility and knighthood, the clerical and lay estates. At the same time, the people of urban condition of that nation were also immediately given their rights and liberties [in return] for their faithful submission and true benevolence.[61]

In this particular interpretation, then, the Ruthenian nation included all strata of the Rus' community except the peasants.

But it is quite apparent from other polemical works of the period that many Ruthenian nobles were not eager to share the rights of the "Ruthenian noble *narod*" with the burghers or the clergy. The above-mentioned speech by Lavrentii Drevynsky and the text of the *Supplication* contained numerous attacks on the Uniate hierarchy for its lowly social origins, which made it illegitimate in the eyes of the Orthodox nobility. The Uniate nobles, for their part, refused to recognize the legitimacy of the newly consecrated Orthodox hierarchy, as they questioned the noble origins of Metropolitan Iov Boretsky and Archbishop Smotrytsky and denied them the right to speak on behalf of the Ruthenian nation. The authors of the *Letter to the Monks of the Monastery of Vilnius*, signed by representatives of prominent Ruthenian families that supported the Union in the Grand Duchy of Lithuania, posed the question: "And who are Smotrytsky and Boretsky in the Ruthenian nation?" and immediately answered it: "Scum of the nation, degenerates of the rabble – what shadow can they cast on the Ruthenian nation?" This was their hostile reaction to Smotrytsky's earlier appeal for national solidarity across religious lines, to which they would not subscribe on social grounds. They utterly rejected the right of non-noble clergymen to represent the Ruthenian nation to the outside world. The *Letter* went on to assert:

You call us born of the same blood as you and relatives of yours and cause great and unseemly detraction to the glory and provenance of our ancient nobility, which you yourselves later – not without sycophancy – concede to us. What is this "one blood" – our blood and that of the plebeians? What relation to the peasantry? You join yourselves by blood and equate yourselves in lineage with the ancient Ruthenian families, [claiming] that you, out of your lowly descent, are also Rus': that is a stupid claim, not in keeping with monastic modesty.[62]

---

[61] Quoted in Hrushevs'kyi, *Istoriia ukraïns'koï literatury*, VI: 295. For an English translation of part of this statement, see Frick, *Meletij Smotryc'kyj*, p. 233. Cf. the reprint of Smotrytsky's *Justification* in *Collected Works of Meletij Smotryc'kyj*, vol. I (Cambridge, Mass., 1986), p. 513.

[62] Quoted in Hrushevs'kyi, *Istoriia ukraïns'koï literatury*, VI: 254. Cf. Plokhy, *The Cossacks and Religion*, pp. 160–61. On the spread of the Union among the Volhynian nobility, many of whose representatives supported Orthodoxy or the Union by turns, depending on prevailing circumstances, see the revisionist essay by Mykhailo Dovbyshchenko, "Realiï ta mify relihiinoho protystoiannia na Volyni v kintsi XVI – pershii polovyni XVII st.," in *Sotsium* (Kyiv) 2 (2003): 57–82.

The nation of "Ruthenian worship"

The debate over the consecration of the new Orthodox hierarchy by Patriarch Theophanes in 1620 indicated a serious contradiction between the two concepts of nation (*narod*) then current in Ruthenian society. The first concept, restricted to princely and nobiliary Rus', was promoted by Ruthenian nobles on both sides of the religious divide. The other was promoted by the church hierarchy, which insisted on a broad interpretation of the Ruthenian nation encompassing both noble and non-noble strata. That "inclusive" model was promoted by the Orthodox hierarchs not merely because the nobiliary status of the new metropolitan and many of his bishops was questionable – after all, their milieu also included people of unquestionable princely origin, such as Bishop Iosyf (Iezekyil) Kurtsevych – but mainly because it was the dominant model of the time. As Althoen has shown, in the Polish-Lithuanian Commonwealth the term "nation" (*narod*) was associated first and foremost with the concept of ethnolinguistic community. As in Kyivan times, the Rus' literati continued to use the term "language" (*iazyk*) to designate what we would now call "people" or "nation."[63] Moreover, as the Orthodox Church had traditionally been associated with Rus' and the Ruthenian nation in the eyes of adherents and "outsiders" alike, the boundaries of the Rus' religious and ethnonational communities were all but identical until the mid-seventeenth century. Because the ecclesiastical community accommodated people of all walks of life, the concept of the national community became equally inclusive. The close correlation between these two models of identity, religious and national, is clearly apparent in the writings of the Orthodox literati. In 1582, for example, Herasym Smotrytsky addressed the Ostrih Bible to the "Orthodox reader of every degree." Forty years later, Metropolitan Iov Boretsky addressed a circular to "the whole community of the faithful of the Eastern Church of the illustrious Ruthenian nation of every clerical and secular order of every degree." Church documents of the period attest that hierarchs normally divided the secular order into princes, nobles, knights, and burghers.[64] Peasants were excluded from the list of Orthodox "degrees," but the townsfolk were certainly there. Indeed, the burghers were not slow to defend their rights in the name of the Ruthenian nation, regardless of the hierarchy's attitude toward them.[65]

[63] Plokhy, *The Cossacks and Religion*, 147–48.   [64] Ibid., pp. 163–64.

[65] In 1609 the Lviv brotherhood complained in a petition to the king that "we, the Ruthenian nation, are oppressed by the Polish nation with a yoke worse than Egyptian bondage" (quoted in Kraliuk, *Osoblyvosti vyiavu*, p. 50). On the history of the brotherhood movement in Ukraine, see Iaroslav Isaievych, "Between Eastern Tradition and Influences from the West: Confraternities in Early Modern Ukraine and Byelorussia," *Ricerche slavistiche* 37 (1990): 269–93.

Thus it appears that in the early seventeenth century the nobility tried hard, but without ultimate success, to claim the exclusive right to represent the Ruthenian nation to the outside world. This failure was due in large part to the opposition of the clergy and the burghers, who had their own views of the Ruthenian nation and its rights. The religious debate gave them an excellent opportunity to present their opinions, as the church was an institution that transcended social boundaries and the administrative borders of palatinates. Even as the Uniate nobility challenged the right of the Orthodox hierarchs to represent the whole Ruthenian nation, the same hierarchs were bringing their new protectors, the Zaporozhian Cossacks, into the ranks of the Ruthenian nation. Very few of the Cossacks, including their hetmans, could claim noble origin, but the old tradition of including knights in the ranks of the "noble nation/estate" opened the door to anyone prepared to make a case in favor of Cossack membership in the Ruthenian nation. Indeed, their formal qualifications were better than those of the burghers. Their chances of acceptance were further improved by the readiness of the Orthodox clergy to list them as members of the "nation of Ruthenian worship."

For the new Orthodox hierarchy that was consecrated under Cossack auspices in 1620, ensuring Cossack involvement in the religious conflict was almost as important as legitimizing its own existence. That is why the "Cossack theme" received special attention in the petitions, protestations, and literary works issued by Orthodox clerics in the years following the consecration. In the *Protestation* – a petition of the Orthodox hierarchy issued in late April 1621 to condemn the persecution of their church in the Commonwealth – the Cossacks were presented as an integral part of the Ruthenian nation:

As for the Cossacks, we know that these military men are our kin, our brothers, and Christians of the true faith. . . . For this is the tribe of the glorious Ruthenian nation, born of Japheth's seed, that campaigned against the Greek Empire across the Black Sea and overland. It is the host of the generation that under Oleh, the monarch of Rus', traveled in its dugouts over land and sea and stormed Constantinople. It was they who, under Volodymyr, the holy monarch of Rus', campaigned against Greece, Macedonia, and Illyria. It was their ancestors who were baptized together with Volodymyr and accepted the Christian faith from the church of Constantinople and are born and baptized and live their lives in that faith to this day.[66]

The authors of the *Protestation* were concerned to establish first and foremost that the Cossacks were Orthodox Christians devoted to their church

---

[66] See P. N. Zhukovich, "'Protestatsiia' mitropolita Iova Boretskogo i drugikh zapadno-russkikh ierarkhov, sostavlennaia 28 aprelia 1621 goda," in *Stat'i po slavianovedeniiu*, ed. V. I. Lamanskii, vyp. 3 (St. Petersburg, 1910), pp. 135–53. This extract is quoted from Hrushevsky, *History of Ukraine-Rus'*, VII: 305–6.

and thus needed no clerical instigation (the accusation made against the hierarchy by the authorities) to rise in its defense. Given the dominant Ruthenian discourse of the time, proving the Cossacks Orthodox was equivalent to proving them Ruthenian, and vice versa. To achieve both goals, it was necessary to incorporate the Cossacks into the historical grand narrative of the Ruthenian nation – the narrative that began with Oleh, the conqueror of Byzantium, and Volodymyr, the baptizer of Rus'. The new element here was that the "old Rus'" of Volodymyr's successors was represented not by the princes but by the low-born Cossacks. In this new atmosphere, Orthodox intellectuals portrayed the Cossack uprising of 1630 not as a conflict between princely Rus' and brigands of indeterminate origin but as a national and religious struggle between the Poles and the Rus', now represented by the Cossacks.[67]

A year after the appearance of the *Protestation*, Kasiian Sakovych, one of the leading Orthodox intellectuals of the time, repeated the hierarchs' statement on the ancient origins of the Cossacks almost verbatim in his *Sorrowful Obsequy for the Worthy Knight Petro Konashevych-Sahaidachny* (1622). In this elegy to Sahaidachny, the Cossack hetman whose intervention had made possible the consecration of the new hierarchy, Sakovych not only mentioned the Kyivan princes Oleh and Volodymyr but also depicted the Cossacks as a knightly order whose military services entitled it to the reward of "golden liberty." He wrote:

> Golden Liberty – so they call it.
> All strive ardently to attain it.
> Yet it cannot be given to everyone,
> Only to those who defend the fatherland and the lord.
> Knights win it by their valor in wars,
> Not with money but with blood do they purchase it.[68]

The notion of liberty was the supreme value of the Commonwealth nobility, and Sakovych was eager to represent the Cossacks as a group whose martial prowess, history, and values made it as noble as could be. The theme of the Cossacks' knightly status and Orthodox affiliation was evoked again and again in Orthodox writings of the period. In his *Elenchus* (1622), Meletii Smotrytsky called the Cossacks "a people educated in the school of faith and in the school of knightly deeds." He elaborated as follows:

---

[67] The coverage of the uprising of 1630 in the Lviv Chronicle is discussed in my *Cossacks and Religion*, pp. 137–39.

[68] See Kasiian Sakovych, "Virshi na zhalosnyi pohreb zatsnoho rytsera Petra Konashevycha Sahaidachnoho," in *Ukraïns'ka literatura XVII st.*, comp. V. I. Krekoten', ed. O. V. Myshanych (Kyiv, 1987), pp. 220–38, here 221. Cf. Plokhy, *The Cossacks and Religion*, p. 168.

They have fear of the Lord and great constancy in faith, and in military discipline and prudence they will not yield even to the most pious, and in courage they excel Roman Scipios and Carthaginian Hannibals! For the Zaporozhian Cossack [as a fighter] for the renowned Kingdom of Poland against border enemies is like a knight of Malta for the Italian land: he stands in good order and gives brave cavaliers to our fatherland.[69]

The Cossacks themselves sought to acquire economic, judicial, and political privileges that would put them on a par with the nobility, and recognition of those claims by the Orthodox clergy was certainly in their interest. The Cossack leaders also regarded themselves as part of the religiously defined nation of Rus'. Back in 1610, they had issued a protestation against the persecution of Orthodoxy that stated: "Like Their Graces the princes, the lords, the dignitaries, the knightly order, the nobility, and the Christian populace . . . we, too, as sons of the universal apostolic Eastern Church . . . protest."[70] In 1620 they demanded that Patriarch Theophanes "consecrate a metropolitan and bishops for the nation of Rus'."[71] Opponents of the Orthodox hierarchs, such as the nobles who wrote the *Letter to the Monks of the Monastery of Vilnius*, did not question the knightly status of the Cossacks, nor did they directly contest their right to serve as protectors of the Orthodox Church. Nevertheless, their denial of the right of the non-noble hierarchy to speak in the name of Rus' clearly gave the low-born Cossacks no opportunity to be considered part of the "Ruthenian noble nation."

In 1632 the Cossack delegation sent to take part in the Diet convoked to elect a new king was turned away, since participation in the election was considered an exclusive privilege of the nobility. On that occasion, the Commonwealth drew a clear line between the nobility and the "knightly warriors."[72]

The "accommodated nation"

In November 1632, after long deliberation, the new Polish king Władysław IV signed the "Measures for the Accommodation of Citizens of the Kingdom of Poland and the Grand Duchy of Lithuania of the Ruthenian Nation and the Greek Faith." They guaranteed the legal existence of the Orthodox Church in the Commonwealth and granted it property rights, some of them at the expense of the Uniate Church. It was the greatest victory of the Orthodox camp in its struggle against

---

[69] Quoted in Hrushevs'kyi, *Istoriia ukraïns'koï literatury*, VI: 265–66.
[70] Quoted in Plokhy, *The Cossacks and Religion*, p. 109.
[71] See Zhukovich, "'Protestatsiia' mitropolita Iova Boretskogo," p. 146.
[72] See Hrushevsky, *History of Ukraine-Rus'*, VIII: 116–17.

the Union and a major triumph for the "Ruthenian nation of the Greek faith." The Orthodox, who had been very quick to shape debate on the legitimacy of church union in terms of national discourse, claiming that the ancient rights of the Ruthenian nation had been violated, had every reason to celebrate the success of their strategy. Yet the Ruthenian nation that was "accommodated" in 1632 was quite different from the one promoted by the Orthodox literati of the 1620s. Very telling in that regard was the above-mentioned refusal to allow a Cossack delegation to take part in electing the king, as was the fact that the "Measures" were addressed to "citizens" of the Kingdom of Poland and the Grand Duchy of Lithuania – a category that included noble landowners alone, excluding all other strata of Ruthenian society. This new deal with the government marked the climax of decades of struggle by the Orthodox nobility at local and Commonwealth diets. Their victory would have been impossible without the efforts of the outlawed Orthodox hierarchy of the 1620s, as well as the support of the religious brotherhoods and the Cossacks, but in the end the nobles alone secured an understanding with the state.[73]

By appeasing the nobles, the government was trying to obtain the loyalty of the whole Ruthenian Orthodox community (not least the Cossacks) in its imminent confrontation with Orthodox Muscovy – the Smolensk War of 1633–34. Additional benefits were the termination of decades of official conflict with much of the nobility in the eastern provinces of the Commonwealth and the disruption of the alliance between the Orthodox and the Protestants, with whose help the compromise of 1632 had been achieved in the first place. While making concessions to the "Ruthenian nation of the Greek faith," the authorities wanted to ensure that the new rights did not fall into the wrong hands. Very important in that regard was the election at the Diet of a new metropolitan of Kyiv and all Rus' to replace the incumbent metropolitan, who was closely allied with the rebellious Cossacks. Symbolic of the government's new policy was the election of the new hierarch by the Ruthenian Orthodox nobles present at the Diet, as well as his own impeccably noble credentials. The new metropolitan was Petro Mohyla, the archimandrite of the Kyivan Cave Monastery and son of the late hospodar of Moldavia, who enjoyed good connections not only with the Ruthenian princes and nobles but also with the leading aristocratic families of Poland.[74] What could better guarantee the "accommodation" of the Ruthenian nation in

---

[73] On the discussion of the Orthodox question at the Diets of 1632 and the "Measures," see Hrushevsky, *History of Ukraine-Rus'*, VIII: 117–55.

[74] The most informative work on Mohyla's activities is still Stepan Golubev, *Kievskii mitropolit Petr Mogila i ego spodvizhniki (Opyt tserkovno-istoricheskogo issledovaniia)*, 2 vols. (Kyiv, 1883–98).

the eyes of the government than a non-Ruthenian aristocrat as head of its principal institution?

Mohyla and his Ruthenian supporters in the ranks of the Orthodox nobility were eager to take back control of their church from the rebellious Cossacks. In so doing, they were trying not so much to appease the government as to take revenge for years of humiliation at the hands of the Cossacks. Cossack interference in church affairs throughout the 1620s had not only shifted the nobles – the traditional patrons of the church – to the periphery but also brought extreme discomfort to those who benefited most from Cossack involvement in religious affairs – the hierarchs and clergy of the Orthodox Church. The authors of the *Protestation* of 1621 had already noted the Orthodox zeal of the Cossacks and their readiness to ensure that the clergy was adhering to the established rules. Subsequent events showed that the hierarchs had not simply made up this claim to avoid responsibility for Cossack actions. The Cossacks indeed proved themselves a highly intrusive element, prepared to resort to violence not only against external enemies of the church but also against perceived enemies within it. In the late 1620s, Cossack pressure forced the hierarchs to condemn one of their own, Meletii Smotrytsky, for what the Cossacks regarded as a pro-Uniate and anti-Orthodox attitude. As if in realization of a self-fulfilling prophecy, the condemned hierarch soon joined the Uniate Church. Cossack hostility also precluded the convocation of an Orthodox-Uniate council intended to reconcile "Rus′ with Rus′." Mohyla himself was so distressed by Cossack interference that at one point he was observed weeping. Now, armed with the new legitimacy imparted by the official appointment, Mohyla and the nobiliary faction in the church were prepared to take their revenge.[75]

They showed no hesitation. Mohyla's first action on entering Kyiv as the new metropolitan in July 1633 was to arrest his predecessor, the pro-Cossack Metropolitan Isaia Kopynsky. He was kept under arrest in the Kyivan Cave Monastery until a rising star in Ruthenian politics, the Orthodox noble Adam Kysil, resolved the crisis by brokering an agreement with the Cossacks. Kopynsky was released in exchange for a promise not to use his title of metropolitan or interfere with Mohyla's administration. The Cossacks also agreed to recognize the authority of the new metropolitan, whom they had earlier accused of being a Polish puppet. That was the end of close cooperation between Cossackdom and the Orthodox metropolitanate. Responding to the growing confessionalization of religious life, Mohyla managed to strengthen the power of bishops

---

[75] On Cossack interference in the affairs of the Kyiv metropolitanate and the reaction of the Orthodox hierarchy, see Plokhy, *The Cossacks and Religion*, pp. 124–33.

in the church, improve clerical discipline, and reduce the influence of lay elements that he did not welcome. Not surprisingly, they included the Cossacks and the burghers. These changes in the leadership, legal status, political orientation, and social basis of the Orthodox Church profoundly influenced the national discourse that the Kyivan literati were constructing and the model of the Ruthenian nation promoted by that discourse.[76]

A good example of emerging trends in the thinking of Orthodox intellectuals is given by two panegyrics welcoming Mohyla's entrance into Kyiv. Reflecting the cultural orientation of the new church leadership, only one of them was in Ruthenian, while the other was in Polish. Both panegyrics welcomed Mohyla to Kyiv as a new leader of Rus' and a successor to the medieval Kyivan princes, especially Yaroslav the Wise, the builder of St. Sophia's Cathedral, which had been taken away from the Uniates on the eve of Mohyla's arrival. The Ruthenian-language panegyric, presented to the new metropolitan on behalf of the printers of the Kyivan Cave Monastery – Mohyla's stronghold – probably best captured the new characteristics of the national discourse. It began with verses about Mohyla's coat of arms, indicating not only his noble origins but also his descent from a family of rulers. This opening stood in clear contradiction to Sakovych's verses on the demise of Hetman Sahaidachny, which began by describing the coat of arms of the Zaporozhian Host. In the Mohyla panegyric, it was not the Cossacks but the new metropolitan who figured as the successor of the Kyivan princes. The connection between the Moldavian prince and his Kyivan predecessors is articulated by St. Sophia's Cathedral, which speaks to Mohyla as follows:

> Now I entrust my walls to you,
> Which I have from Yaroslav,
> It is praiseworthy: be their Atlas,
> Be their Adamant.[77]

---

[76] Concerning the impact of confessionalization on cultural developments, see Heinz Schilling, "Confessionalisation and the Rise of Religious and Cultural Frontiers in Early Modern Europe," in *Frontiers of Faith: Religious Exchange and the Constitution of Religious Identities, 1400–1750*, ed. E. Andor and I. G. Toth (Budapest, 2001), pp. 21–36. On Mohyla's religious reforms, see Georges Florovsky, *Ways of Russian Theology*, pt. 1 (Belmont, Mass., 1979), pp. 64–85; Ivan Wlasowsky, *Outline History of the Ukrainian Orthodox Church*, vol. II, *XVII Century* (New York, 1979), pp. 74–103; Paul Meyendorff, "The Liturgical Reforms of Peter Mogila: A New Look," *St. Vladimir's Theological Quarterly* 29, no. 2 (1985): 101–14; Francis J. Thomson, "Peter Mogila's Ecclesiastical Reforms and the Ukrainian Contribution to Russian Culture: A Critique of Georges Florovsky's Theory of 'the Pseudomorphosis of Orthodoxy,'" *Slavica Gandensia* 20 (1993): 67–119.

[77] See *Ukraïns' ka poeziia. Seredyna XVII st.*, comp. V. I. Krekoten' and M. M. Sulyma, ed. O. V. Myshanych (Kyiv, 1992), p. 64.

Mohyla's panegyrists exalt him as the new protector not just of the church but also of Rus' in general, which he has been summoned to save from its current misery. The personified Cathedral of St. Sophia addresses the new metropolitan in the following words:

> O Petro, long-desired guest
> Given to Rus' (*Rossiia*) for consolation, welcome!
> Give shelter to the ornament of Rus'
>   In a miserable age.
> Do you recall how famous Rus' was before,
> How many patrons it had?
> Now there are few of them; Rus' wants to have you
>   In the Sarmatian world.[78]

Thus, in the eyes of the Orthodox literati, Rus' (and, one might assume, the Ruthenian nation) had acquired a new leader descended from a noble family of rulers, associated with the Kyivan foundation myth and prepared to serve as its new protector. But what was the threat from which he was to protect Rus'? Prince Ostrozky had warded off the church union and the Cossacks had stood firm against the Catholic state. It would seem that Mohyla was now called upon to save the "accommodated" nation from educational and cultural decline vis-à-vis Catholic Poland and Uniate Rus'. The author of the Polish-language panegyric spelled out the task:

> So that, having power from God and the church,
> He wiped away the apostates' soot from Rus',
> Which, unfortunate one, had become very sooty
> When it grew poor in educated men.[79]

Lack of education and the resulting inferiority complex had dogged the Orthodox since the earliest debates on the Union of Brest. The Uniates promised to raise the educational level of their clergy and did so by sending students to papal academies in the West, while the Orthodox remained on the defensive. Some of them, like Vyshensky, took pride in the Ruthenian lack of sophistication. Others, like Sakovych, abandoned Orthodoxy for Uniatism and then Uniatism for Roman Catholicism in their efforts to shed the image of "foolish Rus'."[80] The author of the *Warning*, an early seventeenth-century Orthodox tract, went so far as to

---

[78] Ibid.
[79] See Anonim, "Mnemosyne sławy, prac i trudów," in *Roksolański Parnas. Polskojęzyczna poezja ukraińska od końca XVI do początku XVIII wieku*, pt. 2, *Antologia*, ed. Rostysław Radyszewśkyj [Rostyslav Radyshevs'kyi] (Cracow, 1998), 2: 123–34, here 126.
[80] On Sakovych, see David Frick, "'Foolish Rus'': On Polish Civilization, Ruthenian Self-Hatred, and Kasijan Sakovyč," *Harvard Ukrainian Studies* 18, nos. 3–4 (December 1994): 210–48.

blame the decline of the Kyivan state on the lack of schools and education.[81] The only nation to which the Ruthenians could claim cultural superiority were the Lithuanians, but even in that instance, the Ruthenian claims were limited to the distant past, when the Orthodox Rus′ had introduced the pagan Lithuanian princes to Christianity.[82]

Mohyla was very serious about improving the educational level of his church: his reform of the brotherhood school turned it into a college and made it the outstanding educational institution in the whole Orthodox world. He also sponsored the publishing of religious literature and helped produce the very first *Confession of the Orthodox Faith*. Mohyla assembled a staff of first-rate Orthodox scholars and not only stopped the defection of Orthodox literati to the Uniates but also made Ruthenian Orthodoxy an intellectually attractive confession. The text of Mohyla's will shows that his dedication to raising the educational level of Rus′ was rooted in a conscious choice made very early in his ecclesiastical career. He wrote:

on seeing the decline of pious religiosity in the Rus′ nation for no other reason than its complete lack of education and learning, I took an oath before the Lord my God that I would dedicate all the resources left to me by my parents and apply whatever might remain after due service to the holy places entrusted to me, and income from appropriate estates, partly to restoring ruined houses of God, of which there remain lamentable ruins, and partly to establishing schools in Kyiv [and maintaining] the rights and liberties of the Ruthenian nation, permitted and privileged by the particular favor of His Royal Majesty, our gracious Lord.[83]

Was Mohyla a Ruthenian nation-builder? His raising of educational standards among the Orthodox clergy and in society at large, his transformation of Ruthenian Orthodoxy into an institution capable of meeting the challenges of Protestantism and reformed Catholicism, and his restoration of princely churches in Kyiv certainly make him a suspect in that regard and at least partly justify the assumptions of some modern Ukrainian scholars who represent him not only as a Ukrainian patriot but also as a Ukrainian state-builder.[84] But a more careful examination of his own writings and reforms shows him to have been primarily a devoted Orthodox Christian. In the Commonwealth context that clearly made him a Ruthenian, but, unlike other zealots of Ruthenian Orthodoxy, he was a man acquainted with many cultural worlds. In political terms, he

---

[81] See "Perestoroha," in *Ukraïns′ka literatura XVII st.*, pp. 26–27.

[82] On such claims of Ruthenian superiority, see Igor′ Marzaliuk, "Velikoe kniazhestvo Litovskoe v istoricheskoi pamiati belorusov-rusinov: ot srednevekov′ia k modernu," *Ab Imperio*, 2004, no. 4: 539–60.

[83] See "Zapovit mytropolyta Petra Mohyly," in Arkadii Zhukovs′kyi, *Petro Mohyla i pytannia iednosti tserkov* (Kyiv, 1997), pp. 291–98, here 291.

[84] See Valeriia Nichyk, *Petro Mohyla v dukhovnii istoriï Ukraïny* (Kyiv, 1997), pp. 119–29.

was a patriot of the Polish-Lithuanian Commonwealth and felt much more at home in the Polish cultural setting than in the Ruthenian one. His will was written in Polish, his Ruthenian (not unlike that of other Kyivan authors of the period) was full of Polonisms, and the Orthodox publications of the Kyivan Cave Monastery press were issued mainly in Polish.[85] Mohyla's reform of the Kyivan College and of his metropolitanate followed a program of confessionalization of religious and secular life based on Polish Roman Catholic models. Mohyla made the church and nation he served more competitive, but in the process he also brought them dangerously close to the dominant Polish culture and church.

Understanding Ruthenian identity

In early modern Ukraine and Belarus, the creation of new identities was driven by changes in dominant loyalties. With the advance of confessionalization, loyalty to rulers and lands was marginalized by loyalty to a given religion. Religious debates concerning the Union of Brest thus helped shape the main characteristics of Ruthenian identity. What were those characteristics?

It is quite obvious that the conclusion and implementation of the Union of Brest awakened the broad strata of the Rus' elites – from the princely stratum and the church hierarchy all the way down to village priests, burghers, and Cossacks – from intellectual slumber and forced them to take sides in the religious debate. The unprecedented number of new participants in the debate was a result of rising educational levels in society at large and the appearance of print as an everyday phenomenon in Polish-Lithuanian Rus'. One outcome of this awakening was the creation of a nation-based discourse that postulated the interests of the "Ruthenian nation" as the supreme communal value. The geographical boundaries of the Ruthenian nation constructed by the ongoing ecclesiastical polemics coincided with the boundaries of Rus' settlement in the Polish-Lithuanian Commonwealth and the canonical jurisdiction of the Kyiv metropolitanate. In short, the elites of significant parts of Ukraine and Belarus came under a new structure – an umbrella of early modern national identity – that superseded previously dominant local loyalties circumscribed by the boundaries of towns, palatinates, and the internal border between the Kingdom of Poland and the Grand Duchy of Lithuania.

---

[85] On Mohyla's cultural preferences and policies, see Ihor Ševčenko, "The Many Worlds of Peter Mohyla," in idem, *Ukraine between East and West*, pp. 164–86.

The geographical boundaries in which the public discourse of the period imagined the Ruthenian nation were not set in stone: various types of discourse proposed different boundaries and formulas for the amalgamation of local identities. One such discourse, advanced by the Ruthenian nobility in the 1640s, presented the palatinates of Volhynia, Kyiv, Bratslav, and Chernihiv (to the exclusion of Galicia, Podilia, and the Ruthenian territories of the Grand Duchy of Lithuania) as a unit that should enjoy the same rights and privileges.[86] Another discourse employed by the panegyrists of the Ruthenian princes defined their homeland as a combination of the above-mentioned palatinates with Galicia, thereby restoring the memory of the Galician-Volhynian principality and laying a foundation for the future Ukrainian identity.[87] It appears, however, that the solidarity of the Ruthenian elite in the Commonwealth promoted by the religious polemics of the day was much stronger than solidarity based on historical or legal grounds.

The political upheaval created by the church union consolidated elites irrespective of territorial location, political loyalty, and cultural preferences, forcing them to play on one Ruthenian field. It also linked Lviv, Ostrih, Vilnius, and Kyiv as major centers of a common cultural space. The same process encompassed a variety of social strata active in ecclesiastical politics and polemics throughout the Rus' territories of the Polish-Lithuanian Commonwealth. The princes of Volhynia and Belarus, church hierarchs, clergy and monks of the whole Kyiv metropolitanate, the Ruthenian nobility of the Kingdom of Poland and the Grand Duchy of Lithuania, the burghers of Lviv and Vilnius and, finally, the Cossacks of the Dnipro region all participated in one great debate that ultimately gave them a sense of common belonging and identity. That socially inclusive character of the religious discourse helped promote a model of early modern identity based on the nation as a linguistic and cultural entity. The nobility's efforts to monopolize the right to speak in the name of the Ruthenian nation were only partly successful. The close association of religious and ethnonational identity made it impossible for the nobility to monopolize the national idea in the Rus' territories of the Commonwealth. The religious debate, however, had the potential not only to consolidate the differerent strata of Ruthenian society but also to promote a major split within it if clear social or geographical cleavages began to emerge. In the age of confessionalization, a religious schism could lead

---

[86] See Frank E. Sysyn, "Regionalism and Political Thought in Seventeenth-Century Ukraine: The Nobility's Grievances at the Diet of 1641," *Harvard Ukrainian Studies* 6, no. 2 (1982): 171–85.

[87] See Iakovenko, "Topos 'z'iednanykh narodiv,'" pp. 249–51.

to a national one as well. Smotrytsky's idea of uniting "Rus' with Rus'" through the creation of a Ruthenian patriarchate, which was later supported by Mohyla, did not materialize in the first half of the seventeenth century and left open the possibility of creating two Ruthenian nations, Orthodox and Uniate.

How did the Ruthenian nation of the period position itself against its major "others"? It might be argued that the early modern Ruthenian nation and identity were formed mainly in opposition to Poland, while borrowing from it concepts, methods, and tropes of self-expression and self-assertion. The linguistic and cultural differences between the two early modern nations were underlined by the religious divide, which was deepened by the events of the Reformation and the struggle over church union. The Union of Brest was supposed to close that gap, but those who supported it soon found themselves in the minority, while most of the Ruthenian elites (especially in the Ukrainian lands) joined forces in defense of the violated rights of the "Ruthenian nation of the Greek faith." In general, the religious crisis served to estrange the Catholic Poles and Lithuanians from the Orthodox Ruthenians. To be sure, the membership of the Ruthenian nobility in the ruling class of the Polish-Lithuanian Commonwealth did not allow that trend to go too far. The sense of belonging to a larger entity was manifested, *inter alia*, by the Ruthenian nobility's devotion to the fatherland – a term that polemicists of the late sixteenth and early seventeenth centuries (including Orthodox writers) used exclusively with reference to the Kingdom of Poland, the Grand Duchy of Lithuania, or the whole Commonwealth, not to the individual palatinate or region, as Orzechowski had done half a century earlier. The religious discourse of the early seventeenth century included (and to some degree reconciled) such paramount values as the good of the fatherland (Polish, Lithuanian, or Commonwealth) and the good of the Ruthenian nation. What this tells us is that Ruthenian identity was not exclusive. It often coexisted peacefully with the concept of loyalty to the king and the state. Even so, it is crucial to note that loyalty to the Ruthenian nation, which consisted of various estates, not to the nobiliary political nation of the Commonwealth, prevailed in Ukrainian and Belarusian discourse of the period.

Ruthenian identity appeared on the east European scene at a time when the elites of Muscovite Rus' already possessed a strong and distinct identity of their own. Both identities used the same Rus' linguistic nomenclature to define themselves. In one way or another, both drew on the intellectual, political, and cultural heritage of Kyivan times. Both were closely linked to the Orthodox religious tradition and church structure. Finally, both identities were often weaker than the loyalty of the secular elites to their local homelands and family clans.[88] At the same time, these two identities were very different in origin and structure. For example, state boundaries often performed different functions in shaping the Muscovite and Polish-Lithuanian Rus′ identities. If Muscovite Rus′ imagined itself first and foremost within the borders of the Muscovite state, tending to ignore cultural differences within the tsar's realm, the identity of Polish-Lithuanian Rus′ was formed not only by the eastern border of the Commonwealth but also by the linguistic, cultural, and religious boundary between Ruthenians on the one hand and Poles and Lithuanians on the other. If Muscovite Rus′ identity had at its core the idea of loyalty to the ruling tsar and dynasty, the Ruthenian one, for obvious reasons, could not rely too much on its own Rurikid tradition. Besides, for all noble citizens of the Commonwealth, including Ruthenians, the concept of loyalty to the state-defined *patria* overshadowed the notion of loyalty to the king. The leitmotif of the public debate that shaped the Ruthenian identity was not loyalty to the ruler (as in Muscovy) but the rights of individual institutions, estates, and nations. In the latter context, the Eastern Christian Church – a common building block of identity in Muscovy and Polish-Lithuanian Rus′ – was treated not as the only true religious confession but as one of many that had the right to exist in the Commonwealth. Finally, the discourses that formed the Muscovite and Ruthenian identities differed profoundly in origin: the first was produced at the courts of the tsar and the metropolitan, while the second was shaped by a broad spectrum of secular and religious elites that gained access to the printing press in the last decades of the sixteenth century. These differences of discourse had political, social, and cultural consequences that would become fully apparent in the course of the seventeenth century.

[88] In that sense, the situation in Ukraine and Belarus was not unlike the one prevailing around the same time in Poland and Lithuania (as shown by Althoen) and in Muscovy (as demonstrated by Keenan and Kollmann). On the importance of local identities and clan loyalties among Ukrainian nobles of the seventeenth century, see Natalia Yakovenko's forthcoming paper on the multiple identities of the Ukrainian nobleman Yoakhym Yerlych, initially presented at an international conference on "Ukraine in the Seventeenth Century" (Kyiv, November 2003).

6   Was there a reunification?

Few events of early modern East Slavic history have attracted as much attention or caused such public controversy as the Pereiaslav Agreement of January 1654 between Hetman Bohdan Khmelnytsky of Ukraine and the Muscovite boyars. When the Ukrainian president Leonid Kuchma, apparently trying to please his Russian counterpart Vladimir Putin, signed a decree in March 2002 to commemorate the 350th anniversary of the Pereiaslav Council, which had approved the deal from the Ukrainian side, his opponents immediately accused him of kowtowing to Russia. The decree provoked heated debates in scholarly circles and in the media. In January 2004 the Ukrainian authorities had to scale down the commemoration of the event, to the apparent displeasure of the Russian delegation, headed by President Vladimir Putin, which came to Kyiv to celebrate the "Year of Russia in Ukraine."[1]

What was it about the Pereiaslav Agreement that infuriated so many of Ukraine's academics and politicians, while eliciting such approval from the Russian political and academic elite? At the core of the disagreement is not so much the event itself or the hard facts of its history as its interpretation, especially in the nineteenth-century Russian Empire and its successor state, the USSR. It is no accident that President Kuchma's critics accused him of reviving the Soviet tradition of celebrating the "reunification of Ukraine with Russia" – the official formula that defined

---

[1] On the political ramifications of Kuchma's decree, see Taras Kuzio, "Ukraine's 'Pereiaslav Complex' and Relations with Russia," *Ukrainian Weekly* 50, no. 26 (26 May 2002). For the attitude of the Russian media to the slighting of the Pereiaslav anniversary in Kyiv in January 2004, see the BBC monitoring service transcript of Russian TV news for 23 January 2004. The presenter on Ren TV news in Moscow announced that in the course of his visit to Kyiv Vladimir Putin was planning to take part in celebrations of the anniversary of the Pereiaslav Council, "a symbol of Russo-Ukrainian unity." But a Ren TV correspondent reported from Kyiv that "nothing in the streets of Kiev reminds one either of the 350th anniversary of the Pereiaslav Council, which is described by historians as a moment of union of the two countries, or about the Year of Russia in Ukraine, or about the Russian president's forthcoming visit. Near the monument to Bohdan Khmelnytsky an old man approached us to ask when picketing in protest against Putin's visit would start."

the purpose of the Pereiaslav Agreement in Soviet historiography after World War II. There were two commemorations of the event in the Soviet period. The first, in 1954, was a large-scale event held with great fanfare and accompanied by transfer of sovereignty over the Crimean penin-sula from Russia to Ukraine. The Central Committee of the Communist Party of the Soviet Union approved a collection of "Theses on the Three Hundredth Anniversary of the Reunification of Ukraine with Russia" that shaped the interpretation of Russo-Ukrainian relations until the end of Soviet rule. In 1979, when the 325th anniversary of the Pereiaslav Coun-cil rolled around, the Central Committee of the Communist Party of Ukraine issued a resolution outlining the commemoration program and restating the interpretation established in 1954.[2]

The "reunification" paradigm was the first fixture of Soviet historiogra-phy to be scrapped by professional historians in Ukraine once they began the revision of their communist-era heritage in the late 1980s. Although the presidential decree of 2002 did not use the term "reunification," the very idea of marking the anniversary of an event so deeply colored by the significance it had acquired in Soviet nationality policy could not help but create an uproar in Ukraine. Still, current politics aside, was there indeed a reunification in Pereiaslav? And if there was, who reunited with whom and on what conditions? These are the questions I shall address, approaching them through a study of the construction and evolution of East Slavic ethnonational identities in the first half of the seventeenth century.

From conflict to alliance

The period under consideration witnessed a sequence of events that brought Muscovites and Ruthenians into closer contact than ever before. The conditions for the first encounter between these two groups of Eastern Slavs, by that time quite distinct, were established by the Time of Troubles, a major political, social, and economic crisis that erupted in Muscovy at the turn of the seventeenth century, producing two decades of civil strife and foreign intervention. Nothing seemed to presage such a turn of events in 1589, when the Muscovite author-ities successfully applied pressure to the Eastern patriarchs to elevate the Moscow metropolitanate to the status of a patriarchate. For the first time,

---

[2] On the treatment of the Pereiaslav Agreement in Soviet historiography in connection with the 1954 celebrations of the "reunification of Ukraine with Russia," see John Basarab, *Pereiaslav 1654: A Historiographical Study* (Edmonton, 1982), pp. 179–87, and the intro-duction to the book by Ivan L. Rudnytsky, "Pereiaslav: History and Myth," pp. xi–xxiii. For an English translation of the "Theses," see ibid., pp. 270–87.

references to Moscow as the Third Rome entered official Muscovite discourse. The establishment of the patriarchate also ended the split in the Orthodox world that had begun with the Union of Florence in the mid-fifteenth century. Muscovy was back in the fold of Orthodox nations, and the Muscovite tsardom seemed to be attaining the peak of its power.[3]

The first clear sign of the impending troubles came in 1598, when Fedor Ioannovich, the last tsar of the Rurikid dynasty, died without an heir. But the situation appeared manageable: the Assembly of the Land elected a new tsar, Boris Godunov. The fix turned out to be temporary. In the early 1600s, when the Muscovite economy and society were destabilized by successive years of bad harvest, mass famine, and popular revolts, Godunov died unexpectedly (April 1605), just as an army gathered in Ukraine by Grigorii Otrepev, a former Muscovite monk posing as Dmitrii, the son of Tsar Ivan the Terrible, augmented its ranks with local recruits and crossed the Muscovite border, heading for Moscow. Accompanied by Polish and Ruthenian advisers and troops, the False Dmitrii soon entered Moscow and was installed as the new tsar. To the surprise of many Muscovites, he was not terribly interested in Orthodox church services and surrounded himself with Catholic and Protestant advisers. He also married a Polish Catholic woman. The False Dmitrii's unorthodox behavior prompted a group of Moscow boyars to stage a coup that did away with him and installed their own leader, Vasilii Shuisky, as tsar. Almost immediately Shuisky was challenged by a mass uprising under the leadership of Ivan Bolotnikov, whose power base was in the Chernihiv area. In 1608 the Ruthenian lands of the Commonwealth produced another pretender, the so-called Second False Dmitrii, whose armies, largely composed of Ukrainian Cossacks, moved deep into Muscovite territory.

The Commonwealth invaded Muscovy with its regular army in 1609, and Shuisky was toppled by another internal coup in the following year. What ensued was the rule of seven Moscow boyars, who offered the throne to Royal Prince Władysław of Poland on condition that he convert to Orthodoxy. By that time Commonwealth troops had occupied Moscow, and the installation of the Polish royal prince on the Muscovite throne seemed all but a foregone conclusion. At this juncture, however, King Sigismund III of Poland demanded the throne for himself, with no promise of accepting the Orthodox faith. The Muscovite elites could imagine a foreigner as their ruler but had trouble with the idea of sharing a

[3] On the debate concerning the causes of the Time of Troubles, see Chester Dunning, "Crisis, Conjuncture, and the Causes of the Time of Troubles," *Harvard Ukrainian Studies* 19 (1995): 97–119.

non-Orthodox monarch with another country. Under the circumstances, Patriarch Hermogen of Moscow emerged as the leading opponent of the Polish king and the most vocal agitator against the foreign occupation. His appeals helped create a coalition of forces headed by the provincial leaders Kuzma Minin and Prince Dmitrii Pozharsky, who managed to recapture Moscow from Commonwealth troops in the autumn of 1612. In the following year, the Assembly of the Land elected as the new Muscovite tsar the adolescent Mikhail Romanov, whose father, Metropolitan Filaret Romanov – a former supporter of both False Dmitriis and Royal Prince Władysław – was then in Polish captivity. With the dynastic crisis overcome and the new tsar installed, the slow rebuilding of the Muscovite state, society, and identity began.[4]

Apart from everything else, the Time of Troubles turned out to be a unique opportunity for representatives of two parts of Rus', the Polish-Lithuanian and the Muscovite, to meet each other en masse – certainly not under the best of circumstances, but for the first time in many decades, if not centuries. Ukrainian Cossacks, often accompanied by their families, crossed the Muscovite border in the ranks of the pretenders' armies, while noblemen made their way there under the leadership of Sigismund III of Poland. There were as many as twenty thousand Ukrainian Cossacks in the army of the First False Dmitrii, and up to thirteen thousand in the forces of the second. They entered the heartland of Muscovy, going as far north as Beloozero. The encounter of the two Ruses entailed not only killing and robbery but also the establishment of new families. Some Cossacks stayed in the Muscovite service after the end of the campaigns, creating problems for the authorities with regard to their social and religious assimilation. Such encounters continued during the Commonwealth campaign of 1618 and the Smolensk War of 1632–34. The incorporation into the Commonwealth of the Smolensk and Chernihiv lands, which had been part of the Muscovite state for most of the sixteenth century, gave rise to new situations and allowed both sides to draw comparisons.[5]

---

[4] For the most recent survey of the Time of Troubles, see Chester Dunning, *A Short History of Russia's First Civil War: The Time of Troubles and the Founding of the Romanov Dynasty* (University Park, Pa., 2004). On Grigorii Otrepev and other pretenders to the Russian throne during the Time of Troubles, see Maureen Perrie, *Pretenders and Popular Monarchism in Early Modern Russia: The False Tsars of the Time of Troubles* (Cambridge, 1995). For a treatment of pretenders to kingship as a cultural phenomenon, see Boris Uspenskii, "Tsar' i samozvanets: samozvanchestvo v Rossii kak kul'turno-istoricheskii fenomen," in idem, *Izbrannye trudy*, vol. I, *Semiotika istorii. Semiotika kul'tury* (Moscow, 1994), pp. 75–109.

[5] On Ukrainian Cossack involvement in the Time of Troubles, see Tatiana Oparina, "Ukrainskie kazaki v Rossii: edinovertsy ili inovertsy? (Mikita Markushevskii protiv Leontiia Pleshcheeva)," *Sotsium* (Kyiv) 3 (2003): 21–44.

The mid-century uprising in Ukraine led by Bohdan Khmelnytsky resulted in a major new encounter between Muscovites and Ruthenians. Like many other Cossack uprisings of the period, the one of 1648 began with a rebellion at the Zaporozhian Sich. Its distinguishing feature was that from the very beginning Khmelnytsky was able to obtain support from the Cossacks' traditional enemies, the Crimean Tatars. The combined Cossack-Tatar army proved invincible in fighting the Commonwealth troops. In May 1648, the Polish army suffered two crushing defeats, leaving the entire Dnipro region in the hands of the Cossacks, rebel peasants, and burghers. The jacquerie that began in the summer counted among its victims thousands of Poles, Jews, and Ruthenian nobles, all of whom were associated in the eyes of the rebels with the Commonwealth's oppressive rule in the region. The Kingdom of Poland was left without a standing army, and a levy en masse raised in the autumn of 1648 was soon defeated. The Cossacks, accompanied by the Tatars (who did not distinguish between Ruthenians and non-Ruthenians when it came to robbery and ransom), reached Lviv and Zamość, creating panic as far west as Warsaw. The Diet convened to elect a new king after the unexpected death of Władysław IV in May 1648 chose a candidate favored by Khmelnytsky – the brother of the deceased, John Casimir. The Cossacks retreated, at least temporarily.

Hostilities resumed in the summer of 1649. The Cossack Host, reinforced by tens of thousands of rebellious peasants, besieged the Commonwealth corps in the town of Zbarazh in Volhynia. Troops under Khmelnytsky's command also attacked the main Commonwealth army, led by the new king himself, at the nearby town of Zboriv, forcing the king's army onto the defensive. A new victory of Cossack arms seemed imminent, but the Crimean khan, who benefited from continuing military conflict in the Commonwealth and wanted neither side to gain a decisive advantage, opted for a truce with the king. The subsequent negotiations resulted in compromise. The Zboriv Agreement recognized the existence of the new Cossack state (known in historiography as the Hetmanate) but limited the territory under Cossack control and reduced the size of its army to forty thousand (at Zboriv, contemporary reports gave estimates as high as three hundred thousand). The Commonwealth, for its part, was also unhappy with the deal forced on the king by unfavorable circumstances.

The resumption of open warfare was thus only a matter of time. The next major battle took place in the summer of 1651 at the village of Berestechko in Volhynia. Again the Cossacks and their Tatar allies had a good chance of victory, and again the khan decided the issue, this time by fleeing the battlefield. Abandoned to the mercy of the Commonwealth army, the Cossacks suffered a major defeat. Khmelnytsky managed to recover by autumn, mustering a new army that confronted Crown and Lithuanian troops near the town of Bila Tserkva in Dnipro Ukraine. The agreement signed there significantly reduced the territory of the Hetmanate and the Cossack register, but the Cossack polity survived. In 1652 Khmelnytsky struck again, defeating Commonwealth forces at the village of Batih in Podilia. The next year witnessed an indecisive battle between the Cossack Host, again allied with the Crimean Tatars, and the Commonwealth army at the village of Zhvanets.[6]

By the autumn of 1653, Khmelnytsky and his officers realized that they needed another strong ally. While the Tatars had been essential to the Cossacks' initial victories, they had also proved themselves unreliable. Moreover, the price paid by the Hetmanate for that alliance was counted in tens of thousands of Ukrainian captives taken to the Crimea as slaves. Khmelnytsky had to take the anti-Tatar sentiments of his people into account once they began to flee Ukraine, cross the border with Muscovy and settle there in the territories that became known as Sloboda Ukraine. Khmelnytsky's formal acceptance of Ottoman suzerainty, on which he resolved in the difficult year of 1651, brought no military aid from Istanbul. Under the circumstances, Khmelnytsky intensified his negotiations with the tsar, pressing the Muscovite authorities to enter the war with the Commonwealth. Negotiations between Muscovy and the Cossack hetman led to the conclusion of the Pereiaslav Agreement in January 1654 and the establishment of a Muscovite protectorate over the Hetmanate – developments that became known in imperial Russian and Soviet historiography as "reunification."[7]

The reunification paradigm

The origins of the reunification paradigm, which dominated the Soviet historiography of Russo-Ukrainian relations for decades, can be traced back at least to the end of the eighteenth century. After the second partition of Poland in 1793, Empress Catherine II struck a medal welcoming Polish and Lithuanian Rus' into the empire. The inscription read: "I have recovered what was torn away."[8] The same statist approach

---

[6] Like the Time of Troubles, the Khmelnytsky Uprising has given rise to an enormous literature. For a detailed analysis of the first years of the revolt and references to the most recent work on the subject, see the translation of Mykhailo Hrushevsky's *History of Ukraine-Rus'*, ed. Frank E. Sysyn et al., vols. VIII and IX, bk. 1 (Edmonton and Toronto, 2002–5).

[7] On the Pereiaslav negotiations, see the comprehensive body of research assembled in *Pereiaslavs'ka rada 1654 roku. Istoriohrafiia ta doslidzhennia*, ed. Pavlo Sokhan' et al. (Kyiv, 2003).

[8] See Orest Subtelny, *Ukraine: A History* (Toronto, Buffalo, and London, 1988), p. 203.

to the problem of "reunification" was reflected in the writings of the nineteenth-century Russian historian Mikhail Pogodin, a leader of the pan-Slav movement. He claimed that the leitmotif of Russian history was the reclamation of those parts of the Russian land that had been lost to western neighbors since the times of Yaroslav the Wise. The first scholar to fully merge the statist and nation-based elements of the reunification paradigm in his historical survey of Russia was Nikolai Ustrialov, who maintained that all Eastern Slavs constituted one Russian nation and that the various parts of Rus' professed a "desire for union." Ustrialov's ideas, first articulated in the 1830s, shaped the interpretation of Russia's relations with its East Slavic neighbors for generations of Russian historians. At the turn of the twentieth century, a modified version of the Ustrialov thesis made up the core of Vasilii Kliuchevsky's argument on the nature of all-Russian history.[9] Even some Ukrainian historians, such as Panteleimon Kulish, the author of the *History of the Reunification of Rus'*, bought into the idea. The same is true of nineteenth-century Russophile historiography in Galicia, but most Ukrainian historians, led by Mykhailo Hrushevsky, rejected the reunification paradigm. They regarded Ukraine as a separate nation whose origins reached back to Kyivan Rus': it had not been torn away from any other nation and thus had no need to be reunited with its other parts.[10]

Early Soviet historians concurred with Hrushevsky in regarding Russia, Ukraine, and Belarus as separate nations and kept their historical narratives apart in every period except that of Kyivan Rus' and the 1917 revolution. But in the 1930s, that view was revised and elements of the old imperial approach reintroduced into the interpretation of the Pereiaslav Agreement. The view of the agreement as a product of Russian imperial policy was abandoned in favor of the "lesser evil" formula, whereby Muscovy's annexation of Cossack Ukraine was considered a better alternative than its subordination to the Ottomans or to the Kingdom of Poland. After World War II, when class-based discourse declined and the Russocentric nation-based approach reemerged in Soviet historical works, the concept of "annexation" was dropped altogether and that of "reunification" reintroduced into historical discourse. A new formula was invented to describe the Pereiaslav Agreement, which was now to be called

[9] On the interpretation of Russo-Ukrainian relations in Russian imperial historiography, see Stephen Velychenko, *National History as Cultural Process: A Survey of the Interpretations of Ukraine's Past in Polish, Russian, and Ukrainian Historical Writing from the Earliest Times to 1914* (Edmonton, 1992), pp. 79–140.

[10] On Hrushevsky's "deconstruction" of the Russian imperial narrative, see my *Unmaking Imperial Russia: Mykhailo Hrushevsky and the Writing of Ukrainian History* (Toronto, Buffalo, and London, 2005).

the "reunification of Ukraine and Russia."[11] This new/old paradigm took into account the Soviet treatment of Ukrainian history as a distinct subject and accepted the view that by the mid-seventeenth century there were two separate East Slavic nationalities. But the attempt to merge pre-1917 and post-revolutionary historiographic concepts produced a contradiction. How could Ukraine reunite with Russia when, according to the official line, there had been no Russians, Ukrainians, or Belarusians in Kyivan Rus'?

Soviet historians were discouraged from asking questions of that kind. Nevertheless, the liberal thaw of the 1960s created an atmosphere in which a semi-official challenge to the reunification paradigm became possible. It came in the form of an essay, "Annexation or Reunification," written in 1966 by the Ukrainian historian Mykhailo Braichevsky. Intending to publish his essay in a Soviet scholarly journal, Braichevsky proceeded to delegitimize the reunification paradigm by invoking the class-based Marxist discourse of the 1920s. He also pointed out the contradiction between the Russocentric paradigm and Communist Party declarations on the equality of Soviet nations. Colleagues in the Ukrainian Academy of Sciences initially were very supportive of Braichevsky's argument, and one of them even advised him to look at work done by the Belarusian historian L. S. Abetsedarski, who also questioned the legitimacy of the reunification concept, though in a much more subdued manner. Braichevsky's essay was never published in the USSR, where it circulated only in *samizdat*. It appeared in the West in 1972. The author was dismissed from the Institute of History of the Ukrainian Academy of Sciences in 1968. He worked at the Institute of Archaeology for two years (1970–72) but was also hounded from that position and prevented from taking another for the next six years. Meanwhile, in the summer of 1974 the Institute of History of the Ukrainian Academy of Sciences organized a discussion of the essay behind closed doors. Needless to say, Braichevsky's colleagues, including those who had supported him at the beginning, now solemnly condemned his work.[12]

Scholarly discussion of the meaning and historical importance of the Pereiaslav Agreement resumed only in the late 1980s, following the advent of glasnost. Ukrainian historians overwhelmingly rejected the reunification paradigm, replacing the imperial- and Soviet-era "reunification" with the terms "Ukrainian revolution" and "national-liberation

[11] On the interpretation of Russo-Ukrainian relations in Soviet historiography of the 1940s and 1950s, see Serhy Yekelchyk, *Stalin's Empire of Memory: Russian-Ukrainian Relations in the Soviet Historical Imagination* (Toronto, 2004).

[12] See the text of Braichevsky's essay, the minutes of the closed discussion of 1974, and Braichevsky's response to his critics in *Pereiaslavs'ka rada 1654 roku*, pp. 294–430.

war" to denote the Khmelnytsky Uprising and its aftermath. Both terms stressed the national characteristics of the uprising. No less decisive in rejecting the term and the concept symbolized by it were Belarusian specialists in the early modern history of eastern Europe.[13] Their Russian colleagues remained much more loyal to the old imperial and Soviet interpretations of the Pereiaslav Agreement. The authors of a book on early modern Russian foreign policy published in 1999 continued to argue that Russia became involved in the Polish-Ukrainian conflict in 1654 because of its desire to unite three fraternal peoples.[14] Lev Zaborovsky, one of the best Russian specialists on diplomatic history of the period, supported the continued use of the reunification terminology by arguing that the desire of the Ukrainian population for union with Muscovy was apparent from the historical sources of the period. Yet Zaborovsky had no objection to calling the Khmelnytsky Uprising a "war of national liberation" as long as it was considered to have been anti-Polish.[15] Also not prepared to discard the term "reunification" is Boris Floria, who claims that it reflected the interpretation of the Pereiaslav Agreement by the Muscovite authorities.[16] The reunification terminology seems to have made a comeback in Russian historiography. Is it indeed too early to bid farewell to this old, "proven" term and approach? Let us keep this question in mind as we take a closer look at Muscovite-Ruthenian relations in the first half of the seventeenth century.

The loss of the dynasty

In his review of Sergei Platonov's work on Muscovite tales about the Time of Troubles (1890), Vasilii Kliuchevsky noted that Platonov, preoccupied with the textual analysis of the tales, had entirely ignored the political ideas reflected in them. According to Kliuchevsky, who, for his part, was preoccupied with constitutionalism as a substitute for the monarchical rule of the last Romanovs, the tales were full of such ideas: more specifically, they asserted the primacy of subjects over the dynasty and advocated the principles of constitutional rule in early modern Russia.[17] Platonov,

---

[13] See, for example, Henadz′ Sahanovich, *Neviadomaia vaina, 1654–67* (Minsk, 1995).

[14] See *Istoriia vneshnei politiki Rossii. Konets XV–XVII vv.*, ed. G. A. Sanin et al. (Moscow, 1999), pp. 277–78.

[15] On the treatment of the term "reunification" in contemporary Russian and Ukrainian historiography, see my article "The Ghosts of Pereyaslav: Russo-Ukrainian Historical Debates in the Post-Soviet Era," *Europe-Asia Studies* 53, no. 3 (2001): 489–505.

[16] See Floria's remarks at a round table on the ethnocultural history of the Eastern Slavs (2001) in *Na putiakh stanovleniia ukrainskoi i belorusskoi natsii: faktory, mekhanizmy, sootneseniia*, ed. Leonid Gorizontov (Moscow, 2004), p. 30.

[17] For a critique of Kliuchevsky's thesis, see Daniel Rowland, "The Problem of Advice in Muscovite Tales about the Time of Troubles," *Russian History* 6, no. 1 (1979): 259–83.

who succeeded Kliuchevsky as dean of Russian historiography in the first decades of the twentieth century, and whose works on the Time of Troubles are still numbered among the most authoritative studies of the subject, took note of this criticism but did not adopt Kliuchevsky's view regarding the constitutional aspirations of the authors of the tales. He later regarded the late sixteenth and early seventeenth centuries in Muscovy as a period of confluence of three crises: dynastic, social, and national.[18] More than any other aspect of Platonov's analysis, his insistence on the dynastic crisis as one of the main causes of the Time of Troubles has won the assent of present-day scholars.[19]

Since the mid-fifteenth century, the Muscovite state had not experienced anything comparable to the civil war unleashed by the succession crisis of the Time of Troubles. The new crisis was more difficult to resolve than the previous one because the new state was fully independent, with no overlord to settle the quarrel. It encompassed incomparably larger and more diverse territories, each with its own strong tradition of sovereignty. Nor was competition for the office of tsar limited to members of the Rurikid clan, which complicated the situation even more. The desire of the Muscovite elite to restore the Rurik line was at least partly responsible for the emergence of pretenders to the Muscovite throne, all of whom claimed direct descent from the Rurikid tsars. The extinction of the Rurik line resulted in the disruption and partial delegitimization of the dynastic mythology that linked Muscovite rulers with the Roman emperor Augustus and served as a cornerstone of Muscovite historical identity. Thus, the chronicle once attributed to Prince I. M. Katyrev-Rostovsky, written ca. 1626, informed its readers "about the origins of the . . . lineage of our Muscovite grand princes, the sundering of the tsarist lineage from Emperor Augustus, and the origins of another tsarist lineage."[20] The same author distinguished between the hereditary tsar Ivan the Terrible, who "stood up for his patrimonial realm (otechestvo)," and the elected tsar Boris Godunov, who, in his words, "took great care of his state (derzhava)."[21] The Rurikids temporarily returned to power with the enthronement of Vasilii Shuisky. Not surprisingly, his partisans were eager to stress the Rurikid credentials of the new tsar and traced his genealogy through Aleksandr Nevsky and St. Volodymyr of Kyiv all the

---

[18] See S. F. Platonov, *The Time of Troubles: A Historical Study of the Internal Crisis and Social Struggle in Sixteeenth- and Seventeenth-Century Muscovy*, trans. John T. Alexander (Lawrence, Manhattan and Wichita, 1976).

[19] See Dunning, "Crisis, Conjuncture, and the Causes of the Time of Troubles."

[20] See "*Letopisnaia kniga*, pripisyvaemaia kniaziu I. M. Katyrevu-Rostovskomu," in *Khrestomatiia po drevnei russkoi literature*, comp. N. K. Gudzii (Moscow, 1973), pp. 329–43, here 329.

[21] Ibid., p. 341.

way back to Emperor Augustus.[22] But Shuisky's tenure did not last very long and was followed by the rule of non-Rurikids.

The rapid succession of tsars on the Muscovite throne tended to dissociate the ruler from the state in the popular mind. As the author of the Karamzin Chronograph noted, referring to the enthronement of Vasilii Shuisky, "in Moscow the thief Grishka the Unfrocked Monk [Otrepev] was killed, and Grand Prince Vasilii Ivanovich of all Rus' became sovereign tsar of the Muscovite state."[23] A reader might conclude from this entry that tsars and, more importantly, dynasties could come and go, while the Muscovite state remained. The elite, which feared treason and enemy attack, was also turning the state into its main object of loyalty.[24] In either case, the state was regarded as an institution separate from the office of tsar – a new development in Muscovite political thought. Political, historical, and literary works written during or shortly after the Time of Troubles give us a whole series of names by which the state was known to contemporaries. By the turn of the seventeenth century, Muscovy was usually denoted by the word *gosudarstvo*, which had a double meaning, referring both to the tsar's rule and to his realm.[25] Apart from the term "Muscovite state" (*Moskovskoe gosudarstvo*), the early modern Russian polity was also referred to as *Moskovskoe tsarstvo*, *Rossiiskoe gosudarstvo*, *Rossiiskoe tsarstvo*, and *Rossiiskaia derzhava*. All these terms were used interchangeably. When authors discussed territory and population, those notions could also be rendered by such terms as *Rossiia*, *vsia Rossiia*, *Velikaia Rossiia*, *Russkaia zemlia*, or *Rossiiskaia oblast'*. The semantic difference between the latter terms and those referring to the Muscovite state becomes apparent from the following statement in a contemporary narrative discussing the intentions of the rebels led by Ivan Bolotnikov (1607): "they will attract the whole population of the Russian territory (*Rossiiskaia oblast'*) and take control of the Muscovite state (*Moskovskoe*

[22] See "Povest' o smerti i pogrebenii kniazia Mikhaila Vasil'evicha Skopina-Shuiskogo," in *Khrestomatiia po drevnei russkoi literature*, pp. 314–21, here 315.

[23] See "Iz *Karamzinskogo khronografa*," in *Vosstanie I. Bolotnikova. Dokumenty i materialy* (Moscow, 1959), pp. 109–19, here 109.

[24] "And by now they have handed over to him, the thief, almost all the Rus' tsardom," wrote a contemporary author about the intentions of the Muscovite "traitors." See "Novaia povest' o preslavnom rossiiskom tsarstve i velikom gosudarstve Moskovskom," in *Khrestomatiia po drevnei russkoi literature*, pp. 305–12, here 307. For the complete text of the monument, see N. F. Dobrolenkova, *Novaia povest' o preslavnom rossiiskom tsarstve i sovremennaia ei agitatsionnaia patrioticheskaia pis'mennost'* (Moscow and Leningrad, 1960), pp. 189–209.

[25] See Nancy Shields Kollmann, "Concepts of Society and Social Identity in Early Modern Russia," in *Religion and Culture in Early Modern Russia and Ukraine*, ed. Samuel H. Baron and Kollmann (DeKalb, Ill., 1997), pp. 40–41. Cf. András Zoltán, "Polskie 'państwo' i rosyjskie 'gosudarstvo,'" *Zeszyty naukowe Wydziału Humanistycznego Uniwersitetu Gdańskiego: Filologia rosyjska*, 1982, no. 10: 111–15.

gosudarstvo)."[26] It appears that in this particular context "Russian territory" stood for the land and people, while "Muscovite state" referred to the political institution.

Another important political concept of the time was that of the land (*zemlia*). At the turn of the seventeenth century it emerged as an important term alongside *gosudarstvo*. On the one hand, *zemlia* could be synonymous with *gosudarstvo* (state), as indicated by the following phrase in the *New Narration*: "within our great land, that is, within our great state."[27] On the other hand, it meant the Muscovite community at large as a category separate from the ruler and the central government.[28] The new political circumstances and the new rules of public discourse made the tsar dependent as never before on the will of the land with regard to his election and his subsequent tenure of office. A contemporary author condemned the First False Dmitrii, among other things, for having "asserted himself suddenly and spontaneously against the will of the whole land and installed himself as tsar."[29] In 1606 Patriarch Hermogen claimed that Tsar Vasilii Shuisky had acted against the rebels in the interest of both the sovereign and the land.[30] There was an assumption that the land could even be ruled (or self-ruled) without a tsar (although this was an aberration); thus the special term *zemlederzhtsy* (literally "landholders") was coined to denote the boyar council that assumed power in Moscow in 1610.[31]

The prominence of *zemlia* in the narratives of the period reflected, among other things, the growing importance of an institution that in previous decades had been marginal at best – the Assembly of the Land (*zemskii sobor*).[32] The council was entrusted with the election of new tsars after the Rurikid dynasty died out. Indeed, election by the Assembly of the Land came to be regarded during the Time of Troubles as the only legitimate way to install a new tsar, regardless of lineage. The fact that the Rurikid Vasilii Shuisky was not elected by such an assembly undermined

---

[26] See "Iz *Inogo skazaniia*," in *Vosstanie I. Bolotnikova*, pp. 92–103, here 92.

[27] See "Novaia povest'," p. 307.

[28] Kollmann defines the term as follows: "Generally 'the Land' was envisioned as being separate from the tsar, the privileged military ranks, and the apparatus of government. The usage of the term 'Land' fairly explicitly distinguishes between the tsar's realm and perhaps a vestigial public sphere; this distinction is evident since the mid-sixteenth century" ("Concepts of Society and Social Identity," p. 41).

[29] See "Iz *Vremennika Ivana Timofeeva*," in *Vosstanie I. Bolotnikova*, p. 125.

[30] See an excerpt from Patriarch Hermogen's letter of June 1607 in *Vosstanie I. Bolotnikova*, pp. 215–16.

[31] See "Novaia povest'," p. 311.

[32] Kollmann suggests that assemblies of the land "should probably best be regarded as a consultative process rather than as formal institutions, particularly of a protoparliamentary type" ("Concepts of Society and Social Identity," p. 39).

his legitimacy in the eyes of some of his subjects.[33] Assemblies of the land represented the whole society, including the boyars, clergy, service nobility, burghers, and, in times of unrest, the Cossacks as well. The notion of the "land" was as close as early seventeenth-century Muscovy came to the concepts of "nation" and "fatherland." It also acquired supernatural characteristics: as Valerie Kivelson has recently noted, "The voice of the land was understood as an embodiment of divine choice."[34] If applied broadly, the concept could inspire local communities to pursue an "all-Rus'" political agenda, as was the case with the movement that led to the enthronement of Mikhail Romanov. Understood locally, the same concept could encourage regionalism or even secession. If the views of a particular region were ignored, local elites could claim the right of revolt. According to the narrative of a Dutch merchant, Isaac Massa, the people of the Siverian region (that is, Chernihiv and vicinity) justified their rebellion against Vasilii Shuisky by claiming that the Muscovites (inhabitants of Moscow) had killed the legitimately consecrated tsar (the First False Dmitrii) for no reason and without having consulted them.[35]

As a rule, the term "land" was applied either to a region or to the whole territory of the Muscovite tsardom, but given the prevailing political fragmentation, it could also exceed the boundaries of Muscovy. This applies to the proclamation of a separate Novgorodian state (*gosudarstvo*) under Swedish protection in 1611. The treaty signed between Novgorod and Sweden envisioned the possible annexation of the "Muscovite and Suzdalian states" to the state of Novgorod.[36] Some documents of the period also included references to a Kazan state, and there were mentions of a Vladimir state as well.[37] Under these circumstances, references to "the whole land" and "the Russian land" took on the "supra-state" meaning they had had in the fifteenth and early sixteenth centuries, stressing the cultural unity of the politically fragmented realm. Quite telling in that regard are references in Muscovite tales to Kuzma Minin's miraculous

---

[33] Avraamii Palitsyn wrote in that regard: "After the unfrocked monk was killed on the fourth day by certain petty servants from the tsar's palaces, Vasilii Ivanovich Shuisky was given preference and installed in the tsar's residence, but he was not persuaded [to take office] by any of the magnates or entreated by the rest of the people, and Russia (*Rosia*) was of two minds: those who loved him and those who hated him" ("Iz *Skazaniia* Avraamiia Palitsina," in *Vosstanie I. Bolotnikova*, pp. 126–27, here 126). For the complete text of the monument, see *Skazanie Avraamiia Palitsyna*, ed. O. Derzhavina and E. Kolosova (Moscow and Leningrad, 1955).

[34] See Valerie Kivelson, "Muscovite 'Citizenship': Rights without Freedom," *Journal of Modern History* 74 (September 2002): 465–89, here 474.

[35] See excerpts from Isaac Massa's notes in *Vosstanie I. Bolotnikova*, pp. 134–49, here 134.

[36] See G. M. Kabalenko, "Dogovor mezhdu Novgorodom i Shvetsiei 1611 goda," *Voprosy istorii*, 1988, no. 11: 131–34.

[37] See Kollmann, "Concepts of Society and Social Identity," pp. 40–41.

vision of St. Sergii, the fourteenth-century "protector of the Muscovite realm and the whole Russian land."[38] The old, supra-state meaning of the terms "the whole land" and "all Russia" is revived in Avraamii Palitsyn's narrative. Palitsyn wrote about the revolts in the borderlands, which included the Riazan Land, the Siverian and Smolensk regions, Novgorod and Pskov. Discussing the revolt in the Chernihiv (Siverian) region, he draws a parallel with Novgorod, as both were relatively late additions to the Muscovite realm: "The Siverian region, being well aware of Tsar Ivan Vasilievich's latest destruction of Novgorod, and not waiting for such suffering to be inflicted upon it, soon separated from the Muscovite state, thereby doing great harm to all Russia (*Rosia*) when it elevated the Unfrocked Monk to the Russian tsardom and completely forsook the Christian fraternity, consigning itself to servitude to the Kingdom of Poland."[39] Thus, in Palitsyn's opinion, regional grievances and insecurities vis-à-vis the policy of the Moscow center were among the causes of the Time of Troubles and could prompt certain regions to seek foreign protection. Palitsyn treated the Siverian case as an example of regionalism, not of incipient statehood. In his view, the Siverian Land was part of "all Russia."

The boundaries of Muscovite identity

If the inhabitants of Chernihiv (or Novgorod, for that matter) were not regarded as foreigners or infidels in Muscovy, where did the early seventeenth-century Muscovites draw the line between themselves and the "other"? In seeking an answer to this question, we should begin with the self-image of the Muscovites as it emerges from writings of the first decades of the seventeenth century. The picture presented by contemporary texts is quite confusing. On the one hand, both ecclesiastical and secular authors of the period saw themselves as part of the Muscovite or Russian populace. On the other hand, the ethnonational terms that our authors used to describe themselves and their people (*Moskovskie* or *Russkie liudi*) consisted mostly of adjectives, while nouns were used to denote their neighbors (*liakh*, *nemets*, etc.). The noun *Rusin/Rusyn*, used in earlier Muscovite texts and employed in Ukraine and Belarus to refer to the local population, does not appear in Muscovite texts of the early seventeenth century. The term *narod*, which is occasionally encountered in Muscovite texts of the period, is not used in the sense of "nation" or "ethnocultural community," as in Ukraine and Belarus of the period, but

---

[38] See Kivelson, "Muscovite 'Citizenship,'" pp. 471–72.
[39] See "Iz *Skazaniia* Avraamiia Palitsina," p. 126.

simply means "a number of people." The nouns that Muscovites used to
refer to themselves were not usually ethnonational (the ethnonym *Rus'*
was seldom used in that capacity) but political (*moskvich*, "Muscovite")
or religious ("Orthodox," "Christians").

But let us return to the terms *Moskovskie* or *Russkie liudi*. The first
could refer either to residents of the city of Moscow or to inhabitants of
the whole Muscovite state. *Russkie liudi* usually meant the whole population of Muscovy, including those dwelling in territories lost after 1600.
For example, Ukrainians and Belarusians figured as *inozemtsy* (foreigners)
in official Muscovite documents and historical narratives, as did Lithuanians, but the adjective *russkie* was consistently used with reference to
inhabitants of territories lost to the Commonwealth, such as the Smolensk
and Chernihiv regions.[40] Muscovite authors drew a clear distinction
between Commonwealth and Muscovite subjects in their accounts of
the Time of Troubles. For example, in his description of the siege of
the St. Sergii Trinity Monastery near Moscow, Avraamii Palitsyn distinguished between the "Polish and Lithuanian people" and the "Russian
traitors" (*russkie izmenniki*).[41] Even though there were numerous Ruthenians (including Zaporozhian Cossacks) in the Commonwealth army
and in the forces led by the pretenders, Muscovite authors never called
them "Russian people" or "Orthodox Christians" but referred to them as
Poles, Lithuanians, or Polish and Lithuanian people. Thus the Karamzin
Chronograph refers to the "Lithuanian foreigner Ivan Storovsky."[42] The
Zaporozhians were the only group that Muscovite authors distinguished
from the general category of "Polish and Lithuanian people," and then
only on a social basis, not an ethnonational one.[43] In proclamations to
the Muscovite population, the distinction between Russian subjects of
the Muscovite tsars and Ruthenians in the invasion forces was maintained even in the case of inhabitants of Smolensk, which Lithuania had
lost only in the early sixteenth century. Thus, in a letter sent to Smolensk
in April 1608, the Second False Dmitrii differentiated the inhabitants of
Smolensk, whom he called "our indigenous people" (*nashi prirozhdennye*

[40] See, for example, the report of Muscovite envoys to the Crimea about their encounter
with three prisoners captured by the Tatars on Commonwealth territory: "One introduced himself as a Lithuanian servitor from Olgov named Stepan Yatskov; the second
was the Lithuanian Mishkovsky; and the third, named Fedor, introduced himself as a
Russian from Smolensk . . . taken to Lithuania as a prisoner three years ago." *Dokumenty
rosiis'kykh arkhiviv z istorii Ukrainy*, vol. I, *Dokumenty do istorii ukrains'koho kozatstva
1613–1620 rr.*, comp. Leontii Voitovych et al. (Lviv, 1998), p. 77.
[41] See "*Skazanie* Avraamiia Palitsina," in *Khrestomatiia po drevnei russkoi literature*, pp. 321–
28, here 324.
[42] "Inozemets Litvin Ivan Storovskii" ("Iz *Karamzinskogo khronografa*," in *Vosstanie I. Bolotnikova*), pp. 113–14.
[43] See *Dokumenty rosiis'kykh arkhiviv z istorii Ukrainy*, I: 62, 68, 71–72.

liudi), from "our military Lithuanian people and the Cossacks" (*nashi ratnye litovskie liudi i kazaki*).[44]

The political distinction made by Muscovite authors between the subjects of Muscovy and those of the Polish-Lithuanian Commonwealth was strengthened by the imposition of a clear religious divide. As noted above, religiously based self-designations such as "Orthodox" or "Christian" were among the nouns most often applied by Muscovite authors to their own people. Not surprisingly, then, it was religious rather than political (state- or nation-based) discourse that emerged as the leading rhetorical instrument for the mobilization of the Muscovite populace in its struggle against the foreign presence on Muscovite soil after 1610. As we have seen, that resistance was sparked by Patriarch Hermogen's protest against Sigismund III's decision to prevent the election of Władysław as the new Muscovite tsar and take the throne himself. Some students of the period have pointed out that the presence of Roman Catholics and Protestants in the entourage of the First False Dmitrii and his personal lack of Orthodox piety created dissatisfaction with the new tsar, undermined his legitimacy in the eyes of the Muscovites, and eventually fueled the revolt that ended in his death.[45] These factors played an even larger role in the rejection of Sigismund's bid for the throne. While conversion to Orthodoxy was a condition of the offer to Władysław, Sigismund had no intention whatever of abandoning Roman Catholicism. The prospect of swearing allegiance to a Catholic ruler aroused protest in Moscow, which was fully articulated by the patriarch. It set the tone for a propaganda effort that defined the political, social, and international conflict as a confrontation between true faith and heresy, stressing Muscovite political independence and self-assertion, xenophobia and hatred of invaders.

Since religion provided the Muscovites with their basic inspiration in this essentially political and social conflict, it was religious allegiance that defined the image of their "other." Not only the Catholics (including the Uniates) and the Protestants but also the Orthodox Ruthenians were portrayed as enemies of the true faith, as were those Orthodox Muscovites who supported foreign contenders for the Muscovite throne. As early

---

[44] See *Vosstanie I. Bolotnikova*, p. 231.

[45] For an attempt to treat the fall of the First False Dmitrii as the result of a cultural conflict between the Muscovites and the tsar's Polish entourage, see Vasyl Ulianovsky's doctoral dissertation, *Rosiia na pochatku smuty XVII stolittia: nova kontseptsiia* (Kyiv, 1995). Cf. his *Rossiia v nachale Smuty: Ocherki sotsial'no-politicheskoi istorii i istochnikovedeniia*, 2 pts. (Kyiv, 1993). On the image of the pious tsar in tales about the Time of Troubles, see Rowland, "The Problem of Advice in Muscovite Tales about the Time of Troubles," pp. 264–70. On the sacralization of the person of the tsar in early modern Russia, see Boris Uspenskii and Viktor Zhivov, "Tsar' i Bog," in Uspenskii, *Izbrannye trudy*, vol. I (Moscow, 1994), pp. 110–218.

as the autumn of 1606, Patriarch Hermogen condemned Bolotnikov's supporters, who had taken over "Siverian Ukraine" (*Severskaia Ukraina*) and then made their way to the Riazan Land. Although he did not regard them as foreigners or adherents of another faith, he read them out of the Orthodox Church for killing "their own brethren, Orthodox Christians." In Hermogen's words, they had "abandoned God and the Orthodox faith and submitted to Satan and the devil's hosts. . . . They desecrated holy icons, utterly defiled holy churches and shamelessly dishonored women and girls by fornication, and plundered their homes, and put many to death."[46] Hermogen called on "Orthodox Christians" to fight for "the holy churches of God and for the Orthodox faith and for the Sovereign's kissing of the cross [oath]."[47] Even though the war involved severe conflicts between fellow Orthodox (a fact recognized by the narrators), Muscovite authors regarded casualties on the tsar's side as martyrs for the faith. The *Kazan Narration*, reporting on a battle between government troops and rebels at Tula, describes the grim results as follows: "the broad field was covered with the dead bodies of coreligionists; there was not one infidel at that slaughter, but only the Rus' killing one another. And here they killed in battle the commanding Prince Boris Petrovich, who suffered as a martyr for the true Orthodox faith."[48] With the tsar's authority losing its formerly unquestionable legitimacy and ceasing to serve as the sole object of loyalty, and with the "land" not yet established as a fatherland (the term *otechestvo* still generally meant either patrimony or noble origin), religion became the primary source of legitimacy and a value worth dying for. Consequently, all appeals to the Muscovite populace to defend the regime included references to the Orthodox faith and the churches of God.

If it was so easy for Muscovite authors to find tools of the devil among their own people, it was even easier to portray non-Orthodox foreigners in those terms. According to Avraamii Palitsyn, the defenders of the St. Sergii Trinity Monastery refused to surrender to the Commonwealth army (which consisted largely of Orthodox Ruthenians) because they regarded surrender as a betrayal of the Orthodox Church and a submission to the "new, heretical laws of those who have fallen away from

---

[46] See *Vosstanie I. Bolotnikova*, p. 197. Bolotnikov and his associates were presented as instruments of the devil in *The Other Narration*. See "Iz *Inogo skazaniia*," pp. 92–103, here 92.

[47] See Hermogen's missives in *Vosstanie I. Bolotnikova*, pp. 198, 215–16.

[48] See "Iz *Kazanskogo skazaniia*," in *Vosstanie I. Bolotnikova*, pp. 104–9, here 106. The author of the Piskarev Chronicle treated boyars and nobles killed by the rebels as martyrs, exclaiming: "How are they not martyrs, not saints? Did martyrs not suffer thus at the hands of torturers in days of old?" ("Iz *Piskarevskogo letopistsa*," in *Vosstanie I. Bolotnikova*, pp. 131–33, here 132).

the Christian faith, who have been condemned by the four ecumenical patriarchs." In that context, the adversaries were called "Latins" and infidels (*inovernye*).[49] If the First False Dmitrii was routinely called a heretic in Muscovite texts, the Polish king commonly figured there as an infidel. Subordination to such a ruler meant loss of the true faith and all prospect of salvation. The author of the *New Narration* attacked those who "did not wish to choose a tsar of Christian descent and serve him but preferred to come up with a tsar from among the infidels and the godless and serve him."[50] In the author's opinion, those who joined the enemy had "fallen away from God and the Orthodox faith and adhered wholeheartedly to him, the enemy king, their accursed souls falling and descending to perdition."[51] Joining the foreigners or supporting a non-Muscovite pretender to the throne meant ceasing to be Orthodox. Such authors paid little attention to facts that challenged their preconceptions. In the autumn of 1608, for example, the Commonwealth commander Jan Piotr Sapieha asked Metropolitan Filaret Romanov of Rostov to reconsecrate an Orthodox church desecrated in the course of military operations, but such episodes were conveniently omitted from the Muscovite master narrative of the infidel invasion.[52]

A sense of national solidarity certainly existed in early seventeenth-century Muscovy, but it lacked a self-made vocabulary to express itself. It found its voice not so much in a dynasty- or state-based discourse as in a religiously based one. The complexity of the situation has been well depicted by Nancy Shields Kollmann. On the one hand, she believes that "Muscovites were indeed part of a larger social unit that we would call society, not only because modern Russian nationalism claims its roots in this historical experience but also because of unifying principles in the Russian language, Orthodox religion, or (most salient) political subordination and bureaucratic organization in an empire." On the other hand, in defining Muscovite "national" consciousness, she argues that "the root principle . . . [was] religious, rather than social – elite writers depict the society as the Godly Christian community, not a cohesive political unity of a common people."[53] This conclusion seems to apply particularly to the views expressed by writers of the post-1613 era. The extensive use of religious discourse by Muscovite literati of the period reflected the way in which Muscovite elites regarded themselves during and after the Time

[49] See "*Skazanie* Avraamiia Palitsina," p. 328.
[50] See "Novaia povest'," pp. 305–12, here 307.   [51] Ibid.
[52] See Filaret's positive response to Sapieha's request in *Pamiatniki smutnogo vremeni. Tushinskii vor: lichnost', okruzhenie, vremia. Dokumenty i materialy*, comp. V. I. Kuznetsova and I. P. Kulakova (Moscow, 2001), pp. 358–59.
[53] Kollmann, "Concepts of Society and Social Identity," pp. 38–39.

of Troubles. More than ever before, they confined true "Russianness" to the territory of their tsardom and thought of their state as the last bastion of Orthodoxy.

Despite the problems that Muscovite elites encountered in expressing their ethnonational identity in the first decades of the seventeenth century, there is little doubt that the sources of the period present that identity better than texts from earlier periods of Muscovite history. This is corroborated by Valerie Kivelson's argument for the existence of a Muscovite "nation" or broad political community in the sixteenth and seventeenth centuries – an argument based exclusively on documents associated with the Time of Troubles.[54] In the long run, the historical myth of the Time of Troubles, with its anti-Polish overtones, played an outstanding role in the formation of modern Russian national identity. Prince Dmitrii Pozharsky and the merchant Kuzma Minin, the leaders of the provincial militias that recaptured Moscow, became exemplars of patriotism in the Russian historical imagination. The election of Mikhail Romanov laid the basis for the foundation myth of the Romanov dynasty as the one chosen by the Russian people – a theme well illustrated by the popularity of the opera *Ivan Susanin*, originally entitled *A Life for the Tsar*, which eulogizes a Russian peasant who preferred to die at the hands of the Poles rather than betray the future tsar.[55] Was the Time of Troubles as fundamental to the development of Russian national identity as traditional Russian historiography claims? Indeed it was, but not necessarily in the way suggested by Sergei Platonov and others.[56]

The crisis served to isolate Muscovy from the other Eastern Slavs and the world at large, strengthening the sense of political and cultural solidarity within the Muscovite realm. The Time of Troubles showed that the political, social, and cultural bonds established between Muscovy's various regions and social groups during the reigns of Ivan III, Vasilii III, and Ivan IV were strong enough to withstand a major political and social upheaval. Instead of disintegrating into a dozen or so appanage principalities, the Muscovite state survived the calamities of the period with relatively small territorial losses. Significantly, it held together under

[54] See Kivelson, "Muscovite 'Citizenship,'" pp. 471–75.
[55] On the rise of interest in the history of the Time of Troubles in Russia on the eve of the Napoleonic Wars and the use of early seventeenth-century motifs for the construction of the foundations of modern Russian national identity, with its profoundly anti-Polish stereotypes, see Andrei Zorin, *Kormia dvuglavogo orla . . . Literatura i gosudarstvennaia ideologiia v Rossii v poslednei treti XVIII – pervoi treti XIX veka* (Moscow, 2001), pp. 157–86.
[56] In Platonov's opinion, the general crisis reached its national stage ca. 1609, with the beginning of open foreign intervention, the rise of anti-Polish resistance, and the eventual expulsion of Commonwealth troops from Muscovy. See his *Time of Troubles*.

conditions of severe dynastic crisis, as the Rurikid line expired and a number of domestic and foreign candidates engaged in fierce competition for the throne. The central space in the Muscovite identity traditionally occupied by the tsar became temporarily vacant or contested, but the identity itself did not disintegrate, finding new pillars to support its complex structure. In the end, the system was restored, with a new tsar taking the throne. The Muscovites learned in the process to distinguish the office of the sovereign (*gosudar'*) from his realm (*gosudarstvo*), which helped them preserve the former and restore the latter.

Not so splendid isolation

Most Muscovite accounts of the Time of Troubles were written retrospectively during the rule of Mikhail Romanov and his father, Metropolitan Filaret Romanov, who returned to Moscow in 1619 from Commonwealth captivity to be installed as the next patriarch of Moscow.[57] It was a period of reflection on what had gone so wrong in the land of the tsars. It was a time when all of Muscovite society was licking the wounds inflicted by a prolonged period of chaos, internecine warfare, and foreign intervention. Whole towns and villages were deserted; churches and monasteries lay in ruins.[58] Who was to blame for all that? "Russian traitors," to be sure, but also Muscovy's neighbors to the west – Poles, Lithuanians, Swedes, and Ruthenians – who had helped destroy and humiliate the "Russian Land." A peace treaty with Sweden was signed in 1617 at Stolbovo, but Royal Prince Władysław of Poland continued to claim the Muscovite throne, and there was a new conflict between Muscovy and the Commonwealth in 1618. The armistice of Deulino, which ended nine years of open warfare, assigned Chernihiv and Smolensk to the Commonwealth. The war of 1632–34 that was supposed to win back those territories for Muscovy ended in military disaster for its planners.

It is hardly surprising that the immediate reaction of the Muscovite state and society to early seventeenth-century developments was one of rising anti-Western sentiment and growing cultural isolation, including estrangement from the Orthodox ecumene. In a society that lacked a secular vocabulary to express the full bitterness of its humiliation by foreign

---

[57] On Patriarch Filaret and his policies, see Marius L. Cybulski, "Political, Religious and Intellectual Life in Muscovy in the Age of the Boyar Fedor Nikitich Iur'ev-Romanov a.k.a. The Grand Sovereign The Most Holy Filaret Nikitich, Patriarch of Moscow and All Rus' (ca. 1550–1633)," Ph.D. diss., Harvard University, 1998. The text of the thesis, which remains unpublished, is as informative and extensive as its baroque title suggests.

[58] In 1629 there were 554 inhabited homesteads in Tver as opposed to 1,450 abandoned ones. There were also eleven deserted churches and monasteries within the city limits. See N. N. Ovsiannikov, *Tver' v XVII veke* (Tver, 1889).

invaders, religious discourse embodied the mixture of fear and superiority with which the Muscovites regarded their real and imagined enemies. More than ever, Muscovites considered their brand of Orthodoxy the one true faith, while the rest of the Christian world was perceived as heretical at worst and sinful at best. Even "Russian people" – former subjects of the tsar residing in lands annexed by the Polish-Lithuanian Commonwealth after the Time of Troubles – were considered non-Christian, for they served a non-Orthodox ruler.[59] In writings of the period, the "Christian people of the Muscovite state" were characterized as dwellers in a new Jerusalem, while the difference between Western and Eastern Christendom was presented as a contrast between darkness and light, falsehood and truth, honor and disgrace, freedom and slavery. The Orthodox tsar embodied the positive side of this dichotomy, and Muscovites were supposed to choose between the two.[60]

Nowhere was this sense of Muscovy as the last bastion of Orthodox Christianity expressed more strongly than in the treatment of foreigners residing in the Muscovite state. In 1628 Patriarch Filaret forbade them to hire local servants, as that would affect the latter's capacity to practice the Orthodox religion. Especially despised among fellow Christians were the Catholics. Adam Olearius, who visited Moscow in the 1630s as part of an embassy from Holstein, noted that his hosts were prepared to deal with representatives of all religions, including Protestants and Muslims, but showed intolerance toward Catholics and Jews. But even in the case of Protestants, the degree of tolerance was apparently quite limited: Olearius reported that after the embassy's stay in a peasant house, its owner called for a priest to reconsecrate his icons, which had evidently been tainted by the foreigners' presence.[61] While Protestants had two churches in Moscow, Catholics had none. They were not even allowed to have priests in their households. In 1630 an exception was made for the French in hopes of gaining their support in the impending war with the Commonwealth. While official Orthodox discourse (in the tradition of Ivan the Terrible) continued to treat the Protestants as worse heretics than the Catholics, the demands of realpolitik, especially the search for allies in the war with largely Catholic Poland-Lithuania, forced the Muscovite authorities to treat Protestants more favorably than Catholics. This schizophrenic policy was not called off until 1643, when the government decided to close down the Protestant churches, yielding

---

[59] See Serhii Plokhy, *The Cossacks and Religion in Early Modern Ukraine* (Oxford, 2001), pp. 291–94.

[60] See "Povest' o smerti i pogrebenii," p. 320; "*Skazanie* Avraamiia Palitsina," p. 328.

[61] See *The Travels of Olearius in Seventeenth-Century Russia*, ed. S. H. Baron (Stanford, 1967), pp. 248–54.

to pressure from the patriarchal court and Muscovite merchants who, besides combating impiety, wanted to eliminate their commercial competitors.[62]

Thus Muscovite society isolated itself and vigilantly guarded the borders of its political and cultural identity. The desire to reform and modernize the army so as to challenge the Polish-Lithuanian Commonwealth and regain the lost territories meant that Westerners were welcomed but kept at arm's length from the tsar's subjects. It was relatively easy for a foreigner to enter the tsar's service but difficult to leave it, and virtually impossible to integrate into Muscovite society – unless one was prepared to convert to Orthodoxy. That was the case with the Tatar elite in the sixteenth century.[63] It also applied to Westerners in the Muscovite service. The government encouraged conversion through a system of payments and privileges, leaving short-term visitors like Olearius to complain about Westerners willingly converting to Orthodoxy for material reasons. In 1621 the English government asked the tsar to prevent his English employees from converting. The reply came back that no one was forced to convert, but the tsar could not stop those who wished to become Orthodox.[64] Unlike in the Volga region, where Tatars were often coerced into Orthodoxy, there was indeed no direct pressure on Westerners in the Muscovite service, but there were material incentives, as in the east. For Tatars or Germans who wanted to join the Muscovite elite and desired full membership in Muscovite society (which essentially meant marital ties with the Muscovite clan system), there was no alternative to conversion. Not only was the language of early modern Russian nationalism religious, but religion defined the procedure for becoming Russian.

Conversion was at the heart of a major controversy that developed in Muscovite society in the decades following the Time of Troubles. The issue was not whether to accept new converts but whether non-Muscovite Christians (Catholics, Protestants, and even Orthodox) should be rebaptized in order to make them truly Orthodox. Christian custom forbade

---

[62] See Salomon Arel, "Don't Ask, Don't Tell: Merchant Diasporas, Xenophobia and the Issue of Faith in Muscovite Russia," paper presented at a conference on "The Modern History of Eastern Christianty; Transitions and Problems," Davis Center, Harvard University, 26–27 March 2004. Salomon Arel's data indicate the rise of xenophobic attitudes in Muscovite government and society in the decades following the Time of Troubles. At the same time, her comparison of the treatment of foreigners in Reformation-era England and early modern Russia suggests that Muscovy was a more tolerant or at least less violent society in religious terms. Having been spared the conflicts of the European Reformation, Muscovy still awaited the confessionalization of its church and society.

[63] See Michael Khodarkovsky, "The Conversion of Non-Christians in Early Modern Russia," in *Of Religion and Empire: Missions, Conversion, and Tolerance in Tsarist Russia*, ed. R. P. Geraci and M. Khodarkovsky (Ithaca, NY, 2001), pp. 115–43, here 120–26.

[64] See Salomon Arel, "Don't Ask, Don't Tell."

rebaptism, but only if one regarded the candidate as a Christian in the first place. Muscovite discourse of the time, which limited the term "Christian" to Orthodox subjects of the Muscovite tsar, put the faith of other Christians under suspicion, if not under an outright ban. The question of rebaptizing foreigners first caused controversy in 1620, when the recently consecrated Patriarch Filaret Romanov used it against the former locum tenens of the patriarchal throne, Metropolitan Iona. Filaret accused the latter of having admitted two converts to Orthodoxy by confirmation (both had come from the Commonwealth and were either Catholics or Protestants). Filaret insisted that they should have been rebaptized, and that became the official position of the church, approved by an ecclesiastical council. In fact, the new policy implied that non-Orthodox Christians were not Christians at all: their original baptism was considered invalid. The readiness of converts to go along with the new policy was generously rewarded by the state, especially when those who accepted Muscovite Orthodoxy were of noble origin.[65]

Not surprisingly, the treatment of the non-Orthodox as non-Christians began to create major problems for the Muscovite court on the international scene, hindering the Romanovs' ability to intermarry with foreign rulers and forge international alliances. In the early 1640s, when Royal Prince Waldemar of Denmark came to Moscow to marry the tsar's daughter Irina, he agreed to follow Orthodox ritual but refused to be rebaptized. The Protestant theologians who accompanied the prince tried to convince their Muscovite counterparts of the illegitimacy of the whole procedure and used a Greek dictionary to explain the meaning of the word *baptismo* to the Muscovites, but the latter rejected their argument, claiming that the dictionary was not a sacred text. The tsar, who was eager to strengthen Muscovy's relations with Denmark, wanted to go ahead with the marriage, but strong opposition was inspired by Patriarch Iosif. The pro-marriage faction sought help from one of Muscovy's most open-minded intellectuals of the day, Prince Semen Shakhovskoi, who wrote a treatise full of theological and historical arguments suggesting that as a last resort, the marriage could go ahead without rebaptism of

---

[65] On the rebaptism of Christians in Muscovy, see Oparina, "Ukrainskie kazaki v Rossii." Cf. the appendix to her *Ivan Nasedka i polemicheskoe bogoslovie v Kievskoi mitropolii* (Novosibirsk, 1998), which includes a petition of 1625 to Patriarch Filaret from Franz Farensbach, a Lutheran in the Muscovite service who asked to be admitted to the Orthodox faith (pp. 337–39). Oparina has also published a text that was to be read by catechumens before their conversion. The title of the document gives a good idea of who was converted and of the Muscovite conception of the outside world at the time. It begins: "If a Latin or a Pole or a Lithuanian of the Roman schism or a foreigner of the Lutheran heresy or an evangelical of the Calvinist heresy comes to the true Orthodox Christian faith of the Greek rite, requesting holy baptism . . ." (ibid., pp. 340–42).

the prince. Shakhovskoi was accused of heresy and exiled.[66] The marriage never took place – a striking example of Muscovite isolationism and the self-righteous "piety" of the period. As noted above, Protestant churches in the capital were shut down in 1643. In the eyes of the Muscovite ruling elite, the outside world, including even Muscovy's foreign allies, consisted of non-Christians and was possessed by the devil. The only true Christians were the Russians, that is to say, the multiethnic Orthodox subjects of the Muscovite tsar.

The Ruthenian challenge

By the time Polish-Lithuanian Rus′ met its Muscovite counterpart in the whirlwind of the Time of Troubles, both communities had a clear sense of distinct identity. As noted above, the trauma suffered by the Muscovites only strengthened their alienation from Polish-Lithuanian Rus′. The Ruthenians appear to have become no less alienated from the Muscovites, whether they served in Cossack detachments or in the armies of Sigismund III or Royal Prince Władysław. Loyalty to a common king and fatherland, the Polish-Lithuanian Commonwealth, emerged as the force that bound together Poles, Lithuanians, and Ruthenians – Roman Catholics, Protestants, and Orthodox Christians – and divided them from the Muscovite subjects of the tsar. Polish-Lithuanian Rus′ clearly regarded Muscovite Rus′ as its "other," reserving for it the term *Moskva* (Muscovy) while calling itself "Rus′." That distinction was reflected in numerous Ruthenian writings of the period, including chronicles in which the Rus′ and the Muscovites were identified as separate Slavic nations.[67]

At the same time, Polish-Lithuanian Rus′ was well aware of the commonality of the "Rus′ religion," which included both parts of Rus′. The religious turmoil of the Union of Brest era and the advancing confessionalization of religious and secular life in the Commonwealth alerted the Orthodox side to the existence of the Orthodox Rus′ state to the east. In the last decade of the sixteenth century, Prince Kostiantyn Ostrozky suggested that Moscow be included in the negotiations on church union. The Lviv Orthodox brotherhood sent letters and representatives to Moscow, asking the tsar for financial support of its projects. So did the Vilnius brotherhood. By the turn of the seventeenth century, the advance of the

---

[66] On Shakhovskoi, his writings, and his role in the Waldemar affair, see Edward L. Keenan, "Semen Shakhovskoi and the Condition of Orthodoxy," *Harvard Ukrainian Studies* 12/13 (1988/89): 795–815.

[67] See Aleksandr Myl′nikov, *Kartina slavianskogo mira: vzgliad iz Vostochnoi Evropy. Ėtnogeneticheskie legendy, dogadki, protogipotezy XVI – nachala XVII veka* (St. Petersburg, 2000), pp. 21–45, 95–140 passim.

Union and the pro-Uniate policy of the Polish court were inclining the Ruthenian Orthodox toward Muscovy more than ever before. The Commonwealth authorities tried to put an end to that tendency, accusing the Orthodox of treason, taking their leaders to court, and ordering the arrest of delegations to Moscow. Orthodox complaints about the persecution of their church in the Commonwealth lessened the king's chances of success with his Muscovy project. The Ruthenian Orthodox bishops Hedeon Balaban and Mykhail Kopystensky, who signed an appeal to the Muscovites pointing out the First False Dmitrii's contacts with the Jesuits, were accused of treason. Meletii Smotrytsky faced the same accusation after publishing his anti-Uniate *Threnos* in 1610.[68]

What was really going on in the minds of the Ruthenian Orthodox during the Time of Troubles? How did they reconcile their conflicting loyalties toward their Polish-Lithuanian fatherland on one hand and the Orthodox faith on the other, given that the latter included Muscovite Rus', which was at war with the Commonwealth? This question can be answered on the basis of the Barkalabava Chronicle, composed in the early seventeenth century on the territory of present-day Belarus. Its Orthodox author presents us with a complex picture of competing identities and loyalties. Among the First False Dmitrii's entourage in Moscow, he listed not only Poles and Lithuanians (as did the authors of Muscovite accounts) but also Rus' and Volhynians. He was clearly upset when he described the massacre of Dmitrii's Commonwealth courtiers in Moscow in 1606 – "it was lamentable and frightful to hear of such evil befalling those noble people" – yet he did not blame the Muscovites for it. Instead, he pointed a finger at the Poles and Lithuanians who had provoked the Muscovites by showing disrespect for the "Rus' churches." He wrote:

And that happened to them because of the great Lithuanian abuses and the Polish mockery, for in Moscow Tsar Dmitrii had built a Polish Roman Catholic church for his wife's sake, and monks served the divine liturgy, but they [the Poles and Lithuanians] made great mock of the Rus' churches and abused the Muscovite priests, putting them to scorn. [The Muscovites] considered this a great injustice and a great wrong inflicted upon them; they did not want the Polish faith in their tsardom, for it had not been among them for ages.[69]

Associating himself with the Ruthenians in Dmitrii's army, the author of the chronicle also took the side of his Muscovite coreligionists, who opposed the Roman Catholic Poles and Lithuanians. He was certainly not the only Ruthenian torn by conflicting loyalties. The religious aspect

[68] See Plokhy, *The Cossacks and Religion*, pp. 278–81.
[69] See "Barkulabavskaia khronika," in *Pomniki starazhytnai Belaruskai pis'mennastsi* (Minsk, 1975), pp. 111–55, here 151.

of the Commonwealth's confrontation with Muscovy explains at least in part why the authors of the Lviv and Ostrih chronicles presented the whole history of Commonwealth intervention in Muscovite affairs as a solely Polish undertaking that had nothing to do with Polish-Lithuanian Rus'.[70]

Since there is no evidence of Ruthenian Orthodox protest against the war, nor were there any major religiously motivated desertions of Orthodox Ruthenians to Muscovy, it is fair to say that most Ruthenians found ways of handling their conflicting identities in a manner that did not compromise their loyalty to the Commonwealth. Of particular interest in this connection is the *Trynografe* (1625), a Polish-language poem on the death of Prince Bahdan Ahinski written by a professor of the Orthodox College in Vilnius. Ahinski was a Ruthenian aristocrat who traced his origins back to St. Volodymyr, was active in the Vilnius Orthodox Brotherhood, and signed a protestation in defense of the rights of the Orthodox Church in 1608. He also held high offices in the Commonwealth administration, being subchamberlain of Trakai and starosta of Dorsun. From the verses we learn that he was elected a captain (*rotmistrz*) during the campaign against Muscovy, in which he fully demonstrated his devotion to the Commonwealth as his fatherland:

> Velikie Luki, Kropivna and the Dnipro,
> Full of boyar blood and corpses of musketeers, must attest
> That no one could appease him by being of the same faith;
> They could not ward off the gifts of Mars rendered by his hand.
> He considered foes of the Fatherland enemies of God;
> He venerated the cross, revered the faith and the threshold of the
>   Lord's Church;
> Not for the faith but for space, for the sake of the Fatherland's borders,
> He would gladly have turned the Muscovite lands inside out. [71]

Was the reconciliation of the two loyalties more a problem for the Orthodox cleric who wrote these verses than for Ahinski himself? That is a definite possibility. But there is also good reason to believe that the verses accurately reflected the thinking of the prince, who, as we learn from this source, was known to his contemporaries as a "Ruthenian" (*Rusnak*) and

---

[70] See O. A. Bevzo, *L'vivs'kyi litopys i Ostroz'kyi litopysets'. Dzhereloznavche doslidzhennia*, 2nd edn (Kyiv, 1971), pp. 102–3, 130–31. Both chronicles were written far from the theater of events, which may also have influenced their coverage of those developments.

[71] See *Trynografe*, in *Roksolański Parnas. Polskojęzyczna poezja ukraińska od końca XVI do początku XVIII wieku*, pt. 2, *Antologia*, ed. Rostysław Radyszewśkyj [Rostyslav Radyshevs'kyi] (Cracow, 1998), pp. 97–104, here 100. The author of the verses, Iosyf Bobrykevych, wrote and recited them in Ruthenian but published them in Polish. See Ihar A. Marzaliuk, *Liudzi daŭniai Belarusi: ètnakanfesiinyia i satsyia-kul'turnyia stereotypy (X–XVII st.)* (Mahilioŭ, 2003), p. 76.

regarded himself as one of the leaders of the Orthodox Rus'. In order to deal with their conflicting loyalties, Ahinski and his coreligionists separated religious and political identity.

In the eyes of the Orthodox clergy, the way to balance the two loyalties was, at a minimum, to refrain from attacking Orthodox churches (as distinct from the Orthodox population) on occupied territory. Kasiian Sakovych, for example, praised Hetman Petro Konashevych-Sahaidachny, who led one of the most devastating Cossack attacks on Muscovy in 1618, for having forbidden his Cossacks to attack Orthodox churches during the Moldavian campaign.[72] Sakovych was silent on whether Sahaidachny had done the same in Muscovy, but Meletii Smotrytsky later wrote that the Cossack hetman had repented his participation in the campaign against Muscovy before Patriarch Theophanes.[73] Muscovite sources leave little doubt that there was good reason to repent, for the Orthodox Ruthenian nobles and Cossacks participated equally with their non-Orthodox comrades in atrocities against the Muscovite population. The actions of one of them, the Cossack officer Andrii Nalyvaiko, who impaled Muscovite nobles and took women and children captive, prompted the Second False Dmitrii to issue an order sentencing him to death.[74] There is also no reason to disregard Muscovite documents stating that the Cossacks robbed Orthodox churches of their valuables, which were considered legitimate booty at the time, whatever the denomination of the churches and the religion of the soldiers involved in those acts of blasphemy.[75] It was probably easier for the Cossacks and the rank and file of the Commonwealth army, not yet religiously mobilized, to disregard the denominational affiliation of the churches, while the leaders of the Orthodox nobility, deeply involved in the struggle over church union, found it more difficult to do so.

At a time when the Ruthenian Orthodox elite sought to balance loyalty to the Commonwealth and to the Orthodox Church, which included enemies of its Polish-Lithuanian fatherland, while the rank and file simply exercised the right of conquest in the course of expeditions against

---

[72] See Kasiian Sakovych, "Virshi," in *Ukraïns'ka literatura XVII st.*, comp. V. I. Krekoten', ed. O. V. Myshanych (Kyiv, 1987), p. 230.

[73] Boris Floria, "Narodno-osvoboditel'noe dvizhenie na Ukraine i v Belorussii (20–40-e gody XVII v.). Ego politicheskaia ideologiia i tseli," in Vladimir Pashuto, Floria, and Anna Khoroshkevich, *Drevnerusskoe nasledie i istoricheskie sud'by vostochnogo slavianstva* (Moscow, 1982), pp. 195–226, here 202–3.

[74] See Oparina, "Ukrainskie kazaki v Rossii," p. 22. Nalyvaiko was ultimately executed by his own men.

[75] Ibid, p. 31. For a discussion of the military ethos of the time, see Natalia Iakovenko, "Skil'ky oblych u viiny: Khmel'nychchyna ochyma suchasnykiv," in eadem, *Paralel'nyi svit*, pp. 189–230.

Muscovy, a number of Orthodox intellectuals began to develop a view that prepared the way for what nineteenth-century historiography would call the "reunification of Rus'." That view was based on the notion of the dynastic, religious, and ethnic affinity of the two Rus' nations. The origin of all three elements in Ruthenian discourse of the time can be traced back to a letter of 1592 from the Lviv Orthodox brotherhood requesting alms from the tsar. The letter reintroduced Great Russian/Little Russian terminology, which was important for creating the discourse of Rus' unity. Its argument capitalized on the idea of religious unity between Muscovy and Polish-Lithuanian Rus' and employed the notion of one "Rossian stock" (*rod Rossiiskii*) – a tribe (*plemia*) led by the Muscovite tsar, the heir of St. Volodymyr.[76] Thereafter, the Ruthenian Orthodox constantly employed all three elements in letters to Moscow as they sought ways to strengthen their case for alms and other forms of support from the tsar and the patriarch.

The idea of the ethnic affinity of the two Rus' nations took on special importance in the writings of the new Orthodox hierarchy consecrated by Patriarch Theophanes in 1620. The hierarchs, who were not merely denied recognition but actually outlawed by the Polish authorities, could not take office in their eparchies and found themselves confined to Dnipro Ukraine. They needed all the help they could get, including support from Muscovy, and even contemplated emigration to the Orthodox tsardom – a plan later implemented by Bishop Iosyf Kurtsevych. Thus the famous *Protestation* of the Orthodox hierarchy (1621) asserted that the Ruthenians shared "one faith and worship, one origin, language, and customs" with Muscovy.[77] The author of the Hustynia Chronicle (written in Kyiv in the 1620s, possibly by the archimandrite of the Kyivan Cave Monastery, Zakhariia Kopystensky) established a biblical genealogy for the Slavic nations that listed the Muscovites next to the Rus' and called them *Rus'-Moskva*.[78] The most compelling case for the ethnic affinity of the two Rus' nations was made by Iov Boretsky, the newly consecrated metropolitan himself. In a letter of August 1624 to Mikhail Romanov, he compared the fate of the two Rus' nations to that of the biblical brothers Benjamin and Joseph. Boretsky called upon the Muscovite tsar (Joseph) to help his persecuted brethren. "Take thought for us as well, people of the same

---

[76] See *Akty, otnosiashchiesia k istorii Zapadnoi Rossii*, vol. IV (St. Petersburg, 1854), pp. 47–49.

[77] See P. N. Zhukovich, "'Protestatsiia' mitropolita Iova Boretskogo i drugikh zapadno-russkikh ierarkhov, sostavlennaia 28 aprelia 1621 goda," in *Stat'i po slavianovedeniiu*, ed. V. I. Lamanskii, vyp. 3 (St. Petersburg, 1910), pp. 135–53, here 143. Cf. Plokhy, *The Cossacks and Religion*, p. 291.

[78] See "Hustyns'kyi litopys," in *Ukraïns'ka literatura XVII st.*, pp. 146–66, here 147.

birth as your Rus' (*rosyiskyi*) tribe," wrote the metropolitan, using the latter term to denote both Ruthenians and Muscovites.[79]

A close reading of the texts produced by the Ruthenian Orthodox elites in the first decades of the seventeenth century indicates that the ethnic motif was a supplementary one in letters from Lviv and Kyiv to Moscow, but it is of special interest for our discussion as one of the first instances of the use of early modern national terminology in relations between the two Ruses.

The Muscovite response

How did the Muscovite elites react to the ideas put forward by the Ruthenian seekers of the tsar's alms? As might be expected, given the experience of the Time of Troubles, continuing military conflicts with the Commonwealth, and the general tendency of Muscovite society toward self-righteous isolation, the response was by no means enthusiastic. Patriarch Filaret was reluctant to accept and use in his correspondence the title of Patriarch of Great and Little Rus' attributed to him by the Ruthenian bishop Isaia Kopynsky in 1622. In letters to the Orthodox in the Commonwealth, he would carefully style himself Patriarch of Great Rus' (instead of all Rus'), apparently to avoid provoking a negative reaction from the Commonwealth authorities. The tsar did likewise. In 1634 Muscovite envoys assured Polish diplomats that the reference to "all Rus'" in his title had nothing to do with the Polish-Lithuanian "Little Rus'."[80]

There was more understanding between the two parties on the issue of the Kyivan origins of the Muscovite ruling dynasty. Muscovite diplomacy fought hard with the Polish-Lithuanian authorities to gain recognition of the Romanovs as heirs of the Rurikids. The Ruthenian Orthodox hierarchs, by contrast, whether out of ignorance or for political reasons, preferred to take no notice of the change of dynasty. Their treatment of Mikhail Romanov as an heir of St. Volodymyr followed the pattern established by the Orthodox alms-seekers of the early 1590s. Despite the profound dynastic crisis of the Time of Troubles, St. Volodymyr remained a popular figure in Muscovite political and religious discourse. References to him as a second Constantine appeared in Patriarch Hermogen's letter of 1610 to Royal Prince Władysław, in which the patriarch attempted to convince his addressee to convert to Orthodoxy. Later, in 1625, Semen

---

[79] For the text of the letter, see *Vossoedinenie Ukrainy s Rossiei. Dokumenty i materialy*, 3 vols. (Moscow, 1954), I: 46–48. Cf. Plokhy, *The Cossacks and Religion*, pp. 289–90.

[80] See letters from Kopynsky to Filaret (December 1622) and Filaret's letter to Boretsky (April 1630) in *Vossoedinenie Ukrainy s Rossiei*, 1: 27–28, 81. On the negotiations of 1632, see Sergei Solov'ev, *Istoriia Rossii s drevneishikh vremen*, bk. 5 (Moscow, 1961), pp. 176.

Shakhovskoi included the same references in a draft of the tsar's letter to Shah Abbas of Persia, whom the Muscovite authorities also tried to convert.[81] By all accounts, Ruthenian references to the legacy of St. Volodymyr were appreciated in Moscow. In the 1640s, when Metropolitan Mohyla (not very well disposed toward Muscovy) asked the tsar to help build "a sepulcher for the remains of our forefather [St. Volodymyr]" at St. Sophia's Cathedral, the response was not negative. The tsar's exact answer is not known, but there is evidence that a Muscovite goldsmith worked for Mohyla in Kyiv in 1644–45 on the tsar's orders.[82] It would appear that both sides agreed on the Kyivan origins of the Muscovite dynasty and statehood.

Nevertheless, that agreement did very little to alleviate Muscovite suspicions about the religion of their Ruthenian neighbors. Responding to the challenges of the Reformation and Counter-Reformation, the Ruthenian Orthodox sought to confessionalize their religious and public life; in so doing, they looked to Constantinople and Moscow for support. The Ruthenians were disappointed with the model of reform offered by Constantinople, whose patriarch, Cyril Lukaris, seemed to them excessively influenced by Protestant ideas. Nor did they get any help in Moscow, where they were considered dangerous heretics. A typical indication of that attitude was the reception offered by the Muscovite authorities to the Ruthenian writer Lavrentii Zyzanii, who came to Moscow in 1626 for theological advice and approval of the Orthodox catechism he had drafted. Zyzanii was actually imprisoned in the capital. Accused of harboring heretical and non-Orthodox views, he chose to make concessions on issues that aroused suspicion about the purity of his Orthodoxy. As the Orthodox faith of the Ruthenians was not considered truly Orthodox or even Christian, the Muscovite authorities forbade the import of Orthodox theological literature from Ruthenia, and some books were even burned.[83]

The attitude of the Muscovites toward Orthodox Ruthenians in their midst is fully apparent in their insistence on the rebaptism of the Commonwealth Orthodox. The same Orthodox council of 1620 that condemned Metropolitan Iona (at the initiative of Patriarch Filaret) for the confirmation of two non-Orthodox Christians also issued a pastoral letter

---

[81] See Keenan, "Semen Shakhovskoi and the Condition of Orthodoxy."

[82] See *Vossoedinenie Ukrainy s Rossiei*, 1: 400–401. Cf. Plokhy, *The Cossacks and Religion*, pp. 242–43.

[83] On Zyzanii's mission to Muscovy and Smotrytsky's trip to Constantinople, see David A. Frick, "Zyzanij and Smotryc'kyj (Moscow, Constantinople and Kiev): Episodes in Cross-Cultural Misunderstanding," *Journal of Ukrainian Studies* 17, nos. 1/2 (Summer-Winter 1992): 67–94. On the burning of Kyrylo Tranquillon-Stavrovetsky's *Didactic Gospel* in Muscovy, see Oparina, *Ivan Nasedka*, pp. 162–74, 368–429.

entitled "A Ukase on How to Investigate and on the Belarusians Themselves," which ordained the rebaptism not only of non-Orthodox but also
of Orthodox Ruthenians in Muscovy. According to the "Ukase," those
Ruthenian Orthodox who had been baptized by infusion (the pouring
of water) and not by triple immersion, as was the custom in Muscovy,
were to be rebaptized along with Catholics, Protestants, and Uniates.
The policy was extended to cover those who did not know how they had
been baptized or had received communion in non-Orthodox (including
Uniate) churches. Only those who had been baptized by triple immersion
(excluding confirmation) could be admitted to Orthodoxy by confirmation. The "Ukase" led to the mass rebaptism of Orthodox Ruthenians
who crossed the Muscovite border and entered the tsar's service between
the 1620s and 1640s. Before rebaptism the converts were ordered to read
(or have read to them, if they were illiterate) the text of an oath very similar to the one administered to those who entered the tsar's service. The
convert promised to sacrifice his life, if necessary, for the Orthodox faith
and the health of the tsar. He also swore not to leave the Muscovite state,
not to return to his former faith, and not to instigate any treason in his
new country.[84]

The "Ukase" and the policy promoted by it treated Orthodox Ruthenians not only as foreigners (*inozemtsy*) but also as either non-Christians or
not entirely Orthodox (even those whose baptism was considered impec-
cable were allowed to join the Muscovite church only after making an act
of contrition). But what was the reaction of those who accepted a second
baptism, contrary to the laws of the church? Did they protest or call upon
their fellow Christians and Eastern Slavs to come to their senses? We know
of no such instances. As in the case of Westerners, the reward given by the
tsarist authorities to the new Ruthenian converts apparently silenced the
Christian conscience of those who knew that there was something wrong
with the practice. This, at least, is the impression given by the sources on
the mass rebaptism of almost seven hundred Cossacks who entered the
Muscovite service in 1618–19. The vast majority of them were registered
by Muscovite scribes as "Cherkasians" (meaning Ukrainian Cossacks)
in the Muscovite "table of ranks" and received a stipend commensurate
with their status. But once they realized that the non-Orthodox converts
were getting a stipend twice as large for full rebaptism as the one paid to
the Orthodox joining the Muscovite church by confirmation, more than
half the Cossacks declared themselves non-Orthodox "Poles." Since the
Muscovite scribes did not distinguish between Catholics and Uniates, the

---

[84] On the origins of the "Ukase" and its impact on Muscovite religious policy, see Oparina,
"Ukrainskie kazaki v Rossii," pp. 32–33. Cf. eadem, *Ivan Nasedka*, pp. 60–65.

Cossack declarations were readily accepted. Moreover, declaring oneself a "Pole" entailed a larger salary for joining the tsar's service, because nobles, whom the Muscovite scribes usually treated as "Poles" or Roman Catholics, were paid better than rank-and-file Cossacks. One of the former "Cherkasians" even proclaimed himself a noble of Jewish faith and descent and was registered as such by the Muscovite authorities upon his baptism. It would appear that the Cossacks (because of whom the ukase of 1620 had been adopted – it was also known as the "Ukase on the Baptism of Latins and Cherkasians") did not mind rebaptism as long as they were well paid for it. Besides, quite a few of them were joining the Muscovite service because they were married to Russian women whom they had met during the war, and ratification of their Orthodoxy by the local church also meant the recognition of their marriages, followed by integration into Muscovite society, sometimes with noble rank.[85]

The rebaptism of the Ukrainian Cossacks in Muscovy shows vividly that while the Ruthenian Orthodox hierarchs could obtain alms by stressing religious affinity in their letters to the tsar and the patriarch of Moscow, the Muscovite authorities were by no means persuaded that they belonged to the same faith. Even if properly baptized, the Ruthenian Orthodox were tainted in the eyes of the Muscovites by their allegiance to a non-Orthodox ruler and everyday contact with the non-Orthodox. (Certainly the Ruthenians did not call upon their priests to reconsecrate the icons in their homes after every visit by non-Orthodox, as was the case with the Muscovite peasant described by Olearius.) Not unlike the communist rulers of the Soviet Union in the post-World War II era, the Orthodox rulers of Muscovy after the Time of Troubles tried to support their coreligionists in the West while protecting their own population from the former's corrupting influence. What was desirable from the perspective of their foreign policy agenda was highly undesirable from the viewpoint of domestic policy. Thus the Muscovite authorities were eager to collect information about the persecution of Orthodoxy in the Polish-Lithuanian Commonwealth. They offered help and safe haven for Orthodox clergymen crossing the Muscovite border. They even attempted to use that tactic to turn the Ukrainian Cossacks from enemies into allies during the Smolensk War.[86]

What about the argument of ethnic affinity advanced by the Lviv brotherhood and its biblical interpretation presented by Metropolitan Boretsky in his story of Joseph and Benjamin? Here it would appear that the

---

[85] For a detailed discussion of the rebaptism of Ukrainian Cossacks in Muscovy, see Oparina, "Ukrainskie kazaki v Rossii," pp. 34–44.

[86] See Boris Floria, "Nachalo Smolenskoi voiny i zaporozhskoe kazachestvo," in *Mappa Mundi. Zbirnyk naukovykh prats' na poshanu Iaroslava Dashkevycha z nahody ioho 70-richchia* (Lviv, Kyiv, and New York, 1996), pp. 443–50.

Ruthenian Orthodox had even less chance of being heard, or, if heard, of being understood. With regard to Orthodoxy, while the two Ruses disagreed, at least they spoke the same language and used the same vocabulary. When it came to nationality, the Muscovites apparently lacked the language and vocabulary to deal with the issue. The Muscovite language of the time lacked terms not only for such Ruthenian phenomena as "church brotherhood" and "Uniates" but also for "nation." As noted above, the term *narod*, which served to render that concept in Ruthenian, usually meant just a group of people in Russian. In official correspondence, reference to the Ruthenians was made predominantly in political rather than national or religious terms, and they figured either as Poles or as Lithuanians. The Muscovite scribes who conducted negotiations and disputes with Lavrentii Zyzanii referred to his Ruthenian language as "Lithuanian." An exception was made only for the Cossacks, who were called "Cherkasians," but this was a social rather than an ethnic or national designation.

The situation was somewhat better with regard to ecclesiastical texts. There, as the title of the ukase of 1620 makes apparent, the term "Belarusians" was used to denote the Ruthenian population of the Commonwealth. But was it indeed an ethnic term, as one might assume on the basis of the modern use of the word "Belarusians"? Apparently not. Its use in combination with the term "Cherkasian" indicates that it did not apply to the Ukrainian Cossacks. The context in which it appears in ecclesiastical documents indicates that it was used primarily to designate the Orthodox Ruthenians. It could also be applied to Uniates, as Tatiana Oparina argues, but Uniates often fell into the category of "Poles," the term used to denote either nobles or Catholics and Protestants of the Commonwealth irrespective of national background. Thus "Belarusian" was primarily an ethnoconfessional term. It served an important purpose in distinguishing the East Slavic population of the Commonwealth from its Polish and Lithuanian neighbors. At the same time, it distinguished that population from the East Slavic inhabitants of Muscovy. The invention of a special term for the Ruthenian population of the Commonwealth, the treatment of that population as not entirely Christian, and the reservation of the term "Russians" for subjects of the Muscovite tsar indicate that although the Muscovite elites recognized the Ruthenians as a group distinct from the Poles and Lithuanians, they also made a very clear political, religious, and ethnic distinction between themselves and their relatives to the west.[87]

---

[87] Although the iconographic evidence can be quite tricky, given the uncertain dating of icons, it is worth noting that in early modern Muscovite icons of the Last Judgment, the "Lithuanians" emerge most frequently (after the Jews) as the nation awaiting God's

Cossack nationhood

In the first months of 1648, the Cossack captain Bohdan Khmelnytsky led the people known to the Muscovite elites as Cherkasians in a bold revolt against the Polish-Lithuanian Commonwealth. The revolt, in which the Cossacks initially counted on the assistance of the Crimean Tatars, very soon gained strong support from the popular masses and then from noblemen in the territory of what is now Ukraine. In the long term, the revolt changed the political map of eastern Europe and significantly influenced the nation-building process in the region, becoming an important milestone in the formation of the modern Ukrainian identity and thereby influencing the development of distinct identities in both Russia and Belarus.[88] But what can be said about the impact of the uprising on the construction of national identities in the short term? Was it indeed a "national-liberation war of the Ukrainian people," as some Ukrainian historians call it today?

The very first reports about the uprising appear to have taken it exactly for what it was originally – a Cossack revolt. That perception was shared by the leaders of the rebellion and by those who tried to put it down. Cossack grievances were at the core of the rebels' demands, and given that the government originally planned to curb this uprising of Ruthenian Orthodox Cossacks with the help of detachments composed of other Ruthenian Orthodox Cossacks, there was no reason for either side in the conflict to appeal to the distinct ethnonational or religious loyalties of the combatants.[89] That changed when rebellion broke out in the ranks of the registered Cossacks loyal to the government, who switched sides and joined the Khmelnytsky rebels. Cossack victories over the Polish standing army in May 1648 spread the rebellion across Ukraine and ignited a popular uprising that very soon took on clear ethnic characteristics, turning into a war against Poles and Jews. Both ethnic categories became associated with religious (Catholic and Judaic) and social (landowner and leaseholder) characteristics, although quite often the category of Poles also included Polonized Ruthenian nobles. The leaders of the uprising

judgment, while there is no special category for the Ruthenians. See John-Paul Himka, "On the Left Hand of God: 'Peoples' in Ukrainian Icons of the Last Judgment," in *States, Societies, Cultures, East and West: Essays in Honor of Jaroslaw Pelenski*, ed. Janusz Duzinkiewicz (New York, 2004), pp. 317–49, here 321–26.

[88] For a detailed discussion of the impact of the Khmelnytsky Uprising on the formation of the Ukrainian nation, see Frank E. Sysyn, "The Khmelnytsky Uprising and Ukrainian Nation-Building," *Journal of Ukrainian Studies* 17, nos. 1/2 (Summer-Winter 1992): 141–70.

[89] See a letter of 20 February 1648 from Crown Grand Hetman Mikołaj Potocki to the Cossack rebels in *Dokumenty ob Osvoboditel'noi voine ukrainskogo naroda 1648–1654* (Kyiv, 1965), pp. 15–16, and Khmelnytsky's letter of 3 (13) March 1648 to Potocki in *Dokumenty Bohdana Khmel'nyts'koho* (Kyiv, 1961), pp. 23–27.

took advantage of the new situation and the unprecedented opportunities it offered. Thus, in June 1648, Khmelnytsky began writing to the authorities with demands that pertained to the rights of the Orthodox Church in places as far removed from the Cossack lands as the town of Krasnostav on the far western edge of Ukrainian ethnic territory.[90] By the end of 1648, Cossack detachments reached the Polish-Ukrainian ethnic border and, unexpectedly from the military standpoint, stopped there. The explanation should be sought in the cultural sphere. Khmelnytsky was able to take the Ukrainian territories under his control partly because, as Crown Vice-Chancellor Andrzej Leszczyński noted in June 1648, "All Rus' is defecting from us to him and freely throwing open towns to him."[91] The same reception was by no means guaranteed to the Cossack hetman on Polish territory.

Vice-Chancellor Leszczyński was also alarmed by the news that Khmelnytsky was allegedly calling himself "Prince of Kyiv and Rus'." Polish letters were full of rumors to that effect.[92] But were Khmelnytsky and the Cossack leaders of the uprising actually contemplating a restoration of Rus' statehood in its ancient Kyivan-era boundaries, or did the rumors reflect the thinking of the Polish nobles themselves? We do not have a single authentic document in which Khmelnytsky styles himself "Prince of Rus'." Still, it is worth noting that after the victories of 1648 Khmelnytsky arranged a triumphal entry into Kyiv for himself. There he was greeted by Patriarch Paisios of Jerusalem, who was brought to Kyiv on the hetman's orders and bestowed the title of *illustrissimus princeps* upon him. In February 1649, Khmelnytsky told Polish envoys that he was the "sovereign of Kyiv." At that point he defined the western extent of his "land and principality" by the boundaries of ethnic Ruthenian territory: the cities of Lviv, Kholm, and Halych. He told the envoys that he was counting on the support of the peasantry all the way to Lublin and Cracow and that his goal was to liberate the whole Rus' nation from Polish captivity. Khmelnytsky also stressed the religious dimension of the war when he stated: "And if at first I fought because of the damage and injustice done to me, now I shall also fight for our Orthodox faith."[93]

Allegedly, Khmelnytsky was not entirely sober when he presented the Polish envoys with his new program. He never defined it in any official

---

[90] See *Dokumenty Bohdana Khmel'nyts'koho*, p. 39. Cf. Plokhy, *The Cossacks and Religion*, pp. 186–87.

[91] See *Dokumenty ob Osvoboditel'noi voine*, pp. 43–44, here 43.

[92] For an analysis of these rumors, see Valerii Smolii and Valerii Stepankov, *Ukraïns'ka derzhavna ideia. Problemy formuvannia, evoliutsiï, realizatsiï* (Kyiv, 1997), pp. 25–34.

[93] See *Vossoedinenie Ukrainy s Rossiei*, II: 104–14, here 108–9. On the consistent Cossack demand for territory "up to the Vistula" in the course of the military campaigns of 1654–57, see Smolii and Stepankov, *Ukraïns'ka derzhavna ideia*, pp. 88–94.

document, but the Polish report that recorded the hetman's threats leaves no doubt that the idea of creating a Kyivan principality within the ethnic boundaries of Ukraine was alive and well among the leaders of the uprising, who by that time included not only Cossack officers but also quite a few Ruthenian nobles. The idea of a Kyivan principality that included Galicia was closer to the model advocated by the panegyrists of the early modern Ruthenian princes than to that of the seventeenth-century Ruthenian nobility, which imagined its homeland in terms of the four eastern palatinates of the Kingdom of Poland, with the notable exception of Galicia. The Cossack leader was ambitious indeed. But there were also some geographical limits to his aspirations for Rus' (at least in the way he presented them to the Polish envoys). It would appear that like the princes and nobles, the Cossacks thought of the northern boundary of their polity as extending along the border between the Polish Crown and the Grand Duchy of Lithuania. Although they considered the East Slavic population of the Grand Duchy to be part of the Ruthenian nation,[94] the political realities of the time dictated caution: Khmelnytsky was trying to avoid a war on two fronts and counted on the neutrality of Prince Janusz Radziwiłł, the commander of the Lithuanian army. Khmelnytsky sought to represent the uprising as an internal matter of the Kingdom of Poland. If the Cossacks crossed the Lithuanian border, they did so in order to stir up revolt and keep the Lithuanian troops busy putting down popular uprisings on their own territory instead of encroaching on the Ruthenian lands of the Crown. From very early on, Cossack diplomacy tried to persuade the Muscovite tsar to send his troops to Smolensk in order to open a Lithuanian front, suggesting that at least for the moment they were not interested in Belarus. [95]

---

[94] Both the Cossacks and their opponents in the Grand Duchy of Lithuania considered the Ruthenian population on both sides of the border to belong to the same ethnocultural group. Albert Wijuk Kojałowicz, the author of *Rerum in Magno Ducatu Lithvaniae per tempus rebellionis Russicae gestarum Commentarius* (Regiomonti [Königsberg], 1653), who was close to Radziwiłł, saw the reason for the spread of the uprising in the Grand Duchy in the national unity of Ruthenians on both sides of the Polish-Lithuanian boundary. See my *Osvoboditel'naia voina ukrainskogo naroda 1648–1654 gg. v latinoiazychnoi istoriografii serediny XVII veka* (Dnipropetrovsk, 1983), pp. 21–30.

[95] The situation changed in the second half of the 1650s, when Cossack officers competed with Muscovite voevodas for control of southeastern Belarus, and Khmelnytsky created a separate Belarusian regiment. In 1656–57, Khmelnytsky established a protectorate over the Slutsk principality, Stary Bykhaŭ, Pinsk, Mazyr, and Turaŭ. In October 1657, Vyhovsky signed a treaty with Sweden that recognized the Brest and Navahrudak palatinates as parts of the independent Cossack state. See Hrushevs'kyi, *Istoriia Ukraïny-Rusy*, vol. IX, pt. 2 (New York, 1957), pp. 961–63, 1152–59, 1257–77; A. N. Mal'tsev, *Rossiia i Belorussiia v seredine XVII veka* (Moscow, 1974), pp. 19–134, 218–54; Sahanovich, *Neviadomaia vaina*, pp. 14–82; Smolii and Stepankov, *Ukraïns'ka derzhavna ideia*, pp. 105–7.

Developments in the second year of the uprising led to the recognition of autonomous Cossack statehood in the provisions of the Zboriv Agreement (1649).[96] In many ways the agreement was a major triumph for the rebels, although it fell short of Khmelnytsky's aspirations as reported in a Polish diary for the first months of 1649. The territory that ended up under Cossack control was even smaller than that envisaged as a historical and legal unit by the Ruthenian nobles of the 1640s: it included the Kyiv, Chernihiv, and Bratslav palatinates, but not Volhynia. Still, within the boundaries of the new Cossack state the Ruthenian Orthodox nobility was able to achieve some of the major goals of its original program, which could never have been realized without Cossack intervention. These included special rights for the Orthodox Church (in fact, Jews, Uniates, and members of Catholic religious orders were officially banned from the territory of the Hetmanate). Offices in the royal administration of the Cossack palatinates were reserved for nobles of Ruthenian Orthodox extraction. Thus the key post of palatine of Kyiv went to Adam Kysil, a leader of the Ruthenian nobility and author of an appeal that represented the palatinates of Volhynia, Kyiv, Bratslav, and Chernihiv as part of the same administrative entity. To be sure, the Ruthenian Orthodox nobles did not run the new state, but many of them found their place in it, and some made spectacular careers: one such was the Orthodox nobleman Ivan Vyhovsky, who became general chancellor under Khmelnytsky and succeeded him as hetman in 1657.[97]

On the occasion of the Zboriv Agreement, Vyhovsky or, much more probably, some of his secretaries recruited from the ranks of the Ruthenian nobility composed verses that eulogized the Cossack hetman and thus picked up where Kasiian Sakovych had left off in the early 1620s. Khmelnytsky and his family were presented in the verses as successors to St. Volodymyr. "Under Volodymyr's sons Rus′ fell / With the Khmelnytskys, under Bohdan, it rose to its feet," asserted the unknown author.[98] Cossackdom and its hetman were thus reconnected with the myth of

---

[96] For an account of the Zboriv campaign and the text of the Zboriv Agreement, see Hrushevsky, *History of Ukraine-Rus′*, vol. VIII (Edmonton and Toronto, 2002), pp. 575–654.

[97] On the participation of the Ruthenian nobility in the Khmelnytsky Uprising, see Wacław Lipiński, "Stanisław Michał Krzyczewski. Z dziejów walki szlachty ukraińskiej w szeregach powstańczych pod wodzą Bohdana Chmielnickiego," in *Z dziejów Ukrainy*, ed. idem (Cracow, 1912), pp. 145–513. On Kysil's activities as palatine of Kyiv, see Frank E. Sysyn, *Between Poland and the Ukraine: The Dilemma of Adam Kysil, 1600–1653* (Cambridge, Mass., 1985), pp. 175–214.

[98] *Ukraïns′ka poeziia. Seredyna XVII st.*, comp. V. I. Krekoten′ and M. M. Sulyma, ed. O. V. Myshanych (Kyiv, 1992), pp. 101–4, here 104. Cf. Hrushevs′kyi, *Istoriia Ukraïny-Rusy*, IX, pt. 2: 1523–26, here 1526.

princely Rus', but the 1630s also did not go unnoticed: Metropolitan Petro Mohyla, whose epoch influenced the thinking of the new generation of Orthodox intellectuals, was mentioned in the verses. The Cossack hetman was praised for performing the same functions in Rus' society as those earlier attributed to Mohyla. For example, the author credited Khmelnytsky with solicitude for the "common good of the Rus' stock" and with freeing their mother church from captivity in order to return it to the "Rus' (*Rosiiskym*) sons." Rus' (or *Rosiia* in its Hellenic form) is presented in the verses as the polity led by Khmelnytsky, who is treated as a ruler no less powerful than King John Casimir of Poland.

> The Polish mace in the Ruthenian stock;
> Ruthenian glory in the Polish nation;
> When King Casimir is lord in Poland,
> Bohdan Khmelnytsky is hetman in Rus'

states the author.[99] Although the hetman and the Cossack Host are the main objects of attention in the verses, when it comes to ethnonational discourse the protagonist appears to be Rus' (*Rosiia*), which is featured along with another national entity, Poland. Conflict between Rus' and Poland and its peaceful resolution are a leitmotif of the verses, which present the uprising in clear-cut national terms.

The war was presented as a conflict between Rus' and Poland not only by the Cossack literati but also by Bohdan Khmelnytsky himself in letters to none other than King John Casimir. In a petition dispatched to the king in February 1649 in the name of the Zaporozhian Host, the hetman asked for the return to the "Rus' nation (*narod*)" of the churches taken by the Uniates and the abolition of "the very name of the [church] Union," which had not existed at the time of the "unification of Rus' and Poland" (that is, the Union of Lublin of 1569). He also insisted that the palatine of Kyiv be appointed from among the people "of the Rus' nation and the Greek religion."[100] In February 1652, Khmelnytsky warned the king of a possible new revolt and a breach within the "Rus' nation," noting that such developments could only redound to "the perdition of Rus' or to Polish misfortune."[101]

To be sure, the fact that the ethnonational interpretation of the conflict found its way into the letters of leaders of the uprising and the writings of Ruthenian literati does not mean that in the eyes of the elites the national view prevailed over the legal, social, and especially the religious

---

[99] *Ukraïns'ka poeziia. Seredyna XVII st.*, p. 102. Cf. Hrushevs'kyi, *Istoriia Ukraïny-Rusy*, IX, pt. 2: p. 1525.

[100] See *Dokumenty Bohdana Khmel'nyts'koho*, pp. 105–6.   [101] Ibid., p. 251.

interpretation.[102] What the sources indicate, nevertheless, is that the national factor was always present in the perception of the uprising by its participants and opponents. It also served as an important motive and justification for the actions of individuals and social groups. Given prevailing circumstances, the ethnonational factor did not exist in isolation, and more often than not it was closely linked to – and expressed through – the language of political, legal, social, and religious discourse. The interplay of factors in the thinking of the Cossack officer stratum is well demonstrated in a note written by the Cossack colonel Syluian Muzhylovsky to the tsar in 1649 in order to explain the uprising. Muzhylovsky presented the war as a conflict between the Cossacks and the Poles (Liakhs) in defense of Cossack liberties and the Orthodox faith, both of which the Poles had violated. According to Muzhylovsky, the Poles had burned the town of Korsun, destroyed Orthodox churches and killed Orthodox priests because, as they said, "treason is being committed in Rus' by your people." The Cossacks, on the other hand, had concluded an armistice with the Poles on condition that the newly elected king, John Casimir, be a "Rus' king"; if he failed in that duty, the war would resume.[103] This meant that the king was supposed to represent not only the interests of Poland and Lithuania but also those of Rus', which in this case was regarded as including the Dnipro area and extending to the western border of Ukrainian ethnic territory. Up to that boundary, the king had allegedly permitted the Cossacks to keep all they had conquered by the sword. Muzhylovsky's expectations of the king were undoubtedly informed by the Ruthenian nobility's desire to see Rus' as an equal partner in the Commonwealth and by Khmelnytsky's interpretation of the uprising as a national war.

The continuation of the uprising and the varying fortunes of war significantly altered the Cossack view of the Hetmanate, its geographical extent, and legal status, but the vision of Rus' as a nation endowed with a particular territory and protected by its own political and military institutions remained a constant in the thinking of Cossack elites for generations to come.

The Orthodox alliance

Sylvian Muzhylovsky's mission to Moscow in early 1649 served as the beginning of direct diplomatic exchange between Muscovy and the

---

[102] On the role of the religious factor in the uprising, see Plokhy, *The Cossacks and Religion*, pp. 176–206. On the low priority of religious identities in the pecking order of soldiers' loyalties at the time, see Iakovenko, "Skil'ky oblych u viiny."

[103] *Vossoedinenie Ukrainy s Rossiei*, II: 127–31, here 128, 130.

Hetmanate – an exchange that eventually led to the Pereiaslav Agreement of 1654. Not unlike the Khmelnytsky Uprising itself, this event had a profound impact on the political situation in the region and the process of nation-building among the Eastern Slavs. Here, however, our task is not so much to look into the long-term consequences of the agreement as to understand whether the ethnonational factor was part of the equation from the outset and, if so, how it influenced the course of events.

Contacts between the rebels and the Muscovite authorities began in the summer of 1648 at the initiative of the Cossack hetman. From the very beginning he asked Muscovy to join forces with the Cossacks in the war against the Commonwealth. The situation of 1632 was repeating itself, with the difference that it was now the Cossacks, not the tsar, who were eager to obtain support. After the defeat of 1634, Muscovy was more than cautious. Besides, the specter of a new Cossack-led uprising that might spread to Muscovy and provoke a new Time of Troubles discouraged the Muscovites from becoming openly involved in the conflict. They adopted a compromise tactic: those of the Cossacks and rebels who wanted to cross the border were welcomed in Muscovy (on one occasion, Cossack troops were even allowed to launch a surprise attack on the Grand Duchy of Lithuania from Muscovite territory), but the tsar would not start a new war with the Commonwealth. Not until 1651 was Muscovy finally prepared to change its policy of noninterference in Commonwealth affairs. Preparations were even made to convene an Assembly of the Land to sanction the war, but the Commonwealth army's defeat of the Cossacks at Berestechko put an end to the plan. By 1653, unable to obtain military assistance from the Ottomans and losing the cooperation of the khan, Khmelnytsky insisted that the Muscovite rulers finally make up their mind. That autumn, a special convocation of the Assembly of the Land decided to take Khmelnytsky and the Cossacks "with their towns" (meaning the territory of the Hetmanate) under the tsar's "high hand." An embassy led by the boyar Vasilii Buturlin was sent to Ukraine to administer an oath to the Cossack leadership and the rank-and-file Cossacks. In January 1654, the embassy met with Khmelnytsky in the town of Pereiaslav. After brief negotiations that were not very satisfactory to the Cossack side, a council was convened to formally approve Cossack submission to the tsar.

Historians still differ on what the Pereiaslav Agreement amounted to in legal terms. Was it indeed an agreement? After all, no document was signed in Pereiaslav, and the tsar's approval of the conditions of submission was given much later in Moscow. If it was an agreement, was it a personal union, real union, alliance, federation, confederation, vassalage, protectorate, or outright incorporation? How did that arrangement compare with previous ones, such as the Zboriv Treaty of 1649 with the king, or agreements concluded by Muscovy with previously incorporated territories and peoples?[104]

Of greatest interest to us is not the legal status of the Pereiaslav Agreement but the discourse that accompanied its preparation and legitimized its conclusion. If Muscovy's involvement in the war with the Commonwealth was the main goal of Cossack diplomacy, what ideological arguments did Khmelnytsky and his associates use to convince the tsar to send his troops against Poland-Lithuania? Khmelnytsky's letters to the tsar and to his courtiers and voevodas provide sufficient information to answer this question. They indicate that from the very beginning of that correspondence in the summer of 1648, the religious motif had a prominent place. The tsar emerges from the hetman's letters as first and foremost an Orthodox Christian ruler duty-bound to assist fellow Orthodox Christians rebelling against Catholic persecution of their church. Khmelnytsky also sought to lure the tsar into the conflict by invoking the mirage of a vast Orthodox empire including not only Cossack Ukraine and Polish-Lithuanian Rus' but also the Orthodox Balkans and Greece. All the Orthodox – Greeks, Serbians, Bulgarians, Moldavians, and Wallachians – argued Khmelnytsky in his conversation with Arsenii Sukhanov, a Muscovite monk and onetime secretary of Patriarch Filaret – wanted to be united under the rule of the Muscovite tsar.[105] Khmelnytsky also promised the tsar a rebellion in Belarus: as soon as Muscovy dispatched its troops to the front, the hetman intended to send letters to "the Belarusian people (*liudi*) living under Lithuania" in Orsha, Mahiliou, and other towns, setting off a revolt of forces two hundred thousand strong.[106] If the tsar refused to take the Zaporozhian Host "under his high hand," Khmelnytsky threatened to ally himself out of necessity with the Muslim Turks and Tatars. Since the prospective alliance with the "infidels" would be directed first and foremost against Muscovy, such threats prompted the Muscovite authorities to reach a final decision in the autumn of 1653.[107]

So much for the Cossack claims. How did the Muscovite authorities react to claims of confessional solidarity from people whom they regarded after the Time of Troubles not only as not entirely Orthodox but also as

---

[104] On the legal nature of the Pereiaslav Agreement, see the articles by Mykhailo Hrushevsky, Andrii Yakovliv and Oleksander Ohloblyn in *Pereiaslavs'ka rada 1654 roku*. For the most recent debates on the issue, see my "Ghosts of Pereyaslav."

[105] See *Vossoedinenie Ukrainy s Rossiei*, II: 189.

[106] See the ambassadorial report of Ivan Fomin, the Muscovite emissary to Khmelnytsky, on his discussions with the hetman in August 1653 (*Vossoedinenie Ukrainy s Rossiei*, III: 357).

[107] See the report on Ivan Iskra's embassy to Muscovy in the spring of 1653 in *Vossoedinenie Ukrainy s Rossiei*, III: 209.

not entirely Christian, and whose representatives continued to be rebaptized once they crossed the Muscovite border? Surprisingly, given what we know about Muscovite religious attitudes of the earlier period, those appeals were heard, understood, and even welcomed. In fact, it was the common Orthodox discourse that created the ideological foundation for the Pereiaslav Agreement. How did that happen? First of all, even after the Time of Troubles, Orthodoxy remained a potent weapon in the Muscovite foreign-policy arsenal. As noted earlier, Orthodox connections and rhetoric were put to use by Moscow during the Smolensk War to attract Zaporozhian Cossacks to the tsar's side. Secondly, Muscovy entered into the union with Cossack Ukraine with very different views on Orthodoxy from those it had held in the aftermath of the Time of Troubles. Led by the new and energetic Patriarch Nikon, it was trying to open itself to the Orthodox world: the Kyivan Christianity once condemned by Patriarch Filaret could now serve as a much-needed bridge to that world. Nikon, bombarded by letters from Khmelnytsky, was in favor of extending a Muscovite protectorate to the Cossacks. He emerged as a strong voice at court arguing for Muscovy's intervention in the war for the sake of the Orthodox religion.[108] But changes in the Muscovite attitude toward fellow Orthodox outside the tsar's realm had begun even before Nikon assumed the patriarchal throne in 1652.

An important stimulus for change was the debate over the marriage of Prince Waldemar of Denmark to Grand Princess Irina Mikhailovna. The event that (as noted above) ended the career of that admirer of Kyivan learning, Prince Semen Shakhovskoi, also prompted the Muscovite church to reach out to fellow Orthodox abroad. The debates with Lutheran pastors showed a lack of training, skills, and sophistication on the part of the Muscovite intellectuals. The church was in need of reform, and calls for it were coming not only from the capital but also from the regions. The movement of the Zealots of Piety was gathering strength in the provinces, and the ascension of Aleksei Mikhailovich to the throne in 1645 made its adherents influential at court as well. These new conditions called for a complete overhaul of Orthodox doctrine, and the formerly rejected Greek learning was now regarded as the solution to the problem. But where could one find enough polyglots to translate from the Greek? The eyes of the Muscovite reformers turned to the learned monks of Kyiv. In the autumn of 1648, the tsar wrote to the Orthodox bishop of Chernihiv, asking him to send to Moscow monks who could translate the

---

[108] On Nikon's role in the Muscovite decision-making process concerning the war, see the chapter on the war of religion in Sergei Lobachev, *Patriarkh Nikon* (St. Petersburg, 2003), pp. 130–46.

Bible into Slavonic. In the summer of the following year, with the blessing of Metropolitan Sylvestr Kosov of Kyiv, the learned monks Arsenii
Satanovsky (it would be interesting to know what the Muscovites made
of his "Satanic" surname) and Yepyfanii (Epifanii) Slavynetsky arrived
in Moscow, becoming the founders of the Ruthenian colony there. (It
later counted such luminaries as Simeon Polatsky among its prominent
members.) The years 1648–49 also saw the publication or reprinting in
Moscow of a number of earlier Kyivan works, including the Orthodox
confession of faith (*Brief Compendium of Teachings about the Articles of the
Faith*) composed under the supervision of Petro Mohyla and approved by
the council of Eastern patriarchs. The Muscovite Orthodox were clearly
trying to catch up with their coreligionists abroad. They hoped for enlightenment from Greece, but what they got was the beginning of the Ruth-
enization of Muscovite Orthodoxy.[109]

The elevation to the patriarchal throne of Metropolitan Nikon, who
was close to reformist circles in Moscow, strengthened the hand of those
in the Muscovite church who were prepared to look to Kyiv for inspiration. At the last prewar negotiations with Commonwealth diplomats,
the Poles maintained that the Muscovites and the Orthodox Ruthenians were not in fact coreligionists, for the Muscovite faith was as far
removed from Ruthenian Orthodoxy as it was from the Union and Roman
Catholicism. The Muscovite envoys, who twenty years earlier might readily have agreed with the Poles, now rejected their argument. They also
ignored Polish accusations that Khmelnytsky had abandoned Orthodoxy
and accepted Islam. Indeed, they turned the issue of the tsar's right to
protect the liberties of his coreligionists into the main justification for
his intervention in Commonwealth affairs.[110] When the Assembly of the
Land finally approved the decision to enter the war with the Commonwealth in the autumn of 1653, it did so not only to defend the honor
of the Muscovite tsar, allegedly besmirched by Commonwealth officials'
errors in citing his title (one of them consisted of mistakenly calling the
tsar Mikhail Nikitich Romanov, Mikhail Filaretovich, after the monastic
name of his father), but also "for the sake of the Orthodox Christian faith
and the holy churches of God."[111] The Muscovite embassy dispatched to

---

[109] For a survey of developments in the Muscovite church in the mid-seventeenth century,
see Paul Bushkovitch, *Religion and Society in Russia: The Sixteenth and Seventeenth Centuries* (New York and Oxford, 1992), pp. 51–73, 128–49. On the publication of Kyivan
books in Moscow, see Oparina, *Ivan Nasedka*, pp. 245–86.

[110] On the course of the negotiations of 1653, which took place in Lviv and involved
a Muscovite embassy headed by Boris Repnin-Obolensky, see Hrushevs'kyi, *Istoriia
Ukraïny-Rusy*, IX, pt. 2: pp. 619–41.

[111] See the decisions of the Assembly of the Land in *Vossoedinenie Ukrainy s Rossiei*, III:
414.

Khmelnytsky scarcely missed an opportunity to visit a Ruthenian Orthodox church or take part in a religious procession along its way. It was met not only by Cossacks but also by burghers solemnly led by priests, who welcomed the embassy with long baroque-style speeches, and sermons. The conclusion of the Pereiaslav Agreement itself was accompanied by a solemn church service. In his speech at Pereiaslav, the tsar's envoy Vasilii Buturlin mentioned not only the Muscovite saints to whose support he attributed the success of the whole enterprise but also SS. Antonii and Teodosii of the Kyivan Cave Monastery and St. Barbara, highly venerated in the Kyiv metropolitanate, whose relics were preserved in one of the Kyivan monasteries.[112]

If there was a reunion in Pereiaslav, it was an Orthodox one, declared in numerous religious services, speeches, and pronouncements but not yet implemented. In fact, it was not even a reunion (that did not happen in institutional, liturgical, and other terms until the last decade of the seventeenth century and the first decades of the eighteenth) but an avowal of reconciliation. After the tumultuous struggle against the Union in the Kyiv metropolitanate and the shock of the Time of Troubles in Muscovy, the two sides had agreed to reestablish relations. The churchmen thereby provided the political elites with the common language required to begin a dialogue between the two nations, which by now were very different. In Europe, even after the end of the Thirty Years' War, religion continued to provide legitimization for political alliances, breaches of peace, and declarations of war. Muscovy and the Cossack Hetmanate were no exception to that rule.

The Pereiaslav disagreement

What about ethnic motives for the "reunification"? Were they entirely absent from Cossack negotiations with the tsar? Although Khmelnytsky defined certain elements of the uprising in ethnonational terms in his letters to Muscovy, it appears that the hetman and his secretaries never made the seemingly natural link between the two Rus' nations. In a letter to the voevoda Semen Bolkhovsky in the summer of 1648, Khmelnytsky complained about the persecution of "our Rus' Orthodox Christians," but in his attempt to involve the tsar in the Cossack-Polish conflict he made no use of the theme of ethnic affinity between the two parts of Rus'; instead, he invited the tsar to seek the Polish throne, which was

---

[112] For the texts of the speeches, see the report of Buturlin's embassy in *Vossoedinenie Ukrainy s Rossiei*, III: 423–89. Cf. Plokhy, *The Cossacks and Religion*, pp. 318–25.

vacant at the time.[113] That did not change in Khmelnytsky's subsequent letters to Moscow.[114] What changed was the way in which he referred to his homeland. If at first he called it Rus' (the name he also used in his letters to the Polish king), from the spring of 1653 he began to refer to it as Little Rus', thereby adopting a Muscovy-friendly terminology. In January 1654, he even introduced a corresponding change into the tsar's official title, addressing him not as "Sovereign of All Rus'" but as "Sovereign of Great and Little Rus'."[115] The tsar accepted this change of his title.[116] The beginning of the new war with the Commonwealth clearly freed him from the Muscovite envoys' claim of 1634 that the Polish Little Rus' had nothing to do with the tsar's "all Rus'." Now the tsar claimed Little Rus' as well, and his title was changed accordingly to avoid the ambiguity of 1634.

In accepting the formula of "Great and Little Rus'," did the tsar and his Muscovite entourage also embrace the idea of the ethnic affinity of the two Ruses as an important element in their conceptualization of events? Available sources indicate that this is extremely unlikely. The tsar's ideologists continued to think not just primarily but almost exclusively in dynastic terms. They saw the Cossack territories as just another part of the tsar's patrimony. In December 1653, the tsar's chancellery addressed the voevodas dispatched to Kyiv as "boyars and voevodas of the patrimony of his tsarist majesty, the Grand Principality of Kyiv." In April 1654, Aleksei Mikhailovich referred to Kyiv as his patrimony in a letter to Bohdan Khmelnytsky himself. His full title now included references to the principalities of Kyiv and Chernihiv.[117] We do not know how Khmelnytsky reacted to these manifestations of the tsar's patrimonial thinking. Nor are we certain of the meaning with which the hetman himself invested the terms Little and Great Rus', for even after Pereiaslav he occasionally

---

[113] See Khmelnytsky's letter dated 29 July (8 August) 1648 in *Dokumenty Bohdana Khmel'nyts'koho*, p. 65.

[114] There was also no attempt to play on the theme of ethnic affinity in Khmelnytsky's letter of 29 September (9 October) 1649 to the voevoda Fedor Arseniev, in which the hetman complained about attacks on "the Orthodox Rus' and our faith" (*Dokumenty Bohdana Khmel'nyts'koho*, p. 143). Khmelnytsky's use of the formula "Sovereign of All Rus'" in his letters to the tsar seems to have been fairly insignificant, given that in his letters to Muscovite correspondents (including the missive to Arseniev) the hetman also used the full title of John Casimir, which included a reference to the king as "Prince of Rus'."

[115] See Khmelnytsky's letters in *Dokumenty Bohdana Khmel'nyts'koho*, pp. 286, 298, 316.

[116] On the tsar's new title, see Mykhailo Hrushevs'kyi, "Velyka, Mala i Bila Rus'," *Ukraïna*, 1917, nos. 1–2: 7–19; A. V. Solov'ev, "Velikaia, Malaia i Belaia Rus'," *Voprosy istorii*, 1947, no. 7: 24–38.

[117] See Plokhy, *The Cossacks and Religion*, p. 326.

referred to his homeland as Rus' (*Rosiia*) when writing to the tsar.[118] A further complication is that most of Khmelnytsky's letters to Moscow are not available in the original but only in Muscovite translations "from the Belarusian." What strikes one about those translations is that they contain no references to the "Rus' nation," whose rights Khmelnytsky was eager to defend in his Polish-language letters to the king. We know that Ruthenian authors of the period freely used the term "nation" (*narod*), which had the same meaning in Ruthenian as in Polish. Did Khmelnytsky consciously avoid such references in his letters to Muscovy, replacing them with such formulae as "Rus' Orthodox Christians" or "the whole Rus' Orthodox community of Little Rus'," which were contrary to Ukrainian practice at the time?[119] Or was the term lost in translation? Both possibilities suggest a breakdown of communication between the two parties.

Thus a nation-based dialogue was hardly possible between the Ruthenian and Muscovite elites. It appears that lack of understanding in that regard was not the only disconnection between the two sides, as events in Pereiaslav demonstrated. A major crisis was provoked by Buturlin's refusal to swear in the name of the tsar to the preservation of Cossack freedoms and liberties. Buturlin did his best to assure the Cossack officers that the tsar would not only preserve but actually increase their liberties, but refused to swear an oath in the name of his sovereign. Khmelnytsky left the envoy in church to await the results of his negotiations with the colonels. When it was conveyed to Buturlin that the Polish kings swore oaths to their subjects, the boyar stood his ground. He told his interlocutors that he represented the Orthodox tsar and autocrat, while the Polish king was neither; hence the two monarchs could not be compared.[120] Khmelnytsky and the colonels were eventually obliged to consent. The Cossacks swore allegiance to the tsar without extracting an oath from the representatives of their new sovereign. This was unprecedented in Cossack practice. Although the Polish king had indeed refused to sign agreements with them and recognize them as equals in negotiations, Polish commissioners took an oath in the name of the Commonwealth on whatever agreement they reached with the Cossacks, as was the case at Bila Tserkva in the autumn of 1651. The Cossacks would not swear their own oath otherwise. At Pereiaslav, they did. It was their introduction to the world of Muscovite politics.

---

[118] See Khmelnytsky's petition to the tsar of 17 (27) February 1654 in *Dokumenty Bohdana Khmel'nyts'koho*, p. 323.

[119] See Khmelnytsky's letter to the tsar of 19 (29) July 1654 in *Dokumenty Bohdana Khmel'nyts'koho*, p. 373.

[120] See the description of the disagreement over the oath in Buturlin's ambassadorial report (*Vossoedinenie Ukrainy s Rossiei*, III: 464–66).

Buturlin did not lie: tsars indeed never swore oaths to their subjects. At Pereiaslav the tsar's representative applied to his sovereign's new subjects the rules of steppe diplomacy – a set of principles inherited by Muscovy from the Golden Horde and practiced with regard to its eastern neighbors and vassals. As Andreas Kappeler has argued, these principles entailed "a loose protectorate, which was concluded by means of an oath, by installing a loyal ruler. From the Russian point of view that established a client status to which it could always refer in the future, whereas the other side saw it at the most as a personal and temporary act of submission."[121] Indeed, if the Cossack elite viewed the oath and service to the tsar as conditional ("voluntary" [*povol'ne*], in their language) subordination to the ruler, with subsequent relations depending on the willingness of each party to keep its side of the bargain, Muscovite diplomacy regarded the oath as proof of eternal subjection. After all, the text of the standard oath included the following words: "And not to leave the Muscovite tsardom in treasonable fashion, and not to engage in double-dealing or treason."[122] Subsequent events showed quite conclusively that neither side in the Pereiaslav negotiations fully understood what it was getting into.

---

[121] Andreas Kappeler, *The Russian Empire: A Multiethnic History*, trans. Alfred Clayton (Harlow, 2001), p. 52.
[122] Quoted in Oparina, *Ivan Nasedka*, p. 342.

7   The invention of Russia

The confluence of national and imperial identity in modern Russian consciousness has always puzzled observers of the Russian scene and attracted the attention of historians of Russia. That confluence, which distinguished Russian identity from that of west European imperial nations, was expressed somewhat paradoxically by Geoffrey Hosking, who remarked in one of his review articles: "Britain *had* an empire, but Russia *was* an empire – and perhaps still is."[1] One possible explanation of the peculiarities of the Russian imperial experience noted by Hosking is that, unlike the British and other west European empires, the Russian Empire was not a maritime entity but a land-based one.[2] But geography cannot be regarded as the sole explanation of the peculiarities of Russian national identity. The role of historical experience was not insignificant. In the opinion of Richard Pipes, the phenomenon of Russian identity might be explained by the fact that in Russia "the rise of the national state and the empire occurred concurrently, and not, as in the case of the Western powers, in sequence."[3] If that was indeed the case, then where should one seek the moment in history when the rise of the national state and the empire began? When it comes to the empire, many historians point to the era of Peter I (1689–1725), the founder of the modern Russian state[4] and, coincidentally, the first Muscovite ruler to proclaim himself "all-Russian emperor," inaugurating the history of Russia not only as a modern state but also as an empire. To be sure, many professors of history maintain that Muscovy became an empire much earlier, by the time

[1] Geoffrey Hosking, "The Freudian Frontier," *Times Literary Supplement*, 10 March 1995, p. 27.
[2] On the Russian Empire as a land-based power, see Dominic Lieven, *Empire: The Russian Empire and Its Rivals* (New Haven and London, 2001).
[3] Richard Pipes, "Weight of the Past: Russian Foreign Policy in Historical Perspective," *Harvard International Review* 19, no. 1 (Winter 1996/97): 5–6.
[4] On the establishment of modern governmental institutions in Russia during the rule of Peter I, see James Cracraft, *The Petrine Revolution in Russian Culture* (Cambridge, Mass., and London, 2004), pp. 144–92.

of Ivan the Terrible,[5] but for their students, whose study of the subject is divided into courses on Muscovy, the Russian Empire and Soviet Russia/USSR, Peter's rule marks the beginning of Russian imperial history and the history of the Russian Empire as such.

Whether we start the history of the Russian Empire with the rule of Ivan IV or Peter I, it is important to note that the confluence of national and imperial discourses in Russia can first be identified in the closing decades of the seventeenth century leading up to the era of the Petrine reforms. It was at this time, before Muscovy opened itself to the West and became known as Russia, that it first became receptive to new people and ideas from the recently acquired Cossack Hetmanate, and more specifically from its religious and intellectual capital, the city of Kyiv. The entanglement of the concepts of nationality and imperial statehood that took place during the encounter between Kyivan and Muscovite elites appears to have been crucial for the formation of Russian imperial identity. That entanglement sowed much confusion in the minds of the Eastern Slavs themselves, as well as among those who study their histories and political behaviors. It is this confluence of ideas, discussed within the chronological frame of the years 1654–1730 (from the Pereiaslav Agreement to the end of the Petrine era and the ascension of Anna Ioannovna to the Russian imperial throne), that constitutes the main theme of the present chapter.

Muscovy goes west

The Pereiaslav Agreement marked a turning point in Moscow's relations with its immediate and more distant West. In 1654, the Tsardom of Muscovy began a westward movement that was to be continued by the Russian Empire and the Soviet Union, first with troops and then with political and cultural influence. The end of the seventeenth century saw Muscovy's borders on the Dnipro River; by the end of the eighteenth century they were on the Niemen and the Dnister; the nineteenth century saw the incorporation of Warsaw and the entrance of Russian troops into Paris. In the mid-twentieth century, the Red Army took Berlin and Prague. Only the collapse of the Soviet bloc and the disintegration of the USSR in 1991 seemingly put an end to the westward expansion of Russia, whose western border partly retreated to the boundaries of

---

[5] See, for example, the treatment of the issue in Geoffrey Hosking, *Russia: People and Empire, 1552–1917* (London; 1998), pp. 45–56.

pre-1654 Muscovy. In the process of its westward expansion, Russia changed the world, but it also profoundly changed itself.[6]

After the Pereiaslav Agreement, most of what is now Ukraine and Belarus remained outside Moscow's control. The outbreak of the Russian-Polish conflict in 1654 turned Belarus into a battleground between Muscovite, Polish-Lithuanian, and Ukrainian Cossack armies. Under the terms of the Russo-Polish treaties of 1667 and 1686, the Commonwealth managed to maintain control over all Belarusian territories except the Smolensk region, which passed to Muscovy. Muscovy's direct relations with other Eastern Slavs were often limited to dealings with those Ruthenians who ended up on the territory of the Hetmanate, which was a Muscovite dependency. The tsars' relations with the Cossack Hetmanate can be characterized, using the title of Hans-Joachim Torke's article, as an "unloved alliance."[7] The expression aptly defines the nature of Russo-Ukrainian relations in the second half of the seventeenth century, as the "marriage" of the two parties announced in January 1654 at Pereiaslav was far from happy and worry-free. First there was a contest for Belarus, followed by well-founded suspicions that the tsar was "cheating" on the Cossacks with their worst enemy, the Polish king. Indeed, the year 1656 witnessed the conclusion of the Vilnius Agreement between Muscovy and the Commonwealth at the expense of the Hetmanate. The Cossacks nevertheless continued to fight the king, having allied themselves with two Protestant powers, Transylvania and Sweden. Nor can it be said that Muscovy was happy with its new Cossack partner. Some influential leaders in Moscow, such as the head of the Ambassadorial Office in the 1660s, A. L. Ordin-Nashchokin, considered the protectorate over the Hetmanate a mistake and advocated improving relations with the Polish-Lithuanian Commonwealth by giving up on the Cossacks. The Truce of Andrusovo (1667), with its clause about handing over Kyiv to Poland, was largely the product of his advice and activities.

Whether the makers of Muscovite foreign policy oriented themselves on the Hetmanate or the Commonwealth, Muscovy and its elites were becoming more and more involved in European politics. In so doing, they were opening the door to the penetration of Western culture and ideas into their previously isolated world. It was in the times of Aleksei

---

[6] On the geopolitics of Russian imperial expansion, see John P. LeDonne, *The Russian Empire and the World, 1700–1917: The Geopolitics of Expansion and Containment* (New York and Oxford, 1997).

[7] See Hans-Joachim Torke, "The Unloved Alliance: Political Relations between Muscovy and Ukraine in the Seventeenth Century," in *Ukraine and Russia in Their Historical Encounter*, ed. Peter J. Potichnyj, Marc Raeff, Jaroslaw Pelenski, and Gleb N. Żekulin (Edmonton, 1992), pp. 39–66.

Mikhailovich that theater and ballet were first introduced at court. Western fashions apparently became so popular during his rule that in 1675 he had to issue an edict prohibiting Western clothing and hairstyles. His son and successor Fedor (1676–82), a disciple of Simeon Polatsky, liked Western paintings and prints and commissioned portraits for his court. The Westernization of Muscovite high culture continued under the regent Sofia (1682–89) and reached its pinnacle under Peter I. His reign saw a major transformation of Muscovy along Western lines – a development that could not but dramatically influence the nation-building project in Russia and the way in which the Muscovite elites perceived themselves and the outside world.[8]

Although it is hard to disagree with Max J. Okenfuss's assessment of Muscovite society at large as resistant to the humanistic ideas brought to the realm of the tsars by the learned Kyivans, it would be a mistake to underestimate their impact on the formation of official Russian ideology, culture, and identity in the second half of the seventeenth century and the early decades of the eighteenth.[9] Kyivans were the first to adapt Western religious and political ideas to Orthodox conditions in the early seventeenth century. It was they who began to think in protonational terms, regarding the nation not as a byproduct of the dynasty and the state but as a distinct and self-sufficient phenomenon. Quite often, the alumni of the Kyivan College did not have to go to Moscow or St. Petersburg to influence others and to be influenced themselves. The Chernihiv archbishop Lazar Baranovych, for example, successfully petitioned the tsar for publication subsidies and marketed his publications in Muscovy without leaving Ukraine. Scores of literati educated at the Kyiv Mohyla College, beginning with Yepyfanii Slavynetsky, who founded the Greco-Latin School in Moscow in 1653, and continuing with Simeon Polatsky, the teacher of the tsar's children and an initiator of the Slavo-Greco-Latin Academy in Moscow, and Teofan Prokopovych (Feofan Prokopovich), the main propagandist of Peter I's reforms, were in the forefront of the Westernization and transformation of Russia, its society and its self-image in the formative stage of its history. The Kyivans certainly helped Peter if not to formulate his ideas, then at least to articulate them by creating a discourse that popularized and legitimized his policies.

---

[8] On the politics of Peter's rule, see Paul Bushkovitch, *Peter the Great: The Struggle for Power, 1671–1725* (Cambridge and New York, 2001); on his reforms, see Evgenii V. Anisimov, *The Reforms of Peter the Great: Progress through Coercion in Russia*, trans. with an introduction by John T. Alexander (Armonk, NY, and London, 1993).

[9] On the impact of Polish culture and Kyivan learning on Muscovite high culture, see Max J. Okenfuss, *The Rise and Fall of Latin Humanism in Early-Modern Russia: Pagan Authors, Ukrainians, and the Resiliency of Muscovy* (Leiden, New York, and Köln, 1995).

The major influx of Kyiv-trained intellectuals into the Muscovite and, later, the imperial service occurred after the Battle of Poltava (1709), a disaster for Ukraine. Chafing under the efforts of Tsar Peter I to further limit the Hetmanate's autonomy, Hetman Ivan Mazepa (in office from 1687 to 1709) seized the opportunity presented by the Northern War and joined the invading army of Charles XII of Sweden in 1708. Only part of the Cossack officers followed their hetman in switching sides, and the Russian army's defeat of Charles XII and Mazepa's forces at the Battle of Poltava in July 1709 firmly reestablished Russian control over the Left Bank. Little remained the same in Kyiv and the Cossack Hetmanate after the Poltava battle – the secular and religious elites rapidly changed their political orientation, public stand and discourse, abandoning old loyalties and taking on or actualizing new ones. The post-Poltava Ukrainians skillfully adapted their views to the demands of the Muscovite state and society, but, having been educated under different circumstances, they could not help introducing new and provocative ideas into the minds of their readers. For generations to come, they helped form Russia's perception of its past, its role in the world, and its destiny as a modern nation. Needless to say, in the process the Kyivans also transformed their own identity, as well as the image and, in part, the self-perception of their homeland.[10]

Examining the Petrine epoch

The eighteenth century is the earliest period of Russian history into which most students of nationalism are prepared to venture in search of the roots of Russian national identity. Even the boldest of them must take account of the modernist approach, which holds – to adapt the words of the nineteenth-century Russian minister of the interior, P. A. Valuev – that there "has never been and never can be" a nation prior to the rise of nationalism.[11] Thus historians resort to all sorts of disclaimers to legitimize their search for elements of identity that, according to conventional wisdom, could not have existed in those "ancient" times. The

---

[10] The most extensive account of the influence exercised by the Kyiv-trained clergy in Muscovy is Konstantin Kharlampovich, *Malorossiiskoe vliianie na velikorusskuiu tserkovnuiu zhizn'* (Kazan, 1914). On the activities of the Kyivan literati (Slavynetsky and Polatsky) in Moscow, see Paul Bushkovitch, *Religion and Society in Russia: The Sixteenth and Seventeenth Centuries* (New York and Oxford, 1992), pp. 150–75. For a revisionist view that questions the extent of Kyivan influence on Muscovite society, see Okenfuss, *The Rise and Fall of Latin Humanism*, pp. 45–63.

[11] Such was Valuev's reference to the Ukrainian language in his circular of 1863 prohibiting Ukrainian publications in the Russian Empire. On the origins of the circular and its influence, see Alexei Miller, *The Ukrainian Question: The Russian Empire and Nationalism in the Nineteenth Century* (Budapest and New York, 2003), pp. 97–126.

traditional approach to the topic is well summarized in the opening para-
graph of Hans Rogger's groundbreaking study, *National Consciousness in
Eighteenth-Century Russia* (1960), where we read the following:

Nationalism, most of its students are agreed, is a recent phenomenon, and any use
of the term applied to events or attitudes before the eighteenth century unjustified.
Even then, only some favored few – the English, the French, perhaps the Dutch –
could claim it as their own. The Russians, backward in this as in so many other
things, did not, in the eighteenth century, have a nationalism worthy of that name,
and "real" Russian nationalism did not make its appearance until the nineteenth
century.[12]

Rogger's study proved beyond reasonable doubt the existence of
"national consciousness" in post-Petrine eighteenth-century Russia, but
the reign of Peter himself, and especially the decades leading up to it, long
remained a gray area to most students of Russian history. Only recently
has the situation begun to change. Geoffrey Hosking, for example, introduced the schismatic Old Belief into his discussion of Russian national
mythology, presenting it as a factor "in some ways even more damag-
ing to Russians' confidence about their own national identity" than the
rift between Russia and the West.[13] In her comparative study of European nationalisms, Liah Greenfeld included the Petrine era in a general
discussion of "Russian national consciousness," as did Vera Tolz in her
pioneering work on the invention of the Russian nation. Tolz was nevertheless careful to observe: "It should be said from the very outset that in
the eighteenth century, Russia was not a nation. Nevertheless, concepts
about what Russia was, and especially how it compared to the West, first
began to be elaborated in the eighteenth century."[14]

What are the findings, suppositions, and hypotheses of the most recent
historiography concerning the Petrine "beginnings" of Russian national
identity? Greenfeld's observations deserve particular attention in this
regard. For her, the eighteenth century is the period of the rise of national
consciousness in Russia, as it provided safe haven and gave a new identity to the masses of the nobility and educated non-nobles who were
experiencing a crisis of their old identities and searching for new ones.
Greenfeld credits Peter I, along with Catherine II, with "installing the
idea of the nation in the Russian elite and awakening it to the potent
and stimulating sense of national pride." According to her, the idea of

---

[12] Hans Rogger, *National Consciousness in Eighteenth-Century Russia* (Cambridge, Mass.,
    1960), p. 1.
[13] See Geoffrey Hosking, "The Russian National Myth Repudiated," in *Myths and Nation-
    hood*, ed. Geoffrey Hosking and George Schöpflin (London, 1997), pp. 198–210, here
    198–99.
[14] Vera Tolz, *Russia* (London and New York, 2001), pp. 23–24.

nation "implied the fundamental redefinition of the Russian polity (from the property of the tsar into a commonwealth, an impersonal *patrie* or *fatherland* in which every member had an equal stake and to which everyone was naturally attached)." Greenfeld studied official documents of the Petrine era, looking for the occurrence and usage of such terms as "*gosudarstvo*/state," "common good," and "fatherland." Her conclusion was that the use of such (often Western) terms signaled the arrival in Russia of new, nation-related concepts and ideas. At the same time, Greenfeld noted the contradictory nature of the process, observing that Peter continued to regard the state as an extension of himself and failed to provide his subjects with a sense of individual dignity, but gave them instead a sense of pride in being subjects of a mighty emperor. She also took her lead from Hans Rogger in stressing the importance of the West as a factor in opposition to which Russian identity of the period was formed.[15]

Vera Tolz developed some of Greenfeld's ideas (and was apparently influenced by her selection of source quotations) but refrained from making any reference to Greenfeld's book in her discussion of the Petrine era. Tolz's main argument was that Peter's reforms both "laid the foundation for, and at the same time put constraints on, Russia's subsequent nation-building" and the construction of its national identity. When it comes to the foundations of both, Tolz indicates the secularization of the state and educational system, as well as the creation of an ideology of state patriotism that nurtured the loyalty of imperial subjects to the state. Constraints on nation-building included Peter's consolidation of autocratic rule, the strengthening of the institution of serfdom, and the further extension of the empire. Tolz notes that by the time Peter came to power, traditional Russian identity based on the pillar of Orthodoxy was already crumbling. Taking her lead from Hosking, she includes the Old Belief schism in her discussion and emphasizes the dissenters' opposition to the secularization of the state and their profound anti-Westernism. Unlike Greenfeld, Tolz draws attention not so much to the discourse of the epoch as to those reforms of Peter I that altered the character and structure of Russian society, thereby contributing (mostly in the long run) to the construction of Russian national identity.[16]

Both Greenfeld and Tolz pay substantial attention to the role played in Peter's reform of Russian politics, high culture, and learning by Ruthenian alumni of the Kyiv Mohyla Academy. In both studies they are presented as bearers of new Western ideas and cadres that helped undermine the old Muscovite culture. Who were those Kyivans in the imperial service, what

---

[15] See Liah Greenfeld, *Nationalism: Five Roads to Modernity* (Cambridge, Mass., 1992), pp. 189–274.
[16] See Tolz, *Russia*, pp. 23–44.

kind of identities did they possess, and how did they bear "transplanta-tion" from the intellectual soil of Kyiv to that of St. Petersburg? These questions were first placed on the scholarly agenda by George (Yurii) Shevelov with reference to Peter's leading ideologue, an alumnus and one-time rector of the Kyiv Mohyla Academy, Teofan Prokopovych. In 1954, under the pseudonym Jurij Šerech, he published an article "On Teofan Prokopovič as Writer and Preacher in His Kyiv Period"[17] in which he questioned the practice, dominant in Russian studies, of treating Prokopovych exclusively as an ideologist of the Russian Empire. Shevelov argued that Prokopovych could be properly understood only if one took account of his Kyivan writings. Shevelov believed that during his Kyiv period Prokopovych showed himself to be a local patriot, not a promoter of the idea of the Russian Empire, and that his works of that period belong to the sphere of Ukrainian literature and culture. Prokopovych's tragi-comedy *Vladymyr* (1705) provided most of the ammunition for Shevelov's argument. He rejected the views of the nineteenth-century Russian spe-cialists on Prokopovych, Petr Morozov and N. S. Tikhonravov, as well as the Soviet scholar G. A. Gukovsky, who claimed that the character of Volodymyr embodied the image of Peter. Shevelov found support for his skepticism in the writings of Aleksei Sobolevsky and especially Yaroslav Hordynsky, who saw Volodymyr as embodying the image of Ivan Mazepa, not of the Russian tsar.[18]

Shevelov's views were reexamined almost a quarter century after the publication of his article by the foremost Western specialist on the Petrine era, James Cracraft. In his article "Prokopovyč's Kiev Period Reconsid-ered," Cracraft set out to prove that during his Kyiv period Prokopovych was "not only a proponent of a kind of Ukrainian nationalism, but some-thing of an incipient ideologist of the Petrine empire too."[19] In fact, he made a strong argument in favor of the latter thesis, while completely rejecting the former. Noting the "all-Russian" elements in Prokopovych's writings before 1709, Cracraft traced them back to the *Synopsis* of 1674, effectively placing Prokopovych's Kyiv period into the context of Russian imperial thought. He claimed that Prokopovych's all-Russian views were already present in his Kyivan works. A different approach to the Kyivan

---

[17] First published in *Harvard Slavic Studies*, 2: 211–23. Reprinted in George Y. Shevelov, *Two Orthodox Ukrainian Churchmen of the Early Eighteenth Century: Teofan Prokopovych and Stefan Iavors'kyi* (Cambridge, Mass., 1985).

[18] See Iaroslav Hordyns'kyi, "'Vladymyr' Teofana Prokopovycha," *Zapysky Naukoroho tovarystva im. Shevchenka* 130 (1920): 43–53. For a summary of discussion on the ideo-logical and political message of the play and an assessment of Shevelov's argument, see Francis Butler, *Enlightener of Rus': The Image of Vladimir Sviatoslavich across the Centuries* (Bloomington, Ind., 2002), pp. 117–52.

[19] James Cracraft, "Prokopovyč's Kiev Period Reconsidered," *Harvard Ukrainian Studies* 2, no. 2 (June 1978): 138–57, here 139.

writer's place in Russian culture was developed by Max J. Okenfuss, who indicated "a vast cultural divide between Teofan and most Russians of his day" and depicted Prokopovych as a figure deeply rooted in the humanistic and classicist culture of the Kyivan literati.[20] Clearly, Prokopovych had more than one identity, and scholars are right to indicate a variety of cultural values, as well as ethnonational and political loyalties, in his writings. Given his educational background and talent, Prokopovych was obviously very good at expressing, formulating, and articulating those loyalties. Thus, leaving aside the question of what Prokopovych and other Kyivans in St. Petersburg believed or did not believe, it is much more fruitful to treat their works and pronouncements as statements reflecting a set of political and cultural identities accepted and promoted by the new imperial elite.

My task in this chapter will be twofold. The first is to indicate the pre-1654 origins of many of the concepts that gained currency in Peter's times and to put the era of his reforms into the context of earlier identity projects – something that most scholars studying the Petrine era from the perspective of its impact on later developments have neglected. The second is to explore the interrelation between the national and imperial elements of "all-Russian" identity by examining the contribution of Kyivan intellectuals based both in Kyiv and in St. Petersburg.

The "Slavo-Rossian" project

In October 1663, Ivan Briukhovetsky, one of the best-educated and initially most pro-Muscovite of the Cossack hetmans, issued a circular to the population of Right-Bank Ukraine, calling upon his "dear brethren" to abandon the Polish king and join the Muscovite tsar. In making his case, he used historical, dynastic, religious, and national arguments that established a direct connection between the Ruthenian nation (*Rossiiskyi narod*) and the Russian (*Rossiiskyi*) tsar in Moscow. Briukhovetsky wrote:

Not only all surrounding nations but Your Graces yourselves, dear brethren of ours, should acknowledge that you are abiding in obvious blindness and visible delusion when, bearing the Ruthenian name from your ancestors, you incline not to the monarch whose holy ancestor of blessed memory [St. Volodymyr], the equal of the apostles, brought our whole Ruthenian nation to the Greek Christian faith, but, having defected from the hereditary Russian Orthodox monarch of the one true faith, being Rus', you incline toward one of another faith, to the Liakh side, which is not concordant in name and faith.[21]

---

[20] See Okenfuss, *The Rise and Fall of Latin Humanism*, pp. 110–19.
[21] *Tysiacha rokiv ukraïns'koï suspil'no-politychnoï dumky*, 9 vols., ed. Taras Hunczak et al. (Kyiv, 2001), III, pt. 1, pp. 385–87, here 385.

The set of ideas that informed Briukhovetsky's attempt to associate the
Ruthenian nation with the Russian tsar found its most explicit expression
in the first "textbook" of "Russian history," entitled *Synopsis*. Originally
published in Kyiv in 1674, by the mid-nineteenth century the book had
seen nineteen editions and reprints, becoming the most popular historical work in the premodern Russian Empire.[22] It was originally published under the supervision of Inokentii Gizel, the archimandrite of the
Kyivan Cave Monastery, and was long considered his intellectual product. The true author remains unknown, but the first three editions (1674,
1678, and 1680/81) are considered to be his work. The first edition of
the book was issued during a most turbulent year in the history of the
city of Kyiv and its Cave Monastery. In 1674, the Muscovite army, supported by Cossack formations from the Left Bank, crossed the Dnipro
to attack the Ottomans and pro-Turkish Cossacks led by Hetman Petro
Doroshenko. They besieged the fortress of Chyhyryn but were repelled
and obliged to retreat. By the end of the year they were strengthening the Kyiv fortress in expectation of an Ottoman-led assault on the
city. Inokentii Gizel and the monks of the Cave Monastery thought of
sending their valuables to Muscovy for safekeeping. To make things even
worse, the Polish-Lithuanian Commonwealth demanded that Muscovy
surrender Kyiv, as stipulated in the Truce of Andrusovo between the two
states.[23]

It is hard to imagine how the monks continued their publishing program under these circumstances, but in that difficult year they managed
to issue at least six books and pamphlets. Those that were not exclusively religious had a clear pro-Muscovite orientation. One of them was
a program of the play *Aleksii, a Man of God*, staged by the students of
the Kyiv Mohyla College and dedicated to Tsar Aleksei Mikhailovich
"as a token of loyal submission / on the part of noble student youth."
The program was published at the request of the Muscovite voevoda of
Kyiv, Georgii Petrovich Trubetskoi. The monastery print shop also produced two editions of Lazar Baranovych's *Trumpets of the Homiletic Word*,
one with a set of engravings specially prepared for the publication. The
book was dedicated to the tsar, who supplied the paper, and intended

[22] For a reproduction of the 1680 edition, see *Sinopsis, Kiev 1681: Facsimile mit einer Ein-
leitung*, ed. Hans Rothe (Cologne and Vienna, 1983). On the publishing history and
readership of the *Synopsis*, see A. Iu. Samarin, *Rasprostranenie i chitatel' pervykh pechat-
nykh knig po istorii Rossii (konets XVII–XVIII v.)* (Moscow, 1988), pp. 20–76.
[23] For a discussion of the political conditions that influenced the publication of the *Synopsis* and its content, see Zenon E. Kohut, "The Political Program of the Kyivan Cave
Monastery (1660–80)," unpublished paper prepared for the AAASS Convention in Salt
Lake City (2005).

for the Muscovite market.[24] The author of the *Synopsis* toed the same pro-Muscovite line. The title of the book promised the reader not only the life story of Prince Volodymyr but also of "the successors of his pious Ruthenian state (*rossiskiia derzhava*), even unto our most illustrious and pious sovereign Tsar and Grand Prince Aleksei Mikhailovich [in the second and third editions, Fedor Alekseevich], autocrat of all Great, Little and White Russia."[25]

Why were the Kyivan monks so strongly in favor of the Muscovite tsar? The most obvious answer to this question was given in the program of the student play, where the printer set the words "Orthodox monarch" in capitals. Gizel and his subordinates, who clearly wanted to stay in the Orthodox realm, despised the notion of becoming subjects of a Catholic king or, even worse, of a Muslim sultan. At the same time, Gizel was as ardent a defender of the independence of the Kyiv metropolitanate from Moscow (and its continuing subordination to the patriarchate of Constantinople) as he was a supporter of the tsar's rule over Kyiv. It was the tsar, not the patriarch of Moscow, whom the monks of the Cave Monastery wanted as their protector. The Cave Monastery (and, to a degree, the Kyiv metropolitanate as a whole) can be imagined as a seventeenth-century multinational corporation with its headquarters in Moscow-controlled Kyiv, but with possessions, subjects, and interests extending beyond the Muscovite borders into the Polish-Lithuanian Commonwealth and the Ottoman Empire. For those behind the publication of the *Synopsis,* close Muscovite-Cossack cooperation under the aegis of the Orthodox tsar and a prospective alliance with the Commonwealth against the Ottomans constituted the optimal political program. But for the moment, with the Poles demanding the return of Kyiv and the Ottomans in close proximity to the city, the monks had to persuade the tsar not to yield Kyiv to the Commonwealth and defend it against Turkish attack. They intended to achieve their goal by portraying the Cave Monastery as the most precious jewel in the Kyivan crown, which deserved the tsar's particular attention and protection. Acknowledgment of the special role of Kyiv and the Cave Monastery in Rus' religious history also presupposed the recognition of their special status and rights

[24] For a list and brief description of Kyivan Cave Monastery publications of 1674, see Iakym Zapasko and Iaroslav Isaievych, *Pam'iatky knyzhkovoho mystetstva. Kataloh starodrukiv vydanykh na Ukraïni,* bk. 1, *1574–1700* (Lviv, 1981), pp. 89–90. On the publication of Baranovych's book and the ideological meaning of its engravings, see my *Tsars and Cossacks: A Study in Iconography* (Cambridge, Mass., 2002), pp. 39–43.

[25] See I. V. Zhylenko, "Slovo do chytacha," in idem, *Synopsys Kyïvs'kyi* (Kyiv, 2002), pp. 19–39 (=*Lavrs'kyi al'manakh,* vyp. 6 [special vyp. 2]). Cf. "Synopsis [excerpts]" in *Ukraïns'ka literatura XVII st.,* comp. V. I. Krekoten', ed. O. V. Myshanych (Kyiv, 1987), pp. 167–200, here 167.

within the Orthodox tsardom. The author of the *Synopsis* presented Kyiv as the cradle of the Rus' dynasty, state, nation, and religion. The Orthodox theme was reinforced by the author's profound anti-Muslim bias, as he described the Muslim invasion of the "Orthodox-Russian Land" and the confrontation between the "Orthodox army" and the "infidels."[26]

Of greatest interest to us are the anonymous author's views on the ethnonational history of the world in general and Ruthenia and Muscovy in particular. Those views, on the one hand, are deeply rooted in the earlier tradition of chronicle writing, with its search for the Biblical origins of nations and legendary accounts of the early settlement of the Slavs. On the other hand, the author shows a preoccupation with the idea of nation (*narod*) unprecedented in Rus' chronicle writing. That idea emerges in the *Synopsis*, along with dynasty, state, and religion, as one of the main subjects of the historical narrative. The long title of the work, which is informative about the author's conceptualization of the past, puts the nation as a subject of historical narrative ahead of the Rurikid dynasty, the Kyivan princes, and the "pious state" of St. Volodymyr. The first part of the title reads: "The Synopsis, or brief compendium of various chronicles about the origin of the Slavo-Rossian nation and the first princes of the divinely protected city of Kyiv and the life of the holy, pious grand prince of Kyiv and all Russia, the first autocrat, Volodymyr."[27]

What was the Slavo-Rossian nation (*slavenorossiiskyi narod*) of the *Synopsis*? The anonymous author traces its origins back to the resettlement of the Slavs, familiar to him from the Rus' and Polish chronicles. By using the composite term "Slavo-Rossian," he stresses the Slavic origin and character of the Rus' peoples and their membership in a larger Slavic family of nations. Thus, depending on context, the Slavo-Rossian nation of the *Synopsis* could occasionally include the Poles and other Slavs. Nevertheless, its core appears to have been based in Kyiv; besides the Ruthenian nation, referred to as "Rus'" or "Rossian" (*rus'kyi, rossiiskyi*), it included the Muscovites. The latter were sometimes included in the family of Rus' peoples in the Polish and Ruthenian chronicles and polemical works of the period but never explicitly regarded as part of the same nation (*narod*) as the Ruthenians. Now both branches of Rus' were declared parts of one Slavo-Rossian nation, the historical and spiritual center of which, according to the *Synopsis*, was not in the "ruling" city of Moscow but in the first capital of the Slavo-Rossian nation and state – the city of Kyiv. Behind the concept of the Slavo-Rossian nation stood the idea of a much closer unity of Ruthenians and Muscovites than anything envisioned earlier. The historical tradition rooted in Kyiv, the common

[26] "Synopsis," p. 180.   [27] Ibid., p. 167.

Orthodox religion and the existence of a common state, the Orthodox tsardom, were factors that supported and strengthened that intellectual construct. It was also reinforced by the ethnogenealogical legend that traced the origins of the Slavs in general and the Slavo-Rossians in particular back to the biblical Meshech (East Slavic "Mosokh"), a son of Japheth – the "forefather" of the Muscovite nation (*Moskva-narod*) and "all Slavo-Rossians."[28]

As he introduced the "Slavo-Rossian" nation to his readers, the author of the *Synopsis* still had to deal with the political and cultural realities of his day, as well as with the existing historiographic tradition. Thus, on occasion, he listed Moskva and Rus' (*Rus'/Rossy*) as separate nations along with the Poles, Lithuanians, and Prussians. He also followed the earlier tradition of listing peoples defined in territorial terms – an echo of the previously dominant regional identities – along with politically or culturally defined nations. Thus, along with Moskva and Rus', he listed the Volhynians – an early sixteenth-century *narod* that figured in early modern lists of Slavic nations and was copied from one chronicle to another. Supported by the authority of the *Synopsis*, the Volhynians even made their way into eighteenth-century Russian histories, including the one written by Aleksei Mankiev.[29] At the same time, the anonymous author made an effort to reconcile or update some of the older historiographic legends and concepts. Thus, developing the Kyivan-era legend that the Slavs took their names from their places of settlement, he claimed that although the Muscovite nation derived its name from Mosokh, the "ruling" city of Moscow was named after the Moskva River. As examples of the topographic origin of the names of Slavo-Rossian peoples, he also gave the Zaporozhian Cossacks, who took their name from Zaporizhia (the region beyond the Dnipro rapids), where they settled, and the Don Cossacks (*Dontsy*), named after the Don River.[30] The author's vision of the Slavo-Rossian nation also corresponded to the new historiographic concepts that influenced the Kyivan literati in the second half of the seventeenth century. Those concepts bore the clear imprint of early modern pan-Slavism, which originated among the Southern Slavs, as well as the

---

[28] Ibid., p. 170. For interpretations of the Mosokh legend of Slavic ethogenesis, see Aleksandr Myl'nikov, *Kartina slavianskogo mira: vzgliad iz Vostochnoi Evropy. Étnogeneticheskie legendy, dogadki, protogipotezy XVI – nachala XVII veka* (St. Petersburg, 2000), pp. 21–45; Zenon E. Kohut, "Ot Iafeta do Moskvy: protsess sozdaniia bibleiskoi rodoslovnoi slavian v pol'skoi, ukrainskoi i russkoi istoriografii (XVI–XVII vv.)," in *Ukraina i sosednie gosudarstva v XVII veke. Materialy mezhdunarodnoi konferentsii*, ed. Tatiana Iakovleva (St. Petersburg, 2004), pp. 59–82.

[29] See "Synopsis," pp. 169–70. For references to the Volhynians in East Slavic chronicles and historical works, see Myl'nikov, *Kartina slavianskogo mira*, pp. 29, 30, 33–34, 103.

[30] See "Synopsis," p. 170.

Polish notion of Sarmatism. Thus the Slavo-Rossian nation emerges from the pages of the *Synopsis* both as part of a larger Slavic world and as part of a Sarmatian community of Commonwealth nations.[31] In advocating an anti-Muslim alliance between the Orthodox tsardom and the Catholic-dominated Commonwealth, the author of the *Synopsis* did not bother to hide the Polish roots of his intellectual constructs.

The *Synopsis* continued a long tradition of chronicle writing in the Cave Monastery – one that began in the princely era and included the legendary Nestor the Chronicler among its creators. Apart from the Ruthenian sources of the work, which included the Kyivan Cave Patericon, the author was familiar with some Western sources, including Giovanni Botero's *Le relationi universali,* and Polish chronicles, the most important of which was the work of Maciej Stryjkowski.[32] By employing a cut-and-paste technique to bring all his sources together, the author (not unlike the medieval chroniclers) jumbled together the contradictory theories of his predecessors without attempting to provide a satisfactory explanation of them.[33] What emerges from the seemingly chaotic collection of different and often conflicting concepts and interpretations in the *Synopsis* is a joint Muscovite-Ruthenian narrative – a blueprint for the new nation as envisioned by the Kyivan literati. The third edition of the *Synopsis* included a tale about the Battle of Kulikovo Field (1380) – the founding myth of early modern Muscovy. By merging that tale with the founding myth of the Ruthenian nation – the story of the Kyivan princes and the baptism of Rus' – the author of the *Synopsis* helped create a common "Slavo-Rossian" historical narrative. Interestingly enough, that narrative did not include the founding myth of the Hetmanate. The story of the Khmelnytsky Uprising was absent from the pages of the first "Russian" history textbook. Clearly, the Pereiaslav Council was not as compelling to the author of the *Synopsis* as it became to his continuators.

According to the new narrative, the country called *Rossiia* was the home of the Slavo-Rossian nation. The concept of one nation (*narod*) uniting Ruthenians and Muscovites was a revolutionary element introduced by the author of the *Synopsis* to the field of early modern Slavic ethnology. Rooted in the tradition established by the literati of Kyivan Rus',

---

[31] Ibid., pp. 167–71.

[32] On the sources of the *Synopsis*, see Iurii Mytsyk, *Ukrainskie letopisi XVII veka* (Dnipropetrovsk, 1978), pp. 22–24; Zhylenko, "Slovo do chytacha," p. 40.

[33] The linguistic analysis of the *Synopsis* recently undertaken by Ilona Tarnopolska indicates that a number of authors worked on the book, as one would expect of a work deeply rooted in the tradition of chronicle writing. See Ilona Tarnopol's'ka, "Kyïvs'kyi *Synopsys* v istoriohrafichnomu ta dzhereloznavchomu aspektakh," Candidate thesis, Dnipropetrovsk National University, 1998.

articulated on a new intellectual level, and introduced into public discourse under new political and religious circumstances, the concept of the national unity of the Rus' lands and peoples was advanced after centuries of separate existence and diverse political and cultural experiences had in fact created two very different political and cultural entities on the territories of the former Kyivan realm. Although the Slavo-Rossian nation was imagined within the parameters of the Ruthenian intellectual tradition, it did not include all of Ruthenia but only those parts of it that were attached to the Orthodox tsardom. By contrast, it included Muscovy, which was not part of the imagined geography of early modern Ruthenia. To be sure, in the chronicler's mind the merger of the tsar's Ruthenia with the tsar's Muscovy was far from complete. The Orthodox tsardom/empire had two capitals: Kyiv, which figures as the "ruling city" (*tsarstvennyi hrad*) even with reference to events of the second half of the seventeenth century, and Moscow.[34] It also had two spiritual centers – the seats of the two Rus' metropolitanates, Kyiv and Moscow. There were two armies as well: the tsar's forces and the Zaporozhian Host (*Sily tsarskoho velichestva i voiska zaporozhskie*).[35]

How did the Muscovites receive the ideas put forward by the author of the *Synopsis*? The phenomenal commercial success of the book indicated that they liked the work. The most influential people in the Russian Empire, such as Peter I and D. M. Golitsyn, a former governor of Kyiv, had the book in their libraries, but did they pay attention to its national message? Not necessarily. At the time of its publication, Muscovite court historiography, as represented by the writings of Fedor Griboedov, the author of the *History of the Tsars and Princes of the Rus' Land* (1669), was hopelessly mired in the prenational age, conceptualizing Rus' and Muscovite history primarily in dynastic terms.[36] Originally the *Synopsis* was regarded in Muscovy as not entirely a domestic product, to say the least. In referring to the *Synopsis*, the compilers of the Novgorod Zabelin Chronicle occasionally called it "the Polish printed chronicle."[37]

---

[34] See "Synopsis," p. 177. With reference to princely times, Kyiv was called the principal city of the all-Russian nation (*vseho naroda rosyiskoho holovnoi hrad*). Ibid., p. 172.

[35] Ibid., pp. 182–83.

[36] According to Zenon Kohut, who compared Griboedov's views with those of the author of the *Synopsis*, in Russian historical writing the "dominance of the dynastic-state vision of Russia was not challenged until the 1830s." See Zenon E. Kohut, "A Dynastic or Ethno-Dynastic Tsardom? Two Early Modern Concepts of Russia," in *Extending the Borders of Russian History: Essays in Honor of Alfred J. Rieber*, ed. Marsha Siefert (Budapest and New York, 2003), pp. 17–30, here 26. Quite logically from that point of view, it was in the 1830s that reprints of the *Synopsis* finally ceased to appear.

[37] See A. P. Bogdanov, "Rabota A. I. Lyzlova nad russkimi i inostrannymi istochnikami," in Andrei Lyzlov, *Skifskaia istoriia*, ed. E. V. Chistiakova (Moscow, 1990), pp. 390–447, here 396. Lyzlov used the *Synopsis* as one of his sources. Under the influence of the Polish chronicles, Lyzlov identified *Moskva* and *rossiiane* as distinct peoples, along

The most prominent of the eighteenth-century Russian historians, Vasilii Tatishchev, criticized the *Synopsis*, *inter alia*, for its inclusion of "Polish tales (*basnei*)."[38] Nor was the Church Slavonic language of the work entirely clear to the Muscovite reader. Consequently, the early eighteenth-century Russian publishers of the *Synopsis* not only replaced its Church Slavonic typeface with the modern *grazhdanskii* script introduced by Peter I but also replaced its original title, "Synopsis, or Brief Compendium of Various Chroniclers," with the more understandable "Synopsis, or Brief History Compiled from Various Authors."[39] The St. Petersburg editors also planned to remove Ukrainianisms from the text, replacing the Ukrainian *vezha* (tower), for example, with the Russian *bashnia*, but the project remained unrealized for financial reasons.[40]

The book regarded by a Kyivan as the history of a nation was received by educated readers in St. Petersburg as the history of a state. In the catalogue of the library of Stefan Yavorsky, a former Kyivan and later metropolitan of Riazan and de facto head of the imperial church, the 1718 edition of the book was listed as *Sinopsis ili istoriia o rossiistem narode* (Synopsis, or A History of the Russian Nation), while the St. Petersburg publishers of that edition entered it in their records as *Sinopsis, ili korotkaia istoriia o Rosiiskom gosudarstve* (Synopsis, or a Brief History of the Rus' State).[41] Not surprisingly, the director of the St. Petersburg publishing house, M. P. Avramov, was known for collecting documents on the "history of the Russian state," not of the Russian nation. It was also the history of the Russian state that Peter I ordered Fedor Polikarpov to write in 1708.[42] The topics that interested Ruthenian and Muscovite readers were also quite different. The latter were drawn to subjects taken from Russian history: thus, Iakov Golovin wrote in the margin of the *Synopsis* in September 1805, "Some historical facts are very well presented: for example, about the invasion and subjection of Mamai and others."[43] The *Synopsis* was not, of course, the complete account of the history of Russia and the Russian state needed by the educated elites of the period,

---

with the Lithuanians, Wallachians, and Tatars (Lyzlov, *Skifskaia istoriia*, p. 8). He also readily used the term *narod* in reference to Tatar and other nomadic tribes – the main protagonists of his book.

[38] See Samarin, *Rasprostranenie*, p. 63.

[39] See *Ukraïns' ki pys'mennyky. Bio-bibliohrafichnyi slovnyk*, vol. I, *Davnia ukraïns' ka literatura (XI–XVIII st.)*, comp. Leonid Makhnovets' (Kyiv, 1960), pp. 179–80.

[40] See Samarin, *Rasprostranenie*, pp. 51–53.   [41] Ibid., pp. 47, 44.

[42] See Elena Pogosian, *Petr I – arkhitektor rossiiskoi istorii* (St. Petersburg, 2001), pp. 184, 189. It is difficult to judge Golitsyn's interpretation of the *Synopsis*, although Marc Raeff assumed that his Ukrainian experience as governor of Kyiv might have influenced his attempt to limit the powers of Empress Anna Ioannovna ("Ukraine and Imperial Russia: Intellectual and Political Encounters from the Seventeenth to the Nineteenth Century," in *Ukraine and Russia in their Historical Encounter*, pp. 69–85, here 72).

[43] See Samarin, *Rasprostranenie*, p. 34.

and Tatishchev had every right to complain that the book was too short, and that "much that was needed has been omitted."[44] In his *Iadro Rossiiskoi istorii* (Essence of Russian History, first published in 1770), Mankiev sought to fill the gap by supplementing data taken from the *Synopsis* with an account of Muscovite history. Mikhail Lomonosov, another author inspired by the *Synopsis*, addressed the same problem in his *Kratkii Rossiiskii letopisets* (Brief Russian Chronicle, 1760).[45]

However differently the *Synopsis* was read in Kyiv and in the Russian provinces of the empire, it certainly helped make the history of Kyiv an integral part of the Muscovite and, for that matter, the imperial Russian narrative. The account of Kyivan Rus' history and the description of the Battle of Kulikovo Field presented in the *Synopsis* served as a factual basis for the literary works of such prominent Russian authors of the late eighteenth and early nineteenth centuries as A. P. Sumarokov. The original difficulties with the reception of the national message of the *Synopsis* in Muscovy were due in part to the fact that the old dynastic and later state-based paradigm served the interests of the multiethnic empire much better than the nation-based one. But it certainly corresponded to the views and interests of Kyivans in the imperial service, who attempted to secure their niche in the empire and establish special relations with its rulers by employing the "Slavo-Rossian" national paradigm.

The Kyivan "Rossiia"

The formulation and promotion of the Slavo-Rossian project by the author of the *Synopsis* raises the question of the meaning of the term *Rossiia*, which was often used by the Kyivan literati in the seventeenth and early eighteenth centuries.

In Ukraine, the tradition of using "Rus'" in its Greek form, *Rossiia*, and derivatives of it (for example, *rossiiskii*) with regard to the Ruthenian lands (sometimes including Muscovy) goes back at least to the 1590s.[46]

---

[44] On the Russian elites' reading of the *Synopsis*, see ibid., pp. 46–47, 62–63.

[45] Also heavily influenced by the *Synopsis* was Lomonosov's *Drevniaia Rossiiskaia istoriia ot nachala rossiiskogo naroda* (Old Russian History from the Beginning of the Russian Nation, 1766), in which Lomonosov adopted the anonymous author's approach to his subject as the history of a nation but ignored his preoccupation with the history of the Orthodox Church. On the "successors" of the *Synopsis* in Muscovy and Ukraine, see Zhylenko, "Slovo do chytacha," pp. 10–11.

[46] The term was also used in Muscovy and Poland from the sixteenth century. See Frank E. Sysyn, "The Image of Russia and Russian-Ukrainian Relations in Ukrainian Historiography of the Late Seventeenth and Early Eighteenth Centuries" in *Culture, Nation, and Identity: The Ukrainian-Russian Encounter, 1600–1945*, ed. Andreas Kappeles, Zenon

In 1592, in a letter dispatched with one of the traveling Greek hierarchs from the Lviv Orthodox brotherhood to the Muscovite tsar, the notion of the Russian race (*rod Rossiiskii*) was invoked as an ethnocultural category linking Polish-Lithuanian and Muscovite Rus'.[47] As a rule, however, in Ruthenian and Polish writings of the period, the term *Rossiia* (Polish *Rossyja*) was used exclusively to denote Polish-Lithuanian Rus'. It was in this sense that the terms *narod Rosijski* and *Rosiejska Ziemla* were used by Meletii Smotrytsky in his *Threnos* of 1610.[48] That usage became especially popular in the times of Petro Mohyla. The verses printed in 1633 on the occasion of his entrance into his capital include numerous references to "Russia."[49] The anonymous author of *Mnemosyne of Glory, Works and Deeds*, a Polish-language panegyric to Mohyla, styled him "the Russian Phoebus" and praised his defense of "dear Russia" (*miła Rossyja*), which is reminiscent of Polish authors' references to *miła Polska*.[50] Mohyla's "Russia" certainly included the lands of the Kyiv metropolitanate but not the Muscovite territories that officially acquired that name under Peter I. Polish-Lithuanian Rus' was also called "Russia" and its inhabitants "Russians" in verses written at Bohdan Khmelnytsky's chancellery in late 1649.[51] Although Mohyla used the title "Metropolitan of Little Russia" in his correspondence with Moscow, he otherwise styled himself "Metropolitan of All Russia." The same was true of his heir on the metropolitan throne, Sylvestr Kosov. In verses on Kosov's death, he was

E. Kohut, Frank E. Sysyn, and Mark von Hagen (Edmonton and Toronto, 2003), pp. 108–43, here 117–18. On the use of *Rossiia* in eighteenth-century Russian historiography, see Elena Pogosian, "Rus' i Rossiia v istoricheskikh sochineniiakh 1730–1780-kh gg.," in *Rossiia/Russia* (Moscow and Venice), ed. N. G. Okhotin, no. 3 (1999): 7–19. On the multiple contexts in which "Russia" was used in early modern eastern Europe (and the terminological problems that such usage creates for present-day research), see Giovanna Brogi Bercoff, "Ruś, Ukraina, *Ruthenia*, Wielkie Księstwo Litewskie, Rzeczpospolita, Moskwa, Rosja, Europa środkowo-wschodnia: o wielowarstwowości i polifunkcjonalizmie kulturowym," in *Contributi italiani al XIII congresso internazionale degli slavisti*, ed. Alberto Alberti et al. (Pisa, 2003), pp. 325–87, here 360–64.

[47] See *Akty, otnosiashchiesia k istorii Zapadnoi Rossii*, vol. IV (St. Petersburg, 1854), pp. 47–49.

[48] See excerpts from the *Threnos* in *Roksolański Parnas. Polskojęzyczna poezja ukraińska od końca XVI do początku XVIII wieku*. Pt. 2, *Antologia*, ed. Rostysław Radyszewśkyj [Rostyslav Radyshevs'kyi] (Cracow, 1998), pp. 64–84, here 78.

[49] One of the stanzas reads: "Russia, now at last you have a change / Of fortune; you have the hour of triumph: / This is Petro [Mohyla], the defender of your rights, / the shield of Zion." See *Ukraïns'ka poeziia. Seredyna XVII st.*, comp. V. I. Krekoten' and M. M. Sulyma, ed. O. V. Myshanych (Kyiv, 1992), p. 63.

[50] See "Mnemosyne sławy, prac i trudów," in *Roksolański Parnas*, 2: 123–34, here 128. For references to Poland as *miła Polska*, see "Rozprawa. Przygody starego żołnierza," in *Roksolański Parnas*, 2: 47–58, here 47.

[51] See *Ukraïns'ka poeziia. Seredyna XVII st.*, p. 102.

called the head of "all Russia," and it was "all Russia" that mourned his demise.[52]

The Mohylan tradition of using "Russia" predominantly, if not exclusively, to denote the lands of the Kyiv metropolitanate returned to prominence after the Ruin with the revival of the Kyivan College during the hetmancy of Ivan Samoilovych (1672–87), who restored the practice of making regular donations to the academy.[53] Pavlo Baranetsky, the author of the Polish-language *Trybut*, a panegyric to Samoilovych published in 1687, not only wrote in his verses about the "monuments of Mohyla" and the "Mohylan muses" but also, in the tradition of Mohyla's era, used *Rossyja* and *Rossyjacy* to denote the Ruthenian lands and their population.[54] In his Polish verse composition, *The Pole Star of the Russian Sky* (1690), Stefan Yavorsky, the future leader of the imperial church, also wrote about "Mohylan muses" and applied the terms *Rossyja* and *Rossiaci* to the Rus' (non-Muscovite) land and people.[55] In the tradition of Mohyla and Kosov, Metropolitan Varlaam Yasynsky (1690–1707) was referred to not only as "Metropolitan of Kyiv" and Little Russia but also as "Metropolitan of Kyiv and All Russia," or "Kyivan-Russian Metropolitan."[56]

The *Rossiia*-based terminology was also used in the Latin writings of the Kyiv-educated Cossack elites. The authors of the Latin *Pacta et Constitutiones* – the document composed in exile in 1710 – used such terms as *patriam Rossiacam*, *gente Rossiaca*, *filiis Rossiacis*, and *liberam Rossiacam* to denote Ukraine and Ukrainians.[57] The application of such terms to Ukraine is particularly apparent in the reference to Kyiv as the metropolis of *Rossia* in relation to other Ukrainian towns: *Metropolis Urbs Rossiae, Kiiovia, caeteraeque Ucrainae civitates* (xxv). The terms "Ukraine" and "Ukrainian" (*Ucraina, Ucrainensibus*) were frequently used in the text of the *Pacta* as synonyms of *Rossiia*-based terms. The same is true of terms

[52] Ibid., pp. 68, 94–95.
[53] On Samoilovych's and Mazepa's support of the Kyivan College, see George Gajecky, "The Kiev Mohyla Academy and the Hetmanate," *Harvard Ukrainian Studies* 8, nos. 1/2 (June 1984): 81–92, here 87–89.
[54] See Paweł Baraniecki, "Trybut," in *Roksolański Parnas*, 2: 319–26.
[55] See Stefan Jaworski, "Arctos planet herbowych," in *Roksolański Parnas*, 2: 331–34.
[56] For the use of the first title, see the description of the title page of *Lohyka, perypatetyka* in "Ocherki russkoi khristianskoi ikonografii. 1. Sofiia Premudrost' Bozhiia" in *Vestnik Obshchestva drevne-russkogo iskusstva pri Moskovskom publichnom muzee, 1874–76*, nos. 1–12, ed. G. D. Filimonov (Moscow, 1876), no. 1. For a reference to Yasynsky as Kyivan-Russian metropolitan, see the text of the epitaph for the archimandrite of Novhorod-Siverskyi written by Yasynsky in Samiilo Velychko, *Litopys*, trans. Valerii Shevchuk, vol. II (Kyiv, 1991), p. 593.
[57] See the Latin original of the *Pacta et Constitutiones* in *Konstytutsiia ukraïns' koï het'mans' koï derzhavy* (Kyiv, 1997), pp. iv, vi, viii, x, xi, xii, xiii ff. Further page references to the text of the *Pacta* are given in parentheses in the text.

based on the ethnonym *Roxolani: Roxolana patria nostra* (xxvi), *incolis Roxolanis* (xxix), *Roxolane patriae, Matris Nostrae* (xxxii), etc. The term *Parva Rossia* (Little Russia) was used in the *Pacta* only twice, once with regard to church jurisdiction and once in reference to the Cossack fatherland: *Parva Rossia, patria nostra.* With regard to their northern neighbor, the authors of the *Pacta* used the terms *Moscovitico Imperio* and *iugo Moscorum.*[58] While in the chancellery Ukrainian of the day the Cossack elites referred to their fatherland as Little Russia (*Malorosiia*), not *Rossiia*, in "elevated" languages such as Latin they preferred *Rossiia*-based ethnonyms to those based on the terms "Ukraine" (*Ucraina*) or "Little Russia" (*Parva Rossia*).

Thus, by the turn of the eighteenth century, "Russia" was firmly established in Kyivan writings as a term for the Ruthenian lands in general. Although its use in Kyivan clerical circles was clearly influenced by the Mohylan tradition, the "Russia" of the Mohylan authors of the 1630s–40s and the Kyivan writers of the last decades of that century differed dramatically in geographic extent. As noted above, by the end of the seventeenth century the territory under the jurisdiction of the Kyivan metropolitan had shrunk to the borders of the Kyiv eparchy. Similarly, the "Russia" of Kyivan authors became limited to the lands of the Hetmanate – a phenomenon that allowed the Kyivans to present Hetman Mazepa as a luminary of "Russia." A case in point is the tragicomedy *Vladymyr* (1705) by Teofan Prokopovych, the rector of the Kyiv Mohyla Academy and one of the leading ideologues of the Petrine era.[59] In the prologue to the tragicomedy, it was Hetman Mazepa and not Tsar Peter who figured as heir to the all-Russian heritage of Volodymyr the Great. It was to Mazepa, claimed Prokopovych, that "the care of this patrimony of Volodymyr's has been entrusted by God through the tsar. Proceeding with victories equal to Volodymyr's, with husbandry equal to his in Russia, you show forth his face on your person as a son shows forth his father's face."[60] According to Prokopovych, Volodymyr's patrimony

---

[58] The Ukrainian version of the *Pacta*, which has not been dated precisely, avoids using the term "Russia" with regard to Ukraine, preferring "Little Russia" (*Malorossiia*). Still, it does not apply that term to Russia or the Russian state, which it calls "Muscovy."

[59] For biographies of Prokopovych, see I. Chistovich, *Feofan Prokopovich i ego vremia* (St. Petersburg, 1868); H.-J. Härtel, *Byzantinisches Erbe und Orthodoxie bei Feofan Prokopovič* (Würzburg, 1970); Valeriia Nichik (Nichyk), *Feofan Prokopovich* (Moscow, 1977); Valeriia Nichyk and M. D. Rohovych, "Pro netochnosti v zhyttiepysakh F. Prokopovycha," *Filosofs'ka dumka*, 1975, no. 2: 117–27; James Cracraft, "Feofan Prokopovich and the Kyivan Academy," in *Russian Orthodoxy under the Old Regime*, ed. R. Nicholas and T. Stavrou (Minneapolis, 1978), pp. 44–64. On Prokopovych's role in the planning and realization of the church reform, see James Cracraft, *The Church Reform of Peter the Great* (London and Basingstoke, 1971).

[60] See "Vladimir. Tragikomediia," in Feofan Prokopovich, *Sochineniia*, ed. I. P. Eremin (Moscow, 1961), pp. 149–205, here 152.

was not granted by God to the tsar but through the tsar to Mazepa. It is hardly surprising that Prokopovych counted Mazepa among the "Russian luminaries resplendent with glory."[61]

Could the continuing use of the "Russia"-based terminology by authors associated with the Kyivan Academy have reflected their desire to stress their equality of status with Moscow while also securing Kyiv's autonomy vis-à-vis the center? While that possibility cannot be excluded, what seems much more obvious in retrospect is that this usage facilitated the integration of the Kyivan clergy and its national discourse into the imperial church and discourse. A clear indication of this is to be found in a sermon given by Prokopovych in the presence of Peter I. Prokopovych delivered it a year after he wrote *Vladymyr*, in July 1706, on the occasion of the tsar's visit to Kyiv. Addressing Peter, Prokopovych called him "Tsar and Ruler of All Russia" and "true successor" of Volodymyr.[62] On 24 July 1709, shortly after the Battle of Poltava, Teofan Prokopovych, then prefect of the Kyivan Academy, greeted the victorious Tsar Peter I with a sermon at St. Sophia's Cathedral in Kyiv. In the sermon, entitled *Slovo pokhval'noe o preslavnoi nad voiskami sveiskimi pobede* (A Laudatory Word on the Most Glorious Victory over the Swedish Forces), Prokopovych congratulated the "all-Russian monarch" on his great victory, praised the "Russian military," and warned Russia against such traitors to the fatherland (*otechestvo*) as the defeated Hetman Ivan Mazepa.[63]

The two "Russias" of Teofan Prokopovych

It would be hard to find a better source for studying the transformation of old identities and the formation of new loyalties among the Kyivan elites in the Russian Empire than the sermons and writings of Teofan Prokopovych, one of the leading spokesmen of the new Russia, whose works embodied the formation of the new all-Russian imperial identity and helped forge new political and cultural loyalties for its elites. Apart from shedding light on the construction of new loyalties by the empire's political elites, Prokopovych's sermons are of great interest as a specific literary genre that served as one of the most effective transmitters of elite

---

[61] Ibid. On the image of Mazepa in the panegyrics of the period, see Lidiia Sazonova, "Getman Mazepa kak obraz panegiricheskii: iz poètiki vostochnoslavianskogo barokko," in *Mazepa and His Time: History, Culture, Society*, ed. Giovanna Siedina (Alessandria, 2004), pp. 461–87; Rostysław Radyszewski (Rostyslav Radyshevs'kyi), "Hetman Mazepa w polskojęzycznych panegirykach Jana Ornowskiego i Filipa Orłyka," in *Mazepa and his Time*, pp. 489–502; Serhij Jakowenko, "Panegiryk *Krzyż. Początek mądrości . . .* i mecenacka działalność Mazepy w Czernihowie," in *Mazepa and his Time*, pp. 517–27.

[62] See Cracraft, "Prokopovyč's Kiev Period Reconsidered," pp. 149–50.

[63] For the text of the *Slovo*, see Feofan Prokopovich, *Sochineniia*, pp. 23–38.

ideas to broader strata of society, allowing us to make some cautious projections regarding their dissemination among the population at large.[64]

How did Prokopovych's "Russia" of the pre-Poltava era differ from the post-1709 "Russia"? The question may be answered by comparing the use of that term in Prokopovych's tragicomedy *Vladymyr*, dedicated to Hetman Mazepa, and in his sermon on the Poltava victory, delivered in the presence of Peter I in July 1709. Let us first examine the geographic limits of Prokopovych's Russia of 1705. Kyiv and the Dnipro River, the Cave Monastery, and the Mohyla Academy clearly emerge from the epilogue of the tragicomedy as the most important centers of his Russia, but it was not limited to the capital city. Prokopovych was also excited about the restoration of the Pereiaslav bishopric, to which he refers in the epilogue, thereby extending the limits of his Russia to that town and eparchial center, which was subject to the metropolitan of Kyiv. Prokopovych's indirect reference to Metropolitan Varlaam Yasynsky supports the assumption that in writing about Russia, he was in fact referring to the territory of the Kyiv metropolitanate. As noted above, another "Russian luminary" (*rossiiskoe svetilo*) to whom Prokopovych referred indirectly in the prophecy of St. Andrew was Hetman Ivan Mazepa, whose virtues he discussed in much greater detail than those of the metropolitan. "For over all these temples," wrote Prokopovych, referring to the churches and buildings of Kyiv and Pereiaslav, "one sees the image of the eminent builder Ioann [Mazepa]."[65] Thus it is safe to assume that Prokopovych's Russia included not only the territory of the Kyiv metropolitanate, which had shrunk significantly by the turn of the eighteenth century, but also the rest of the Hetmanate; for example, the eparchy of Chernihiv, which constituted an integral part of the Hetmanate. These were the territories Prokopovych had in mind first and foremost when referring to Russia. According to him, they were the home of the Russian churches. In the tragicomedy, the students of the Kyivan Academy were termed "noble Russian sons," while the audience that came to the performance of *Vladymyr* was referred to as people of the Russian race (*rossiiskii rod*).

Was Prokopovych unique in limiting the concept of Russia to the territory of the Kyiv metropolitanate or the Hetmanate? The very fact that he did so in a tragicomedy publicly produced in Kyiv indicates that he

---

[64] On the role of sermons in promoting political ideas in England, see T. Claydon, "Sermons, the 'Public Sphere,' and the Political Culture of Late-Seventeenth Century England" in *The English Sermon Revised: Religion, Literature, and History 1600–1750*, ed. Lori Anne Ferrell and Peter McCullough (Manchester, 2000), pp. 208–34. See also James Cracraft, "Feofan Prokopovich: A Bibliography of His Works," *Oxford Slavonic Papers* 8 (1975): 1–36.

[65] Prokopovich, *Sochineniia*, p. 206.

used the term and construed its meaning in accordance with the usage prevalent at the time among the educated circles of the Hetmanate. Prokopovych was not proposing anything particularly new here, as is shown by the text of Yan Ornovsky's panegyric to Mazepa, which was written in 1705, the same year as Prokopovych's *Vladymyr*. Ornovsky referred to Mazepa as the Camillus of Russia.[66]

A very different image of Russia emerges from Prokopovych's post-Poltava writings. As in the tragicomedy *Vladymyr*, so in his Poltava sermon of 1709 Prokopovych often referred to Russia as his interlocutor. Referring to the tsar's military victories, Prokopovych exclaimed: "O thy powers and glory, Russia!" and called upon her to celebrate the Poltava victory: "Exult, O Russia."[67] The Russia of the Poltava sermon turns out to have different geographical boundaries from the Russia of the tragicomedy. Referring in the sermon to the victories of the Russian armies, Prokopovych stated: "All that was taken from many towns and peoples was granted to Russia."[68] The territories given to Russia in recognition of her military victories are enumerated elsewhere in the sermon. Prokopovych describes the geographical limits of the Russian monarch's power as follows:

starting from our Dnipro River to the shores of the Euxine in the south, from there eastward to the Caspian or Khvalinian Sea, even to the borders of the Persian kingdom, and from there to the farthest reaches of the Sino-Chinese kingdom, of which only the barest rumors reach us, and from there to the far north to Novaia Zemlia and to the shores of the Arctic Ocean, and from there to the west, to the Baltic Sea, until one returns again by a long land and water route to the above-mentioned Dnipro. For these are the boundaries of our monarch.[69]

The sermon goes on to indicate that the "limits" of the monarch were also the limits of the "Russian monarchy," the "Russian state," and consequently Russia. Thus, in his Poltava sermon, Prokopovych abandoned his earlier application of the term to the Kyivan ecclesiastical realm or the Cossack polity and reserved it for the territory of the entire Muscovite state, including the Hetmanate.

If the term "Russia" was reserved in the sermon of 1709 to denote the tsar's whole realm, the land that Prokopovych called "Russia" in the tragicomedy was now referred to as "Little Russia" – a term absent from the play.[70] According to the sermon, it was Little Russia to which Mazepa had

[66] See Jan Ornowski, "Muza Roksolańska," in *Roksolański Parnas*, 2: 377–94, here 380.
[67] Prokopovich, *Sochineniia*, pp. 31, 34.   [68] Ibid., p. 33.   [69] Ibid., pp. 24–25.
[70] In the sermon, the patrimony of St. Volodymyr, which, according to the tragicomedy, was given to Mazepa by God through the tsar, becomes a region given to Mazepa by the tsar, as Prokopovych accuses Mazepa of daring "to advance on the kingdom of one from whom he had accepted a territory equal to some kingdoms" (ibid., p. 28).

invited Charles XII: "by insidious persuasion and secret direction he was led into the depths of Little Russia itself."[71] It was from Little Russia that the "servants of the devil" intended to expel the Orthodox faith and introduce the church union – a standard accusation leveled against Mazepa in Russian propaganda of 1708–9 and duly repeated by Prokopovych in his sermon.[72] Thus the Russia of the tragicomedy was transformed into the Little Russia of the sermon, while the terms "Russia" and "Russian" were used to denote East Slavic entities. In the sermon, Peter's army at Poltava, which included Cossack regiments, was termed the Russian army (*rossiiskoe voinstvo*), with no differentiation between Cossacks and regular Muscovite regiments. The outcome of the battle was deemed to be the source of "common all-Russian joy" (*obshchei vserossiiskoi radosti*)[73] – a formula indicating that the inhabitants of Little Russia were as glad of the victory as the monarch himself and his entire realm.

Quite different, in Prokopovych's writings of 1705 and 1709, was not only the delineation of Russia's territorial limits but also the interpretation of its relation to the person of the tsar. In *Vladymyr* Russia is presented as an entity autonomous of the monarch, if not absolutely independent, linked to him through the hetman, while in the sermon of 1709 it emerges as a polity directly associated with the person of the monarch. Referring to the episode in the Battle of Poltava when an enemy bullet struck Peter's hat, Prokopovych wrote that if it had been on target, "all Russia would have been wounded as a result of its [Peter's head] wound."[74] In Prokopovych's opinion, Russia was blessed to have such a tsar as Peter ("O prosperous in your tsar, Russia"). Russia, allegedly, was both glad and apprehensive on seeing Peter's direct participation in the battle: "On seeing this, Russia both rejoiced and trembled."[75] In the verses attached to the speech, Prokopovych encouraged Russia to glorify the tsar: "To you, sovereign monarch, / What will your Russia bring as a gift and what songs will it sing?"[76] Thus the Russia of the 1709 sermon not only changed its boundaries but also lost its contextual autonomy and the absolute priority in the hierarchy of social, religious, and political

---

[71] Ibid., p. 26.
[72] Ibid., p. 37. "The holy Orthodox Catholic [universal] faith, which the diabolical servitors wished to drive out of Little Russia, will expand successfully into other lands."
[73] Ibid., p. 23.
[74] Ibid., p. 31. Prokopovych's presentation of Tsar Peter as the head, whose wound or demise affects the whole body, is reminiscent of the depiction of Peter Mohyla by Yosyp Kalimon in the verses on Mohyla's obsequy entitled *Żal Ponowiny*. There, Kalimon writes: "An arrow brought death to my head. Peter was my head; Peter was wounded by death; Peter was my head: what befalls the head / Is transmitted from the head to the other members" (*Roksolański Parnas*, 2: 200).
[75] Prokopovich, *Sochineniia*, pp. 29, 31.   [76] Ibid., p. 213.

loyalties that it had possessed in the tragicomedy *Vladymyr*. Betraying the monarch in this context was equivalent to betraying Russia, and it is in this infamous role that Mazepa, the luminary of Russia in *Vladymyr*, appears in the sermon of 1709. "For he lies in calling himself a son of Russia – her enemy and a lover of the Liakhs. Beware of such, O Russia, and banish them from your bosom."[77]

Was Prokopovych the only author and preacher who observed the developments at Poltava through all-Russian eyes? Apparently not. Metropolitan Stefan Yavorsky, another product of the Kyivan educational system, marked the events of 1708–9 in the Hetmanate not only with sermons that feted the occasion but also with verses on "Mazepa's treason" in which he depicted the former hetman as a poisonous snake that had betrayed Russia. The whole poem was constructed as a lament of Mother Russia condemning her treacherous son. Its title indicated that the poem was published in the name of "all Russia," leaving no doubt which Russia the author had in mind.[78] In his *Slovo o pobede nad korolem Shvedskim pod Poltavoi* (Word on the Victory over the Swedish King at Poltava), another work devoted to the events of 1708–9, Yavorsky envisioned the Orthodox Church and Russia singing hymns in Peter's honor. Although Yavorsky, not unlike Prokopovych, saw Mazepa as a traitor to all of Russia, not just to his Little Russian fatherland, he was somewhat confused (like Hetman Ivan Skoropadsky) as to whether the tsar's state (*derzhava*) was a "Russian" or "Great Russian" formation and used both appellations in referring to it.[79] Yavorsky's use of "Russia" reflected the broader, "all-Russian" meaning of the term and contributed to the confusion brought about by the indiscriminate use of the same term with reference to the Russian state and Cossack Ukraine. While the secular elites of the Hetmanate, writing in Ruthenian, Polish, or Russian, clearly distinguished their homeland – Ukraine or Little Russia – from Muscovy, increasingly referred to as Great Russia, the high style of Kyivan verses and sermons preserved the old Mohylan tradition of using *Rossiia*

---

[77] Ibid., p. 28.

[78] For the text of the verses, see *Propovedi Blazhennyia pamiati Stefana Iavorskogo*, pt. 3 (Moscow, 1805), pp. 241–49. On Yavorsky's anathematization of Mazepa at the behest of Peter I, see Giovanna Brogi Bercoff, "Mazepa, lo zar e il diavolo. Un inedito di Stefan Javorskij," *Russica Romana* 7 (2000): 167–88; Elena Pogosian, "I. S. Mazepa v russkoi ofitsial'noi kul'ture 1708–1725 gg.," in *Mazepa and His Time*, pp. 315–32, here 316–18.

[79] For the text of the *Slovo*, see *Propovedi Blazhennyia pamiati Stefana Iavorskogo*, 3: 299–302. Russia also emerges as a major point of reference in the text of the church service celebrating the Poltava victory attributed to Teofilakt Lopatynsky (1711). On the origin and fate of the service, whose composition was ordered by Peter I, see Pogosian, *Petr I*, p. 177; idem, "I. S. Mazepa," pp. 327–28.

as though there were no other Russia beyond the borders of the Kyiv metropolitanate. In changing the meaning of the term, Prokopovych was opening the door to a shift of loyalty (and thus identity) from the Hetmanate and its ecclesiastical and civic institutions to the Russian tsar and his state.

Throughout most of his St. Petersburg career, Prokopovych was a strong promoter of the idea of one united Russian nation, which he called *rossiiskii narod, rossiistii rod, rossiane*, and *rosiistii synove*. Like many of his contemporaries, Prokopovych used *narod* in two senses. The first referred to the population of the tsar's realm in general. As a rule, Prokopovych spoke and wrote about the *narod* as a community that was supposed to be grateful to its ruler, but also as one whose happiness and prosperity were among the ruler's main concerns. Most of the time, when speaking about the *narod* in this first sense, Prokopovych apparently had in mind social elites, but at times he also referred to the "simple people," which included the lower strata of society.[80] The second meaning of *narod* pertained to the ethnocultural and political organization of the world, which consisted of nations, states, countries, and realms – Prokopovych used all these terms interchangeably. (Thus, for Prokopovych, the Kazan khanate was a *narod*.)[81] *Narod* as a subject of international relations was also occasionally rendered by Prokopovych as *natsiia*.[82] His sermons contain references to foreign peoples (*inostrannye* – those residing in other countries) and Russian peoples (*rossiistii narody*), but the latter term, which was common in Muscovite political discourse of the time, was not favored by Prokopovych.[83] Clearly, he saw the world in terms of political communities (nations) and apparently believed that in Russia there was supposed to be one Russian nation. The Slavo-Rossian nation of the author of the *Synopsis*, ambiguously rooted in the broader Slavic world, was giving way to a nation largely defined by the borders of the Muscovite state. That view was quite concordant with the worldview of Samuel Pufendorf,

---

[80] For examples of the use of *narod* as a social category in Prokopovych's sermons of 1709–25, see his *Sochineniia*, pp. 25, 36, 38, 43, 44, 46, 47, 83, 98, 102, 138.

[81] Ibid., p. 36.

[82] Ibid., p. 133. Here, Prokopovych used *natsiia* to denote a foreign polity, as opposed to what he called "our fatherland."

[83] For a rare example of Prokopovych's use of the term *rossiistii narody*, see ibid., p. 57. Among other authors, Patriarch Adrian of Moscow used *narod* in the plural to denote the tsar's subjects. See, for example, his letter of 19 May 1696 to Peter in *Pis'ma imperatora Petra Velikogo k bratu svoemu Tsariu Ioannu Alekseevichu i patriarkhu Adrianu* (St. Petersburg, 1788), pp. 18–23, here 19. A church service following the Poltava victory, allegedly conducted by another Kyivan, Teofilakt Lopatynsky, also differentiated between *okrestnye* and the Russian *narody*.

whose works, translated into a heavily Slavonicized Russian by the Kyivan Samuil Buzhynsky, were well known to Prokopovych.[84]

In his sermon of 1709 on the Poltava victory, Prokopovych used the term "people" (*narody, iazytse*) only in relation to foreign countries or those conquered by Muscovite monarchs. He did not mention either the Great Russian or the Little Russian nation, or, for that matter, the Russian nation, preferring to speak of the Russian military (*voinstvo*) or forces (*sily*).[85] If he used *narod* with regard to the inhabitants of the tsar's realm, the word denoted the population in general, which was either the object of Mazepa's intrigues – by raising his hand against his master, Mazepa had "shaken the people with such confusion" – or was behind the "nectar of popular rejoicing" in connection with the Poltava victory.[86] That population acquired much clearer ethnonational characteristics in the first sermon that Prokopovych delivered after his transfer to St. Petersburg in October 1716. In *Slovo pokhval'noe* (A Word of Praise), presented on the first birthday of the tsar's son Petr Petrovich, the Kyivan preacher called upon the *rossiiskii narod* to celebrate the birth of the tsar's son, spoke about the *rossiistii rod* of the times of Boris Godunov, and addressed his audience as *rossiiane*.[87] Subsequently, Prokopovych often used these terms in his St. Petersburg sermons and writings. He refused to see the Mazepa affair as a conflict between two different nations and reaffirmed his view of it as an internal Russian matter in *Slovo na pokhvalu . . . pamiati Petra Velikogo* (A Word in Praise of the Memory of Peter the Great, June 1727), where he summarized the main developments and accomplishments of Peter's rule. There Mazepa's "treason" was treated on a par with the Don and Astrakhan revolts, all of which were deemed internal Russian conflicts (*terzaniia*).[88]

Prokopovych did not regard Russia as a multinational or multiethnic state. He generally avoided using the term "empire" in relation to Russia, preferring "state" or "monarchy." Thus he imposed on the essentially imperial state the concept of an ethnically and religiously homogeneous Russian (Ruthenian) people constructed by the Kyivan literati of the

---

[84] See Cracraft, *The Petrine Revolution in Russian Culture*, pp. 212–16. The interest of Petrine society in the Slavic origins of the Muscovite state found expression in a Slavonicized Russian translation of Mauro Orbini's book on the history of the Slavs (1722). In the context of the present discussion, it is of interest that the author of the foreword to the book, Teofilakt Lopatynsky, apparently used the *Synopsis* to rebut some of Orbini's pro-Catholic statements (ibid., pp. 217–19). On Orbini and his work, see Giovanna Brogi Bercoff, *Królestwo Słowian. Historiografia Renesansu i Baroku w krajach słowiańskich* (Izabelin, 1998), pp. 43–98.

[85] See Prokopovich, *Sochineniia*, pp. 24, 26, 29–30, 33–36, 38.   [86] Ibid., pp. 35–36.

[87] For the text of the *Slovo pokhval'noe*, see ibid., pp. 38–48.

[88] See the text of *Slovo na pokhvalu . . . pamiati Petra Velikogo*, ibid., pp. 129–46, here 33.

seventeenth century. The Kyivan *Rossiia* lacked a "Russian monarch," since it was ruled by the Polish king, and Prokopovych found the perfect realization of the Kyivan national ideal in the transformed and renamed Muscovy of Peter's day. Such a strategy helped set Russia on the path to modern nationhood, and Prokopovych was a tireless builder and promoter of the national image of the Russian Empire.

The search for a fatherland

In his post-Poltava sermons and writings, Prokopovych often referred to Russia as "fatherland" (*otechestvo*). The term itself was not new to him. In the tragicomedy, he used one of its forms, *otchestvo*, to denote St. Volodymyr's patrimony as inherited by Mazepa.[89] After 1709, however, Prokopovych used *otechestvo* to render a different concept, defined by the Latin *patria* – a term linked to the development of patriotism and "nationalism" in the lands of early modern Europe. The notion of "fatherland" as an equivalent of *patria* was not entirely new to Muscovite political discourse, but Prokopovych was one of the first writers to stress loyalty to the fatherland as one of the highest civic virtues.[90]

The term "fatherland" was as ambiguous in Prokopovych's writings as was "Russia." What were the boundaries of his fatherland? Where did it begin and end? For an answer to this question, we may look to the role played by that concept in the pre-Poltava ideological duel or, as a student of the period put it, the "war of manifestos" between Mazepa and Peter.[91] The tsar, who had seldom if ever used that term in his official documents prior to Mazepa's defection in the autumn of 1708, now emerged in his manifestos to the Cossacks as the true champion of their fatherland and the Little Russian nation.[92] In his circular of 28 October 1708, issued immediately after Peter learned about Mazepa's defection

---

[89] Prokopovich, *Sochineniia*, p. 152.

[90] This particular meaning of the term *otechestvo* can be traced back to fifteenth-century texts and is directly linked to Bulgarian cultural influence. See the discussion of the use of the terms *otchina* and *otechestvo* in V. V. Kolesov, *Mir cheloveka v slove drevnei Rusi* (Leningrad, 1986), pp. 242–46.

[91] For the texts of Peter's manifestos, as well as texts and excerpts from the letters of Peter, Mazepa, and Aleksandr Menshikov, see *Pis'ma i bumagi imperatora Petra Velikogo*, 19 vols. (St. Petersburg and Moscow, 1887–1992), VIII, vyp. 1, nos. 2760–94; Oleksandr Rigel'man, *Litopysna opovid' pro Malu Rosiiu ta ii narod i kozakiv uzahali* (repr. of 1847 edn. of *Letopisnoe povestvovanie o Maloi Rossii*, Kyiv, 1994), pp. 531–74; and Sergei Solov'ev, *Istoriia Rossii s drevneishikh vremen*, bk. 8 (Moscow, 1962), pp. 240–52. For a discussion of the "war of manifestos," see Bohdan Kentrschynskyj, "Propagandakriket i Ukraina, 1708–1709" in *Karolinska Förbundets Årsbok* (Stockholm, 1958), pp. 181–224.

[92] See the discussion of that terminological innovation in Peter's propaganda in Greenfeld, *Nationalism*, pp. 195–96.

to the Swedes,[93] the tsar presented the hetman's actions as a betrayal of his oath of personal loyalty. Apart from accusing the hetman of treason, Peter employed two other political arguments. The first was related to the conditions of the Muscovite protectorate over the Hetmanate established in the days of Bohdan Khmelnytsky. According to those conditions, the tsar took it upon himself to protect "Little Russia" from the Polish threat to the Orthodox religion. Now that King Stanisław Leszczyński of Poland was assisting Charles XII in his war with Muscovy, Peter exploited that motif to the fullest. He accused Mazepa of attempting to subjugate the "Little Russian land" (*krai*) to the Poles and turn the Orthodox churches over to the Union. As the protector of the "Little Russian land," the tsar declared his determination to prevent the enslavement and destruction of Little Russia and the desecration of God's churches. The other motif that Peter employed to discredit his opponent was related to the image of the Muscovite tsar as protector of the "Little Russian nation" against abuses of power by the Cossack administration. Alleged betrayal of the tsar's interests and ill-treatment of the Zaporozhian Host and the "Little Russian nation" were among the reasons cited by Moscow for the removal in 1687 of Mazepa's predecessor in the office of hetman, Ivan Samoilovych.[94] Now it was Mazepa's turn to be accused of imposing unfair and heavy taxes on the "Little Russian nation" for his own enrichment. All three motifs were present in one form or another and further developed in the numerous manifestos and circulars that Peter issued in late October and early November 1708.[95]

Peter's first use of the term "fatherland" probably occurred in his manifesto of 6 November 1708, by far the longest document presenting the tsar's case against the hetman. It was issued in response to letters to the "Little Russian nation" from Charles XII and Mazepa that were intercepted by the tsar's troops. Peter's manifesto sought to discredit Charles XII and Mazepa as enemies of the "Little Russian nation" who wanted to exploit Ukraine economically and then either deliver it to Poland

---

[93] See the text of Peter's circular of 28 October 1708 in Rigel'man, *Litopysna opovid'*, pp. 531–32.

[94] See the text of the tsar's letter of 3 December 1690 to Colonel Yakiv Lyzohub of Chernihiv, ibid., pp. 501–2.

[95] See the texts of Peter's letters of that period, ibid., pp. 531–35. The idea of using manifestos to enumerate Mazepa's abuses of his own people so as to secure the support of the "simple folk" and prove that Mazepa was acting in his own interests rather than for the good of Ukraine was suggested to Peter by Menshikov on 26 October in the same letter in which he informed the tsar about Mazepa's "treason." See Solov'ev, *Istoriia Rossii*, bk. 8, p. 244. On Peter's accusing Mazepa of treason and the antagonists' opposing interpretations of the conditions of the Pereiaslav Agreement, see Orest Subtelny, "Mazepa, Peter I, and the Question of Treason," *Harvard Ukrainian Studies* 2, no. 2 (June 1978): 158–83.

or establish Mazepa's autocratic rule, introducing Lutheranism and the Union in order to destroy Orthodoxy. These claims were supported by references to the devastation of territories occupied by the Swedes and the alleged plunder of Orthodox churches in Belarus by Swedish troops.[96] Peter also assured his addressees that the ancient rights granted them by the tsar in the days of Bohdan Khmelnytsky had never been violated. He claimed that Moscow had not taken a penny from Little Russia and that "no nation under the sun can boast such liberties, privileges, and freedom as the Little Russian nation, by the Grace of Our Tsarist Majesty." Responding to Mazepa's charge that the tsar had stationed his troops in Ukraine in order to take complete control of it after the war, Peter wrote that he had no intention of leaving Great Russian troops in Ukrainian towns after the campaign. He claimed that the troops had already left some of the towns, while those soldiers responsible for unruliness and abuse of the local population had already been executed. In conclusion, the tsar called on his subjects of the "Little Russian nation" to support his effort to liberate "their fatherland" – the "Little Russian land."[97]

In a letter to the Zaporozhian Cossacks, Peter not only promised to increase the yearly stipend for every detachment (kurin') of the Sich by 1,500 rubles but also expressed his hope that the Cossacks would "stand up for their fatherland and for the Orthodox faith and for us, and not give ear to the blandishments of the apostate traitor Mazepa."[98] In his manifesto of 21 January 1709, Peter set out to undermine Mazepa's claim that he wanted to establish Ukraine as an independent polity, claiming that the hetman had gone over to the Swedes not "for the benefit of the Little Russian land and for the preservation of liberties and so that they might be neither under Our nor under Polish rule but remain free and independent" but in order to deliver Ukraine into the hands of the Poles. The tsar

[96] Apart from developing the themes introduced in the first manifesto, the tsar and his assistants felt that they had to respond to the accusations leveled against them by their opponents. The manifestos issued by Charles and Mazepa asserted in particular that Peter was corresponding with the pope in order to establish Roman Catholicism in place of Orthodoxy in his tsardom. Other charges were related to the nature of Peter's war with Sweden, his violation of the ancient privileges and freedoms of the "Little Russian nation," and the pillaging and destruction of Ukrainian possessions by Great Russian troops. In response, Peter listed his reasons for the war, indicating the need to reclaim former Muscovite territories, liberate the churches forcibly taken over by the Lutherans, and defend the tsar's honor, allegedly violated by the Swedish king and his envoys. For a discussion of some of the accusations against Peter and his responses to them, see Solov'ev, *Istoriia Rossii*, bk. 8, pp. 250–52.
[97] For the text of the manifesto, see *Pis'ma i bumagi imperatora Petra Velikogo*, VIII, pt. 1, no. 2816: 276–84. Cf. Rigel'man, *Litopysna opovid'*, pp. 539–45. In his circular, Peter mentioned "fatherland" twice; in both cases it was "their" fatherland, referring to the Little Russian addressees of the letter.
[98] Cited in Solov'ev, *Istoriia Rossii*, bk. 8, p. 250.

called upon his Little Russian subjects to pay no heed to Mazepa and the Swedes but to support the Great Russian troops and oppose their enemy, "seeing this open treason on the part of the apostate Mazepa, seeking the betrayal of your fatherland into unbearable Polish bondage."[99] Peter was clearly changing emphasis from characterizing Mazepa's actions as a betrayal of the tsar – the leitmotif of his first manifesto – to a betrayal of the fatherland. Not surprisingly, in all the manifestos and letters known to us, Peter wrote only about "your," not "our," fatherland – a clear indication that *otechestvo* was associated in his mind with the specific character of Ukrainian political discourse and not directly related to the "all-Russian" political culture and vocabulary.[100]

The war of manifestos between Peter and Mazepa during the months leading up to the Poltava battle constitutes the ideological background against which we can properly assess the meaning of the concepts, ideas and images employed by Prokopovych in his sermon before the tsar on 24 July 1709. The war directly affected the Kyivan Academy, as all "foreign" students – that is, those born outside the Hetmanate – were sent back across the Polish-Lithuanian border by the local Muscovite voevoda on the orders of the tsar's chancellor.[101] Prokopovych could not but have known the content of at least some of Mazepa's manifestos and the responses to them by Peter and Skoropadsky: in fact, his sermon contains a reference to Peter's manifesto on the Zaporozhians.[102] Clearly, Prokopovych developed some of the ideas expressed in the manifestos, including the motif of Mazepa's betrayal of both the tsar and the fatherland. And yet, despite clear parallels between Prokopovych's sermon and the circular letters of the tsar and the new hetman, there were some important differences in the treatment of the issue by Prokopovych and his royal predecessor in the propaganda war against Mazepa. One of the most important concerns the notion of the fatherland – the entity allegedly betrayed by Mazepa. If Peter had in mind the Little Russian fatherland, Prokopovych considered that his own fatherland and the one betrayed by Mazepa was not Little Russia but the entity to which Peter referred

[99] For the text of Peter's manifesto, see *Pis'ma i bumagi imperatora Petra Velikogo*, VIII, pt. 1, no. 299: 38–41. Cf. Rigel'man, *Litopysna opovid'*, pp. 565–67. On the image of Mazepa in the tsar's official and private correspondence of the autumn of 1708 and the winter of 1709, see Pogosian, "I. S. Mazepa," pp. 315–23.

[100] In a letter of 30 October 1708 to Fedor Apraksin, Peter characterized Mazepa as a "turncoat and traitor to his nation" (*izmennik i predatel' svoego naroda*) (Pogosian, "I. S. Mazepa," p. 320).

[101] Solov'ev, *Istoriia Rossii*, bk. 8, p. 268.

[102] In his manifesto of 26 May 1709, the tsar accused the Zaporozhian Cossacks, among other things, of wishing to bring about the "destruction of their fatherland, the Little Russian land" (*razorenie otchizny svoei, Malorossiiskogo kraia*). See the text of the manifesto in *Pis'ma i bumagi imperatora Petra Velikogo*, IX, pt. 2: 907–14, here 912.

in one of his manifestos as the "Russian state" (Prokopovych generally called it "Russia").

The concept of the Russian fatherland constructed by Prokopovych was a major ideological innovation, for it not only implied a prospective change of loyalty on the part of the "Little Russian nation" from the Hetmanate to the "all-Russian" state but also introduced a new object of loyalty for the rest of the population of that state. For Prokopovych, unlike Peter, there were no Little Russian and Great Russian troops at Poltava – there were only Russian troops; there were no Little Russian and Great Russian nations but one united Russian nation; no Little Russia and Great Russia as constituents of one "all-Russian" state but Little Russia as part of a greater Russia – the new fatherland and the new object of loyalty of the tsar's subjects. That new source of legitimacy was closely linked to the old one – the person of the tsar – but henceforth the tsar had to share his place in the hierarchy of loyalties with the concept of Russia as a fatherland. The appellation "father of the fatherland," earlier applied by Kyivan literati to Mazepa, was now reserved, with the change of the fatherland's political boundaries, exclusively for the person of the tsar. Not surprisingly, in his sermon of 1709, Prokopovych called Peter the "father of the fatherland."

Was Prokopovych alone in attempting to turn the Russian state into a nationally defined fatherland called "Russia"? Probably not, but the proof of that is not easy to find. One indication that Prokopovych had a powerful ally and protector in this undertaking – the tsar himself – is to be found in the text of the tsar's order to his troops on the eve of the Poltava battle. There, in an apparent departure from his earlier manifestos, Peter addressed his country as both "Russia" and "fatherland." "Let the Russian (rossiiskoe) army know," reads the text of the order, "that the hour has drawn nigh in which the very existence of the whole fatherland (otechestvo) is placed in their hands; either Russia (Rossiia) will perish completely or she will be reborn for the better."[103] The problem with this order is that its original text has not survived, and the one known today originates with a manuscript entitled "The History of Emperor Peter the Great," whose authorship is attributed to none other than Teofan Prokopovych.[104] Whether Peter indeed addressed his troops before the battle in the manner indicated above, using the words "Russia" and "fatherland," cannot be known for certain. Research on the use of the

---

[103] Pis'ma i bumagi imperatora Petra Velikogo, IX, pt. 1: 980–83. Quoted in James Cracraft, "Empire versus Nation: Russian Political Theory under Peter I," Harvard Ukrainian Studies 10, nos. 3–4 (December 1986): 524–41, here 529.

[104] For a discussion of the textual history of the order, see Pis'ma i bumagi imperatora Petra Velikogo, IX, pt. 2: 980–81.

term "fatherland" in Muscovy and the Russian Empire still lies ahead, but it seems highly appropriate to find these terms in the work of one of the original promoters of the concept of Russia as a common fatherland of the two nations that the pre-Poltava propagandists called Little Russia and Great Russia.

The notion of the fatherland was associated in Prokopovych's mind with a particular polity, and he saw it as constituting a natural object of loyalty for its sons from the most ancient times. The Trojans had their own fatherland, as did the Romans and, later, the Poles.[105] Apparently the borders of the fatherland could change with those of the state. For example, in Prokopovych's opinion, Aleksandr Nevsky had "revived Russia and these members of it, Ingria, I say, and Karelia, which were then about to be cut off; he preserved and consolidated them in the body of his fatherland."[106] Thus, as was often the case in Prokopovych's sermons, the notions of the fatherland and Russia merged into one concept. As noted above, the notion of Russia had a clear national connotation in Prokopovych's sermons, for he considered Russia a "national name" (obshchenarodnoe imia), often compared it to other nations, and occasionally called it a narod.[107] The concept of Russia as a fatherland linked the concept of the Russian monarch (all-important to Prokopovych) with the concepts of the Russian state (gosudarstvo, derzhava) and the Russian nation.

The new meaning of such terms as "Russia" and "fatherland" employed in Prokopovych's sermons and writings of the post-1709 period manifested the emergence of a novel identity in the Romanovs' realm – one based on loyalty not to the ruler alone or to his state but to a new type of protonational entity. Prokopovych actively promoted these new terms and concepts in his numerous speeches and sermons. In so doing, he echoed the Protestant preachers on the Swedish side of the Northern War, as well as their colleagues elsewhere in northern Europe. All of them were busy promoting the notion of the fatherland and the concept of loyalty to it in their own sermons and writings.[108] The concept of Russia as a fatherland and object of loyalty for the subjects of the tsar made spectacular progress in the Muscovite realm during the age of Peter, and

---

[105] For references to the Trojan, Roman, and Polish fatherlands, see Prokopovich, Sochineniia, pp. 26, 137.

[106] See "Slovo v den' sviatogo blagovernogo kniazia Aleksandra Nevskogo," in Prokopovich, Sochineniia, p. 100.

[107] See Prokopovich, Sochineniia, pp. 52, 91, 133, 137.

[108] On the development and promotion of the concept of fatherland in northern Europe, see Pasi Ihalainen, "The Concepts of Fatherland and Nation in Swedish State Sermons from the Late Age of Absolutism to the Accession of Gustavus III," Scandinavian Journal of History 28 (2003): 37–58.

in that progress it is not difficult to see the hand of Prokopovych. On the eve of the proclamation of the Russian state as an empire, Prokopovych was consciously or unconsciously promoting the "nationalization" of the patrimony of the Muscovite tsars. As that process gained momentum in the course of the eighteenth century, along with the "imperialization" of the Muscovite state, the confluence of the two trends could not but create a good deal of confusion, first in the minds of the subjects of the Russian emperors and subsequently in the interpretations of students of Russian imperial history.

The Russian Empire

On 22 October 1721, during the official ceremony held at Holy Trinity Cathedral in St. Petersburg to celebrate the Peace of Nystadt with Sweden, which ended the Northern War, the Senate awarded Peter I the title "all-Russian emperor" and two appellations, "Great" and "Father of the Fatherland." According to the official version of events, it was the Senate that gave the tsar his new title, but in fact the initiative came from the Holy Synod. Most likely it was Teofan Prokopovych who came up with the idea of awarding Peter I his new title and appellations. The award has long been regarded as a significant milestone in Russian history.[109] The appellation "Peter the Great" is firmly established in both Russian and Western historiography, and his rule is considered to have inaugurated a new, imperial period in his country's history. No less important was the designation of the Russian ruler as "father of the fatherland."[110] Recently, close attention has been paid to the fact that Peter was proclaimed a "national" emperor, the ruler of all Russia, which distinguished him from his Byzantine and Holy Roman predecessors, whose titles had no ethnonational connotations.[111] The tsar's new title and appellations brought together two very different concepts of political loyalty that were current at Peter's court during the first quarter of the eighteenth century and linked them in a complex entanglement. The first of these was the concept of Russia as a nation-state, and the second was the notion of Russia as an empire.

Let us take a closer look at all three elements of the tsar's new title – "all-Russian emperor," "father of the fatherland," and "great" – in an effort to discover the precise meaning that Peter and his entourage attributed to the inauguration of what is now known as Russian imperial history. Were

[109] See Pogosian, *Petr I*, pp. 220–29. Historians have traditionally regarded the ceremony of 22 October 1721 as marking the inception of the Russian Empire. See, e.g., Anisimov, *The Reforms of Peter the Great*, pp. 143–44.
[110] See Greenfeld, *Nationalism*, pp. 195–96.   [111] Tolz, *Russia*, p. 41.

they empire-builders or nation-builders, and what did the term "empire" really mean to them?

As we have seen, the terms "emperor" and "empire" were hardly the most popular in the vocabulary of Prokopovych, the likely initiator of the events of October 1721, but they certainly were among the most cherished ones in Peter's book. Foreign observers noted that after the Battle of Poltava, those who wanted to flatter the tsar addressed him as "emperor." As Elena Pogosian has shown, Peter began to toy with the idea of declaring himself emperor during the Azov campaigns against the Ottomans in the late seventeenth century, returned to it after his victories over the Swedes in 1708–9, and finally made up his mind ca. 1717, delaying his official acceptance of the title until the end of the Northern War with Sweden.[112] The chronology of Peter's interest in the title shows that in his mind the imperial title and, it would seem, the concept of empire itself were closely associated with war, military victory, and acquisition of new territories. The same idea is highlighted in the Russian word used in official documents and publications of the period to render the Latin "imperator" – *prisnopribavitel'*, which may be translated as "one who constantly augments or increases." This meant that Peter had attached new territories to the old tsardom, which would now be known as an empire. Peter's additions to the old state in the Baltic region were indeed of enduring strategic importance, but in terms of territorial aggrandizement, he was a distant fourth as compared with his predecessors: Ivan III, with his victories over Tver and Novgorod; Ivan IV, with his incorporation of the Volga khanates and the "conquest" of Siberia; and his father, Aleksei Mikhailovich, with his "additions" of Smolensk, Kyiv, and Left-Bank Ukraine. These facts must have been obvious to Peter and his ideologues; hence they preferred to justify the new title by reference to old Muscovite tradition, allegedly obscured by the Time of Troubles. At the ceremonial conferral of Peter's new title, it was asserted that he had in fact inherited it from his ancestors, since it had first been applied to the Muscovite rulers centuries earlier by the Holy Roman Emperor Maximilian I.[113]

What was behind the thinking of Prokopovych, who apparently put this argument into the resolutions of the Synod; of Pavel Shafirov, who wrote the speech for the ceremony; and of the Reverend Feodosii Yanovsky (another Kyivan), who delivered the speech featuring this argument? It would appear that they were conforming to the beliefs and trying to anticipate the desires of the tsar himself. Back in 1708, when Peter thought

---

[112] For a discussion of the process of bestowing the new title and appellations on the tsar, see Pogosian, *Petr I*, pp. 220–29.

[113] See an English translation of an excerpt from the petition asking the tsar to accept the new title in Greenfeld, *Nationalism*, p. 196.

that the Northern War was nearing its end and was again considering the adoption of the imperial title, he ordered the preparation of a history of the "Russian state" beginning with the rule of Vasilii III. Why did Peter attribute such importance to the tenure of Vasilii, which is normally squeezed into historical narratives between the rule of Vasilii's much more famous father, Ivan III, and that of his son, Ivan IV the Terrible? The reason lies in the contemporary belief that Vasilii III had been the first Muscovite ruler to assume the title of tsar and had been recognized as such in a letter from Maximilian I. Peter's historiographic initiative yielded scant results, but in 1718 Maximilian's letter, originally issued in 1514, was reprinted in St. Petersburg, and copies were sent to foreign ambassadors in the capital.[114] Since Peter was preparing to assume a title then possessed only by the Habsburg emperor, Maximilian's historical recognition of the tsar's title took on extraordinary importance. To be sure, no one questioned Peter's title of tsar, but what he wanted was the imperial title. He therefore claimed that they were one and the same and that the first title had been granted to his ancestors (no matter that he was a Romanov, while they were Rurikids) in the early sixteenth century and lost during the calamities of the Time of Troubles. Now, by recovering lands lost at that time (such was his justification for annexing Ingria), Peter was restoring not only the battle-scarred empire but the imperial title itself. For all the Westernization of Russian political thought during this period, the principal justification of the new territorial acquisitions remained patrimonial.

The conferral on Peter of the title "emperor of all Russia" was another bow to the Muscovite political tradition and a refusal to surrender the old status of the rulers of Moscow as sovereigns of all Rus'. The adoption of this title marked a return to the tsars' pre-1654 tradition of calling themselves sovereigns of all Rus' – a practice they had abandoned in favor of a bipartite form (Great and Little Rus') and then a tripartite one (Great, Little, and White Rus'). Now all the Ruses were merged into one and extended to cover all the new acquisitions of the empire, including the Baltic provinces. The traditional term "Rus'" was merely replaced with its Hellenized form, *Rossiia*, which reflected the new usage of the day. The foreign-sounding *Rossiia* was in keeping with the foreign-sounding *imperiia* (empire), which now replaced *tsarstvo* (tsardom) as the official name of the state. Thus, along with the Holy Roman Emperor there emerged an all-Russian one whose title was something of a novelty, since it defined the empire in ethnonational terms, but apparently not without historical parallel in Peter's mind. In his acceptance speech

---

[114] On Peter's interpretation of Russian history, see Pogosian, *Petr I*, pp. 183–206.

at the ceremony, Peter warned his subjects that while hoping for peace they had best prepare for war, so that "what had happened to the Greek monarchy would not happen to us" – a reference to the Byzantine Empire defined as a Greek polity. The tsar was an avid reader of popular Muscovite translations of historical works about Alexander of Macedonia and the fall of Constantinople. Both works, which originally circulated in manuscript, were published on his orders. The latter work was issued twice, and images derived from it even appeared in the tsar's dreams.[115]

As for the appellation "father of the fatherland," there is little doubt what fatherland Peter and his entourage had in mind. As noted above, tsarist ideologues such as Prokopovych readily applied the new term to the whole Muscovite state: gone were the days when the tsar had written to the Cossacks about their fatherland. Gone, but not entirely forgotten. In the draft of the speech prepared by Shafirov and delivered by Yanovsky at the ceremony of the granting of the new title, the Kyiv-trained cleric took care to change "our fatherland," a form that probably reminded him of the city of Kyiv, to "the whole fatherland."[116] In the Holy Synod's proposal, the rationale given for bestowing that particular appellation on the tsar was the desire to recognize Peter's work for the good of Russia, which through his efforts had been "brought out of the darkness of ignorance into the theater of worldwide glory and born into existence out of nonexistence and introduced into the society of political nations." In the speech delivered at the ceremony, it was claimed that the appellation was being offered to the tsar according to the example of the Greek and Roman senates.[117] While it was indeed rooted in the ancient concept of *patria*, it had even more to do with ideas current among the European "political nations" that Russia aspired to join. The concept of fatherland was among the first signs of the advance of modern nationalism, with its discourse of "nation" and the "common good,"[118] and the tsar showed his aptitude for the new rhetoric when in his acceptance speech he called upon those in attendance to "work for the common good and profit that God sets before your eyes, both at home and abroad, which will ease the nation's burden."[119]

The tsar was fluent in the language of the European "political nations," but did he mean what he said? Imitating foreign examples, he routinely ordered his subjects to build triumphal arches to mark his victories, creating the impression of popular enthusiasm for him. As for the title, Peter ordered the Senate to bestow it on him. A foreign diplomat wrote in 1721

---

[115] Ibid., pp. 226–43.   [116] Ibid., p. 222.
[117] Ibid., pp. 221, 224–25. Cf. Greenfeld, *Nationalism*, p. 196.
[118] See Greenfeld, *Nationalism*, pp. 193–94.   [119] Quoted in Pogosian, *Petr I*, p. 226.

that the tsar gave the Senate rights equal to those of the Roman Senate so that it could grant him the title of emperor, but took them away after the ceremony. Wanting the fatherland to glorify him as its father and benefactor, he deliberately planned the "spontaneous" outpouring of his subjects' love and admiration. He certainly achieved a measure of success in that regard, at least when it came to official propaganda. Prokopovych glorified him not only in life but also after his death. On 8 March 1725, he delivered a eulogy for the deceased emperor in the Church of SS. Peter and Paul, addressing his former patron as "Responsible for countless successes and joys of ours, having resurrected Russia from the dead and raised it to such power and glory or, even more, having borne and raised Russia – this directly descended son of the fatherland and its father."[120] But how lasting and widely accepted was that praise? Opportunist that he was, Prokopovych readily discontinued his praise for the deceased emperor in the 1730s, while the elite in general had mixed feelings about the emperor from the very beginning, to say the least. Vasilii Kliuchevsky revealed the core of Peter's contradictions when he wrote that the emperor "hoped through strong power to provoke independent activities in the enslaved society, wanted a slave, remaining a slave, to act as a responsible free man."[121]

The appellation "great," bestowed on Peter for his personal accomplishments,[122] according to Yanovsky's speech, further stressed the unquestionable centrality of the person of the ruler for the Russian political system and identity. The new title and appellations heralded the arrival in Russia of the age of secular absolutism. After all, even though the initiative to award the new title came from the Holy Synod, Peter entrusted the Senate with the task. It was ratified not by the church, which had conferred the tsar's titles and consecrated every new ruler until the end of the seventeenth century, but by a secular government body. Peter did a great deal to secularize the Russian state, from abolishing the office of patriarch to firmly subordinating the church to the state along the lines of Prokopovych's *Ecclesiastical Regulations* (1721). He also did much to secularize his court and society at large, introducing a new, mostly secular and dynastically oriented official calendar to replace the predominantly religious one of his predecessors. Personally, however, Peter remained a religious man. References to God and God's will and grace appear as

---

[120] Feofan Prokopovich, "Slovo na pogrebenie Vsepresvetleishago Derzhavneishago Petra Velikago," in idem, *Sochineniia*, p. 126.

[121] Quoted in Tolz, *Russia*, p. 36.

[122] The Synod papers contain a parallel with Julius Caesar and a reference to foreigners who used that appellation in addressing Peter, but these were not incorporated into the text of the Shafirov-Yanovsky speech.

frequently in his private correspondence as in his official papers and pronouncements, while his edicts required the populace to attend church services on Sundays and major holidays and to make regular confession. On the other hand, during his reign religion in general and Orthodoxy in particular disappeared from the list of principal markers of Russian identity as defined vis-à-vis foreigners.[123] In fact, Peter had to hold back his Kyiv-trained ideologues, who tried to present not only the Mazepa affair but also the whole war with Sweden in religious terms. He suggested corrections to the text of the *Service on the Poltava Victory*, composed by the Kyiv alumnus Teofilakt Lopatynsky, who compared Peter to Constantine the Great. The emperor noted that the war with Sweden was "not for the faith but for space" (*ne o vere, a o mere*) and that the Swedes revered the same cross as the Russians.[124] Peter regarded Protestant Sweden as belonging to the same Christian tradition as his own Orthodox subjects and refused to justify the major undertaking of his reign in religious terms. This was a dramatic departure from Muscovite tradition, which had framed not only the conflicts of the Time of Troubles but also the Pereiaslav Agreement in religious terms.

All of a sudden wars ceased to be confessional, and religion no longer constituted the core of Russian identity vis-à-vis the Christian West. What, then, took the place of seventeenth-century religious discourse when it came to constructing Russia's main "other"? In his *Rassuzhdenie* (Consideration, 1717) on the reasons for the war with Sweden, Pavel Shafirov listed the tsar's desire to recover lost territories, the personal insult to the tsar on the part of the Swedish governor of Riga, and the plot of the Western powers to prevent Russia from gaining military might. The tsar, who certainly approved this interpretation of the causes of the war, later wrote that "all other nations follow a policy of maintaining a balance of power among their neighbors, and particularly of keeping us from the light of reason in all matters, especially military ones."[125] If the first two of Shafirov's reasons for war find parallels in seventeenth-century Muscovite claims to the tsar's patrimony and the need to avenge insults to his honor (both figured in one way or another with regard to the Pereiaslav Agreement), the third argument is based on entirely different

---

[123] On Peter's personal religious beliefs and his policies toward the church, see Cracraft, *The Church Reform of Peter the Great*.

[124] See Pogosian, *Petr I*, p. 242. The author of the eulogy to Prince Bahdan Ahinski (1625) used the same words, though under different circumstances and with a different meaning, with reference to the war between the Commonwealth and Muscovy. See chapter 6 of the present work.

[125] Pogosian, *Petr I*, p. 278; cf. p. 272.

grounds, as it presupposes the right of every nation to acquire knowledge and rise up against those who conspire to prevent it from doing so. The tsar was opening a window on Europe so as to bring Continental expertise and thinking to Russia not because he wished to subordinate Russia to the West but, on the contrary, because he wanted to make it the equal of the other nations of Europe. As Ivan Nepliuev, Peter's one-time envoy to Istanbul, wrote in his memoirs, "This monarch made our fatherland comparable with others; taught us to recognize that we too are people (*liudi*)."[126]

The Russian Empire as imagined and built by Peter was not intended to be a multiethnic commonwealth. It was supposed to be devoted to the pride and honor of its ruler, his military victories, and territorial acquisitions, high status for Russia in the hierarchy of European nations, and the common good of its people, who remained subjects of the tsar. That vision of the empire was no obstacle to the "nationalization" of the emperor's realm; indeed, it promoted that goal. Along with military expertise, the West was exporting to Russia the concepts of nation, fatherland, and the common good. Muscovy was turning itself into a nation-state, a process reflected in its official discourse. That discourse originated in the experience and thinking of the Kyivan literati, was adapted to the political traditions of Muscovy (with its focus on the dynasty and the state), and was sharpened by direct and sustained military confrontation with the West. It offered a new identity to the subjects of the newly proclaimed empire.

The Schism

The territories of the Russian Empire were vast, its society was far from homogeneous, and the official imperial discourse was not dominant in every part of the tsar's realm. Kyivan learning and the elements of Westernization associated with it came into conflict with powerful forces within the Muscovite church and society as soon as they began to be promoted by the Muscovite court in the times of Aleksei Mikhailovich and Patriarch Nikon. In institutional terms, the resistance of traditional Muscovite society to the religious and cultural change promoted by the Kyivans was embodied in the Old Belief, which divided the Russian church and society into two warring camps. The official secularization of the state and the thoroughgoing Westernization of Muscovite society, most vividly

---

[126] Tolz, *Russia*, p. 23.

expressed in Peter's prohibition against the wearing of beards and his introduction of Western costume, only added insult to injury.[127]

Peter was of course at the center of the controversy. There were even rumors to the effect that the real Peter had been replaced at birth by a German child and that Russia was being ruled by a German, not by the legitimate Russian tsar. The Old Believers regarded the tsar as the Antichrist who betrayed his true nature by using the Latin name *Peter* (which the tsar liked to do) instead of the Russian *Petr*. According to an Old Believer text of 1710, "Just as in transforming the name of Jesus the devil presents a different Jesus, so the newly applied Latin name of Peter points to a hellish devil presiding over and through him."[128] Peter, for his part, treated the Old Believers with unprecedented tolerance and pragmatism, halting the campaign to do away with them that had been undertaken by the government of the regent Sofia. The tsar needed Old Believer cooperation for his war effort, and instead of persecuting them he imposed double taxation on Old Believer communities, isolated their settlements, and allowed them to wear their beards and old-fashioned clothes, making them a visible embodiment of the old Muscovite Rus'. Peter's Westernization stopped at the gates of the Old Believer communities.[129]

Who were the Old Believers, and why did they become the symbol of society's resistance to Peter's Westernization? The origins of the movement went back to the protest provoked by the reforms of Patriarch Nikon in the mid-seventeenth century. Nikon's goal was to introduce a degree of uniformity into Russian religious practices and bring them closer to those of the rest of the Orthodox world – Kyivan Christianity and the Greek church. The most prominent signs of change were corrections in the texts of liturgical books and the new practice of making the sign of the cross not with two fingers, as was customary in Muscovy, but with three. The church council of 1666–67 removed Nikon from the office

---

[127] Some scholars have argued that in the late seventeenth and early eighteenth centuries the Kyivans replaced Muscovite high culture with their own, deepening the chasm between the educated elites and the people. See Nikolai Trubetzkoy, "The Ukrainian Problem," in idem, *The Legacy of Genghis Khan and Other Essays on Russian Identity*, ed. Anatoly Liberman (Ann Arbor, 1991), pp. 245–67.

[128] Quoted in Boris A. Uspensky, "Schism and Cultural Conflict in the Seventeenth Century," in *Seeking God: The Recovery of Religious Identity in Orthodox Russia, Ukraine and Georgia*, ed. Stephen K. Batalden (DeKalb, Ill., 1993), pp. 106–43, here 115.

[129] The illustration on the cover of Anisimov's *The Reforms of Peter the Great* – a Russian *lubok* (woodcut) depicting a barber in Western dress attempting to cut the beard of an Old Believer over the latter's protests – is therefore misleading. The *lubok* actually dates from 1770, long after the end of Peter's rule. See the reproduction of the woodcut and its dating in Robin Milner-Gulland, *The Russians* (Oxford, 1997), p. 127. On Peter's policy toward the Old Belief, see Cracraft, *The Church Reform of Peter the Great*, pp. 74–79.

of patriarch following his personal conflict with the tsar, but it also condemned those who opposed his reforms. The council ruled that not only the church but also the tsar had the right to persecute the dissenters, who became known as *raskol′niki* (schismatics) or adherents of the *staraia vera* (Old Believers). In 1681 another church council decided to turn over all unrepentant "schismatics" to the jurisdiction of state courts, which had the power to sentence them to execution. The Westernizing government of the regent Sofia obliged by issuing a decree in 1684 authorizing the use of torture against the most stubborn Old Believers, as well as their execution by burning at the stake. The "schismatics" retreated into the most remote areas of the country, and some of them committed acts of self-immolation. In the traditional historiography, based on data collected from hagiographies of founders of the Old Belief, their movement is often characterized as massive and well organized, but recent reexamination of the sources points rather to the absence of a coordinated mass movement in the second half of the seventeenth century. Moreover, the aspirations of rank-and-file spiritual rebels were often at odds with the views of the leaders of the Old Belief, which became a formidable movement only in the first half of the eighteenth century, partly as a result of Peter's ban on open persecution. By that time, the leaders of the Old Belief had also adopted educational models from their Kyivan opponents that helped them train their own missionaries and propagate their new "old religion."

Traditional interpretations of the Old Belief range from Georges Florovsky's view of the schism as a "grievous spiritual disease" to the Soviet-era assessment of it as a social movement in religious guise.[130] Georg Michels has recently argued that the schism was a social reaction to the unprecedented interference of the central authorities in the life of the church. As such, the Old Belief provided an umbrella for a variety of religious trends and types of popular disobedience.[131] One might also argue that it was a reaction on the part of traditional society to the confessionalization of religious life, which originated in the West and began to be promoted by Moscow in the mid-seventeenth century. Confessionalization involved the standardization of the liturgy and religious practices, the introduction of central control over parish life,

---

[130] See Florovsky, *Ways of Russian Theology*, pt. 1 (Belmont, Mass., 1979), pp. 97–104; V. S. Rumiantseva, *Narodnoe antitserkovnoe dvizhenie v Rossii v XVII veke* (Moscow, 1986). For a brief survey of the literature on the subject, see Robert O. Crummey, "Interpreting the Fate of Old Believer Communities in the Eighteenth and Nineteenth Centuries," in *Seeking God*, pp. 144–59, here 144–47.

[131] For a summary of Georg Michels's argument, see the conclusions to his *At War with the Church: Religious Dissent in Seventeenth-Century Russia* (Stanford, 1999), pp. 217–29.

and the raising of the clergy's educational standards. Among those who brought this new agenda to Muscovy were Kyivan clerics whose church had already undergone confessionalization in the times of Peter Mohyla and who were now eager to impose the new models of church life on their Orthodox brethren. It was probably no accident that at the church council of 1666–67, which proved all-important for the outcome of the controversy over the Old Belief, it was Simeon Polatsky who represented the official line in the dispute with the Archpriest Avvakum, the leader of the Old Believers. It was also Polatsky who gave the phenomenon its official name. In the Kyiv metropolitanate, the term "schism" was applied to those who left the Orthodox Church to join the Union. Polatsky used it to denote all (real or imagined) manifestations of opposition to the religious policies of the center, thereby creating the image of a powerful centralized movement. In Georges Florovsky's opinion, there were two factions among the Kyivans residing in Muscovy, with the "Latinizers," represented most prominently by Polatsky and Yavorsky, fighting the Protestant-leaning clerics such as Prokopovych. What seems obvious, however, is that all the Kyivans were united in vehement opposition to the Old Belief. One of them, St. Dymytrii (Dmitrii) Tuptalo, summoned by Peter from Ukraine and appointed first to Tobolsk and then to the vacant Rostov see, was eventually canonized by the church for his efforts in battling the Old Belief.

If the Old Belief of the seventeenth and early eighteenth centuries was not a well-organized mass movement, what was it? Robert Crummey has noted the existence of a complex cultural system (or systems) within the world of the Old Believers, sustained by texts and icons produced in such major centers of the movement as the Vyg community in the Russian North.[132] That "textual community," which shared, exchanged, and copied the same texts, created a discourse that helped construct an alternative to the official culture and identity. Of particular interest in that regard is Boris Uspensky's interpretation of the Old Belief as a manifestation of cultural conflict between two systems of thought – one represented by the Kyivans in the imperial service and the other advocated by defenders of the old Muscovite folkways. In Uspensky's opinion, this was a conflict between the rigid, inflexible understanding of sacred signs and sacred texts as ones received from God – a view embedded in Muscovite culture – and the conventional treatment of sacred texts

---

[132] See Crummey, "Interpreting," pp. 147–48; idem, "The Miracle of Martyrdom: Reflections on Old Believer Hagiography," in *Religion and Culture in Early Modern Russia and Ukraine*, ed. Samuel H. Baron and Nancy Shields Kollmann (DeKalb, Ill., 1997), pp. 132–45. Cf. Crummey, *The Old Believers and the World of Antichrist: The Vyg Community and the Russian State, 1694–1855* (Madison, Wis., 1970).

and signs professed by the Kyivans in the new learning that they helped bring to Muscovy. Uspensky writes: "Old Believers preserved the attitude toward the sacred sign that was characteristic of Muscovy. Followers of the new rituals were influenced by the Polish baroque through Ukrainian culture. Hence the conflict between Old Believers and the followers of the new rituals reflected a conflict between Eastern and Western cultural traditions."[133]

As attested by the discussion of Kyryl Tranquillon-Stavrovetsky's *Didactic Gospel* in Moscow in 1627, the conflict between the two approaches was long in the making. The book was condemned and burned partly because of the Ukrainianisms found in Kyryl's Church Slavonic, which the Muscovites regarded as distortions not just of the biblical text but of the words of Christ himself. The Old Believers took the same attitude toward changes in grammatical forms, spelling, and even pronunciation of words introduced into liturgical books by Patriarch Nikon, whose corrections were based on Meletii Smotrytsky's grammar of Church Slavonic. Simeon Polatsky called upon his opponents to read the grammar before raising objections, but grammatical arguments had little influence on the Old Believers, especially as Polatsky himself used the rules of Latin grammar. The leaders of the Old Belief were also completely opposed to the metaphorical use of words, especially those that conveyed sacred meaning. Consequently, they rejected as blasphemous the traditions of baroque literature and theater that the Kyivans brought to Muscovy. In the context of traditional Muscovite culture, changes of form were directly related to changes of content,[134] and thus debate over the form of Christian teaching rather than the substance of dogma brought about the greatest ecclesiastical schism since the division of Christendom into Eastern and Western churches in the eleventh century.[135]

If the leaders of the Old Belief took such an "unconventional" attitude to Church Slavonic texts, what did they think of foreign-language translations? As one might expect, their attitude was unfavorable, especially if the language involved was Latin. As noted above, the Latin form of Peter's name sufficed for some of them to declare him possessed by the devil. Even as the government busied itself with opening the Slavonic-Greco-Latin School (at Polatsky's initiative), the leaders of the Old Belief denounced Latin as a heretical language that distorted not only the form but also the content of Christian teaching. Hatred of the Latin West was

---

[133] Uspensky, "Schism and Cultural Conflict," p. 110.
[134] This was an attitude foreign to Western Christendom and the rest of the Orthodox world. Peter Mohyla claimed that errors in church texts were of no consequence for the salvation of souls.
[135] See Uspensky, "Schism and Cultural Conflict," pp. 110–27.

not, of course, an invention of the Old Believers. In this case, as in many others, they appeared merely to be continuing deeply ingrained Muscovite ecclesiastical tradition.[136] They strongly believed that the truth, especially the truth about the faith, could not be rendered in any language other than Church Slavonic. In adopting this attitude, they were taking a page from the late sixteenth- and early seventeenth-century writings of Ivan Vyshensky: in debating the Polish Jesuit Piotr Skarga, who claimed that Church Slavonic could not serve as a language of religious discussion, Vyshensky maintained that there was no salvation except through the Church Slavonic script. To be sure, since Vyshensky's time Ruthenian Orthodoxy had done much to embrace Western learning and develop Church Slavonic into a language suitable for early modern religious debate, but the Old Believers were more attuned to the Ruthenian culture of the turn of the seventeenth century, which recoiled from Western threats, than to its more confident manifestation at the end of the century.

Archpriest Avvakum, the most prominent early leader of the Old Belief,[137] gave vivid evidence of its characteristic anti-Western attitude in his comments on new trends in Muscovite icon painting. Under the influence of Kyiv and as a result of direct contacts with the West, Muscovite icon painting underwent a profound transformation in the last decades of the seventeenth century. Realistically portrayed iconic images gained in popularity among residents of Moscow, and, ironically enough, one of the first expressions of public discontent with Nikon's "standardization" of church practices was caused by his order to confiscate Western sacred images and Western-influenced icons in the possession of Muscovites. With the passage of time, both the patriarch and the tsar's court succumbed to Western influence; the Armory became the center of the new icon painting and employed such luminaries of the new Russian art as Simon Ushakov.[138] Now it was the turn of Nikon's opponents to protest against "corrupt" Western influences. Avvakum discredited the new trends by pointing out their foreign origin:

---

[136] This tradition also made its way into modern Russian theology, as attested by Fr. Florovsky, who regarded the late seventeenth century as a period of "pseudomorphosis of Muscovite Orthodoxy" marked by the triumph of Kyivan "latinophilism." See Florovsky, *Ways of Russian Theology*, pt. 1, pp. 111–13.

[137] For a psychological portrait of Avvakum, who apparently suffered from some form of mental illness, see Edvard Kinan (Edward Keenan), "Avvakum: istoriia bezumstva," in idem, *Rosiis' ki istorychni mity*, 2nd expanded edn (Kyiv, 2003), pp. 274–88.

[138] On Ushakov, see Engelina S. Smirnova, "Simon Ushakov – 'Historicism' and 'Byzantinism': On the Interpretation of Russian Painting from the Second Half of the Seventeenth Century," in *Religion and Culture in Early Modern Russia and Ukraine*, pp. 169–83.

They paint the image of Emmanuel the Savior with a swollen face, red lips, curly hair, fat arms and hands, and plump fingers, legs and thighs – his whole body fat and bloated. Like a foreigner (*nemchin*), only without the sword at his hip . . . And that dirty dog Nikon, the enemy, has designed it so that one should paint the saints as though they were living and arrange everything in a Frankish, foreign (*po nemetskomu*) way. . . . Oh, oh, poor Rus', for some reason you have acquired a taste for foreign (*nemetskikh*) ways and customs![139]

For the Old Believers, their Rus' identity still wore the same predominantly religious garb as in the days of Patriarch Filaret Romanov, when the early leaders of what later came to be known as the Old Belief embarked on their careers. The sophisticated nationalism of Peter, who proposed to embrace Western knowledge and ways in order to make Russia better able to compete with the West, was foreign to them. In many ways, the Old Belief represented not only the old forms of Muscovite worship but also the old ways of defining Russian identity. If in Ukraine and Belarus the religious polemics provoked by the Union of Brest helped create the discourse that articulated and mobilized Ruthenian identity, the controversy over the Old Belief divided Muscovite society. One camp united Kyivan ecclesiastical culture with the culture of the Muscovite elites, while the other continued to uphold premodern Muscovite religious and cultural practices, carefully insulated from the outside world. Ironically, it was the latter that produced the more democratic model of Russian identity. Semen Denisov, one of the leaders of the Old Belief, presented in his writings an alternative vision not only of the Russian faith but also of Russian society and identity. No longer centered on the tsar and the official church, both of which had betrayed the true faith, that identity had at its core the image of the Russian land and communities.[140] Peter isolated this alternative Russian identity on the "reservations" of the Old Believers. Although it did not disappear, it was sidelined by the new Westernized culture and identity of imperial Russia.

Reassessing the Petrine impact

What was the new element that Peter and his era brought to the construction site of Russian identity? On examining Peter's contribution to Russian identity formation, one sees relatively little in the ideological background of his nation-building initiatives that could qualify as a

---

[139] See "Sochineniia protopopa Avvakuma," in *Khrestomatiia po drevnei russkoi literature*, comp. N. K. Gudzii (Moscow, 1973), pp. 477–90, here 489–90. Cf. Uspensky, "Schism and Cultural Conflict," p. 124.

[140] See Geoffrey Hosking, "The Russian National Myth Repudiated," in *Myths and Nationhood*, ed. Hosking and George Schöpflin (London, 1997), pp. 207–208.

"first." Seeking such "firsts," Vera Tolz, for example, lists among Peter's contributions the "revolutionary . . . idea, imported from Europe that the state was separate from and superior to the personality of the tsar." She notes the rise of the West as the future constituent "other" for the formation of Russian national identity and mentions Peter's expansion of the empire as another significant factor.[141] But when one considers the Muscovite experience of the seventeenth century, none of these factors can be regarded as a unique contribution to the Russian nation-building effort. As discussed in the previous chapter, the separation of the state from the person of the ruler first appeared in Russian political writings during the Time of Troubles. It was also during that turbulent period that the Muscovites began to define themselves in opposition to the Catholic and Protestant West, although it was then represented by the Poles and Lithuanians, not by the western and central Europeans. As for the extension of the empire, Ivan IV's contribution to the "imperialization" of the Russian psyche looms much more prominently than that of Peter I. Also debatable are Liah Greenfeld's observations on the shift in the meaning of *gosudarstvo* from "lordship" and "kingdom" to "state" during the Petrine epoch. It might be argued that that shift took place in Muscovite texts soon after the Time of Troubles, if not earlier. Besides, as Greenfeld notes elsewhere, Peter continued to see his state as an extension of himself.[142] To this one might add that Peter's panegyrists, such as Teofan Prokopovych, could not imagine Russia without its glorious *pater patriae*. What does seem beyond doubt, however, is that all these ideas, which first entered official Muscovite discourse in the sixteenth century, took on new importance and meaning during Peter's reign.

The claims on behalf of Peter's ideological innovations that set them apart from the ideas of the earlier period pertain to the secularization of the state (Tolz) and the "nationalization" of official discourse (Greenfeld). What did these "firsts" mean for the identity-construction project? Tolz suggests that the Russian secular elite ceased to define itself against the West primarily in religious terms and began to do so predominantly in secular ones. Greenfeld indicates that while seeking a way to define itself in secular terms, the Russian elite had developed the vocabulary required to articulate its new identity not only in the context of loyalty to the ruler but also with regard to such notions as state and fatherland. Of particular importance for the present discussion is that both these developments would be difficult to imagine without the active participation of the Kyiv-trained clergy. The Kyivans contributed to the first project by

---

[141] See Tolz, *Russia*, pp. 42–43.
[142] See Greenfeld, *Nationalism*, p. 193; cf. also pp. 196–97.

isolating the most anti-secular and anti-Western elements of Muscovite
society as "schismatics" (a label applied to them by Polatsky) and then by
subordinating the church to the state by means of the *Ecclesiastical Regulations* of 1721, drafted by Teofan Prokopovych and other Kyivans, such
as Havryil Buzhynsky. Through his translations of Pufendorf, Buzhynsky
helped introduce such notions as "citizen" (*grazhdanin*) and "society"
(*obshchestvo*) into Russian political discourse.[143] The Kyivans also led the
way in creating a "nationalized" discourse, although the identity that they
shaped by means of it was not "Great Russian," as Greenfeld suggests,[144]
but "all-Russian" or imperial. As argued above, they took the concepts of
nation and fatherland that they had developed for the Hetmanate in Kyiv
and applied them with little reflection or hesitation to the multiethnic and
multireligious empire. In so doing, they further blurred the line between
the Slavic Orthodox core of the tsardom/empire and its non-Slavic and
non-Christian (or at least non-Orthodox) periphery. The new Russian
imperial identity developed with the help of the Kyivans was designed
to include the Little Russian and Muscovite elites, as well as Westerners who were joining the imperial service. It failed, however, to include
Ruthenians west of the Russian imperial boundary and non-Slavs in the
borderlands of the empire.

The non-Christians of the East were referred to as foreigners
(*inozemtsy*) both by the authorities and by the dissenters of the Old Belief.
Archpriest Avvakum, one of the first "political" exiles in Siberia, who left
memoirs of his travels there, referred to the indigenous peoples as foreigners and barbarians (*strana varvarskaia, inozemtsy nemirnye*). Nor did
he consider Siberia to be part of Rus'; when summoned back to Moscow,
he was happy to return to Rus' and the "Russian towns."[145] Like the
Old Believers in general, Avvakum showed no interest in preaching to
the "barbarians." His attitude was very different from the one adopted
by the tsarist government, which was eager to turn the "foreigners" and
"barbarians" into Christian and thus Russian subjects of the tsar with
the help of Kyiv-trained clergymen.[146] The tsar thought of his empire as
a unitary state created as a result of conquest, not as a diverse collection of territories, peoples, and religions. Peter's contemporaries did not
necessarily share his outlook. Through the "window" that Peter had cut

---

[143] On the vocabulary of Buzhynsky's translations, see Cracraft, *The Petrine Revolution in
Russian Culture*, pp. 214–16.
[144] See ibid., p. 239.   [145] See "Sochineniia protopopa Avvakuma," pp. 486–87.
[146] Peter became personally involved in appointing Kyiv-trained clerics to Siberia. On
Moscow's efforts to convert the indigenous population of the eastern borderlands to
Christianity in the last decades of the seventeenth century, see Cracraft, *The Church
Reform of Peter the Great*, pp. 64–70.

onto Europe, new ideas about the empire as a multiethnic entity were entering Russia. By the 1730s, Anna Ioannovna was already celebrating the "multiculturalism" of her empire, bringing representatives of the conquered peoples (including Cossacks) in traditional costume to the capital for festivities.[147] Times were changing, indeed. Nevertheless, for all the imperial rulers' positive notice of the internal "foreigners," they remained outside the bounds of imperial Russian identity.

[147] See Jelena Pogosjan (Elena Pogosian), "'O zakone svoem i sami nedoumevaiut': Narody Rossii v etnograficheskikh opisaniiakh, sostavlennykh i izdannykh v 1770–1790-e gg." Unpublished manuscript.

8   Ruthenia, Little Russia, Ukraine

The outcome of the Khmelnytsky Uprising forever changed the fate and identity of the land called Ruthenia and its inhabitants, the Ruthenians. The Cossack state, which came into existence in the first months of the Khmelnytsky Uprising and received international recognition during the Zboriv negotiations in the summer of 1649, became known in historiography as the Hetmanate, a term based on its later, eighteenth-century name, which is used throughout this book. But for most of the seventeenth century and the first decades of the eighteenth it was known primarily as the Zaporozhian Host, a term derived from the official name of the Cossack army, which was initially based at the Zaporozhian Sich and later in the settled area as well. It is the Zaporozhian Host that figures as an official entity in the treaties concluded by the Cossack hetmans with Muscovy, the Ottoman Empire, and the Polish-Lithuanian Commonwealth in the second half of the seventeenth century. It became the legal name of the Ukrainian state and territory, which also acquired other names related to a variety of social and national projects that were under way in the Cossack polity during the seventeenth and eighteenth centuries. One of those names was *Ukraïna* (Ukraine), which was preferred by middle-rank Cossack officers and, apparently, by the Cossack masses in general. Another was *Rosiia*, used in the literary works of the Kyivan clergy. Then there was *Malorosiia* (Little Russia), which the Cossack and ecclesiastical elites used in their correspondence with Muscovy and, increasingly, among themselves. The Grand Duchy of Ruthenia served to identify another political initiative undertaken by Cossack officers of noble descent who oriented themselves on the Commonwealth. Each of these terms stood for a particular political concept, cultural vision and, potentially, a distinct identity, which is the focus of our discussion in this chapter.

Ukraine or Little Russia?

A manuscript bearing this title was written in the 1920s by Nikolai Fitilev, an ethnic Russian who became a prominent Ukrainian publicist under

299

the name of Mykola Khvyliovy. The manuscript, which consisted of a number of pamphlets, was confiscated by the Soviet secret police shortly after it was written, spent more than half a century in the KGB archives, and became available to the general public only in 1990, a year before the collapse of the Soviet Union. What did the Bolshevik regime find so dangerous in that pamphlet? First and foremost, it was Khvyliovy's answer to the question posed in the title. In choosing between Ukraine and Little Russia, he opted for Ukraine. In the context of his time, this meant that Khvyliovy conceived of Ukraine as independent of Russia, possessing – or entitled to possess – a literature and culture of its own. For Khvyliovy's generation, the term "Little Russia" stood for the tradition of treating the Ukrainian people, language, and culture as branches of the Russian nation, language, and culture, while "Ukraine" symbolized the political and cultural independence of their homeland from Russia.[1]

In his attack on "Little Russianism," Khvyliovy was influenced by the writings of Mykhailo Drahomanov, Serhii Shelukhyn, and Viacheslav Lypynsky, as well as by the works of other Ukrainian activists outside the Russian Empire and the USSR who saw the Little Russian mentality as the result of centuries of Russian political and cultural control over Ukraine.[2] But Khvyliovy's viewpoint was by no means universally shared in his homeland. The title of his pamphlet was a reverse mirror image of Andrei Storozhenko's "Little Russia or Ukraine?" (1918). Storozhenko, a Little Russian par excellence, thought of Ukraine as an integral part of a larger Russian political and cultural space. He traced the origins of the controversy over its name back to the late eighteenth and early nineteenth centuries. As Storozhenko saw it, the use of the term "Ukraine" to denote what he believed to be essentially Rus' or Little Russia was nothing but an attempt by Polish intellectuals to reverse the partitions of Poland. Their strategy was to claim that the Ruthenian lands of the Commonwealth attached to the Russian Empire by Catherine II were not in fact Rus' lands but those of a territory distinct from Russia that they called "Ukraine." According to Storozhenko, the first to reject those claims was the anonymous author of the "History of the Rus'," a historical work that had circulated in Ukraine in manuscript since the late 1820s. Its author protested against the practice (allegedly Polish) of calling the Dnipro region "Ukraine" and opted for "Little Russia" instead.[3]

---

[1] For an interpretation of the political and cultural message of Khvyliovy's pamphlets, see Myroslav Shkandrij, *Russia and Ukraine: Literature and the Discourse of Empire from Napoleonic to Post-Colonial Times* (Montreal and Kingston, 2001), pp. 223–31.

[2] See the entry "Little Russian Mentality" by Bohdan Kravtsiv in *Encyclopedia of Ukraine*, vol. III (Toronto, 1993), p. 166.

[3] See A. V. Storozhenko, "Malaia Rossiia ili Ukraina?" First appeared in 1918 in the journal *Malaia Rus'*; repr. in *Ukrainskii separatizm v Rossii. Ideologiia natsional'nogo raskola*, comp. M. B. Smolin (Moscow, 1998), pp. 280–90.

Storozhenko's treatment of "Ukraine" as a subversive Polish term intended to undermine the unity of the Russian nation was far from original. Debates over a politically correct name for Ukraine intensified in the Russian Empire during the Revolution of 1905. In Austria-Hungary that issue came to the fore in 1907, when the Russophile members of the Austrian parliament in Vienna decided to refer to the Ruthenian caucus there as the "Little Russian Club." They rejected the name "Ukraine" as a Polish invention to denote the borderland of the historical Commonwealth. In 1908, at the Russian Archaeological Congress in Chernihiv, a Ukrainian activist from Odesa named Serhii Shelukhyn delivered a paper on the origins of the term "Ukraine," claiming that it had been the original name of the land. The paper sparked a polemic in the Russian press, and Professor Ivan Linnichenko of the University of New Russia in Odesa endorsed the theory, shared by the majority of Ukraine's historians, that "Ukraine" essentially meant "borderland."[4]

Shelukhyn's claim that the name "Ukraine" had preceded "Rus'" helped attract the attention of scholars and the public at large to the late medieval usage of the term but failed to convince the specialists – not only proponents of the Little Russian identity like Storozhenko but also Ukrainian scholars. Most of them followed the example of Mykhailo Hrushevsky (often attacked in Shelukhyn's publications), who believed that the term "Ukraine" derived from the notion of borderland. Hrushevsky avoided "Little Russia" but often used "Rus'" to denote the Ukrainian lands. In the late nineteenth and early twentieth centuries, he frequently used the compound "Ukraine-Rus'" to stress the continuity of Ukrainian history from the times of Kyivan Rus' to his own days and the unity of the Ukrainian lands, including Galicia, where "Rus'" and "Ruthenian" were often applied to Ukrainian territory and its population.[5] Hrushevsky claimed that "Little Russia" had first been used with regard to the Galician-Volhynian principality in the fourteenth century. It had later fallen out of use but was reintroduced into official discourse in the seventeenth century to define the Ukrainian lands under Muscovite control. According to Hrushevsky, the term did not become popular among the masses, which preferred to call their land "Ukraine." That term, applied since the sixteenth century to the middle Dnipro region, was chosen as

---

[4] See Serhii Shelukhyn, *Ukraïna – nazva nashoï zemli z naidavnishykh chasiv* (Prague, 1936; repr. Drohobych, 1992), pp. 19–32. Cf. Ivan Linnichenko, "Malorusskii vopros i avtonomiia Malorossii. Otkrytoe pis'mo professoru M. S. Grushevskomu" (Petrograd and Odesa, 1917; repr. in *Ukrainskii separatizm v Rossii*), pp. 253–79, here 271.

[5] On Hrushevsky's usage of "Ukraine-Rus'" and "Ukraine," see my *Unmaking Imperial Russia: Mykhailo Hrushevsky and the Writing of Ukrainian History* (Toronto, Buffalo, and London, 2005), pp. 166–71.

the national name by leaders of the nineteenth-century Ukrainian literary revival.[6]

The outbreak of World War I brought accusations of treason against Ukrainians in the Russian Empire. So did the Revolution of 1917. Suggestions that the name "Ukraine" was of Polish origin only encouraged the notion that the Ukrainian movement was little more than the product of foreign intrigue. That argument inspired many articles in the journal *Malaia Rus'*, which published Storozhenko's essay "Little Russia or Ukraine?" The essay in turn provoked a response from Shelukhyn, who continued publishing on the topic in the Ukrainian emigration during the interwar period.[7] The Soviet era suspended the use of the term "Little Russia" with regard to Ukraine, but the revival of Russian nationalism after 1991 resurrected the term. The Russian writer Mikhail Smolin, who reprinted Storozhenko's essay and other anti-Ukrainian works of the period in Moscow in 1998, advocated the revival of the "Little Russian" terminology and decried the use of "Ukraine" and "Ukrainians" as an attempted "dismemberment of the all-Russian body by depriving it of the Little Russians, arbitrarily defining them as 'Ukrainians,' who are unknown to history."[8] Today, it is clear that the terms "Ukraine" and "Little Russia" represent very different East Slavic identities. But is there good reason to believe that they also denoted different national identities in early modern times?

The fate of Ruthenia

The outbreak of the Khmelnytsky Uprising shook the Polish-Lithuanian Commonwealth to its foundations and opened the door to foreign intervention, first by Muscovy and then by Transylvania and Sweden. The Swedish invasion of 1655, known in historiography as the Deluge, even raised the possibility that the Commonwealth might be partitioned by its neighbors, but Muscovy, apprehensive about the rising power of Sweden, changed its attitude, and so the Polish-Lithuanian state managed to survive and eventually recover most of its losses. In the east, the front line was pushed back from Lviv and Vilnius – the westernmost cities reached by Muscovite and Cossack troops in 1654–55 – to the borders of the Smolensk palatinate and the banks of the Dnipro. Under the terms of the Truce of Andrusovo (1667) between Muscovy and the Commonwealth,

---

[6] See Mykhailo Hrushevsky, *History of Ukraine-Rus'*, vol. I, *From Prehistory to the Eleventh Century* (Edmonton and Toronto, 1997), pp. 1–2.

[7] See Shelukhyn, *Ukraïna*, pp. 34–40.

[8] See Mikhail Smolin, "Ukrainskii tuman dolzhen rasseiat'sia, i russkoe solntse vzoidet," in *Ukrainskii separatizm v Rossii*, pp. 5–22, here 6.

the latter lost Smolensk and Left-Bank Ukraine to its eastern neighbor. This was by no means the catastrophe that might have been anticipated during the Deluge: Poland-Lithuania merely returned to its eastern borders of the turn of the seventeenth century, when Smolensk and Chernihiv belonged to Muscovy and the Left Bank of the Dnipro was not yet fully settled. The only major exception was the city of Kyiv, which was supposed to remain temporarily under Muscovite control and revert to Poland after two years. That did not happen. According to the Eternal Peace of 1686, Kyiv was confirmed as a Muscovite possession. After a devastating war, the land that we now call Belarus was returned to the Grand Duchy of Lithuania. Most of Ukraine remained under the rule of the Kingdom of Poland. Both lands were parts of the Polish-Lithuanian Commonwealth.[9]

By the conclusion of the Eternal Peace of 1686, the Ruthenian nation of the Commonwealth had become a shadow of its former self. The main reasons for this were the continuous wars waged on the territory of Ukraine and Belarus and the decline of Cossackdom as a political, social, and military force that had protected the Orthodox Church and the rights of the Ruthenian nation throughout the Commonwealth. The entrance of Muscovy into the war with the Polish-Lithuanian Commonwealth on the side of the Cossacks, as well as the tsar's recognition of the distinct status of the Hetmanate, greatly strengthened the Cossack position vis-à-vis Warsaw. There was of course a price to be paid for Muscovite support. The Crimean Tatars, on whom the Cossacks had hitherto depended, were alarmed by the new Orthodox alliance of Cossackdom with Muscovy and turned against the Cossacks. Muscovite voevodas and troops were stationed in the Hetmanate, restricting the freedom of the hetman, and the Hetmanate itself became the hostage of Muscovite policy toward the Commonwealth. In 1656, Tsar Aleksei Mikhailovich decided to halt his offensive against the Commonwealth, saving the Polish-Lithuanian state from complete collapse (it was then being hammered by Muscovite and Cossack forces from the east and Swedish and Transylvanian forces from the north and south). Khmelnytsky refused to follow suit and continued his military operations against the Commonwealth. He also sought new protectors and allies, establishing close relations with Sweden. Khmelnytsky's policy of promoting the Hetmanate's interests rather than those of the Muscovite sovereign in international relations was continued after his

---

[9] There were no major adjustments to the border until the first partition of Poland in 1772. On the history of the Polish-Lithuanian Commonwealth in the late seventeenth and eighteenth centuries, see Daniel Stone, *The Polish-Lithuanian State, 1386–1795*, A History of East Central Europe, vol. IV (Seattle and London, 2001), and Richard Butterwick, ed., *The Polish-Lithuanian Monarchy in European Context, c. 1500–1795* (Basingstoke, 2001).

death by the new hetman, Ivan Vyhovsky. Disappointed with Muscovite policy, Vyhovsky provoked dissent in the Cossack ranks when he signed an agreement with the Polish-Lithuanian Commonwealth at Hadiach in September 1658. According to its terms, the "Ruthenian nation" was to become a third partner in the Commonwealth along with the Poles and Lithuanians. This suited the Ukrainian nobility, which had been aspiring to an arrangement of that kind since the 1620s, but did not sit well with the Cossack officers or the rank and file, who stood to lose a great deal if the social order embodied in the Union of Hadiach were to become a reality. Nor were the Poles prepared to accept the rebellious Ruthenians as their equals. Both factors led to the collapse of the Hadiach Agreement and Vyhovsky's loss of the hetmancy in 1659.[10]

The new hetman, Bohdan Khmelnytsky's son Yurii, was elected to office with the approval of Muscovy but switched sides in 1660, joining the Commonwealth. His about-face split the Cossack officer stratum, part of which, led by Colonel Yakym Somko, remained loyal to the tsar. What followed was a period known in Ukrainian historiography as the Ruin. Muscovite armies fought Polish-Lithuanian ones for control of the Dnipro region, and both sides were assisted by competing groups of Cossack officers led by opposing hetmans. The Truce of Andrusovo (1667) between Muscovy and the Commonwealth divided the Hetmanate into two parts: territories on the Left Bank of the Dnipro, together with Kyiv (first temporarily and then permanently) went to Muscovy, while the rest of Cossack territory remained under Polish rule. An attempt to reestablish Cossack control over both parts of the Hetmanate was led by Hetman Petro Doroshenko (1665–76), who relied on Ottoman assistance. Although Istanbul promised military support, it was not strong enough to enable Doroshenko to defeat the Muscovite army and Left-Bank Cossack regiments that supported it. In 1676 Doroshenko was obliged to surrender to the hetman of Left-Bank Ukraine and go into exile in Muscovy. Decades of unremitting warfare devastated the Dnipro lands, especially parts of the Right Bank, which were depopulated and treated as a no-man's-land – a neutral zone between the competing states and the Cossack groupings.[11]

The signing of the Eternal Peace in 1686 was a clear signal to the Ruthenian elites in the Commonwealth that the period of continuous warfare between Warsaw and Moscow was drawing to a close, and the

[10] For a survey of political developments in Ukraine in the years 1654–59, see Tetiana Iakovleva, Het'manshchyna v druhii polovyni 50-kh rr. XVII stolittia. Prychyny i pochatok Ruïny (Kyiv, 1998).
[11] On the Truce of Andrusovo and Doroshenko's policies, see Dmytro Doroshenko, Het'man Petro Doroshenko. Ohliad ioho zhyttia i politychnoï diial'nosty (New York, 1985).

border along the Dnipro River was there to stay. The elites now had to accommodate themselves to new conditions or move to the Left-Bank Hetmanate. In the 1620s, when the Orthodox nobility began to demand equal rights for the Ruthenians with the Polish and Lithuanian nations – the founding members of the Commonwealth – it introduced a highly particular model of the nation into the political discourse of the time. In the documents pertaining to the Union of Lublin (1569), "nation" meant the (noble) population of the two states that constituted the union – the Kingdom of Poland and the Grand Duchy of Lithuania. Out of this dual polity the Ruthenian leaders managed to carve a third nation, defined not in terms of state structure but by culture, religion, and language. In the course of the Khmelnytsky Uprising, the explosive mixture of Cossack military power, Ruthenian solidarity, and Orthodox piety shook the foundations of the Commonwealth, depriving it of its prized possessions in the east. Little wonder, then, that after the end of the uprising Ruthenian culture, religion, and language found themselves under attack. The abolition of Cossackdom in Right-Bank Ukraine, the conversion of the Ruthenian Orthodox to the Union, and the progressive decline of the Ruthenian language and culture led to the gradual Polonization of the Ruthenian elites. To be sure, the leaders of the Polish-Lithuanian state did not think in terms of creating a positive program for the Ruthenian elites, hoping instead to undermine and eliminate them lest they be exploited against the Commonwealth by its powerful Muscovite neighbor. For most of the period, Polonization was a "natural" process in the sense that the vacuum created by the destruction of one culture and tradition was filled by another. The first "positive" programs consciously designed to promote the Polonization of the Ruthenian masses were not formulated until the final decades of the eighteenth century.

The most vulnerable stratum of the Ruthenian community turned out to be its backbone of the previous era, the nobility. Gone were the times when Orthodox magnates and their noble clients advanced the Ruthenian political and cultural agenda at local and Commonwealth diets. When it came to their political outlook, culture, and religion, there were no champions of the Ruthenian cause among the new crop of magnates. After the death in 1667 of the Orthodox castellan of Trakai, Aliaksandr Ahinski, there was no one left in the Commonwealth Senate to defend the rights of the Ruthenians.[12] Descendants of Ruthenian princely and noble families no longer sought to trace their lineage back to St. Volodymyr, as Prince Kostiantyn Ostrozky had done in the sixteenth century. Instead, the scions of the Sapiha, Polubinsky, Sanhushko, Oransky, Voina, Tryzna,

---

[12] See Henadz' Sahanovich, *Narys historyi Belarusi* (Minsk, 2001), p. 291.

and other formerly Orthodox families tried to associate themselves with the ancient Romans and Lithuanian princes of the house of Gediminas. In the Kingdom of Poland and the Grand Duchy of Lithuania, the Ruthenian elites were developing a supplementary loyalty to their Polish or Lithuanian fatherland, not to the nation of Rus'. That process started long before 1648, but it was the Khmelnytsky Uprising and its consequences that accelerated the political and cultural Polonization of the Ruthenian elites in the Polish-Lithuanian Commonwealth.[13]

The Orthodox Ruthenian nobility, which was otherwise part of the political class of the Commonwealth and generally shared the way of life and ideals of the noble estate, was often prepared to abandon its ancestral religion when faced with discrimination on religious grounds. In 1673, the Orthodox of the Commonwealth were prohibited from acquiring noble status. In 1717 and 1733, religious dissenters were banned from participating in Diets. Under these circumstances, the Orthodox nobles preferred to join the dominant Roman Catholic Church. They bypassed the Uniate "purgatory," leaving the non-noble segments of the Ruthenian community to suffer there. The concept of the Ruthenian nation as a community united by loyalty to the Orthodox Church and comprising nobles, clergy, burghers, and Cossacks, which had become so prominent during the Khmelnytsky Uprising and still constituted the major parameter of national identity in the Hetmanate, was clearly out of place in the eighteenth-century Commonwealth. The identity of the Ruthenian nobility of the period has yet to be studied in depth, but it is clear that in the eighteenth century most of its members joined the Polish-Lithuanian "nation" not only in political but also in religious, linguistic, and cultural terms. During the partitions of Poland they demonstrated true Polish patriotism, as exemplified by Ruthenian members of the ultra-Catholic Confederation of Bar in 1768, or by the leader of the uprising of 1794, Tadeusz Kosciuszko, a native of the Brest region of Belarus. Their regional patriotism (Lithuanian, or Ukrainian in the narrow sense of the term) did not prevent them from being true members of the new Polish nation.[14]

Ruthenian burghers also could not avoid discrimination on the part of the Polish-Lithuanian state and society. In 1699 Orthodox burghers were prohibited from holding council offices in the royal towns. In general

---

[13] On the genealogical legends of the noble elites of the Grand Duchy of Lithuania, see Arturas Tereskinas, "The Imperfect Body of the Community: Formulas of Noblesse, Forms of Nationhood in the Seventeenth-Century Grand Duchy of Lithuania," Ph.D. diss., Harvard University, 1999, pp. 309–91.

[14] See Sahanovich, *Narys historyi Belarusi*, p. 29; Iakovenko, *Narys istoriï Ukraïny*, pp. 266–67.

terms, however, the status of Ruthenian burghers differed from one town to another. In what is now Belarus, Ruthenians constituted approximately 80 percent of the urban population, which made it difficult to discriminate against them. Thus there were joint guilds headed by elders of the "Catholic," "Ruthenian," or Protestant religion.[15] More difficult was the situation of Ruthenian burghers in such well-established centers of international trade as the city of Lviv, where Ruthenians were not allowed to have their representatives on the city council until the mid-eighteenth century. The royal decree of 1572 that granted the Lviv Ruthenians equal rights with Polish Catholics was largely ignored by the city council, which argued that the decree contravened the city's rights and privileges. The conversion of the Lviv Orthodox community to the Union in 1709 seemed to circumvent the restriction on holding city council offices, as a Diet ruling of 1699 specifically guaranteed that right to Uniates. But their conversion to the Union changed nothing. Religion (or, rather, rite) continued to bar the Lviv Ruthenians from civic office. The Ruthenians continued to be called a "nation" (*natio*) in royal privileges and civic decrees, a designation that usually set them apart from the Polish Catholic majority and, in their opinion, implied discrimination. In 1749 the Ruthenian members of the (now Uniate) brotherhood complained that the city council, in denying them the right to hold civic office, was "alienating itself from us, calling us a 'nation' and not incorporated persons equal to itself."[16] Ironically, the discrimination of which the Lviv Ruthenian community complained (it included nobles as well as burghers) helped preserve a strong sense of distinct Ruthenian identity – the same identity that Ruthenian nobles who did not belong to religious brotherhoods were losing at an alarming rate.

The Cossacks turned out to be the stratum of Ruthenian society most resistant to Polonization. Cossack leaders of the late seventeenth century still dabbled in geopolitics, allying themselves with the Commonwealth, the Ottomans, the Crimea, or Moldavia, or casting themselves as possible unifiers of Ukraine on both banks of the Dnipro, like Hetman Petro Doroshenko. Those who lived in the Commonwealth still dreamed of establishing the western border of the Cossack polity along

[15] See A. S. Kotliarchuk, *Prazdnichnaia kul'tura v gorodakh Rossii i Belorussii XVII v.* (St. Petersburg, 2001), pp. 39–45. Cf. Ihar A. Marzaliuk, *Liudzi daŭniai Belarusi: ètnakanfesiinyia i satsyia-kul'turnyia stereotypy (X–XVII st.)* (Mahilioŭ, 2003), p. 104.

[16] See Myron Kapral', *Natsional'ni hromady L'vova XVI–XVIII st. (Sotsial'no-pravovi vzaiemyny)* (Lviv, 2003), p. 153. On the Ruthenian community of Lviv in the late seventeenth and eighteenth centuries, see ibid., pp. 131–57. For the privileges of the Ruthenian community of Lviv, see idem, comp., *Pryvileï natsional'nykh hromad mista L'vova (XIV–XVIII st.)* (Lviv, 2000), pp. 39–119.

the river Sluch and saw themselves as protectors of the whole Ruthenian nation. Nevertheless, the conditions offered to the Cossacks by the Polish authorities at Hadiach in 1658 remained an unattainable ideal for the new generations of Cossack leaders in the Commonwealth. Indeed, while the Cossacks remained a powerful social group in the Left-Bank Hetmanate, the precipitous decline of their strength on the Right Bank rendered them almost obsolete in the Commonwealth. The rule of Hetman Petro Doroshenko in Right-Bank Ukraine marked the twilight of Cossack power in Poland-Lithuania. When Doroshenko failed to establish control over the Left-Bank Hetmanate, he sought a way out of his precarious situation in an alliance with the Ottomans. His recognition of the suzerainty of the Ottoman Sultan led to direct interference in Ukrainian affairs by the Porte. In 1672, after the fall of Kamianets to the Ottomans, the Commonwealth was constrained to sign the Peace of Buchach, which established an Ottoman protectorate over Podilia and Right-Bank Ukraine.

The treaty triggered a mass exodus from those areas that continued until the mid-1680s, when the new Polish king, Jan Sobieski, began a resettlement of the area by reviving Cossackdom on the Right Bank. The Cossack colonels appointed by the king were quite successful in attracting new colonists to the territory, which the Commonwealth had no legal right to settle. They operated in a gray zone between the Commonwealth and the Ottomans, which made them indispensable to the Polish-Lithuanian state. But after 1699, when the Ottomans renounced their claim to the territory and the Poles could openly proceed to settle it, they ordered the disbandment of Right-Bank Cossackdom. Led by Colonel Semen Palii (Hurko), a native of the Hetmanate, the Cossacks refused to comply and began an uprising that lasted until 1704, when Left-Bank Cossacks took over the region, taking advantage of the incursion of Russian troops into the Commonwealth during the Northern War. Population shifts resulting from wars and transfers of territory between the Commonwealth, Muscovy and the Ottomans left Right-Bank Cossackdom without an elite of its own. Only occasional uprisings indicated that the population of Right-Bank Ukraine preserved Cossack ideals and aspired to the same kind of self-rule as that enjoyed by the Cossacks of the Hetmanate. But they lacked leaders of the stature they had had in the seventeenth century, and the Ruthenian nobility steadily abandoned the Cossack masses.[17]

---

[17] On the ethnic composition of the population of Right-Bank Ukraine and migratory processes there, see Oleksandr Hurzhii and Taras Chukhlib, *Het'mans'ka Ukraïna*, vol. VIII of *Ukraïna kriz' viky* (Kyiv, 1999), pp. 272–77. On Cossack political programs between 1676 and 1715, see Valerii Smolii and Valerii Stepankov, *Ukraïns'ka derzhavna ideia. Problemy formuvannia, evoliutsiï, realizatsiï* (Kyiv, 1997), pp. 175–235.

Among the major factors that contributed to the Polonization of the Ruthenian elites was the decline in the use of the Ruthenian language. In 1696, when the Commonwealth Diet adopted a resolution making the use of Polish obligatory in jurisprudence and administration, the nobility of the Grand Duchy of Lithuania submitted a proposal to the Diet to introduce Polish instead of Ruthenian as the language of the local courts. The proposal was one of a number of petitions intended to extend the rights possessed by the nobility of the Kingdom of Poland to their peers in the Grand Duchy of Lithuania.[18] Thus the equalization of noble rights in the Commonwealth went hand in hand with linguistic and cultural Polonization. The process was "voluntary" in the sense that by the turn of the eighteenth century there was a lack of qualified people to conduct and record court proceedings in Ruthenian. By the end of the seventeenth century, the higher and elementary education of the children of Ruthenian nobles and burghers was largely in the hands of the Jesuits. In their schools, students learned Latin and Greek as well as Polish, but not Ruthenian. While Orthodox Ruthenians were not barred from attending Jesuit-run colleges, they had difficulty in maintaining their religion while enrolled there. That was certainly the case at Lviv University, where in the late seventeenth century the Orthodox were allowed to take only one year of philosophy and barred from other courses unless they converted to the Union. In 1725 Orthodox students were denied housing at the university. Similar practices were adopted in other educational institutions of the region. By the mid-eighteenth century, the Ruthenian lands of the Commonwealth were covered with a network of Jesuit colleges and schools reaching as far east as Ovruch and Zhytomyr. Around that time, the Jesuits began teaching Polish history in their colleges. They were not only educating young Ruthenians but also turning them into political, religious, and cultural Poles.[19]

As the Ruthenian language was squeezed out of the public sphere, its existence was confined to the premises of the Orthodox and Uniate churches, but even there it had to compete with other languages. The Uniate clergy was encouraged to preach to the people in their own language, but the language taught in the Uniate schools was Church Slavonic – the language of ecclesiastical liturgy – not Ruthenian. The schools organized and run by the Basilian fathers included Church Slavonic in their curriculum. Latin and Church Slavonic were obligatory subjects in the monastery schools, while the secular schools run by the Basilians stressed Latin, Polish, and German, with Church Slavonic as an optional subject.

---

[18] See Sahanovich, *Narys historyi Belarusi*, pp. 294–95.
[19] On Jesuit schools and colleges in Ukraine, see *Istoriia ukraïns′koï kul′tury*, ed. V. A. Smolii et al., vol. III (Kyiv, 2003), pp. 471–81.

The condition of the printed word was no better. The Basilians undertook an impressive publishing program based at the Univ and Pochaiv monasteries. Most of their publications were issued in Church Slavonic, and only a few were written in a language close to spoken Ruthenian.[20] But even among the Basilians, linguistic and cultural Polonization was making dramatic progress.

The Uniate Janus

From the second half of the seventeenth century to the end of the eighteenth, the close connection between religion and ethnonational identity continued to define the distinction between "us" and "them" in the Ukrainian and Belarusian lands of the Commonwealth. Under these circumstances, as in the first half of the seventeenth century, it was the division of Ruthenians between the Orthodox and Uniate churches that created the greatest confusion. Those Ruthenians (generally nobles and members of the urban elite) who joined the Roman Catholic Church, either directly or through the Union, were regarded by their contemporaries as Poles and were not taken into account when it came to the discussion of Ruthenian issues. That tendency, already quite apparent in sources of the earlier period, became especially pronounced in the late seventeenth and eighteenth centuries. From the first decades of the eighteenth century, the term "Ruthenian" was increasingly associated with the Union rather than with Orthodoxy, as Catholicism in its Uniate form was steadily becoming the dominant religion of most of the Ukrainian and Belarusian population. Its road to dominance, however, was by no means easy.

The outbreak of the Khmelnytsky Uprising dealt a major blow to the Uniate Church throughout the Polish-Lithuanian Commonwealth. This was especially true in Ukraine and the lands of eastern Belarus, which were occupied by Muscovite and Cossack forces after the Pereiaslav Agreement of 1654. The Uniate Church as an institution was among the main victims of the Cossack revolt and was subsequently banned in the Hetmanate. The Zboriv Agreement of 1649 obliged the king to return to the Orthodox a number of eparchies located far beyond the territory controlled by the Cossack Host. The Hadiach Agreement of 1658, while bringing the Cossacks back under the jurisdiction of the Commonwealth, threatened to put an end to the Union on the whole territory of the Polish-Lithuanian state. Its conditions provided not only for Senate seats for the Orthodox metropolitan and bishops but also for

---

[20] Ibid., pp. 450–54, 777–83. Cf. Iakovenko, *Narys istoriï Ukraïny*, pp. 278–79.

the return to the Orthodox of all church properties that had belonged to them before 1596. Additionally, a ban was introduced on the funding of new Uniate churches and monasteries. The provisions of the agreement were never implemented by the Polish-Lithuanian authorities, but the Uniate Church, which was left without a metropolitan between 1655 and 1665, could hardly be expected to survive under such conditions. If prior to 1648 discussions had been held on a "universal union" of Uniates and Orthodox under the auspices of Rome, now the leaders of the Uniate Church were looking for a face-saving way to amalgamate with the Orthodox. The decline in the number of Uniate parishes serves to indicate the depth of the crisis in which the church found itself in the mid-1660s. In the Lutsk eparchy in Volhynia, the Uniates were left in possession of only a hundred parishes, which amounted to 10 percent of all the Eastern Christian communities in the area. Their situation in some parts of Belarus was no better: in the Pinsk eparchy, for example, only ten Uniate parishes remained. The Orthodox accounted for two-thirds or, by some estimates, up to three-quarters of all Eastern Christian parishes of the Commonwealth.[21]

Conditions improved for the Uniates with the conclusion of the Truce of Andrusovo between Muscovy and the Commonwealth, which divided Ukraine along the Dnipro and left all the Belarusian eparchies, apart from Smolensk, within the boundaries of the Polish-Lithuanian Commonwealth. The Uniate Church was allowed to elect a new metropolitan, the king restored its rights in Poland and Lithuania, and the separation of Kyiv and Left-Bank Ukraine from the other Ruthenian territories undermined the influence of the Orthodox in the Commonwealth. The subordination of the Kyiv metropolitanate to the patriarch of Moscow in 1686 coincided with the conclusion of the Eternal Peace between Muscovy and the Commonwealth. One of its provisions gave the metropolitan of Kyiv the right to oversee Orthodox parishes in the Commonwealth and ultimately made the Polish authorities more interested in supporting the Uniate Church as an alternative to the Moscow-controlled Orthodox Church. The continuing subordination of the Commonwealth Orthodox to the patriarch of Constantinople, who was under the control of Warsaw's other enemy, the Ottoman Porte, also did not appeal to the Commonwealth authorities. The powerful Orthodox eparchies of

---

[21] See Ludomir Bieńkowski, "Organizacja Kościoła Wschodniego w Polsce," in *Kościół w Polsce*, ed. Jerzy Kłoczowski, vol. II, *Wieki XVI–XVIII* (Cracow, 1969), pp. 781–1049, here 849–51. On the situation of the Uniate Church in the first post-Pereiaslav decade, see J. Praszko, *De Ecclesia Ruthena Catholica sede metropolitana vacante (1655–1665)* (Rome, 1944). Cf. Antoni Mironowicz, *Prawosławie i unia za panowania Jana Kazimierza* (Białystok, 1997).

Ukraine – Lviv, Peremyshl, and Lutsk – looked especially troublesome to the state. During the rule of Jan III Sobieski (1674–96), the Orthodox came under strong official pressure to convert to the Union. The Coronation Diet of 1676 issued a prohibition on Orthodox contacts with the patriarch of Constantinople. Sobieski also exploited conflicts among Orthodox bishops to support those who indicated their willingness to join the Union. One such was the Orthodox bishop of Lviv, Yosyf Shumliansky, whom Sobieski appointed administrator of the Commonwealth portion of the Kyiv metropolitanate in 1675. In the same year, Shumliansky secretly accepted the Union. In 1679 the bishop of Peremyshl, Inokentii Vynnytsky, also secretly joined the Union. He became the first hierarch to convert his eparchy to the Union in 1691–93. The Lviv eparchy followed suit in 1700, as did the Lutsk eparchy in 1702. Ten years later, the monks of the largest Orthodox monastery in the region, the Pochaiv Lavra, also joined the Union. The only Orthodox bishopric surviving on the territory of the Commonwealth was that of Mahiliou, with jurisdiction over the Orthodox in the former Polatsk eparchy, but even there, by 1777, the Orthodox were in possession of only 22 percent of all non-Protestant churches. Uniate parishes accounted for 68 percent and Roman Catholic ones for 10 percent. By the late 1780s, the Orthodox accounted for a mere 3.5 percent of the entire population of the Commonwealth.[22]

In the first decades of the eighteenth century, Uniate eparchies and parishes in the Commonwealth differed little from Orthodox ones. The main distinction was jurisdictional, which made conversion to the Union a relatively easy process. The reform of the newly converted parishes along Counter-Reformation lines began with the Zamość synod of 1720. Its decisions not only required that Uniate priests and faithful adopt the *filioque* as part of their new credo and mention the pope in their liturgy but also forbade them to receive the sacraments from Orthodox priests. Instead, they were allowed to receive the sacraments from the Roman Catholic clergy.[23] The Zamość synod drew a clear confessional line between Uniates and Orthodox, who otherwise continued to employ the same rite and use the same liturgical language – features that clearly set them apart from the Roman Catholics. In the opinion of many scholars, the Zamość synod also set the Uniate Church on course for Latinization, introducing numerous Roman Catholic rituals and traditions into

[22] See Sahanovich, *Narys historyi Belarusi*, pp. 292–94, 404. On the conversion of the Orthodox eparchies of Ukraine to the Union, see Hryhorii Luzhnyts'kyi, *Ukraïns'ka tserkva mizh Skhodom i Zakhodom* (Philadelphia, 1954), pp. 396–406; Atanasii Velykyi, *Z litopysu khrystyians'koï Ukraïny*, bk. 5 (Rome, 1972), pp. 229–72; bk. 6 (Rome, 1973), pp. 29–56.

[23] On the decisions of the Zamość synod, see Atanasii Velykyi, *Z litopysu khrystyians'koï Ukraïny*, bk. 6 (Rome, 1973), pp. 129–54.

its practices. Latinization implied the cultural Polonization of the Uniate hierarchy, especially its bishops and monks, who in 1743 were organized in one Basilian Order governed from Rome. As noted above, the Basilians were in charge of publishing and education, contributing to the preservation of the traditional book culture and Church Slavonic language. But they were not immune to Polonization and often took the lead in adopting Latin practices. This applied particularly to Belarus, where the Union took hold much earlier than in Ukraine, and both tendencies were more pronounced among the Basilians. In 1636, when the Vilnius Basilians decreed that they would conduct church services in Ruthenian, that decision was recorded in Polish.[24] In 1684 the monks of the Zhirovichi Monastery in Belarus requested permission to follow the Gregorian calendar and celebrate the Latin mass. Quite a few of the Belarusian Basilians were former Roman Catholics. They included not only Ruthenians but also Poles and Lithuanians. Not surprisingly, by the mid-eighteenth century reports on visitations of Belarusian monasteries included information on knowledge of the Ruthenian language among the monks. Combined with Latinization, the advancing Polonization of the Uniate clergy could not help but make the few remaining Orthodox think of the Uniate Church as a "Catholic" and "Polish" organization.[25]

Needless to say, the Uniates disagreed with that designation of their church, for they regarded themselves as Ruthenians and were perceived as such by the Poles. By the mid-seventeenth century Ruthenian identity, formulated in the course of debates about the Union of Brest, had clearly taken root throughout the Ukrainian and Belarusian lands of the Commonwealth. It was also strongly established in the self-identification matrix of the Ruthenian population of the state, irrespective of region, palatinate, and social group. The Eastern rite shared by Orthodox and Uniates alike served as a clear indication of nationality, and vice versa. To be sure, the old competition for exclusive ownership of the Ruthenian "brand" continued within these subgroups. Judging by documents of the second half of the seventeenth century, the Orthodox continued

---

[24] See Marzaliuk, *Liudzi daŭniai Belarusi*, p. 76.

[25] On the history of the Basilian Order, see M. Vavryk, *Narys rozvytku i stanu Vasyliians' koho Chyna XVII–XX st.: Topohrafichno-statystychna rozvidka z kartoiu monastyriv* (Rome, 1979); Sophia Senyk, *Women's Monasteries in Ukraine and Belorussia to the Period of Suppressions*, Orientalia Christiana Analecta, vol. 222 (Rome, 1983); Maria Pidłypczyk-Majerowicz, *Bazylianie w Koronie i na Litwie: szkoły i książki w działalności zakonu* (Warsaw, 1986); eadem, "Kulturalna spuścizna zakonów męskich na Białorusi," in *U schyłku tysiąclecia: księga pamiątkowa z okazji sześćdziesiątych urodzin Prof. Marcelego Kosmana* (Poznań, 2001), pp. 211–25. On the gradual Latinization and Polonization of the Uniate Church in the eighteenth century, see Sophia Senyk, "The Ukrainian Church and Latinization," *Orientalia Christiana Periodica* 56 (1990): 165–87, here 180–82.

to regard themselves as the sole possessors of the Rus' name and identity. The Cossack authors of the Union of Hadiach made certain that the treaty guaranteed the freedom of the Orthodox religion "as far as the language of the Ruthenian nation reaches."[26] The authors of Orthodox tracts lumped Uniates and Catholics together under the names "Roman," "Latin," and "Liakh" (Pole), excluding the Uniates from Rus' identity defined in confessional terms. But even Orthodox polemicists had to admit the existence of another, non-Orthodox Rus', if only because the Poles treated the Orthodox and Uniates differently. One Orthodox author of the period described that unquestionable reality in the following words: "The Liakhs call the Uniates Ruthenians and Greeks, although the Uniates hold to the Roman faith, but incessantly refer to us Orthodox, who are actually Ruthenians and Greeks, as pagans, schismatics, unbelievers, and apostates to the pope."[27]

The conversion to the Union of Orthodox bishops and most of the Orthodox clergy and faithful residing in the Commonwealth in the late seventeenth and early eighteenth centuries greatly reduced the importance of the quarrel between the Orthodox and the Uniates for the right to be called Ruthenians. The Uniate Church, which now became the largest Ruthenian institution in those lands, took on the task of representing the Rus' tradition. Conversion to the Union, which took place so smoothly in part because the Orthodox were promised that "holy days, fasts and rites will remain among you as before, and there will be no change in any respect (as some fancy),"[28] meant that the converts continued to be regarded by the Polish elites as members of a quintessentially Ruthenian or "Greek" church. This also meant that the freshly converted Uniates continued to perceive the Roman Catholic Church as essentially Polish. Nothing changed in that regard after 1680, when a Ruthenian addressed a Roman Catholic priest as follows: "Just as my father did not venerate the Liakh God, so shall I refuse to do so."[29] In the eyes of the Uniates, Roman Catholicism was closely linked not only to Polish identity but also to the nobiliary stratum, since it was often Polish or Polonized nobles who encouraged the conversion of their Ruthenian subjects to Catholicism – a

---

[26] See Bieńkowski, "Organizacja Kościoła Wschodniego w Polsce," p. 850.

[27] See excerpts from this Orthodox tract, written in the Polish-Lithuanian Commonwealth in the late 1660s or early 1670s, in *Pravda pro Uniiu. Dokumenty i materialy*, 2nd edn (Lviv, 1968), pp. 67–71, here 71.

[28] See an extract from a decree of 25 August 1700 issued by the starosta of Halych, Józef Potocki, to the inhabitants of Zbarazh county (ibid., p. 76).

[29] See the account of the conflict between a Roman Catholic priest and members of the "Ruthenian church" in Zhydachiv (*Pravda pro Uniiu*, p. 74). The document does not specify whether the church was Orthodox or Uniate, but the fact that it was visited by a Catholic priest indicates that it must have been Uniate.

process that the latter regarded as a transformation from Ruthenian to Polish identity. "Andrii Basii in Ostriv," reported a Uniate priest in 1763, "who was taken to the lord's household, turned from a Ruthenian into a Pole at the instigation of people from the lord's household. Ilko Pekara in Chernytsia turned from a Ruthenian into a Pole at the lord's command."[30]

The Polish elites, for their part, not only closely associated the Union with Ruthenians in general but also questioned the loyalty of the Uniate Ruthenians, as well as that of the Orthodox. Given the growing interference of Muscovy and, later, the Russian Empire in the internal affairs of the Polish-Lithuanian state, the Polish elites considered the Uniate Ruthenians a potential fifth column, regardless of St. Petersburg's support for the Orthodox and hostility to the Uniates, whom it regarded as worse enemies than the Catholics. The anonymous author of a pamphlet written ca. 1717 that argued for the conversion of the Uniate Ruthenians to Roman Catholicism concluded his work with the following statement: "Finally, one should also take account of the axiom that if Rus' were left with its rite and . . . that schism were joined to the Union, it would threaten the fall of Poland. Thus, if we make it Roman Catholic, we will first of all deprive the Muscovites of the hope of annexing it and, in time, by firmly binding it to ourselves, we shall make it [Rus'] a land hostile and unconquerable to Moscow."[31] Thinking in religious and social terms, the author of the pamphlet argued for eradicating the rite of the "common people," since it was foreign to Polish Catholicism; he called that rite "Ruthenian," making no distinction between the Orthodox and Uniate churches. He also advocated a public campaign to intimidate and ridicule Ruthenians, creating an atmosphere in which "anyone would prefer to change his faith and renounce his existence as a Ruthenian than suffer so much grief and trouble throughout his life that it would be better to die."[32] Ruthenians were to be barred from government posts and their priests denied opportunities to study or to purchase "Ruthenian books"; priests' sons were to be enserfed and peasants kept illiterate. According to the plan, Jews were to be employed to undermine the economic status of Ruthenian burghers, while Tatars were to be used against the populace of Right-Bank Ukraine, Podilia, and Volhynia if it rose in defense of its faith. The devastated lands would then be settled by migrants from Poland.

To modern eyes, the pamphlet reads like a conspiracy theorist's dream come true, proving "beyond a reasonable doubt" that there was a Polish plot against the Ruthenian nation. It also reads like an ultimate expression

---

[30] See an excerpt from the report, ibid., p. 88.
[31] See ibid., pp. 79–86, here 85–86.   [32] Ibid., p. 80.

of sectarian hatred, reflecting the mutual distrust between the Catholic Poles and the Ruthenians who had recently converted to the Union. Clearly, the union of churches was insufficient to heal the deep split in Commonwealth society between the Catholic Poles and Lithuanians on the one hand and the Orthodox Ruthenians on the other.

The rise of Ukraine

The Left Bank of Ukraine, which was under Muscovite control, avoided the Polonization of politics and culture that was taking place on the Right Bank. In the Left-Bank Hetmanate, Cossack institutions survived much better than on the Right Bank, and the relative political and economic stability of the region allowed the elites to consolidate their power, while the intellectuals came up with a new model of Ruthenian identity. Its principal marker was the term "Ukraine," which received particular attention in the historical, political, and cultural debates of the modern era. The name "Ukraine" and the concept behind it were first introduced to a broader Western public in 1660 through the publication in Rouen of Guillaume Le Vasseur de Beauplan's *Description d'Vkranie*. The book's long title explained to the reader that Ukraine consisted of "several provinces of the Kingdom of Poland lying between the borders of Muscovy and the frontiers of Transylvania."[33] *Description d'Vkranie* was in fact the title of the second edition of the book, which had first appeared in 1651 in a print run of one hundred copies and without the name "Ukraine" in its title (it referred instead to lands of the Kingdom of Poland). The nine years that passed between the two editions apparently made "Ukraine" more recognizable to the French public. That certainly applied to readers of the *Gazette de France*, as the newspaper gave substantial coverage to the Cossack wars of the period. Indeed, Beauplan's book caught the attention of the public and was reprinted in 1661, 1662 and 1663. It was published in Latin in 1662, in Dutch in 1664, in Spanish in 1665 and 1672, and in English in 1680. There were numerous reprints in all these languages throughout the rest of the seventeenth century and all of the eighteenth.[34] Certainly there were few authors more qualified than Beauplan to write about Ukraine. A military engineer and architect, he spent the 1630s working on the construction of fortifications and planning settlements in

---

[33] For an English translation of the book, see Guillaume Le Vasseur, Sieur de Beauplan, *A Description of Ukraine*, introduction, trans., and notes by Andrew B. Pernal and Dennis F. Essar (Cambridge, Mass., 1993).

[34] For descriptions of the numerous editions of the book, see Andrew B. Pernal and Dennis F. Essar, "Introduction" to de Beauplan, *A Description of Ukraine*, pp. xix–xcvi, here lxvi–xcvi.

the Ukrainian lands, from Kamianets in the west to the Kodak fortress in the southeast. He also produced a number of excellent maps of Ukraine that, like his book, were often reprinted until the end of the eighteenth century.

What was the "Ukraine" that Beauplan presented to the Western public in his writings and maps? Although the title of the 1660 edition described Ukraine as a group of Polish provinces extending from Transylvania to the Muscovite border, the narrative focused on the Dnipro region, from Kyiv in the north to Zaporizhia and the territory controlled by the Crimean Tatars in the south. Thus, most of the reprints and translations of Beauplan's book appeared under titles that highlighted the Dnipro River, the Zaporozhian Cossacks, and the Crimean Tatars – the main markers of Beauplan's "Ukraine." The Frenchman's broader definition of Ukraine was reflected in his maps, all of which used that name. His map of 1650, titled "Delineatio Specialis et Accurata Ukrainae," showed the palatinates of Kyiv, Bratslav, Podilia, Volhynia and, in part, Rus' (Pokutia). Another map, dated 1658, bears the title "Typus Generalis Ukrainae sive Palatinatuum Podoliae, Kioviensis et Braczlaviensis terras nova delineatione exhibens." It covers the territories of the three palatinates mentioned in the title.[35] Why did Beauplan consider them part of Ukraine? A possible answer is to be found in another of his maps, produced in 1648 and titled "Delineatio Generalis Camporum Desertorum vulgo Ukraina. Cum adjacentibus Provinciis."[36] Thus Beauplan was using the term "Ukraine" to denote all the provinces of the Kingdom of Poland that bordered on the uninhabited steppe areas (*campus desertorum*) in one way or another and constituted the steppe frontier of the Commonwealth. "Ukraine" had been used in that sense in official Polish documents at least since 1580, when a decree issued by King Stefan Batory made mention of Ruthenian, Kyivan, Volhynian, Podolian, and Bratslavian Ukraine. In so doing, Batory was merely subscribing to a tradition that went back at least to the twelfth century, when a Rus' chronicler entered a note referring to Pereiaslav Ukraine under the year 1187. "Ukraine" came to mean "steppe frontier" not only in the Ukrainian and Polish languages but also in Russian, for the Muscovites referred to their steppe borderland as "Ukraine," while reserving different names for areas bordering on the settled territories of the Grand Duchy of Lithuania and the Kingdom of Poland.[37]

Such were the historical roots of the term "Ukraine," popularized in western Europe by numerous reprints and editions of Beauplan's book

---

[35] Ibid., pp. xxxii, xxxvi.   [36] Ibid., p. xxix.
[37] The term "Ukraine" was also used to define other, non-steppe, borderlands. For examples of its use in seventeenth-century sources, see Shelukhyn, *Ukraïna*, pp. 156–62.

and maps. In Beauplan's case, it was based predominantly on the knowledge and experience that he acquired in the 1630s, but to what extent did it reflect rapidly changing reality? In 1660, when Beauplan's book was published in Rouen, the new hetman of the Zaporozhian Host, Yurii Khmelnytsky, set out to define the geographical boundaries of Ukraine in a letter to the tsar of Muscovy.[38] The question had been raised in connection with the peace negotiations between Sweden and the Commonwealth, and the tsar wanted to know the exact borders of his Cossack dependency. In the instructions given to Cossack envoys headed for negotiations with Commonwealth representatives in May 1660, Yurii Khmelnytsky suggested as the starting position that "His Tsarist Majesty's Ukraine is divided from the Kingdom of Poland by the (Western) Buh River." The fallback position was the border defined by the Treaty of Zboriv – the one described by the hetman in his letter to the tsar.[39]

The term "Ukraine," meaning the Hetmanate, had been used with increasing frequency in Cossack correspondence with Muscovy since the times of Bohdan Khmelnytsky. Thus, for Yurii Khmelnytsky and the Cossack officers of his day, the tsar's question concerned the borders of Ukraine as they used that term to define the Cossack polity.[40] Judging by the younger Khmelnytsky's letter, the Cossack officers thought of Ukraine as the Cossack state defined by the Treaty of Zboriv (1649), which included neither Rus' nor Volhynia nor the part of Podilia around Kamianets-Podilskyi (even though they bordered on the steppe). It did, however, include the palatinate of Chernihiv, which was not considered part of Ukraine by Beauplan and the Polish tradition that influenced him. The single factor most responsible for the dramatic shift in the meaning of "Ukraine" was of course the Khmelnytsky Uprising and the rise of the Zaporozhian Host as a distinct political entity recognized in the Zboriv Agreement. Even though the Polish side clearly regarded the agreement as a temporary concession and generally refused to recognize the Zboriv boundaries (the Bila Tserkva Agreement of 1651 reduced Cossack territory to the Kyiv palatinate), the Cossacks kept insisting on the Zboriv borders. So did their allies – the Muscovite envoys at negotiations with the Commonwealth in the summer of 1653 and the Crimean khan at Zhvanets in the autumn of that year. Eventually the Poles, too, found themselves obliged to treat the Zboriv line as the official border of the

---

[38] See *Tysiacha rokiv ukraïns'koï suspil'no-politychnoï dumky*, vol. III, bk. 1 (Kyiv, 2001), pp. 373–74.

[39] See *Universaly ukraïns'kykh het'maniv vid Ivana Vyhovs'koho do Ivana Samoilovycha (1657–1687)* (Kyiv and Lviv, 2004), pp. 155–56.

[40] In his letter to the tsar, Yurii Khmelnytsky wrote that the tsar's envoy had come to see "us in Ukraine."

Cossack polity. The Hadiach Agreement between Hetman Ivan Vyhovsky and Commonwealth representatives (1658) provided for the creation of a Cossack-led Rus' principality within the Zboriv boundaries of 1649.[41]

From a pre-1648 term applied to the steppe borderland of the Kingdom of Poland, "Ukraine" turned into a name for the Cossack polity formed on the territory of the kingdom's three eastern palatinates – Kyiv, Bratslav, and Chernihiv. For all the importance attached to the Zboriv line in the 1650s as the "natural" boundary between the Commonwealth and Cossack Ukraine, it had originated as a negotiated compromise after the Battle of Zboriv. By the end of 1648, Bohdan Khmelnytsky found himself in control of most of Ukrainian ethnic territory, extending as far as Zamość in the west. That was the territory he claimed during negotiations with Commonwealth commissioners at Pereiaslav in February 1649. He later settled for a smaller territory with boundaries defined by the Prypiat River in the north and the Horyn River down to Kamianets-Podilskyi in the west. At Zboriv the Cossacks began negotiations by offering to move that border eastward from the Horyn to the Sluch and from Kamianets to Bar and Starokostiantyniv, but the final agreement drove it even farther east, to Vinnytsia and Bratslav.[42] The Cossacks also had to give up their claim to the right bank of the Prypiat in the Grand Duchy of Lithuania.[43] Such was the "Zboriv border" described by Yurii Khmelnytsky in his letter of 1660 to the tsar. His instructions regarding the Western Buh border with the Commonwealth show that the Cossack elites did not abandon their aspirations of the first years of the uprising.

Ironically, the next decade saw the Cossack Host and its territory divided along the Dnipro River by the Truce of Andrusovo (1667). The Cossack elite's reaction to the agreement showed that in a relatively brief period (between 1649 and 1667) the Zboriv territory and the name "Ukraine" associated with it had developed into a central element of Cossack identity and an object of ultimate political loyalty. When the Right-Bank hetman Petro Doroshenko set out to reunite Ukraine in the boundaries defined at Zboriv, the Left-Bank hetman Ivan Briukhovetsky supported the idea after some hesitation, calling for the restoration of the

---

[41] For the text of the Hadiach Agreement, see *Universaly ukraïns' kykh het' maniv*, pp. 33–39. For a discussion of the agreement, see Iakovleva, *Het' manshchyna v druhii polovyni 50-kh rr.*, pp. 305–23.

[42] As a result, Cossack political discourse of the late seventeenth century never showed the same level of attachment to Kamianets or Bar in Podilia as it did to such towns in Podilia as Yampil or Vinnytsia, which were on the Cossack side of the Zboriv line and were considered part of Cossack Ukraine long after the territory was lost to the Poles and then to the Ottomans.

[43] See Serhii Plokhy, *The Cossacks and Religion in Early Modern Ukraine* (Oxford, 2001), pp. 54–55.

unity of Cossack Ukraine, which had been violated by Moscow and Warsaw. In February 1668, in a letter to the citizens of Novhorod-Siverskyi,
he called upon the Cossack officers and the populace at large "also to
desire the unity of your fatherland, Ukraine, and lend your efforts along
with us on its behalf."[44] The same motif appeared in the letters of Petro
Doroshenko, who lauded the unification of Ukraine in his proclamation
of January 1669: "the Lord God gladdened our Ukraine, which was in
decline, so that it has again united both banks of the Dnipro in their
previous concord and loving fraternal union under the ancient regimen
of our hetmancy."[45] By the time Doroshenko issued that proclamation,
the short-lived unity of Cossack Ukraine had again been broken by the
Left-Bank Cossack officers' election of Demian Mnohohrishny as a new
pro-Muscovite hetman. But the idea of the unity of the Zaporozhian Host
on both banks of the Dnipro, which was so prominent in the events and
discourse of 1667–69, did not vanish because of Doroshenko's unavailing
effort and remained on the agenda of Cossack politics until the second
half of the eighteenth century.

Assessing the changes in the application of the term "Ukraine" in
the second half of the seventeenth century in relation to the Ruthenian
projects of the pre-1648 era, it is important to note that all those unrealized projects, clerical, princely, and nobiliary, exerted their influence
on the new Ukrainian project. Like the princes of Rus', Khmelnytsky
claimed Ukrainian ethnic territory as far as Zamość in early 1649. Elements of the Orthodox clergy's vision of Ruthenia are apparent in Khmelnytsky's claim to Belarusian territories south of the Prypiat River and in
the Right-Bank hetmans' demand for guarantees of Orthodox ecclesiastical rights throughout the Commonwealth.[46] As for nobiliary projects,
Cossack Ukraine included the Chernihiv palatinate, which was part of
Ruthenia as imagined by Adam Kysil in the early 1640s. Conversely, it
did not include Volhynia, which was a crucial part of Kysil's Ruthenian
vision. What differentiated Cossack Ukraine from all the earlier projects
was its possession of Zaporizhia, the ultimate steppe borderland, with its
symbolic role as cradle and virtual capital of the whole Cossack land. But
the most important difference lay elsewhere: if the pre-1648 Ruthenian
projects were virtual, the new Ukrainian project was very real, enhanced
by the existence of a separate polity, administrative structure, and army.

[44] For the text of Briukhovetsky's letter, see *Universaly ukraïns'kykh het'maniv*, p. 353.
[45] *Tysiacha rokiv*, III, pt. 2 (Kyiv, 2001), pp. 13–14.
[46] See, e.g., Hetman Petro Doroshenko's instructions of May 1670 to Cossack representatives at negotiations with the Commonwealth authorities in Ostrih (*Universaly
ukraïns'kykh het'maniv*, pp. 383–91).

Between Ukraine and Ruthenia

The Khmelnytsky Uprising and the rise of the Cossack polity gave birth to a new Ukrainian identity but did not abolish the old Ruthenian one constructed by Orthodox publicists before 1648. Among the Cossack elites under Polish control, the Ruthenian identity remained dominant. As late as 1668, Petro Doroshenko was thinking not only of reuniting the Cossack lands on both banks of the Dnipro but also about extending Cossack control all the way to the Vistula, as in the times of Bohdan Khmelnytsky. In his negotiations with the Ottomans, Doroshenko defined the western borders of the Cossack polity in religious terms (as far as the Orthodox religion reached) and the eastern borders in social terms (as far as Cossack settlements reached).[47] Doroshenko grasped the unity of Ruthenian ethnic space, even if he lacked a modern vocabulary to define the borders of the nation.

Clear proof that Ruthenian identity did not disappear overnight in the Moscow-controlled part of the Hetmanate is to be found in a chronicle written by the archimandrite of St. Michael's Monastery in Kyiv, Feodosii Sofonovych. A native of Kyiv and a graduate of the Kyiv Mohyla College, he wrote his work "so that I myself might know and tell other sons of Rus' when Rus' began and how the Rus' state (*panstvo ruskoe*), having risen from its beginnings, has proceeded to the present time. For everyone needs to have knowledge of his fatherland and tell it to those who ask."[48] The geographical scope of Sofonovych's Rus' fatherland becomes clear from his focus on the Ruthenian lands of the Commonwealth. The chronicle ends with a description of the events of 1672, and even though its concluding sections are increasingly concerned with the Hetmanate, with more frequent mentions of "Ukraine" than of "Rus'," Ruthenia dominates the work. For Sofonovych, the Polish historical context remains the most important one. Thus he discusses the Hetmanate in the third part of his work, titled "Chronicle of the Polish Land," as well as in sections on the rule of the Polish kings Władysław IV and John Casimir.[49] Nor did he give any attention to Muscovy in his account of the past. As Frank E. Sysyn has noted, Sofonovych divided his chronicle into sections concerned with Rus', Lithuania, and Poland, but not with Muscovy, apparently because he considered Muscovite rule too recent or too

---

[47] See Petro Doroshenko's draft treaty with the Ottomans, ibid., p. 381.

[48] Feodosii Sofonovych, *Khronika z litopystsiv starodavnikh*, ed. Iurii Mytsyk and Volodymyr Kravchenko (Kyiv, 1992), p. 56.

[49] Under the year 1670, Sofonovych writes about the election of the new Polish king Michał Wiśniowiecki but does not begin a new section and soon ends the narrative altogether (ibid., pp. 240–42).

uncertain.[50] He probably thought of the Cossack hetmans in similar fashion – too new or too unstable. Despite the dramatic political changes of the period 1648–72, Sofonovych's worldview continued to be defined by the political and cultural realities of the pre-Khmelnytsky era.

Also lagging behind the political changes of the era were the opinions of Sofonovych's fellow student at the Kyiv Mohyla College, Archbishop Lazar Baranovych of Chernihiv. Based in the Hetmanate and seeking the protection of the Muscovite tsar, this "former Ruthenian," as David A. Frick has called him, "was still seeking answers to the old problems caused by Polish-Lithuanian-Ruthenian cohabitation of one Commonwealth."[51] In the early 1670s, when Sofonovych was finishing his chronicle, which treated the history of the Hetmanate as part of the development of the Kingdom of Poland, Baranovych wrote Polish verses in which he imagined his fatherland as the home of Lech (a Pole) and Rus (a Ruthenian). He referred to the Poles and Ruthenians as "Sarmatian sons," echoing the Ruthenian nobility's project of transforming the Commonwealth from a land of two nations into the home of three and manifesting the influence of Polish Sarmatism on his world view. His writings, published in 1680, advocated Polish-Ruthenian cooperation against the Ottomans – an idea also promoted by the author of the *Synopsis*.

Baranovych's attitude toward Muscovy largely depended on the audience to which he addressed his works. In the panegyrics devoted to the Muscovite tsar, Baranovych demonstrated his subservience to the Orthodox ruler – the protector of his homeland from the Muslim and Catholic danger. But a reading of Baranovych's works addressed to a Ruthenian audience leaves the impression that it was not Muscovy that took control of part of Ruthenia but Ruthenia that absorbed Muscovy and continued its old contest with Poland. Baranovych shared the Polish inferiority complex vis-à-vis the West (Italy in particular) and a feeling of superiority over "barbaric" Muscovy; he also discussed the common features of Poland and Rus'. Still, it was against the Polish "other" that he constructed his own Ruthenian identity. Feeling at home in Polish culture, Baranovych playfully suggested that the Polish language was as foreign to Ruthenia as Latin and asserted that "As long as the world is the world, the Ruthenian will not be brother to the Pole."[52] Whether Baranovych imagined his

---

[50] See Frank E. Sysyn, "The Image of Russia and Russian-Ukrainian Relations in Ukrainian Historiography of the Late Seventeenth and Early Eighteenth Centuries," in *Culture, Nation, and Identity: The Ukrainian-Russian Encounter, 1600–1945*, ed. Andreas Kappeler, Zenon E. Kohut, Frank E. Sysyn, and Mark von Hagen (Edmonton and Toronto, 2003), p. 114.

[51] David A. Frick, "Lazar Baranovych, 1680: The Union of Lech and Rus," in *Culture, Nation, and Identity*, pp. 19–56, here 31.

[52] Quoted ibid., p. 30.

Ruthenia as politically linked with Muscovy or with Poland-Lithuania, he wanted it to be accommodated in a Commonwealth-type federation. Baranovych obviously cared about his Ukrainian homeland and wished it peace and prosperity, but he remained a Commonwealth-era Ruthenian to the end of his days, even though his actual world had shrunk to the size of the Cossack Hetmanate. Although Baranovych occasionally referred to his compatriots as "Ukrainian," his usual name for them was "Ruthenian." Admittedly, the meaning of the terms "Rus'" and "Ruthenian" in his works was becoming limited to the territory controlled by the Left-Bank Cossack hetman.

For the educated elite of the Hetmanate, "Ruthenian" continued to serve as the primary ethnocultural marker. But what terms and concepts were popular among the population at large? Sources produced on both sides of the Dnipro indicate that for those lacking the Renaissance-inspired education offered by the Kyiv Mohyla College, local identities and loyalties (including the "Ukrainian" or borderland identity) were more important than the Ruthenian identity constructed by the Orthodox clergy after the Union of Brest. That is certainly the impression one gets from reading the chronicle/diary of the Ruthenian nobleman Yoakhym Yerlych, a Commonwealth loyalist who was highly critical of the Khmelnytsky Uprising and Cossack politics in general. In the text of Yerlych's chronicle, "Ukraine" appears much more often than "Rus'," which he uses mainly in reference to Orthodox church affairs. Ukraine and Volhynia are the focus of Yerlych's narrative and define the geographical base of his identity. Yerlych began to compile his chronicle while taking shelter in the Kyivan Cave Monastery after the outbreak of the Khmelnytsky Uprising, but his worldview was formed long before the Cossack revolt – he was born in 1598 and died after 1673 – and reflected the image of Ukraine familiar to us from the writings and maps of Beauplan. Judging by Yerlych's chronicle, in the course of the seventeenth century Ukraine emerged in the minds of the Ruthenian nobility, which was accustomed to thinking in local terms, as a new geographical entity on a par with such historical regions as the Rus' palatinate or Volhynia. Unlike those regions, however, it included the borderlands of a number of palatinates.[53] Treating Ukraine as a distinct region opened the possibility of developing a local loyalty and identity attached to it, and the establishment of a separate polity in some of the Ukrainian lands helped turn that possibility into a reality.

[53] For the text of the chronicle, see "Letopis' Ioakhima Erlicha," in *Iuzhno-russkie letopisi*, ed. Orest Levyts'kyi (Kyiv, 1916), pp. 32–456. For a brief biography of Yerlych and a bibliography on the subject, see *Bibliografia literatury polskiej. Nowy Korbut. Piśmiennictwo staropolskie*, vol. II (Warsaw, 1964), pp. 292–93.

The formation of a distinct Ukraine-based identity can be reconstructed on the basis of the Eyewitness Chronicle, which covers Cossack history from 1648 to the early eighteenth century. The chronicle is generally believed to have been written by a Cossack officer turned Orthodox priest, Roman Rakushka-Romanovsky. It is of particular interest to scholars as the first work of Cossack historical writing. The chronicle is especially valuable for our purposes because its entries, from the 1670s at least, were written year by year, not retrospectively. The bulk of the chronicle was written in the town of Starodub, where Rakushka spent the last decades of his life (he died in 1703). Closely involved in many contemporary developments, Rakushka took part in the Khmelnytsky Uprising and briefly served as acting colonel in the Zaporozhian Host. He also held the office of general treasurer under Hetman Ivan Briukhovestsky. After Briukhovetsky's demise, Rakushka spent a few years in Polish-controlled Right-Bank Ukraine and served as Hetman Pavlo Teteria's envoy to Istanbul. From what we know of Rakushka-Romanovsky's life, he never attended the Kyiv Mohyla College, and his thinking was only minimally "corrupted" by the humanistic education and ideas of the time. The chronicle is thus *sui generis* in its account of the period and gives us a good idea of the opinions and identities of the Cossack officers on both banks of the Dnipro.[54]

The Eyewitness Chronicle leaves no doubt that by the early 1670s (when Rakushka began to write annual entries and Cossack Ukraine was divided between Muscovy and the Commonwealth), the concept of Ukraine and Ukrainian identity had taken hold in the minds of Cossack officers – indeed, it seems to have all but eliminated whatever elements of Ruthenian identity they had. Rakushka uses "Rus'" and "Ruthenian" even less frequently than Yerlych. In his case, these terms are limited to the sphere of the Orthodox Church and such related matters as the liturgical calendar. What we see instead are strong manifestations of Cossack identity and a firm attachment to Ukraine as the land of the Cossacks. The borders of Ukraine (whether in retrospective coverage of the events of 1648–71 or in entries for the years 1672–1702) are clearly defined by the Zboriv treaty of 1649. In fact, the author never uses "Ukraine" in reference to any territory outside those borders and clearly distinguishes Ukraine from Volhynia and Podilia. His work leaves the impression that the pre-1648 use of the term with reference to all the border palatinates of the Kingdom of Poland was all but forgotten by the Cossack elite of the Hetmanate. The unity of Cossack Ukraine seems to be high on the list of

---

[54] On Roman Rakushka-Romanovsky, see Iaroslav Dzyra, "Vstup," in *Litopys Samovydtsia* (Kyiv, 1971), pp. 9–42, here 20–22.

the author's loyalties and values. Rakushka clearly did not welcome the conditions of the Truce of Andrusovo, whereby the Right Bank was ceded to Poland, and showed sympathy for the opposition to the truce voiced by his late superior, Hetman Briukhovetsky. According to the Eyewitness Chronicle, the hetman had been tempted by Doroshenko's promise "to give up the hetmancy entirely, as long as Cossackdom remained united." Thus, continued the chronicler, "Hetman Briukhovetsky allowed himself to be persuaded and began to conceive a hatred for Muscovy."[55]

The division of Ukraine along the Dnipro River did not prevent Rakushka-Romanovsky from using the name "Ukraine" to refer to both parts of Cossack territory, but the devastation of the Right Bank in the 1670s and the onset of the Ruin, which impelled many Cossacks (including Rakushka himself) to migrate to the Left Bank, could not but affect his perception of events. Under the year 1675, describing the fate of the Right Bank, he wrote, "And so that Ukraine became desolate, for the remaining people from the [Southern] Buh region and the merchants went beyond the Dnipro."[56] Rakushka occasionally wrote of "all Ukraine." Most often, however, he used "Ukraine" without qualification to denote Left-Bank Ukraine, which he also called *Zadnipria* (the lands beyond the Dnipro) and *sehobochna Ukraina* (Ukraine on this side of the river). Rakushka-Romanovsky's Ukraine also included his own Siverian land, with Starodub as its center, and Zaporizhia with its Cossack headquarters, the Sich. Thus Rakushka's Ukraine was slowly shifting eastward to the territory under the tsar's protectorate. The Right Bank did not cease to be part of Ukraine, but that was the broader meaning of the term, while the narrow one, meaning the Left-Bank Hetmanate, became dominant in the chronicle.

The shifting of territorial identity is well illustrated by Rakushka's use of the terms "our" and "ours." If in earlier entries, such as those for the years 1649, 1662, and 1663, the chronicler uses expressions such as "our land" and "our people" to describe the territory and population of all Cossack Ukraine, in later entries he applies them almost exclusively to the population and Cossack troops of Left-Bank Ukraine. In the entry for 1692, for example, he clearly distinguishes between Left-Bank and Right-Bank Cossacks, applying the word "our" only to the former: "having divided [the troops], [Semen] Palii sent his to the king and our troops to His Majesty the Tsar."[57] As a rule, Rakushka used different terms for Muscovite forces (mentioned in the chronicle as *Moskva*, the Muscovite army, or the tsar's people) and Cossacks, whom he called "our army," "the Cossack army," or "our Cossack troops." He also distinguished Ukrainian

[55] See *Litopys Samovydtsia*, p. 103.   [56] Ibid., p. 121.   [57] Ibid., p. 153.

and Muscovite culture. Under the year 1682, he commented on the death of Tsar Fedor Alekseevich as follows: "[the tsar] had great love for our people, for he both ordained that divine services be sung in the churches and monasteries of Muscovy in our chant and Muscovite costumes were abolished, but he allowed them to dress according to our fashion."[58] It should be noted nevertheless that Rakushka also increasingly referred to Muscovite troops as "ours," for example when Left-Bank Cossacks and the tsar's forces took part in joint campaigns against the Ottomans or the Tatars. Beginning with the 1680s, the chronicler included detailed descriptions of events in Moscow in his narrative, while Warsaw all but disappeared from his field of vision. At least once he referred to the Muscovite rulers as "our Muscovite monarchs."[59]

A careful reading of the Eyewitness Chronicle shows how the author's focus, and even his loyalty, were shifting more and more to the east, eventually becoming almost completely identified with the Left-Bank Hetmanate. But because Rakushka-Romanovsky had been raised to think of Ukraine as a united country encompassing both banks of the Dnipro, he had little desire to articulate that new reality. Moreover, lacking the humanistic education offered by the Kyiv Mohyla College and Polish schools and academies, he did not think in national terms (to him, *narod* meant a group of people, not a nation). His dominant identity, like the main focus of his narrative, remained largely social (Cossack), not national. That identity served the useful purpose of distinguishing the elites of the Hetmanate from the Ruthenian elites of the Commonwealth on the one hand and the inhabitants of the Muscovite state on the other. What it lacked, however, was a clearly articulated ethnonational designation.

Little Russia

From the Rus′ tradition Cossack Ukraine inherited the concept of the "Ruthenian nation," as well as a strong elite attachment to Orthodoxy. If these elements had differentiated the Left-Bank Cossacks from the Poles, they could not serve the same purpose with regard to the Muscovites, who were also Orthodox and conscious of their own Rus′ origins. To be sure, their Orthodoxy was not identical to that of Kyiv, nor was their Muscovite identity the same as that of the Rus′ in the Commonwealth, but the new situation created potential problems for the Ruthenian- and Orthodox-based nation-building project in the Hetmanate. The Little Russian terminology originally developed by the Kyivan clergy in the 1620s offered

[58] Ibid., p. 135.   [59] Ibid., p. 145.

a solution to the problems faced by the humanistically educated elites of the Hetmanate. By employing that terminology, the Ukrainian secular and clerical elites could articulate their own identity vis-à-vis Moscow, avoiding the extremes of the "Russia"-based discourse, which afforded little opportunity to differentiate Ruthenians from Muscovites. It also opened an avenue of compromise between Ukrainian Cossack identity and the Ruthenian identity of the Kyivan intellectuals by imposing limitations on Ukrainian Cossack discourse, which favored social categories over national ones.

As discussed in the previous chapters, the term "Little Russia" reentered East Slavic public discourse with the growth in relations between the persecuted Orthodox clergy and faithful in the Commonwealth and the Orthodox tsar in Moscow. It was used to distinguish Polish-Lithuanian Rus' and the Kyiv metropolitanate from Muscovite Rus' and the metropolitanate (later patriarchate) of Moscow, which were called Great Russia or Great Rus' in that context. This ecclesiastically based terminology, which Bohdan Khmelnytsky and his associates employed at Pereiaslav in 1654, was accepted by the Muscovite side with such alacrity that the tsar's short title, "sovereign of all Rus'," was soon replaced with a new one, "sovereign of Great and Little Russia." While the confines of Great Russia were clear and coincided with the pre-1654 borders of Muscovy (with the notable exception of Smolensk), the borders of Little Russia were open to interpretation. They were as uncertain as the western and northern boundaries of the Cossack polity itself. The Pereiaslav Agreement and the subsequent "Articles of Bohdan Khmelnytsky" failed to define them. Most likely, the Muscovite authorities considered Little Russia to have been defined by the Zboriv boundaries of 1649. As noted earlier, Muscovy's official pretext for entering the war with the Commonwealth in 1654 was a demand for the restoration of the Zboriv Agreement.

The western boundaries of Little Rus' were certainly regarded differently in the Cossack Hetmanate. The metropolitan of Kyiv, who styled himself metropolitan of Little Russia in his dealings with Moscow, claimed jurisdiction over all the Ruthenian territories of the Commonwealth. In 1654–55, Cossack detachments encroached on the Grand Duchy of Lithuania, which Muscovy considered its own. The Muscovite authorities decided to set the record straight not only by adjusting the tsar's title to include a reference to him as prince of Volhynia and Podilia but also by adding "White Russia" or Belarus to his short title, which now read "sovereign of Great, Little and White Russia."[60] The whole

---

[60] See Mykhailo Hrushevs'kyi, "Velyka, Mala i Bila Rus'," *Ukraïna*, 1917, nos. 1–2; repr. in *Ukraïns'kyi istorychnyi zhurnal*, 1991, no. 2: 77–85.

exercise was intended to curb Khmelnytsky's ambitions and stress that Belarus – that is, the Ruthenian territories in the Grand Duchy of Lithuania conquered by the tsar's forces – could not claim the rights granted to the Zaporozhian Host. Thus the Muscovite scribes effectively reduced the territory denoted by the term "Little Russia" from Polish-Lithuanian Rus′ and the Kyiv metropolitanate to that of the Zaporozhian Host, so that in Muscovite usage it meant the same as the Cossack and Polish term "Ukraine."

Even so, the multiple meanings of "Little Russia" continued to haunt Muscovite and Cossack politicians, as well as Orthodox hierarchs, for decades to come. The "second" Pereiaslav Agreement of 1659 between the Muscovite boyars and Hetman Yurii Khmelnytsky includes references to Little Russia that attest to different understandings of the term. On the one hand, references to schools on "both banks of Little Russia" suggest that it was synonymous with "Ukraine." The prohibition against Cossacks in Belarus calling themselves Zaporozhians indicated that Belarus was not part of Little Russia, where the Cossacks, known to Muscovite scribes as Zaporozhians, held special rights and privileges from the tsar. On the other hand, references to the jurisdictional status of the Little Russian clergy manifested the old sense of the term, which was originally used to define the territory of the Kyiv metropolitanate. The same broad meaning can be assumed in the phrases "Cherkasian towns of Little Russia" and "Zaporozhian Host of Little Russia," where the term seems to refer to a larger entity than the Cossack polity and its towns.[61]

Gradually the official Muscovite line of limiting the territory of Little Russia to that of the Cossack state took hold in Cossack documents, and in their correspondence with Moscow Cossack scribes replaced "Ukraine" with "Little Russia" and "Muscovy" with "Great Russia." As the correspondence of Hetman Ivan Briukhovetsky indicates, the scribes adopted this practice only in their correspondence and treaties with the Muscovite authorities, while letters sent to the Don Cossacks, to say nothing of addressees outside Muscovy, were free of that terminology.[62] Members of Ruthenian elites outside the Hetmanate, who had fewer dealings with Muscovy, seem to have been unaware of the change taking place in the meaning of the term "Little Russia." For example, the Orthodox of Polatsk who asked the tsar not to forget them after the Truce of Andrusovo (1667) and protect the rights of the Orthodox in the Commonwealth when he negotiated with the king regarded their town as

---

[61] See the text of the Treaty of Pereiaslav (1659) in *Tysiacha rokiv*, III, pt. 1: 345–63.
[62] See the text of Briukhovetsky's letter to the Don Cossacks in *Universaly ukraïns′kykh het′maniv*, p. 456.

part of Little Russia.[63] While clerical elites, faithful to the old tradition, continued to use "Little Russia" in its original broader sense, political developments made it necessary to adjust the meaning of the term once again and further reduce the territory defined by it. Since the Truce of Andrusovo left only the Left-Bank territories under Muscovite control, a tendency emerged to limit not only the notions of the Zaporozhian Host and Ukraine but also that of Little Russia to the confines of the Left Bank.

In order not to be accused by the Poles of violating the agreement or advancing illegitimate claims to the Right Bank, Muscovite diplomats were careful to establish that their new agreements with Left-Bank hetmans pertained only to the Zaporozhian Host on "this side of the Dnipro" and generally avoided referring to the Right Bank as "Little Russia." The Cossacks, on the other hand, were reluctant to abandon the concept of Little Russia on both banks of the Dnipro when they negotiated with the Muscovite authorities, just as they were unwilling to forsake the vision of Ukraine on both banks of the river.[64] Only in 1674, when Muscovite forces and Left-Bank Cossacks crossed to the Right Bank and Ivan Samoilovych was proclaimed hetman of both banks of the Dnipro, did the Muscovite authorities dare to include the "trans-Dnipro regiments" in the category of Little Russian towns.[65] The extension of the tsar's authority to the Right Bank turned out to be short-lived, and the usage of "Little Russia" soon reverted to pre-1674 practice. The Left-Bank Cossacks, whose hetmans maintained references to both banks of the Dnipro in their titles, continued to think of Little Russia/Ukraine as extending to both banks of the river, while Muscovite diplomats generally limited the notion of "Little Russia" to the Left Bank and the city of Kyiv.

While the territorial dimension of Little Russia was obviously shrinking, the popularity of the term among the Cossack elites was gaining new ground during the second half of the seventeenth century. If at first the Cossack officers used it only in their relations with Moscow, by the end of the century they were also using it in dealings with other powers in the region. An indication of this usage occurs in the text of a treaty signed in May 1692 between the Crimean khan and Hetman Petro Ivanenko, better known as Petryk, one of the challengers to Ivan Mazepa in the Hetmanate. According to the treaty text, the parties to the agreement

---

[63] See the text of the letter in *Tysiacha rokiv*, III, pt. 1: 474.

[64] See, e.g., Ivan Briukhovetsky's circular letters to the inhabitants of the Right Bank (1663) in *Universaly ukraïns'kykh het'maniv*, pp. 291–93, and a Muscovite report of 1668 on negotiations with representatives of Hetman Petro Doroshenko in *Tysiacha rokiv*, III, pt. 1, pp. 445–51.

[65] See, e.g., the text of the Pereiaslav Articles (1674), which established conditions according to which Right-Bank Cossackdom accepted the authority of Samoilovych and the supremacy of the tsar (ibid., III, pt. 2: 118–29).

resided in the Crimean and Little Russian states. The latter was also called the Principality of Kyiv and Cherhihiv. Its boundaries were largely restricted to the Left Bank, but Petryk contemplated eastward and westward extensions of its territory, as he planned to include the regiments of Sloboda Ukraine (then under the direct rule of Moscow) and resettle part of the Sloboda population to the Right Bank.[66] Petryk's use of Little Russian terminology clearly demonstrated that it had become popular among the top elite of the Hetmanate and was accepted in the General Chancellery, where Petryk served as senior secretary before escaping to the Crimea.

Little Russian terminology, fully accepted by the Muscovite scribes, aroused no suspicions in Moscow about the loyalty of the Cossack elites. Thus the term "Little Russia" and many of its derivatives were constantly used in Cossack and Muscovite documents. Nevertheless, given that Rakushka-Romanovsky used "Little Russia" in his chronicle only when it occurred in the tsar's official title, it might be assumed that the term was not popular among the middle-rank Cossack officers and clergy of the Hetmanate, who did not have direct contacts with Muscovy. This was certainly not the case with the new and better-educated representatives of the Hetmanate secular and religious elite. The Cossack literati of the new generation were influenced by the Muscovite political and historical thinking of the time and were also unhappy with the limitations imposed on them by the short chronological span of the Cossack historical narrative, as exemplified by Rakushka-Romanovsky's Eyewitness Chronicle. As Petryk's references to Little Russia and the Kyiv-Chernihiv principality indicated, the Muscovite view of the Hetmanate as constituting the lands of the Rurikid principalities could be useful in connecting their immediate Cossack past with the much more ancient history of Rus', reaching all the way back to Kyivan times. That terminology could also give the new generation of the Cossack elite an opportunity (denied by the Cossack-based discourse) to articulate its vision of itself as a separate Rus' nation. Judging by the text of the agreement, Petryk's Little Russian principality consisted of the Zaporozhian Host and the Little Russian people/nation.

The latter notion had gained broad popularity long before Petryk's times. Back in 1663, Ivan Briukhovetsky, in all likelihood an alumnus of the Kyiv Mohyla Academy and one of the most articulate and innovative political propagandists among the Cossack hetmans, had addressed a circular letter to "the Little Russian nation," replacing the term "Ruthenian

---

[66] See the text of the treaty, ibid., pp. 332–36.

nation," which we encounter in the documents of his predecessors.[67] Briukhovetsky did not stop using the old term in his own documents but reserved it largely for circulars addressed to the population of the Right Bank, where he wanted to stress the unity of Little Russia and Polish Ukraine.[68] In 1669 Hetman Demian Mnohohrishny, or more probably one of his secretaries, came up with the formula "Orthodox Christian Little Russian nation of the whole people."[69] In 1685 his successor, Hetman Ivan Samoilovych, issued instructions to his envoys to Moscow in the name of "the hetman, the Cossack officers, the whole Zaporozhian Host and the Little Russian nation."[70] While the Cossack side readily employed the term "Little Russian nation," the Muscovite authorities generally avoided it in their documents, preferring to speak of the Little Russian towns or, alternatively, inhabitants of Little Russia or the Little Russian towns. In the articles granted to Briukhovetsky by the tsar in 1663, there was an awkward formulation to the effect that the hetman was supposed to be elected from among the Zaporozhian Host and not from any other nation, while the term "Little Russian nation," used by the hetman himself on other occasions, was avoided.[71] The latter concept was all but indispensable to the Cossack identity-building project. It continued the established tradition of thinking in terms of the Ruthenian nation but adjusted it to new circumstances; furthermore, it drew a boundary between the Cossacks on the one hand and Ruthenians outside the Hetmanate on the other. It also drew a line between the Cossack elites and the Muscovites, who were admittedly involved with Little Russia but clearly positioned outside the boundaries of the Little Russian nation.

The Little Russian terminology was by no means the only rhetorical instrument available to the architects of the Hetmanate's identity. The close connection between the Little Russian terminology and Cossack political discourse and tradition found expression in the term "Little Russian Ukraine," which was used by Cossack hetmans of various political orientations. Yurii Khmelnytsky, for example, called himself prince of "Little Russian Ukraine" in a circular letter of the 1670s. In 1682 Ivan Samoilovych wrote about "Little Russian Ukraine on the other side [of the Dnipro]." Petryk included a reference to "Little Russian Ukraine" in his agreement of 1692 with the Crimea. Petryk's enemy Ivan Mazepa also used that term, expressing concern with regard to Muscovy's plans

---

[67] See the text of the circular, ibid. pt. 1: 385.
[68] See *Universaly ukraïns'kykh het'maniv*, pp. 291–308.
[69] See his instructions to the envoys, *Tysiacha rokiv*, III, pt. 2: 7–12, here 8.
[70] Ibid., pp. 191–97, here 191.   [71] See the text of the articles, ibid., pt. 1: 409.

for "Little Russian Ukraine."[72] The same term was widely used after Mazepa's defeat, as is attested by Samiilo Velychko's chronicle, written in the 1720s.[73] Since "Little Russian Ukraine" was applied to the same territory as the terms "Ukraine" and "Little Russia," it helped combine both terminological traditions and reconcile the estate-based concept of Cossack Ukraine with the ethnoculturally based concept of Little Russia.

One indication that a separate political structure and distinct historical experience was turning the population of the Hetmanate into a particular social group, known in sources of the time as the Little Russian nation, is the emergence of stereotypical perceptions of that nation at home and abroad. One such stereotype, advanced by the Muscovite administration, was that of the Hetmanate's elites as unreliable allies. According to standard Muscovite discourse of the time, anyone who opposed Moscow or rebelled against Muscovite rulers was perceived as a traitor and accused of violating the oath he had sworn to the Muscovite sovereign. It did not matter to Muscovite officials that the person in question might never have given such an oath, or that the Cossacks understood allegiance to the tsar as a contract subject to annulment if one side violated its conditions. Thus official Muscovite documents included references to the unreliability of the "Little Russian inhabitants," who were neither "good" nor "faithful." Muscovite officials routinely referred to hetmans who rebelled against the tsar and the Little Russian population in general as "traitors." That practice provoked complaints on the part of those who remained faithful to Moscow and went so far as to ask the Muscovite authorities not to apply the term to Cossacks in general.[74] Ironically, with the passage of time, the Hetmanate's elites themselves began to adopt the Muscovite terminology and accept the stereotypes of their countrymen circulated by Muscovite officialdom. This began in official treaties with the tsars and correspondence with Muscovite officials, who encouraged denunciations of all kinds, and then penetrated domestic correspondence and writings in the Hetmanate. Ivan Briukhovetsky's "Articles" of 1665 referred to the "inconstancy of the inhabitants of Little Russia."[75] In 1669 the archpriest Symeon Adamovych complained to Moscow about the "unsteadiness" of his "brothers, inhabitants of Little Russia" and denounced Hetman Demian Monohohrishny.[76]

---

[72] For references to "Little Russian Ukraine" by Yurii Khmelnytsky, Petryk and Mazepa, see ibid., pt. 2: 319, 333, 429; *Universaly ukraïns'kykh het'maniv*, pp. 184, 776.

[73] For Velychko's references to "Little Russian Ukraine," see Shelukhyn, *Ukraïna*, pp. 148–50.

[74] See, for example, the request in Briukhovetsky's "Articles" of 1665 that "in disputes, Russians not slander Cossacks as traitors" (*Universaly ukraïns'kykh het'maniv*, p. 266).

[75] See *Universaly ukraïns'kykh het'maniv*, p. 266.   [76] See *Tysiacha rokiv*, III, pt. 2: 16.

"Unreliability" was also one of the features ascribed to "our people" by the author of the Eyewitness Chronicle. Interestingly enough, Rakushka-Romanovsky associated that "unreliability" with the failure of the Cossack elites to remain loyal to their hetmans, not to the tsars.[77] The constant need for political maneuvering among three neighboring powers, each of which claimed the Cossack polity for itself, left an imprint on the character of Hetmanate politics and of the emerging nation. Unable to restore the unity of their homeland, which had been devastated by decades of warfare and internal conflict, the Cossack elites in different parts of Ukraine were mastering the art of political and physical survival on their own. Hetman Ivan Mazepa regarded the lack of unity among the Cossack officers and their readiness to serve the Ottomans, Poland, and Muscovy as Ukraine's principal curse. In a *duma* attributed to him by his foes, Mazepa called upon the Almighty: "O God, take pity on Ukraine, / Whose sons are not in concord."[78] Lazar Baranovych made an almost identical plea in one of his poems: "O God, grant concord to holy Ukraine." If Baranovych considered the Ruthenians no less devoted to their faith than the Poles, and praised their readiness to fight for it, he regretted the readiness of Ruthenian peasants to rebel against the nobility and of Ruthenians in general to fight one another. Once again, he appealed to the deity: "It happens that the father does not believe the son, or the son the father / Lord, extinguish the fire that is burning in Ukraine."[79]

The fatherland

The definition of one's homeland in ethnocultural terms and the formulation of the concept of loyalty to one's *patria* (fatherland) were among the most important factors in the formation of national identity in eighteenth-century Europe, and their study presents a unique opportunity to trace changes in the identity of the Cossack Hetmanate's elite.

"Fatherland" (*otchyzna*) was an important term in the Ruthenian and, later, Ukrainian political vocabulary of the seventeenth and early eighteenth centuries. The word was a borrowing from Polish, with which Ukrainian political discourse shared a number of important characteristics.[80] In the Commonwealth, the fatherland (*ojczyzna*) was conceived as independent of the ruler, or even of a particular state; the word could be

---

[77] See *Litopys Samovydtsia*, pp. 87, 91.
[78] See *Tysiacha rokiv*, III, pt. 2: 238–40, here 239.
[79] See the Ukrainian translation of Baranovych's poem, ibid., pp. 81–93, here 85.
[80] On the use of the term "fatherland" in Polish political discourse, see Ewa Bem, "Termin 'ojczyzna' w literaturze XVI i XVII wieku. Refleksje o języku," *Odrodzenie i Reformacja w Polsce* 34 (1989): 131–57.

applied to a constituent part of a state as easily as to the whole. The Commonwealth, the Polish Crown, and the Grand Duchy of Lithuania could be considered fatherlands of their inhabitants.[81] For example, in the Polish verses recited by students of the Kyivan College in May 1648 in honor of Prince Jeremi Wiśniowiecki (Yarema Vyshnevetsky), two fatherlands – the Kingdom of Poland and the Grand Duchy of Lithuania – vied for the right to call the scions of the princely families of the Sanhushkos, Chartoryiskys, and Koretskys their sons. Notably, Polish-Lithuanian Rus′ was not mentioned as a possible fatherland of the Rus′ elites, even though Vyshnevetsky, descended from a Rus′ princely line, was the first representative of his Orthodox family to convert to Catholicism.[82]

All this would change with the outbreak of the Khmelnytsky Uprising (1648), which was gathering momentum even as the students of the Kyivan College recited their verses in honor of Wiśniowiecki. The Cossack state produced by the uprising created new loyalties in the region and established political, cultural, and geographical boundaries for the new fatherland of the Rus′ elites. But the change was slow in coming. Pro-Polish hetmans, or those who sought accommodation with Poland, continued to refer to the Commonwealth as a "common fatherland" shared with the Poles.[83] As far as we can tell today, the shift in the reference of "fatherland" from the Kingdom of Poland or the Commonwealth to Cossack Ukraine began in the Hetmanate. Ivan Briukhovetsky, by all accounts a talented demagogue, was probably the first Cossack leader to introduce the topos of loyalty to Ukraine as the Cossacks′ new fatherland into political discourse.[84] References to Ukraine as a fatherland appeared in his letters even before his election to the hetmancy in 1663 and became more pronounced afterwards.[85] By contrast, Briukhovetsky's principal

---

[81] For the use of the terms "nation," "state," and "fatherland" in the Grand Duchy of Lithuania, see Tereskinas, "The Imperfect Body of the Community," pp. 47–60.

[82] See "Maiores Illustrissimorum Principum Korybut Wiszniewiecciorum" in *Roksolański Parnas. Polskojęzyczna poezja ukraińska od końca XVI do początku XVIII wieku*, pt. 2, *Antologia*, ed. Rostysław Radyszewśkyj (Cracow, 1998), pp. 215–30, here 225–26. The verses were most probably written by Lazar Baranovych or Teodosii Vasylevych-Baievsky, professors who taught courses of poetics and rhetoric in the Kyivan Academy at that time.

[83] See the references to the "common fatherland" in the text of the Hadiach Union (1658) and Vyhovsky's circular letter of 1660, as well as in Petro Doroshenko's instructions to his negotiators with the Commonwealth (1670), in *Universaly ukraïns′kykh het′maniv*, pp. 34, 98, 384.

[84] Muscovite documents also record earlier references by the Cossack elites to their *otchyzna*. A case in point is the report of a conversation between a Russian merchant and General Chancellor Ivan Vyhovsky in January 1652 (see *Vossoedinenie*, II: 199). Given the ambiguity of the word *otchizna* in Muscovite political vocabulary of the time, it is difficult to say whether these were references to the fatherland or to the Cossack patrimony and possessions in general.

[85] See Briukhovetsky's letter of April 1662 to Bishop Metodii in *Tysiacha rokiv*, III, pt. 1: 383.

opponent, the Right-Bank hetman Pavlo Teteria, was still referring to the Commonwealth as the Cossack fatherland and "our mother."[86] The Muscovite political elites had no concept of "fatherland" with which to challenge Cossack usage and probably did not understand what was at stake. Although their word *otchina* closely resembled the Polish *ojczyzna* and the Ruthenian *otchyzna*, its meaning – the tsar's patrimony – was entirely different. Briukhovetsky paid tribute to this Muscovite notion as well when he referred to the Ukrainian lands (including the Right Bank) as the tsar's patrimony.[87]

The development that removed much of the ambiguity concerning the Cossack usage of "fatherland" was the Truce of Andrusovo, which divided Ukraine along the Dnipro not only de jure but also de facto. After that, the Cossacks used "fatherland" to refer to their divided country, whether Little Russia or Ukraine. Calls to unite the fatherland and save it from further destruction became common in Cossack leaders' appeals to their countrymen. In 1668 Briukhovetsky explained his own rebellion against the tsar as a reaction against the plans of the Commonwealth and Muscovy to destroy Ukraine, "our dear fatherland."[88] At about the same time, Hetman Doroshenko rallied support in Left-Bank Ukraine with references to the "fatherland, our Ukraine." In the 1670s, the now pro-Ottoman Yurii Khmelnytsky and the pro-Polish hetman Mykhailo Khanenko followed suit.[89] While this "fatherland" was no longer the Commonwealth or the Kingdom of Poland and clearly excluded Muscovy, in other respects its boundaries were as ambiguous and indefinite as those of Ukraine, Little Russia, or Ruthenia. The "old Ruthenian" intellectuals in Kyiv continued to think in pre-1648 categories and regarded not only Cossack Ukraine but also Ruthenia as their fatherland. In the 1670s, such chroniclers of the Hetmanate as Mykhailo Losytsky and Feodosii Sofonovych pledged their loyalty to the Rus' fatherland.[90] But as early as 1683, Dymytrii Tuptalo wrote an epitaph for the deceased general judge of the Hetmanate, Ivan Domontovych, characterizing him as a "true son of the fatherland,"[91] which most probably meant the Hetmanate, given the office that Domontovych had held. So

---

[86] See references to "fatherland" in Teteria's letters in *Universaly ukraïns'kykh het'maniv*, p. 232; *Tysiacha rokiv*, III, pt. 1: 381–90.
[87] See *Universaly ukraïns'kykh het'maniv*, pp. 318, 330.
[88] See Briukhovetsky's letter of 10 February 1668 in *Tysiacha rokiv*, III, pt. 1: 454–55.
[89] See *Universaly ukraïns'kykh het'maniv*, pp. 184–87, 425, 579–81.
[90] See Frank E. Sysyn, "Fatherland in Early Eighteenth-Century Political Culture," in *Mazepa and His Time: History, Culture, Society*, ed. Giovanna Siedina (Alessandria, 2004), pp. 39–53.
[91] For the text of the epitaph, see Pavlo Zholtovs'kyi, *Ukraïns'kyi zhyvopys XVII–XVIII st.* (Kyiv, 1978), p. 220.

did the reference to the fatherland in one of the panegyrics to Hetman Ivan Samoilovych.[92] By the early 1690s, as will be shown below, Kyivan intellectuals were exalting Bohdan Khmelnytsky, the founder of the Hetmanate, as the "father of the fatherland." Here again, the reference to the Hetmanate (or at least primarily to the Cossack state) was quite obvious to the reader.

In a eulogy to Khmelnytsky contained in a textbook of rhetoric published in 1693, the hetman emerges as a European Mars, a Rossian Leonidas and Phoebus, a Ukrainian Tamerlane, and the father of his fatherland. The Cossack fatherland is depicted as an entity absolutely distinct from and even opposed to the Polish fatherland, as well as the object of highest loyalty of its sons, who are duty-bound to glorify the heroic acts of the "knight Khmelnytsky." The hetman is praised for his victories over the Poles, which included "the Thermopylae of Korsun," "the Cannae of Pyliavtsi," and the battles of Zbarazh, Zboriv, and Batih. By means of these battles Khmelnytsky prepared Rus' for freedom and himself for eternity, wrote the unknown author.[93] The fact that, according to Polish usage, the word "fatherland" could mean not only a state but also one of its constituent parts and was relatively independent of the person of the monarch probably helped those intellectuals who wanted to define the Cossack Hetmanate as their fatherland. By the turn of the eighteenth century, we see references to the "Little Russian fatherland" (i.e., the Hetmanate) in Hetman Mazepa's official circulars.[94] Some panegyrists even went so far as to call Mazepa (like Khmelnytsky before him) the "father of the fatherland."[95]

It is not surprising that the emotive term "fatherland" was of major importance in efforts to legitimize or, alternatively, to discredit Ivan Mazepa's rebellion against Peter I in 1708. Mazepa's first public act on joining forces with Charles XII was to take an oath before the Cossack officers who accompanied him, claiming that he had acted not for his

---

[92] See an excerpt from Ivan Velychkovsky's panegyric to the hetman in Natalia Iakovenko, "'Hospodari vitchyzny': uiavlennia kozats'koï ta tserkovnoï elity Het'manatu pro pryrodu, reprezentatsiiu i obov'iazky vlady (druha polovyna XVII–pochatok XVIII st.)," in *Mazepa and His Time*, pp. 7–37, here 25. See also references to Ukraine or to the Little Russian Land as fatherland in the circular letters of Samoilovych (*Universaly ukraïns'kykh het'maniv*, pp. 697, 808, 811, 821).

[93] For a Ukrainian translation of the panegyric, see *Tysiacha rokiv*, III, pt. 2: 366–72.

[94] See *Universaly Ivana Mazepy, 1687–1709*, comp. Ivan Butych (Kyiv and Lviv, 2002), nos. 344, 433.

[95] In the text of an engraving produced at the Kyivan Academy in 1708, Mazepa was called "the protecting father of the fatherland, defender of the church, cultivator and patron of the home in war and peace." See Konstantyn Bida, *Soiuz het'mana Ivana Mazepy z Karlom XII* (Winnipeg, 1959), p. 38.

own sake but for the good of the whole fatherland and the Zaporozhian Host.[96] In a letter to Colonel (and future hetman) Ivan Skoropadsky, Mazepa called upon him to attack the Muscovite troops as a "true son of the fatherland."[97] As noted in the previous chapter, Mazepa was the first to employ the notion of loyalty to the fatherland in the course of the "war of manifestos" with Peter I in 1708–9.

In his manifesto of 8 December 1708, Mazepa asserted that "Moscow, that is, the Great Russian nation, has always been hateful to our Little Russian nation; in its malicious intentions it has long resolved to drive our nation to perdition." Ivan Skoropadsky, the new hetman installed in Mazepa's place with the tsar's approval, responded in a circular of 10 November that the "Little Russian nation . . . with our whole fatherland" should be grateful to the "Great Sovereigns, our Orthodox Monarchs" for the protection they offered and for the prosperous condition of "Ukraine, our fatherland" (*Ukraina, otchyzna nasha*) following the protracted wars of the late seventeenth century. He added that Mazepa had committed treason not in order to protect "our fatherland" but for his own gain; never having been its true son, "now he has become all the more manifest an enemy and destroyer." Skoropadsky also asserted that "in general, our Little Russian fatherland must beware of that self-styled son, or, one should say, degenerate, the infamous Mazepa" and accused Charles XII of wanting to hand over "our fatherland" to the Polish king. The new hetman called upon his followers to support the Great Russian troops in the name of the Orthodox faith, the true churches, and "their fatherland."[98] A letter from the "Little Russian hierarchs," distributed in Ukraine at the insistence of the tsar, similarly portrayed Mazepa not only as a traitor who had abandoned the Orthodox tsar for a heretical monarch but also as one who had "alienated himself from his Little Russian fatherland," sought to subject it to the Polish yoke, and intended to turn the Orthodox churches into Uniate ones.[99]

The theme of the good of the fatherland as the highest value and object of loyalty, which Mazepa introduced into the propaganda war, clearly sidelined the concept of personal loyalty to the monarch, which had been paramount in Peter's first letter on Mazepa's treason. By invoking the

---

[96] See Sergei Solov′ev, *Istoriia Rossii s drevneishikh vremen*, bk. 8 (Moscow, 1962), pp. 243–44.

[97] For the text of the letter, see ibid., pp. 246–47.

[98] For the text of Skoropadsky's manifesto, see Oleksandr Rigel′man, *Litopysna opovid′ pro Malu Rosiiu ta ïï narod i kozakiv uzahali* (repr. of 1847 edn of *Letopisnoe povestvovanie o Maloi Rossii* (Kyiv, 1994)), pp. 555–62.

[99] See an excerpt from the letter in Solov′ev, *Istoriia Rossii*, bk. 8, p. 250.

notion of loyalty to the fatherland, Mazepa effectively questioned and rejected the notion that his primary loyalty was owed to the monarch, and Peter's propagandists had little choice but to accept that logic if they wanted to win the hearts and minds of the "Little Russian people." Another significant innovation of Mazepa's was the presentation of the ongoing conflict not as an act of personal treason but as a confrontation between two nations (peoples), Little Russian and Great Russian. Again, Peter's and Skoropadsky's responses to Mazepa's accusations demonstrate that they had to accept his logic and adopt the rules of the national discourse imposed on them. They were obliged to write not only about the "Little Russian nation" and "Little Russian" and "Great Russian" troops, as the Muscovite authorities had been prepared to do all along,[100] but also about the Great Russian subjects of the tsar and the Great Russian nation. If these terms were not entirely novel, they were by no means usual in the tsar's manifestos, which normally preferred statist to national discourse and legitimized the tsar's actions by invoking the interests of the Russian state (*Rossiiskoe gosudarstvo*).

While all parties involved in the war of manifestos concordantly referred to the inhabitants of the Hetmanate as "Little Russians," they could not agree on a terminology for the tsar's army and state. The definition of the Muscovite forces as Great Russians, which we encounter in the manifestos of Peter I and Hetman Ivan Skoropadsky, was clearly rejected by the rebel Mazepa and his entourage. In his letter to Skoropadsky, Mazepa opposed the Little Russian fatherland not to Great Russia but to tyrannical "Muscovite power" and the Muscovite army. The point was repeated in Mazepa's letter to the Zaporozhian Cossacks and in the manifesto of Charles XII, composed with the help of Cossack advisers.[101] Mazepa was repudiating the Great Russian terminology that he and his Left-Bank predecessors had used in correspondence with Muscovy and was reverting to terms customary in the Polish tradition, which, judging by the text of the Eyewitness Chronicle, were popular among middle-rank Cossack officers and the population at large. Without abandoning Little Russian terminology, Mazepa avoided references to Great Russia in his anti-Muscovite propaganda so as not to suggest any association between the two nations.

---

[100] The tsar's chancellery used both concepts in negotiations with the Cossack officers long before Mazepa's hetmancy. In his letter of 20 July 1696 to Patriarch Adrian, Peter distinguished Great Russian and Little Russian troops taking part in the Azov campaign. See *Pis'ma imperatora Petra velikogo k bratu svoemu Tsariu Ioannu Alekseevichu i patriarkhu Adrianu* (St. Petersburg, 1788), p. 31.

[101] See the text of Mazepa's letter to Skoropadsky, the response of the Sich otaman Kost Hordiienko to Mazepa's circular letter, and the manifesto of Charles XII in *Tysiacha rokiv*, III, pt. 2: 449–50, 461–68.

The Cossack nation

The political language and ideological concepts employed by Mazepa in his confrontation with the tsar are further clarified by the writings of his followers, especially his successor in exile, Hetman Pylyp Orlyk, who served as Mazepa's general chancellor and apparently penned many of his manifestos in the autumn and winter of 1708. In a letter of 1721 to another Kyivan, Metropolitan Stefan Yavorsky, who was then de facto head of the Russian imperial church, Orlyk wrote that when Mazepa confided his intention to rebel against the tsar, he claimed to be doing so "for all of you who are under my rule and command, for your wives and children, for the common welfare of my mother, my fatherland, poor unfortunate Ukraine, for the whole Zaporozhian Host and the Little Russian people, for the elevation and expansion of the Host's rights and privileges."[102] The authors of the *Pacta et Conditiones* (1710), the conditions on which the exiled Cossack officers and Zaporozhians elected Orlyk to succeed the deceased Mazepa, also explained the latter's actions as motivated by his concern for the unity and welfare of the fatherland. They claimed that he had been continuing the cause of Bohdan Khmelnytsky, who allied himself with Charles X of Sweden in the mid-seventeenth century in order to liberate his fatherland from the foreign yoke. As Mazepa's successor, Orlyk in turn was to promote the welfare of the fatherland, whose name was given in the Latin text of the *Pacta* as *Ucraina* or *Parva Rossia*.[103]

In its historical section, the text of the *Pacta* indicated a major reconceptualization of the Cossack elite's relations with Muscovy. The document begins with a brief introduction presenting the history of the Cossacks and their relations with Poland, Muscovy, and Sweden. The introduction breaks with the Ruthenian historiographic tradition in many ways, establishing a non-Rus' genealogy for the Cossacks and thereby cutting all historical and ethnocultural links between them and Muscovy. A distinct Cossack nation (*narod* in the Ukrainian variant of the document; *gens* in the Latin version) thus emerges. It is also occasionally called "Little Russian" in the Ukrainian text and *Rossiaca* in the Latin version, but its primary name is "Cossack." Both Cossack and Little Russian terminology helped to differentiate the inhabitants of the Hetmanate from the

---

[102] See the English translation of Orlyk's letter of June 1721 to Stefan Yavorsky in Orest Subtelny, *The Mazepists: Ukrainian Separatism in the Early Eighteenth Century* (Boulder, Colo., 1981), pp. 178–205, here 190. Cf. the original text in idem, *Mazepyntsi. Ukraïns'kyi separatyzm na pochatku XVIII st.* (Kyiv, 1994), pp. 158–82, here 170.

[103] See the Latin original of the *Pacta*, the Ruthenian version, and translations into contemporary Ukrainian and English in *Konstytutsiia ukraïns'koï het'mans'koï derzhavy* (Kyiv, 1997).

Muscovites and the Ruthenian population of the Commonwealth. The concept of Rus', which linked all three communities together, was clearly marginalized. The authors of the *Pacta* used the terms "Cossack" and "Little Russian" interchangeably, leaving no doubt that they had in mind both the Zaporozhian Host and the "Little Russian nation," traditionally separate categories in the official discourse of the time. Now they were united in the concept of the Cossack nation – a major breakthrough in defining the new community created within the boundaries of the Hetmanate. While the term "Cossack nation" fused these two categories, it did not equate them: the commoners were by no means regarded as equal to the Cossacks. Instead, the term suggested the leading role of the Cossack element in the Little Russian nation – a clear echo of the special rights enjoyed by the nobility in the Ruthenian and Polish nations of the period. In fact, while using the Cossack name and referring to the historical rights once granted to the Cossacks, the new elite of the Hetmanate was quickly turning into an exclusive social estate, characterized by Zenon Kohut as a "gentry." It was this gentry that fully emerged as the leading stratum of the Cossack or Little Russian nation of the Hetmanate in the decades following the Poltava battle.[104]

The etymology of the word "Cossack" was used by the authors of the *Pacta* to establish a historical genealogy for the new nation. According to the *Pacta*, the Cossacks were known in earlier times as Khazars and became famous for their military expeditions against various powers, including Byzantium (*Imperia Orientalis*). In order to make peace with them, the Byzantine emperor even agreed to marry his son to the daughter of Kagan, the prince of the Khazars. The Cossack nation – so went the story – was later conquered by the Polish kings Bolesław the Brave and Stefan Batory, but in their pursuit of freedom the Cossacks overthrew Polish rule under the leadership of Hetman Bohdan Khmelnytsky, whom God had anointed to be the defender of holy Orthodoxy, the rights of the fatherland, and the freedoms of the Host. With the support of Sweden and the Crimea, Khmelnytsky liberated the Zaporozhian Host and the Little Russian nation. The Cossacks accepted the protection of the Muscovite state (*Imperio Muscovitico*), hoping that as coreligionists the Muscovites would preserve their freedoms, but these were violated after the death of Khmelnytsky, and Mazepa had to accept the protection of the Swedish king for the sake of the unity of the fatherland and the rights and liberties of the Host.[105]

---

[104] See Zenon E. Kohut, *Russian Centralism and Ukrainian Autonomy: Imperial Absorption of the Hetmanate, 1760s–1830s* (Cambridge, Mass., 1986).

[105] See *Konstytutsiia ukraïns'koï het'mans'koï derzhavy*, pp. iii–vii.

Such was the history of the Cossack nation as presented by Mazepa's followers in exile. The section concerning Poland had much in common with the earlier, Ruthenian accounts of Ukrainian history. But there were also major differences between the two approaches. The authors of the *Pacta* abandoned the efforts of Orthodox intellectuals of the 1620s to link the Cossacks with the Kyivan princes. The Kyivan period, which was ambiguous in ethnonational terms because it lumped together Muscovite and Ruthenian history (even in narratives produced by such Ruthenian-oriented authors as Sofonovych), was now dropped, completely dissociating the Cossacks from the Rurikids. The story of the baptism of Rus′, which had been all-important to Ruthenian historiography, was also dropped, along with Volodymyr the Great, and replaced with one that featured a Khazar-Cossack prince establishing matrimonial ties with Byzantium. If Volodymyr was claimed as an ancestor by the Muscovite tsars, the Cossacks could not regard him as their own forefather. The architects of the Cossack nation of the early eighteenth century were trying to disentangle themselves from the politically dangerous Rus′ name and history, much as their successors, the architects of the modern Ukrainian nation in the early nineteenth century, would sacrifice the traditional name of their Ruthenian homeland for the then controversial name "Ukraine."

The authors of the *Pacta* were certainly influenced by the tradition of Polish Sarmatism, with its tendency to seek ancestors among the glorious peoples of the past. If the Poles found them in the Sarmatians, the Ukrainian Cossacks found them in the Khazars. Polish historiography, especially the chronicle of Maciej Stryjkowski, who regarded the Khazars as a Rus′ people, also provided historiographic ammunition for "Cossack Sarmatism." As early as 1676, Ioanikii Galiatovsky was already referring to Stryjkowski and the Khazar theory of Cossack origins, but ultimately he was not convinced by the arguments of its proponents and preferred the theory that traced the Cossacks back to the mysterious Aries (*Kozerozhets*).[106] While the "old Ruthenians" of Kyiv had their learned doubts, Cossack authors embraced the Khazar theory, which stressed the importance of the Cossack element in defining the nation of the Hetmanate and established a completely independent genealogy for it. The text of the Eyewitness Chronicle attests that Cossackdom was generally reluctant to partake of the Great Russian/Little Russian or even Ruthenian discourse created by the clerical intellectuals of the period and sought a different vocabulary to express its estate-based identity and political agenda. The historical paradigm presented in the *Pacta* allowed Cossack

---

[106] See the text of the introduction to Galiatovsky's *Skarbnytsia* in *Tysiacha rokiv*, III, pt. 2: pp. 136–41, here 138.

intellectuals to project their Cossack identity into the past and clothe it in national dress.

While Orlyk and his comrades in exile certainly had sufficient political motivation and opportunity to formulate a historical justification for the existence of a distinct Cossack nation, the groundwork for their project appears to have been done in the Hetmanate before 1708, as Galiatovsky's writings attest. The historical introduction to the *Pacta* also looks very much like the summary of the history of the Cossacks presented in the early eighteenth-century chronicle attributed to the Cossack officer Hryhorii Hrabianka. The Hrabianka chronicle is a highly sophisticated historical narrative that depends more than any other work of the period on the accomplishments of previous historiography. It is thus highly likely that Hrabianka and the author of the *Pacta* used the same historical sources. Hrabianka's account of the Khazar theory of Cossack origins is probably the most comprehensive one available. Indeed, Hrabianka completes the "nationalization" of the Cossacks undertaken in the *Pacta* by establishing the biblical origins of the Cossack nation. His account links the Khazars to the Alans and the latter to the Scythians, who in turn are traced back to Japheth, the eldest son of the biblical Gomer.[107] Thus the Cossacks ("the people of the Little Russian land called Cossacks") emerge on the pages of the chronicle as a nation with a biblical status in no way inferior to that of the Muscovites or the Ruthenians, whom the author of the *Synopsis* had traced back to one common ancestor, Mosoch. Hrabianka goes on to amalgamate the Khazar and Rus' past in the history of the "Little Russian Cossacks." Both the *Pacta* and Hrabianka's narrative reflect the tendency of Cossack intellectuals of the period to present Cossackdom as an entity more ancient than its immediate neighbors and thereby to establish its credentials as a separate nation.

The Cossack nation is presented in the *Pacta* as a brave, freedom-loving, and law-abiding entity, quite unlike its principal neighbors, the Polish-Lithuanian Commonwealth and Muscovy. Poland and its kings emerge in the historical introduction as conquerors and oppressors of the Cossacks, who rebelled against them because of the violation of their religious and other rights. The text of the *Pacta* shows quite clearly that all of Peter's accusations against Mazepa and his associates concerning their alleged plans to turn Ukraine over to Poland and introduce the Union instead of Orthodoxy were a propaganda ploy. Orthodoxy remained important to the authors, who wanted the Kyiv metropolitanate

---

[107] See *Hryhorij Hrabjanka's "The Great War of Bohdan Xmel′nyc′kyj"* (Cambridge, Mass., 1990), p. 300.

to be withdrawn from the jurisdiction of Moscow and returned to the authority of Constantinople. If Poland is treated in the *Pacta* as a different nation, Muscovy is not differentiated from the Cossacks on ethnonational grounds but is treated as a separate state. In a tradition going back to Hetman Ivan Vyhovsky's manifesto of 1658 to European rulers explaining the Cossack breach with Muscovy, the authors of the *Pacta* stress that the Muscovites violated their rights instead of protecting them and thus forced Mazepa to accept Swedish protection. What makes the breach legitimate is the interpretation of the original agreement between the tsar and the Cossacks as one binding on both sides, not one in which the Cossacks are mere subordinates to the tsar. As in Mazepa's manifestos, loyalty to the fatherland is rated higher than loyalty to the monarch, especially one who violates the original agreement. Muscovy emerges in the *Pacta* as a tyrannical state whose power and example corrupted the hetmancy, turning hetmans into autocrats who encroached on the rights of the Host and the whole nation. Thus the *Pacta*, concluded between the newly elected hetman and the Cossack officers, the Host, and the Little Russian nation, were intended to curb authoritarian tendencies on the part of future hetmans and guarantee the rights of the nation.

Little Russian Ukraine

Peter took advantage of the defeat of Charles XII and Mazepa at the Battle of Poltava (1709) to launch a decisive attack on the Hetmanate's autonomy. Its capital was moved closer to the border with Russia, the tsar took over the right to appoint Cossack colonels, his resident was installed at the hetman's court, and the office of hetman itself was abolished and replaced in 1722 by the Little Russian College. The Cossack elites protested but did not rebel. Instead they sent a delegation to St. Petersburg to lobby for the restoration of the office of hetman. The members of the delegation were arrested. The leaders of the Hetmanate were silenced. Literary and iconographic works produced at the time show convincingly that the Cossack elites who fought for the preservation of their rights and privileges also possessed a distinct cultural identity that was threatened by the Muscovite offensive. But what was that identity?

Among the most important sources on the post-Poltava views of the Hetmanate's elites are the above-mentioned chronicle by Hryhorii Hrabianka, judge and later colonel of the Hadiach regiment, and a long *Relation* by Samiilo Velychko, a former secretary in the general chancellery.[108] Both works were most probably written or revised in the course of the 1720s. Even though the Hrabianka chronicle ends with the events of 1709, its author was familiar with the Russian translation of a work of Samuel Pufendorf that appeared in print in 1718; he also employed the term "all-Russian emperor," which Peter I adopted in the autumn of 1721. Velychko also knew the Russian translation of Pufendorf, and the text of his chronicle suggests that he outlived Peter I. The fact that two major works of Cossack historiography appear to have been completed no earlier than the 1720s permits the assumption that the Cossack elite's vision of the past was influenced not so much by Mazepa's defeat at Poltava as by its long-term political consequences, especially Peter's abolition of the office of hetman in 1722 and the subsequent incorporation of the Hetmanate into the imperial administration through the direct rule of the Little Russian College.

Both Cossack chroniclers had personal reasons as well as ideological ones to oppose the incorporation. Hrabianka, for example, was a member of the Cossack delegation, led by Acting Hetman Pavlo Polubotok, that went to St. Petersburg in 1723 to appeal for the restoration of the hetman's office. Like Polubotok, he was imprisoned by the tsar; unlike him, he survived imprisonment, was released after the death of Peter I, and had a successful career after the restoration of the hetmancy under Danylo Apostol. In 1730 Hrabianka became colonel of Hadiach; he died during the Cossack assault on the Crimea in 1737.[109] Sometime after the Battle of Poltava, Velychko was also imprisoned for reasons unknown. It is thus hardly surprising that as historians, both Hrabianka and Velychko were strong advocates of maintaining traditional Cossack liberties and freedoms. Given the political circumstances of the day, unlike Mazepa and Orlyk, they naturally tried to achieve that goal within the Russian Empire. The abolition of the hetmancy, unlike the removal of individual hetmans in the past, was a clear threat to the very existence of Cossack statehood. There was no better way to respond than to develop a historical argument to prove the "ancient" and therefore legitimate origins of Cossack rights, privileges, and freedoms. Unlike the seventeenth-century Cossacks, however, the post-Poltava elites whose attitudes were reflected

---

[108] For texts of the Hrabianka chronicle, see *Hryhorij Hrabjanka's "The Great War of Bohdan Xmel′nyc′kyj."* For a scholarly edition of the first volume of the Velychko chronicle, see *Samiila Velychka Skazaniie o voini kozatskoi z poliakamy*, ed. Kateryna Lazarevs′ka (Kyiv, 1926); the complete text was published under the title *Letopis′ sobytii v Iugo-Zapadnoi Rossii v XVII veke*, 4 vols. (Kyiv, 1848–64).

[109] On Hrabianka, see Yurii Lutsenko's introduction to *Hryhorij Hrabjanka's "The Great War,"* pp. xviii–xxii.

in the historical works of Hrabianka and Velychko were not seeking to extend their once broad political autonomy but merely to preserve it. A reading of their chronicles shows that the Petrine reforms and the resounding defeat of Cossack independentist aspirations gave rise to a new type of identity in the Hetmanate.

The meaning of Hrabianka's and Velychko's works is best understood against the background of the historical, political, and ideological debate initiated by the war of manifestos between Mazepa and Peter in 1708–9 and echoed in Orlyk's writings in exile. Whose side, Peter's or Mazepa's, did the chroniclers of post-Poltava Ukraine take? Judging by what we know today, the Cossack elites generally had little reason to cherish Mazepa. At first they criticized him for kowtowing to the tsar, and then they were more than reluctant to support him in his rebellion. Even his supporters could hardly wait for his demise to compose the *Pacta*, which was a reaction to Mazepa's authoritarian rule and was intended to limit the powers and aspirations of his successor, Pylyp Orlyk. And one of our chroniclers, Samiilo Velychko – a protégé of Mazepa's enemy, General Chancellor Vasyl Kochubei – was also no friend or admirer of the late hetman. But it was one thing to withhold support from Mazepa and quite another to endorse Peter's encroachment on the Hetmanate's autonomy, which culminated in the abolition of the hetmancy.

One of the major issues discussed in the manifestos was that of loyalty and treason. As noted above, Peter accused Mazepa of violating his oath to the tsar, and Mazepa responded that he was bound by a higher loyalty – to his fatherland, the liberties of the Host, and the welfare of the Little Russian nation. Orlyk sustained Mazepa's line of argument in exile (probably with the hetman's active participation), but intellectuals in the Hetmanate do not appear to have followed suit. As Frank E. Sysyn has argued, Hrabianka adopted the idea of loyalty to the tsar as his main criterion for judging the activities of individual hetmans.[110] Velychko, informing the reader about the death of his patron, Vasyl Kochubei, noted that he had served God, his sovereign, his fatherland, and the Cossack Host.[111] In this hierarchy of loyalties, fatherland followed the sovereign. Although Velychko gave substantial attention in his chronicle to the idea of loyalty to the fatherland, he basically subscribed to the tsar's propagandistic thesis of 1708–9: love of the fatherland could trump a Cossack's duty to serve a hetman acting against the interests of the fatherland, but it could not justify rebellion against the Muscovite monarch. In general, Velychko tried to avoid counterposing loyalties to the Muscovite

---

[110] See Sysyn, "The Image of Russia," p. 131.   [111] Ibid., p. 139.

tsar and to the Cossack fatherland.[112] While Velychko might criticize the individual actions of monarchs, including Peter, he stopped short of putting loyalty to Ukraine, his Little Russian fatherland, ahead of loyalty to the sovereign. In that regard, Velychko turned out to be less consistent than either Mazepa or Orlyk: he recognized Khmelnytsky's right to rebel against the Polish king in the name of the fatherland but apparently denied that right to his successors who rebelled against the Russian tsar. To be sure, the Polish monarchs were non-Orthodox, while the Muscovite sovereigns were first and foremost Orthodox tsars and protectors of the Orthodox Church. Yet one need not search for an ideological justification: as Sysyn notes, Velychko's support for the Orthodox tsar may have been based on his mere acknowledgment of "the political reality resulting from the late seventeenth-century struggles and the Battle of Poltava."[113]

While both Velychko and Hrabianka took the tsar's side in the loyalty debate between Peter and Mazepa, there are clear indications that they leaned toward the latter when it came to the liberties and freedoms of the Cossack Host and the Little Russian nation. Velychko particularly criticized Peter for surrendering Right-Bank Ukraine and introducing the rule of the Little Russian College, despite the tsar's claim that the Little Russians enjoyed more rights than any other nation on earth.[114] While that critique of the tsar was provoked by Peter's actions after Poltava, it was nothing if not a direct response to the tsar's manifestos of 1708–9, in which he claimed that the Cossacks were more privileged than any other nation under the sun. It was also an echo of the accusations leveled against the tsar by Mazepa, who justified his rebellion by invoking his desire to protect the unity of the fatherland. The authors of both Cossack chronicles, like the author of the Eyewitness Chronicle before them, were highly critical of the Truce of Andrusovo, which had divided Ukraine, and continued to treat the Right Bank of the Dnipro as part of their homeland.

Crucial to the "rights" argument of both Cossack chroniclers was the interpretation of the Pereiaslav Agreement of 1654 as the Magna Carta of the Hetmanate's liberties. Velychko defined Pereiaslav as a mutually binding treaty between two equal partners. That interpretation was of course contrary to the views of the Muscovite authorities, who treated the rights and privileges of the Host as a grant from the tsar to his subjects and thus liable to revocation at the tsar's whim. The Muscovite side never acknowledged the binding character of the Pereiaslav Agreement and the

---

[112] On the meaning and importance of "fatherland" in the Velychko chronicle, see Sysyn, "Fatherland in Early Eighteenth-Century Political Culture."
[113] See Sysyn, "The Image of Russia," p. 138.   [114] Ibid., p. 140.

subsequent Khmelnytsky Articles, but, in negotiations with his successors, it also denied having violated them. In 1708, at a time of crisis, Peter denied any violation of the Pereiaslav Agreement by the tsars. In reality he continued the policy of his predecessors and significantly curtailed Cossack privileges, first by issuing new articles that drastically reduced the powers of the newly elected Hetman Ivan Skoropadsky and then by abolishing the hetmancy altogether in 1722. In their interpretation of the Pereiaslav Agreement as a contract binding on both parties, the Cossack chroniclers, not unlike their predecessors of 1654, were projecting the legal and political practices of the Polish-Lithuanian Commonwealth onto Muscovy. Treating that autocratic tsardom as if it conformed to Commonwealth traditions was a clear misunderstanding of political reality for which one might forgive such "former Ruthenians" as Sofonovych or Baranovych, but not Hetmanate intellectuals of the 1720s. Yet they, too, were ultimately victims of political circumstance. Acknowledging the realities of the tsarist autocracy would not have helped them make a better argument for the restoration of Cossack rights taken away by Peter and his predecessors. In the end, despite everything, they stubbornly reiterated their defense of Cossack rights.

Neither chronicler discussed Mazepa's choice in any detail. Hrabianka simply mentions the fact of the hetman's "treason," while Velychko's chronicle ends with the events of the late seventeenth century. The latter's response to Mazepa's revolt can be detected only on the basis of his reaction to arguments in favor of the rebellion staged by Petryk, who sided with the Crimea in 1693. In his account of Petryk's appeal to the Host, Velychko presented the same arguments as those that appeared in Mazepa's manifestos of 1708: the war against Muscovy was conducted for the sake of Cossack liberties and the common good of the nation, with the goal of returning to the idealized times of Bohdan Khmelnytsky. Petryk's letter is countered in the text of the chronicle by the alleged response of Velychko's own Poltava Cossack regiment. The Poltava letter refused to admit that the Muscovite authorities had wronged the Cossacks and Little Russia in any way but suggested that if something like that should ever happen, a remedy should be sought by wise leaders, not by rebels like Petryk. Since Velychko did not consider Petryk a wise leader, it may be assumed that he was no more favorably disposed toward Mazepa.[115] While Velychko appears to have thought that the rebels had raised valid concerns, he did not endorse rebellion as a means of redress.

---

[115] For the text of Petryk's proclamation and the response of the Poltava regiment, see *Letopis' sobytii*, III: 111–16. The exchange of letters is discussed in Sysyn, "The Image of Russia," p. 138.

Not unlike Mazepa himself and his possible proxy in Velychko's chronicle, the unfortunate Petryk, the Cossack chroniclers envisioned a solution to their problems in a return to the times of Bohdan Khmelnytsky, who emerges from the pages of both chronicles as the ideal hetman. In the Hetmanate, the Khmelnytsky era was generally regarded as a "golden age" against which the failures and accomplishments of new Cossack leaders were judged. References to the "Articles" of Bohdan Khmelnytsky were almost obligatory in the texts of treaties drafted for his successors by the Muscovite authorities. The Ottomans certainly wanted to exploit the popularity of the old hetman when they installed his son Yurii Khmelnytsky as "prince of Little Russian Ukraine" in 1678. The Muscovites, for their part, drew a clear distinction between the father and the son, whom they branded as a traitor along with Ivan Vyhovsky and Ivan Briukhovetsky in the "Konotop Articles" granted to Hetman Ivan Samoilovych in 1672.[116]

The first signs of Khmelnytsky's evolution into a cult figure can be traced back to the era of Ivan Samoilovych, when the professors of the restored Kyiv Mohyla Academy began to represent him as the foremost hero of the Hetmanate. Khmelnytsky appears in the above-mentioned eulogy of 1693 as the leader of an anti-Polish struggle and has no connection to Muscovy and the Pereiaslav Articles, for which he was known in agreements between Muscovy and the Cossacks in the second half of the seventeenth century.[117] He also emerges untainted by his ties with Moscow in the historical introduction to the *Pacta*. His name was raised in the war of manifestos in late 1708 and early 1709 in connection with the rights granted him by the tsars. Khmelnytsky's main function in the *Pacta* seems to be that of legitimizing the political choice made by Mazepa and Orlyk in 1708. He is portrayed as the hetman who not only liberated his fatherland but also initiated alliances with Sweden and the Crimea, the two nations on whose support the exiles counted. Khmelnytsky's acceptance of the Muscovite protectorate is treated as an honest mistake. After Poltava, this interpretation of Khmelnytsky's role in relation to Muscovy could only be advanced in writings produced outside the Hetmanate, which came under increasingly stringent Muscovite control. In the Hetmanate itself, there developed a very different image of Khmelnytsky and his historical role. Hrabianka's and Velychko's image of Khmelnytsky differs very significantly from the one in Orlyk's *Pacta*. If they retained the characterization of Khmelnytsky as the leader of an anti-Polish uprising and protector of the Orthodox faith, the rights of the

---

[116] See the text of the articles in *Universaly ukraïns'kykh het'maniv*, pp. 587–600.
[117] See *Tysiacha rokiv*, III, pt. 2: 374.

Host, and the welfare of the fatherland, they rejected the image of him as a forerunner of the hetmans who oriented themselves on the Crimea or Sweden. They went on to present Khmelnytsky as a pro-Muscovite hetman who had not only liberated Ukraine from the Polish yoke but also brought it under Muscovite protection and guaranteed Little Russian liberties under the tsar's rule.[118]

The 1720s saw the transformation of Bohdan Khmelnytsky from a popular historical personage into a cult figure who was regarded as the founder and, more importantly, the protector of the whole nation. In writings of the period he emerged as a clear alternative to Ivan Mazepa, who was anathematized by the imperial church. If Mazepa was officially accused of having plotted to subjugate Ukraine to the Poles, Khmelnytsky was portrayed as the savior of Little Russia from Polish oppression. If Mazepa had allegedly conspired to bring all of Ukraine under the Union of Brest, Khmelnytsky was the protector of Orthodoxy. If Mazepa was branded a traitor to the tsar and to Little Russia, Khmelnytsky was portrayed as a loyal subject and the father, protector, and benefactor of his fatherland. It was the pro-Muscovite motifs of the new cult that made Khmelnytsky's image drastically different from the one created by Orlyk, or even by the authors of the eulogy of 1693 discussed above. This new image of the hetman was of course indispensable to the Cossack elites' campaign to restore the office of Cossack hetman and its prerogatives. When that restoration took place in 1728, the election of the new hetman was allowed by St. Petersburg, unsurprisingly, "in accordance with the Articles of Bohdan Khmelnytsky," and the veneration of Khmelnytsky in the Hetmanate reached its peak. The chronicles of Velychko and Hrabianka fully attest to Khmelnytsky's new cult status in the political culture of the Hetmanate. So do numerous contemporary verses celebrating his anti-Polish and pro-Muscovite orientation preserved in the textbooks and notes of professors and students of the Kyiv Mohyla Academy. There is also reason to believe that it was around that time that the woodcut portrait of Khmelnytsky etched by Wilhelm Hondius in the mid-seventeenth century was rediscovered in Kyiv. It was used as the basis for the depiction of Khmelnytsky on the wall of the Dormition Cathedral in the Kyivan Cave Monastery, as well as in icons and secular paintings.[119] All this activity celebrated the restoration of some of the rights granted by the tsar to Khmelnytsky in 1654 and now returned to the nation that he had established. Pereiaslav served as the founding myth of that nation, and

---

[118] See *Hryhorij Hrabjanka's "The Great War,"* pp. 296–97.
[119] On the cult of Khmelnytsky and its iconographic reflections, see my *Tsars and Cossacks: A Study in Iconography* (Cambridge, Mass., 2002), pp. 45–54.

Khmelnytsky emerged after Poltava as the most prominent symbol and embodiment of that myth and of the nation itself.

The boundaries of Little Russian identity

In 1728, twenty-three years after the performance of Prokopovych's *Vladymyr*, Kyivans attended another play staged by students of the Kyivan Academy. Entitled *Mylost' Bozhiia* (The Grace of God), it celebrated the restoration of the hetman's office, which had been abolished by Peter in 1722. It was clearly influenced by Prokopovych's play, and its epilogue included an appeal to God to bestow his grace on the tsar (now Peter II) and his faithful chief (*virnyi vozhd'*), the hetman (now Danyil). Nevertheless, the ideological messages of these plays showed more differences than similarities. The drama of 1728 made no attempt to link the power of the hetmans to that of the Kyivan princes. It compared the new hetman, Danylo (Danyil) Apostol, not to Volodymyr, as did Prokopovych in the case of Mazepa, but to Khmelnytsky. The playwright's main interlocutor was not "Russia" but "Ukraine." He called upon Ukraine to celebrate Khmelnytsky's victories: "do not weep, o Ukraine, cease to grieve, / It is time to turn your sorrow into joy."[120] The confusing sequence of "all-Russian" terms was now abandoned in favor of clearly defined "Ukrainian" ones that promoted local Ukrainian patriotism and identity. The Cossacks were presented as patriots of Mother Ukraine, while the main character, Bohdan Khmelnytsky, was portrayed as a true patriot of his Ukrainian fatherland: "Having come to love the fatherland above all else, and for its sake having scorned all / Luxuries, peace, advantages, and all private gain."[121] Everyone who loved his fatherland was encouraged to love Khmelnytsky as well.[122] The fatherland of the play was clearly delineated by the boundaries of Ukraine or Little Russia – an interpretation that indicated the Hetmanate's attachment to the traditions of Mazepa and Orlyk. While Prokopovych continued to promote his new imperial fatherland in St. Petersburg, his successors at the Kyivan Academy apparently preferred to remain loyal to their old one.

What were the main features of the new identity celebrated by the author of *The Grace of God*? A reading of the Cossack chronicles and other sources of the period indicates that the attempt to root the Cossack nation in a Khazar historical mythology (as in the *Pacta*) and thereby distinguish it clearly from Muscovy to the east and Ruthenia and Poland to the west

---

[120] "Mylost' Bozhiia" in *Ukraïns'ka literatura XVIII st.*, comp. O. V. Myshanych, ed. V. I. Krekoten' (Kyiv, 1983), pp. 306–24, here 314.
[121] Ibid., p. 323.   [122] Ibid., p. 317.

ultimately prevailed in the Hetmanate – a fact attested by the popularity of Hrabianka's chronicle.[123] The notion of the rights and liberties of the Little Russian nation remained central to all models of Hetmanate identity, and the Treaty of Pereiaslav took on overriding importance in the political culture of the Hetmanate. The myth of Pereiaslav became the founding myth of the whole Little Russian nation, which, of course, was embodied in the Cossack estate or, more precisely, in the officer stratum that led and controlled the Cossack polity. The cult of Khmelnytsky came to embody that myth in the early eighteenth century, when the officer stratum and its followers among the populace accepted him as their founding father and protector, to whom all faithful sons of Ukraine/Little Russia should be loyal.

The elites of the Hetmanate continued to project the image of Little Russia/Ukraine as a society led and represented by the Cossack estate. Other social strata might have their own rights and privileges, but it was the leading Cossack estate that defined the rights of the polity and its inhabitants. Less clear was the distinction between rank-and-file Cossacks and the officer elite. The notion that the Cossack officer stratum enjoyed special rights was never developed in the Hetmanate, even though it was that stratum, not the Cossack estate as a whole, that became dominant in the Cossack polity very early in its history and consolidated its status in the early decades of the eighteenth century. The ideology and discourse of the Hetmanate remained officially egalitarian, including the Cossack estate as a whole. For all the officer stratum's aspirations to the status of a new nobility, it maintained its original Cossack image, partly because the Muscovite tsar had granted special rights and privileges to the Zaporozhian Host, not to the Little Russian nobility. The elites of the Hetmanate had a variety of names for their Cossack homeland, with Velychko producing perhaps the widest array, including "Ukraine," "Little Russia," and "Little Russian Ukraine." Even after Poltava, the Cossack elites continued to regard the Hetmanate, not the Russian Empire, as their fatherland. To be sure, the boundaries of that fatherland were changing: "Little Russia" and "Ukraine" were becoming more and more identified with the Moscow-controlled territories of the Left Bank. The boundary with Poland was becoming more pronounced, and close relations with the Right Bank were now viewed with suspicion. Peter's accusations that Mazepa was acting in the interests of Poland unleashed a fierce campaign against admirers of Polish ways in the Hetmanate.

---

[123] On the popularity of the Hrabianka chronicle and its multiple copies, see Elena Apanovich, *Rukopisnaia svetskaia kniga XVIII veka na Ukraine. Istoricheskie sborniki* (Kyiv, 1983), pp. 137–86.

Wherever you go, they praise the Poles,
They all but burn the faithful,
They stuff the ears of commoners,
Tainting them with deadly poison.
Not a word passes without praise of the Poles –
Eating or drinking, they speak of them . . .
All spirit, all enthusiasm is devoted to the Poles.
So much for wisdom and virtue

reads the poem "Lament of Little Russia," recorded in the notebook of a student of the Kyiv Mohyla Academy for the academic year 1719–20.[124] The image presented there is of course tainted by the polemics of the day and probably exaggerated. Mazepa, Orlyk, and their supporters were as far from idealizing Poland as were the Cossack elites after Poltava; indeed, all of them preferred Muscovite rule to that of Poland in view of the complete elimination of Cossackdom on the Right Bank. At the same time, not unlike Baranovych, they remained products of the Polish educational system (insofar as it influenced the curriculum of the Kyiv Mohyla Academy). The Polish-Ruthenian encounter of the early modern period brought not only conflicts but also negotiations, and the latter helped the Cossack elites master and appropriate the concepts and values shared by their Polish adversaries. Not surprisingly, then, the Cossack officers of Mazepa's time felt themselves intellectually more at home in the Polish cultural tradition than in the Muscovite one. Yet political realities were overcoming that cultural connection and turning the Poles into foreigners and ultimate "others" of the emerging Little Russian nation.[125] Poems of the period that followed the tradition of Baranovych and depicted the Liakhs (Poles), Lithuanians, and Rus' as children of one mother, Poland, no longer advocated an alliance between them but complained that the first two brothers had turned against their younger brother, Rus, and their mother.[126]

If the boundary between "Little Russia" and the Polish-Lithuanian Commonwealth (with its own Ruthenians) was becoming more pronounced, the one between the Hetmanate and Muscovy was becoming less clear. Peter's administrative and military reforms, which began the integration of the Hetmanate into the imperial administrative system, were making it more difficult to see the Hetmanate and Muscovy

---

[124] See *Ukraïns'ka literatura XVIII st.*, p. 290.
[125] That is how the image of the Poles evolved in the Velychko chronicle. See Frank E. Sysyn, "'The Nation of Cain': Poles in Samiilo Velychko's Chronicle," in *Synopsis: A Collection of Essays in Honour of Zenon E. Kohut* (Edmonton and Toronto, 2005), pp. 443–55.
[126] The poem "Poland Speaks" comes from an early eighteenth-century manuscript. For its text, see *Ukraïns'ka literatura XVII st.*, p. 284.

as two independent entities, linked only by the person of the ruler – the image projected by the Cossack chronicles. Even before the abolition of the hetmancy, Mazepa's successor, Ivan Skoropadsky, had to ask the tsar to make couriers pay for services received in the Hetmanate, invoking not the rights of the Host but standard practice in other parts of the empire.[127] The changing vocabulary used by Cossack intellectuals to describe themselves, their country, and the Muscovite "other" also pointed to an advancing change in attitudes. Not only were Ruthenians and Cossacks more often called Little Russians, but their Muscovite counterparts were now referred to as Great Russians or simply Russians. These terms suggested affinity between the two groups. "Russia" and "Russians" could now refer either to the Hetmanate and its inhabitants or to Muscovy and its inhabitants, or to both entities and populations at the same time. This change of nomenclature made it easier for representatives of the Hetmanate elites to serve the imperial authorities, as demonstrated by the careers of Teofan Prokopovych and other Kyivans in the service of St. Petersburg. In many ways, the Cossack chroniclers were the last defenders of the traditional definitions and values, reminding readers of the old-fashioned terminology that stressed the distinctive character of the Hetmanate. As Frank E. Sysyn has noted, "With the decline of differences in culture and nomenclature that had once so sharply divided Ukraine and Russia, political theory and history writing came to the fore to distinguish the two peoples."[128]

It might be added that in the short run their capacity to draw those distinctions was quite limited, but in the long run political theory and historiography were crucial in forming the historical basis for the new Ukrainian identity. In the nineteenth century the Cossack historical myth became central to the modern Ukrainian national project, which revolutionized the East Slavic nation-building process and helped establish the present-day distinction between the three East Slavic nations.[129]

---

[127] See *Tysiacha rokiv*, IV, pt. 1: 292.   [128] Sysyn, "The Image of Russia," p. 141.

[129] On the importance of Cossack mythology for the Ukrainian nation-building project, see Frank E. Sysyn, "The Reemergence of the Ukrainian Nation and Cossack Mythology," *Social Research* 58, no. 4 (Winter 1991): 845–64; Serhii Plokhy, "Historical Debates and Territorial Claims: Cossack Mythology in the Russian-Ukrainian Border Dispute," in *The Legacy of History in Russia and the New States of Eurasia*, ed. S. Frederick Starr (Armonk, NY, and London, 1994), pp. 147–70; idem, "The Ghosts of Pereyaslav: Russo–Ukrainian Historical Debates in the Post-Soviet Era," *Europe-Asia Studies* 53, no. 3 (2001): 489–505.

Conclusions

"And they said, Go to, let us build us a city, and a tower, whose top may reach unto heaven; and let us make us a name, lest we be scattered abroad upon the face of the whole earth." Such, according to the Old Testament (Gen. 11: 4), were the intentions of those who built the Tower of Babel. But their audacious disregard of God's will angered the Almighty, who punished the human race by dividing it into different lands and languages – an affliction that He considered second only to the Flood. The story of the Tower of Babel was a pillar of historical narrative throughout medieval Christendom. It also found its way into the Primary Chronicle, composed in the city of Kyiv at the turn of the twelfth century. The Kyivan princes were making a name for themselves in neighboring lands (the name was "Rus'") and had a construction project of their own that involved the land, religion, and people of Rus'. If they hoped to reach heaven, it was by adopting and supporting Christianity in their realm. But the fate of their enterprise was not very different from that undertaken by the builders of the tower. In the mid-thirteenth century their state, weakened by internal strife, fell victim to Mongol invaders from the East. The Kyivan realm was divided, and in the long run its people developed literary languages and nations of their own.

The crucial issue that has continued to provoke controversy among historians of Eastern Slavdom over the last two hundred years is whether the Kyivan rulers and elites managed to complete their project before the destruction of the Rus' state. Did they succeed in shaping a coherent Rus' nationality that later gave birth to the three modern nations of Russia, Ukraine, and Belarus? Or was the East Slavic world divided from the very beginning, and did the three nations already exist in Kyivan times? The evidence presented in this book supports a negative answer to both questions. A study of changes in the collective identities of people who defined themselves primarily by reference to the name "Rus'" until the advent of modernity makes it possible to suggest a new model of East Slavic ethnonational development and raises the prospect of a general reconceptualization of East Slavic history. This model interprets the growth of

354

East Slavic identities as a succession of identity-building projects. Such projects served as blueprints for the construction of new identities, which in turn are prerequisites for the existence of self-conscious communities, whether they be polities, religious groups, ethnicities, nations, or entire civilizations. This does not mean, however, that every project closely corresponds to a given identity and each identity to an ethnonational or other type of community. In every case, the former is a necessary but not sufficient condition for the existence of the latter. As the preceding discussion of the problems related to the (non)existence of the Old Rus' nationality demonstrates, a well-developed identity-building project does not suffice, in and of itself, to bring a particular ethnicity into existence. This is especially true for the medieval period.

The foregoing investigation of the medieval and early modern identity-building projects of the Eastern Slavs indicates that the development of Rus' ethnicities and nations cannot be treated as a history of one pan-Russian ethnos or three primordial East Slavic nations. The builders of the East Slavic Tower of Babel were not able to create one ethnicity out of the diverse subjects of the Kyivan princes. If ethnicity is defined by commonality of language, customs, and religion, the Kyivan Rus' population clearly did not measure up to that criterion. Not all Kyivan subjects were Slavs, to say the least, and not all Slavs were Christians, while those who were never developed East Slavic identity to a level clearly discernible in the literary sources of the time. What the Rus' literati did manage to establish, however, was an elite Rus' identity that became closely associated with the Rus' dynasty, law, and church, as well as a Rus' literature written in Church Slavonic. The post-Kyivan elites adopted the political name "Rus' Land," which originally denoted the territory of the Kyiv-Chernihiv-Pereiaslav triangle – the patrimony of the Rurikid dynasty – but then became an appellation for other regions at various times. After the Mongol invasion, the elites retained the Rus' name as their self-designation but proceeded to develop separate identities in their appanage principalities, steadily distancing themselves from the Rus' model constructed by the Kyivan bookmen of the eleventh and twelfth centuries. Although the sense of a Rus' community never fully disappeared from East Slavic texts of the premodern period, it was clearly fading with the passage of time.

The first distinct East Slavic identities bore little relation to the three future East Slavic nations. Instead, they were called into existence by the Rurikid elites living under the suzerainty of the Mongol khans in the east and the Lithuanian princes in the west of the former Kyivan realm. The emergence of a clear political boundary between the two Ruses created a strong sense of belonging to a given political space and, in time, promoted loyalty to local political institutions and practices. On their external border, the two Rus' communities of the time, Lithuanian and Mongol, had clearly defined linguistic and cultural markers that distinguished them from the pagan Lithuanians on the one hand and the shamanist Mongols on the other. The internal border between the two Ruses became more pronounced with the unification of the lands of Mongol Rus' under the auspices of Moscow in the second half of the fifteenth century and the prolonged warfare between Muscovy and Lithuania in the late fifteenth and early sixteenth centuries. My analysis of the structure and content of post-Kyivan Rus' identity, which developed on the basis of the political and cultural heritage of Mongol Rus', points to the formation of a separate Muscovite identity (and ethnicity) in the fifteenth and sixteenth centuries. Built around the idea of loyalty to the tsar, based on the view of Muscovite Orthodoxy as the only true religion, and limited to the boundaries of the grand-princely (subsequently tsarist) state, Muscovite identity may be regarded as a distant but still direct precursor of the Russian imperial and national projects of the modern era.

The first East Slavic entity that might be called an early modern nation is the Ruthenian community formed on the Ukrainian and Belarusian lands of the Polish-Lithuanian Commonwealth in the late sixteenth and seventeenth centuries. Ruthenian identity grew out of the identities of Lithuanian and Polish Rus' of the pre-1569 (Union of Lublin) period. To become national in the early modern sense of the word, Ruthenian identity had not only to bridge the division between Polish and Lithuanian Rus' but also to overcome the dominance of local identities in the Rus' lands of the Grand Duchy of Lithuania. Ruthenian identity was constructed under the influence of Renaissance ideas and the "national" discourse of the Polish and Lithuanian elites of the time. It was fully formed during the struggle of the Orthodox Ukrainian and Belarusian elites against the forcible union of the Kyiv metropolitanate with Rome that was concluded at the Synod of Brest in 1596. That identity was based on the concept of the nation (*narod*). As understood in the Orthodox Church, the Ruthenian nation included in its ranks not only princes and nobles but also Cossacks, burghers, and sometimes even peasants. The discourse that shaped the new identity was produced by the authors of polemical religious tracts, which mushroomed in the Ukrainian and Belarusian lands because of the controversy over the church union. Thus the print revolution helped create the Ruthenian nation, which acquired a developed literature of its own almost overnight. Its readership included relatively broad segments of the nobility, clergy, and burghers. The Ruthenian nation and identity cannot be considered direct predecessors of the modern Ukrainian or Belarusian nations and identities to the degree that early modern Muscovite identity can be so regarded vis-à-vis the Russian nation. At the time of its formation, Ruthenian identity emerged victorious from competition with identity projects that restricted the loyalties of local elites to the Ukrainian or Belarusian territories divided by the internal Commonwealth border between the Kingdom of Poland and the Grand Duchy of Lithuania. The victory of Ruthenian identity was temporary: in the long run, it was superseded by distinct Ukrainian and Belarusian national identities among the East Slavic population of the former Crown lands and the territories of the Grand Duchy.

When it comes to Muscovy, there are indications that the Muscovite ethnicity fully developed into an early modern nation in the wake of the Time of Troubles. The shock of foreign intervention made Muscovite society much more self-conscious than ever before. Resistance to invasion strengthened the external boundaries of the community, forced it to take cognizance of itself independently of the image of its ruler, and consolidated its internal solidarity. With the dissemination of historical and literary texts devoted to the Time of Troubles, a new identity was created and a new nation was born. The difference between the seventeenth-century Muscovite and Ruthenian nations and identities was nowhere more apparent than in the depth of cultural misunderstanding that accompanied the "reunification" of the two Ruses at mid-century. A study of the sources related to the Pereiaslav Agreement of 1654 between Muscovy and the Ukrainian Cossacks indicates that ethnonational motifs were virtually absent from the accompanying discourse. Although in his letters to Muscovy the Cossack hetman Bohdan Khmelnytsky defined certain elements of the Ukrainian uprising in ethnonational terms, the Muscovite side continued to view the world primarily in religious terms and thus lacked the vocabulary required to conduct a dialogue based on the concept of ethnonational unity. Even the idea of religious unity, which became the basis of the diplomatic dialogue between the two parties, was merely proclaimed at Pereiaslav: by that time, the two ecclesiastical traditions had diverged too radically to provide a stable basis for "reunification." Not surprisingly, it was the metropolitan of Kyiv who became the first opponent and critic of the Muscovite presence in Ukraine.

The Pereiaslav Agreement not only helped manifest the differences between Ruthenians and Muscovites but also created political preconditions for the formation of a new identity that came into existence as a result of more than half a century of "negotiation" between the Muscovite and Cossack elites. A leading role in its construction was played by natives of the Hetmanate, such as Teofan Prokopovych, a close associate of Peter I, who left their homeland to serve the tsar. Having been trained at the Kyivan Academy in the Renaissance tradition of Polish and central European scholarship, they brought to Muscovy the concepts of "nation" and "fatherland," which revolutionized Muscovite political discourse in the Petrine era. That discourse helped shape the new identity of the Russian imperial elites, which was formed in strong opposition to the old Muscovite identity represented by the leaders of the Old Belief. The problem with eighteenth-century Russian identity was that Russia's self-realization as a nation developed simultaneously with the growth of its imperial image and identity. The entanglement of the concepts of nationality and imperial statehood during the encounter between the Ruthenian (Ukrainian and Belarusian) and Muscovite elites was crucial to the formation of Russian imperial identity. From the outset, it was based on the assumption that the Eastern Slavs constituted one "Russo-Slavic" nation. In the long run, that belief created a great deal of confusion among modern Russians, Ukrainians, and Belarusians with regard to their identities and greatly complicated the task of those who study their histories and political behaviors.

Although the formation of Russian imperial identity had a clear impact on the development of early modern identities in the Ukrainian and Belarusian territories, it did not compromise their distinct character. This pertains especially to Ruthenian identity, which remained dominant among the Ukrainian and Belarusian population of the Polish-Lithuanian Commonwealth. More profound was the imperial influence on identity and nation-building projects in the Hetmanate, where a new Ukrainian or Little Russian identity took shape in the late seventeenth and early eighteenth centuries. The Ukrainian elites of the Hetmanate produced the first model of collective identity that clearly differentiated them from the elites of neighboring Belarus. The Cossack officers successfully transferred the concept of "fatherland," applied by their predecessors to the Kingdom of Poland, to the territory of the Hetmanate (which initially reached as far west as Lviv and covered both Left- and Right-Bank Ukraine). The Hetmanate elites turned that fatherland – Ukrainian or Little Russian, as it was alternatively called at the time – into the object of their highest political loyalty. As indicated by documents pertaining to the revolt of Hetman Ivan Mazepa in 1708, the concept of a distinct fatherland helped distinguish Ukrainian elites in the Hetmanate from those of their counterparts in the Polish-Lithuanian Commonwealth and Muscovy. The Ukrainian identity of the period was deeply rooted in Cossack practices and traditions, and the elites of the Hetmanate imagined Ukraine as a society led and represented by the Cossack estate. Other social strata might have their own rights and privileges, but it was the leading Cossack estate that defined the rights of the polity and its inhabitants. Although the Ukrainian (Little Russian) identity of the period did not claim all of the modern Ukrainian territories, it established the foundations of modern Ukrainian identity and supplied it with legends, myths, and symbols that became indispensable to the national awakeners of the nineteenth century.

What were the crucial factors in the formation of these new identity constructs? Clearly, as in premodern communities elsewhere in the world, myths of origin, historical narratives, language, culture, and religious beliefs played an important role in the development, maintenance, and reconstruction of East Slavic identities. What should be stressed in this regard is the mediating function of institutions, which often determined the mix of factors that formed a given ethnonational identity. Even limited familiarity with the historical sources indicates that the ethnonational projects of the premodern era originated with the political and intellectual elites associated with polities and religious institutions. It would be difficult to exaggerate the role of the state, its boundaries and institutions in the formation and promotion of political loyalties. The legacy of Kyivan Rus' included the Rus' dynasty, language, law, and religion – factors that helped distinguish the Rus' community from the rest of the world. An important role in identity formation and ethnicity/nation-building was played not only by the states of the Eastern Slavs themselves, which, apart from Kyivan Rus', included such polities as Muscovy and the Cossack Hetmanate, but also by "foreign" states dominated by the Mongols, Poles, and Lithuanians, and, in relation to the Ukrainians and Belarusians, by the Great Russians. Thus the role of the state as an institution was not limited to the promotion of certain projects; it could also hinder their development.

Apart from the state, another important institutional actor in the formation and reshaping of local cultural and political identities was the church, with its complement of learned authors. The acceptance and (often forcible) introduction of Christianity in Kyivan Rus' was highly significant in establishing a sense of Rus' commonality. The division of the Rus' metropolitanate into several jurisdictions in the course of the fourteenth and fifteenth centuries undermined that awareness and strengthened the centrifugal tendencies associated with the formation of new political and ecclesiastical boundaries. It would be hard to exaggerate the role played in the identity-building process by the Uniate Church, whose establishment in the late sixteenth century launched the public debate that helped define the boundaries and identity of the Ruthenian nation. By the mid-eighteenth century, the Uniate Church had become the organizational and cultural mainstay of the distinct Ruthenian community in the Polish-Lithuanian Commonwealth, but the division of the Ukrainian and Belarusian population into Orthodox and Uniate factions was a hindrance to their respective nation-building projects. On the other hand, the Orthodox discourse that developed in Moscow, fully exploited by the tsars and modernized by the Russian imperial court, contributed significantly to the formulation of the Russian imperial project of the period.

The succession of premodern identity-building projects presented above can serve as a starting point for the discussion of a new history of the Eastern Slavs. But the relations between project, identity, and particular type of community must be investigated more deeply if the study of East Slavic history is to be based not only on the successive identity projects left by producers of political and cultural texts but also on popular identities and the communities that they shaped. The new interpretation of the history of East Slavic identities during the Middle Ages and the early modern period also opens new prospects for the understanding of modern national identities in the region. Not only were the premodern East Slavic identities influenced by the identity-building projects that preceded them, but their own influence shaped the national projects of the modern era. Anthony D. Smith has noted the close connection between premodern and modern national identities, arguing that "it becomes important to enquire into the 'state of cultural identity' of the given community on the eve of its exposure to the new revolutionary forces, in order to locate the bases of its subsequent evolution into a fully fledged nation."[1] The present study of East Slavic identities not only refutes "primordialist" attempts to nationalize the premodern past but helps identify the roots of many features that define the "national character" of modern-day Russians, Ukrainians, and Belarusians.

The achievements and setbacks of contemporary nation-building among the Eastern Slavs can be traced back to premodern times. The modern Russian nation grew out of the Russian imperial project and preserved many of its characteristics, including the blurred boundary between the Great Russians per se and the non-Russian subjects of the empire. The modern Ukrainian identity developed out of the Ukrainian/Little Russian project of the Hetmanate, excluding Russians and Belarusians and taking over not only the formerly Polish-ruled Right-Bank Ukraine but also Austrian Galicia, Bukovyna, and eventually Transcarpathia, providing legitimacy for the creation of one nation out of historically, culturally, and religiously diverse regions. The Belarusian national project was based on the Ruthenian identity that had previously developed in the Grand Duchy of Lithuania but failed to produce

---

[1] Anthony D. Smith, *The Ethnic Origins of Nations* (Oxford, 1986), p. 3.

a distinct identity in early modern times, given the lack of a proto-Belarusian polity comparable to the Cossack Hetmanate in Left-Bank Ukraine. Ultimately, the Ruthenian name was claimed by the Rusyns of Transcarpathia, whose leaders insist today that they are distinct from the Ukrainians.

Today the three East Slavic nations are still haunted and often led by ghosts of the past: Russia's imperial legacy is apparent in its continuing war with Chechnia; Ukraine finds it difficult to reconcile the political culture and orientation of its formerly Cossack, Polish, and Austrian west-central lands with its eastern and southern territories, settled in the days of the Russian Empire; Belarus struggles to define a place for itself in a world of developed nation-states.

Existing national identities, like their distant and immediate predecessors, are affected by particular historical circumstances and thus subject to constant change. For now, though, it may safely be assumed that the three post-Soviet states will develop distinct national identities that promote their continued existence. Even the "anti-national" Belarusian state, simply by maintaining a boundary with its nationalizing neighbors to the east and south, is constructing an identity that distinguishes modern Belarusians from modern Russians and Ukrainians to a degree unmatched in Soviet times. Talk of an East Slavic civilization and a common Orthodox or East Slavic moral tradition, encouraged in different degrees by politicians in Moscow, Kyiv, and Mensk, seems ineffective as an antidote to the ongoing nationalization of the post-Soviet societies.

Author index

General index